The Horizontal Line Synopsis of the Gospels

First Edition, All Rights Reserved.
Library of Congress Catalog Card Number: 75-20997
International Standard Book Number (ISBN)   0-915948-01-X
Copyright © 1975 by Reuben Joseph Swanson

Manufactured in the United States of America
by Washburn Press, Inc.
Charlotte, North Carolina

The Horizontal Line Synopsis of the Gospels

Reuben J. Swanson, S.T.M., Ph.D.
Professor of Philosophy and Religion
Western Carolina University
Cullowhee, North Carolina

Western North Carolina Press, Inc.
Dillsboro, North Carolina

To Edna Maria
Partner and Co-Worker in this Venture of Faith

ACKNOWLEDGEMENTS

Constructive criticisms and helpful suggestions have been made by a number of persons who have aided in moving this work along to completion in an improved form. Among those who deserve special mention are John Reumann who gave the work a more appropriate name; Bruce Metzger for a number of helpful suggestions with reference to format; Dean Luther Weigle for encouragement and assistance in securing permission for the use of the Revised Standard Version text; James Pugh for supplying the first Greek typewriter; D. P. Rudisill for monumental efforts in behalf of the formation of Western North Carolina Press; James Ballard for his wise business counsel in behalf of the company; Western Carolina University for encouraging my research and writing and for supplying necessary equipment and materials; Susan Swanson for proofreading the manuscript; and finally above all to Edna Maria who has born with patience and fortitude the loss of a husband to a vision of parallel lines. These few names by no means exhaust the list of those to whom I owe a debt of gratitude for kind assistance in the pursuit of this goal. May their reward be great!

THE SYNOPSIS

The idea of a new Synopsis of the Gospels evolved out of a classroom experience with undergraduates in a course entitled, "The Life of Jesus." It soon became apparent that students had great difficulty identifying similarities and differences in the gospel materials.   How can similarities and differences be meaningful to students if they are unable to identify them quickly and readily?   How can there be time for thoughtful consideration of the similarities and differences if it is used up in searching out those similarities and differences?   Evidently a new arrangement of the gospel materials was necessary to facilitate their study in depth.

One difficulty to overcome was, How to rearrange the gospel materials in columns so as to make it possible for the student to identify similarities and differences immediately.   At this stage the columnar model was the sacred cow that commended itself for want of a better idea. So the writer began laboriously to rearrange the materials to show the parallelism by matching lines across four columns.   The new Synopsis, as first conceived, was to take each gospel in turn as the lead gospel and arrange all parallels from the other three to it. The rationale for this procedure was: each gospel must be read consecutively in its natural order to preserve the original context and content. All Synopses in print disturb the natural order, since no gospel is followed consecutively in its natural sequence without interruption.   Furthermore, gospel materials in current Synopses are juxtaposed only approximately, for frequently the organization of the materials varies within the pericopes themselves.

The organization of the materials in this new format was completed and the final draft about to be typed when suddenly the idea of a parallel line arrangment came as a bolt from the blue.   Immediately it became apparent that arranging the material in parallel lines would eliminate many of the technical difficulties inherent in any columnar arrangement.   Further, a parallel line arrangement was flexible enough to preserve the integrity of each gospel and yet make possible the closest comparisons among them.

So the work began and the arrangement proceeded over a period of more than ten years.   The master plan called for editions in both Greek and English, each edition to be arranged in four parts, one part for each gospel.   There was encouragement from a number of friends and associates in New Testament studies who saw the value of the new arrangement.   There was discouragement from those who saw no need for a new tool, but said 'The old is good enough.'

It also became apparent that finding a publisher would be difficult, for the parallel line arrangement with the precise spacing within the lines offers overwhelming difficulties to the typesetter.   The cost would be enormous. Meeting rebuff from publisher after publisher led to the conclusion that an alternative method must be determined to reproduce the material in an economical form that would make it available to everyone who has an interest in the study of the gospels. This led to the formation of WESTERN NORTH CAROLINA PRESS, INC., for the precise purpose of publishing THE HORIZONTAL LINE SYNOPSIS OF THE GOSPELS in the English and Greek editions as the initial offerings of what we anticipate will be other valuable tools for all areas of study. This company, organized by the author, is owned by stockholders who have seen a vision of the usefulness of this arrangement of the gospel materials on all levels of Christian education.

The preparation of the text for reproduction likewise represented a hurdle to be overcome. Several printing companies in the Western North Carolina area were consulted, resulting in the determination that photo offest printing was a viable and economic method for the reproduction of the text. Washburn Press was selected because of the imaginative ideas they projected for the book. Finally, an arrangement was made with International Business Machines to secure a Memory Typewriter on a rental basis for typesetting the copy. Since the actual typing is rather an involved operation and, since it was possible to make changes and improvements in the original manuscript, it was apparent that the author himself must type the entire copy. So the work has progressed to completion and it is offered to the public in the hope that it will be a most useful resource for the study of our gospels. If this book in either or both the English or Greek editions contributes anything to an increased knowledge and understanding of our Lord's life and message, then its birthpains have indeed been worthwhile.

Sola Dei Gloria!

THE USE OF THE SYNOPSIS

The Horizontal Line Synopsis is a neutral source for the study of the gospels and their interrelationships. It does not prejudge the question of relationships by giving priority to one gospel over another. Each gospel is given an opportunity to tell its own story and at the same time the relationships of the other gospels to it are immediately apparent. Thus the Synopsis consists of four parts beginning with Matthew and continuing through John. The lead gospel is almost always the gospel in boldface type on the top line of the blocks of lines. Exceptions occur only when there is material in the supporting gospels not found in the lead gospel. Such material is included, since it is important to see what the other gospel writers are saying which is not repeated in the lead gospel. The lead gospel is always underlined consecutively, so that the reader may follow its text independently from the other gospels. Exact parallels in the supporting gospels are always underlined too, so that the eye can pick up the similarities between the lead gospel and the supporting texts.

The parallel material arranged to the lead gospel are of two kinds: first, the primary parallels which are printed in boldface type and, second, the secondary parallels which are printed in light italic except when the text is in exact agreement with the lead gospel. Light italic is also used to identify materials in the primary parallels which are not found in the lead gospel. The material is presented in context, so that the reader does not need to turn to that gospel to determine what it is saying which is not found in the lead gospel.

The chapter and verse identifications are always found in the left-hand margin. The chapter and verse of the lead gospel will always occur consecutively. The chapter and verse of the supporting gospels will not occur consecutively, but will be rearranged to conform to the lead gospel. Sometimes this means that individual verses will be out of their order in the pericope; sometimes portions of the verse will be rearranged to the exemplar. When this occurs, the portion of the verse will be referred to as a, b, c, or d. The chapter and verse of secondary parallels are always indented two spaces so that the reader may identify the material immediately as secondary.

The Horizontal Line Synopsis is to be read in blocks of lines. The similarities and differences among the gospel accounts stand out immediately. The arrangement and the underlining are all intended to aid the reader to visualize the relationships among the gospels. Now it is possible for the first time to see all the similarities and differences in synoptic form. The student of the gospels is released from the mechanical task of identifying similarities and differences and can devote his attention to the interpretation of the phenomena. The Greek and English editions will parallel one another, so that they can be used alternately, or even simultaneously, in the classroom.

The flexibility of The Horizontal Line Synopsis is immediately apparent. The difficulty of showing more than the primary parallels in synoptic form has been overcome. Whereas the columnar arrangement only sets the primary parallels in an approximate parallel form, the horizontal line arrangement can include as many primary and secondary parallels as exist, not only in the gospels, but when such parallels occur in other parts of the New Testament. For example, Paul's account of the Lord's Supper is shown in comparison to the gospel accounts (note pages 161 - 163).

Each gospel is organized into pericopes representing the natural order of that gospel, so that organization of the material by one gospel writer, e.g., Matthew, is not imposed upon the others. Thus the atomistic tendency of breaking down the gospels into the smallest possible units to accommodate a columnar arrangement is avoided. The pericope titles, which appear in Bookface type, along with the chapter and verse identifications are correlated throughout the four parts whenever possible. The Tables of Contents for each section cite cross references for the pericopes, so that the reader can turn to the other gospels if he wants to view the pericope from the perspective of another gospel writer.

THE DIVISION INTO PARTS

It is widely maintained that Mark provides the framework and basis outline for the Synoptic Gospels. The consensus is that Mark was the earliest gospel and was used by the authors of Matthew and Luke as a main source in the preparation of their gospels. The Horizontal Line Synopsis will serve as a tool to test this hypothesis in a more comprehensive and precise way than previous arrangements of the gospel materials. The inclusion of the Gospel of John and the paralleling of all materials, primary and secondary, will give a more solid base for whatever conclusions can be formulated pertaining to this and to other synoptic questions. Gospel materials are truly paralleled by the horizontal format. Identical words and phrases are shown directly above and below one another. So the basic relationships among the four gospels are demonstrated conceptually, contextually, and verbally. The ease of visualizing the similarity and dissimilarity among the gospels is facilitated, for the reader views groups of parallel lines across the page, rather than three or four separate columns in which the material is paralleled only approximately. This in the opinion of the author is the noteworthy contribution of The Horizontal Line Synopsis to the study of the gospels.

The very nature of the gospel materials demands that the work be presented in four parts. The close juxtaposition of parallel materials makes it necessary to disturb the order of the three gospels to compare them to the one. Each gospel must appear in its natural order to preserve its integrity. This has its advantages. The student can study one gospel at a time and yet view its relationship to the others at the same time. He does not lose the theme or the progression of the Gospel of Mark, for example, as in a columnar harmony just because Matthew or Luke insert non-Markan material into the Markan framework. One is able to visualize each of the gospels as a whole and at the same time consider the interrelationships of the gospels to one another.

The author has chosen not to present variant readings in the English edition. These will be presented in the Greek edition and will be compiled from original collations of manuscripts by the author. This will make possible the correction of the many errors now extant in current critical editions of the Greek New Testament. Furthermore, these variant readings will also be presented in parallel lines, so that the interplay among them in the transmission of the text will be clearly demonstrated. The current method of presenting the textual data offers a great mass of variant readings, highly condensed, but largely ignores the relationships of these variants from one gospel to another and the influence which readings in one gospel have had in producing textual variations in the parallel passages in the other gospels. It may be that something of this should be done for future editions of the English edition as well, so that those students of the gospels who depend solely on the English text may have some understanding and appreciation of the discipline of textual criticism.

SIGLA AND ABBREVIATIONS

The sigla and abbreviations used are few. The gospels are abbreviated as follows: M = Matthew, Mk = Mark, L = Luke, and J = John. In addition, A = The Acts of the Apostles and 1 C = 1 Corinthians. The mark, |, indicates a new verse start, or the start of a part of a verse when the verse is divided into two or more sections for comparative purposes.

TABLE OF CONTENTS

PART I.   THE GOSPEL ACCORDING TO MATTHEW   1

PART II.   THE GOSPEL ACCORDING TO MARK   187

PART III.   THE GOSPEL ACCORDING TO LUKE   327

PART IV.   THE GOSPEL ACCORDING TO JOHN   513

PART I

THE GOSPEL ACCORDING TO MATTHEW

CONTENTS AND CROSS REFERENCES: MATTHEW

| | | Page | Parallel Sections in |||
			Mark	Luke	John
1. The Genealogy of Jesus	1.1-17	1		11	
2. The Birth of Jesus	1.18-25	3		6	
3. The Wise Men and the Descent into Egypt	2.1-23	3			
4. John the Baptist	3.1-12	5	2	9	2
5. The Baptism of Jesus	3.13-17	8	3	10	
6. The Temptation	4.1-11	9	4	12	
7. Jesus Announces the Kingdom of Heaven	4.12-17	11	5	13	
8. The First Disciples	4.18-22	12	6	17	3
9. Preaching and Healing in Galilee	4.23-25	13	8	16	
10. First Discourse: Sermon on the Mount	5.1-7.29	14			
a. Setting	5.1-2	14			
b. The Beatitudes	5.3-12	15		25a	
c. Salt and Light	5.13-16	16	43,19	68,32,54	
d. The Old Law and the New	5.17-48	17		59,71,25b	
e. The New Righteousness	6.1-7.23	21	19	51,58,25b 25c,25d,63	
f. The Two Houses	7.24-27	28		25e	
g. Summary	7.28-29	29			
11. A Leper Cleansed	8.1-4	29	9	18	
12. The Centurion's Servant	8.5-13	30		26	9
13. Healings at Capernaum	8.14-17	32	7	15	
14. The Demands of Discipleship	8.18-22	33		46	
15. The Storm at Sea	8.23-27	33	23	34	
16. The Two Demoniacs	8.28-9.1	35	24	35	
17. A Paralytic Healed	9.2-8	37	10	19	10
18. Matthew the Tax Collector	9.9-13	39	11	20	
19. Question of Fasting	9.14-17	41	12	21	
20. Jairus' Daughter and a Woman with a Hemorrhage	9.18-26	42	25	36	
21. Two Blind Men and a Dumb Demoniac	9.27-34	45	49	81	

		Page	Mark	Luke	John
22. Second Discourse: Mission of the Twelve 9.35-11.1		47			
a. Setting	9.35-38	47		47	
b. The Twelve	10.1-4	48	15	23	
c. The Mission	10.5-15	50	27	37,47	
d. The Instruction	10.16-42	52	57b	56,89b	
e. Summary	11.1	58			
23. John the Baptist and the 'Coming One'	11.2-19	58		28	
24. Woes and Thanksgivings	11.20-30	61		48	
25. Question of Sabbath Observance	12.1-8	62	12	21	
26. A Withered Hand	12.9-21	63	13	22,65	
27. How Can Satan Cast Out Satan?	12.22-37	65	16	52	
28. An Evil Generation Seeks a Sign	12.38-45	69	36	53	
29. His Mother and Brothers	12.46-50	71	17	33	
30. Third Discourse: Parables of the Kingdom	13.1-53	71			
a. Setting	13.1-3a	71			
b. The Soils	13.3b-23	72	18	31	
c. Weeds Among the Wheat	13.24-30	76	20		
d. The Mustard Seed and Leaven	13.31-33	77	21	62	
e. The Use of Parables	13.34-35	78	22		
f. The 'Weeds' Interpreted	13.36-43	78			
g. Hidden Treasure and the Pearl	13.44-46	79			
h. The Net	13.47-50	79			
i. The Householder	13.51-52	80			
j. Summary	13.53	80			
31. Jesus Rejected by His Own	13.54-58	80	26	14	17
32. Death of John the Baptist	14.1-12	81	28	9	
33. The Five Thousand Fed	14.13-21	83	29	38	12
34. Walking on the Water	14.22-33	87	30		13
35. Healing at Gennesaret	14.34-36	88	31		
36. A Question of Defilement	15.1-20	88	32	54	
37. The Canaanite Woman	15.21-28	91	33		
38. Many Sick are Healed	15.29-31	92	34		

		Page	Mark	Luke	John
39. The Four Thousand Fed	15.32–39	93	35		
40. Pharisees Seek a Sign and a Warning	16.1–12	97	36	53	
41. Peter's Confession and First Prediction of the Passion	16.13–23	99	38	39	15
42. Cost of Discipleship	16.24–28	100	39	40	26
43. The Transfiguration	17.1–13	102	40	41	
44. The Epileptic Boy	17.14–21	104	41	42	
45. Second Prediction of the Passion	17.22–23	107	42	43	
46. The Temple Tax	17.24–27	107			
47. Fourth Discourse: The New Community	18.1–19.2	108			
a. Setting	18.1–3a	108			
b. Who is the Greatest?	18.3b–4	108	43	44	
c. Receiving Children	18.5–14	109	43	73,69	
d. Forgiveness	18.15–22	111		73	
e. The Unmerciful Servant	18.23–35	112			
f. Summary	19.1–2	113			
48. Marriage and Divorce	19.3–12	113	44	71	
49. Let the Children Come	19.13–15	114	45	78	
50. The Peril of Riches	19.16–30	115	46	79	
51. The Laborers in the Vineyard	20.1–16	118			
52. Third Prediction of the Passion	20.17–19	118	47	80	
53. The Sons of Zebedee	20.20–28	119	55	98	27
54. Blind Bartimaeus	20.29–34	121	56	81	
55. Jesus Enters Jerusalem	21.1–11	122	50	84	25
56. Cleansing the Temple	21.12–17	125	52	85	5
57. The Withered Fig Tree	21.18–22	126	51,53	60	
58. Controversies in Jerusalem	21.23–22.46	128			
a. The Authority of Jesus	21.23–27	128	54a	86a	
b. The Two Sons	21.28–32	129			
c. The Wicked Tenants	21.33–46	129	54b	86b	
d. The Marriage Feast	22.1–14	132			
e. Render to God	22.15–22	133	54c	86c	

		Page	Mark	Luke	John
f. The God of the Living	22.23-33	135	54d	86d	
g. The Great Commandment	22.34-40	136	54e	49	
h. The Son of David	22.41-46	137	54f	86e	17
59. Woes Against Scribes and Pharisees	23.1-36	138	55	87,55	
60. Lament over Jerusalem	23.34-39	142		64	
61. Fifth Discourse: The End of the Age	24.1-26.2	143			
a. Setting: Destruction of the Temple	24.1-2	143	57a	89a	
b. Signs of the End	24.3-44	144	57b	89b	
c. The Faithful and Wise Servant	24.45-51	150		58	
d. The Ten Maidens	25.1-13	151			
e. The Talents	25.14-30	152		83	
f. The Last Judgment	25.31-46	155			
g. Summary	26.1-2	156			
62. The Plot to Kill Jesus	26.3-5	156	58	91	23
63. Jesus Anointed for Burial	26.6-13	157	59	29	24
64. Judas Plans the Betrayal	26.14-16	159	60	91	15
65. The Passover Meal	26.17-29	159	61	92	28,14
66. Peter's Denial Foretold	26.30-35	163	62	94	29
67. Gethsemane	26.36-46	164	63	96	
68. Jesus Arrested	26.47-56	166	64	97	35
69. Before the High Priest	26.57-68	168	65	98	36
70. Peter's Denial	26.69-75	170	66	98	36
71. Jesus Brought Before Pilate	27.1-2	172	67	99	37
72. Death of the Betrayer	27.3-10	172			
73. The Trial before Pilate	27.11-26	173	67	99,101	37
74. Crucifixion and Death	27.27-56	176	68	102	38
75. The Burial	27.57-61	181	69	103	39
76. The Guard Posted at the Tomb	27.62-66	183			
77. The Empty Tomb	28.1-10	183	70	104	40
78. Bribing the Guard	28.11-15	185			
79. Go and Make Disciples	28.16-20	186	72		

1. THE GENEALOGY OF JESUS

Matthew 1.1-17

M	1.1	The book	of the genealogy	of Jesus	Christ,
Mk	1.1	The beginning of the gospel		of Jesus	Christ,
L	3.23				Jesus, when he began
J	*20.31*	*but these are written that you may believe that*		Jesus *is the*	Christ,

M	1.1		the son
Mk	1.1		the Son
L	3.23	his ministry, was about thirty years of age, being	the son (as was
J	*20.31*		the Son

M	1.1	of David,	the son of Abraham.
Mk	1.1	of God.	
L	3.34c	supposed) of Joseph,	the son of Abraham, *the son of Terah, the son of*
J	*20.31*	*of God, and that believing you may have life in his name.*	

L	*3.35*	*Nahor, |the son of Serug, the son of Reu, the son of Peleg, the son of*
L	*3.36*	*Eber, the son of Shelah, |the son of Cainan, the son of Arphaxad, the*
L	*3.37*	*son of Shem, the son of Noah, the son of Lamech, |the son of Methuselah,*
L	*3.37*	*the son of Enoch, the son of Jared, the son of Mahalaleel, the son of*
L	*3.38*	*Cainan, |the son of Enos, the son of Seth, the son of Adam, the son of*
L	*3.38*	*God.*

M	1.2	Abraham was the father of Isaac, and Isaac the father of Jacob, and
L	3.34b,a	the son of Isaac, the son of Jacob,

M	1.3	Jacob the father of Judah and his brothers, |and Judah the father of
L	3.33f,e	the son of Judah, the son of

M	1.3	Perez and Zerah by Tamar, and Perez the father of Hezron, and Hezron
L	3.33d	Perez, the son of Hezron,

M	1.4	the father of Ram, |and Ram the father of Amminadab, and
L	3.33c,b,a	the son of Arni, the son of Admin, the son of Amminadab,

M	1.5	Amminadab the father of Nahshon, and Nahshon the father of Salmon, |and
L	3.32e,d	the son of Nahshon, the son of Sala,

M	1.5	Salmon the father of Boaz by Rahab, and Boaz the father of Obed by Ruth,
L	3.32c,b	the son of Boaz, the son of Obed,

M	1.6	and Obed the father of Jesse, |and Jesse the father of David the king.
L	3.32a,31e	the son of Jesse, the son of David,

M	1.7	And David was the father of Solomon by the wife of Uriah, |and Solomon
L	3.31d	the son of Nathan,

M	1.7	the father of Rehoboam, and Rehoboam the father of Abijah, and Abijah
L	3.31c,b	the son of Mattatha, the son of Menna,

1

```
M   1.8        the father of Asa, |and Asa the father of Jehoshaphat, and Jehoshaphat
L   3.31a,30e  the son    of Melea,        the son    of Eliakim,


M   1.9        the father of Joram, and Joram the father of Uzziah, |and Uzziah the
L   3.30d,c,b  the son    of Jonam,         the son    of Joseph,            the


M   1.9        father of Jotham, and Jotham the father of Ahaz, and Ahaz the father
L   3.30a,29e  son    of Judah,          the son    of Simeon,         the son


M   1.10       of Hezekiah, |and Hezekiah the father of Manasseh, and Manasseh the
L   3.29d,c    of Levi,            the son    of Matthat,          the


M   1.11       father of Amos, and Amos the father of Josiah, |and Josiah the father
L   3.29b,a    son    of Jorim,        the son    of Eliezer,         the son


M   1.11       of Jechoniah and his brothers, at the time of the deportation to
L   3.28e,d,c  of Joshua, |the son of Er, the son of Elmadam, the son of Cosam,


M   1.11       Babylon.
L   3.28b,a,27e the son of Addi, the son of Melchi, the son of Neri,


M   1.12       And after the deportation to Babylon: Jechoniah was the father of
L   3.27d                                            the son    of


M   1.13       Shealtiel, and Shealtiel the father of Zerubbabel, |and Zerubbabel
L   3.27c      Shealtiel,           the son    of Zerubbabel,


M   1.13       the father of Abiud, and Abiud the father of Eliakim, and Eliakim
L   3.27b,a    the son    of Rhesa,         the son    of Joanan,


M   1.14       the father of Azor, |and Azor the father of Zadok, and Zadok the
L   3.26e,d,c  the son    of Joda,          the son    of Josech,         the


M   1.15       father of Achim, and Achim the father of Eliud, |and Eliud the father
L   3.26b,a    son    of Semein,        the son    of Mattathias,       the son


M   1.15       of Eleazar, and Eleazar the father of Matthan,
L   3.25e,d,c  of Maath,           the son    of Naggai, the son of Esli, the


L   3.25b,a,24e  son of Nahum, the son of Amos, the son of Mattathias, |the son of
L   3.24d,c,b  a  Joseph, the son of Jannai, the son of Melchi, the son of Levi, the


M   1.16       and Matthan  the father of Jacob, |and Jacob the father
L   3.23c,b    son of Matthat, |the son    of Heli,      being the son (as was


M   1.16              of Joseph the husband of Mary, of whom Jesus was born, who
L   3.23a      supposed) of Joseph,                   |Jesus, when he began


M   1.16       is called Christ.
L   3.23a      his ministry, was about thirty years of age,
```

2

M	1.17	So all the generations from Abraham to David were fourteen genera-
M	1.17	tions, and from David to the deportation to Babylon fourteen genera-
M	1.17	tions, and from the deportation to Babylon to the Christ fourteen
M	1.17	generations.

2. THE BIRTH OF JESUS

Matthew 1.18-25

M	1.18	Now the birth of Jesus Christ took place in this way.
L	1.26	*In the sixth month the angel Gabriel was sent from God to a city of*

M	1.18	When his mother Mary had been betrothed to
L	1.27	*Galilee named Nazareth,* |*to a virgin* betrothed to *a man whose name*

M	1.18	Joseph, before they came together she was found to be with child of
L	1.28	*was* Joseph, *of the house of David; and the virgin's name was Mary. And*

M	1.19	the Holy Spirit; and her husband Joseph, being a just man and unwilling
L	1.28	*he came to her and said, "Hail, O favored one, the Lord is with you!"*

M	1.20	to put her to shame, resolved to divorce her quietly. But as he considered
L	1.29	*But she was greatly troubled at the saying,* *and* considered

M	1.20	this, behold, an angel of the
L	1.30	*in her mind what sort of greeting this might be. And the* angel

M	1.20	Lord appeared to him in a dream, saying, "Joseph, son of David, do not
L	1.30	said *to her,* "Do not be

M	1.20	fear to take Mary your wife, for that which
L	1.31	afraid, Mary, *for you have found favor with God. And behold, you*

M	1.21	is conceived in her is of the Holy Spirit; she will bear a son, and you
L	1.31	*will* conceive *in your womb* *and* bear a son, and you

M	1.21	shall call his name Jesus, for he will save his people from their sins."
L	1.31	shall call his name Jesus.

M	1.22	All this took place to fulfil what the Lord had spoken by the prophet:
M	1.23	"Behold, a virgin shall conceive and bear a son,
M	1.23	and his name shall be called Emmanuel"
M	1.24	(which means, God with us). When Joseph woke from sleep, he did as the
M	1.25	angel of the Lord commanded him; he took his wife, |but knew her not until
M	1.25	she had borne a son; and he called his name Jesus.

3. THE WISE MEN AND THE DESCENT INTO EGYPT

Matthew 2.1-23

M	2.1	Now when Jesus was born in Bethlehem of Judea in the days of Herod the
M	2.2	king, behold, wise men from the East came to Jerusalem, saying, |"Where

| M | 2.2 | is he who has been born king of the Jews? For we have seen his star in |
| M | 2.3 | the East, and have come to worship him." When Herod the king heard this, |

| M | 2.4 | he was troubled, and all Jerusalem with him; and assembling all the |
| J | 7.41 | *Others said, "This is the Christ." But some said, "Is* |

| M | 2.4 | chief priests and scribes of the people, he inquired of them where the |
| J | 7.42 | *the Christ to come from Galilee? Has not the scripture said that* the |

M	2.5	Christ was to be born. They told him, "In Bethlehem of Judea; for
L	2.11	*for to you is* born *this day in the city of David a*
J	7.42	Christ *is descended from David, and comes from* Bethlehem, *the village*

M	2.5	so it is written by the prophet:
L	2.11	*Savior, who is Christ the Lord.*
J	7.42	*where David was?"*

M	2.6	'And you, O Bethlehem, in the land of Judah,
M	2.6	are by no means least among the rulers of Judah;
M	2.6	for from you shall come a ruler
M	2.6	who will govern my people Israel.'"

M	2.7	Then Herod summoned the wise men secretly and ascertained from them
M	2.8	what time the star appeared; and he sent them to Bethlehem, saying, "Go
M	2.8	and search diligently for the child, and when you have found him bring
M	2.9	me word, that I too may come and worship him." When they had heard the
M	2.9	king they went their way; and lo, the star which they had seen in the
M	2.9	East went before them, till it came to rest over the place where the
M	2.10	child was. When they saw the star, they rejoiced exceedingly with great
M	2.11	joy; and going into the house they saw the child with Mary his mother,
M	2.11	and they fell down and worshiped him. Then, opening their treasures,
M	2.12	they offered him gifts, gold and frankincense and myrrh. And being
M	2.12	warned in a a dream not to return to Herod, they departed to their own
M	2.12	country by another way.

M	2.13	Now when they had departed, behold, an angel of the Lord appeared to
M	2.13	Joseph in a dream and said, "Rise, take the child and his mother, and
M	2.13	flee to Egypt, and remain there till I tell you; for Herod is about to
M	2.14	search for the child, to destroy him." And he rose and took the child
M	2.15	and his mother by night, and departed to Egypt, |and remained there
M	2.15	until the death of Herod. This was to fulfil what the Lord had spoken
M	2.15	by the prophet, "Out of Egypt have I called my son."

M	2.16	Then Herod, when he saw that he had been tricked by the wise men, was
M	2.16	in a furious rage, and he sent and killed all the male children in Beth-
M	2.16	lehem and in all that region who were two years old or under, according
M	2.17	to the time which he had ascertained from the wise men. Then was ful-
M	2.17	filled what was spoken by the prophet Jeremiah:

M	2.18	"A voice was heard in Ramah,
M	2.18	wailing and loud lamentation,
M	2.18	Rachel weeping for her children;
M	2.18	she refused to be consoled,
M	2.18	because they were no more."

M	2.19	But when Herod died, behold, an angel of the Lord appeared in a dream
M	2.20	to Joseph in Egypt, saying, |"Rise, take the child and his mother, and
M	2.20	go to the land of Israel, for those who sought the child's life are
M	2.21	dead." And he rose and took the child and his mother, and went to the
M	2.22	land of Israel. But when he heard that Archelaus reigned over Judea in

4

```
M    2.22    place of his father Herod, he was afraid to go there, and being warned
   L  2.39         And when they had performed everything according to the law of the


M    2.23    in a dream he   withdrew   to the district of Galilee.  And he went and
   L  2.39    Lord,        they returned into              Galilee,


M    2.23    dwelt in a        city called Nazareth, that what was spoken by the
   L  2.40         to their own city,          Nazareth.  And the child grew and


M    2.23    prophets might be fulfilled, "He shall be called a Nazarene."
   L  2.40    became strong, filled with wisdom; and the favor of God was upon him.
```

4. JOHN THE BAPTIST

Matthew 3.1-12

```
M    3.1     In    those      days
L    3.1     In    the fifteenth year of the reign of Tiberius Caesar, Pontius Pilate
   M  4.17    From that         time


   L  3.1    being governor of Judea, and Herod being tetrarch of Galilee, and his
   L  3.1    brother Philip tetrarch of the region of Ituraea and Trachonitis, and
   L  3.2    Lysanias tetrarch of Abilene, |in the high-priesthood of Annas and


M    3.1                              came                    John the Baptist,
Mk   1.4                                                      John the baptizer
L    3.2     Caiaphas, the word of God came          to John the son of
   M  4.17                                                  Jesus began to
   M  10.7                                                            And
   J  1.6         There was a man sent from God, whose name was John.
   J  1.19        And this is the testimony          of John, when the


M    3.1     preaching in the wilderness                        of
Mk   1.4     appeared  in the wilderness,
L    3.3     Zechariah in the wilderness; and he went into all the region about the
   M  4.17    preach,
   M  10.7    preach    as you go,
   J  1.19    Jews sent priests and Levites from Jerusalem to ask him, "Who are you?"


M    3.2     Judea,                    "Repent,    for the kingdom of heaven is
Mk   1.4              preaching a baptism of repentance for the forgiveness of sins.
L    3.3     Jordan, preaching a baptism of repentance for the forgiveness of sins.
   M  4.17    saying,                   "Repent,    for the kingdom of heaven is
   M  10.7    saying,                              'The kingdom of heaven is


M    3.3     at hand."  For this is he who was spoken of                by
Mk   1.2               As  it  is           written              in
L    3.4               As  it  is           written in the book of the words of
J    1.23b             as
   M  4.17    at hand."
   M  10.7    at hand.'


M    3.3     the prophet Isaiah when he said,
Mk   1.2     Isaiah the prophet,
L    3.4     Isaiah the prophet,
J    1.23a   the prophet Isaiah           said."  He said, "I am
```

```
Mk   1.2              "Behold, I send my messenger before thy face,
Mk   1.2               who shall prepare thy way;


M    3.3              "The voice of one crying in the wilderness:
Mk   1.3               the voice of one crying in the wilderness:
L    3.4              "The voice of one crying in the wilderness:
J    1.23a            the voice of one crying in the wilderness,


M    3.3              Prepare        the way of the Lord,
Mk   1.3              Prepare        the way of the Lord,
L    3.4              Prepare        the way of the Lord,
J    1.23a            'Make straight the way of the Lord,'


M    3.3              make his paths straight."
Mk   1.3              make his paths straight--"
L    3.4              make his paths straight.


L    3.5              Every valley shall be filled,
L    3.5              and every mountain and hill shall be brought low,
L    3.5              and the crooked shall be made straight,
L    3.5              and the rough ways shall be made smooth;
L    3.6              and all flesh shall see the salvation of God."


M    3.4              Now John wore a garment of camel's hair, and     a leather girdle around
Mk   1.6              Now John was  clothed with camel's hair, and had a leather girdle around


M    3.5              his waist; and his food was locusts and wild honey.  Then      went out
Mk   1.5              his waist, and        ate     locusts and wild honey.  And there went out
J    1.24                                                                   Now they had been


M    3.5              to him Jerusalem and all           Judea  and all the region about
Mk   1.5              to him              all the country of Judea, and all the people of
J    1.25            sent from the Pharisees.                            They asked


M    3.6              the Jordan, |and they were baptized by him in the river Jordan, confessing
Mk   1.5              Jerusalem;  |and they were baptized by him in the river Jordan, confessing
J    1.25            him, "Then why are   you baptizing, if you are neither the Christ, nor


M    3.6              their sins.
Mk   1.5              their sins.
J    1.25            Elijah, nor the prophet?"


M    3.7              But when he saw many of the Pharisees and Sadducees coming for
L    3.7              He said therefore    to the multitudes          that came   out to be


M    3.7              baptism, he said to them, "You brood of vipers!  Who warned you to flee
L    3.7              baptized by him,         "You brood of vipers!  Who warned you to flee


M    3.8,9            from the wrath to come?  Bear fruit  that befits repentance, |and do not
L    3.8              from the wrath to come?  Bear fruits that befit  repentance,  and do not


M    3.9              presume to say to yourselves, 'We have          Abraham as our
L    3.8              begin   to say to yourselves, 'We have          Abraham as our
J    8.33            They answered him, "We are descendants of Abraham, and have
J    8.39            They answered him,                        "Abraham is our
```

6

```
M    3.9      father'; for I tell you, God is able from these stones to raise up
L    3.8      father'; for I tell you, God is able from these stones to raise up
  J  8.33     never been in bondage to any one. How is it that you say, 'You will
  J  8.39     father."                        Jesus said to them, "If you were


M    3.10     children to Abraham.  Even now the axe is laid to the root of the trees;
L    3.9      children to Abraham.  Even now the axe is laid to the root of the trees;
  J  8.33     be made free'?"
  J  8.39     Abraham's children, you would do what Abraham did,


M    3.10     every tree therefore that does not bear good fruit is cut down and
L    3.9      every tree therefore that does not bear good fruit is cut down and
  M  7.19     Every tree          that does not bear good fruit is cut down and


M    3.10     thrown into the fire.
L    3.9      thrown into the fire."
  M  7.19     thrown into the fire.


  L  3.10,11  And the multitudes asked him, "What then shall we do?" And he answered
  L  3.11     them, "He who has two coats, let him share with him who has none; and he
  L  3.12     who has food, let him do likewise." Tax collectors also came to be bap-
  L  3.13     tized, and said to him, "Teacher, what shall we do?" And he said to them,
  L  3.14     "Collect no more than is appointed you." Soldiers also asked him, "And
  L  3.14     we, what shall we do?" And he said to them, "Rob no one by violence or
  L  3.14     by false accusation, and be content with your wages."


  L  3.15        As the people were in expectation, and all men questioned in their
  L  3.15     hearts concerning John, whether perhaps he were the Christ,


M    3.11                                               "I    baptize  you with water
Mk   1.7a,8a    And he    preached, saying, |I have baptized you with water;
L    3.16                 John answered them all, "I    baptize  you with water;
J    1.26               John answered them, "I    baptize    with water;
J    1.33     I myself did not know him; but he who sent me to baptize    with water


M    3.11     for repentance,                                       but he
Mk   1.7b                                        "After me comes he
L    3.16                                                           but he
J    1.15     (John bore witness to him, and cried, "This was he of whom I said, 'He
J    1.27     but among you stands one whom you do not know,        |even he
J    1.33     said to me,                                           'He on


M    3.11     who is coming after me is mightier than I,         whose sandals
Mk   1.7b     who         is mightier than I, the thong of whose sandals
L    3.16     who is mightier than I is coming,      the thong of whose sandals
J    1.15     who    comes after me ranks before me, for he was before me.'")
J    1.27     who    comes after me,                the thong of whose sandal
J    1.33     whom you see the Spirit descend and remain,


M    3.11     I am not worthy to                carry;    he will baptize you with
Mk   1.8b     I am not worthy to stoop down and untie. |but he will baptize you with
L    3.16     I am not worthy to           untie;       he will baptize you with
J    1.27     I am not worthy to           untie."
J    1.33                                      this is he who baptizes    with


M    3.12     the Holy Spirit and with fire.  His winnowing fork is in his hand, and
Mk   1.8b     the Holy Spirit."
L    3.17     the Holy Spirit and with fire.  His winnowing fork is in his hand,
J    1.33     the Holy Spirit.'
```

7

```
M    3.12    he will clear his threshing floor  and    gather his wheat into the
L    3.17             to clear his threshing floor, and to gather the wheat into his


M    3.12    granary, but the chaff he will burn with unquenchable fire."
L    3.17    granary, but the chaff he will burn with unquenchable fire."
```

5. THE BAPTISM OF JESUS

Matthew 3.13-17

```
M    3.13    Then          Jesus came from              Galilee to the Jordan to
Mk   1.9     In those days Jesus came from Nazareth of Galilee


M    3.14    John, to be baptized by him.  John would have prevented him, saying, "I
M    3.15    need to be baptized by you, and do you come to me?"  But Jesus answered
M    3.15    him, "Let it be so now; for thus it is fitting for us to fulfil all


M    3.16    righteousness."  Then he consented. |And when Jesus          was
Mk   1.9                                          and                    was
L    3.21    Now when all the people were baptized, and when Jesus also had been
 J   1.33                   I myself did not know him; but he who sent me to


M    3.16    baptized,                                he went up  immediately from
Mk   1.10    baptized by John in the Jordan.  And when he came up out of the water,
L    3.21    baptized                          and          was praying,
 J   1.33    baptize with water said to me,


M    3.16    the water, and behold, the heavens were opened  and he saw the
Mk   1.10    immediately     he saw  the heavens     opened  and         the
L    3.22                            the heaven was  opened, |and         the Holy
 J   1.32                      And John bore witness, "I   saw the
 J   1.33                      'He on whom  you see the


M    3.16    Spirit of God descending                  like a dove,
Mk   1.10    Spirit        descending upon him         like a dove;
L    3.22    Spirit        descended  upon him in bodily form, as a dove,
 J   1.32    Spirit        descend                      as a dove from heaven,
 J   1.33    Spirit        descend
 M  17.5             He was still speaking, when lo, a bright cloud
Mk   9.7                                       And     a        cloud
 L   9.34            As he           said this,        a        cloud came


M    3.16    and     alighting on him;
 J   1.32    and it remained  on him.
 J   1.33    and     remain,
 J  12.28                                       Father, glorify thy name."
 M  17.5         overshadowed them,
Mk   9.7         overshadowed them,
 L   9.34    and overshadowed them; and they were afraid as they entered the cloud.


M    3.17    and lo, a voice     from     heaven, saying,   "This is  my beloved
Mk   1.11    and     a voice came from    heaven,           "Thou art my beloved
L    3.22    and     a voice came from    heaven,           "Thou art my beloved
 J   1.33                                          this is he who
 J   1.34    And I have seen         and have borne witness that this is  the
 J  12.28    Then    a voice came from      heaven,          "I have glorified it,
 M  17.5     and     a voice      from  the cloud  said,     "This is  my beloved
Mk   9.7     and     a voice came out of the cloud,          "This is  my beloved
 L   9.35    And     a voice came out of the cloud, saying,  "This is  my
```

8

```
M    3.17     Son, with whom I am well pleased."
Mk   1.11     Son; with thee I am well pleased."
L    3.22     Son; with thee I am well pleased."
  J  1.33     baptizes with the Holy Spirit.'
  J  1.34     Son of God."
  J 12.28     and I will glorify it again."
M   17.5      Son, with whom I am well pleased;  listen to him."
  Mk  9.7     Son;                               listen to him."
  L   9.35    Son, my Chosen;                    listen to him!"
```

6. THE TEMPTATION

Matthew 4.1-11

```
M    4.1        Then Jesus                                                was
L    4.1        And  Jesus, full of the Holy Spirit, returned from the Jordan, and was


M    4.1        led up by the Spirit                        into the wilderness
Mk   1.12,13         The Spirit immediately drove him out into the wilderness.  And
L    4.2        led   by the Spirit         |for forty days in   the wilderness,


M    4.2                                    to be tempted by the devil.  And he
Mk   1.13       he was in the wilderness forty days, tempted by    Satan;
L    4.2                                    tempted by the devil.  And he


M    4.2        fasted         forty days and forty nights, and afterward
L    4.2        ate nothing in those days;          and when they were ended,


M    4.3        he was hungry.  And the tempter came and said to him, "If you are the
L    4.3        he was hungry.      The devil       said to him, "If you are the


M    4.4        Son of God, command these stones to become loaves of bread."  But he
L    4.4        Son of God, command this  stone  to become        bread."  And Jesus


M    4.4        answered,    "It is written,
L    4.4        answered him, "It it written,


M    4.4            'Man shall not live by bread alone,
L    4.4            'Man shall not live by bread alone.'"


M    4.4                'but by every word that proceeds from the mouth of God.'"


M    4.5        Then the devil took him to the holy city, and set him on the pinnacle of
L    4.9        And      he   took him to    Jerusalem, and set him on the pinnacle of


M    4.6        the temple, |and said to him, "If you are the Son of God, throw yourself
L    4.9        the temple,  and said to him, "If you are the Son of God, throw yourself


M    4.6        down;           for it is written,
L    4.10       down from here; for it is written,


M    4.6            'He will give his angels charge of you,'
L    4.10           'He will give his angels charge of you, to guard you,'
```

```
M    4.6      and
L    4.11    | and


M    4.6                'On their hands they will bear you up,
L    4.11               'On their hands they will bear you up,


M    4.6                   lest you strike your foot against a stone.'"
L    4.11                  lest you strike your foot against a stone.'"


M    4.7        Jesus said to  him, "Again it is written, 'You shall not tempt the
L    4.12   And Jesus answered him,          "It is said,   'You shall not tempt the


M    4.8    Lord your God.'"  Again, the devil took him to a very high mountain, and
L    4.5    Lord your God.'"  And    the devil took him up,                      and


M    4.8    showed him all  the kingdoms    of    the  world and the glory of them;
L    4.5    showed him all  the kingdoms    of    the  world in a moment of time,
  J  18.36  Jesus answered, "My kingship is not of    this world;


  J  18.36                  if my kingship were   of    this world, my servants would
  J  18.36  fight, that I might not be handed over to the Jews;
  J  18.36                  but my kingship is not from the  world."


M    4.9    and he said to him, "All these I will give you,
L    4.6    and     said to him, "To you   I will give all this authority and their


M    4.9                                                                          if
L    4.7    glory; for it has been delivered to me, and I give it to whom I will. If


M    4.10   you      will fall down and worship me."                         Then
L    4.8    you, then, will            worship me, it shall all be yours." And


M    4.10   Jesus said  to him, "Begone, Satan!  for it is written,
L    4.8    Jesus answered him,          "It is written,


M    4.10               'You shall worship the Lord your God
L    4.8                'You shall worship the Lord your God,


M    4.10               and him only shall you serve.'"
L    4.8                and him only shall you serve.'"


M    4.11   Then the devil                             left      him, and
Mk   1.13                                   and he was with the wild beasts; and
L    4.13   And when the devil had ended every temptation, he departed from him until
  J  1.51   And he said to him, "Truly, truly, I say to you, you will see heaven


M    4.11   behold,      angels came and ministered to him.
Mk   1.13            the angels        ministered to him.
L    4.13   an opportune time.
  J  1.51   opened, and the angels of God ascending and descending upon the Son of
  J  1.51   man."
```

Matthew 4.12-17

```
M     4.12     Now when he heard that
Mk    1.14     Now after
L     4.14     And
J     1.43a    The next day
  M   14.3     For Herod
  L   3.19     But Herod the tetrarch, who had been reproved by him for Herodias, his
  J   4.43     After the two days


  L   3.20     brother's wife, and for all the evil things that Herod had done, |added


M     4.12                                                John had been arrested, he
Mk    1.14                                                John     was  arrested, Jesus
L     4.14                                                                       Jesus
J     1.43a                                                                      Jesus decided
  M   14.3                                 had seized John and bound him and put him in
  L   3.20     this to them all, that he shut up John               in
  J   4.3                                                                   he left Judea
  J   4.43                                                                  he


M     4.13     withdrew                              into Galilee; and leaving Nazareth
Mk    1.14     came                                  into Galilee,
Mk    1.21                                                          And
L     4.14     returned in the power of the Spirit into Galilee,
L     4.31                                                          And
J     1.43a    to  go                                to Galilee.
  M   14.3     prison, for the sake of Herodias, his brother Philip's wife;
  L   3.20     prison.
  J   2.12                                                       After this
  J   4.3      and departed again                   to Galilee.
  J   4.43        departed                           to Galilee.


M     4.13     he   went and dwelt in   Capernaum by the sea, in the territory of
Mk    1.21     they went            into Capernaum;
L     4.31     he   went down          to Capernaum, a city of Galilee.
  J   2.12     he   went down          to Capernaum, with his mother and his brothers


M     4.14     Zebulun and Naphtali, |that what was spoken by the prophet Isaiah might
  J   2.12     and his disciples; and there they stayed for a few days.


M     4.14     be fulfilled:
M     4.15         "The land of Zebulun and the land of Naphtali,
M     4.15          toward the sea, across the Jordan,
M     4.15          Galilee of the Gentiles--
M     4.16          the people who sat in darkness
M     4.16              have seen a great light,
M     4.16              and for those who sat in the region
M     4.16                      and shadow of death
M     4.16          light has dawned."


M     4.17     From that time               Jesus           began to preach,
Mk    1.14                                                           preaching
Mk    1.21     and immediately on the sabbath he entered the synagogue and taught.
L     4.14     and a report concerning him went out through all the surrounding
  M   3.1      In those days came            John the Baptist,        preaching
  M   10.7     And                                                    preach
  L   4.43     but                           he said to them,   "I must preach
```

11

```
M    4.17                          saying, "Repent,                for the kingdom
Mk   1.15    the gospel of God, |and saying, "The time is fulfilled, and the kingdom
L    4.15    country.  And he taught in their synagogues, being glorified by all.
 M   3.2     in the wilderness of Judea,       "Repent,                for the kingdom
 M   10.7    as you go,              saying,                          'The kingdom
 L   4.43    the good news                                        of  the kingdom
```

```
M    4.17    of heaven is at hand."
Mk   1.15    of God      is at hand; repent, and believe in the gospel."
 M   3.2     of heaven is at hand."
 M   10.7    of heaven is at hand.'
 L   4.43    of God to the other cities also; for I was sent for this purpose."
```

8. THE FIRST DISCIPLES

Matthew 4.18-22

```
M    4.18    As                                                          he
Mk   1.16    And
L    5.1     While the people pressed upon him to hear the word of God, he was
```

```
M    4.18    walked      by the Sea of Galilee,      he saw two brothers,
Mk   1.16    passing along by the Sea of Galilee,      he saw
L    5.2     standing      by the lake of Gennesaret.  And he saw two boats by the
 J   1.41                              He first found his brother
```

```
M    4.18    Simon who is called
Mk   1.16    Simon
L    5.2     lake;
 J   1.41    Simon, and said to him, "We have found the Messiah" (which means Christ).
```

```
 J   1.42    He brought him to Jesus.  Jesus looked at him, and said, "So you are
 J   1.42    Simon the son of John?  You shall be called Cephas" (which means
```

```
M    4.18    Peter and                                            Andrew
Mk   1.16          and                                            Andrew
L    5.2                                              but the fishermen
 J   1.40    Peter). One of the two who heard John speak, and followed him, was Andrew,
```

```
M    4.18              his brother,      casting a    net into the sea; for they
Mk   1.16              the brother of Simon casting a    net in   the sea; for they
L    5.3     had gone out of them and were washing their nets.  Getting into one of
 J   1.40    Simon Peter's brother.
```

```
M    4.18    were fishermen.
Mk   1.16    were fishermen.
 L   5.3     the boats, which was Simon's, he asked him to put out a little from the
```

```
 L   5.4     land.  And he sat down and taught the people from the boat. |And when he
 L   5.4     had ceased speaking, he said to Simon, "Put out into the deep and let down
 L   5.5     your nets for a catch."  And Simon answered, "Master, we toiled all night
 L   5.6     and took nothing!  But at your word I will let down the nets." |And when
 L   5.6     they had done this, they enclosed a great shoal of fish; and as their nets
 L   5.7     were breaking, |they beckoned to their partners in the other boat to come
 L   5.7     and help them.  And they came and filled both the boats, so that they be-
 L   5.8     gan to sink.  But when Simon Peter saw it, he fell down at Jesus' knees,
 L   5.9     saying, "Depart from me, for I am a sinful man, O Lord."  For he was as-
 L   5.9     tonished, and all that were with him, at the catch of fish which they had
```

M	4.19		And he	said to them,	"Follow me, and I will make you
Mk	1.17		And Jesus	said to them,	"Follow me and I will make you become
L	5.10b	taken;	And Jesus	said to Simon,	"Do not be afraid; henceforth you will be

M	4.20	fishers of men."	Immediately they left their nets and followed him.	
Mk	1.18	fishers of men."	And immediately they left their nets and followed him.	
L	5.10b	catching men."		

M	4.21	And going on from there	he saw two other brothers, James	the
Mk	1.19	And going on a little farther,	he saw	James the
L	5.10a		and so also were	James and John,

M	4.21	son of Zebedee and John his brother,	in the boat with Zebedee
Mk	1.19	son of Zebedee and John his brother, who were in their boat	
L	5.10a	sons of Zebedee, who were partners with Simon.	

M	4.21	their father,	mending their nets,	and he called them.
Mk	1.20		mending the nets.	And immediately he called them;
L	5.11			And when they had brought their

M	4.22	Immediately	they left the boat and their father,
Mk	1.20	and	they left their father Zebedee in the boat
L	5.11	boats to land,	they left everything

M	4.22		and followed him.
Mk	1.20	with the hired servants,	and followed him.
L	5.11		and followed him.

9. PREACHING AND HEALING IN GALILEE

Matthew 4.23-25

M	4.23	And	he	went about
Mk	1.39	And	he	went throughout
L	4.44	And	he	was
M	*9.35*	*And*	*Jesus*	*went about*
Mk	*1.14*	*Now after John was arrested,*	*Jesus*	*came into*
Mk	*6.6b*	*And*	*he*	*went about among*
L	*4.14*	*And*	*Jesus*	*returned in the power of the Spirit*
L	*4.15*	*And*	*he*	
L	*5.17a*	*On one of those days,*	*as he*	*was*
L	*8.1a*	*Soon afterward*	*he*	*went on through*

M	4.23	all	Galilee,	teaching	in their synagogues and preaching
Mk	1.39	all	Galilee,	preaching	in their synagogues
L	4.44			preaching	in the synagogues of Judea.
M	*9.35*	*all the cities and villages,*		*teaching*	*in their synagogues and preaching*
Mk	*1.14*		*Galilee,*		*preaching*
Mk	*6.6b*	*the*	*villages*	*teaching.*	
L	*4.14*	*into*	*Galilee,*		
L	*4.15*			*taught*	*in their synagogues, being*
L	*5.17a*			*teaching,*	*there were Pharisees and teachers*
L	*8.1a*	*cities and villages,*			*preaching*

```
M     4.23                    the gospel      of the kingdom  and healing every disease and
  M   9.35                    the gospel      of the kingdom, and healing every disease and
  Mk  1.14                    the gospel      of      God,
  L   4.15    glorified by all.
  L   5.17a   of the law sitting by,
  L   8.1a    and bringing the good news of the kingdom of God.


M     4.24    every infirmity among the people.  So his fame                    spread
  M   9.35    every infirmity.
  L   4.14                                                and a report concerning him went out


M     4.24    throughout all Syria, and they brought him all the sick, those afflicted
  L   4.14    through     all the surrounding country.
  L   6.18                                              and those who were troubled


M     4.24    with various diseases and pains, demoniacs, epileptics, and paralytics,
  Mk  1.39                    and casting out demons.
  L   5.17c                             and the power of the Lord was with
  L   6.17a              And he came down with them and stood on a level
  L   6.17b                                      who came to hear him
  L   6.18    with                      unclean spirits
  L   6.19      And all the crowd sought to touch him, for power came forth from him


M     4.25    and he           healed them.          And   great crowds
  Mk  3.7     Jesus withdrew with his disciples to the sea, and a great multitude
  L   5.17b        him to     heal.                              who had come
  L   6.17a   place,  with a great crowd of his disciples  and a great multitude
  L   6.17b   and     to be   healed of their diseases;
  L   6.18             were cured.
  L   6.19   and              healed them all.


M     4.25    followed him      from Galilee and the Decapolis and Jerusalem
  Mk  3.8     from Galilee           followed;       also from    Judea      |and
  L   5.17b   from every village of Galilee          and        Judea and from
  L   6.17a   of people                              from all Judea and


M     4.25    and Judea        and from beyond the Jordan.
  Mk  3.8     Jerusalem and Idumea and from beyond the Jordan and from about Tyre and
  L   5.17b   Jerusalem;
  L   6.17a   Jerusalem                           and the seacoast of     Tyre and


  Mk  3.8     Sidon a great multitude, hearing all that he did, came to him.
  L   6.17a   Sidon,
```

10. FIRST DISCOURSE: SERMON ON THE MOUNT

Matthew 5.1-7.29

a. Setting

Matthew 5.1-2

```
M     5.1     Seeing the crowds, he   went up                    on the mountain,
  L   6.17    And                 he   came down with them and stood on a level place,
  J   6.3                     Jesus went up                      on the mountain,
```

M	5.1	and when he sat down his disciples came to him.
L	6.17	with a great crowd of his disciples and a great multitude of people
J	6.3	and there sat down with his disciples.

L	6.17	*from all Judea and Jerusalem and the seacoast of Tyre and Sidon, who came*
L	6.18	*to hear him and to be healed of their diseases; and those who were*
L	6.19	*troubled with unclean spirits were cured. And all the crowd sought to*
L	6.19	*touch him, for power came forth from him and healed them all.*

M	5.2	And he opened his mouth and taught them, saying:
L	6.20	And he lifted up his eyes on his disciples, and said:

b. The Beatitudes

Matthew 5.3-12

M	5.3	"Blessed are the poor in spirit, for theirs is the kingdom of heaven.
L	6.20	"Blessed are you poor, for yours is the kingdom of God.

M	5.4	"Blessed are those who mourn, for they shall be comforted.
L	6.21b	"Blessed are you that weep now, for you shall laugh.

M	5.5	"Blessed are the meek, for they shall inherit the earth.

M	5.6	"Blessed are those who hunger and thirst for righteousness,
L	6.21a	"Blessed are you that hunger now,

M	5.6	for they shall be satisfied.
L	6.21a	for you shall be satisfied.

M	5.7	"Blessed are the merciful, for they shall obtain mercy.
L	6.24	*"But woe to you that are rich, for you have received your consolation.*

M	5.8	"Blessed are the pure in heart, for they shall see God.
L	6.25	*"Woe to you that are full now, for you shall hunger.*

M	5.9	"Blessed are the peacemakers, for they shall be called sons of God.
L	6.25	*"Woe to you that laugh now, for you shall mourn and weep.*

M	5.10	"Blessed are those who are persecuted for righteousness' sake,
L	6.26	*"Woe to you, when all men speak well of you,*

M	5.10	for theirs is the kingdom of heaven.
L	6.26	*for so their fathers did to the false prophets.*

M	5.11	"Blessed are you when men
L	6.22	"Blessed are you when men hate you, and when they exclude you and

M	5.11	revile you and persecute you and utter all kinds of evil against you
L	6.22	revile you, and cast out your name as evil,

15

```
M   5.12    falsely on my account.                              Rejoice              and be
L   6.23             on    account of the Son of man! Rejoice in that day, and leap


M   5.12          glad, for        your reward is great in heaven, for so
L   6.23    for joy,  for behold, your reward is great in heaven; for so their


M   5.12    men      persecuted the prophets who were before you.
L   6.23    fathers did    to the prophets.
```

c. Salt and Light

Matthew 5.13-16

```
M   5.13         "You           are the salt  of the earth;         but if
Mk  9.49,50  For every one will be       salted with fire.  Salt is good; but if the
L   14.34                                   "Salt is good; but if


M   5.13    salt has lost its taste,   how shall its saltness be restored? It is
Mk  9.50    salt has lost its saltness, how will  you season it?            Have
L   14.35    salt has lost its taste,   how shall its saltness be restored? It is


M   5.13    no longer good for anything          except to be thrown out and
Mk  9.50    salt in yourselves, and be at peace with one another."
L   14.35       fit neither for the land nor for the dunghill; men throw it away.


M   5.13    trodden under foot by men.
L   14.35    He who has ears to hear, let him hear."
J    8.12                                  Again Jesus spoke to them, saying,


M    5.14       "You are the light of the world.  A city set on a hill cannot be hid.
Mk   4.22                                        For there is nothing hid,
L    8.17                                        For       nothing is hid
J    8.12       "I   am  the light of the world; he who follows me will not walk in


Mk   4.22    except     to be made manifest; nor is anything secret, except
L    8.17    that shall not be made manifest, nor  anything secret  that shall not
J    8.12    darkness, but will have the light of life."


Mk   4.23              to come to light.  If any man has ears to hear, let him hear."
L    8.18    be known and come to light.  Take heed then how you hear; for to him who


L    8.18    has will more be given, and from him who has not, even what he thinks
L    8.18    that he has will be taken away."


M    5.15    Nor do men      light   a lamp         and put    it
Mk   4.21    And he said to them, "Is a lamp brought in to be put
L    8.16    "No     one after lighting a lamp             covers it
L    11.33   "No     one after lighting a lamp             puts  it in a cellar


M    5.15       under a bushel,                    but       on a stand, and
Mk   4.21       under a bushel, or       under a bed, and not  on a stand?
L    8.16       with  a vessel, or puts it under a bed, but puts it on a stand, that
L    11.33   or under a bushel,                       but       on a stand, that
```

M	5.16	it gives light to all in the house. Let your light so shine before men,
L	8.16	those who enter may see the light.
L	11.33	those who enter may see the light.

M	5.16	that they may see your good works and give glory to your Father who is
M	5.16	in heaven.

d. The Old Law and the New

Matthew 5.17-48

M	5.17	"Think not that I have come to abolish the law and the prophets; I have
L	16.16	"The law and the prophets were

M	5.17	come not to abolish them but to fulfil them.
L	16.16	until John; *since then the good news of the kingdom of God is preached,*

M	5.18	For truly, I say to you, till
L	16.17	*and every one enters it violently.* But it is easier for
M	*24.34*	Truly, I say to you,
M	*13.30*	Truly, I say to you,
L	*21.32*	Truly, I say to you,

M	5.18	heaven and earth pass away, not an iota, not a dot, will
L	16.17	heaven and earth to pass away, than for one dot
M	*24.34*	*this generation will not* pass away
Mk	*13.30*	*this generation will not* pass away
L	*21.32*	*this generation will not* pass away
M	*24.35*	Heaven and earth will pass away, *but my words* will
Mk	*13.31*	Heaven and earth will pass away, *but my words* will
L	*21.33*	Heaven and earth will pass away, *but my words* will

M	5.18	pass from the law until all is accomplished.
L	16.17	of the law to become void.
M	*24.34*	*till* all *these things take place.*
Mk	*13.30*	*before* all *these things take place.*
L	*21.32*	*till* all *has taken place.*
M	*24.35*	*not* pass *away.*
Mk	*13.31*	*not* pass *away.*
L	*21.33*	*not* pass *away.*

M	5.19	Whoever then relaxes one of the least of these commandments and teaches
M	5.19	men so, shall be called least in the kingdom of heaven; but he who does
M	5.19	them and teaches them shall be called great in the kingdom of heaven.
M	5.20	For I tell you, unless your righteousness exceeds that of the scribes
M	5.20	and Pharisees, you will never enter the kingdom of heaven.

M	5.21	"You have heard that it was said to the men of old, 'You shall not
M	5.22	kill; and whoever kills shall be liable to judgment.' But I say to you
M	5.22	that every one who is angry with his brother shall be liable to judgment;
M	5.22	whoever insults his brother shall be liable to the council, and whoever
M	5.22	says, 'You fool!' shall be liable to the hell of fire.

M	5.23	So if you are offering your gift at the altar, and there remember that
Mk	11.25	And whenever you stand praying, forgive, if

17

M	5.24	your brother has something against you, |leave your gift there before
Mk	11.25	you have anything against any one; so that your Father also who

M	5.24	the altar and go; first be reconciled to your brother, and then come and
Mk	11.25	is in heaven may forgive you your trespasses."
L	12.57	*"And why do you not judge for yourselves*

M	5.25	offer your gift. Make friends quickly with your accuser, while you are
L	12.58	*what is right?* As you go with your accuser

M	5.25	going with him to court,
L	12.58	before the magistrate, make an effort to settle with him

M	5.25	lest your accuser hand you over to the judge, and the judge
L	12.58	on the way, lest he drag you to the judge, and the judge

M	5.25	to the guard, and you be put in prison;
L	12.58	hand you over to the officer, and the officer put you in prison.

M	5.26	truly, I say to you, you will never get out till you have paid the
L	12.59	I tell you, you will never get out till you have paid the very

M	5.26	last penny.
L	12.59	last copper."

M	5.27	"You have heard that it was said, 'You shall not commit adultery.'
M	5.28	But I say to you that every one who looks at a woman lustfully has

M	5.29	already committed adultery with her in his heart. If your right eye
Mk	9.47	And if your eye
M	*18.9*	*And if your eye*

M	5.29	causes you to sin, pluck it out and throw it away; it is better that you
Mk	9.47	causes you to sin, pluck it out; it is better for you
M	*18.9*	causes you to sin, pluck it out and throw it away; it is better for you

M	5.29	lose one of your members than that your whole body be thrown
Mk	9.47	to enter the kingdom of God with one eye than with two eyes to be thrown
M	*18.9*	*to enter life with one eye than with two eyes to* be thrown

M	5.29	into hell.
Mk	9.48	into hell, where their worm does not die, and the fire is not quenched.
M	*18.9*	into *the* hell *of fire.*

M	5.30	And if your right hand causes you to sin, cut it off and
Mk	9.43	And if your hand causes you to sin, cut it off;
M	*18.8*	And if your hand *or your foot* causes you to sin, cut it off and

M	5.30	throw it away; it is better that you lose one of your members than
Mk	9.43	it is better for you to enter life maimed than
M	*18.8*	throw it away; it is better *for* you *to enter life maimed or lame* than

18

```
M    5.30     that your whole body        go        into hell.
Mk   9.43     with two hands                   to go          to hell,  to the unquenchable
  M  18.8     with two hands or two feet to be thrown into              the eternal


 Mk  9.43     fire.
  M  18.8     fire.


M    5.31                                              "It was also said,
Mk   10.2     And Pharisees came up        and in order to test   him     asked,  "Is it
  M  19.3     And Pharisees came up to him and                 tested him by asking,  "Is it


M    5.31              'Whoever divorces his   wife,
Mk   10.3     lawful for a man to divorce  his   wife?" He answered them,  "What did
  M  19.3     lawful            to divorce  one's wife for any cause?"


M    5.31                                                             let
Mk   10.4     Moses command you?"  They said,              "Moses allowed a
  M  19.7                           They said to him,  "Why then did Moses command


M    5.32     him   give her a certificate of divorce.'                But
Mk   10.11    man to write    a certificate of divorce, and to put her away."  And
  M  19.9     one to give     a certificate of divorce, and to put her away?"  And


M    5.32     I  say  to you that every one who divorces his wife, except on the
Mk   10.11    he said to them,        "Whoever divorces his wife
L    16.18                       "Every one who divorces his wife
  M  19.9     I  say  to you:      whoever divorces his wife, except


M    5.32     ground of unchastity,                    makes her an adulteress;
Mk   10.11                    and marries another, commits      adultery
L    16.18                    and marries another  commits      adultery,
  M  19.9     for unchastity, and marries another, commits      adultery."


M    5.32                    and whoever marries a divorced woman
Mk   10.12    against her; and if she          divorces         her husband
L    16.18                 and he who  marries a woman divorced from her husband


M    5.32                         commits adultery.
Mk   10.12    and marries another, she commits adultery."
L    16.18                         commits adultery.


M    5.33     "Again you have heard that it was said to the men of old, 'You shall
M    5.33     not swear falsely, but shall perform to the Lord what you have sworn.'


M    5.34     But I say to you, Do not swear at all, either by heaven, for it is the
  M  23.22               and he who swears        by heaven, swears by the


M    5.35     throne of God, |or by the earth, for it is his footstool, or by Jerusalem,
  M  23.22    throne of God and by him who sits upon it.


M    5.36     for it is the city of the great King.  And do not swear by your head,
M    5.37     for you cannot make one hair white or black.  Let what you say be simply
M    5.37     'Yes' or 'No'; anything more than this comes from evil.


M    5.38     "You have heard that it was said, 'An eye for an eye and a tooth for
M    5.39     a tooth.'  But I say to you, Do not resist one who is evil.  But
```

```
M     5.39    if any one strikes you on the right cheek, turn to him the other also;
L     6.29    To him who strikes you on the        cheek, offer      the other also;


M     5.40    and if   any one would sue you and take        your coat, let him have
L     6.29    and from him who                takes away your coat  do not withhold


M     5.41         your cloak as well; and if any one forces you to go one mile, go
L     6.29    even your shirt.


M     5.42    with him two miles.  Give to      him who begs from you, and do not
L     6.30                         Give to every one who begs from you; and


M     5.42    refuse him who would borrow from you.
L     6.30         of him who      takes away your goods do not ask them again.


M     5.43    "You have heard that it was said, 'You shall love
  M  22.39              And a second is like it, You shall love
  Mk 12.31              The    second is this,  You shall love
  L  10.27              And he answered,        "You shall love the Lord your God


  L  10.27    with all your heart, and with all your soul, and with all your strength,


M     5.44                              your neighbor and hate your enemy.' But I
L     6.27                                                                   "But I
L     6.35                                                                   But
  M  22.39                      your neighbor as yourself.
  Mk 12.31                      your neighbor as yourself.' There is no
  L  10.27    and with all your mind; and your neighbor as yourself."


M     5.44    say to you,        Love your enemies
L     6.27    say to you that hear, Love your enemies,     do good to those who hate
L     6.35                         love your enemies, and do good, and lend, expecting
  Mk 12.31    other commandment greater than these."


M     5.45                        and pray for those who persecute you, |so
L     6.28    you, |bless those who curse you, pray for those who abuse    you.
L     6.35    nothing in return;      and your reward will be great,        and


M     5.45    that you may be sons of your Father who is in heaven; for he makes his
L     6.35         you will be sons of the  Most High;        for he is kind


M     5.45    sun rise on the evil     and on the good, and sends rain on the just
L     6.35         to the ungrateful and    the selfish.


M     5.46    and on the unjust.  For if you love those who love you, what reward have
L     6.32                        "If you love those who love you, what credit is


M     5.46         you? Do not even the tax collectors do the same?
L     6.32    that to you?    For even    sinners    love those who love them.


M     5.47    And if you salute  only your brethren,              what more
L     6.33    And if you do good to those    who  do good  to you,  what credit
L     6.34    And if you lend    to those from whom you hope to receive, what credit
```

20

```
M    5.48    are you doing than others?  Do not even the Gentiles do the same?  |You,
L    6.33    is  that to you?                        For even    sinners  do the same.
L    6.34    is  that to you?                            Even    sinners  lend to sinners, to


M    5.48    therefore, must be perfect,        as your heavenly Father is perfect.
L    6.34    receive as much again.
L    6.36              Be merciful, even as your              Father is merciful.
```

e. The New Righteousness

Matthew 6.1–7.23

```
M    6.1     "Beware of practicing your piety before men in order to be seen by them;
  M  23.5a                                   They do all their deeds to be seen by men;


M    6.1     for then you will have no reward from your Father who is in heaven.


M    6.2       "Thus, when you give alms, sound no trumpet before you, as the hypo-
M    6.2     crites do in the synagogues and in the streets, that they may be praised
M    6.3     by men. Truly, I say to you, they have received their reward.  |But when
M    6.3     you give alms, do not let your left hand know what your right hand is
M    6.4     doing, |so that your alms may be in secret; and your Father who sees in
M    6.4     secret will reward you.


M    6.5       "And when you pray, you must not be like the hypocrites; for they love
M    6.5     to stand and pray in the synagogues and at the street corners, that


M    6.5     they                     may be seen by men.  Truly, I say to you, they
  M  23.5a   They do all their deeds to be seen by men;


M    6.6     have received their reward.  But when you pray, go into your room and
M    6.6     shut the door and pray to your Father who is in secret; and your Father
M    6.6     who sees in secret will reward you.


M    6.7       "And in praying do not heap up empty phrases as the Gentiles do; for
M    6.8     they think that they will be heard for their many words.  Do not be like
M    6.8     them, for your Father knows what you need before you ask him.


  L  11.1     He was praying in a certain place, and when he ceased, one of his
  L  11.1     disciples said to him, "Lord, teach us to pray, as John taught his


M    6.9                                            Pray then like this:
L    11.2    disciples."  And he said to them, "When you pray, say:


M    6.9              Our Father who art in heaven,
L    11.2               "Father,


M    6.9              Hallowed be thy name.
L    11.2            hallowed be thy name.


M    6.10             Thy kingdom come.
L    11.2             Thy kingdom come.


M    6.10             Thy will be done,
M    6.10               On earth as it is in heaven.
```

```
M    6.11                    Give us this day our daily bread;
L   11.3                     Give us each day our daily bread;


M    6.12                    And forgive us our debts,
L   11.4                     And forgive us our sins,


M    6.12                        As  we also have forgiven              our debtors;
L   11.4                         for we ourselves forgive every one who is indebted to us;


M    6.13                    And lead us not into temptation,
L   11.4                     and lead us not into temptation."


M    6.13                    But deliver us from evil.


M    6.14        For if      you                forgive  men their trespasses,
Mk  11.25        And whenever you stand praying, forgive, if you have anything against


M    6.14                        your heavenly Father also              will forgive
Mk  11.25        any one; so that your           Father also who is in heaven may  forgive
 M  18.35            So also my  heavenly Father                        will do to


M    6.15                    you;              but if you do not forgive
Mk  11.26                    you your trespasses."  But if you do not forgive,
 M  18.35        every one of you,                  if you do not forgive your


M    6.15        men their trespasses, neither will your Father              forgive
Mk  11.26                              neither will your Father who is in heaven forgive
 M  18.35        brother from your heart."


M    6.15        your trespasses.
Mk  11.26        your trespasses."


M    6.16         "And when you fast, do not look dismal, like the hypocrites, for they
M    6.16        disfigure their faces that their fasting may be seen by men.  Truly, I
M    6.17        say to you, they have received their reward.  But when you fast, anoint
M    6.18        your head and wash your face, |that your fasting may not be seen by men
M    6.18        but by your Father who is in secret; and your Father who sees in secret
M    6.18        will reward you.


M    6.19         "Do not lay up for yourselves treasures on earth,
 L  12.32         "Fear not, little flock, for it is your Father's good pleasure to give
 M  19.21                                                     Jesus
Mk  10.21                                        And       Jesus looking upon
 L  18.22                                        And when Jesus heard it,


M    6.19                     where moth and rust consume and where thieves break in
L   12.33        you the kingdom.    Sell your possessions, and give alms; provide yourselves
 M  19.21                        said to him, "If you would be perfect, go, sell     what
Mk  10.21        him loved him, and said to him, "You lack     one thing; go, sell     what
 L  18.22                    he said to him, "One thing you still lack.    Sell all that


M    6.20        and steal,            |but lay up for yourselves     treasures in
L   12.33        with purses             that do not grow old,  with a treasure  in
 M  19.21        you possess and give    to the poor, and you will have treasure  in
Mk  10.21        you have,    and give    to the poor, and you will have treasure  in
 L  18.22        you have    and distribute to the poor, and you will have treasure  in
```

22

```
M    6.20          heaven,                              where neither moth nor rust consumes and
L    12.33    the heavens that does not fail, where no        thief approaches          and
  M  19.21          heaven; and come, follow me."
  Mk 10.21          heaven; and come, follow me."
  L  18.22          heaven; and come, follow me."


M    6.21     where thieves do not break in and steal.  For where your treasure is,
L    12.34    no    moth    destroys.                    For where your treasure is,


M    6.21     there will your heart be also.
L    12.34    there will your heart be also.


M    6.22        "The eye is the lamp of the body.  So, if  your eye is sound, your
L    11.34        Your eye is the lamp of your body;       when your eye is sound, your


M    6.23     whole body will be full of light; but if your eye is not sound, your
L    11.34    whole body      is full of light; but when   it is not sound, your


M    6.23     whole body will be full of darkness.  If then                    the
L    11.35          body   is full of darkness.  Therefore be careful lest the


M    6.23     light in you is darkness, how great is the darkness!
L    11.36    light in you be darkness.  If then your whole body is full of light,


  L  11.36    having no part dark, it will be wholly bright, as when a lamp with its
  L  11.36    rays gives you light."


M    6.24        "No one    can serve two masters; for either he will hate the one and
L    16.13        No servant can serve two masters; for either he will hate the one and


M    6.24     love the other, or he will be devoted to the one and despise the other.
L    16.13    love the other, or he will be devoted to the one and despise the other.


M    6.24     You cannot serve God and mammon.
L    16.13    You cannot serve God and mammon."


M    6.25                               "Therefore I tell you, do not be anxious
L    12.22    And he said to his disciples, "Therefore I tell you, do not be anxious


M    6.25     about your life, what you shall eat or what you shall drink, nor about
L    12.22    about your life, what you shall eat,                       nor about


M    6.25     your body, what you shall put on.  Is not life more than food, and the
L    12.23    your body, what you shall put on.  For life is more than food, and the


M    6.26     body more than clothing?  Look at the birds of the air: they neither sow
L    12.24    body more than clothing.  Consider the ravens:          they neither sow


M    6.26     nor reap              nor    gather    into barns, and yet your heavenly
L    12.24    nor reap, they have neither storehouse nor barn,   and yet
```

23

```
M   6.26    Father feeds them.  Are you not of              more value        than
L   12.24   God    feeds them.                 Of how much more value are you than the
  M  10.31  Fear not, therefore;  you are      of            more value        than many
  L  12.7b  Fear not;             you are      of            more value        than many


M   6.27    they?  And which of you by being anxious can add one cubit to his span
L   12.25   birds! And which of you by being anxious can add a   cubit to his span
  M  10.31  sparrows.
  L  12.7b  sparrows.


M   6.28    of life?                                                        And why
L   12.26   of life?  If then you are not able to do as small a thing as that, why


M   6.28    are you anxious about clothing?  Consider the lilies of the field, how
L   12.27   are you anxious about the rest?  Consider the lilies,            how


M   6.29    they grow; they neither toil nor spin; |yet I tell you, even Solomon in
L   12.27   they grow; they neither toil nor spin;  yet I tell you, even Solomon in


M   6.30    all his glory was not arrayed like one of these.  But if God so clothes
L   12.28   all his glory was not arrayed like one of these.  But if God so clothes


M   6.30    the grass of the field, which today is alive and tomorrow is thrown into
L   12.28   the grass which is alive  in the field today and tomorrow is thrown into


M   6.30    the oven, will he not much more clothe you, O men of little faith?
L   12.28   the oven, how much more will he clothe you, O men of little faith!


M   6.31    Therefore do.not be anxious, saying, 'What shall   we eat?' or 'What
L   12.29   And          do not seek           what you are to eat   and what


M   6.32    shall   we drink?' or 'What shall we wear?'  For     the Gentiles
L   12.30   you are to drink, nor  be of anxious mind.  For all the nations of the


M   6.32           seek all these things; and your heavenly Father knows that you
L   12.30   world seek      these things; and your          Father knows that you


M   6.33    need them all.  But      seek first his kingdom and his righteousness,
L   12.31   need them.  Instead, seek        his kingdom,


M   6.33    and all these things shall be yours as well.
L   12.31   and       these things shall be yours as well.


M   6.34    "Therefore do not be anxious about tomorrow, for tomorrow will be
M   6.34    anxious for itself.  Let the day's own trouble be sufficient for the day.


M   7.1     "Judge not, that you      be not judged.
L   6.37    "Judge not, and  you will not be judged; condemn not, and you will not

  L  6.38   be condemned; forgive, and you will be forgiven; |give, and it will be
  L  6.38   given to you; good measure, pressed down, shaken together, running over,
```

M	7.2	For with the judgment you pronounce you will be judged, and the measure
Mk	4.24	And he said to them, "Take heed what you hear; the measure
L	6.38	*will be put into your lap.* For the measure

M	7.2	you give will be the measure you get.
Mk	4.24	you give will be the measure you get, *and still more will be given you.*
L	6.39	you give will be the measure you get *back." He also told them a parable:*

| Mk | 4.25 | *For to him who has will more be given; and from him who has not, even* |
| L | 6.39 | *"Can a blind man lead a blind man? Will they not both fall into a pit?* |

| Mk | 4.25 | *what he has will be taken away."* |
| L | 6.40 | *A disciple is not above his teacher, but every one when he is fully* |

| M | 7.3 | Why do you see the speck that is in |
| L | 6.41 | *taught will be like his teacher.* Why do you see the speck that is in |

| M | 7.3 | your brother's eye, but do not notice the log that is in your own eye? |
| L | 6.41 | your brother's eye, but do not notice the log that is in your own eye? |

| M | 7.4 | Or how can you say to your brother, 'Let me take the speck out |
| L | 6.42 | Or how can you say to your brother, 'Brother, let me take out the speck |

| M | 7.4 | of your eye,' when there is the log in |
| L | 6.42 | that is in your eye,' when you yourself do not see the log that is in |

| M | 7.5 | your own eye? You hypocrite, first take the log out of your own eye, |
| L | 6.42 | your own eye? You hypocrite, first take the log out of your own eye, |

| M | 7.5 | and then you will see clearly to take the speck out of your |
| L | 6.42 | and then you will see clearly to take out the speck that is in your |

| M | 7.5 | brother's eye. |
| L | 6.42 | brother's eye. |

| M | 7.6 | "Do not give dogs what is holy; and do not throw your pearls before |
| M | 7.6 | swine, lest they trample them under foot and turn to attack you. |

L	11.9	*And I tell you,*
M	18.19	*Again I say to you, if two of you agree on earth about anything*
M	21.22	*And whatever you*
Mk	11.24	*Therefore I tell you, whatever you*
J	14.13	*Whatever you*
J	14.14	*if you*
J	15.7	*If you abide in me, and my words*
J	16.23b	*Truly, truly, I say to you, if you*
J	16.24	*Hitherto you have asked nothing in my*

M	7.7	"Ask, and it will be given you;
L	11.9	Ask, and it will be given you;
M	18.19	*they* ask, it will be done for them
M	21.22	ask *in prayer,*
Mk	11.24	ask *in prayer, believe that*
J	14.13	ask *in my name,* I will do *it,*
J	14.14	ask *anything in my name,* I will do *it.*
J	15.7	*abide in you,* ask *whatever you will, and* it shall be done *for* you.
J	16.23b	ask *anything of the Father,* he will give *it to* you
J	16.24	*name;* ask,

25

```
M      7.8    seek, and you will find; knock, and it will be opened to you.  For every
L     11.10   seek, and you will find; knock, and it will be opened to you.  For every
  M   18.19   by   my  Father in heaven.
  J   14.13   that the Father may be glorified in the Son;
  J   16.23b  in   my  name.


M      7.8    one who asks receives, and he who seeks finds, and to him who knocks it
L     11.10   one who asks receives, and he who seeks finds, and to him who knocks it
  M   21.22        you will receive,    if  you have faith."
  Mk  11.24        you have received it, and it will be yours.
  J   16.24   and you will receive,    that your joy may be full.


M      7.9    will be opened.  Or what man    of    you, if his son asks him for
L     11.11   will be opened.     What father among you, if his son asks     for a


M      7.10   bread, will                 give him a stone?  Or if he asks for a
L     11.12   fish, will instead of a fish give him a serpent; or if he asks for an


M      7.11   fish, will give him a serpent?  If you then, who are evil, know how to
L     11.13   egg,  will give him a scorpion?  If you then, who are evil, know how to


M      7.11   give good gifts to your children, how much more will your Father who is
L     11.13   give good gifts to your children, how much more will the  heavenly


M      7.11   in heaven give    good things to those who ask him!
L     11.13      Father give the Holy Spirit to those who ask him!"


M      7.12   So whatever you wish that men would do to you, do so to them; for this
L      6.31   And as      you wish that men would do to you, do so to them.


M      7.12   is the law and the prophets.


M      7.13                                          "Enter   by the narrow
L   13.23b,24 And he         said to them,   |"Strive to enter  by the narrow
  J   10.7    So Jesus again said to them, "Truly, truly, I say to you, I am the
  J   10.9                       I am the door; if any one enters by me,


M      7.13   gate; for the gate is wide and the way is easy, that leads to destruction,
L     13.24   door;                                    for many, I tell you,
  J   10.7    door of the sheep.


M      7.14   and those who enter by it are many.  For the gate is narrow and the way
L     13.24   will seek  to enter and will not be able.


M      7.14   is hard,    that leads to life, and those who find it   are few.
L     13.23a  And some one said to him, "Lord, will those who are saved be few?"
  J   10.9                       he will          be saved, and will


M      7.15   "Beware of false prophets, who come to you in sheep's clothing but
  J   10.9    go in and out and find pasture.
```

M	7.16	inwardly are ravenous wolves. You will know them by their fruits.
L	6.44	for each tree is known by its own fruit.
M	12.33b	*for the tree is* known by its fruit.

M	7.16	Are grapes gathered from thorns, or figs from
L	6.44	For figs are not gathered from thorns, nor are grapes picked from a

M	7.16	thistles?
L	6.45	bramble bush. *The good man out of the good treasure of his heart pro-*

L	6.45	*duces good, and the evil man out of his evil treasure produces evil;*
L	6.45	*for out of the abundance of the heart his mouth speaks.*

M	7.17	So, every sound tree bears good fruit, but the
L	6.43	"For no good· tree bears bad fruit, nor again does a
M	12.33	*"Either make the tree good, and its fruit good; or make the*

M	7.18	bad tree bears evil fruit. A sound tree cannot bear evil fruit,
L	6.43	bad tree bear good fruit; "For no good tree bears bad fruit,
M	12.33	tree bad, *and its* fruit bad;

M	7.19	nor can a bad tree bear good fruit. Every tree
L	6.43	nor again does a bad tree bear good fruit;
M	3.10	*Even now the axe is laid to the root of the trees; every tree therefore*
L	3.9	*Even now the axe is laid to the root of the trees; every tree therefore*

M	7.19	that does not bear good fruit is cut down and thrown into the fire.
M	3.10	that does not bear good fruit is cut down and thrown into the fire.
L	3.9	that does not bear good fruit is cut down and thrown into the fire."

M	7.20	Thus you will know them by their fruits.
L	6.44a	for each tree is known by its own fruit.
M	12.33	*for the tree is* known by its fruit.

M	7.21	"Not every one who says to me, 'Lord, Lord,' shall enter the kingdom
L	6.46	"Why do you call me 'Lord, Lord,'
L	13.25	*When once the householder*

M	7.22	of heaven, but he who does the will of my Father who is in heaven. On
L	6.46	and not do what I tell you?
M	25.11	*Afterward the other*
L	13.25	*has risen up and shut the door, you will begin to stand outside and to*
L	13.26	*Then*

M	7.22	that day many will say to me, 'Lord, Lord, did we not prophesy in your
M	25.11	*maidens came also, saying, 'Lord, lord, open to us.'*
L	13.25	*knock at the door, saying, 'Lord, open to us.'*
L	13.26	*you will begin to say, 'We ate and drank in your*

M	7.22	name, and cast out demons in your name, and do many mighty works in
L	13.26	*presence, and you taught in our streets.'*

```
M    7.23   your name?'  And then      will I declare to them,               'I never
  M  25.12                    But        he         replied, 'Truly, I say to you, I do not
  M  25.41                         Then he will     say     to those at his left hand,
  L  13.25                              He will     answer  you,                    'I do not
  L  13.27                    But        he will    say,            'I tell  you, I do not


M    7.23   knew      you;           depart from me,      you evildoers.'
  M  25.12   know      you.'
  M  25.41                            'Depart from me,      you cursed, into the
  L  13.25   know where you come from.'
  L  13.27   know where you come from; depart from me, all you workers of iniquity!'


  M  25.41   eternal fire prepared for the devil and his angels;
  L  13.28   There you will weep and gnash your teeth, when you see Abraham and Isaac


  L  13.28   and Jacob and all the prophets in the kingdom of God and you yourselves
  L  13.29   thrust out.  And men will come from east and west, and from north and
  L  13.30   south, and sit at table in the kingdom of God.  And behold, some are
  L  13.30   last who will be first, and some are first who will be last."
```

f. The Two Houses

Matthew 7.24-27

```
M    7.24   "Every one then who                    hears these words of mine and does
L    6.47    Every one      who comes to me and hears my      words      and does


M    7.24   them                           will be like a wise man who
L    6.48   them, I will show you what he is like:  he is like a      man


M    7.24   built   his house                              upon the rock;
L    6.48   building a house, who dug deep, and laid the foundation upon      rock;


M    7.25   and the rain fell, and    the floods came, and the winds blew and beat
L    6.48                      and when a flood  arose,    the stream          broke


M    7.25   upon    that house, but it did not fall,    because it had been founded
L    6.48   against that house, and  could not shake it, because it had been well


M    7.26   on the rock.  And every one who hears these words of mine and does not
L    6.49   built.     But      he who hears                      and does not


M    7.26   do them will be like a foolish man who built his house upon the sand;
L    6.49   do them      is like a      man who built a  house   on the ground


M    7.27               and the rain fell, and the floods came, and the winds blew
L    6.49   without a foundation; against which the stream broke,


M    7.27   and beat against that house, and         it fell; and      great
L    6.49                               and immediately it fell, and the ruin of


M    7.27   was  the fall  of it."
L    6.49   that house was great."
```

Matthew 7.28-29

M	7.28	And when Jesus finished	these sayings, the crowds were astonished
Mk	1.22	And	they were astonished
L	7.1	After he had ended all his	sayings in the hearing of the people
L	*4.32*	and	*they were astonished*

M	7.29	at his teaching,	for he taught them as one who had authority, and
Mk	1.22	at his teaching,	for he taught them as one who had authority, and
L	7.1	he entered Capernaum.	
L	*4.32*	at his teaching,	for *his word was with* authority.

M	7.29	not as their scribes.
Mk	1.22	not as the scribes.

11. A LEPER CLEANSED

Matthew 8.1-4

M	8.1	When he came down from the mountain, great crowds followed him;
Mk	1.45b	and people came to him
L	5.12	While he was in one of the cities,
L	5.15b	and great multitudes gathered to
L	*17.12*	*And as he entered a village,*

M	8.2	and behold, a leper came to him
Mk	1.40	from every quarter. And a leper came to him beseeching him,
L	5.12	there came a man full of leprosy; and when
L	5.15b	hear and to be healed of their infirmities.
L	*17.12*	*he was met by ten lepers, who stood at a distance*

M	8.2	and knelt before him, saying, "Lord, if you will,
Mk	1.40	and kneeling said to him, "If you will,
L	5.12	he saw Jesus, he fell on his face and besought him, "Lord, if you will,
L	*17.13*	*and lifted up their voices and said, "Jesus, Master,*

M	8.3	you can make me clean." And he stretched out his hand
Mk	1.41	you can make me clean." Moved with pity, he stretched out his hand
L	5.13	you can make me clean." And he stretched out his hand,
L	*17.13*	*have mercy on us."*

M	8.3	and touched him, saying, "I will; be clean." And immediately
Mk	1.42	and touched him, and said to him, "I will; be clean." And immediately
L	5.13	and touched him, saying, "I will; be clean." And immediately
L	*17.14b*	*And as they went*

M	8.3	his leprosy was cleansed.
Mk	1.43	the leprosy left him, and he was made clean. *And he sternly charged*
L	5.14	the leprosy left him. *And he charged*
L	*17.14b*	*they were cleansed.*

M	8.4	And Jesus said to him, "See that you
Mk	1.44	*him, and sent him away at once,* and said to him, "See that you
L	5.14	*him* to
L	*17.14a*	*When he saw them he said to them,*

29

```
M    8.4     say nothing to any one; but  go,    show yourself   to the priest, and
Mk   1.44    say nothing to any one; but  go,    show yourself   to the priest, and
L    5.14    tell              no one; but "go and show yourself   to the priest, and
  L  17.14a                                  "Go and show yourselves to the priests."
```

```
M    8.4             offer        the  gift      that Moses commanded, for a proof
Mk   1.44            offer    for your cleansing what Moses commanded, for a proof
L    5.14    make an offering for your cleansing,  as Moses commanded, for a proof
```

```
M    8.4     to the people."
Mk   1.45    to the people."  But he went out and began to talk freely about it, and
L    5.15a   to the people."  But so much the more the report went abroad concerning
```

```
Mk   1.45    to spread the news, so that Jesus could no longer openly enter a town,
L    5.15a   him;
```

```
Mk   1.45      but    was out  in the country;              and       people
L    5.16,15b  But he withdrew to the wilderness and prayed. |and great multitudes
```

```
Mk   1.45    came    to him from every quarter.
L    5.15b   gathered to hear and to be healed of their infirmities.
```

12. THE CENTURION'S SERVANT

Matthew 8.5-13

```
M    8.5      As                                                            he
Mk   2.1      And when                                                      he
L    7.1      After he had ended all his sayings in the hearing of the people he
J    4.46b    And
```

```
M    8.5      entered     Capernaum,        a  centurion came forward to him,
Mk   2.1      returned to Capernaum after some days, it was reported that he was
L    7.2      entered     Capernaum.    Now a  centurion had
J    4.46b            at Capernaum there was an official
```

```
M    8.6      beseeching him |and saying, "Lord, my servant
Mk   2.1      at home.
L    7.2                                    a  slave who was dear to him, who
J    4.46b                          whose son
```

```
M    8.6      is lying paralyzed at home, in terrible distress."
L    7.3      was sick and at the point of death.  When he heard of   Jesus,
J    4.47     was ill.                             When he heard that Jesus had come
```

```
L    7.3                             he sent to him elders of the Jews, asking him to
  J  4.47     from Judea to Galilee, he went                    and begged him to
```

```
L    7.4      come    and heal his slave.  And when they came to Jesus, they besought
  J  4.47     come down and heal his son, for he was at the point of death.
```

```
L    7.5      him earnestly, saying, "He is worthy to have you do this for him, |for
L    7.5      he loves our nation, and he built us our synagogue."
```

30

```
M    8.7      And he                      said to    him, "I will come and heal him."
L    7.6      And Jesus                   went with them.  When he was not far from the house,
J    4.48         Jesus therefore said to    him, "Unless you see signs and wonders you


M    8.8                          But the centurion               answered  him,
L    7.6                          the centurion sent friends to him, saying to him,
J    4.49     will not believe." The official                    said   to him,


M    8.8      "Lord,                            I am not worthy to have you come under
L    7.6      "Lord, do not trouble yourself, for I am not worthy to have you come under
J    4.49     "Sir,


M    8.8      my roof;                                            but only say the
L    7.7      my roof; |therefore I did not presume to come to you.  But      say the


M    8.9      word, and    my servant will be healed.  For I am a man     under
L    7.8      word, and let my servant      be healed.  For I am a man set under
J    4.50b       come down before my child dies."  The man believed the word


M    8.9      authority, with soldiers under me; and I say to one, 'Go,' and he goes,
L    7.8      authority, with soldiers under me: and I say to one, 'Go,' and he goes;
J    4.51     that Jesus spoke to him and went his way.  As he was going down, his


M    8.9      and to another, 'Come,' and he comes, and to my slave, 'Do this,' and
L    7.8      and to another, 'Come,' and he comes; and to my slave, 'Do this,' and
J    4.52     servants met him and told him that his son was living.  So he asked


M    8.10     he does it."  When Jesus heard him, he marveled,                and
L    7.9      he does it."  When Jesus heard this he marveled at him, and turned and
J    4.52     them the hour when he began to mend, and they said to him, "Yesterday


M    8.10     said to    those    who followed him, "Truly, I say to you, not even
L    7.9      said to the multitude that followed him,       "I tell   you, not even
J    4.53     at the seventh hour the fever left him."  The father knew that was the


M    8.11     in Israel have I found such faith.    I tell you, many will come from
L    7.9      in Israel have I found such faith."
J    4.53     hour when Jesus had said to him, "Your son will live"; and he himself
   L  13.29                                        And   men   will come from


M    8.11     east and west                           and sit at table
J    4.54     believed, and all his household.  This was now the second sign that
   L  13.29   east and west, and from north and south, and sit at table in the kingdom


M    8.11                        with Abraham,     Isaac, and Jacob
J    4.54     Jesus did when he had come from Judea to Galilee.
   M  13.49   So it will be at the close of the age.  The angels will come out and
   M  22.13                                   Then the king said to the attendants,
   L  13.28b  of God.  |when you see Abraham and Isaac and Jacob and all the prophets


M    8.11     in the kingdom of heaven,            |while the sons of the kingdom will
   M  13.42                                        |and
   M  13.50   separate the evil from the righteous, |and
   M  22.13   'Bind him hand and foot,              |and
   M  24.51                     and will punish him, |and
   M  25.30                                         |And
   L  13.28b  in the kingdom of God               |and      you  yourselves
```

31

M	8.12	be thrown			into the outer darkness;	there men will
M	*13.42*	*throw*	*them*		into the *furnace of fire;*	there men will
M	*13.50*	*throw*	*them*		into the *furnace of fire;*	there men will
M	*22.13*	*cast*	*him*		into the outer darkness;	there men will
M	*24.51*	*put*	*him*		with the *hypocrites;*	there men will
M	*25.30*	*cast the worthless*	*servant*		into the outer darkness;	there men will
L	*13.28a*	*thrust out.*				There *you* will

M	8.13	weep and gnash their teeth." And to the centurion Jesus said, "Go;
L	7.10	And when those who had been sent returned to
J	4.50a	Jesus said to him, "Go;
M	*13.42*	weep and gnash their teeth.
M	*13.50*	weep and gnash their teeth.
M	*22.13*	weep and gnash their teeth.'
M	*24.51*	weep and gnash their teeth.
M	*25.30*	weep and gnash their teeth.'
L	*13.28a*	weep and gnash *your* teeth,

M	8.13	be it done for you as you have believed." And the servant was healed at
L	7.10	the house, they found the slave well.
J	4.50a	your son will live."

M	8.13	that very moment.

13. HEALINGS AT CAPERNAUM

Matthew 8.14-17

M	8.14	And when Jesus left the synagogue, and entered Peter's
Mk	1.29	And immediately he left the synagogue, and entered the house
L	4.38	And he arose and left the synagogue, and entered Simon's

M	8.14	house, he saw his mother-in-law
Mk	1.30	of Simon and Andrew, with James and John. Now Simon's mother-in-law
L	4.38	house. Now Simon's mother-in-law

M	8.14	lying sick with a fever;
Mk	1.30	lay sick with a fever, and immediately they told him of her.
L	4.38	was ill with a high fever, and they besought him for her.

M	8.15	he touched her hand, and the
Mk	1.31	And he came and took her by the hand and lifted her up, and the
L	4.39	And he stood over her and rebuked the fever, and

M	8.16	fever left her, and she rose and served him. That evening
Mk	1.32	fever left her; and she served them. That evening,
L	4.40	it left her; and immediately she rose and served them. Now when the

M	8.16	they brought to him many who were possessed
Mk	1.32	at sundown, they brought to him all who were sick or possessed
L	4.40	sun was setting, all those who had any that were sick with various

M	8.16	with demons;
Mk	1.33	with demons. *And the whole city was gathered together about the door.*
L	4.40	diseases brought them to him;

M	8.16	and he cast out the spirits with a word,
Mk	1.34b	and cast out many demons; *and he would not permit the demons to speak,*
L	4.40	and he laid his hands on every one of them
L	4.41	And demons also came out of many, crying, "You are the

M	8.17	<u>and</u> <u>healed all</u> who were sick. <u>This was to</u>
Mk	1.34a	*because they knew him.* <u>And</u> he <u>healed</u> many who were sick with various
L	4.40	<u>and</u> <u>healed</u> them.
L	4.41	Son of God!" *But he rebuked them, and would not allow them to speak,*

M	8.17	<u>fulfil what was spoken by the prophet Isaiah, "He took our infirmities</u>
L	4.41	*because they knew that he was the Christ.*

M	8.17	<u>and bore our diseases."</u>
Mk	1.34a	<u>diseases,</u>

14. THE DEMANDS OF DISCIPLESHIP

Matthew 8.18-22

M	8.18	<u>Now when Jesus saw great crowds around him,</u> he gave orders
Mk	4.35	On that day, when evening had come, he said to them,
L	8.22	One day he got into a boat with his disciples, and he said to them,

M	8.18	<u>to go over</u> to the other side.
Mk	4.35	"Let us <u>go</u> across <u>to the other side.</u>"
L	8.22	"Let us <u>go</u> across <u>to the other side</u> of the lake." So they set out,
L	9.57	As they were going along the

M	8.19	<u>And</u> a scribe came up and said to him, "Teacher, <u>I will follow you</u>
L	9.57	road, a man <u>said to him,</u> "<u>I will follow you</u>

M	8.20	<u>wherever you go.</u>" <u>And Jesus said to him,</u> "<u>Foxes have holes, and birds</u>
L	9.58	<u>wherever you go.</u>" <u>And Jesus said to him,</u> "<u>Foxes have holes,</u> and birds

M	8.20	<u>of the air have nests; but the Son of man has nowhere to lay his head.</u>"
L	9.58	<u>of the air have nests; but the Son of man has nowhere to lay his head.</u>"

M	8.21	<u>Another of the disciples</u> <u>said to him,</u> "<u>Lord, let me</u>
L	9.59	|To <u>another</u> he said, "Follow me." But he <u>said,</u> "<u>Lord, let me</u>

M	8.22	<u>first go and bury my father.</u>" <u>But Jesus said to him,</u> "<u>Follow me, and</u>
L	9.60	<u>first go and bury my father.</u>" <u>But he</u> <u>said to him,</u>

M	8.22	<u>leave the dead to bury their own dead.</u>"
L	9.60	"<u>Leave the dead to bury their own dead</u>; *but as for you, go and proclaim*

L	9.61	*the kingdom of God." Another said, "I will follow you, Lord; but let*
L	9.62	*me first say farewell to those at my home." Jesus said to him, "No one*
L	9.62	*who puts his hand to the plow and looks back is fit for the kingdom of*
L	9.62	*God."*

15. THE STORM AT SEA

Matthew 8.23-27

Mk	4.35	*On that day, when evening had come, he said to them, "Let us go across*

```
M    8.23                                    And when he got                      into
Mk   4.36    to the other side."  And leaving the crowd, they took him with them  in
L    8.22                         One day  he got                                 into


M    8.23    the boat,                      his disciples followed  him.
Mk   4.36    the boat, just as he was.  And other boats were with him.
L    8.22    a   boat               with his disciples, and he said to them, "Let us


M    8.24                                                          And behold,
Mk   4.37                                                          And
L    8.23b   go across to the other side of the lake."  So they set out, |And


M    8.24    there arose        a great storm    on the sea,
Mk   4.37            a great storm of wind arose,    and the waves beat into the boat,
L    8.23b       a        storm of wind came down on the lake,


M    8.24    so that the boat was being  swamped by the waves;
Mk   4.37    so that the boat was already filling.
L    8.23b   and         they were       filling with water, and were in danger.


M    8.25        but            he was        asleep.           And they
Mk   4.38        But            he was in the stern, asleep on the cushion; and they
L    8.23a,24a |and as they sailed he fell    asleep.           And they


M    8.25    went and woke him,    saying, "Save,  Lord;              we are
Mk   4.38              woke him and said to him,   "Teacher, do you not care if we
L    8.24a   went and woke him,    saying, "Master, Master,          we are


M    8.26    perishing."  And he said to them, "Why  are you afraid, O men of little
Mk   4.40    perish?"         He said to them, "Why  are you afraid?  Have you no
L    8.25a   perishing!"      He said to them, "Where is  your


M    8.26    faith?"  Then he rose  and rebuked the winds and       the      sea;
Mk   4.39    faith?"  And  he awoke and rebuked the wind, and said to the      sea,
L    8.24b   faith?"  And  he awoke and rebuked the wind  and       the raging waves;


M    8.26                                     and there was a great calm.
Mk   4.39    "Peace! Be still!"  And the wind ceased, and there was a great calm.
L    8.24b                       and     they ceased, and there was a    calm.


M    8.27    And               the men  marveled, saying,          "What
Mk   4.41    And they were filled with awe,    and  said  to one another, "Who
L    8.25b   And they were afraid, and they marveled, saying to one another, "Who


M    8.27    sort of man is this, that       even winds and sea
Mk   4.41    then        is this, that       even wind  and sea
L    8.25b   then        is this, that he commands even wind  and water, and they


M    8.27    obey him?"
Mk   4.41    obey him?"
L    8.25b   obey him?"
```

16. THE TWO DEMONIACS

Matthew 8.28-34

M	8.28	And when he <u>came to the other side</u>, <u>to the country of the</u>
Mk	5.1	They <u>came to the other side</u> of the sea, <u>to the country of the</u>
L	8.26	Then they arrived <u>at the country of the</u>

M	8.28	<u>Gadarenes,</u>
Mk	5.2	<u>Gerasenes.</u> And when he had come out of the
L	8.27	<u>Gerasenes,</u> which is opposite Galilee. And as he stepped out on

M	8.28	<u>two demoniacs met him,</u>
Mk	5.2	boat, there <u>met him</u>
L	8.27	land, there <u>met him</u> a man from the city who had demons; for a long

M	8.28	<u>coming out of the</u>
Mk	5.2	<u>out of the</u>
L	8.27	time he had worn no clothes, and he lived not in a house but among <u>the</u>

M	8.28	<u>tombs, so fierce that no one could pass that way.</u>
Mk	5.3	<u>tombs</u> a man with an unclean spirit, |*who lived among the tombs; and no*
L	8.27	<u>tombs.</u>

Mk	5.4	*one could bind him any more, even with a chain; for he had often been*
Mk	5.4	*bound with fetters and chains, but the chains he wrenched apart, and the*
Mk	5.4	*fetters he broke in pieces; and no one had the strength to subdue him.*
Mk	5.5	*Night and day among the tombs and on the mountains he was always crying*
Mk	5.6	*out, and bruising himself with stones. And*

M	8.29	<u>And behold, they</u>
Mk	5.7	*when he saw Jesus from afar, he ran and worshiped him;* |*and*
L	8.28	*When he saw Jesus,* *he*

M	8.29	<u>cried</u> out,
Mk	5.7	crying <u>out</u> with a loud voice, he said,
L	8.28	<u>cried</u> <u>out</u> and fell down before him, and said with a loud voice,

M	8.29	"<u>What have you to do with us,</u> O Son of <u>God?</u>
Mk	5.7	"<u>What have you to do with</u> me, Jesus, <u>Son of</u> the Most High <u>God</u>? I
L	8.28	"<u>What have you to do with</u> me, Jesus, <u>Son of</u> the Most High <u>God</u>? I

M	8.29	<u>Have you</u> come here to torment us before the time?"
Mk	5.8	adjure <u>you</u> by God, do not <u>torment</u> me." *For he had said to*
L	8.29	beseech <u>you</u>, do not <u>torment</u> me." *For he had commanded the unclean*

Mk	5.8	*him, "Come out of the man, you unclean spirit!"*
L	8.29	*spirit to come out of the man. (For many a time it had seized him; he was*

L	8.29	*kept under guard, and bound with chains and fetters, but he broke the*

Mk	5.9	*And Jesus asked*
L	8.30	*bonds and was driven by the demon into the desert.) Jesus then asked*

Mk	5.9	*him, "What is your name?" He replied, "My name is Legion; for we*
L	8.30	*him, "What is your name?" And he said, "Legion"; for*

Mk	5.10	*are many." And he begged him eagerly not to*
L	8.31	*many demons had entered him. And they begged him not to*

M	8.30			Now a	herd of many swine
Mk	5.11	send them	out of the country.	Now a great	herd of swine
L	8.32	command them to depart into the abyss.		Now a large	herd of swine

M	8.31	was feeding at some distance from them.	And the demons begged him, "If
Mk	5.12	was feeding there on the hillside;	and they begged him,
L	8.32	was feeding there on the hillside;	and they begged him

M	8.31	you cast us out, send us away into the herd of swine."
Mk	5.12	"Send us to the swine, let us enter
L	8.32	to let them enter

M	8.32	And he said to them, "Go." So they came out
Mk	5.13	them." So he gave them leave. And the unclean spirits came out,
L	8.33	these. So he gave them leave. Then the demons came out of

M	8.32	and went into the swine; and behold, the whole herd
Mk	5.13	and entered the swine; and the herd, numbering
L	8.33	the man and entered the swine, and the herd

M	8.32	rushed down the steep bank into the sea, and
Mk	5.13	about two thousand, rushed down the steep bank into the sea, and were
L	8.33	rushed down the steep bank into the lake and were

M	8.33	perished in the waters. The herdsmen fled,
Mk	5.14	drowned in the sea. The herdsmen fled,
L	8.34	drowned. When the herdsmen saw what had happened, they fled,

M	8.33	and going into the city they told everything, and
Mk	5.14	and told it in the city and in the country. And people came to
L	8.35	and told it in the city and in the country. Then people went out to

M	8.34	what had happened to the demoniacs. And behold, all the
Mk	5.15	see what it was that had happened. And they
L	8.35	see what had happened, and they

M	8.34	city came out to meet Jesus; and when they saw him,
Mk	5.15	came to Jesus, and saw the demoniac
L	8.35	came to Jesus, and found the man from whom the

Mk	5.15	sitting there, clothed and in his right
L	8.35	demons had gone, sitting at the feet of Jesus, clothed and in his right

Mk	5.16	mind, the man who had had the legion; and they were afraid. And those
L	8.36	mind; and they were afraid. And those

Mk	5.16	who had seen it told what had happened to the demoniac
L	8.36	who had seen it told them how he who had been possessed with demons

M	8.34	they
Mk	5.17	and to the swine. And they began
L	8.37	was healed. Then all the people of the surrounding country of the

M	8.34	<u>begged him</u> <u>to leave</u> <u>their neighborhood.</u>
Mk	5.17	to beg Jesus <u>to depart</u> from <u>their neighborhood.</u>
L	8.37	Gerasenes asked him <u>to</u> depart from them; *for they were seized with*

Mk	5.18	*And as he was getting into the boat,* *the man*
L	8.37	*great fear; so he got into the boat and returned. The man from*

Mk	5.18	*who had been possessed with demons begged him that he might be*
L	8.38	*whom the demons had gone begged that he might be*

Mk	5.19	*with him. But he refused, and said to him, "Go home to*
L	8.39	*with him; but he sent him away, saying, |"Return to your home,*

Mk	5.19	*your friends, and tell them how much the Lord has done for you, and how*
L	8.39	*and declare how much God has done for you."*

Mk	5.20	*he has had mercy on you." And he went away and began to proclaim*
L	8.39	*And he went away, proclaiming*

Mk	5.20	*in the Decapolis how much Jesus had done for him; and all men*
L	8.39	*throughout the whole city how much Jesus had done for him.*

Mk	5.20	*marveled.*

17. A PARALYTIC HEALED

Matthew 9.1-8

M	9.1	<u>And</u> <s>getting into a</s> <u>boat</u>
Mk	2.1	<u>And</u> when
Mk	5.18	<u>And</u> as he was <u>getting into</u> the <u>boat</u>, the man who had been possessed
Lk	5.17	On one of those days, *as he was teaching, there were Pharisees and*
Lk	8.37b	so he got <u>into</u> the <u>boat</u> and
J	5.1	After this there was a feast of the Jews, and

Lk	5.17	*teachers of the law sitting by, who had come from every village of*
Lk	5.17	*Galilee and Judea and from Jerusalem; and the power of the Lord was*

M	9.1	<u>he</u>
Mk	2.1	<u>he</u>
Mk	5.21	with demons begged him that he might be with him. And when Jesus had
L	5.17	*with him to heal.*
J	5.1	Jesus

M	9.1	<u>crossed over</u> and came to his own city.
Mk	2.1	returned <u>to</u> Capernaum after some days, *it was*
Mk	5.21	<u>crossed</u> again in the boat <u>to</u> the other side, *a great crowd gathered*
L	8.37b	returned.
J	5.2	went up <u>to</u> Jerusalem. *Now there is in Jerusalem*

Mk	2.2	*reported that he was at home. And many were gathered together, so that*
Mk	5.21	*about him; and he was beside the sea.*
J	5.2	*by the Sheep Gate a pool, in Hebrew called Bethzatha, which has five*

Mk	2.2	*there was no longer room for them, not even about the door; and he was*
J	5.2	*porticoes.*

M	9.2	And behold, they brought to him a
Mk	2.3	*preaching the word to them.* And they came, bringing to him a
L	5.18	And behold, men were bringing on a bed a
J	5.3	In these lay a multitude of invalids,

M	9.2	paralytic, lying on his bed;
Mk	2.3	paralytic carried by four men.
L	5.18	man who was paralyzed, *and they sought to bring him in and lay him before*
J	5.5	blind, lame, paralyzed. *One man was there, who had been ill for thirty-*

Mk	2.4	*And when they could not get near him because of the crowd, they*
L	5.19	*Jesus; but finding no way to bring him in, because of the crowd, they*
J	5.5	*eight years.*

Mk	2.4	*removed the roof above him; and when they had made an opening, they*
L	5.19	*went up on the roof and*

Mk	2.4	*let down the pallet on which the paralytic lay.*
L	5.19	*let him down with his bed through the tiles into the midst before Jesus.*

M	9.2	and when Jesus saw their faith
Mk	2.5	And when Jesus saw their faith,
L	5.20	And when he saw their faith
J	5.6	When Jesus saw him and knew that he had been lying there a long time,

M	9.2	he said to the paralytic, "Take heart, my son; your sins are forgiven."
Mk	2.5	he said to the paralytic, "My son, your sins are forgiven."
L	5.20	he said, "Man, your sins are forgiven
J	5.6	he said to him, "Do you want to be healed?"

M	9.3	And behold, some of the scribes
Mk	2.6	Now some of the scribes were sitting there,
L	5.21	you." And the scribes and the Pharisees began to
J	5.7	*The sick man answered him, "Sir, I have no man to put me into the*
J	10.33	*The Jews*

M	9.3	said to themselves, "This man is
Mk	2.7	questioning in their hearts, |"Why does this man speak thus? It is
L	5.21	question, saying, "Who is this that speaks
J	5.7	*pool when the water is troubled, and while I am going another steps down*
J	10.33	*answered him, "It is not for a good work that we stone you but*

M	9.4	blaspheming." But
Mk	2.8	blasphemy! Who can forgive sins but God alone?" And immediately
L	5.22	blasphemies? Who can forgive sins but God only?" When
J	5.7	*before me."*
J	10.33	*for blasphemy; because you, being a man, make yourself God."*

M	9.4	Jesus, knowing their thoughts,
Mk	2.8	Jesus, perceiving in his spirit that they thus questioned within themselves,
L	5.22	Jesus perceived their questionings, he

M	9.5	said, "Why do you think evil in your hearts? For which is
Mk	2.9	said to them, "Why do you question thus in your hearts? Which is
L	5.23	answered them, "Why do you question in your hearts? Which is

M	9.5	easier, to say, 'Your sins are forgiven,' or to say,
Mk	2.9	easier, to say to the paralytic, 'Your sins are forgiven,' or to say,
L	5.23	easier, to say, 'Your sins are forgiven you,' or to say,

M	9.6	'Rise and walk'? But that you may know that the Son
Mk	2.10	'Rise, take up your pallet and walk'? But that you may know that the Son
L	5.24	'Rise and walk'? But that you may know that the Son

M	9.6	of man has authority on earth to forgive sins"--he then said to the
Mk	2.10	of man has authority on earth to forgive sins"--he said to the
L	5.24	of man has authority on earth to forgive sins"--he said to the man
J	5.8	Jesus said to

M	9.6	paralytic-- "Rise, take up your bed and go
Mk	2.11	paralytic--|"I say to you, rise, take up your pallet and go
L	5.24	who was paralyzed-- "I say to you, rise, take up your bed and go
J	5.8	him, "Rise, take up your pallet, and walk."

M	9.7	home." And he rose
Mk	2.12	home." And he rose, and immediately took up the
L	5.25	home." And immediately he rose before them, and took up that
J	5.9	And at once the man was healed, and he took up his

M	9.8	and went home. When the crowds saw it,
Mk	2.12	pallet and went out before them all; so that
L	5.26	on which he lay, and went home, glorifying God. And
J	5.9	pallet and walked.

M	9.8	they were afraid, and they glorified God,
Mk	2.12	they were all amazed and glorified God,
L	5.26	amazement seized them all, and they glorified God and were

M	9.8	who had given such authority to men.
Mk	2.12	saying, "We never saw anything like this!"
L	5.26	filled with awe, saying, "We have seen strange things today."

18. MATTHEW THE TAX COLLECTOR

Matthew 9.9-13

Mk	2.13	*He went out again beside the sea; and all the crowd gathered about him,*

M	9.9	As Jesus passed on from there, he saw a man
Mk	2.14	*and he taught them.* And as he passed on, he saw
L	5.27	After this he went out, and saw a tax

M	9.9	called Matthew sitting at the tax office; and
Mk	2.14	Levi the son of Alphaeus sitting at the tax office, and
L	5.27	collector, named Levi, sitting at the tax office; and

```
M     9.9     he said to him, "Follow me."  And he                    rose and
Mk    2.14    he said to him, "Follow me."  And he                    rose and
L     5.28    he said to him, "Follow me."  And he left everything, and rose and


M     9.9     followed him.
Mk    2.14    followed him.
L     5.28    followed him.


M     9.10    And as        he  sat  at table in the house,                    behold,
Mk    2.15    And as        he  sat  at table in his house,
L     5.29    And Levi made him a great feast in his house; and there was a large


M     9.10    many       tax collectors and sinners came and sat down        with
Mk    2.15    many       tax collectors and sinners were      sitting        with
L     5.29    company of tax collectors and others            sitting at table with
  L  15.1     Now the    tax collectors and sinners were all drawing near to hear


M     9.11    Jesus and his disciples.                                         And when
Mk    2.16    Jesus and his disciples; for there were many who followed him.   And the
L     5.30    them.                                                            And
  L  15.2     him.                                                             And
  L  19.7                                                                      And when


M     9.11            the Pharisees         saw this,
Mk    2.16    scribes of the Pharisees, when they saw that he was eating with sinners
L     5.30            the Pharisees and their scribes
  L  15.2            the Pharisees and the  scribes
  L  19.7            they                   saw it


M     9.11        they        said to      his disciples,       "Why does your
Mk    2.16    and tax collectors, said to      his disciples,       "Why does
L     5.30              murmured against his disciples, saying, "Why do
  L  15.2          murmured,                            saying,       "This
  L  19.7      they all murmured,                               "He has gone in


M     9.12    teacher    eat           with tax collectors and sinners?"  But when
Mk    2.17    he         eat           with tax collectors and sinners?"  And when
L     5.31    you        eat and drink with tax collectors and sinners?"  And
  L  15.2     man      receives                              sinners and eats with
  L  19.7     to be the guest       of a man       who is a sinner."


M     9.12    he    heard it, he said,        "Those who are well have no need of
Mk    2.17    Jesus heard it, he said to them, "Those who are well have no need of
L     5.31    Jesus           answered them, "Those who are well have no need of
  L  15.2     them."


M     9.13    a physician, but those who are sick.  Go and learn what this means, 'I
Mk    2.17    a physician, but those who are sick;
L     5.31    a physician, but those who are sick;
  M  12.7                              And if you had known what this means, 'I


M     9.13    desire mercy, and not sacrifice.'  For I      came not to call the
Mk    2.17                                          I      came not to call the
L     5.32                                          I have not come to call the
  M  12.7     desire mercy, and not sacrifice,'  you would not have condemned the
```

40

```
M     9.13    righteous, but sinners."
Mk    2.17    righteous, but sinners."
L     5.32    righteous, but sinners to repentance."
  M  12.7     guiltless.
```

19. QUESTION OF FASTING

Matthew 9.14-17

```
M     9.14    Then the disciples of John
Mk    2.18    Now       John's  disciples and the Pharisees were fasting; and people
L     5.33    And       they


M     9.14    came            to him, saying, "Why do we
Mk    2.18    came and said to him,          "Why do John's disciples
L     5.33         said to him,          "The    disciples of John fast often and


M     9.14                    and                    the Pharisees fast, but your
Mk    2.18                    and         the disciples of the Pharisees fast, but your
L     5.33    offer prayers, and so do the disciples of the Pharisees,      but yours


M     9.15    disciples do not fast?"    And Jesus said to them, "Can      the wedding
Mk    2.19    disciples do not fast?"    And Jesus said to them, "Can      the wedding
L     5.34          eat and drink."   And Jesus said to them, "Can you make wedding


M     9.15    guests mourn as long as the bridegroom is with them?
Mk    2.19    guests fast  while     the bridegroom is with them?  As long as they
L     5.34    guests fast  while     the bridegroom is with them?
   J  3.29    He who has the bride is the bridegroom;


M     9.15                                                The days will come,
Mk    2.20    have the bridegroom with them, they cannot fast. The days will come,
L     5.35                                                The days will come,
   J  3.29                                                    the friend


M     9.15    when the bridegroom is taken away from them, and then they will fast.
Mk    2.20    when the bridegroom is taken away from them, and then they will fast in
L     5.35    when the bridegroom is taken away from them, and then they will fast in
   J  3.29    of   the bridegroom, who stands and hears him, rejoices greatly at the


M     9.16                                        And no one puts  a piece of
Mk    2.21    that  day.                            No one sews  a piece of
L     5.36    those days." He told them a parable also: "No one tears a piece from
   J  3.29    bridegroom's voice; therefore this joy of mine is now full.


M     9.16    unshrunk cloth          on an old garment, for      the patch
Mk    2.21    unshrunk cloth          on an old garment; if he does, the patch
L     5.36    a new  garment and puts it upon an old garment; if he does,  he will


M     9.16    tears away from the garment,
Mk    2.21    tears away from      it,                the new          from  the
L     5.36    tear         the new, and the piece from the new will not match the


M     9.17        and a worse tear is made. Neither   is   new wine put into old
Mk    2.22    old, and a worse tear is made. And no one puts new wine     into old
L     5.37    old.                          And no one puts new wine     into old
```

M	9.17	wineskins; if it is, the skins burst, and the wine
Mk	2.22	wineskins; if he does, the wine will burst the skins, and the wine
L	5.37	wineskins; if he does, the new wine will burst the skins and it

M	9.17	is spilled, and the skins are destroyed; but new wine
Mk	2.22	is lost, and so are the skins; but new wine
L	5.38	will be spilled, and the skins will be destroyed. But new wine

M	9.17	is put into fresh wineskins, and so both are preserved."
Mk	2.22	is for fresh skins."
L	5.39	must be put into fresh wineskins. *And no one after drinking old wine*

L	*5.39*	*desires new; for he says, 'The old is good.'"*

20. JAIRUS' DAUGHTER AND A WOMAN WITH A HEMORRHAGE

Matthew 9.18-26

Mk	*5.21*	*And when Jesus had crossed again in the boat to the other side, a*
L	*8.40*	*Now when Jesus returned, the*

M	9.18	* While*
Mk	5.22	*great crowd gathered about him; and he was beside the sea.* Then
L	8.41	*crowd welcomed him, for they were all waiting for him.* And

M	9.18	he was thus speaking to them, behold, a ruler
Mk	5.22	came one of the rulers of the synagogue,
L	8.41	there came a man named Jairus, who was a ruler of the synagogue;

M	9.18	came in and knelt before him,
Mk	5.23	Jairus by name; and seeing him, he fell at his feet, |and besought
L	8.41	and falling at Jesus' feet he besought

M	9.18	saying, "My daughter
Mk	5.23	him, saying, "My little daughter
L	8.42	him to come to his house, |for he had an only daughter, about twelve

M	9.18	has just died; but come and lay your
Mk	5.23	is at the point of death. Come and lay your
L	8.42	years of age, and she was dying.

M	9.19	hand on her, and she will live." And Jesus rose
Mk	5.24	hands on her, so that she may be made well, and live." And he
L	8.42	As he

M	9.19	and followed him, with his disciples.
Mk	5.24	went with him. And a great crowd followed him and thronged about
L	8.42	went, the people pressed round

M	9.20	And behold, a woman who had suffered from a hemorrhage for
Mk	5.25	him. And there was a woman who had had a flow of blood for
L	8.43	him. And a woman who had had a flow of blood for

M	9.20	twelve years
Mk	5.26	twelve years, |*and who had suffered much under many physicians, and had*
L	8.43	twelve years and could not be healed by any one,

```
Mk  5.27   spent all that she had, and was no better but rather grew worse.  She had
Mk  6.56             And wherever he came, in villages, cities, or country, they laid


M   9.20                                      came up behind him                  and
Mk  5.27   heard the reports about Jesus, and came up behind him in the crowd and
L   8.44a                                    |came up behind him,                 and
  M  14.36                              and besought him that they might only
  Mk  3.10   for he had healed many, so that all who had diseases pressed upon him to
  Mk  6.56   the sick in the market places,   and besought him that they might
  L   6.19                     And      all the crowd        sought          to


M   9.21   touched    the fringe of his garment;  for she said to herself, "If I
Mk  5.28   touched                   his garment.  For she said,              "If I
L   8.44a  touched    the fringe of his garment;
  M  14.36  touch      the fringe of his garment;
  Mk  3.10   touch                    him.
  Mk  6.56   touch even the fringe of his garment;
  L   6.19   touch                 him, for power came forth from him and healed


M   9.22   only touch      his garment,  I shall be made well."      Jesus
Mk  5.30         touch even his garments, I shall be made well."  And Jesus, perceiving
L   8.45                                                           And Jesus
  L   6.19   them all.


M   9.22                                                               turned,
Mk  5.30   in himself that power had gone forth from him, immediately turned about


Mk  5.31   in the crowd, and said, "Who              touched my garments?"  And
L   8.45                 said, "Who was it that touched me?"          When all


Mk  5.31           his disciples said to him, "You see the crowd
L   8.45   denied it, Peter      said,          "Master, the multitudes surround you


M   9.22                                                                    and
Mk  5.32      pressing around you, and yet you say, 'Who        touched me?'"  And he
L   8.46   and press     upon    you!"  But Jesus said, "Some one touched me; for


M   9.22                             seeing her
Mk  5.33   looked around to see   who had done it.       But      the woman, knowing
L   8.47   I perceive that power has gone forth from me."  And when the woman  saw


Mk  5.33   what had been done to her,   came in fear and trembling  and fell      down
L   8.47   that she was not hidden, she came                    trembling, and falling down


Mk  5.33   before him, and told     him the whole truth.
L   8.47   before him          declared in the presence of all the people why she had


M   9.22                                                         he     said,
Mk  5.34                                                     And he     said to
L   8.48   touched him, and how she had been immediately healed. And he     said to
  Mk 10.52                                                     And Jesus said to
  L   7.50                                                     And he     said to
  L  17.19                                                     And he     said to
  L  18.42                                                     And Jesus said to
```

```
M     9.22              "Take heart, daughter; your faith has made  you well."
Mk    5.34        her,         "Daughter, your faith has made  you well; go in
L     8.48        her,         "Daughter, your faith has made  you well; go in
  Mk 10.52        him,       "Go your way; your faith has made  you well."
  L   7.50   the woman,                "Your faith has saved you;        go in
  L  17.19        him,  "Rise and go your way; your faith has made  you well."
  L  18.42        him,  "Receive your sight; your faith has made  you well."


M     9.22                                              And instantly   the woman was
Mk    5.29   peace, and be healed of your disease."     And immediately the hemorrhage
L     8.44b  peace."                                    and immediately her flow of blood
  M  14.36                                              and as many as touched it were
  Mk  6.56                                              and as many as touched it were
  Mk 10.52                                              And immediately     he received
  L   7.50   peace."


M     9.22   made well.
Mk    5.29   ceased; and she felt in her body that she was healed of her disease.
L     8.44b  ceased.
  M  14.36   made well.
  Mk  6.56   made well.
  Mk 10.52   his sight and followed him on the way.


Mk    5.35      While he was still speaking, there came from the ruler's house some who
L     8.49      While he was still speaking,    a man from the ruler's house came and


Mk    5.35   said, "Your daughter is dead.  Why    trouble the Teacher any further?"
L     8.49   said, "Your daughter is dead;  do not trouble the Teacher any more."


Mk    5.36   But            ignoring what they said, Jesus said to the ruler of the
L     8.50   But Jesus on hearing   this                    answered him,


Mk    5.37   synagogue, "Do not fear, only believe." And he allowed no one to follow
L     8.50              "Do not fear; only believe, and she shall be well."


Mk    5.37   him except Peter and James and John the brother of James.


M     9.23   And when Jesus came to the ruler's      house,            and     saw
Mk    5.38        When they  came to the house of the ruler of the synagogue, he saw
L     8.51   And when he     came to the            house, he permitted no one to


M     9.23   the flute players,
Mk    5.38   a    tumult,
  L   8.51   enter with him, except Peter and John and James, and the father and


M     9.23                     and the crowd   making            a tumult,
Mk    5.39                     and     people  weeping and   wailing loudly.  And
L     8.52   mother of the child.  And     all were weeping and bewailing her;


M     9.24                       |he said,      "Depart;
Mk    5.39   when he had entered, he said to them, "Why do you make a tumult and weep?
L     8.52                   but he said,       "Do                    not weep;


M     9.24   for the girl is not dead but sleeping."  And they laughed at him.
Mk    5.40     The child is not dead but sleeping."  |And they laughed at him.
L     8.53   for     she is not dead but sleeping."   And they laughed at him,
```

44

M	9.25	But when the crowd had been put outside,
Mk	5.40	But he put them all outside, and took the child's
L	8.53	knowing that she was dead.

M	9.25	
Mk	5.40	father and mother and those who were with him, and went in where the

he went in

M	9.25	and took her by the hand,
Mk	5.41	child was. Taking her by the hand he said to her, "Talitha
L	8.54	But taking her by the hand he called, saying,

Mk	5.41	cumi"; which means, "Little girl, I say to you, arise."
L	8.55	"Child, arise." And her spirit

M	9.25	and the girl arose.
Mk	5.42	And immediately the girl got up and walked (she was twelve
L	8.55	returned, and she got up at once; and he directed that

M	9.26	And the report of this went through
Mk	5.42	years of age), and they were immediately
L	8.56	something should be given her to eat. And her parents were

M	9.26	all that district.
Mk	5.43	overcome with amazement. And he strictly charged them that no one
L	8.56	amazed; but he charged them to tell no one

Mk	5.43	should know this, and told them to give her something to eat.
L	8.56	what had happened.

21. TWO BLIND MEN AND A DUMB DEMONIAC

Matthew 9.27-34

M	9.27	And as Jesus passed on from there,
M	20.29	And as they went out of Jericho,
Mk	10.46	And they came to Jericho; and as he was leaving Jericho with his
L	18.35	As he drew near to Jericho,

M	9.27	two blind men
M	20.30	a great crowd followed him. And behold, two blind men
Mk	10.46	disciples and a great multitude, Bartimaeus, a blind beggar,
L	18.35	a blind man

M	9.27	followed him,
M	20.30	sitting by the roadside,
Mk	10.46	the son of Timaeus, was sitting by the roadside.
L	18.36	was sitting by the roadside begging; and hearing a

L	18.37	multitude going by, he inquired what this meant. They told him, "Jesus

M	20.30	when they heard that Jesus was
Mk	10.47	And when he heard that it was Jesus of
L	18.38	of Nazareth is passing by." And

```
M     9.27                    crying aloud,          "Have mercy on us,
  M  20.30    passing by,         cried   out,        "Have mercy on us,
  Mk 10.47    Nazareth, he began to cry   out and say, "Jesus, Son of David,
  L  18.38             he         cried,              "Jesus, Son of David,


M     9.28        Son of David."  When he entered the house,
  M  20.31        Son of David!"  The crowd                    rebuked them, telling
  Mk 10.48    have mercy on me!"  And many                     rebuked him,  telling
  L  18.39    have mercy on me!"  And those who were in front rebuked him,  telling


M     9.28                        the blind men came to him;
  M  20.31    them to be silent;  but they cried out     the more, "Lord,        have
  Mk 10.48    him  to be silent;  but he   cried out all the more, "Son of David, have
  L  18.39    him  to be silent;  but he   cried out all the more, "Son of David, have


M     9.28                        and Jesus
  M  20.32    mercy on us, Son of David!"  And Jesus stopped and         called    them,
  Mk 10.49    mercy on me!"       And Jesus stopped and said, "Call     him."
  L  18.40    mercy on me!"       And Jesus stopped, and          commanded him


  Mk 10.49    And they called the blind man, saying to him, "Take heart; rise, he is
  L  18.40    to be brought to him;


  Mk 10.50    calling you." And throwing off his mantle he sprang up and came to
  L  18.40                 and when                 he            came near,


M     9.28                        said to them,   "Do you believe that I am able to
  M  20.32                        saying,     "What do you       want me        to
  Mk 10.51    Jesus.  And Jesus said to him, "What do you       want me        to
  L  18.41             he       asked    him, "What do you       want me        to


M     9.28    do this?"                    They said to him, "Yes, Lord."
  M  20.33    do for you?"                 They said to him,       "Lord,   let our
  Mk 10.51    do for you?" And the blind man  said to him,        "Master, let me
  L  18.41    do for you?"              He    said,            "Lord,   let me


M     9.29                    Then he         touched their eyes, saying,
  M  20.34    eyes be opened."  And  Jesus in pity touched their eyes,
  Mk 10.52    receive my sight." And Jesus                          said to him,
  L  18.42    receive my sight." And Jesus                          said to him,


M     9.30    "According to      your faith be it done to you."  And
  M  20.34                                                      and immediately
  Mk 10.52    "Go your way;      your faith has made you well."  And immediately
  L  18.43    "Receive your sight; your faith has made you well." And immediately


M     9.30    their eyes were opened.  And Jesus sternly charged them, "See that no
  M  20.34    they received their sight and followed him.
  Mk 10.52    he   received his   sight and followed him on the way.
  L  18.43    he   received his   sight and followed him, glorifying God; and all


M     9.31    one knows it."  But they went away and spread his fame through all that
  L  18.43    the people, when they saw it, gave praise to God.


M     9.31    district.
```

M	9.32	As they were going away, behold,
M	12.22	*Then*
M	15.30	*And great crowds came to him, bringing with them the lame, the maimed,*
L	11.14	*Now he was casting out*

M	9.33	a	dumb demoniac was brought to him.	And when the demon had
M	12.22	a *blind and* dumb demoniac was brought to him,		*and*
M	15.30	*the blind, the* dumb, *and many others, and they put them at his feet, and*
L	11.14	a	demon that was dumb;	when the demon had

M	9.33	been cast out,		the dumb man
M	12.22	*he healed him,* so that		the dumb man
M	15.31	*he healed them,* |*so that the throng wondered, when they saw* the dumb
L	11.14	*gone* out,		the dumb man

M	9.33	spoke;	and	the crowds	marveled,
M	12.23	spoke *and saw.*	*And all the people were amazed, and*
M	15.31	speaking, *the maimed whole, the lame walking, and the blind seeing;*
L	11.14	spoke,	and	the *people*	marveled.

M	9.34	saying, "Never was anything like this seen in Israel."	But	the
M	12.24	said, *"Can this be the Son of David?"*	But *when* the
M	15.31.	*and they glorified the God*	*of* Israel.
Mk	3.22		And	the
L	11.15		But

M	9.34	Pharisees	said, "He casts out demons by
M	12.24	Pharisees *heard it they*	said, *"It is only* by
Mk	3.22	*scribes who came down from Jerusalem* said, "He *is possessed* by
L	11.15	*some of them*	said, "He casts out demons by

M	9.34		the prince of demons."
M	12.24	*Beelzebul,*	the prince of demons, *that this man casts out* demons."
Mk	3.22	*Beelzebul, and by* the prince of demons	*he casts out the demons."*
L	11.15	*Beelzebul,*	the prince of demons";

22. SECOND DISCOURSE: MISSION OF THE TWELVE

Matthew 9.35–11.1

a. Setting

Matthew 9.35–38

M	9.35	And	Jesus	went about
Mk	6.6b	And	he	went about *among*
L	8.1	Soon afterward he	went on	*through*
M	4.23	And	he	went about
L	10.1	*After this the Lord appointed seventy others, and sent them on ahead*

M	9.35	all the cities and villages, teaching in their
Mk	6.6b	the villages teaching.
L	8.1	cities and villages, preaching
M	4.23	all *Galilee,* teaching in their
L	10.1	*of him, two by two, into every town and place where he himself was*

47

```
M      9.35    synagogues and preaching the gospel       of the kingdom,
L      8.1                     and bringing   the good news of the kingdom of God.   And the
  M    4.23    synagogues and preaching the gospel       of the kingdom


M      9.35                                  and                          healing every
L      8.2     twelve were with him,  |and also some women who had been healed of evil
  M    4.23                                  and                          healing every


M      9.36    disease and every infirmity.  When he saw the       crowds,      he had
Mk     6.34                         As he went ashore he saw a great throng, and he had
L      8.2     spirits and            infirmities: Mary, called Magdalene, from whom seven
  M    4.23    disease and every infirmity among the people.
  M   14.14                         As he went ashore he saw a great throng; and he had


M      9.36    compassion for them, because they were harassed and helpless, like sheep
Mk     6.34    compassion on  them, because they were                         like sheep
L      8.3     demons had gone out,  |and Joanna, the wife of Chuza, Herod's steward, and
  M   14.14    compassion on  them, and healed their sick.


M      9.37    without a shepherd.  Then he      said to his disciples,
Mk     6.34    without a shepherd; and he began to teach them many things.
L      8.3     Susanna, and many others, who provided for them out of their means.
L     10.2     about to come.      And  he      said to     them,
  J    4.35                        Do   you not say, 'There are yet four months, then


M      9.38        "The harvest is plentiful, but the laborers are few;  |pray therefore
L     10.2         "The harvest is plentiful, but the laborers are few;   pray therefore
  J    4.35     comes the harvest'?  I tell you, lift up your eyes, and see


M      9.38    the Lord of the harvest to send out laborers into his harvest."
L     10.2     the Lord of the harvest to send out laborers into his harvest.
  J    4.35                     how the fields are already white for harvest.
```

b. The Twelve

Matthew 10.1-4

```
  L    6.12      In these days he went out to the mountain to pray; and all night he
  L    6.12      continued in prayer to God.


M     10.1     And                         he                         called to him
Mk     3.13    And                         he went up on the mountain, and called to him those
L      6.13    And when it was day,        he                         called
  Mk   6.7     And                         he                         called to him
  L    9.1     And                         he                         called
  L   10.1     After this        the Lord


M     10.1                                                             his twelve
Mk     3.14    whom he desired; and they came to him.  And he appointed     twelve, to
L      6.13                                                            his
  Mk   6.7                                                             the twelve,
  L    9.1                                                             the twelve
  L   10.1                                                appointed       seventy
```

48

```
M   10.1    disciples                                                                and
Mk  3.15    be with him, and      to be sent        out to preach                    |and
L   6.13    disciples,    and chose from them twelve,
  Mk 6.7                    and began to      send them out              two by two, and
  L  9.1    together                                                                 and
  L  10.1   others,    and                sent them on ahead of him, two by two, into
```

```
M   10.1    gave them          authority over     unclean spirits, to cast them
Mk  3.15    have               authority                            to cast
  Mk 6.7    gave them          authority over the unclean spirits.
  L  9.1    gave them power and authority over     all     demons
  L  10.1   every town and place where he himself was about to come.
```

```
M   10.2    out, and to heal every disease and every infirmity.  The      names of
Mk  3.15    out demons:
L   6.13                                                  whom he named
  L  9.1          and to cure      diseases,
  J  1.42                          He brought him to Jesus.  Jesus
  A  1.13         and when they had entered, they went up to the
```

```
M   10.2    the twelve apostles are these:  first, Simon,              who
Mk  3.16                                            Simon              whom
L   6.14                    apostles;               Simon,             whom
  J  1.40                                One of the two who heard John speak,
  J  1.41             He first found his brother Simon, and said to him, "We have
  J  1.42    looked at him, and said, "So you are Simon the son of John?  You shall
  A  1.13    upper room, where they were staying,
```

```
M   10.2        is called            Peter, and Andrew his
Mk  3.16    he surnamed              Peter;
L   6.14    he     named             Peter, and Andrew his
  J  1.40    and followed him,              was Andrew, Simon Peter's
  J  1.41    found the Messiah" (which means Christ).
  J  1.42    be called Cephas" (which means Peter).
  A  1.13                             Peter
```

```
M   10.2    brother;     James the son of Zebedee, and John his brother;
Mk  3.17                 James the son of Zebedee  and John the brother of James, whom
L   6.14    brother, and James                     and John,
  J  1.40    brother,
  A  1.13         and John                         and James
```

```
M   10.3                                                               Philip    and
Mk  3.18    he surnamed Boanerges, that is, sons of thunder; |Andrew, and Philip, and
L   6.14                                                      and Philip, and
  J  1.43    The next day Jesus decided to go to Galilee.     And he found Philip  and
  J  1.44                                              Now Philip    was
  A  1.13                                 and Andrew,          Philip    and
```

```
M   10.3    Bartholomew;      Thomas       and Matthew the tax collector; James the
Mk  3.18    Bartholomew, and Matthew,      and Thomas,         and James the
L   6.15    Bartholomew, |and Matthew,     and Thomas,         and James the
  J  1.43    said to him, "Follow me."
  J  1.44    from Bethsaida, the city of Andrew and Peter.
  A  1.13    Thomas,          Bartholomew and Matthew,               James the
```

```
M   10.4    son of Alphaeus, and Thaddaeus;                       |Simon the
Mk  3.18    son of Alphaeus, and Thaddaeus,               and Simon the
L   6.16    son of Alphaeus, and Simon who was called the Zealot, |and Judas the
  A  1.13   son of Alphaeus  and Simon              the Zealot  and Judas the
```

M	10.4	Cananaean, <u>and Judas Iscariot</u>, <u>who betrayed him</u>.
Mk	3.19a	Cananaean, │<u>and Judas Iscariot</u>, <u>who betrayed him</u>.
L	6.16	son of James, <u>and Judas Iscariot</u>, <u>who</u> became a traitor.
A	*1.13*	*son of James.*

c. The Mission

Matthew 10.5-15

M	10.5	These <u>twelve</u>
Mk	6.7	And he called to him the <u>twelve</u>,
L	9.1	And he called the <u>twelve</u> together *and gave them power and*
L	*10.1*	*After this the Lord appointed seventy others,*

M	10.5	Jesus sent
Mk	6.7	and began to send them
L	9.2	*authority over all demons and to cure diseases,* │and he <u>sent</u> them
L	*10.1*	*and* <u>sent</u> *them*

M	10.5	<u>out</u>,
Mk	6.8	<u>out</u> *two by two, and gave them authority over the unclean spirits.* He
L	9.2	<u>out</u>
L	*10.1*	*on ahead of him, two by two,*

M	10.5	<u>charging them</u>, "Go nowhere among the Gentiles, <u>and enter no town of the</u>
Mk	6.8	charged <u>them</u>
L	*10.1*	*into every* <u>*town*</u> *and place*

M	10.6	<u>Samaritans</u>, │<u>but go rather to the lost sheep of the house of Israel</u>.
M	*15.24*	*He answered, "I was sent only* <u>to the lost sheep of the house of Israel</u>."
L	*10.2*	*where he himself was about to come. And he said to them, "The harvest*

L	*10.2*	*is plentiful, but the laborers are few; pray therefore the Lord of the*
L	*10.3*	*harvest to send out laborers into his harvest. Go your way; behold, I*
L	*10.3*	*send you out as lambs in the midst of wolves.*

M	10.7	<u>And</u> <u>preach</u> <u>as you</u>
L	9.2	to <u>preach</u>
M	*3.1*	*In those days* *came John the Baptist,* <u>preaching</u> *in the*
M	*4.17*	*From that time* *Jesus began* *to* <u>preach</u>,
Mk	*1.14*	*Now after John was arrested, Jesus came into Galilee,* <u>preaching</u> *the*

M	10.7	<u>go</u>, <u>saying</u>, '<u>The kingdom of</u>
L	9.2	<u>the kingdom of</u>
M	*3.2*	*wilderness of Judea,* │"*Repent,* *for* <u>the kingdom of</u>
M	*4.17*	<u>*saying*</u>, "*Repent,* *for* <u>the kingdom of</u>
Mk	*1.15*	*gospel of God,* │*and* <u>saying</u>, "*The time is fulfilled, and* <u>the kingdom of</u>
L	*10.9b*	*and say to them,* '<u>The kingdom of</u>
L	*10.11b*	*nevertheless know this,* *that* <u>the kingdom of</u>

M	10.8	<u>heaven is</u> <u>at hand</u>.' <u>Heal the sick, raise the dead, cleanse</u>
L	9.2	God and to <u>heal</u>.
M	*3.2*	<u>heaven is</u> <u>at hand</u>."
M	*4.17*	<u>heaven is</u> <u>at hand</u>."
Mk	*1.15*	*God* *is* <u>at hand</u>; *repent, and believe in the gospel.*"
L	*10.9a*	*God* *has come near to you.'* │<u>heal the sick</u> *in it*
L	*10.11b*	*God* *has come near.'*

```
M    10.8     lepers, cast out demons.  You received without paying, give without pay.
L     9.3                                                        And he said to them,


M    10.9        Take
Mk    6.8     to take nothing for their journey except a staff; no  bread, no  bag,
L     9.3     "Take nothing for your  journey,        no staff, nor bag, nor bread,
  L  10.4     Carry


M    10.10    no  gold, nor silver, nor copper in your  belts, |no bag for your
Mk    6.8     no  money                        in their belts;
L     9.3     nor money;
  L  10.4     no  purse,                                    no bag,


M    10.10    journey, nor       two tunics,      nor         sandals, nor a staff;
Mk    6.9                but to wear sandals and not put on two tunics.
L     9.3     and  do  not have two tunics.
  L  10.4                                        no          sandals; and salute no


  L  10.5     one on the road.  Whatever house you enter, first say, 'Peace be to this
  L  10.6     house!'  And if a son of peace is there, your peace shall rest upon him;
  L  10.7     but if not, it shall return to you.  And remain in the same house, eating
  L  10.7     and drinking what they provide,


M    10.11    for the laborer deserves his food.                          And
  L  10.7     for the laborer deserves his wages; do not go from house to house.


M    10.11    whatever            town or village you enter, find out who is worthy in
  L  10.8     Whenever you enter a town and they receive you, eat what is set before you;


M    10.11    it, and stay with him    until you depart.
Mk   6.10b,a         stay there       until you leave the place.  And he said to them,
L     9.4b,a         stay there, and from there depart.        And


M    10.12,13  As       you enter the house, salute it.  And if the house is worthy, let
Mk    6.10a   "Where    you enter a  house,
L     9.4a    whatever house you    enter,


M    10.13    your peace come upon it; but if it is not worthy, let your peace return
  L  10.10                                             But whenever you enter


M    10.14    to you.  And if     any one  will not receive you or
Mk    6.11            And if     any place will not receive you and they refuse to
L     9.5            And wherever they     do   not receive you,
  L  10.10    a town  and         they     do   not receive you,


M    10.14    listen to your words,                      shake off the dust
Mk    6.11    hear      you,        when you leave,       shake off the dust
L     9.5                           when you leave that town shake off the dust
  L  10.11a                         go into its streets and say, |'Even the dust of your


M    10.14         from          your feet as you leave that house or town.
Mk    6.12         that is    on your feet for a testimony against them."  So  they
L     9.6          from          your feet as a testimony against them."  And they
  L  10.11a   town that clings to our  feet, we wipe off     against you;
```

                                51

M	10.15	<u>Truly,</u> <u>I say to you,</u>　　　<u>it shall be more tolerable on the</u>　<u>day of</u>
Mk	6.12	*went out*　　　　　　*and preached that men should repent.*
L	9.6	*departed and went through the villages, preaching the gospel*
M	11.24	*But*　　<u>I</u> *tell*　<u>you</u> *that* <u>it shall be more tolerable on the</u>　<u>day of</u>
L	10.12	<u>I</u> *tell*　<u>you,</u>　　<u>it shall be more tolerable on</u> *that* <u>day</u>

M	10.15	<u>judgment for the land of Sodom and Gomorrah than for that town.</u>
Mk	6.13	*And they cast out many demons, and anointed with oil many that were sick*
M	11.24	<u>judgment for the land of Sodom</u>　　　<u>than for</u>　　<u>you."</u>
L	10.12	<u>for</u>　　<u>Sodom</u>　　　<u>than for that town.</u>

Mk	6.13	*and healed　them.*
L	9.6	*and healing everywhere.*

d. The Instruction

Matthew 10.16-42

M	10.16	"Behold, <u>I send you out as sheep in the midst of wolves;</u>
L	10.3	Go your way; <u>behold,</u> <u>I send you out as</u> lambs <u>in the midst of wolves.</u>

M	10.17	<u>so be wise as serpents and innocent as doves.</u>　<u>Beware of men;</u> <u>for they</u>
Mk	13.9	"But take heed to yourselves; <u>for they</u>
M	24.9	"Then <u>they</u>
L	21.12	*But before all this*　　　<u>they</u>

M	10.17	<u>will deliver you up to councils,</u>　<u>and</u>　　　　　flog　<u>you</u>
Mk	13.9	<u>will deliver you up to councils;</u>　<u>and</u>　you will be beaten
L	12.11	<u>And</u> when they　　bring　<u>you</u>
M	24.9	<u>will deliver you up to</u> *tribulation,* <u>and</u>　　put　<u>you</u>
L	21.12	<u>will</u> *lay their hands on you and persecute you,*　delivering <u>you</u>
J	16.2a	*They will*　put　<u>you</u>

M	10.18	<u>in</u>　　their <u>synagogues,</u>　|<u>and you will be dragged before</u>
Mk	13.9	<u>in</u>　　　<u>synagogues;</u>　<u>and you will</u>　stand　<u>before</u>
L	12.11	before the　<u>synagogues</u>　　<u>and</u>　　　　　the
M	24.9	*to*　　　*death; and you will be hated by all nations for my name's*
L	21.12	*up to　the*　<u>synagogues</u> *and prisons,* <u>and you will be</u> *brought* <u>before</u>
J	16.2a	*out of the*　<u>synagogues;</u>

M	10.18	<u>governors and kings for my</u>　　<u>sake,</u>　　　　<u>to</u>
Mk	13.9	<u>governors and kings for my</u>　　<u>sake,</u>　　　　<u>to</u>
L	12.11	<u>rulers and the authorities,</u>
M	24.9	*sake.*
L	21.13	<u>kings and governors</u> *for my* name's <u>sake.</u>　*This will be a time for you* <u>to</u>

M	10.18	<u>bear testimony before them and the Gentiles.</u>
Mk	13.10	<u>bear testimony before them.</u>　*And the gospel must first be preached to all*
L	21.13	<u>bear testimony</u>.

M	10.19	<u>When they</u>　　　　<u>deliver you up,</u> <u>do not be</u>
Mk	13.11	*nations.*　And <u>when they</u> bring you to trial and <u>deliver you up,</u> <u>do not be</u>
L	12.11	<u>do not be</u>
L	21.14	*Settle it therefore in your minds,*　　<u>not</u> *to*

52

```
M    10.19    anxious                  how              you are to speak  or what you are to say;
Mk   13.11    anxious   beforehand                                        what you are to say;
L    12.11    anxious                  how or what  you are to answer  or what you are to say;
  L  21.14    meditate beforehand how                    to answer;


M    10.20    for       what you are to say will be given to you in that hour;  |for it is
Mk   13.11    but say whatever                   is given     you in that hour,  for it is
  L  21.15    for           I          will      give      you a mouth and wisdom, which


M    10.20    not you who speak, but                the        Spirit    of your Father
Mk   13.11    not you who speak; but                the Holy Spirit.
L    12.12                         for             the Holy Spirit
  L  21.15    none of your adversaries will be able to withstand or contradict.
  J  14.26                         But the Counselor, the Holy Spirit, whom the Father


  L  12.12                                   will teach you in that very hour
  J  14.26    will send in my name, he will teach you all things, and bring to your


M    10.20                                 speaking through you.
L    12.12                                      what       you ought to say."
  J  14.26    remembrance all that I have said     to     you.


M    10.21          Brother    will    deliver   up                      brother to death,
Mk   13.12    And brother    will    deliver   up                      brother to death,
  M  24.10    And then many will fall away, and betray one another,
  L  21.16          You       will be delivered up even by parents and brothers and
  J  15.19                                              If you were of the
  J  16.2b    indeed, the hour is coming when whoever kills you will think he is


M    10.21    and the father his child, and children will rise against parents and
Mk   13.12    and the father his child, and children will rise against parents and
  L  21.16    kinsmen and friends,                                           and
  J  15.19    world, the world would love its own; but because you are not of the
  J  16.2b    offering service to God.


M    10.22    have          them       put to death;   |and you will be hated by all
Mk   13.13    have          them       put to death;   |and you will be hated by all
  M  24.9b                                              and you will be hated by all
  M  24.10                                              and          hate       one
  L  6.22     "Blessed are you when men            hate       you,
  L  21.17    some of you they will put to death;      you will be hated by all
  J  15.18    "If the world hates you, know that it has hated me before it hated    you.
  J  15.19    world, but I chose you out of the world, therefore the world hates    you.


  M  24.9b    nations
  M  24.10    another.
  L  6.22     and when they exclude you and revile you, and cast out your name as evil,


M    10.22    for           my name's sake.
Mk   13.13    for           my name's sake.
  M  24.9b    for           my name's sake.
  L  6.22     on account of the Son of man!
  L  21.18    for           my name's sake. But not a hair of your head will perish.
```

```
M   10.22,23  But he who endures    to the end will be          saved.    When they persecute
Mk  13.13     But he who endures    to the end will be          saved.
 M  24.13     But he who endures    to the end will be          saved.
 L  21.19     By  your   endurance        you will gain your lives.
 J  16.1      "I have said all this to you to keep you from falling away.


M   10.23     you in one town, flee to the next; for truly, I say to you, you will not
M   10.23     have gone through all the towns of Israel, before the Son of man comes.


 L  6.39          He also told them a parable: "Can a blind man lead a blind man?  Will


M   10.24                                   "A disciple is not above his teacher,
L   6.40      they not both fall into a pit?  A disciple is not above his teacher,
 J  13.16                                     Truly, truly,        I say  to you,
 J  15.20                                     Remember the word that I said to you,


M   10.25     nor   a servant       above        his master; |it is enough for the
L   6.40                                                      but every one when he is
 J  13.16             a servant is not greater than his master;  nor is he who is sent
 J  15.20     'A servant is not greater than his master.'  If they persecuted me,


M   10.25     disciple    to  be like his teacher, and the servant like his master.
L   6.40      fully taught will be like his teacher.
 J  13.16     greater than he who sent him.
 J  15.20     they will persecute you; if they kept my word, they will keep yours also.


M   10.25                                      If they have called the master of
 M  9.34      But       the Pharisees                    said, "He casts out
 M  12.24     But when the Pharisees heard it they       said, "It is only
Mk  3.22      And       the scribes who came down from Jerusalem said, "He is possessed
 L  11.15     But           some of them                 said, "He casts out


M   10.25     the house Beelzebul, how much more will they malign those of his
 M  9.34      demons by                    the prince of demons."
 M  12.24            by Beelzebul,         the prince of demons, that this man casts
Mk  3.22            by Beelzebul, and by the prince of demons         he  casts
 L  11.15     demons by Beelzebul,         the prince of demons";


M   10.25     household.
 M  12.24     out      demons."
Mk  3.22      out the demons."


M   10.26      "So have no fear of them;
L   12.1        In the meantime, when so many thousands of the multitude had gathered


 L  12.1      together that they trod upon one another, he began to say to his disciples
 L  12.1      first, "Beware of the leaven of the Pharisees, which is hypocrisy.


M   10.26     for     nothing is covered    that will  not be        revealed, or
Mk  4.22      For there is nothing hid,     except to        be made manifest; nor is
L   8.17      For     nothing is hid        that shall not be made manifest, nor
L   12.2              Nothing is covered up that will  not be        revealed, or
```

```
M    10.27              hidden that will  not be known.                What      I
Mk    4.22   anything secret,
L     8.17   anything secret that shall  not be known
L    12.3               hidden that will  not be known.  Therefore whatever you have


M    10.27   tell you in the dark,          utter in the light; and what you hear
Mk    4.22                   except to come to      light.
L     8.17                        and      come to      light.
L    12.3    said        in the dark shall be heard in the light, and what you have


M    10.27   whispered,                         proclaim   upon the housetops.
L    12.4    whispered in private rooms shall be proclaimed upon the housetops.   "I


M    10.28                   And do not fear those who kill the body  but
L    12.4    tell you, my friends, do not fear those who kill the body, and after that


M    10.28      cannot        kill the soul;  rather                       fear
L    12.5    have no more that they can do.  But I will warn you whom to fear: fear


M    10.28   him who           can destroy both soul and body in    hell.
L    12.5    him who, after he has killed, has power to cast  into hell; yes, I tell


M    10.29               Are not two   sparrows sold for a    penny?  And not one
L    12.6    you, fear him! Are not five sparrows sold for two pennies?  And not one


M    10.30   of them will fall to the ground without your Father's will.  But   even
L    12.7    of them is     forgotten         before        God.      Why,  even
     L  21.18                                                          But   not


M    10.31   the hairs of your head are all numbered.  Fear not, therefore; you are
L    12.7    the hairs of your head are all numbered.  Fear not;              you are
     L  21.18  a   hair  of your head will perish.


M    10.32   of more value than many sparrows.   So            every one who
L    12.8    of more value than many sparrows.  "And I tell you, every one who


M    10.32   acknowledges me before men,     I         also will acknowledge before
L    12.8    acknowledges me before men, the Son of man also will acknowledge before


M    10.33              my Father who is in heaven; but    whoever    denies    me
L    12.9    the angels of God;                    but he who       denies    me
     Mk  8.38                                        For    whoever is ashamed of me
     L   9.26                                        For    whoever is ashamed of me


M    10.33          before men,
L    12.9           before men
     Mk  8.38  and of my words in this adulterous and sinful generation, of him will the
     L   9.26  and of my words,                                          of him will the


M    10.33   I         also will    deny
L    12.9               will be denied
     Mk  8.38  Son of man also     be ashamed, when he comes in the glory
     L   9.26  Son of man          be ashamed  when he comes in his glory and the glory
```

55

```
M    10.33    before              my  Father who is in heaven.
L    12.10    before the angels of    God.  And every one who speaks a word against the
  Mk  8.38    of                      his Father with   the holy angels."
  L   9.27    of                      the Father and of the holy angels.  But I tell you truly,


  L  12.10    Son of man will be forgiven; but he who blasphemes against the Holy Spirit
  L   9.27    there are some standing here who will not taste death before they see the


  L  12.10    will not be forgiven.
  L   9.27    kingdom of God."


  L  12.49       "I came to cast fire upon the earth; and would that it were already
  L  12.50    kindled!  I have a baptism to be baptized with; and how I am constrained
  L  12.50    until it is accomplished!


M    10.34    "Do not think that I have come to bring peace on earth;      I have
L    12.51    Do you think that I have come to give  peace on earth?  No, I tell


M    10.34    not come to bring peace, but a      sword.
L    12.52    you,                      but rather division; for henceforth in one house


  L  12.52    there will be five divided, three against two and two against three;


M    10.35    For I have come to set           a man against his father,
L    12.53    they will be divided, father against son and son against      father,


M    10.35                   and a daughter against her mother,
L    12.53    mother against daughter and   daughter against her mother, mother-in-law


M    10.35                        and a daughter-in-law against her mother-in-
L    12.53    against her daughter-in-law and   daughter-in-law against her mother-in-
  M  16.24                                        Then Jesus
  Mk  8.34    And he called to him the multitude  with his disciples,      and
  L   9.23                                        And  he
  L  14.25    Now           great multitudes accompanied him; and he turned and


M    10.36,37  law; and a man's foes will be those of his own household.  He who loves
L    12.53    law."
  M  16.24    told his disciples, "If any man would come  after me,
  Mk  8.34    said to them,      "If any man would come  after me,
  L   9.23    said to all,       "If any man would come  after me,
  L  14.26    said to them,     |"If any one      comes to   me and does not hate
  J  12.26                       If any one      serves    me,


M    10.37            father or mother more than me is not worthy of me; and he who
  L  14.26    his own father and mother and wife and children and brothers and sisters,
  J  12.26                                  he must follow me; and where I


M    10.38    loves son or daughter more than me is not worthy of me; and he who   does
  M  16.24                         let him deny himself  and
  Mk  8.34                         let him deny himself  and
  L   9.23                         let him deny himself  and
  L  14.27    yes, and even his own life, he cannot be my disciple.      Whoever does
  J  12.26    am, there shall my servant be also; if any one serves me, the Father
```

```
M    10.38   not take      his        cross        and follow      me   is not worthy of me.
 M   16.24        take up his        cross        and follow      me.
 Mk   8.34        take up his        cross        and follow      me.
 L    9.23        take up his        cross daily and follow      me.
 L   14.27   not bear      his own cross          and come after me, cannot be my disciple.
 J   12.26   will honor him.


M    10.39       He who              finds his life will lose it, and he who  loses his
 M   16.25   For whoever would       save  his life will lose it, and whoever loses his
 Mk   8.35   For whoever would       save  his life will lose it; and whoever loses his
 L    9.24   For whoever would       save  his life will lose it; and whoever loses his
 L   17.33       Whoever seeks to gain his life will lose it, but whoever loses his
 J   12.25       He who              loves his life       loses it, and he who hates his


M    10.39   life for my sake                      will find   it.
 M   16.25   life for my sake                      will find   it.
 M    8.35   life for my sake and the gospel's     will save   it.
 L    9.24   life for my sake,              he will save   it.
 L   17.33   life                                  will preserve it.
 J   12.25   life in this world                    will keep   it for eternal life.


M    10.40                                          "He who  receives
 M   18.5                                           "Whoever receives one such
 Mk   9.37                                          "Whoever receives one such
 L    9.48   and                           said to them, "Whoever receives     this
 L   10.16                                           "He who  hears
 J   12.44   And        Jesus cried out and said,   "He who  believes
 J   13.20   Truly, truly, I          say to you,   he who   receives any one


M    10.40   you             receives me,                              and he
 M   18.5    child in my name receives me;
 Mk   9.37   child in my name receives me;                             and
 L    9.48   child in my name receives me,                             and
 L   10.16   you             hears   me, and he who rejects you rejects me, and he
 J   12.44              in me,
 J   12.45                                                           And he
 J   13.20   whom I send     receives me;                             and he


M    10.41   who      receives me  receives               him who sent me. He who
 Mk   9.37   whoever receives me, receives not    me but  him who sent me."
 L    9.48   whoever receives me  receives                him who sent me; for he
 L   10.16   who      rejects  me  rejects                him who sent me."
 J   12.44                        believes not in me but in him who sent me.
 J   12.45   who      sees     me  sees                   him who sent me.
 J   13.20   who      receives me  receives               him who sent me."


M    10.41   receives a prophet because he is a prophet shall receive a prophet's
 L    9.48   who is least among you all is the one who is great."


M    10.41   reward, and he who receives a righteous man because he is a righteous


M    10.42   man shall receive a righteous man's reward.  And
 Mk   9.41                                          For truly, I say to you,


M    10.42   whoever gives to one of these little ones even a cup of cold water
 Mk   9.41   whoever gives     you               a cup of      water to


M    10.42        because he is   a disciple, truly, I say to you, he shall   not
 Mk   9.41   drink because you bear the name of Christ,          will by no
```

```
M    10.42            lose his reward."
Mk    9.41    means   lose his reward.
```

e. Summary

Matthew 11.1

```
M    11.1     And when Jesus had finished instructing his twelve disciples, he went
M    11.1     on from there to teach and preach in their cities.
```

23. JOHN THE BAPTIST AND THE 'COMING ONE'

Matthew 11.2-19

```
M    11.2       Now when       John heard in prison about the deeds of the Christ,
L    7.18,19    The disciples of John told him of all these things.            And


M    11.2       he                                    sent word by his disciples
L    7.19       John, calling to him two of his disciples, sent them to the Lord,


M    11.3       |and said to him, "Are you he who is to come, or shall we look for
L    7.19            saying,      "Are you he who is to come, or shall we look for


M    11.3       another?"
L    7.20       another?"  And when the men had come to him, they said, "John the Baptist


   L   7.20     has sent us to you, saying, 'Are you he who is to come, or shall we look
   L   7.21     for another?'"  In that hour he cured many of diseases and plagues and
   L   7.21     evil spirits, and on many that were blind he bestowed sight.


M    11.4       And Jesus answered them, "Go and tell John what you    hear and see:
L    7.22       And he    answered them, "Go and tell John what you have seen and heard:


M    11.5       the blind receive their sight and the lame walk, lepers are cleansed
L    7.22       the blind receive their sight,    the lame walk, lepers are cleansed,


M    11.5       and the deaf hear, and the dead are raised up, and the poor have good
L    7.22       and the deaf hear,    the dead are raised up,    the poor have good


M    11.6       news preached to them.  And blessed is he who takes no offense at me."
L    7.23       news preached to them.  And blessed is he who takes no offense at me."


M    11.7       As       they             went away, Jesus began to speak to the
L    7.24       When the messengers of John had gone,    he   began to speak to the


M    11.7       crowds concerning John:  "What did you go out into the wilderness to
L    7.24       crowds concerning John:  "What did you go out into the wilderness to


M    11.8       behold?  A reed shaken by the wind? |Why  then did you go out?  To see
L    7.25       behold?  A reed shaken by the wind? What then did you go out   to see?
```

M	11.8	a man clothed in soft raiment? Behold, those who wear soft
L	7.25	A man clothed in soft clothing? Behold, those who are gorgeously

M	11.9	raiment are in kings' houses. Why then did you
L	7.26	appareled and live in luxury are in kings' courts. What then did you

M	11.9	go out? To see a prophet? Yes, I tell you, and more than a prophet.
L	7.26	go out to see? A prophet? Yes, I tell you, and more than a prophet.

M	11.10	This is he of whom it is written,
L	7.27	This is he of whom it is written,
Mk	1.2	As it is written in Isaiah the prophet,

M	11.10	'Behold, I send my messenger before thy face,
L	7.27	'Behold, I send my messenger before thy face,
Mk	1.2	"Behold, I send my messenger before thy face,

M	11.10	who shall prepare thy way before thee.'
L	7.27	who shall prepare thy way before thee.'
Mk	1.2	who shall prepare thy way;

M	11.11	Truly, I say to you, among those born of women there has risen no one
L	7.28	I tell you, among those born of women none is

M	11.11	greater than John the Baptist; yet he who is least in the kingdom of
L	7.28	greater than John; yet he who is least in the kingdom of

M	11.11	heaven is greater than he.
L	7.29	God is greater than he." (When they heard this all the people and the

L	7.29	tax collectors justified God, having been baptized with the baptism of
L	7.30	John; but the Pharisees and the lawyers rejected the purpose of God for
L	7.30	themselves, not having been baptized by him.)

M	11.12	From the days of John the Baptist until now
L	16.16	"The law and the prophets were until John; since then the
M	17.10	And
Mk	9.11	And

M	11.12	the kingdom of heaven has suffered violence, and men
L	16.16	good news of the kingdom of God is preached, and every one
M	17.10	the disciples asked him, "Then why do the scribes say that first Elijah
Mk	9.11	they asked him, "Why do the scribes say that first Elijah

M	11.13	of violence take it by force. For all the prophets and the law
L	16.17	enters it violently. But it is easier for heaven and earth to pass
M	17.11	must come?" He replied, "Elijah does come, and he is to restore
Mk	9.12	must come?" And he said to them, "Elijah does come first to restore

M	11.13	prophesied until John;
L	16.17	away, than for one dot of the law to become void.
M	17.11	all things;
Mk	9.12	all things; and how is it written of the Son of man, that he should suf-

```
M    11.14                                      and if you are willing to accept it, he is Elijah
 M   17.12                                                       but I tell you that Elijah
 Mk   9.13        fer many things and be treated with contempt?  But I tell you that Elijah


M    11.14    who is  to      come.
 M   17.12            has already come, and they did not know him, but did to him whatever
 Mk   9.13            has           come, and they                     did to him whatever


 M   17.12    they pleased.  So also the Son of man will suffer at their hands."
 Mk   9.13    they pleased,  as it is written of him."


M    11.15                                   He  who has ears to hear, let him hear.
 M   13.9                                    He  who has ears,         let him hear."
 M   13.43b                                  He  who has ears,         let him hear.
 Mk   4.9     And he said,                  "He  who has ears to hear, let him hear."
 Mk   4.23                               If any man has ears to hear, let him hear."
 Mk   7.16                              "If any man has ears to hear, let him hear."
 L    8.8b    As  he said this, he called out,"He  who has ears to hear, let him hear."
 L   14.35b                                  He  who has ears to hear, let him hear."


M    11.16    "But to what     shall I compare               this generation?
 L    7.31       "To what then shall I compare the men of this generation, and what


M    11.16                     It  is  like children sitting in the market places and
 L    7.32    are they like?  They are like children sitting in the market place  and


M    11.16    calling to their playmates,
 L    7.32    calling to one another,


M    11.17               'We piped to you, and you did not dance;
 L    7.32               'We piped to you, and you did not dance;


M    11.17               we wailed, and you did not mourn.'
 L    7.32               we wailed, and you did not weep.'


M    11.18    For John               came neither eating        nor drinking,
 L    7.33    For John the Baptist has come      eating no bread and drinking no


M    11.19           and they say, 'He has a demon';  the Son of man  came eating
 L    7.34    wine; and you  say,  'He has a demon.'  The Son of man has come eating


M    11.19    and drinking, and they say, 'Behold, a glutton and a drunkard, a friend
 L    7.34    and drinking; and you  say, 'Behold, a glutton and a drunkard, a friend


M    11.19    of tax collectors and sinners!'  Yet wisdom is justified by     her
 L    7.35    of tax collectors and sinners!'  Yet wisdom is justified by all her


M    11.19    deeds."
 L    7.35    children."
```

24. WOES AND THANKSGIVINGS

Matthew 11.20-30

M	11.20	Then he began to upbraid the cities where most of his mighty works had
J	12.37	*Though he had done so many signs*

M	11.21	been done, because they did not repent. "Woe to you, Chorazin! woe to
L	10.13	"Woe to you, Chorazin! woe to
J	12.37	*before them, yet* they did not *believe in him;*

M	11.21	you, Bethsaida! for if the mighty works done in you had been done in
L	10.13	you, Bethsaida! for if the mighty works done in you had been done in

M	11.21	Tyre and Sidon, they would have repented long ago in sackcloth
L	10.13	Tyre and Sidon, they would have repented long ago, sitting in sackcloth

M	11.22	and ashes. But I tell you, it shall be more tolerable on the day of
L	10.14	and ashes. But it shall be more tolerable in the

M	11.23	judgment for Tyre and Sidon than for you. And you, Capernaum, will you
L	10.15	judgment for Tyre and Sidon than for you. And you, Capernaum, will you

M	11.23	be exalted to heaven? You shall be brought down to Hades. For if the
L	10.15	be exalted to heaven? You shall be brought down to Hades.

M	11.23	mighty works done in you had been done in Sodom, it would have remained

M	11.24	until this day. But I tell you that it shall be more tolerable on
L	10.12	I tell you, it shall be more tolerable on
M	10.15	*Truly, I say to you,* it shall be more tolerable on

M	11.24	the day of judgment for the land of Sodom than for
L	10.12	that day for Sodom than for that
M	10.15	the day of judgment for the land of Sodom *and Gomorrah* than for *that*

M	11.24	you."
L	10.12	town.
M	10.15	*town.*

M	11.25	At that time Jesus declared, "I thank
L	10.21	In that same hour he rejoiced in the Holy Spirit and said, "I thank

M	11.25	thee, Father, Lord of heaven and earth, that thou hast hidden these
L	10.21	thee, Father, Lord of heaven and earth, that thou hast hidden these

M	11.26	things from the wise and understanding and revealed them to babes; yea,
L	10.21	things from the wise and understanding and revealed them to babes; yea,
J	3.35	
J	13.3	*the*
J	17.25	*Jesus, knowing that the*
		0 righteous

```
M    11.27    Father, for such was thy gracious will.  All things have been delivered
L    10.22    Father, for such was thy gracious will.  All things have been delivered
J     3.35    Father loves the Son,   and has given   all things into his hand.
J    10.14                            I am the good shepherd; I know my own and my own know
J    13.3     Father                    had given     all things into his hands, and
J    17.25    Father,
```

```
M    11.27    to me by my Father; and no one knows       the Son    except the Father,
L    10.22    to me by my Father; and no one knows who the Son is except the Father,
J    10.15    me, | as the Father              knows        me
J    13.3     that he had come from God and was going to God,
J    17.25                         the world has not known thee, but I have known    thee;
```

```
M    11.27    and no one knows the Father      except the Son and any one to whom the
L    10.22    or     who         the Father is except the Son and any one to whom the
J     7.29         I   know     him, for I come from him, and he        sent me."
J    10.15    and    I   know  the Father; and I lay down my life for the sheep.
J    17.25    and these know                           that thou hast sent me.
```

```
M    11.28    Son chooses to reveal him.  Come to me, all who labor and are heavy
L    10.22    Son chooses to reveal him."
```

```
M    11.29    laden, and I will give you rest.  Take my yoke upon you, and learn from
M    11.29    me; for I am gentle and lowly in heart, and you will find rest for your
M    11.30    souls.  For my yoke is easy, and my burden is light."
```

25. QUESTION OF SABBATH OBSERVANCE

Matthew 12.1-8

```
M    12.1     At that time        Jesus   went  through the grainfields on the sabbath;
Mk    2.23    One   sabbath       he was going through the grainfields; and as they
L     6.1     On a sabbath, while he was going through the grainfields,
```

```
M    12.1                    his disciples were hungry, and they began to pluck
Mk    2.23    made their way his disciples            began to pluck
L     6.1                    his disciples                        plucked and
```

```
M    12.2               heads of grain and to eat.          But when     the
Mk    2.24              heads of grain.                     And          the
L     6.2     ate some heads of grain, rubbing them in their hands.  But some of the
```

```
M    12.2     Pharisees saw it, they said to him, "Look, your disciples are     doing
Mk    2.24    Pharisees            said to him, "Look, why           are they doing
L     6.2     Pharisees            said,              "Why           are you  doing
```

```
M    12.3     what is not lawful to do on the sabbath."   He   said to them, "Have
Mk    2.25    what is not lawful      on the sabbath?"  And he   said to them, "Have
L     6.3     what is not lawful to do on the sabbath?"  And Jesus answered,     "Have
```

```
M    12.3     you not    read what David did, when he              was hungry,
Mk    2.25    you never read what David did, when he was in need and was hungry, he
L     6.3     you not   read what David did  when he               was hungry, he
```

62

M	12.4	and those who were with him: how he entered the house of God
Mk	2.26	and those who were with him: how he entered the house of God, when
L	6.4	and those who were with him: how he entered the house of God,

M	12.4	and ate the bread of the Presence, which it
Mk	2.26	Abiathar was high priest, and ate the bread of the Presence, which it
L	6.4	and took and ate the bread of the Presence, which it

M	12.4	was not lawful for him to eat nor for
Mk	2.26	is not lawful for any but the priests to eat, and also gave it to
L	6.4	is not lawful for any but the priests to eat, and also gave it to

M	12.5	those who were with him, but only for the priests? Or have you not
Mk	2.26	those who were with him?"
L	6.4	those with him?"

M	12.5	read in the law how on the sabbath the priests in the temple profane
M	12.6	the sabbath, and are guiltless? I tell you, something greater than the
M	12.6	temple is here.

M	9.12	But when he heard it, he said, "Those who are well have no need of a
M	9.12	physician, but those who are sick.

M	12.7	And if you had known what this means, 'I desire mercy, and not sacrifice,'
Mk	2.27	And he said to them, "The sabbath
L	6.5	And he said to them,
M	9.13	Go and learn what this means, 'I desire mercy, and not sacrifice.'

M	12.8	you would not have condemned the guiltless. For the Son of man is lord
Mk	2.28	was made for man, not man for the sabbath; so the Son of man is lord
L	6.5	"The Son of man is lord
M	9.13	For I came not to call the righteous, but sinners."

M	12.8	of the sabbath."
Mk	2.28	even of the sabbath."
L	6.5	of the sabbath."

26. A WITHERED HAND

Matthew 12.9-21

M	12.9	And he went on from there, and entered their synagogue.
Mk	3.1	Again he entered the synagogue,
L	6.6	On another sabbath, when he entered the synagogue
L	14.1	One sabbath when he went to dine at the house of a

M	12.10	And behold,
Mk	3.1	and
L	6.6	and taught,
L	14.2	ruler who belonged to the Pharisees, they were watching him. And behold,

M	12.10	there was a man with a withered hand. And
Mk	3.2	a man was there who had a withered hand. And
L	6.7	a man was there whose right hand was withered. And
L	14.3	there was a man before him who had dropsy. And Jesus spoke to the

```
M    12.10    they                            asked    him, "Is it lawful              to heal
Mk   3.2      they                            watched  him,  to see whether he would  heal him
L    6.7      scribes and the Pharisees       watched  him,  to see whether he would  heal
  L  14.3     lawyers and        Pharisees, saying,         "Is it lawful              to heal


M    12.10    on the sabbath?"  so that they might              accuse         him.
Mk   3.2      on the sabbath,   so that they might              accuse         him.
L    6.8      on the sabbath,   so that they might find an accusation against  him.  But
  L  14.3     on the sabbath,   or not?"


Mk   3.3                                            And he said to the man who had the withered hand,
 L   6.8                he knew their thoughts, and he said to the man who had the withered hand,


M    12.11                                                                    He    said to
Mk   3.4      "Come          here."                                   And he  said to
L    6.9      "Come and stand here."  And he rose and stood there.  And Jesus  said to
  L  14.5                                                             And he   said to


M    12.11    them, "What man of you, if he has    one sheep    and it         falls
Mk   3.4      them,
L    6.9      them,
  L  14.5     them, "Which    of you,       having a    son or an ox that has fallen


M    12.11    into a pit on the sabbath, will not lay hold of it and lift it   out?
  L  14.5     into a well,               will not immediately          pull him out


M    12.12    Of how much more value is a man than a sheep!  So it is lawful to do good
Mk   3.4                                                "Is it lawful on the sab-
L    6.9                                        "I ask you, is it lawful on the sab-


M    12.12    on the sabbath."
Mk   3.4      bath to do good or to do harm, to save life or to kill?"  But they were
L    6.9      bath to do good or to do harm, to save life or to destroy it?"
  L  14.6,4   on a     sabbath day?"  And they could not reply to this.  But they were


M    12.13                      Then he
Mk   3.5      silent.  And   he looked around at them with anger, grieved at their hard-
L    6.10              And   he looked around on them all,
  L  14.4     silent.  Then he took him


M    12.13                    said to the man, "Stretch out your hand."  And the man
Mk   3.5      ness of heart, and said to the man, "Stretch out your hand."            He
L    6.10              and said to    him, "Stretch out your hand."  And        he


M    12.14    stretched it out, and    it  was restored, whole like the other.  But
Mk   3.5      stretched it out, and his hand was restored.
L    6.11     did so,           and his hand was restored.                       But
  L  14.4                       and             healed him, and let him go.


M    12.14    the Pharisees went out           and           took counsel
Mk   3.6      The Pharisees went out,          and immediately held counsel with the
L    6.11       they were filled with fury and               discussed    with one


M    12.14              against him, how      to destroy  him.
Mk   3.6      Herodians against him, how      to destroy  him.
L    6.11     another              what they might do to Jesus.
```

64

M	12.15	<u>Jesus</u>, <u>aware of this</u>, <u>withdrew</u> <u>from there.</u>
Mk	3.7	<u>Jesus</u> <u>withdrew</u> with his disciples to the sea,
L	6.17	And he came down with them and stood on a level place,

M	12.15	And <u>many</u>
Mk	3.7	<u>and</u> a great multitude from Galilee
L	6.17	with a great crowd of his disciples <u>and</u> a great multitude of people

M	12.15	<u>followed him,</u>
Mk	3.8	<u>followed</u>; also from Judea *|and Jerusalem and Idumea and from beyond*
L	6.17	from all Judea *and Jerusalem*

Mk	3.8	*the Jordan and from about* *Tyre and Sidon a great multitude, hearing*
L	6.17	*and the seacoast of Tyre and Sidon, who came* *to hear*

Mk	3.9	*all that he did, came to him. And he told his disciples to have a boat*
L	6.17	*him*

Mk	3.9	*ready for him because of the crowd, lest they should crush him;*

M	12.15	<u>and he</u> <u>healed them</u> <u>all</u>,
Mk	3.10	for <u>he</u> had <u>healed</u> many, so that <u>all</u> who had diseases pressed upon him
L	6.17	<u>and</u> to be <u>healed</u> of their diseases;

Mk	3.11	*to touch him. And whenever* *the unclean spirits beheld*
L	6.18	*and those who were troubled with unclean spirits were*

Mk	3.11	*him, they fell down before him and cried out, "You are the Son of God."*
L	6.19	*cured. And all the crowd sought to touch him,*

M	12.16	|and <u>ordered them not to make him known.</u>
Mk	3.12	<u>And</u> he strictly <u>ordered them not to make him known.</u>
L	6.19	for power came forth from him and healed them all.

M	12.17	<u>This was to fulfil what was spoken by the prophet Isaiah:</u>
M	12.18	<u>"Behold, my servant whom I have chosen,</u>
M	12.18	<u>my beloved with whom my soul is well pleased.</u>
M	12.18	<u>I will put my Spirit upon him,</u>
M	12.18	<u>and he shall proclaim justice to the Gentiles.</u>
M	12.19	<u>He will not wrangle or cry aloud,</u>
M	12.19	<u>nor will any one hear his voice in the streets;</u>
M	12.20	<u>he will not break a bruised reed</u>
M	12.20	<u>or quench a smoldering wick,</u>
M	12.20	<u>till he brings justice to victory;</u>
M	12.21	<u>and in his name will the Gentiles hope."</u>

27. HOW CAN SATAN CAST OUT SATAN?

Matthew 12.22-37

M	12.22	<u>Then</u>
Mk	3.19b,20	<u>Then</u> *he went home; and the crowd came together again, so that they*
L	11.14	Now he was casting out
M	9.32	*As they were going away, behold,*

65

Mk	3.21	could not even eat. And when his family heard it, they went out to
Mk	3.21	seize him, for people were saying, "He is beside himself."

M	12.22	a blind and dumb demoniac was brought to him, and he
L	11.14	a demon that was dumb; when the demon
M	9.33	a dumb demoniac was brought to him. And when the demon

M	12.23	healed him, so that the dumb man spoke and saw. And all
L	11.14	had gone out, the dumb man spoke, and
M	9.33	had been cast out, the dumb man spoke; and
J	7.31	Yet many of

M	12.23	the people were amazed, and said, "Can this be the Son of
L	11.14	the people marveled.
M	9.33	the crowds marveled, saying, "Never was anything like
J	7.31	the people believed in him; they said, "When the Christ appears,

M	12.24	David?" But when the Pharisees heard it they
Mk	3.22	And the scribes who came down from Jerusalem
L	11.15	But some of them
M	9.34	this seen in Israel." But the Pharisees
J	7.20	The people
J	7.31	will he do more signs than this man has done?"
J	8.48	The Jews
J	8.49	Jesus
J	8.52	The Jews
J	10.20	Many of them
J	10.21	Others

M	12.24	said, "It is only by Beelzebul, the
Mk	3.22	said, "He is possessed by Beelzebul, and by the
L	11.15	said, "He casts out demons by Beelzebul, the
M	9.34	said, "He casts out demons by the
J	7.20	answered, "You
J	8.48	answered him, "Are we not right in saying that you are a Samaritan and
J	8.49	answered, "I
J	8.52	said to him, "Now we know that you
J	10.20	said, "He
J	10.21	said, "These are not the sayings of one who

M	12.24	prince of demons, that this man casts out demons."
Mk	3.22	prince of demons he casts out the demons."
L	11.16	prince of demons": while others, to test him, sought from him a sign
M	9.34	prince of demons."
J	7.20	have a demon! Who is seeking to kill you?"
J	8.48	have a demon?"
J	8.49	have not a demon; but I honor my Father, and you dishonor me.
J	8.52	have a demon. Abraham died, as did the prophets; and you say, 'If
J	10.20	has a demon, and he is mad; why listen to him?"
J	10.21	has a demon. Can a demon open the eyes of the blind?"

M	12.25	Knowing their thoughts, he said to them,
Mk	3.23	And he called them to him, and said to them in
L	11.17	from heaven. But he, knowing their thoughts, said to them,
J	8.52	any one keeps my word, he will never taste death.'

M	12.25	"Every kingdom divided against
Mk	3.24	parables, "How can Satan cast out Satan? If a kingdom is divided against
L	11.17	"Every kingdom divided against

M	12.25	itself is laid waste,	and no city or house	divided
Mk	3.25	itself, that kingdom cannot stand.	And if	a house is divided
L	11.17	itself is laid waste,	and	a divided household

M	12.26	against itself	will	stand;	and if Satan casts
Mk	3.26	against itself, that house will not be able to	stand.	And if Satan has
L	11.18		falls.	And if Satan also

M	12.26	out Satan,	he is divided against himself; how then will
Mk	3.26	risen up against himself and is divided,
L	11.18	is divided against himself, how will

M	12.26	his kingdom stand?
Mk	3.26	he cannot stand, but is coming to an end.
L	11.18	his kingdom stand? For you say that I cast out demons by Beelzebul.

M	12.27	And if I cast out demons by Beelzebul, by whom do your sons cast them out?
L	11.19	And if I cast out demons by Beelzebul, by whom do your sons cast them out?

M	12.28	Therefore they shall be your judges.	But if it is by the Spirit of God
L	11.20	Therefore they shall be your judges.	But if it is by the finger of God

M	12.28	that I cast out demons, then the kingdom of God has come upon you.
L	11.20	that I cast out demons, then the kingdom of God has come upon you.

M	12.29	Or how can one enter a strong man's	house
Mk	3.27	But no one can enter a strong man's	house
L	11.21	When a strong man, fully armed, guards his own palace,

M	12.29	and plunder his goods,	unless he first
Mk	3.27	and plunder his goods,	unless he first
L	11.22	his goods are in peace; but when one stronger than he

M	12.29	binds the strong man?	Then
Mk	3.27	binds the strong man;	then
L	11.22	assails him and overcomes him, he takes away his armor in which he

M	12.29	indeed he may plunder his house.
Mk	3.27	indeed he may plunder his house.
L	11.22	trusted, and divides his spoil.
Mk	9.38	*John said to him, "Teacher, we say a man casting out demons in your*
L	9.49	*John answered, "Master, we saw a man casting out demons in your*

Mk	9.39	*name, and we forbade him, because he was not following us." But*
L	9.50	*name, and we forbade him, because he does not follow with us." But*

Mk	9.39	*Jesus said, "Do not forbid him; for no one who does a mighty*
L	9.50	*Jesus said to him, "Do not forbid him;*

Mk	9.39	*work in my name will be able soon after to speak evil of me.*

M	12.30	He who is not with me is against me, and he who does not gather
Mk	9.40,41	For he that is not against us is for us. *For truly, I say to you,*
L	11.23	He who is not with me is against me, and he who does not gather
L	9.50	*for he that is not against you is for you."*

67

M	12.31	with me scatters. <u>Therefore I tell</u> <u>you</u>, <u>every sin and blasphemy will</u>
Mk	3.28	"Truly, <u>I</u> say to <u>you</u>, all sins <u>will</u>
Mk	9.41	*whoever gives you a cup of water to drink because you bear the name of*
L	11.23	<u>with me scatters.</u>
L	*12.8*	*"And* <u>I tell</u> <u>you</u>, <u>every</u> *one who acknowledges me*

M	12.31	<u>be forgiven</u> <u>men</u>,
Mk	3.28	<u>be forgiven</u> the sons of <u>men</u>, and whatever blasphemies they utter;
Mk	9.41	*Christ, will by no means lose his reward.*
L	*12.8*	*before men, the Son of man also will acknowledge before the angels of God;*

M	12.31	<u>but</u> the blasphemy <u>against the</u> <u>Spirit will not</u> be <u>forgiven.</u>
Mk	3.29	<u>but</u> whoever blasphemes <u>against the</u> Holy <u>Spirit</u> never has forgiveness,
L	*12.9*	<u>but</u> *he who denies me before men will be* <u>denied</u> *before the angels of God.*

M	12.32	<u>And whoever</u> <u>says</u> <u>a word against the Son of man will be forgiven;</u>
L	12.10	<u>And</u> every one who <u>speaks</u> <u>a word against the Son of man will be forgiven;</u>

M	12.32	<u>but whoever speaks</u> <u>against the Holy Spirit will not be forgiven,</u>
L	12.10	<u>but</u> he who <u>blasphemes</u> <u>against the Holy Spirit will not be forgiven.</u>

M	12.32	<u>either in this age or in the age to come.</u>
Mk	3.30	but is guilty of an eternal sin"--*for they had said, "He has an unclean*
L	*12.11*	*And when they bring you before the synagogues and the rulers and the*

Mk	*3.30*	*spirit."*
L	*12.11*	*authorities, do not be anxious how or what you are to answer or what you*

L	*12.12*	*are to say; for the Holy Spirit will teach you in that very hour what*
L	*12.12*	*you ought to say."*

M	12.33	<u>"Either make the tree</u> <u>good,</u> <u>and its fruit good;</u> <u>or</u> <u>make</u>
L	6.43	*"For* no good tree bears bad fruit, nor again does
M	*7.17*	*So,* *every sound tree* *bears* *good fruit,* *but*
M	*7.18*	*A* *sound tree cannot bear* *evil fruit,* *nor* *can*

M	12.33	<u>the tree bad</u>, <u>and its fruit</u> <u>bad</u>; <u>for the</u> <u>tree is</u> <u>known</u> <u>by its</u>
L	6.44	a <u>bad tree</u> bear <u>good fruit</u>; <u>for each</u> <u>tree is</u> <u>known</u> <u>by its</u> own
M	*7.16*	<u>the</u> *bad tree* *bears* *evil fruit.* *You will* know *them* <u>by their</u>
M	*7.18*	<u>a</u> *bad tree* *bear* *good fruit.*

M	12.34	<u>fruit.</u> <u>You brood of vipers! how can you speak good</u>, <u>when you are evil</u>?
L	6.44	<u>fruit.</u> *For figs are* not *gathered from thorns,* *nor are grapes picked*
M	*7.16*	<u>fruits.</u> *Are grapes* *gathered from thorns,* *or* *figs*

M	12.34	<u>For out of the abundance of the heart the mouth</u>
L	6.45b	*from a bramble bush.* <u>for out of the abundance of the heart</u> *his* <u>mouth</u>
M	*7.16*	*from* *thistles?*

M	12.35	speaks. <u>The good man out of his good treasure</u> <u>brings forth</u>
L	6.45a	speaks. <u>The good man out of</u> the <u>good treasure</u> of his heart produces

M	12.36	<u>good, and the evil man out of his evil treasure brings forth evil.</u> <u>I</u>
L	6.45a	<u>good, and the evil man out of his evil treasure</u> produces <u>evil</u>;

M   12.36   <u>tell you</u>, <u>on the day of judgment men will render account for every</u>
 M   7.19   *Every tree that does not bear good fruit is cut down and*

M   12.37   <u>careless word they utter; for by your words you will be justified, and</u>
 M   7.20   *thrown into the fire. Thus you will know them by their fruits.*

M   12.37   <u>by your words you will be condemned."</u>

28. AN EVIL GENERATION SEEKS A SIGN

Matthew 12.38-45

M   12.38   <u>Then some of the scribes and</u>   <u>Pharisees</u>
Mk   8.11   The <u>Pharisees</u>   came   and
L   11.29   When   the crowds   were
 M   16.1   And *the* <u>Pharisees</u> *and Sadducees came, and*
 L   11.16   *while   others,*
 J   2.18   *The Jews   then*
 J   6.30   *So   they*

M   12.38   <u>said</u>   <u>to</u>   <u>him</u>, "Teacher, we wish to
Mk   8.11   began to argue with him,   seeking from <u>him</u>
L   11.29   increasing,
 M   16.1   *to test   him they asked   him   to*
 L   11.16   *to test   him,   sought from him*
 J   2.18   *said   to   him,*   *"What*
 J   6.30   *said   to   him,*   *"Then what*

M   12.39   <u>see</u>   <u>a sign from you."</u>   But he
Mk   8.12   <u>a sign from</u> heaven, to test him.   And he sighed
L   11.29   he began
 M   16.3   *show them* <u>a sign from</u> *heaven.*   He
 L   11.16   <u>a sign from</u> *heaven.*
 J   2.19   <u>sign</u> *have* <u>you</u> *to show us for doing this?"*   *Jesus*
 J   6.30   <u>sign</u> *do* <u>you</u> *do, that we may see, and believe you? What*

M   12.39   <u>answered them,</u>
Mk   8.12   deeply in his spirit, and said,
L   11.29   to say,
 M   16.2   <u>answered them,</u> *"When it is evening, you say,*
 J   2.19   <u>answered them,</u>
 J   6.30   *work do you perform?*

 M   16.3   *'It will be fair weather; for the sky is red.' And in the morning, 'It*
 M   16.3   *will be stormy today, for the sky is red and threatening.' You know how*
 M   16.3   *to interpret the appearance of the sky, but you cannot interpret the signs*

M   12.39   "An evil and adulterous generation   <u>seeks for a</u>
Mk   8.12   "Why does this   <u>generation</u>   seek   <u>a</u>
L   11.29   "This generation is <u>an evil</u>   <u>generation</u>; it seeks   <u>a</u>
 M   16.4   *of the times.*   An evil and adulterous <u>generation</u>   seeks for a

M   12.39   <u>sign;</u> <u>but</u>   <u>no sign shall be given to</u>   <u>it except the</u>
Mk   8.12   <u>sign?</u> Truly, I say to you, <u>no sign shall be given to</u> this generation."
L   11.29   <u>sign,</u> <u>but</u>   <u>no sign shall be given to</u>   <u>it except the</u>
 M   16.4   <u>sign,</u> <u>but</u>   <u>no sign shall be given to</u>   <u>it except the</u>

69

```
M   12.40    sign of the prophet Jonah.    For as Jonah was              three days and
Mk   8.13                                  And he left them, and getting into the boat
L   11.30    sign of            Jonah.    For as Jonah became           a sign to the
  M 16.4     sign of            Jonah."   So he left them and
  J  2.19                                 "Destroy this temple, and in three days I


M   12.40    three nights in the belly of the whale, so will the Son of man be three
Mk   8.13    again he departed to the other side.
L   11.30    men of Nineveh,                          so will the Son of man be to this
  M 16.4              departed.
  J  2.20    will raise it up."  The Jews then said, "It has taken forty-six years to


M   12.41    days and three nights in the heart of the earth.  The men of Nineveh will
L   11.32    generation.                                       The men of Nineveh will
  J  2.20    build this temple, and will you raise it up in three days?"


M   12.41    arise at the judgment with this generation and condemn it; for they
L   11.32    arise at the judgment with this generation and condemn it; for they


M   12.41    repented at the preaching of Jonah, and behold, something greater than
L   11.32    repented at the preaching of Jonah, and behold, something greater than


M   12.42    Jonah is here.  The queen of the South will arise at the judgment with
L   11.31    Jonah is here.  The queen of the South will arise at the judgment with the


M   12.42            this generation and condemn it;   for she came from the ends of the
L   11.31    men of this generation and condemn them;  for she came from the ends of the


M   12.42    earth to hear the wisdom of Solomon, and behold, something greater than
L   11.31    earth to hear the wisdom of Solomon, and behold, something greater than


M   12.42    Solomon is here.
L   11.31    Solomon is here.


M   12.43    "When the unclean spirit has gone out of a man, he passes through
L   11.24    "When the unclean spirit has gone out of a man, he passes through


M   12.44    waterless places seeking rest, but he finds  none.  Then he says, 'I
L   11.24    waterless places seeking rest; and      finding none      he says, 'I


M   12.44    will return to my house from which I came.'  And when he comes he finds
L   11.25    will return to my house from which I came.'  And when he comes he finds


M   12.45    it empty, swept, and put in order.  Then he goes and brings with him
L   11.26    it         swept  and put in order.  Then he goes and brings


M   12.45    seven other spirits more evil than himself, and they enter and dwell
L   11.26    seven other spirits more evil than himself, and they enter and dwell


M   12.45    there; and the last state of that man becomes worse than the first.  So
L   11.26    there; and the last state of that man becomes worse than the first."


M   12.45    shall it be also with this evil generation."
```

29. HIS MOTHER AND BROTHERS

Matthew 12.46-50

M	12.46	While he was still speaking to the people, behold, his mother and his
Mk	3.31	And his mother and his
L	8.19	Then his mother and his

M	12.46	brothers stood outside, asking to speak to him.
Mk	3.31	brothers came; and standing outside they sent to him and called him.
L	8.19	brothers came to him, but they could not reach him for the crowd.

M	12.47	Some one told him, "Your
Mk	3.32	And a crowd was sitting about him; and they said to him, "Your
L	8.20	And he was told, "Your

M	12.47	*mother and your brothers are standing outside, asking to speak to*
Mk	3.32	mother and your brothers are outside, asking for
L	8.20	mother and your brothers are standing outside, desiring to see

M	12.48	*you."* But he replied to the man who told him, "Who is my mother, and
Mk	3.33	you." And he replied, "Who are my mother and
L	8.20	you."

M	12.49	who are my brothers?" And stretching out his hand toward his disciples,
Mk	3.34	my brothers?" And looking around on those who sat about him,
L	8.21	But

M	12.50	he said, "Here are my mother and my brothers! For whoever
Mk	3.35	he said, "Here are my mother and my brothers! Whoever
L	8.21	he said to them, "My mother and my brothers are those who hear the
M	*7.21*	*"Not every one who says to me, 'Lord, Lord,' shall enter the kingdom of*

M	12.50	does the will of my Father in heaven is my
Mk	3.35	does the will of God is my
L	8.21	word of God and do it."
M	*7.21*	*heaven, but he who* does the will of my Father *who is* in heaven.

M	12.50	brother, and sister, and mother."
Mk	3.35	brother, and sister, and mother."

30. THIRD DISCOURSE: PARABLES OF THE KINGDOM

Matthew 13.1-53

a. Setting

Matthew 13.1-3a

M	13.1	That same day Jesus went out of the house and sat beside the sea.
Mk	4.1	Again he began to teach beside the sea.
Mk	*2.13*	*He went out again beside the sea;*
L	*5.1b*	*he was standing by the lake*

```
M    13.2                         And                    great crowds gathered
Mk   4.1                          And       a very large crowd   gathered
L    8.4                          And when a             great crowd  came together and people
  Mk 2.13            of Gennesaret. and   all  the               crowd   gathered
  L  5.1a                         While     the           people pressed


M    13.2                                  about him,
Mk   4.1                                   about him,
L    8.4            from town after town came to  him,
  Mk 2.13                                  about him,
  L  5.2                                   upon  him to hear the word of God,  |And he saw


  L  5.2            two boats by the lake; but the fishermen had gone out of them and were


M    13.2                     so that he got    into      a  boat and    sat there;
Mk   4.1                      so that he got    into      a  boat and    sat in it on
  L  5.3            washing their nets.  Getting into one of the boats, which was Simon's,


  L  5.3            he asked him to put out a little from the land.   And he sat down


M    13.3a                    and the whole crowd stood          on the beach.  And he
Mk   4.2            the sea;  and the whole crowd was beside the sea on the land.  And he
L    8.4                                                                                he
  Mk 2.13                                                                         and he
  L  5.3                                                                          and


M    13.3a         told      them   many things in   parables,
Mk   4.2           taught    them   many things in   parables, and in his teaching he
L    8.4           said                            in a parable:
  Mk 2.13          taught    them.
  L  5.3           taught the people from the boat.


M    13.3a         saying:
Mk   4.2           said to them:
```

b. The Soils

Matthew 13.3b-23

```
M    13.3b,4          "A sower went out to sow.          And as he sowed, some seeds
Mk   4.3,4     "Listen!  A sower went out to sow.          And as he sowed, some seed
L    8.5                  "A sower went out to sow his seed; and as he sowed, some


M    13.4          fell along the path,                       and the birds came and
Mk   4.4           fell along the path,                       and the birds came and
L    8.5           fell along the path, and was trodden under foot, and the birds of the air


M    13.5          devoured them.   Other seeds fell on    rocky ground, where they had
Mk   4.5           devoured it.     Other seed  fell on    rocky ground, where it    had
L    8.6           devoured it.  And some       fell on the rock;


M    13.5          not much soil, and immediately they sprang up,            since
Mk   4.5           not much soil, and immediately it   sprang up,            since
L    8.6                          and as          it   grew  up, it withered away, because
```

72

M   13.6   they had no depth of soil, |but when the sun rose they were scorched; and
Mk   4.6   it   had no depth of soil; and when the sun rose it   was scorched, and
L   8.6   it   had no moisture.

M   13.7   since they had no root they withered away. Other seeds fell upon   thorns,
Mk   4.7   since it   had no root it   withered away. Other seed fell among thorns
L   8.7   And some   fell among thorns;

M   13.7   and the thorns grew up   and choked them.
Mk   4.8   and the thorns grew up   and choked it, and it yielded no grain. And
L   8.8   and the thorns grew with it and choked it.   And

M   13.8   Other seeds fell on   good soil and brought forth grain,
Mk   4.8   other seeds fell into good soil and brought forth grain, growing up and
L   8.8   some   fell into good soil and   grew,

M   13.8   some a hundredfold, some sixty,   some   thirty.
Mk   4.8   increasing and yielding   thirtyfold   and sixtyfold and a hundredfold."
L   8.8   and yielded a hundredfold."

M   13.9   He who has ears,   let him hear."
Mk   4.9   'And he said,   "He who has ears to hear, let him hear."
L   8.8   As he said this, he called out, "He who has ears to hear, let him hear."
   M 11.15   He who has ears to hear, let him hear.
   M 13.43b   He who has ears,   let him hear.
   Mk 4.23   If any man has ears to hear, let him hear."
   Mk 7.16   "If any man has ears to hear, let him hear."
   L 14.35b   He who has ears to hear, let him hear."

M   13.10   Then   the disciples came
Mk   4.10   And when he was alone, those who were about him with the twelve
L   8.9   And when   his disciples

M   13.11   and said to him, "Why do you speak to them in parables?" And he answered
Mk   4.11   asked   him   concerning the parables. And he said to
L   8.10   asked   him   what   this parable meant, |he said,

M   13.11   them, "To you it has been given to know the secrets of the kingdom of
Mk   4.11   them, "To you   has been given   the secret   of the kingdom of
L   8.10   "To you it has been given to know the secrets of the kingdom of

M   13.12   heaven, but to them it has not been given. For to him   who has
Mk   4.11   God,   but for those outside
L   8.10   God;   but for others
   M 25.29   For to every one who has
   Mk 4.25   For to him   who has
   L 8.18   Take heed then how you hear; for to him   who has
   L 19.26   'I tell you, that to every one who has

M   13.12   will more be given, and he will have abundance; but from him who has
   M 25.29 will more be given, and he will have abundance; but from him who has
   Mk 4.25   will more be given;   and from him who has
   L 8.18   will more be given,   and from him who has
   L 19.26 will more be given;   but from him who has

73

```
M    13.13    not, even what he              has will be taken away.  This is why
 M   25.29    not, even what he              has will be taken away.
 Mk  4.25     not, even what he              has will be taken away."
 L   8.18     not, even what he thinks that he has will be taken away."
 L   19.26    not, even what he              has will be taken away.


M    13.13    I speak to them in parables, because              seeing they do  not
Mk   4.12       everything is in parables; so that they may indeed see    but   not
L    8.10       they       are in parables, so that             seeing they may not
 Mk  8.18                                              Having eyes   do  you  not
 J   9.39     Jesus said,  "For judgment I came into this world, that those who do  not


M    13.13    see,      and        hearing they do not   hear, nor do they
Mk   4.12     perceive, and may indeed hear                  but not
L    8.10     see,      and        hearing                       they
 Mk  8.17b                                Do  you not yet perceive  or
 Mk  8.18     see,      and  having ears  do  you not   hear? And do you
 J   9.39     see may see, and that those who see may become blind."


M    13.14              understand.  With them indeed  is fulfilled the prophecy of
Mk   4.12               understand;
L    8.10     may not  understand.
 Mk  8.17b              understand?  Are your hearts hardened?
 Mk  8.18          not remember?
 J   12.38                           it was that the word spoken by the prophet


M    13.14    Isaiah which says:
 J   12.38    Isaiah might be fulfilled:


 J   12.38              "Lord, who has believed our report,
 J   12.38               and to whom has the arm of the Lord been revealed?"
 J   12.39    Therefore they could not believe.  For Isaiah again said,


M    13.14              'You shall indeed hear but never understand,


M    13.14              and you shall indeed see but never perceive.
 J   12.40              "He has blinded their eyes


M    13.15              For this people's  heart has grown dull,
 J   12.40              and hardened their  heart,


M    13.15              and their ears are heavy of hearing,
M    13.15              and their eyes they have closed,


M    13.15              lest they should perceive with their eyes,
Mk   4.12               lest they should
 J   12.40              lest they should see    with their eyes


M    13.15              and hear with their ears,


M    13.15              and understand with their heart,
 J   12.40              and perceive   with their heart,


M    13.15              and turn for me   to heal them.'
Mk   4.12                     turn again, and be forgiven."
 J   12.40              and turn for me   to heal them."
```

74

M	13.16	But blessed are your eyes,
L	10.23	Then turning to the disciples he said privately, "Blessed are the eyes
J	12.41	*Isaiah said this*

M	13.17	for they see, and your ears, for they hear. Truly, I say to you,
L	10.24	which see what you see! For I tell you that
J	12.41	*because he saw his glory and spoke of him.*

M	13.17	many prophets and righteous men longed to see what you see, and did not
L	10.24	many prophets and kings desired to see what you see, and did not
J	8.56	*Your father Abraham rejoiced that he was to see my day; he*

M	13.17	see it, and to hear what you hear, and did not hear it.
L	10.24	see it, and to hear what you hear, and did not hear it."
J	8.56	*saw it and was glad."*

M	13.18	"Hear then the parable
Mk	4.13	And he said to them, "Do you not understand this parable? How then will
L	8.11	Now the parable is this:

M	13.19	of the sower. When any one
Mk	4.14,15b	you understand all the parables? The sower sows the word. when they
L	8.11	The seed is the word of God.

M	13.19	hears the word of the kingdom and does not understand it, the evil one
Mk	4.15b	hear, Satan
L	8.12b	then the devil

M	13.19	comes and snatches away what is sown in his
Mk	4.15b	immediately comes and takes away the word which is sown in
L	8.12b	comes and takes away the word from their

M	13.19	heart; this is what was sown along the
Mk	4.15a	them. And these are the ones along the
L	8.12a	hearts, that they may not believe and be saved. The ones along the

M	13.20	path. As for what was
Mk	4.16	path, where the word is sown; And these in like manner are the ones
L	8.13	path are those who have heard; And the ones

M	13.20	sown on rocky ground, this is he who hears the word and
Mk	4.16	sown upon rocky ground, who, when they hear the word,
L	8.13	on the rock are those who, when they hear the word,

M	13.21	immediately receives it with joy; yet he has no root in himself,
Mk	4.17	immediately receive it with joy; and they have no root in themselves,
L	8.13	receive it with joy; but these have no root,

M	13.21	but endures for a while, and when tribulation or persecution
Mk	4.17	but endure for a while; then, when tribulation or persecution
L	8.13	they believe for a while and in time of temptation

M	13.22	arises on account of the word, immediately he falls away. As for
Mk	4.18	arises on account of the word, immediately they fall away. And others
L	8.14	fall away. And as for

```
M    13.22            what was sown among         thorns, this is he    who hears the
Mk   4.18   are the ones        sown among        thorns; they are those who hear   the
L    8.14            what        fell among the   thorns, they are those who hear,


M    13.22   word,  but                                                 the cares of the
Mk   4.19   word, |but                                                  the cares of the
L    8.14           but as they go on their way they are choked by the cares


M    13.22   world  and the delight in riches
Mk   4.19   world,  and the delight in riches,  and the desire for other things, enter
L    8.14           and                riches  and        pleasures of life,


M    13.23          choke the word, and it    proves    unfruitful.       As for
Mk   4.20   in and  choke the word, and it    proves    unfruitful.  But those
L    8.15                           and their fruit does not mature.  And as for


M    13.23   what was  sown on      good soil, this is  he    who  hears   the
Mk   4.20   that were sown upon the good soil       are the ones who  hear    the
L    8.15   that          in   the good soil, they are those who, hearing the


M    13.23   word and understands it;                                    he indeed
Mk   4.20   word and accept     it                               and
L    8.15   word,      hold     it fast in an honest and good heart, and


M    13.23   bears      fruit, and yields, in one case a hundredfold, in another
Mk   4.20   bear       fruit,                              thirtyfold and
L    8.15   bring forth fruit  with patience.


M    13.23   sixty,    and in another thirty."
Mk   4.20   sixtyfold and    a       hundredfold."
```

c. Weeds Among the Wheat

Matthew 13.24-30

```
M    13.24   Another parable he put before them, saying, "The kingdom of heaven
 Mk  4.26   And                  he                said,    "The kingdom of God


M    13.25   may be compared to a man who sowed good seed in  his field;  but while
 Mk  4.27      is as if        a man should scatter seed upon the ground, |and


M    13.25   men were   sleeping, his enemy came and sowed weeds among the wheat,
 Mk  4.27            should sleep and rise night and day,


M    13.26   and went away.  So when the plants came up and bore grain, then the
 Mk  4.27                   and     the seed should sprout and grow, he knows


M    13.27   weeds appeared also.  And the servants of the householder came and said
 Mk  4.28   not how.  The earth produces of itself, first the blade, then the ear,


M    13.27   to him, 'Sir, did you not sow good seed in your field?  How then has it
 Mk  4.28   then the full grain in the ear.
```

M	13.28	weeds?' He said to them, 'An enemy has done this.' The servants said
M	13.29	to him, 'Then do you want us to go and gather them?' But he said, 'No;
M	13.29	lest in gathering the weeds you root up the wheat along with them.

| M | 13.30 | Let both grow together until the harvest; and   at harvest time |
| Mk | 4.29 | *But when the grain is ripe,* |

| M | 13.30 | I will tell the reapers, Gather the weeds first and bind them in bundles |
| Mk | 4.29 | *at once he puts in the sickle, because the harvest has come."* |

| M | 13.30 | to be burned, but gather the wheat into my barn.'" |

d. The Mustard Seed and Leaven

Matthew 13.31-33

M	13.31	Another parable he put before them, saying,
Mk	4.30	And he said, "With what can we
L	13.18	He said therefore, "What

M	13.31	"The kingdom of heaven
Mk	4.30	compare the kingdom of God, or what parable shall we use
L	13.18	is the kingdom of God like? And to what shall I compare

M	13.31	is like a grain of mustard seed which a man took and sowed
Mk	4.31	for it? It is like a grain of mustard seed, which, when sown
L	13.19	it? It is like a grain of mustard seed which a man took and sowed

M	13.32	in his field; it is the smallest of all seeds, but when
Mk	4.32	upon the ground, is the smallest of all the seeds on earth; yet when
L	13.19	in his garden; and

M	13.32	it has grown it is the greatest of shrubs and
Mk	4.32	it is sown it grows up and becomes the greatest of all shrubs, and
L	13.19	it grew and

M	13.32	becomes a tree, so that the birds of the air come and make
Mk	4.32	puts forth large branches, so that the birds of the air can make
L	13.19	became a tree, and the birds of the air made

M	13.32	nests in its branches."
Mk	4.32	nests in its shade."
L	13.19	nests in its branches."

| M | 13.33 | He told them another parable. "The kingdom of heaven is |
| L | 13.20,21 | And again he said, "To what shall I compare the kingdom of God? It is |

| M | 13.33 | like leaven which a woman took and hid in three measures of flour, till |
| L | 13.21 | like leaven which a woman took and hid in three measures of flour, till |

| M | 13.33 | it was all leavened." |
| L | 13.21 | it was all leavened." |

e. The Use of Parables

Matthew 13.34-35

M	13.34	All this Jesus said to the crowds in parables;
Mk	4.33	With many such parables he spoke the word to them, as they were

M	13.35	indeed he said nothing to them without a parable. This was
Mk	4.34	able to hear it; he did not speak to them without a parable, but pri-

M	13.35	to fulfil what was spoken by the prophet:
Mk	4.34	vately to his own disciples he explained everything.

M	13.35	"I will open my mouth in parables,
M	13.35	I will utter what has been hidden since the foundation
M	13.35	of the world."

f. The 'Weeds' Interpreted

Matthew 13.36-43

M	13.36	Then he left the crowds and went into the house. And his disciples
M	13.36	came to him, saying, "Explain to us the parable of the weeds of the
M	13.37	field." He answered, "He who sows the good seed is the Son of man;
M	13.38	the field is the world, and the good seed means the sons of the kingdom;
M	13.39	the weeds are the sons of the evil one, and the enemy who sowed them
M	13.39	is the devil; the harvest is the close of the age, and the reapers are
M	13.40	angels. Just as the weeds are gathered and burned with fire,

M	13.41	so will it be at the close of the age. The Son of man will send his
M	*13.49*	*So it will be at the close of the age. The*

M	13.41	angels, and they will gather out of his kingdom all causes
M	*13.49*	*angels will come out and separate*
M	*22.13*	*Then the king said to the attendants,*
L	*13.28b*	*when you see Abraham and Isaac and Jacob and all the prophets*

M	13.42	of sin and all evildoers,	and	throw
M	*8.12*	*while the sons of the kingdom will be*		thrown
M	*13.50*	*the evil from the righteous,*	and	throw
M	*22.13*	*'Bind him hand and foot,*	and	*cast*
M	*24.51*	*and will punish him,*	and	*put*
M	*25.30*		And	*cast the worthless*
L	*13.28b*	*in the kingdom of God*	and	*you yourselves thrust out.*

M	13.42	them	into the furnace of fire;	there men will weep and
M	*8.12*		into the *outer darkness;*	there men will weep and
M	*13.50*	them	into the furnace of fire;	there men will weep and
M	*22.13*	*him*	into the *outer darkness;*	there men will weep and
M	*24.51*	*him*	*with the hypocrites;*	there men will weep and
M	*25.30*	*servant*	into the *outer darkness;*	there men will weep and
L	*13.28a*			There *you* will weep and

```
M    13.43    gnash their teeth.    Then the righteous will shine like the sun in the
  M   8.12    gnash their teeth."
  M  13.50    gnash their teeth.
  M  22.13    gnash their teeth.'
  M  24.51    gnash their teeth.
  M  25.30    gnash their teeth.'
  L  13.28a   gnash your   teeth,


M    13.43    kingdom of their Father.              He  who has ears,           let him hear.
  M  11.15                                          He  who has ears to hear,   let him hear.
  M  13.9                                           He  who has ears,           let him hear."
  Mk  4.9     And he said,                         "He  who has ears to hear,   let him hear."
  Mk  4.23                             If any man has ears to hear,   let him hear."
  Mk  7.16                            "If any man has ears to hear,   let him hear."
  L   8.8b    As  he said this, he called out,  "He  who has ears to hear,   let him hear."
  L  14.35b                                          He  who has ears to hear,   let him hear."
```

g. Hidden Treasure and the Pearl

Matthew 13.44-46

```
M    13.44       "The kingdom of heaven is like treasure hidden in a field, which a man
M    13.44    found and covered up; then in his joy he goes and sells all that he has
M    13.44    and buys that field.

M    13.45       "Again, the kingdom of heaven is like a merchant in search of fine
M    13.46    pearls, |who, on finding one pearl of great value, went and sold all
M    13.46    that he had and bought it.
```

h. The Net

Matthew 13.47-50

```
M    13.47       "Again, the kingdom of heaven is like a net which was thrown into the
M    13.48    sea and gathered fish of every kind;  when it was full, men drew it
M    13.48    ashore and sat down and sorted the good into vessels but threw away the


M    13.49    bad.  So it will be at the close of the age.
  M 13.40b,41       so will it be at the close of the age.   The Son of man will send


M    13.49    The angels will come out and           separate
  M 13.41     his angels,              and they will gather out of his kingdom all
  M 22.13                              Then the king said to the attendants,
  L 13.28b        when you see Abraham and Isaac and Jacob and all the prophets


M    13.50          the evil from the righteous, |and              throw
  M  8.12     while the sons of the kingdom will be              thrown
  M 13.42     causes of  sin  and  all evildoers, |and           throw
  M 22.13     'Bind him hand and foot,            and           cast
  M 24.51     and will punish him,                and           put
  M 25.30                                         And           cast the worthless
  L 13.28b    in the kingdom of God               and you yourselves thrust out.


M    13.50    them   into the furnace of fire; there men will weep and gnash
  M  8.12            into the outer darkness;  there men will weep and gnash
  M 13.42     them   into the furnace of fire; there men will weep and gnash
  M 22.13     him    into the outer darkness;  there men will weep and gnash
  M 24.51     him    with the hypocrites;      there men will weep and gnash
  M 25.30     servant into the outer darkness; there men will weep and gnash
  L 13.28a            There you will weep and gnash
```

```
M    13.50      their teeth.
  M   8.12      their teeth."
  M  13.42      their teeth.
  M  22.13      their teeth.'
  M  24.51      their teeth.
  M  25.30      their teeth.'
  L  13.28a     your  teeth,
```

i. The Householder

Matthew 13.51-52

```
M   13.51,52    "Have you understood all this?"  They said to him, "Yes."  And he said
M   13.52       to them, "Therefore every scribe who has been trained for the kingdom
M   13.52       of heaven is like a householder who brings out of his treasure what is
M   13.52       new and what is old."
```

j. Summary

Matthew 13.53

```
M   13.53      And when Jesus had finished these parables, he went away from there,
Mk   6.1a                                                   He went away from there
```

31. JESUS REJECTED BY HIS OWN

Matthew 13.54-58

```
M   13.54      and       coming to his own country
Mk   6.1b,2    and       came   to his own country; and his disciples followed him.  And
  L  4.16a     And he came      to Nazareth, where he had been brought up;          and
```

```
M   13.54                       he         taught them in their synagogue,
Mk   6.2       on the sabbath he began to teach       in the   synagogue;
  L  4.16a                      he went                to the   synagogue, as his custom
```

```
M   13.54                                   so that they             were astonished, and
Mk   6.2                                    and       many who heard him were astonished,
  L  4.22       was, on the sabbath day.  And all spoke well of him, and  wondered at the
  J  6.42                                             They
  J  7.15                                     The Jews                    marveled at it,
```

```
M   13.54      said,  "Where did    this man get    this          wisdom
Mk   6.2       saying, "Where did    this man get all this?  What is the wisdom given
  L  4.22       gracious words which proceeded out of his mouth;
  J  6.42       said,
  J  7.15       saying, "How is it that this man has learning, when he has never studied?"
```

```
M   13.55      and these     mighty works?                        Is not this
Mk   6.3       to him?  What mighty works are wrought by his hands!  Is not this
  L  4.22                                        and they said, "Is not this
  J  6.42                                                        "Is not this Jesus,
```

```
M   13.55      the carpenter's son?      Is not his mother called Mary?  And are not
Mk   6.3       the carpenter,                        the son of Mary    and
  L  4.22           Joseph's     son?"
  J  6.42       the son  of  Joseph, whose father and mother we know?  How does he now
```

M	13.56	<u>his brothers</u> James and Joseph and Simon and Judas? <u>And are not all</u>
Mk	6.3	brother of <u>James and</u> Joses <u>and</u> Judas <u>and</u> Simon, <u>and are not</u>
J	6.42	*say, 'I have come down from heaven'?"*

M	13.57	<u>his sisters</u> <u>with us?</u> <u>Where then did this man get all this?"</u> <u>And</u>
Mk	6.3	<u>his sisters</u> here <u>with us?"</u> <u>And</u>
L	4.28	*When they heard this,*

M	13.57	<u>they</u> <u>took offense</u> <u>at him.</u> <u>But Jesus</u> <u>said to</u>
Mk	6.4	<u>they</u> <u>took offense</u> <u>at him.</u> And <u>Jesus</u> <u>said to</u>
L	4.24	*all in the synagogue were filled with wrath.* And <u>he</u> <u>said,</u>
J	4.44	*For* <u>Jesus</u> *himself testified*

M	13.57	<u>them,</u> "<u>A</u> <u>prophet is</u> <u>not without honor</u> <u>except in his</u>
Mk	6.4	<u>them,</u> "<u>A</u> <u>prophet is</u> <u>not without honor,</u> <u>except in his</u>
L	4.24	*"Truly, I say to you, no* <u>prophet is</u> *acceptable* <u>in his</u>
J	4.44	*that* <u>a</u> <u>prophet</u> *has no* <u>honor</u> <u>in his</u>

M	13.58	<u>own country</u> <u>and in his own house."</u> <u>And he did</u>
Mk	6.5	<u>own country</u>, and among his own kin, <u>and in his own house."</u> <u>And he could</u>
L	4.24	<u>own country.</u>
J	4.44	<u>own country.</u>

M	13.58	<u>not do many mighty works there,</u>
Mk	6.5	<u>do no</u> <u>mighty</u> work <u>there,</u> except that he laid his hands upon a

M	13.58	<u>because of their</u>
Mk	6.6a	few sick people and healed them. And he marveled <u>because of their</u>

M	13.58	<u>unbelief.</u>
Mk	6.6a	<u>unbelief.</u>

32. DEATH OF JOHN THE BAPTIST

Matthew 14.1-12

M	14.1	At that time <u>Herod the tetrarch heard</u> about the fame of Jesus;
Mk	6.14	King <u>Herod</u> <u>heard</u> of it; for <u>Jesus'</u> name
L	9.7	Now <u>Herod the tetrarch heard</u> of all that was done, and he was

M	14.2	<u>and</u> <u>he</u> <u>said to his servants,</u> "<u>This is John the</u>
Mk	6.14	had become known. Some <u>said,</u> "<u>John the</u>
L	9.7	perplexed, because it was <u>said</u> by some that <u>John</u>

M	14.2	<u>Baptist,</u> he has <u>been raised from the dead;</u> <u>that is why these powers are</u>
Mk	6.14	baptizer has <u>been raised from the dead;</u> <u>that is why these powers are</u>
L	9.7	had <u>been raised from the dead,</u>

M	14.2	<u>at work in him."</u>
Mk	6.15	<u>at work in him."</u> *But others said, "It is Elijah."* *And*
L	9.8	*|by some that Elijah had appeared, and by*

Mk	6.15	*others said, "It is a prophet, like one of the prophets of old."*
L	9.8	*others that one of the old prophets had risen.*

81

Mk	6.16	*But when Herod heard of it he said, "John, whom I beheaded, has been*
L	9.9	*Herod said, "John I beheaded; but who is*

Mk	6.16	*raised."*
L	9.9	*this about whom I hear such things?" And he sought to see him.*

M	14.3	For Herod had seized John and bound him and put him in prison,
Mk	6.17	For Herod had sent and seized John, and bound him in prison
L	3.19	*But* Herod *the tetrarch, who had been reproved by him*

M	14.3	for the sake of Herodias, his brother Philip's wife;
Mk	6.17	for the sake of Herodias, his brother Philip's wife; because he had married
L	3.19	for Herodias, his *brother's wife, and for all the evil*

M	14.4	because John said to him, "It is not lawful for you to have
Mk	6.18	her. For John said to Herod, "It is not lawful for you to have your
L	3.20	*things that Herod had done, |added this to them all, that he shut up John*

M	14.5	her." And though he wanted
Mk	6.19	brother's wife." And Herodias had a grudge against him, and wanted
L	3.20	*in prison.*

M	14.5	to put him to death, he feared the people, because
Mk	6.20	to kill him. But she could not, |for Herod feared John, knowing that he

M	14.5	they held him to be a prophet.
Mk	6.20	was a righteous and holy man, and kept him safe. *When he heard him, he*

M	14.6	But
Mk	6.21	*was much perplexed; and yet he heard him gladly.* But an opportunity came

M	14.6	when Herod's birthday came,
Mk	6.21	when Herod on his birthday gave a banquet for his courtiers and officers

M	14.6	the daughter of Herodias
Mk	6.22	and the leading men of Galilee. For when Herodias' daughter came in and

M	14.7	danced before the company, and pleased Herod, |so that he
Mk	6.22	danced, she pleased Herod and his guests; and the king

M	14.7	promised with an oath to give her whatever she might ask.
Mk	6.22	said to the girl, "Ask me for whatever you wish, and I will grant

Mk	6.23	it." *And he vowed to her, "Whatever you ask me, I will give you, even half*

M	14.8	Prompted by her mother,
Mk	6.24	*of my kingdom."* And she went out, and said to her mother, "What shall I

M	14.8	she said, "Give me the head of John the Baptist here
Mk	6.25	ask?" And she said, "The head of John the baptizer." *And she came*

Mk	6.25	*in immediately with haste to the king, and asked, saying, "I want you to*

| M | 14.9 | | | | on a platter." | And the king |
| Mk | 6.26 | *give me at once the head of John the Baptist* | on a platter." | And the king |

| M | 14.9 | was | sorry; | but because of his oaths and his guests |
| Mk | 6.26 | was exceedingly sorry; | but because of his oaths and his guests he did not |

| M | 14.9 | | | he |
| Mk | 6.27 | want to break his word to her. And immediately the king sent a soldier of |

| M | 14.10 | | commanded | it to be given; | he sent and had John beheaded |
| Mk | 6.27 | the guard and gave orders to bring his head. | He went and | beheaded |

| M | 14.11 | in the prison, | and his head was brought on a platter | and given | to |
| Mk | 6.28 | him in the prison, | and brought | his head on a platter, | and gave it to |

| M | 14.12 | the girl, and | she brought it to her mother. And | his disciples |
| Mk | 6.29 | the girl; and the girl gave | it to her mother. When his disciples heard |

| M | 14.12 | | came and took the body | and buried it; and they went and told |
| Mk | 6.29 | of it, they | came and took his body, and laid it | in a tomb. |

| M | 14.12 | Jesus. |

33. THE FIVE THOUSAND FED

Matthew 14.13-21

M	14.13	Now when			Jesus	heard this,
Mk	6.30		The apostles returned to Jesus, and	told him all that
L	9.10	On their return the apostles		told him	what

| Mk | 6.31 | they had done and taught. *And he said to them, "Come away by yourselves* |
| L | 9.10 | they had done. |

| Mk | 6.31 | *to a lonely place, and rest a while." For many were coming and going,* |
| Mk | 6.31 | *and they had no leisure even to eat.* |

M	14.13		he		withdrew from there in a	boat to a	lonely
Mk	6.32	And	they		went away	in the boat to a	lonely
L	9.10	And	he took them and withdrew apart		to a	city
J	6.1	After this Jesus		went		to the other

M	14.13	place	apart.		But
Mk	6.33	place by themselves.		Now
L	9.10	called Bethsaida.
J	6.2	side of the Sea of Galilee, which is the Sea of Tiberias. And
Mk	8.1		*In those days,*

M	14.13	when	the	crowds heard	it,		they followed
Mk	6.33			many saw them going, and knew them, and	they ran there
L	9.11	When	the	crowds learned	it,		they followed
J	6.2		a	multitude			followed
Mk	8.1	when *again a great* crowd *had*			*gathered,*

```
M    14.14   him on foot from    the towns.                                        As he
Mk    6.34       on foot from all the towns, and got there ahead of them.   As he
L     9.11   him;
J     6.2    him,
  M    9.36                                                              When
  M   15.32                                        Then Jesus called his
  Mk   8.1   and they had nothing to eat,                 he    called his


M    14.14   went ashore he saw a great throng; and he had  compassion on        them,
Mk    6.34   went ashore he saw a great throng, and he had  compassion on        them,
L     9.11                                       and he      welcomed             them
  M    9.36            he saw the      crowds,   he had  compassion for       them,
  M   15.32   disciples to him   and said,    "I  have compassion on the  crowd,
  Mk   8.2    disciples to him,  and said to them, |"I  have compassion on the crowd,


M    14.14                                               and healed their sick.
Mk    6.34   because they were                           like sheep without a shepherd;
L     9.11   and spoke to them of the kingdom of God, and cured  those who had need
J     6.2    because they saw the signs which he did on those who were diseased.
  M    9.36   because they were harassed and helpless, like sheep without a shepherd.
  M   15.32   because they have been with me now three days, and have nothing to eat;
  Mk   8.2    because they have been with me now three days, and have nothing to eat;


  J    6.3    Jesus went up on the mountain, and there sat down with his disciples.
  J    6.4    Now the Passover, the feast of the Jews, was at hand.


M    14.15                                           When it was            evening,
Mk    6.35   and he began to teach them many things. And when it grew              late,
L     9.12a  of healing.                           Now the day began to wear away;
J     6.5                                           Lifting up his eyes, then, and seeing


M    14.15        the disciples    came   to him and  said,      "This is
Mk    6.35        his disciples    came   to him and  said,      "This is
L     9.12c  and the twelve        came          and  said to him, |for we are
J     6.5    that a  multitude was coming to him, Jesus said to Philip,


M    14.15        a lonely place, and the day  is now over; send the crowds away
Mk    6.36        a lonely place, and the hour is now late; send        them  away,
L     9.12b  here in a lonely place."                         |"Send the crowd away,
  M   15.32                 and   I am unwilling to  send        them  away
  Mk   8.3                  and if I                 send        them  away


M    14.15   to go into the               villages
Mk    6.36   to go into the country and  villages                round about
L     9.12b  to go into the              villages and country round about, to lodge
  M   15.32   hungry,            lest they      faint on the way."
  Mk   8.3    hungry to their homes, they will faint on the way; and some of them have


M    14.15                                                       and buy
Mk    6.36                                                       and buy
L     9.12b                                                      and get
J     6.5                                   "How    are we  to  buy
  M   15.33          And the disciples said  to him, "Where are we  to  get
  Mk   8.4    come a long way." And his disciples answered him, "How   can one feed


M    14.16              food for themselves."                Jesus said,
Mk    6.37                   themselves something to eat." But  he      answered
L     9.13a             provisions;                          But  he      said  to
J     6.6               bread, so that these people  may eat?" This he    said
  M   15.33          bread enough in the desert to feed so great a crowd?"
  Mk   8.4    these men with bread here   in the desert?"
```

84

```
M    14.16      "They need not go away; you give them something to eat."
Mk   6.37       them,                "You give them something to eat."  And they
L    9.13a      them,                "You give them something to eat."
J    6.7        to test him, for he himself knew what he would do.        Philip


  Mk  6.37      said  to him, "Shall  we       go and buy two hundred denarii
  L   9.13c                             |unless we are to go and buy
  J   6.7       answered him,                        "Two hundred denarii would not


  Mk  6.38          worth of bread, and give it to them to eat?"     And he    said to
  L   9.13c                     -food   for all these people."
  J   6.7       buy enough    bread for each of them to get a little."
  M   15.34                                                       And Jesus said to
  Mk  8.5                                                         And he    asked


  Mk  6.38      them, "How many loaves have you? Go and see." And when they had found
  M   15.34     them, "How many loaves have you?"
  Mk  8.5       them, "How many loaves have you?"


M    14.17          They                                         said to him.
Mk   6.38      out, they                                         said,
L    9.13b          They                                         said,
J    6.8            One of his disciples, Andrew, Simon Peter's brother, said to him,
  M  15.34          They                                         said,
  Mk 8.5            They                                         said,


M    14.17     "We    have only           five          loaves here and      two
Mk   6.38                                  "Five,                   and       two
L    9.13b     "We    have no more than    five      loaves        and       two
J    6.9       |"There is a lad here who has five barley loaves    and       two
  M  15.34                                  "Seven,                 and       a few
  Mk 8.7a                                   "Seven."          And they had a few


M    14.18,19      fish." And he said, "Bring them here to me."  Then he    ordered
Mk   6.39          fish."                                        Then he    commanded
L    9.14b         fish---  but what are they among so many?"    |And  he   said to his
J    6.10a         fish;                                         Jesus said,
  M  15.35   small fish."                                        And        commanding
  Mk 8.6     small fish;                                         And  he    commanded


M    14.19                     the crowds  to sit down              on the
Mk   6.39                      them all to sit down by companies upon the green
L    9.14b     disciples, "Make     them      sit down in companies, about fifty
J    6.10a          "Make the people      sit down."     Now there was much
  M  15.35              the crowd  to sit down              on the
  Mk 8.6                the crowd  to sit down              on the


M    14.19     grass;
Mk   6.40      grass.           So    they                      sat down in
L    9.15      each."           And   they did so, and made them all sit down.
J    6.10a     grass in the place; so the men                   sat down,
  M  15.35     ground,
  Mk 8.6       ground;


M    14.19                             and    taking the five  loaves  and
Mk   6.41      groups, by hundreds and by fifties.  And  taking the five  loaves  and
L    9.16                             And    taking the five  loaves  and
J    6.11                        Jesus then    took    the         loaves,
  M  15.36                          |he took    the seven loaves  and
  Mk 8.6                           and he took    the seven loaves,
```

85

```
        M    14.19      the two fish he looked up to heaven, and                    blessed,
Mk      6.41      the two fish he looked up to heaven, and                    blessed,
L       9.16      the two fish he looked up to heaven, and                    blessed
J       6.11                                          and when he had    given thanks,
  M    15.36      the      fish,                      and         having given thanks
  Mk    8.6                                           and         having given thanks


M       14.19     and broke and gave the loaves                      to the disciples, and
Mk      6.41      and broke        the loaves, and gave        them to the disciples
L       9.16      and broke             them,   and gave        them to the disciples
J       6.11      he                          distributed them to
  M    15.36      he broke         them    and gave       them to the disciples, and
  Mk    8.6       he broke         them    and gave       them to his disciples


M       14.19     the disciples gave them to     the crowds.
Mk      6.41                  to set        before the people; and he divided the two fish
L       9.16                  to set        before the crowd.
J       6.11                     those who were seated; so also      the      fish,
  M    15.36      the disciples gave them to     the crowds.
  Mk    8.6              to set       before the people; and they set them before the


  Mk    8.7       crowd.  And they had a few small fish; and having blessed them, he
  Mk    8.7       commanded that these also should be set before them.


M       14.20                                And     they all ate  and were satisfied.
Mk      6.42      among them all.            And     they all ate  and were satisfied.
L       9.17                                 And        all ate    and were satisfied.
J       6.12      as much as they wanted.    And when they had eaten their    fill, he told
  M    15.37                                 And     they all ate  and were satisfied;
  Mk    8.8                                  And     they    ate,  and were satisfied;


  J    6.12       his disciples, "Gather up the fragments left over, that nothing may be


M       14.20             And they took        up                              twelve
Mk      6.43             And they took        up                              twelve
L       9.17             And they took        up what          was left over, twelve
J       6.13      lost." So they gathered them up and filled                  twelve
  M    15.37             and they took        up                              seven
  Mk    8.8              and they took        up the broken pieces left over, seven


M       14.20     baskets full of the broken pieces                   left over.
Mk      6.43      baskets full of     broken pieces and of the fish.
L       9.17      baskets      of     broken pieces.
J       6.13      baskets      with fragments from the five barley loaves, left
  M    15.37      baskets full of the broken pieces                   left over.
  Mk    8.8       baskets full.


M       14.21     And those who     ate          were about five thousand men, besides
Mk      6.44      And those who     ate the loaves were      five thousand men.
L       9.14a     For there                      were about five thousand men.
J       6.10b     by those who had eaten.   |in number about five thousand.
  M    15.38          Those who     ate          were      four thousand men, besides
  Mk    8.9        And there                     were about four thousand people.


M       14.21     women and children.
J       6.14      When the people saw the sign which he had done, they said, "This is
  M    15.39      women and children.  And   sending   away the crowds,      he got into
  Mk    8.10                                 And he sent them away; and immediately he got into


                                      86
```

J   6.14   indeed the prophet who is to come into the world!"
M 15.39   the boat   and went to the region   of Magadan.
Mk 8.10   the boat with his disciples, and went to the district of Dalmanutha.

34. WALKING ON THE WATER

Matthew 14.22-33

M	14.22	Then	he made the disciples	get into
Mk	6.45	Immediately	he made his disciples	get into
J	6.16b,17a		his disciples went down to the sea,	got into

M   14.22   the boat and go before him to the other side,   while he
Mk   6.45   the boat and go before him to the other side, to Bethsaida, while he
J   6.15   a   boat, and started   across the sea   to Capernaum. Perceiving

M   14.23   dismissed the crowds.   And after he had dismissed   the crowds,
Mk   6.46   dismissed the crowd.   And after he had taken leave of them,
J   6.15   then that they were about to come and take him by force to make him king,
L   6.12   In these days

M   14.23   he   went up   on the mountain by himself to pray.   When
Mk   6.47a   he   went up   on the mountain   to pray. And when
J   6.16a   Jesus withdrew again to the mountain by himself.   When
L   6.12   he   went out   to the mountain   to pray; and all

M   14.24   evening came,   he was there alone, |but the boat by this time
Mk   6.47c,b evening came, |and he was   alone on the, land. |the boat
J   6.16a   evening came,
L   6.12   night   he continued in prayer to God.

M   14.24   was many furlongs distant from the land,
Mk   6.48   was   out   on   the sea, |And he saw that they were

M   14.25   beaten by the waves;   for the   wind was against them. And
Mk   6.48   making headway painfully, for the   wind was against them. And
J   6.18   The sea rose because a strong wind was blowing.

M   14.25   in   the fourth watch of the night   he   came to them,
Mk   6.48   about the fourth watch of the night   he   came to them,
J   6.17b   It was now dark, and Jesus had not yet come to them.

M   14.26   walking on the sea.   But when the disciples
Mk   6.49a   walking on the sea. He meant to pass by them, |but when   they
J   6.19   When they had rowed about three or four miles, they

M   14.26   saw him   walking on the sea,   they were
Mk   6.50a   saw him   walking on the sea |for they all saw him, and   were
J   6.19   saw Jesus walking on the sea and drawing near to the boat. They were

M   14.26   terrified,   saying, "It is a ghost!" And they cried out for
Mk   6.49b   terrified. |they thought it was a ghost,   and   cried out;
J   6.19   frightened,

M   14.27   fear. But immediately he spoke to them,   saying, "Take heart, it is I;
Mk   6.50b   But immediately he spoke to them and said,   "Take heart, it is I;
J   6.20   but   he said to them,   "It is I;

M	14.27	have no fear."
Mk	6.50b	have no fear."
J	6.20	do not be afraid."

M	14.28	And Peter answered him, "Lord, if it is you, bid me come to you on the
M	14.29	water." He said, "Come." So Peter got out of the boat and walked on
M	14.30	the water and came to Jesus; but when he saw the wind, he was afraid,
M	14.31	and beginning to sink he cried out, "Lord, save me." Jesus immediately
M	14.31	reached out his hand and caught him, saying to him, "O man of little
M	14.31	faith, why did you doubt?"

M	14.32	And when they got into the boat,
Mk	6.51	And he got into the boat with them and
J	6.21	Then they were glad to take him into the boat, and immedi-

M	14.33	the wind ceased. And those in the boat worshiped him, saying,
Mk	6.52	the wind ceased. And they were utterly astounded, |for they
J	6.21	ately the boat was at the land to which they were going.

M	14.33	"Truly you are the Son of God."
Mk	6.52	did not understand about the loaves, but their hearts were hardened.

35. HEALING AT GENNESARET

Matthew 14.34-36

M	14.34	And when they had crossed over, they came to land at Gennesaret.
Mk	6.53	And when they had crossed over, they came to land at Gennesaret, and

M	14.35	And when
Mk	6.54	moored to the shore. And when they got out of the boat, immediately

M	14.35	the men of that place recognized him, they sent round to all that
Mk	6.55	the people recognized him, |and ran about the whole neigh-

M	14.35	region and brought to him all that were sick,
Mk	6.55	borhood and began to bring sick people on their

Mk	6.56	*pallets to any place where they heard he was. And wherever he came, in*
Mk	6.56	*villages, cities, or country, they laid the sick in the market places,*

M	14.36	and besought him that they might only touch the fringe of his
Mk	6.56	and besought him that they might touch even the fringe of his

M	14.36	garment; and as many as touched it were made well.
Mk	6.56	garment; and as many as touched it were made well.

36. A QUESTION OF DEFILEMENT

Matthew 15.1-20

M	15.1	Then Pharisees
Mk	7.1	Now when the Pharisees gathered together to him, with some
L	11.37	While he was speaking, a Pharisee asked him to dine with him; so he

M	15.1	<u>and</u> <u>scribes</u> came to Jesus from Jerusalem
Mk	7.2	of the <u>scribes</u>, who had come <u>from Jerusalem</u>, |*they saw that*
L	11.37	went in and sat at table.

Mk	*7.3*	*some of his disciples ate with hands defiled, that is, unwashed. (For*
Mk	*7.3*	*the Pharisees, and all the Jews, do not eat unless they wash their hands,*
Mk	*7.4*	*observing the tradition of the elders; and when they come from the*
Mk	*7.4*	*market place, they do not eat unless they purify themselves; and there*
Mk	*7.4*	*are many other traditions which they observe, the washing of cups and*
Mk	*7.4*	*pots and vessels of bronze.)*

M	15.2	<u>and</u> <u>said</u>, |<u>"Why do your disciples</u>
Mk	7.5	<u>And</u> the Pharisees and the scribes asked him, <u>"Why do your disciples</u>
L	11.38	The Pharisee was astonished to see

M	15.2	<u>transgress</u> <u>the tradition of the elders?</u> <u>For they do</u> <u>not</u>
Mk	7.5	not live according to <u>the tradition of the elders</u>, but
L	11.38	that he did <u>not</u>

M	15.3	<u>wash their hands when they eat</u>." <u>He</u> <u>answered them</u>,
Mk	7.9	eat with <u>hands</u> defiled?" And <u>he</u> said to <u>them</u>,
L	11.39	first <u>wash</u> before dinner. And the Lord said to him,

M	15.3	<u>"And why do you</u> <u>transgress the commandment of God</u>
Mk	7.9	<u>"You</u> have a fine way of rejecting <u>the commandment of God</u>,
L	11.39	"Now <u>you</u> Pharisees cleanse the outside of the cup and

M	15.4	<u>for the sake</u> of <u>your tradition?</u> <u>For God</u> commanded, <u>'Honor your father</u>
Mk	7.10	in order to keep <u>your tradition</u>! <u>For</u> Moses said, <u>'Honor your father</u>
L	11.39	of the dish, but inside you are full of extortion and wickedness.

M	15.4	<u>and your mother</u>,' and, <u>'He who speaks evil of father or mother</u>, <u>let him</u>
Mk	7.10	<u>and your mother</u>'; and, <u>'He who speaks evil of father or mother</u>, <u>let him</u>

M	15.5	<u>surely die</u>.' <u>But you say</u>, <u>'If</u> any one tells his father or his mother,
Mk	7.11	<u>surely die</u>'; <u>but you say</u>, <u>'If</u> a man tells his father or his mother,

M	15.5	<u>What you would have gained from me is</u> <u>given to God</u>,
Mk	7.11	<u>What you would have gained from me is</u> Corban' (that is, <u>given to God</u>)--

M	15.6	<u>he</u> <u>need</u> <u>not honor</u> <u>his father</u>.' <u>So, for</u>
Mk	7.12	|then you no longer permit <u>him to do</u> anything for <u>his father</u> or mother,

M	15.6	<u>the sake of your tradition, you have made</u> <u>void the word of God</u>.
Mk	7.13	|thus making <u>void the word of God</u> through

Mk	*7.13*	*your tradition which you hand on. And many such things you do."*

M	15.7	<u>You hypocrites!</u> <u>Well did Isaiah prophesy of you</u>, <u>when</u>
Mk	7.6	And he said to them, <u>"Well did Isaiah prophesy of you</u> hypocrites, as it

M	15.7	<u>he said</u>:
Mk	7.6	is written,

```
M    15.8            'This people honors me with their lips,
Mk   7.6             'This people honors me with their lips,


M    15.8            but their heart is far from me;
Mk   7.6             but their heart is far from me;


M    15.9            in vain do they worship me,
Mk   7.7             in vain do they worship me,


M    15.9            teaching as doctrines the precepts of men.'"
Mk   7.7             teaching as doctrines the precepts of men.'


  Mk  7.8      You leave the commandment of God, and hold fast the tradition of men."


M    15.10    And he called the people to him      and said to them, "Hear
Mk   7.14     And he called the people to him again, and said to them, "Hear me, all


M    15.11             and understand:          not           what      goes
Mk   7.15     of you, and understand: there is nothing outside a man which by going


M    15.11    into the mouth   defiles a man, but           what   comes out of the
Mk   7.15     into       him can defile      him; but the things which come  out of a


M    15.12    mouth,  this defiles a man."                             Then
Mk   7.17     man are what defile     him."  And when he had entered the house, and


M    15.12                     the disciples came and said to him, "Do you know that
Mk   7.17     left the people, his disciples          asked       him
  J   9.40                                                                  Some of


M    15.13    the Pharisees were offended when they heard this saying?"  He answered,
  J   9.40     the Pharisees near him


M    15.13    "Every plant  which my heavenly Father has not planted will be rooted up.
  J   15.2     Every branch of    mine      that bears no fruit,     he takes away,


M    15.14    |Let them alone; they are blind guides.  And if a blind man leads a
L    6.39                  He also told them a parable: "Can a blind man lead  a
  M  23.16              "Woe to  you,    blind guides, who say, 'If any one swears
  M  23.24                   You      blind guides, straining out a gnat and
  J   9.40     heard this, and they said to him,  "Are we also blind?"
  J   15.2     and every branch that does bear fruit he prunes, that it may bear


M    15.15    blind man,  both           will fall into a pit."  But Peter said to him,
L    6.39     blind man?  Will they not both fall into a pit?
  M  23.16     by the temple, it is nothing; but if any one swears by the gold of the
  M  23.24     swallowing a camel!
  J   15.2     more fruit.


M    15.16    "Explain the parable to us."  And he said,          "Are you also
Mk   7.18     about    the parable.       And he said to them, "Then are you also
  M  23.16     temple, he is bound by his oath.'


M    15.17    still without understanding?  Do you not see that whatever goes into
Mk   7.18           without understanding?  Do you not see that whatever goes into
```

90

M	15.17	the mouth passes
Mk	7.19	a man from outside cannot defile him, |since it enters, not his heart

M	15.17	into the stomach, and so passes on?
Mk	7.19	but his stomach, and so passes on?" (Thus he declared all foods clean.)

M	15.18	But what comes out of the mouth proceeds from the heart, and
Mk	7.20	And he said, "What comes out of a man is

M	15.19	this defiles a man. For out of the heart come evil
Mk	7.21	what defiles a man. For from within, out of the heart of man, come evil

M	15.19	thoughts, murder, adultery, fornication, theft,
Mk	7.21	thoughts, fornication, theft, murder, adultery,

M	15.19	false witness, slander.
Mk	7.22	|coveting, wickedness, deceit, licentiousness, envy, slander, pride,

M	15.20	These are what defile a
Mk	7.23	foolishness. All these evil things come from within, and they defile a

M	15.20	man; but to eat with unwashed hands does not defile a man."
Mk	7.23	man."

37. THE CANAANITE WOMAN

Matthew 15.21-28

M	15.21	And Jesus went away from there and withdrew to the
Mk	7.24	And from there he arose and went away to the

M	15.21	district of Tyre and Sidon.
Mk	7.24	region of Tyre and Sidon. *And he entered a house, and would not have*

M	15.22	And behold, a Canaanite
Mk	7.25	*any one know it; yet he could not be hid.* But immediately a
Mk	7.26	Now the

M	15.22	woman from that region came out and cried, "Have mercy
Mk	7.25	woman,
Mk	7.26	woman was a Greek, a Syrophoenician by birth. And she begged him to cast

M	15.22	on me, O Lord, Son of David; my daughter is severely possessed
Mk	7.25	whose little daughter was possessed
Mk	7.26	the demon out of her daughter.

M	15.23	by a demon." But he did not answer her a word. And his
Mk	7.25	by an unclean spirit, heard of him,
M	10.5	*These*

M	15.23	disciples came and begged him, saying, "Send her away, for she is
M	10.5	*twelve Jesus sent out, charging them, "Go nowhere among the Gentiles, and*

91

M	15.24	crying after us." He answered, "I was sent only to the lost sheep
Mk	7.27	And he said to her, "Let the children first be fed,
M	10.6	*enter no town of the Samaritans,* |*but go rather* to the lost sheep

M	15.25	of the house of Israel." But she came and knelt before him, saying,
Mk	7.25	and came and fell down at his feet.
M	10.6	of the house of Israel.

| M | 15.26 | "Lord, help me." And he answered, "It is not fair to take the children's |
| Mk | 7.27 | for it is not right to take the children's |

M	15.27	bread and throw it to the dogs." She said, "Yes, Lord, yet
Mk	7.28	bread and throw it to the dogs." But she answered him, "Yes, Lord; yet
M	7.6	*"Do not give dogs what is holy; and do not throw your pearls*

M	15.27	even the dogs eat the crumbs that fall from
Mk	7.28	even the dogs under the table eat the children's crumbs."
M	7.6	*before swine, lest they trample them under foot and turn to attack you.*

M	15.28	their masters' table." Then Jesus answered her, "O woman,
Mk	7.29	And he said to her, "For this
M	8.13	*And to the centurion* Jesus *said, "Go; be it done*

M	15.28	great is your faith! Be it done for you as you desire." And
Mk	7.30	saying you may go your way; the demon has left your daughter." And
M	8.13	*for you as you have believed."* And
L	7.10	*And when those who had been sent*

M	15.28	her daughter was healed
Mk	7.30	she went home, and found the child lying in bed, and the
M	8.13	*the servant* was healed *at that*
L	7.10	*returned to the house, they found the slave* well.

M	15.28	instantly.
Mk	7.30	demon gone.
M	8.13	*very moment.*

38. MANY SICK ARE HEALED

Matthew 15.29-31

| M | 15.29 | And Jesus went on from there and passed along |
| Mk | 7.31 | *Then he returned* from *the region of Tyre,* and *went through Sidon to* |

| M | 15.29 | the Sea of Galilee. And he went up on the mountain, and sat down there. |
| Mk | 7.31 | the Sea of Galilee, *through the region of the Decapolis.* |

| M | 15.30 | And great crowds came to him, bringing with them the lame, the maimed, |
| Mk | 7.32 | And *they* brought *to him a man who was* |

| M | 15.30 | the blind, the dumb, and many others, and they put them at |
| M | 7.32 | *deaf and had an impediment in his speech;* and they *besought him to lay* |

M	15.30	<u>his feet,</u>
Mk	7.33	<u>his</u> *hand upon him. And taking him aside from the multitude privately, he*

Mk	7.34	*put his fingers into his ears, and he spat and touched his tongue; and*
Mk	7.34	*looking up to heaven, he sighed, and said to him, "Ephphatha," that is,*

M	15.30	<u>and he</u> <u>healed them,</u>
Mk	7.35	*"Be opened." And <u>his</u> ears were opened, his tongue was released, and he*

Mk	7.36	*spoke plainly. And he charged them to tell no one; but the more he*
Mk	7.36	*charged them, the more zealously they proclaimed it.*

M	15.31	<u>so that the throng</u> <u>wondered,</u>
Mk	7.37	<u>And</u> *they were astonished beyond measure, saying, "He has done*

M	15.31	<u>when they saw the dumb speaking,</u> <u>the</u>
Mk	7.37	*all things well; he even makes the <u>deaf hear</u> and <u>the dumb</u> speak."*

M	15.31	<u>maimed whole,</u> <u>the lame walking,</u> and <u>the blind seeing;</u> and <u>they glorified</u>
M	15.31	<u>the God of Israel.</u>

39. THE FOUR THOUSAND FED

Matthew 15.32-39

M	15.32	<u>Then</u>
Mk	8.1	<u>In those days, when again a great crowd had gathered, and they had</u>

M	15.32	<u>Jesus called his disciples to him</u> <u>and said,</u>
Mk	8.1	<u>nothing to eat,</u> <u>he</u> <u>called his disciples to him,</u> <u>and said</u> to them,
M	9.36	*When* *he* *saw the* *crowds,*
M	14.14	*As he went ashore he* *saw a great throng;* *and*
Mk	6.34	*As he went ashore he* *saw a great throng,* *and*
L	9.11	*When the crowds learned it, they followed him;* *and*
J	6.2	*And* *a* *multitude followed him,*

M	15.32	<u>"I</u> <u>have compassion on the crowd,</u> <u>because they</u> <u>have been with me</u> now
Mk	8.2	<u>"I</u> <u>have compassion on the crowd,</u> <u>because they</u> <u>have been with me</u> now
M	9.36	*he had* <u>compassion</u> *for* *them,* <u>because they</u> *were harassed and help-*
M	14.14	*he had* <u>compassion</u> *on* *them,*
Mk	6.34	*he had* <u>compassion</u> *on* *them,* <u>because they</u> *were*
L	9.11	*he* <u>welcomed</u> *them* *and spoke to them of the kingdom of*
J	6.2	<u>because they</u> *saw the signs which he*

M	15.32	<u>three days,</u> and have <u>nothing to eat;</u>
Mk	8.2	<u>three days,</u> and have <u>nothing to eat;</u>
M	9.36	*less, like sheep without a shepherd.*
M	14.14	*and healed their sick.*
Mk	6.34	*like sheep without a shepherd; and he began to teach them many things.*
L	9.11	*God, and cured those who had need of healing.*
J	6.3	*did on those who were diseased. Jesus went up on the mountain, and there*

J	6.4	*sat down with his disciples. Now the Passover, the feast of the Jews, was*

```
M   14.15                       When it was          evening,      the disciples
Mk  6.35                     And when it grew         late,        his disciples
L   9.12a                       Now the day began to wear away; and the twelve
J   6.5           at hand.  Lifting up his eyes, then, and seeing that a   multitude was


M   14.15     came   to him and   said,       "This   is         a lonely place,
Mk  6.35      came   to him and   said,       "This   is         a lonely place,
L   9.12c     came          and   said to him, |for we are here in a lonely place."
J   6.5       coming to him, Jesus said to Philip,


M    15.32    and   I am unwilling to   send      them   away hungry,
Mk   8.3      and if I                  send      them   away hungry to their homes,
 M   14.15    and the day  is now over; send  the crowds away  to go into the
 Mk  6.36     and the hour is now late; send  the crowd them   away,  to go into the country
 L   9.12b                             "Send the crowd  away,  to go into the


M    15.32    lest they        faint on the way."
Mk   8.3           they will faint on the way; and some of them have come a long way."
 M   14.15         villages
 Mk  6.36     and villages                    round about
 L   9.12b         villages and country round about, to lodge


M    15.33    And the disciples said  to him, "Where are we  to  get
Mk   8.4      And his  disciples answered him, "How   can one     feed these men with
 M   14.15                                                    and buy
 Mk  6.36                                                     and buy
 L   9.12b                                                    and get
 J   6.5                                       "How   are we  to  buy


M    15.33    bread enough in the desert to feed so great a crowd?"
Mk   8.4      bread here   in the desert?"
 M   14.16    food for themselves."                    Jesus said,   "They need
 Mk  6.37              themselves something to eat." But  he    answered them,
 L   9.13a    provisions;                            But  he    said  to them,
 J   6.6      bread, so that these people may eat?" This  he    said  to test him,


 M   14.16    not go away; you give them something to eat."
 Mk  6.37              "You give them something to eat." And they   said  to him,
 L   9.13a             "You give them something to eat."
 J   6.7      for he himself knew what he would do.        Philip answered him,


 Mk  6.37     "Shall  we       go and buy two hundred denarii             worth of
 L   9.13c    unless we are to go and buy
 J   6.7                              "Two hundred denarii would not buy enough


M    15.34                                      And Jesus said to them, "How
Mk   8.5                                        And he    asked  them, "How
 Mk  6.38     bread, and give it to them to eat?" And he  said to them, "How
 L   9.13c    food  for all these people."
 J   6.7      bread for each of them to get a little."


M    15.34    many loaves have you?"                                      They
Mk   8.5      many loaves have you?"                                      They
 M   14.17                                                                They
 Mk  6.38     many loaves have you? Go and see." And when they had found out, they
 L   9.13b                                                                They
 J   6.8                                                                  One of
```

```
M    15.34                                                    said,
Mk    8.5                                                     said,
  M  14.17                                                    said to him,    "We       have
  Mk  6.38                                                    said,
  L   9.13b                                                   said,           "We       have
  J   6.9       his disciples, Andrew, Simon Peter's brother, said to him,  |"There is a


M    15.34                        "Seven,                     and           a few small fish."
Mk    8.7a                        "Seven."                    And they had  a few small fish;
  M  14.17       only              five       loaves here     and           two          fish."
  Mk  6.38                        "Five,                       and           two          fish."
  L   9.13b      no more than      five       loaves           and           two          fish--
  J   6.9        lad here who has five barley loaves           and           two          fish;


M    15.35                                           And           commanding
Mk    8.6                                            And    he     commanded
  M  14.18,19  And he said, "Bring them here to me." Then   he     ordered
  Mk  6.39                                           Then   he     commanded
  L   9.14b                                          And    he     said to his disciples,
  J   6.10a      but what are they among so many?"          Jesus said,


M    15.35              the crowd    to sit down                on the        ground,
Mk    8.6               the crowd    to sit down                on the        ground;
  M  14.19              the crowds   to sit down                on the        grass;
  Mk  6.39                them all   to sit down by companies upon the green grass.
  L   9.14b      "Make      them       sit down in companies, about fifty each."
  J   6.10a      "Make the people      sit down."          Now there was much grass in the


  Mk  6.40            So       they                          sat down in groups, by
  L   9.15            And      they did so, and made them all sit down.
  J   6.10a      place; so the men                           sat down,


M    15.36                              he took   the seven loaves   and the
Mk    8.6                      and he took   the seven loaves,
  M  14.19                        and    taking the five  loaves  and the two
  Mk  6.41      hundreds and by fifties. And    taking the five  loaves  and the two
  L   9.16                        And    taking the five  loaves  and the two
  J   6.11                Jesus then     took    the            loaves,


M    15.36      fish,                     and        having given thanks   he broke
Mk    8.6                                 and        having given thanks   he broke
  M  14.19      fish he looked up to heaven, and                blessed, and broke
  Mk  6.41      fish he looked up to heaven, and                blessed, and broke
  L   9.16      fish he looked up to heaven, and                blessed  and broke
  J   6.11                                 and when he had   given thanks, he


M    15.36            them    and gave       them to the disciples, and the
Mk    8.6             them    and gave       them to his disciples
  M  14.19      and gave the loaves                to the disciples, and the
  Mk  6.41          the loaves, and gave     them to the disciples
  L   9.16           them,   and gave        them to the disciples
  J   6.11           distributed them to


M    15.36      disciples gave them to    the crowds.
Mk    8.6             to set      before the people; and they set them before the crowd.
  M  14.19      disciples gave them to    the crowds.
  Mk  6.41          to set     before the people; and he divided the two fish
  L   9.16          to set     before the crowd.
  J   6.11           those who  were seated; so also      the      fish,
```

Mk 8.7   And they had a few small fish; and having blessed them, he commanded
Mk 6.41 among them all.
J 6.11 as much as they wanted.

M 15.37 that these also should be set before them. And | they all ate | and
Mk 8.8   And | they | ate, | and
M 14.20   And | they all ate | and
Mk 6.42   And | they all ate | and
L 9.17   And | all ate | and
J 6.12   And when they had eaten their

M 15.37 were satisfied;
Mk 8.8   were satisfied;
M 14.20 were satisfied.
Mk 6.42   were satisfied.
L 9.17   were satisfied.
J 6.12   fill, he told his disciples, "Gather up the fragments left over, that

M 15.37   and they took   up
Mk 8.8   and they took   up the broken pieces left
M 14.20   And they took   up
Mk 6.43   And they took   up
L 9.17   And they took   up what   was left
J 6.13   nothing may be lost." So they gathered them up and filled

M 15.37   seven baskets full of the broken pieces
Mk 8.8   over, seven baskets full.
M 14.20   twelve baskets full of the broken pieces
Mk 6.43   twelve baskets full of   broken pieces and of the fish.
L 9.17   over, twelve baskets   of   broken pieces.
J 6.13   twelve baskets   with   fragments from the five barley loaves,

M 15.38 left over.   Those who   ate   were   four thousand
Mk 8.9   .   And there   were about four thousand
M 14.21 left over. And those who   ate   were about five thousand
Mk 6.44   And those who   ate the loaves were   five thousand
L 9.14a   For there   were about five thousand
J 6.10b left   by those who had eaten. |in number about five thousand.

M 15.39 men, besides women and children. And   sending away the crowds,
Mk 8.10   people.   And he sent them away; and immediately
M 14.21 men, besides women and children.
Mk 6.44   men.
L 9.14a men.
J 6.14   When the people saw the sign which he had done, they said, "This is

M 15.39 he got into the boat   and went to the region   of
Mk 8.10   he got into the boat with his disciples, and went to the district of
J 6.14   indeed the prophet who is to come into the world!"

M 15.39 Magadan.
Mk 8.10   Dalmanutha.

40. PHARISEES SEEK A SIGN AND A WARNING

Matthew 16.1-12

```
M    16.1    And                                  the Pharisees and Sadducees came, and
Mk   8.11    The Pharisees                                             came   and began
  M  12.38   Then some of the scribes and Pharisees
  L  11.16   while                                        others,
  L  11.29   When                             the crowds                were increasing,
  J   2.18                                     The Jews       then


M    16.1    to test       him they asked           him                 to show them
Mk   8.11    to argue with him,      seeking from him
  M  12.38                 said      to   him, "Teacher, we wish to see
  L  11.16   to test       him,      sought from him
  J   2.18                 said      to   him,      "What
  J   6.30   So they said            to   him, "Then what


M    16.2    a sign from heaven.                        He
Mk   8.12    a sign from heaven, to test him. And he sighed deeply in his spirit,
  L  12.54                                          He also
  M  12.39   a sign from you."                    But he
  L  11.16   a sign from heaven.
  L  11.29                                         he began
  J   2.18    sign have you to show us for doing this?"
  J   6.30    sign do   you do, that we may see, and believe you?  What work do you


M    16.2         answered    them,       "When it is evening,
Mk   8.12    and said,
  L  12.54        said to the multitudes, "When you see a cloud rising in the west,
  M  12.39        answered    them,
  L  11.29    to  say,
  J   6.30    perform?


M    16.3    you say,        'It will be fair weather; for the sky is red.'  And
L    12.55   you say at once, 'A shower is coming';    and so  it happens.  And


M    16.3    in the morning,                          'It    will be stormy
L    12.55   when you see the south wind blowing, you say, 'There will be scorching


M    16.3    today, for the sky is red and threatening.'  You know how to interpret
L    12.56   heat';and it happens.    You hypocrites!  You know how to interpret


M    16.3    the appearance of      the sky, but      you cannot
L    12.56   the appearance of earth and sky; but why do you    not know how to


M    16.4    interpret the signs of the times.  An evil and adulterous generation
Mk   8.12                                      "Why does this            generation
L    12.56   interpret the present     time?
  M  12.39                                      "An evil and adulterous generation
  L  11.29              "This generation is an evil            generation;


M    16.4    seeks for a sign,                but  no sign shall be given to
Mk   8.12    seek      a sign?  Truly, I say to you, no sign shall be given to
  M  12.39   seeks for a sign;                but  no sign shall be given to
  L  11.29   it seeks   a sign,               but  no sign shall be given to
```

```
M    16.4              it except the sign of              Jonah."  So he left them  and
Mk    8.13    this generation."                                    And he left them,  and
  M  12.39              it except the sign of the prophet Jonah.
  L  11.29              it except the sign of              Jonah.


M    16.4                                        departed.
Mk    8.13    getting into the boat again he departed to the other side.


M    16.5    When the disciples reached the other side, they had forgotten to bring
Mk    8.14    Now                                         they had forgotten to bring
L    12.1    In the meantime                    when so many thousands of the


M    16.6    any bread.                                                      Jesus
Mk    8.15       bread; and they had only one loaf with them in the boat.  And he
L    12.1    multitude had gathered together that they trod upon one another,  he


M    16.6                      said to    them, "Take heed and beware of the leaven
Mk    8.15    cautioned them, saying,          "Take heed,   beware of the leaven
L    12.1    began       to  say  to his disciples first,  "Beware of the leaven


M    16.7    of the Pharisees and             Sadducees."  And they discussed it
Mk    8.16    of the Pharisees and the leaven of Herod."    And they discussed it
L    12.1    of the Pharisees, which is hypocrisy.


M    16.8    among themselves, saying, "We brought no bread."  But Jesus, aware of
Mk    8.17    with one another, saying, "We have   no bread."  And being   aware of


M    16.8    this,      said, "O men of little faith, why do you discuss among your-
Mk    8.17    it, Jesus said to them,                 "Why do you discuss


M    16.9    selves the fact that you have no bread?  Do you not yet perceive?
Mk    8.17           the fact that you have no bread?  Do you not yet perceive or


  Mk  8.18    understand?  Are your hearts hardened?  |Having eyes do you not see,
  Mk  8.18    and having ears do you not hear?  And


M    16.9    Do you not remember              the five loaves of  the five thousand,
Mk    8.19    do you not remember?  When I broke the five loaves for the five thousand,


M    16.9    and how many baskets                   you gathered?
Mk    8.19        how many baskets full of broken pieces did you take up?"  They said


M    16.10              Or  the seven loaves of  the four thousand, and how
Mk    8.20    to him, "Twelve." "And the seven   for the four thousand,      how


M    16.10    many baskets                      you gathered?
Mk    8.20    many baskets full of broken pieces did you take up?"  And they said to


M    16.11                      How is it that you fail to perceive that I did
Mk    8.21    him, "Seven."  And he said to them, "Do you not yet understand?"


M    16.11    not speak about bread?  Beware of the leaven of the Pharisees and Sad-
M    16.12    ducees."  Then they understood that he did not tell them to beware of the
M    16.12    leaven of bread, but of the teaching of the Pharisees and Sadducees.
```

41. PETER'S CONFESSION AND FIRST PREDICTION OF THE PASSION

Matthew 16.13-23

M	16.13	<u>Now when</u> <u>Jesus came</u> <u>into the district</u>
Mk	8.27	<u>And</u> <u>Jesus</u> went on with his disciples, to the villages
L	9.18	<u>Now it happened that as he was praying alone the disciples were</u>
J	*6.66*	*After this many of his disciples drew back and no longer went about*

M	16.13	<u>of Caesarea Philippi,</u> <u>he asked</u> <u>his disciples,</u> "Who do
Mk	8.27	<u>of Caesarea Philippi</u>; and on the way <u>he asked</u> <u>his disciples,</u> "Who do
L	9.18	<u>with him;</u> and <u>he asked</u> them, "Who do
J	*6.67*	*with him.* *Jesus said to the twelve,* "Do

M	16.14	<u>men</u> <u>say that the Son of man is</u>?" <u>And they said,</u> "Some say John
Mk	8.28	<u>men</u> <u>say that</u> I am?" <u>And they</u> told him, "John
L	9.19	the people <u>say that</u> I am?" <u>And they</u> answered, "John
J	*6.67*	*you also wish to go away?"*

M	16.14	<u>the Baptist,</u> <u>others say</u> Elijah, <u>and others</u> Jeremiah or one of the
Mk	8.28	<u>the Baptist</u>; and <u>others say</u>, <u>Elijah</u>; <u>and others</u> one of the
L	9.19	<u>the Baptist</u>; but <u>others say</u>, <u>Elijah</u>; <u>and others</u>, that <u>one of the</u>

M	16.15	<u>prophets.</u>" <u>He said to them,</u> "But who do you say that
Mk	8.29	<u>prophets.</u>" And <u>he asked</u> them, "But who do you say that
L	9.20	old <u>prophets</u> has risen." And <u>he said to them,</u> "But who do you say that

M	16.16	<u>I am?</u>" <u>Simon Peter</u> replied,
Mk	8.29	<u>I am?</u>" <u>Peter</u> answered him,
L	9.20	<u>I am?</u>" And <u>Peter</u> answered,
J	*1.49*	*Nathanael answered him,* *"Rabbi,*
J	*6.68*	*Simon Peter answered him,* *"Lord, to whom shall we go? You*
J	*11.27*	*She* *said to him, "Yes, Lord; I believe*

J	*6.69*	*have the words of eternal life; and we have believed, and have come to*

M	16.17	"<u>You are the Christ, the Son of the living God.</u>" <u>And Jesus</u>
Mk	8.29	"<u>You are the Christ.</u>"
L	9.20	"<u>The Christ</u> <u>of</u> <u>God.</u>"
J	*1.49*	*you are* the Son of God! You are the
J	*6.69*	know, that <u>you are</u> the Holy One of God."
J	*11.27*	that <u>you are the Christ,</u> the Son of God, he who is

M	16.17	<u>answered him,</u> "Blessed are you, Simon Bar-Jona! For flesh and blood has
J	*1.49*	*King of Israel!"*
J	*11.27*	*coming into the world."*

M	16.18	<u>not revealed this to you, but my Father who is in heaven.</u> <u>And I tell</u>
M	16.18	<u>you, you are Peter,</u> and on this rock I will build my church, and the

M	16.19	<u>powers of death shall not prevail against it.</u> <u>I will give you the keys</u>
J	*20.22*	*And when he had said this, he breathed on them, and said to them,*

M	16.19	<u>of the kingdom of heaven, and whatever you bind on earth</u> <u>shall</u>
M	*18.18*	*Truly, I say to you,* whatever you bind on earth shall
J	*20.23*	*"Receive the Holy Spirit.* If <u>you</u> forgive the sins of any, they

```
M   16.19    be  bound in heaven, and whatever you loose on earth          shall be
  M  18.18    be  bound in heaven, and whatever you loose on earth          shall be
  J  20.23    are forgiven;                    if you retain the sins of any, they are


M   16.20    loosed in heaven."  Then he strictly charged          the disciples to
Mk   8.30                         And   he           charged          them       to
L    9.21                         But   he           charged and commanded them       to
  M  18.18    loosed in heaven.
  J  20.23    retained."


M   16.20    tell          no one that  he was the Christ.
Mk   8.30    tell          no one about him.
L    9.21    tell this to  no one,


M   16.21    From that time Jesus began to show his disciples that     he
Mk   8.31    And            he    began to teach    them     that the Son of man
L    9.22                                          |saying, "The Son of man


M   16.21    must go to Jerusalem and suffer many things          from the
Mk   8.31    must                   suffer many things, and be rejected by   the
L    9.22    must                   suffer many things, and be rejected by   the


M   16.21    elders and     chief priests and     scribes, and be killed, and on the
Mk   8.31    elders and the chief priests and the scribes, and be killed, and after
L    9.22    elders and     chief priests and     scribes, and be killed, and on the


M   16.22    third day  be raised.                              And Peter took him
Mk   8.32    three days rise again.  |And he said this plainly. And Peter took him,
L    9.22    third day  be raised."


M   16.22    and began to rebuke him, saying, "God forbid, Lord!  This shall never
Mk   8.32    and began to rebuke him.


M   16.23    happen to you."  But he turned                    and said to
Mk   8.33                     But   turning and seeing his disciples, he rebuked


M   16.23    Peter,            "Get behind me, Satan!  You are a hindrance to me; for
Mk   8.33    Peter, and said, "Get behind me, Satan!                             For


M   16.23    you are not on the side of God, but of men."
Mk   8.33    you are not on the side of God, but of men."
```

42. COST OF DISCIPLESHIP

Matthew 16.24-28

```
M   16.24    Then Jesus told                          his disciples,
Mk   8.34    And  he    called to him the multitude with his disciples, and said to
L    9.23    And  he                                                           said to


M   16.24         "If any man would come after me, let him deny himself and take up
Mk   8.34    them, "If any man would come after me, let him deny himself and take up
L    9.23    all,  "If any man would come after me, let him deny himself and take up
  M  10.38                                           and he who does not take
  L  14.27                                           Whoever does not bear
```

```
M    16.25   his        cross           and follow    me.                          For whoever
Mk    8.35   his        cross           and follow    me.                          For whoever
L     9.24   his        cross  daily    and follow    me.                          For whoever
  M  10.39   his        cross           and follow    me is not worthy of me.    He  who
  L  14.27   his  own   cross                and come after me, cannot be my disciple.
  L  17.33                                                                         Whoever
  J  12.25                                                                       He  who


M    16.25   would    save   his life will lose   it, and whoever loses his life for
Mk    8.35   would    save   his life will lose   it; and whoever loses his life for
L     9.24   would    save   his life will lose   it; and whoever loses his life for
  M  10.39            finds  his life will lose   it, and he  who loses his life for
  L  17.33   seeks to gain   his life will lose   it, but whoever loses his life
  J  12.25            loves  his life     loses   it, and he  who hates his life in


M    16.26   my sake                      will find    it.  For what will it profit a
Mk    8.36   my sake and the gospel's     will save    it.  For what does it profit a
L     9.25   my sake, he                  will save    it.  For what does it profit a
  M  10.39   my sake                      will find    it.
  L  17.33                                will preserve it.
  J  12.26   this world                   will keep    it for eternal life.  If any one


M    16.26   man, if he gains the whole world and          forfeits his life?  Or
Mk    8.37   man,   to gain  the whole world and          forfeit his life?  For
L     9.25   man  if he gains the whole world and loses or forfeits himself?
  J  12.26   serves me, he must follow me; and where I am, there shall my servant


M    16.27   what shall a man give in return for his life?  For
Mk    8.38   what can    a man give in return for his life?  For whoever is ashamed
L     9.26                                                   For whoever is ashamed
  J  12.26   be also; if any one serves me, the Father will honor him.


 Mk  8.38   of me and of my words in this adulterous and sinful generation, of him
  L   9.20   of me and of my words,                                          of him


M    16.27        the Son of man              is to come with his angels in
Mk    8.38   will the Son of man also be ashamed, when he comes           in
L     9.26   will the Son of man      be ashamed  when he comes           in


M    16.27        the glory of his Father, and then he will repay every man
Mk    8.38        the glory of his Father  with the holy angels."
L     9.26   his glory and the glory of the Father and of the holy angels.


M    16.28   for what he has done.  Truly, I say to you,
Mk    9.1    And he said  to them, "Truly, I say to you,
L     9.27                    But    I tell   you truly,
  J   8.51               Truly, truly, I say to you,
  J   8.52   The Jews said to him, "Now we know that you have a demon.  Abraham died,


M    16.28                                   there are some standing here who will
Mk    9.1                                    there are some standing here who will
L     9.27                                   there are some standing here who will
  J   8.51                       if any one      keeps my word, he will
  J   8.52   as did the prophets; and you say, 'If any one      keeps my word, he will
```

```
M    16.28    not   taste death before they see        the Son of man coming in his
Mk    9.1     not   taste death before they see that  the
L     9.27    not   taste death before they see        the
  J   8.51    never see    death."
  J   8.52    never taste death.'


M    16.28    kingdom."
Mk    9.1     kingdom of God has come with power."
L     9.27    kingdom of God."
```

43. THE TRANSFIGURATION

Matthew 17.1-13

```
M    17.1     And after six    days                  Jesus took with him Peter and
Mk    9.2     And after six    days                  Jesus took with him Peter and
L     9.28    Now about eight  days after these sayings he took with him Peter and


M    17.1     James and John his brother, and led them up    a high mountain apart.
Mk    9.2     James and John,              and led them up    a high mountain apart
L     9.28    John  and James,             and went      up on the   mountain to pray.


M    17.2                         And    he was transfigured before them, and his face shone
Mk    9.2     by themselves; and         he was transfigured before them,
L     9.29                        And as he was praying, the appearance    of his countenance


M    17.2     like the sun, and his garments became                    white  as
Mk    9.3                   |and his garments became glistening, intensely white, as
L     9.29    was altered,   and his raiment  became dazzling          white.


M    17.3     light.                                And behold, there   appeared to
Mk    9.4     no fuller on earth could bleach them. And         there   appeared to
L     9.30                                          And behold, two men talked with


M    17.3     them Moses  and  Elijah,                              talking
Mk    9.4     them Elijah with Moses;                and they were talking
L     9.31     him, Moses  and  Elijah, |who appeared in glory and  spoke


M    17.3     with him.
Mk    9.4     to    Jesus.
L     9.32    of    his departure, which he was to accomplish at Jerusalem.  Now Peter


  L   9.32    and those who were with him were heavy with sleep, and when they wakened
  L   9.32    they saw his glory and the two men who stood with him.


M    17.4     And                           Peter said to Jesus, "Lord,   it
Mk    9.5     And                           Peter said to Jesus, "Master, it
L     9.33    And as the men were parting from him, Peter said to Jesus, "Master, it


M    17.4     is well that we are here; if you wish, I will make three booths here,
Mk    9.5     is well that we are here;        let us    make three booths,
L     9.33    is well that we are here;        let us    make three booths,
```

```
M    17.5    one for you and one for Moses and one for Elijah."      He was
Mk   9.6     one for you and one for Moses and one for Elijah." For he did not
L    9.33    one for you and one for Moses and one for Elijah"--            not


M    17.5             still   speaking, when lo,                    a bright
Mk   9.7     know     what to say, for they were exceedingly afraid. And a
L    9.34    knowing what he said.    As he said this,                   a
  J  12.27   "Now is my soul troubled. And what shall I say? 'Father, save me from


M    17.5    cloud           overshadowed them,
Mk   9.7     cloud           overshadowed them,
L    9.34    cloud came and overshadowed them; and they were afraid as they entered
  J  12.28   this hour'? No, for this purpose I have come to this hour. Father,


M    17.5                          and    a voice     from   the cloud  said,
Mk   9.7                           and    a voice came out of the cloud,
L    9.35    the cloud.            And    a voice came out of the cloud, saying,
  J  12.28   glorify thy name."    Then   a voice came from      heaven,
  M  3.17                          and lo, a voice        from    heaven, saying,
  Mk 1.11                          and    a voice came from      heaven,
  L  3.22b                         and    a voice came from      heaven,


M    17.5    "This is  my beloved Son, with whom I am well pleased; listen to him."
Mk   9.7     "This is  my beloved Son;                             listen to him."
L    9.35    "This is  my       Son, my Chosen;                    listen to him!"
  J  12.28   "I have glorified it, and I will glorify it again."
  M  3.17     "This is  my beloved Son, with whom I am well pleased."
  Mk 1.11     "Thou art my beloved Son; with thee I am well pleased."
  L  3.22b    "Thou art my beloved Son; with thee I am well pleased."


M    17.6    When the disciples          heard this, they fell on their faces, and
  J  12.29         The crowd standing by heard it and said that it had thundered.


M    17.7    were filled with awe.                But Jesus came and touched them,
  J  12.30    Others said, "An angel has spoken to him."  |Jesus


M    17.8    saying, "Rise, and have no fear." And when they lifted up their eyes,
Mk   9.8                                       And suddenly looking around
L    9.36                                      And when the voice had spoken,
  J  12.30   answered, "This voice has come for your sake, not for mine.


M    17.8    they         saw no  one         but Jesus         only.
Mk   9.8     they no longer saw any one with them but Jesus      only.
L    9.36                               Jesus was found alone.


M    17.9    And            as  they were coming down    the mountain, Jesus
Mk   9.9     And            as  they were coming down    the mountain, he
L    9.36    And                they kept silence
  L  9.37    On the next day, when they had come  down from the mountain, a great


M    17.9    commanded them, "Tell no one                   the vision,
Mk   9.9     charged    them to tell no one                 what they had
L    9.36             and told no one in those days anything of what they had
  L  9.37    crowd met him.


M    17.9            until the Son of man    is   raised from the dead."
Mk   9.10    seen, until the Son of man should have risen from the dead. So they
L    9.36    seen.
```

103

Mk 9.10   *kept the matter to themselves, questioning what the rising from the dead*

M   17.10   And the disciples asked him, "Then why do the scribes say that
Mk 9.11   *meant.* And   they   asked him,   "Why do the scribes say that

M   17.11 first Elijah must come?"   He replied,   "Elijah does come, and he
Mk 9.12a first Elijah must come?" And he said to them, "Elijah does come first
M   11.13   *For all the prophets and the law prophesied*

M   17.12 is to restore all things;   but I tell you that Elijah has already
Mk 9.13   to restore all things;   But I tell you that Elijah has
M   11.14 *until John; and if you are willing to accept it, he is Elijah who is to*

M   17.12 come, and they did not know him, but did to him whatever they pleased.
Mk 9.13   come, and they   did to him whatever they pleased,
M   11.14 *come.*

M   17.12   So also   the Son of man
Mk 9.12b as it is written of him." |and how is it written of the Son of man,

M   17.13   will   suffer at their hands." Then the disciples understood   .
Mk 9.12b that he should suffer many things and be treated with contempt?

M   17.13 that he was speaking to them of John the Baptist.

44. THE EPILEPTIC BOY

Matthew 17.14-21

M   17.14 And   when they   came   to the
Mk 9.14   And   when they   came to the disciples, they saw a great
L   9.37   On the next day, when they had come down from the mountain,   a great

M   17.14 crowd,
Mk 9.15   crowd about them, and scribes arguing with them. *And immediately all*
L   9.37   crowd met   him.

Mk 9.15   *the crowd, when they saw him, were greatly amazed, and ran up to him and*
Mk 9.16   *greeted him. And he asked them, "What are you discussing with them?"*

M   17.14   a man came up to him and kneeling before him said,
Mk 9.17   And   one of   the crowd   answered him,
L   9.38   And behold, a man from the crowd   cried,

M   17.15 |"Lord,   have mercy   on my son,   for he is   an epileptic
Mk 9.17   "Teacher, I brought   my son to you, for he has a dumb
L   9.38   "Teacher, I beg you to look upon my son,   for he is my only child;

M   17.15   and   he suffers terribly; for   often
Mk 9.18   spirit; and wherever it seizes him,
Mk 9.22a   And it has often
L   9.39   and behold, a spirit   seizes him, and he suddenly cries

```
M    17.15            he falls     into the fire, and often into the water.
Mk    9.18            it dashes           him down; and  he foams  and grinds his teeth and
Mk    9.22a                    cast him into the fire  and          into the water, to destroy him;
L     9.39      out; it convulses him             till he foams, and shatters him,      and


M    17.16                         And I brought him to your disciples,
Mk    9.18      becomes rigid;      and I asked         your disciples to cast it
L     9.40      will hardly leave him.  And I begged        your disciples to cast it


M    17.17            and they could not heal him."  And Jesus answered,    "O faithless
Mk    9.19      out, and they were  not able."      And he      answered them, "O faithless
L     9.41      out, but they could not."            Jesus answered,     "O faithless
     J  14.9                                          Jesus said  to him,  "Have I been


M    17.17      and perverse generation, how long am I to be with you?  How long am I to
Mk    9.19                     generation, how long am I to be with you?  How long am I to
L     9.41      and perverse generation, how long am I to be with you              and
     J  14.9      with you              so  long, and yet you do not know me, Philip?


M    17.17      bear with you?  Bring     him here to me."
Mk    9.20      bear with you?  Bring     him     to me."  And they brought the boy
L     9.41      bear with you?  Bring your son here."
     J  14.9      He who has seen me has seen the Father; how can you say, 'Show us the


Mk   9.20      to him; and when          the spirit saw him, immediately it convulsed
L    9.42           While he was coming,  the demon tore him          and convulsed
J    14.9      Father'?


Mk   9.20      the boy, and he fell on the ground and rolled about, foaming at the mouth.
L    9.42          him.


Mk   9.21      And Jesus asked his father, "How long has he had this?"  And he said,
Mk   9.22      "From childhood.  And it has often cast him into the fire and into the
Mk   9.22      water, to destroy him; but if you can do anything, have pity on us and
Mk   9.23      help us."  And Jesus said to him, "If you can!  All things are possible
Mk   9.24      to him who believes."  Immediately the father of the child cried out
Mk   9.24      and said, "I believe; help my unbelief!"


M    17.18      And     Jesus                                    rebuked
Mk    9.25      And when Jesus saw that a crowd came running together, he rebuked the
L     9.42      But     Jesus                                    rebuked the


M    17.18            him,
Mk    9.25      unclean spirit, saying to it, "You dumb and deaf spirit, I command you,
L     9.42      unclean spirit,


M    17.18                                      and
Mk    9.26      come out of him, and never enter him again."  And after crying out and


M    17.18                         the demon came out of him,
Mk    9.26      convulsing him terribly, it    came out, and the boy was like a corpse;


Mk   9.27      so that most of them said, "He is dead."  But Jesus took him by the hand
```

```
M    17.18                        and            the boy was cured instantly.
Mk    9.27   and lifted him up, and              he          arose.
L     9.42                        and healed the boy, and gave him back to his father.


M    17.19   Then                              the disciples came to Jesus privately
Mk    9.28   And when he had entered the house, his disciples asked   him    privately,
L     9.43a  And all were astonished at the majesty of God.
L    17.5                            The apostles


M    17.20   and said, "Why could we not cast it out?"      He    said  to them,
Mk    9.29             "Why could we not cast it out?"  And he    said  to them,
L    17.5        said to the Lord,
 M   21.21                                           And Jesus answered them,
 Mk  11.22                                           And Jesus answered them,


M    17.20   "Because of your little faith.   For truly, I say to you, if you have
L    17.6           "Increase our faith!"   And the Lord said,   "If you had
 M   21.21                                    "Truly, I say to you, if you have
 Mk  11.23        "Have          faith in God.  Truly, I say to you,


M    17.20   faith as a grain of mustard seed,
L    17.6    faith as a grain of mustard seed,
 M   21.21   faith and never doubt, you will not only do what has been done to the


M    17.20                         you will  say  to this mountain,    'Move from
L    17.6                          you could say  to this sycamine tree, 'Be rooted
 M   21.21   fig tree, but even if you       say  to this mountain,    'Be taken
 Mk  11.23                          whoever  says to this mountain,    'Be taken


M    17.20   here              to      there,'  and
L    17.6    up, and be planted in  the sea,'   and
 M   21.21   up  and      cast     into the sea,'
 Mk  11.23   up  and      cast     into the sea,' and does not doubt in his heart, but


M    17.20                                          it will move; and nothing
L    17.6                                           it would obey you.
 M   21.21                                          it will be done.
 Mk  11.23   believes that what he says will come to pass, it will be done for him.


M    17.21   will be impossible to you."  "But this kind never    comes  out except
Mk    9.29                                 "This kind cannot be driven out
 M   21.22                                 And              whatever you ask
 Mk  11.24                          Therefore I tell you, whatever you ask


M    17.21   by               prayer and fasting."
Mk    9.29   by anything but  prayer."
 M   21.22   in               prayer,              you will receive,    if  you have
 Mk  11.24   in               prayer, believe that you have received it, and it  will


 M   21.22   faith."
 Mk  11.24   be yours.
```

106

45. SECOND PREDICTION OF THE PASSION

Matthew 17.22-23

```
M    17.22    As          they were gathering                      in Galilee,
Mk   9.30                 They went on from there and passed through Galilee.  And he
L    9.43b    But while  they were all marveling at everything he did,
 J   7.1      After this Jesus went                        about in Galilee;       he
```

```
M    17.22                                          Jesus
Mk   9.31     would not have any one know it; for he was teaching his disciples,
L    9.43b                                           he
 J   7.1      would not go about in Judea, because the Jews sought to kill him.
```

```
M    17.22    said    to    them,                                              "The
Mk   9.31     saying to    them,                                              "The
L    9.44     said    to his disciples, |"Let these words sink into your ears; for the
```

```
M    17.23    Son of man is to be delivered into the hands of men, |and they will kill
Mk   9.31     Son of man will be delivered into the hands of men,  and they will kill
L    9.44     Son of man is to be delivered into the hands of men."
```

```
M    17.23    him, and    he                                 will be raised on the
Mk   9.31     him; and when he is killed, after three days he will     rise."
 J   16.6                                                          But because
```

```
M    17.23    third day."  And they were greatly distressed.
Mk   9.32                  But they did not     understand the  saying,
L    9.45                  But they did not     understand this saying, and it was
 J   16.6     I have said these things to you,   sorrow has filled your hearts.
```

```
Mk   9.32                                                     and they were
 L   9.45     concealed from them, that they should not perceive it; and they were
```

```
Mk   9.32     afraid to ask him.
 L   9.45     afraid to ask him about this saying.
```

46. THE TEMPLE TAX

Matthew 17.24-27

```
M    17.24    When they came to Capernaum, the collectors of the half-shekel tax
M    17.25    went up to Peter and said, "Does not your teacher pay the tax?"  He
M    17.25    said, "Yes."  And when he came home, Jesus spoke to him first, saying,
M    17.25    "What do you think, Simon?  From whom do kings of the earth take toll
M    17.26    or tribute?  From their sons or from others?" |And when he said, "From
M    17.27    others," Jesus said to him, "Then the sons are free.  However, not to
M    17.27    give offense to them, go to the sea and cast a hook, and take the first
M    17.27    fish that comes up, and when you open its mouth you will find a shekel;
M    17.27    take that and give it to them for me and for yourself."
```

Matthew 18.1-19.2

a. Setting

Matthew 18.1-3a

M	18.1	At that time the disciples came to Jesus,
Mk	9.33	And they came to Capernaum; *and when he was in the*

Mk	9.34	*house he asked them, "What were you discussing on the way?" But they*

M	18.1	saying, "Who
Mk	9.34	*were silent;* for on the way they had discussed with one another who
L	9.46	And an argument arose among them as to which

M	18.1	is the greatest in the kingdom of heaven?"
Mk	9.35	was the greatest. *And he sat down and called the twelve; and*
L	9.46	of them was the greatest.

Mk	9.35	*he said to them, "If any one would be first, he must be last of all and*

M	18.2	And
Mk	9.36	*servant of all."* And
L	9.47	But *when Jesus perceived the thought of their hearts,*

M	18.3a	calling to him a child, he put him in the midst of them, |and
Mk	9.36	he took a child, and put him in the midst of them; and
L	9.48a	he took a child and put him by his side, |and

M	18.3a	said,
Mk	9.36	taking him in his arms, he said to them,
L	9.48a	said to them,

b. Who is the Greatest?

Matthew 18.3b-4

M	18.3b	"Truly, I say to you, unless you turn and become
Mk	10.15	Truly, I say to you, whoever does not receive the kingdom of
L	18.17	Truly, I say to you, whoever does not receive the kingdom of
J	3.3b	"Truly, *truly,* I say to you, unless *one is born anew,*
J	3.5b	"Truly, *truly,* I say to you, unless *one is born of water and the*

M	18.3b	like children, you will never enter the kingdom of heaven.
Mk	10.15	God like a child shall not enter it."
L	18.17	God like a child shall not enter it."
J	3.3b	he cannot see the kingdom of God."
J	3.5b	*Spirit,* he cannot enter the kingdom of God.

M	18.4	Whoever humbles himself like this child, he is the greatest in the
M	23.11	He who is greatest *among*
L	22.26	*But not so with you; rather let* the greatest *among*

```
M    18.4     kingdom of heaven.
  M   23.11   you                                              shall be your servant;
  L   22.26   you become as the youngest, and the leader as one who serves.
```

c. Receiving Children

Matthew 18.5–14

```
M    18.5                                              "Whoever receives one such
Mk    9.37                                             "Whoever receives one such
L     9.48     and                      said to them, "Whoever receives      this
  M  10.40                                             "He who  receives
  L  10.16                                             "He who  hears
  J  12.44     And        Jesus cried out and said,   "He who  believes
  J  13.20     Truly, truly, I               say  to you,  he who  receives any one


M    18.5     child in my name receives me;
Mk    9.37    child in my name receives me;
L     9.48    child in my name receives me,                          and
  M  10.40    you             receives me,                           and
  L  10.16    you                   hears  me, and he who rejects you rejects me, and he
  J  12.44          in          me,
  J  12.45                                                           And he
  J  13.20    whom I send        receives me;                        and he


Mk   9.37    whoever receives me, receives not    me but    him who sent me."
L    9.48    whoever receives me  receives                  him who sent me; for he
M   10.40    who     receives me  receives                  him who sent me.
L   10.16    who     rejects me  rejects                    him who sent me."
J   12.44                         believes not in me but in him who sent me.
J   12.45    who     sees    me  sees                       him who sent me.
J   13.20    who     receives me receives                   him who sent me."


M    18.6                                                but whoever causes
Mk    9.42                                               "Whoever causes
L     9.48    who is least among you all is the one who is great."
L    17.2b                                      than that he should cause


M    18.6     one of these little ones who believe in me to sin, it would be better
Mk    9.42    one of these little ones who believe in me to sin, it would be better
L    17.2a    one of these little ones                   to sin. It would be better


M    18.6     for him to have a great millstone fastened  round his neck and to be
Mk    9.42    for him if      a great millstone were hung round his neck and he were
L    17.2a    for him if      a         millstone were hung round his neck and he were


M    18.6     drowned in the depth of the sea.
Mk    9.42    thrown  into          the sea.
L    17.2a    cast    into          the sea,


M    18.7     "Woe to the world         for temptations to sin! For it is  necessary
L    17.1      And he said to his disciples, "Temptations to sin      are sure


M    18.7     that temptations come, but woe to the man by whom the temptation comes!
L    17.1     to               come; but woe to    him by whom    they     come!
```

M	18.8	And if your hand or your foot causes you to sin, cut it off and
Mk	9.43	And if your hand causes you to sin, cut it off;
Mk	9.45	And if your foot causes you to sin, cut it off;
L	17.3	*Take heed to yourselves; if your brother sins, rebuke him, and if he*
M	*5.30*	And if your *right* hand causes you to sin, cut it off and

M	18.8	throw it away; it is better for you to enter life maimed or lame than
Mk	9.43	it is better for you to enter life maimed than
Mk	9.45	it is better for you to enter life lame than
L	17.4	*repents, forgive him; and if he sins against you seven times in the day,*
M	*5.30*	throw it away; it is better *that you lose one of your members* than

M	18.8	with two hands or two feet to be thrown into the eternal
Mk	9.43	with two hands to go to hell, to the unquenchable
Mk	9.45	with two feet to be thrown into
L	17.4	*and turns to you seven times, and says, 'I repent,' you must forgive him."*
M	*5.30*	*that your whole body* go into

M	18.9	fire. And if your eye causes you to sin, pluck it out and throw
Mk	9.43	fire.
Mk	9.47	hell. And if your eye causes you to sin, pluck it out;
M	*5.29*	hell. If your *right* eye causes you to sin, pluck it out and throw

M	18.9	it away; it is better for you to enter life with one eye
Mk	9.47	it is better for you to enter the kingdom of God with one eye
M	*5.29*	it away; it is better *that you lose one of your members*

M	18.9	than with two eyes to be thrown into the hell of
Mk	9.48	than with two eyes to be thrown into hell, ⌐*where their worm does*
M	*5.29*	than *that your whole body* be thrown into hell.

M	18.9	fire.
Mk	9.49	*not die, and the* fire *is not quenched. For every one will be salted*

Mk	9.50	*with fire. Salt is good; but if the salt has lost its saltness, how*
Mk	9.50	*will you season it? Have salt in yourselves, and be at peace with one*
Mk	9.50	*another."*

M	18.10	"See that you do not despise one of these little ones; for I tell you
M	18.10	that in heaven their angels always behold the face of my Father who is

M	18.11	in heaven. *For the Son of man came* *to save the lost.*
L	19.10	*For the Son of man came* to seek and *to save the lost."*

M	18.12	What do you think? If a man has a hundred sheep,
L	15.3,4	So he told them this parable: "What man of you, having a hundred sheep,

M	18.12	and one of them has gone astray, does he not leave the ninety-
L	15.4	if he has lost one of them, does not leave the ninety-

M	18.12	nine on the mountains and go in search of the one that went astray?
L	15.4	nine in the wilderness, and go after the one which is lost, until

M	18.13	And if he finds it, truly, I say to you, he
L	15.5	he finds it? And when he has found it, he lays it

| M | 18.13 | <u>rejoices over it more than over the ninety-nine</u> |
| L | 15.6 | on his shoulders, rejoicing. And when he comes home, he calls together |

| L | 15.6 | *his friends and his neighbors, saying to them, 'Rejoice with me, for I* |

| M | 18.14 | <u>that never went astray.</u> <u>So</u> <u>it is not the will</u> |
| L | 15.7 | *have found my sheep* which   was lost.' Just <u>so</u>, I tell you, there |

| M | 18.14 | <u>of my Father who is in heaven that one of these little ones should</u> |
| L | 15.7 | will be more joy   <u>in heaven</u> over one sinner who repents than over |

| M | 18.14 | <u>perish.</u> |
| L | 15.7 | ninety-nine righteous persons who need no repentance. |

d. Forgiveness

Matthew 18.15-22

| M | 18.15 | "If your <u>brother sins against you</u>, <u>go and</u> |
| L | 17.3 | Take heed to yourselves; <u>if your brother sins</u>, |

| M | 18.15 | <u>tell</u> <u>him his fault, between you and him alone.</u> <u>If he listens to you,</u> |
| L | 17.3 | rebuke <u>him</u>,   and <u>if he</u> repents, |

| M | 18.16 | <u>you have gained your brother.</u> <u>But if he does not listen</u>, <u>take one or</u> |
| L | 17.3 | forgive   him; |

| M | 18.16 | <u>two others along with you</u>, <u>that every word may be confirmed by the</u> |
| J | 8.17 | *In your law it is written* <u>that</u>   <u>the</u> |

M	18.17	<u>evidence</u> of two or three witnesses. <u>If he refuses to listen to them,</u>
M	16.18	*And I tell you, you are Peter, and on this rock I*
J	8.17	*testimony* of two *men is true;*

| M | 18.17 | <u>tell it to the church;</u> <u>and if he refuses to listen even to the church</u>, |
| M | 16.18 | *will build my* church, *and the powers of death shall not prevail* |

| M | 18.18 | <u>let him be to you as a Gentile and a tax collector.</u> <u>Truly,</u> <u>I say to</u> |
| M | 16.19 | *against it.* *I will give you the keys of the kingdom of heaven,* |

M	18.18	you, <u>whatever you bind on earth</u> <u>shall be</u> <u>bound in heaven,</u>
M	16.19	*and* <u>whatever you bind on earth</u> <u>shall be</u> <u>bound in heaven,</u>
J	20.23	*If* <u>you</u> *forgive the sins of any, they are* <u>forgiven;</u>

M	18.18	<u>and whatever you loose on earth</u> <u>shall be</u> <u>loosed in heaven.</u>
M	16.19	<u>and whatever you loose on earth</u> <u>shall be</u> <u>loosed in heaven.</u>"
J	20.23	*if* <u>you</u> *retain the sins of any, they are retained."*

M	18.19	<u>Again</u> I say to you, if two of you agree on earth about <u>anything</u>
Mk	11.24	*Therefore* <u>I tell</u> <u>you</u>, *whatever*
J	16.24	*Hitherto* *you have asked* *nothing in*

```
M    18.19      they  ask,                                                                    it  will
Mk  11.24       you   ask in prayer, believe that you have received it, and it  will
J   14.23                       Jesus answered him, "If a man loves me, he  will
J   16.24       my name; ask,                                                    and you  will
```

```
M    18.20      be done for them  by my Father in heaven.  For where two or three are
Mk  11.24       be yours.
J   14.23          keep my word, and my Father will love him,
J   16.24       receive, that your joy may be full.
```

```
M    18.20      gathered in my name, there  am I in the midst of them."
M   28.20b                       and lo, I am        with      you always, to the
J   14.23                        and         we will  come  to him and make our home
```

```
M   28.20b      close of the age."
J   14.23       with him.
```

```
M    18.21      Then Peter came up and said to him, "Lord, how often shall my brother
L   17.4                                              and if                      he
```

```
M    18.22      sin  against me, and I forgive him?  As many as seven times?"  Jesus
L   17.4        sins against you                                seven times in the day,
```

```
M    18.22      said to him, "I do not say to you seven times, but
L   17.4                        and turns to you seven times, and says, 'I repent,'
```

```
M    18.22      seventy times seven.
L   17.4        you must forgive him."
```

e. The Unmerciful Servant

Matthew 18.23-35

```
M    18.23      "Therefore the kingdom of heaven may be compared to a king who wished
M    18.24      to settle accounts with his servants.  When he began the reckoning, one
M    18.25      was brought to him who owed him ten thousand talents; and as he could
M    18.25      not pay, his lord ordered him to be sold, with his wife and children
M    18.26      and all that he had, and payment to be made.  So the servant fell on
M    18.26      his knees, imploring him, 'Lord, have patience with me, and I will pay
M    18.27      you everything.'  And out of pity for him the lord of that servant
M    18.28      released him and forgave him the debt.  But that same servant, as he
M    18.28      went out, came upon one of his fellow servants who owed him a hundred
M    18.28      denarii; and seizing him by the throat he said, 'Pay what you owe.'
M    18.29      So his fellow servant fell down and besought him, 'Have patience with
M    18.30      me, and I will pay you.'  He refused and went and put him in prison
M    18.31      till he should pay the debt.  When his fellow servants saw what had
M    18.31      taken place, they were greatly distressed, and they went and reported
M    18.32      to their lord all that had taken place. Then his lord summoned him and
M    18.32      said to him, 'You wicked servant!  I forgave you all that debt because
```

```
M    18.33      you besought me; and should not you have had mercy on your fellow servant,
M    5.7                               "Blessed are the merciful,
L    6.36                              Be              merciful,               even
```

```
M    18.34      as    I       had   mercy on you?'  And in anger his lord delivered
M    5.7        for   they shall obtain mercy.
L    6.36       as your Father   is    merciful.
```

112

M	18.35	him to the jailers, till he should pay all his debt. So also my
M	6.14b	*your*
M	6.15b	*neither will your*

M	18.35	heavenly Father will do to every one of you, if you do not
M	6.14a	heavenly Father *also* will *forgive* you; *For* if you
M	6.15a	Father *forgive your trespasses. but* if you do not

M	18.35	forgive your brother from your heart."
M	6.14a	forgive *mon their trespasses,*
M	6.15a	forgive *men their trespasses,*

f. Summary

Matthew 19.1-2

M	19.1	Now when Jesus had finished these sayings, he went away
Mk	10.1	And he left there and went

M	19.2	from Galilee and entered the region of Judea beyond the Jordan; and
Mk	10.1	to the region of Judea and beyond the Jordan, and

M	19.2	large crowds followed him, and he
Mk	10.1	crowds gathered to him again; and again, as his custom was, he

M	19.2	healed them there.
Mk	10.1	taught them.

48. MARRIAGE AND DIVORCE

Matthew 19.3-12

M	19.3	And Pharisees came up to him and tested him by asking, "Is
Mk	10.2	And Pharisees came up and in order to test him asked, "Is

M	19.4	it lawful to divorce one's wife for any cause?" He answered,
Mk	10.3	it lawful for a man to divorce his wife?" He answered

M	19.4	"Have you not read that he who made them from the beginning
Mk	10.6	them, "What did Moses command you?" But from the beginning of

M	19.5	made them male and female, |and said, 'For this reason a
Mk	10.7	creation, 'God made them male and female.' 'For this reason a

M	19.5	man shall leave his father and mother and be joined to his wife, and
Mk	10.8	man shall leave his father and mother and be joined to his wife, |and

M	19.6	the two shall become one flesh'? |So they are no longer two but one
Mk	10.8	the two shall become one flesh.' So they are no longer two but one

113

M	19.6	flesh. What therefore God has joined together, let not man put asunder."
Mk	10.9	flesh. What therefore God has joined together, let not man put asunder."
M	*5.31*	*"It was*

M	19.7	They said to him, "Why then did Moses command one to give a
Mk	10.4	They said, "Moses allowed a man to write a
M	*5.31*	*also* said, *'Whoever divorces his wife, let him* give *her* a

M	19.8	certificate of divorce, and to put her away?" He said to them,
Mk	10.5	certificate of divorce, and to put her away." But Jesus said to them,
M	*5.31*	certificate of divorce.'

M	19.8	"For your hardness of heart Moses allowed you to divorce your wives, but
Mk	10.10	"For your hardness of heart he wrote you this commandment. And in

M	19.9	from the beginning it was not so. And I say
Mk	10.11	the house the disciples asked him again about this matter. And he said
M	*5.32*	*But* I say

M	19.9	to you: whoever divorces his wife, except for
Mk	10.11	to them, "Whoever divorces his wife
L	16.18	"Every one who divorces his wife
M	*5.32*	to you *that every one who* divorces his wife, except *on the ground of*

M	19.9	unchastity, and marries another, commits adultery."
Mk	10.12	and marries another, commits adultery against her; *and*
L	16.18	and marries another commits adultery, *and*
M	*5.32*	unchastity, *makes her an* adulteress; *and*

Mk	*10.12*	*if she divorces her husband and marries another,*
L	*16.18*	*he who marries a woman divorced from her husband*
M	*5.32*	*whoever marries a divorced woman*

Mk	*10.12*	*she commits adultery."*
L	*16.18*	*commits adultery.*
M	*5.32*	*commits adultery.*

M	19.10	The disciples said to him, "If such is the case of a man with his wife,
M	19.11	it is not expedient to marry." But he said to them, "Not all men can
M	19.12	receive this saying, but only those to whom it is given. For there are
M	19.12	eunuchs who have been so from birth, and there are eunuchs who have been
M	19.12	made eunuchs by men, and there are eunuchs who have made themselves
M	19.12	eunuchs for the sake of the kingdom of heaven. He who is able to receive
M	19.12	this, let him receive it."

49. LET THE CHILDREN COME

Matthew 19.13-15

M	19.13	Then children were brought to him that he might lay
Mk	10.13	And they were bringing children to him, that he might touch
L	18.15	Now they were bringing even infants to him that he might touch

M	19.13	his hands on them and pray. The disciples rebuked the
Mk	10.13	them; and the disciples rebuked
L	18.15	them; and when the disciples saw it, they rebuked

M	19.14	people; but Jesus said, "Let
Mk	10.14	them. But when Jesus saw it he was indignant, and said to them, "Let
L	18.16	them. But Jesus called them to him, saying, "Let

M	19.14	the children come to me, and do not hinder them; for to such belongs the
Mk	10.14	the children come to me, do not hinder them; for to such belongs the
L	18.16	the children come to me, and do not hinder them; for to such belongs the

M	19.14	kingdom of heaven."
Mk	10.15	kingdom of God. *Truly, I say to you, whoever does not receive the kingdom*
L	18.17	kingdom of God. *Truly, I say to you, whoever does not receive the kingdom*

M	19.15	And he
Mk	10.16	*of God like a child shall not enter it."* And he took them in his arms and
L	18.17	*of God like a child shall not enter it."*

M	19.15	laid his hands on them and went away.
Mk	10.16	blessed them, laying his hands upon them.

50. THE PERIL OF RICHES

Matthew 19.16-30

M	19.16	And behold, one came up
Mk	10.17	And as he was setting out on his journey, a man ran up and knelt
L	18.18	And a ruler
L	10.25	And behold, *a lawyer stood up to put*

M	19.16	to him, saying, "Teacher, what good deed must
Mk	10.17	before him, and asked him, "Good Teacher, what must
L	18.18	asked him, "Good Teacher, what shall
L	10.25	*him to the test,* saying, "Teacher, what *shall*

M	19.17	I do, to have eternal life?" And he said to him, "Why do you ask
Mk	10.18	I do to inherit eternal life?" And Jesus said to him, "Why do you call
L	18.19	I do to inherit eternal life?" And Jesus said to him, "Why do you call
L	10.26	I do *to inherit* eternal life?" He said to him,

M	19.17	me about what is good? One there is who is good. If you
Mk	10.19	me good? No one is good but God alone. You
L	18.20	me good? No one is good but God alone. You
L	10.26	*"What is written*

M	19.18	would enter life, keep the commandments." He said to him,
Mk	10.19	know the commandments:
L	18.20	know the commandments:
L	10.27	*in the law? How do you read?" And he answered,*

M	19.18	"Which?" And Jesus said, "You shall not kill, You shall not
Mk	10.19	'Do not kill, Do not
L	18.20	'Do not commit adultery, Do not
L	10.27	"You shall *love the Lord your God with all*

M	19.18	commit adultery, You shall not steal, You shall not bear false witness,
Mk	10.19	commit adultery, Do not steal, Do not bear false witness,
L	18.20	kill, Do not steal, Do not bear false witness,
L	10.27	*your heart, and with all your soul, and with all your strength, and*

115

```
M    19.19               |Honor your father and mother, and, You shall love your
Mk   10.19    Do not defraud, Honor your father and mother.'"
L    18.20                Honor your father and mother.'"
  M  22.39                         And a second is like it, You shall love your
  Mk 12.31b                                           'You shall love your
  L  10.27    with all your mind;                              and              your


M    19.20    neighbor as yourself."  The young man said to him,        "All these
Mk   10.20                            And      he  said to him, "Teacher, all these
L    18.21                            And      he  said,                 "All these
  M  22.39    neighbor as yourself.
  Mk 12.31b   neighbor as yourself.'
  L  10.28    neighbor as yourself."  And     he  said to him,        "You have


M    19.21    I have observed; what do I still lack?"      Jesus
Mk   10.21    I have observed  from my youth."             Jesus looking upon him loved
L    18.22    I have observed  from my youth."  And when Jesus heard it,
  L  10.28    answered right; do this, and you will live."


M    19.21                said to him, "If      you would be perfect,      go, sell
Mk   10.21    him, and said to him,        "You      lack one thing; go, sell
L    18.22         he said to him, "One thing you still lack.            Sell all


M    19.21    what you possess and give      to the poor, and you will have treasure
Mk   10.21    what you have,    and give     to the poor, and you will have treasure
L    18.22    that you have     and distribute to the poor, and you will have treasure


M    19.22    in heaven; and come, follow me."    When the young man heard this
Mk   10.22    in heaven; and come, follow me."  At that saying his countenance fell,
L    18.23    in heaven; and come, follow me."  But when        he  heard this


M    19.22        he went away sorrowful; for he had great possessions.
Mk   10.22    and he went away sorrowful; for he had great possessions.
L    18.23        he became     sad,      for he  was very  rich.


M    19.23    And Jesus               said to his disciples, "Truly, I say to
Mk   10.23    And Jesus looked  around and said to his disciples,
L    18.24         Jesus looking at him    said,


M    19.23    you, it will be hard        for              a rich man to enter
Mk   10.23    "How      hard it will be for those who have riches   to enter
L    18.24    "How      hard it      is for those who have riches   to enter


M    19.23    the kingdom of heaven.
Mk   10.24    the kingdom of God!"   |And the disciples were amazed at his words.  But
L    18.24    the kingdom of God!


M    19.24               Again I tell you,
Mk   10.24    Jesus said to them again, "Children, how hard it is to enter the kingdom


M    19.24        it is easier for a camel to go through the eye of a needle than
Mk   10.25    of God! It is easier for a camel to go through the eye of a needle than
L    18.25       For it is easier for a camel to go through the eye of a needle than


M    19.25    for a rich man to enter the kingdom of God."  When the disciples heard
Mk   10.26    for a rich man to enter the kingdom of God."  And
L    18.26    for a rich man to enter the kingdom of God."            Those who heard
```

M	19.25	this they were greatly astonished, saying, "Who then can
Mk	10.26	they were exceedingly astonished, and said to him, "Then who can
L	18.26	it said, "Then who can

M	19.26	be saved?" But Jesus looked at them and said to them, "With men this
Mk	10.27	be saved?" Jesus looked at them and said, "With men it
L	18.27	be saved?" But he said, "What

M	19.26	is impossible, but with God all things are possible."
Mk	10.27	is impossible, but not with God; for all things are possible with God."
L	18.27	is impossible with men is possible with God."

M	19.27	Then Peter said in reply, "Lo, we have left everything and
Mk	10.28	Peter began to say to him, "Lo, we have left everything and
L	18.28	And Peter said, "Lo, we have left our homes and

M	19.28	followed you. What then shall we have?" Jesus said to them, "Truly, I
Mk	10.29	followed you." Jesus said, "Truly, I
L	18.29	followed you." And he said to them, "Truly, I
L	22.28	"You are those

M	19.28	say to you, in the new world, when the Son of man shall sit on his
Mk	10.29	say to you,
L	18.29	say to you,
L	22.29	who have continued with me in my trials; and I assign to you, as my

M	19.28	glorious throne, you who have followed me
L	22.30	Father assigned to me, a kingdom, |that you may eat and drink at my table

M	19.28	will also sit on twelve thrones, judging the twelve tribes of
L	22.30	in my kingdom, and sit on thrones judging the twelve tribes of

M	19.29	Israel. And every one who has left houses or brothers or sisters
Mk	10.29	there is no one who has left house or brothers or sisters
L	18.29	there is no man who has left house or wife or brothers
L	14.26	"If any one comes to me and does not hate his own
L	22.30	Israel.

M	19.29	or father or mother or children or lands, for my name's sake,
Mk	10.29	or mother or father or children or lands, for my sake
L	18.29	or parents or children, for the sake
L	14.26	father and mother and wife and children and brothers and sisters, yes,

M	19.29	will receive a hundredfold,
Mk	10.30	and for the gospel, |who will not receive a hundredfold now in
L	18.30	of the kingdom of God, |who will not receive manifold more in
L	14.26	and even his own life, he cannot be my disciple.

Mk	10.30	this time, houses and brothers and sisters and mothers and children and
L	18.30	this time,

M	19.29	and inherit eternal life.
Mk	10.30	lands, with persecutions, and in the age to come eternal life.
L	18.30	and in the age to come eternal life."
Mk	9.35	And he sat down and called the twelve; and he said to them,

```
M    19.30   But              many that      are first    will be last,  and        the last
Mk   10.31   But              many that      are first    will be last,  and        the last
 M   20.16   So                              the last     will be first, and         the first
 Mk  ·9.35   "If        any one would  be    first,  he   must be last of all and servant
 L   13.30   And behold, some                are last  who will be first, and some are first
```

```
M    19.30                    first.
Mk   10.31                    first."
 M   20.16                    last."
 Mk  9.35    of all."
 L   13.30   who will be last."
```

51. THE LABORERS IN THE VINEYARD

Matthew 20.1-16

```
M    20.1     "For the kingdom of heaven is like a householder who went out early in
M    20.2     the morning to hire laborers for his vineyard.  After agreeing with the
M    20.3     laborers for a denarius a day, he sent them into his vineyard.  And going
M    20.3     out about the third hour he saw others standing idle in the market place;
M    20.4     and to them he said, 'You go into the vineyard too, and whatever is right
M    20.5     I will give you.'  So they went.  |Going out again about the sixth hour
M    20.6     and the ninth hour, he did the same.  And about the eleventh hour he went
M    20.6     out and found others standing; and he said to them, 'Why do you stand here
M    20.7     idle all day?'  They said to him, 'Because no one has hired us.'  He said
M    20.8     to them, 'You go into the vineyard too.'  And when evening came, the owner
M    20.8     of the vineyard said to his steward, 'Call the laborers and pay them their
M    20.9     wages, beginning with the last, up to the first.'  And when those hired
M    20.10    about the eleventh hour came, each of them received a denarius.  Now when
M    20.10    the first came, they thought they would receive more; but each of them
M    20.11    also received a denarius.  And on receiving it they grumbled at the
M    20.12    householder, |saying, 'These last worked only one hour, and you have made
M    20.12    them equal to us who have borne the burden of the day and the scorching
M    20.13    heat.'  But he replied to one of them, 'Friend, I am doing you no wrong;
M    20.14    did you not agree with me for a denarius?  Take what belongs to you, and
M    20.15    go; I choose to give to this last as I give to you.  Am I not allowed to
M    20.15    do what I choose with what belongs to me?  Or do you begrudge my
M    20.15    generosity?'
```

```
M    20.16    So                              the last     will be first, and       the
 M   19.30    But            many that        are first    will be last,  and       the
 Mk  9.35b    "If      any one would  be      first,  he   must be last of all and servant
 Mk  10.31    But            many that        are first    will be last,  and       the
 L   13.30    And behold, some                are last  who will be first, and some are
```

```
M    20.16    first            last."
 M   19.30    last             first.
 Mk  9.35b    of all."
 Mk  10.31    last             first."
 L   13.30    first who will be last."
```

52. THIRD PREDICTION OF THE PASSION

Matthew 20.17-19

```
M    20.17    And as Jesus was                going up to Jerusalem,
Mk   10.32    And      they were on the road, going up to Jerusalem, and Jesus was
```

M	20.17	he took the twelve disciples aside, and on the way he
Mk	10.32	*were afraid.* And taking the twelve again, he
L	18.31	And taking the twelve, he

M	20.18	said to them, |"Behold, we
Mk	10.33	began to tell them what was to happen to him, |saying, "Behold, we
L	18.31	said to them, "Behold, we

M	20.18	are going up to Jerusalem; and the Son of
Mk	10.33	are going up to Jerusalem; and the Son of
L	18.31	are going up to Jerusalem, and everything that is written of the Son of

M	20.18	man will be delivered to the chief priests and
Mk	10.33	man will be delivered to the chief priests and the
L	18.31	man by the prophets will be accomplished.

M	20.19	scribes, and they will condemn him to death, |and deliver
Mk	10.33	scribes, and they will condemn him to death, and deliver
L	18.32	For he will be delivered

M	20.19	him to the Gentiles to be mocked
Mk	10.34	him to the Gentiles; and they will mock him, and
L	18.32	to the Gentiles, and will be mocked and shamefully treated and

M	20.19	and scourged and crucified, and
Mk	10.34	spit upon him, and scourge him, and kill him; and after three days
L	18.33	spit upon; they will scourge him and kill him, and on the third day

M	20.19	he will be raised on the third day."
Mk	10.34	he will rise."
L	18.34	he will rise." *But they understood none of these things; this saying*

L	18.34	*was hid from them, and they did not grasp what was said.*

53. THE SONS OF ZEBEDEE

Matthew 20.20-28

M	20.20	Then the mother of the sons of Zebedee came up to him, with
Mk	10.35	And James and John, the sons of Zebedee, came forward to him, and

M	20.20	her sons, and kneeling before him she
Mk	10.35	said to him, "Teacher, we want you to do for us whatever we

M	20.21	asked him for something. And he said to her, "What do you want?"
Mk	10.36	ask of you." And he said to them, "What do you want me to

M	20.21	She said to him, "Command that these two sons of
Mk	10.37	do for you?" And they said to him, "Grant us

M	20.21	mine may sit, <u>one at your right hand and one at your left</u>, <u>in your</u>
Mk	10.37	to <u>sit, one at your right hand and one at your left</u>, <u>in your</u>

M	20.22	kingdom." But Jesus answered, <u>"You do not know what you are asking.</u>
Mk	10.38	glory." <u>But Jesus said to them, "You do not know what you are asking.</u>

M	20.22	<u>Are you able to drink the cup that I am to drink?"</u>
Mk	10.38	<u>Are you able to drink the cup that I</u> drink, or to be baptized

M	20.22	<u>They said to him</u>, "We
Mk	10.39	with the baptism with which I am baptized?" And <u>they said to him</u>, "We

M	20.23	<u>are able</u>." He said to them, <u>"You will drink</u>
Mk	10.39	<u>are able</u>." And Jesus <u>said to them</u>, "The cup that I drink <u>you will drink</u>;

M	20.23	my cup, <u>but</u>
Mk	10.40	and with the baptism with which I am baptized, you will be baptized; <u>but</u>

M	20.23	<u>to sit at my right hand and at my left is not mine to grant</u>, <u>but it is</u>
Mk	10.40	<u>to sit at my right hand</u> or at <u>my left is not mine to grant</u>, <u>but it is</u>

M	20.24	<u>for those for whom it has been prepared</u> by my Father." <u>And when the</u>
Mk	10.41	<u>for those for whom it has been prepared</u>." <u>And when the</u>
L	22.24	A dispute also arose

M	20.25	<u>ten heard it, they</u> were <u>indignant at</u> the two brothers. But
Mk	10.42	<u>ten heard it, they</u> began to be <u>indignant at</u> James and John. And
L	22.25	among them, which of them was to be regarded as the greatest. And

M	20.25	<u>Jesus called them to him and said</u>, <u>"You know that</u>
Mk	10.42	<u>Jesus called them to him and said</u> to them, <u>"You know that</u> those who are
L	22.25	he <u>said</u> to them,

M	20.25	<u>the rulers of the Gentiles</u> <u>lord it</u> <u>over them</u>, <u>and</u>
Mk	10.42	supposed to rule over <u>the Gentiles</u> <u>lord it</u> <u>over them</u>, <u>and</u>
L	22.25	<u>"The</u> kings <u>of the Gentiles</u> exercise lordship <u>over them</u>; <u>and</u>

M	20.25	<u>their great men exercise authority over them.</u>
Mk	10.42	<u>their great men exercise authority over them.</u>
L	22.25	those in <u>authority over them</u> are called benefactors.

M	20.26	<u>It shall not be so among you; but whoever would be</u> great
Mk	10.43	But <u>it shall not be so among you; but whoever would be</u> great
L	22.26	But not so with you; rather let the greatest
M	*23.11*	*He who is* greatest
J	*13.16*	*Truly, truly, I say to you, a servant is not* greater

M	20.26	<u>among you</u> must <u>be your servant</u>,
Mk	10.43	<u>among you</u> must <u>be your servant</u>,
L	22.26	<u>among you</u> become as the youngest, and the leader as one who serves.
M	*23.11*	<u>among you</u> *shall* <u>be your servant</u>;
J	*13.16*	*than his master; nor is he who is sent greater than* <u>*he who sent him.*</u>

```
Mk   9.35      And he sat down and called the twelve; and he said to them,
L    9.48b     "Whoever receives this child in my name receives me, and whoever receives


M    20.27                                      and whoever would be first    among you must
Mk   10.44                                      and whoever would be first    among you must
Mk    9.35                                  "If any one would be first,            he   must
L     9.48b    me receives him who sent me; for he who       is least    among you all


M    20.28     be                 your slave;       even as the Son of man       came
Mk   10.45     be                 slave   of all.   For    the Son of man also came
L    22.27                                          For which is the greater, one who
Mk    9.35     be last of all and servant of all."
L     9.48b    is the one who is    great."
J    13.15                                          For      I               have


M    20.28     not to be served   but to serve,  and to give his life as a ransom for
Mk   10.45     not to be served   but to serve,  and to give his life as a ransom for
L    22.27     sits at table, or one who serves?  Is it not the one who sits at table?
J    13.15     given you an example, that you also should do as I have done to you.


M    20.28     many."
Mk   10.45     many."
L    22.27     But I am among you as one who serves.
```

54. BLIND BARTIMAEUS

Matthew 20.29-34

```
M    20.29                                      And as they  went out  of    Jericho,
Mk   10.46     And they came       to Jericho; and as he    was leaving   Jericho
L    18.35     As he    drew near to Jericho,
M     9.27                                      And as Jesus passed on from there,


M    20.30                          a great crowd followed him.  And behold, two
Mk   10.46     with his disciples and a great multitude,            Bartimaeus, a
L    18.35                                                             a
M     9.27                                                             two


M    20.30     blind men                              sitting by the roadside,
Mk   10.46     blind beggar, the son of Timaeus, was sitting by the roadside.
L    18.35     blind man                        was sitting by the roadside begging;
M     9.27     blind men                            followed him,


M    20.30         when they heard
Mk   10.47     And when he    heard
L    18.36     and        hearing a multitude going by, he inquired what this meant.


M    20.30     that           Jesus           was passing by,
Mk   10.47     that it was    Jesus of Nazareth,                    he began to
L    18.37,38  They told him, "Jesus of Nazareth is  passing by."  And he


M    20.30     cried  out,                        "Have mercy on us, Son of
Mk   10.47     cry    out and say, "Jesus, Son of David, have mercy on me!"
L    18.38     cried,            "Jesus, Son of David, have mercy on me!"
M     9.27     crying aloud,                       "Have mercy on us, Son of
```

```
M    20.31    David!"  The crowd                    rebuked them, telling them to be
Mk   10.48             And many                     rebuked him,  telling him  to be
L    18.39             And those who were in front  rebuked him,  telling him  to be
  M   9.28    David."  When he entered the house,


M    20.31    silent; but they cried out    the more, "Lord,           have mercy on
Mk   10.48    silent; but he   cried out all the more, "Son of David, have mercy on
L    18.39    silent; but he   cried out all the more, "Son of David, have mercy on
  M   9.28             the blind men came to him;


M    20.32    us, Son of David!"  And Jesus stopped  and            called   them,
Mk   10.49    me!"                And Jesus stopped  and said, "Call          him."  And
L    18.40    me!"                And Jesus stopped, and            commanded him to be
  M   9.28                        and Jesus


Mk 10.49    they called the blind man, saying to him, "Take heart; rise, he is calling
Mk 10.50    you."  And throwing off his mantle he sprang up and came to Jesus.


M    20.32                                              saying,        "What do you
Mk   10.51                              And Jesus said to him,         "What do you
L    18.41    brought to him; and when he came near, he asked    him,  |"What do you
  M   9.28                                           said to them,         "Do you


M    20.33    want me to do for you?"                 They said to him,      "Lord,
Mk   10.51    want me to do for you?"  And the blind man  said to him,       "Master,
L    18.41    want me to do for you?"                 He  said,             "Lord,
  M   9.28    believe that I am able to do this?"     They said to him, "Yes, Lord."


M    20.34    let our eyes be opened."  And  Jesus in pity touched their eyes,
Mk   10.52    let me receive my sight." And  Jesus said to him, "Go your way;
L    18.42    let me receive my sight." And  Jesus said to him, "Receive your sight;
  M   9.29                              Then he                 touched their eyes, saying,


M    20.34                                          and immediately they
Mk   10.52              your faith has made you well." And immediately he
L    18.43              your faith has made you well." And immediately he
  M   9.30    "According to your faith be it done to you." And              their eyes


M    20.34    received their sight and followed him.
Mk   10.52    received his   sight and followed him on the way.
L    18.43    received his   sight and followed him, glorifying God; and all the people,
  M   9.30    were opened.  And Jesus sternly charged them, "See that no one knows it."


L  18.43    when they saw it, gave praise to God.
M   9.31    But they went away and spread his fame through all that district.
```

55. JESUS ENTERS JERUSALEM

Matthew 21.1-11

```
L  19.28    And when he had said this, he went on ahead, going up to Jerusalem.


M    21.1     And when                                                   they
Mk   11.1     And when                                                   they
L    19.29        When                                                   he
J    12.12    The next day a great crowd who had come to the feast heard that Jesus
```

```
M    21.1     drew near  to Jerusalem  and came  to Bethphage,                    to the Mount
Mk   11.1     drew near  to Jerusalem,                        to Bethphage and Bethany, at the Mount
L    19.29    drew near                                       to Bethphage and Bethany, at the mount
J    12.12    was coming to Jerusalem.


M    21.2                      of Olives, then Jesus sent two            disciples,   |saying
Mk   11.2                      of Olives,      he    sent two of his disciples,  |and said
L    19.30    that is called Olivet,          he    sent two of the disciples,   |saying,


M    21.2     to them, "Go into the village opposite you, and immediately
Mk   11.2     to them, "Go into the village opposite you, and immediately as you
L    19.30             "Go into the village opposite,                   where on


M    21.2                 you will find an ass  tied, and a colt with her;
Mk   11.2     enter it you will find a  colt tied, on which no one has ever     sat;
L    19.30    entering you will find a  colt tied, on which no one has ever yet sat;


M    21.3     untie them and bring them to me.  If any one says anything to you,
Mk   11.3     untie it   and bring it.          If any one says            to you, 'Why
L    19.31    untie it   and bring it   here.   If any one asks            you, 'Why


M    21.3                          you shall say,      'The Lord has need of them,'
Mk   11.3     are you doing this?'           say,      'The Lord has need of it
L    19.31    are you untying it?' you shall say this, 'The Lord has need of it.'"


M    21.4     and he will send them            immediately."  This took place to fulfil
Mk   11.3     and    will send it   back here immediately.'"


M    21.4     what was spoken by the prophet, saying,
J    12.14b   as it is written,


M    21.5                  "Tell the  daughter of Zion,
J    12.15                 "Fear not, daughter of Zion;


M    21.5                  Behold, your king is coming to you,
J    12.15                 behold, your king is coming,


M    21.5                  humble, and mounted on an ass,
J    12.15                         sitting on an ass's


M    21.5                  and on a colt, the foal of an ass."
J    12.15                     colt!"


M    21.6     The disciples         went     and did          as Jesus had
Mk   11.4     And they              went away, and found a colt tied at the door out
L    19.32    So  those who were sent went away, and found   it   as he      had


M    21.6     directed them;
Mk   11.5     in the open street; and they untied it.  And
L    19.33    told      them.                          And as they were untying the


Mk 11.5               those who stood there said to them, "What are you doing, untying
 L 19.33    colt, its   owners         said to them, "Why  are you          untying
```

```
Mk 11.6     the colt?"  And they told them what Jesus had said; and they let them go.
L  19.34     the colt?"  And they said, "The Lord has need of it."


M   21.7           they  brought the     ass and the colt,       and put      their
Mk  11.7     And  they  brought              the colt to Jesus, and threw    their
L   19.35    And  they  brought                  it  to Jesus, and throwing their
J   12.14a   And Jesus found     a young ass


M   21.8     garments on      them, and he    sat       thereon.          Most of the
Mk  11.8     garments on      it;   and he    sat       upon it.  And        many
L   19.36    garments on the colt       they set Jesus upon it.  And as he rode along,
J   12.14a                         and       sat       upon it;


M   21.8     crowd spread their garments on the road, and others cut           branches
Mk  11.8           spread their garments on the road, and others spread leafy branches
L   19.37    they spread their garments on the road.  As he was now drawing near, at
J   12.13                                             So  they   took          branches


M   21.9     from the trees and spread them on the road.  And the        crowds that
Mk  11.9     which they had cut from the fields.          And          those who
L   19.37    the descent of the Mount of Olives,             the whole multitude of the
J   12.13    of  palm trees                                 and


M   21.9     went before      him and that     followed him shouted,    "Hosanna to
Mk  11.9     went before          and those who followed    cried out, "Hosanna!
L   19.37    disciples began to rejoice and praise God with a loud voice for all the
J   12.13    went out to meet him,                          crying,    "Hosanna!


M   21.9     the Son of David!                        Blessed is      he   who comes
Mk  11.9                                              Blessed is      he   who comes
L   19.38    mighty works that they had seen, |saying, "Blessed is the King who comes
J   12.13                                              Blessed is      he   who comes


M   21.9     in the name of the Lord!
Mk  11.10    in the name of the Lord!  Blessed is the kingdom of our father David
L   19.38    in the name of the Lord!                          Peace in
J   12.13    in the name of the Lord, even the King of Israel!"


M   21.10              Hosanna in the highest!"  And when he entered Jerusalem,
Mk  11.11    that is coming! Hosanna in the highest!"  And       he entered Jerusalem,
L   19.39    heaven       and glory   in the highest!"  And some of the Pharisees in
J   12.16                                      His disciples did not under-


M   21.11    all the city was stirred, saying, "Who is this?"  And the crowds said,
Mk  11.11    and went into the temple; and when he had looked round at everything,
L   19.40    the multitude said to him, "Teacher, rebuke your disciples."  He answered,
J   12.16    stand this at first; but when Jesus was glorified, then they remembered


M   21.11    "This is the prophet Jesus from Nazareth of Galilee."
Mk  11.11    as it was already late, he went out to Bethany with the twelve.
L   19.40    "I tell you, if these were silent, the very stones would cry out."
J   12.17    that this had been written of him and had been done to him.  The crowd


J   12.17    that had been with him when he called Lazarus out of the tomb and raised
J   12.18    him from the dead bore witness.  The reason why the crowd went to meet
J   12.19    him was that they heard he had done this sign.  The Pharisees then said
J   12.19    to one another, "You see that you can do nothing; look, the world has
J   12.19    gone after him."
```

56. CLEANSING THE TEMPLE

Matthew 21.12-17

J 2.13 *The Passover of the Jews was at hand, and Jesus went up to Jerusalem.*

M   21.12   And Jesus entered the temple of God
Mk 11.15   And they came to Jerusalem.   And he   entered the temple
L   19.45   And he   entered the temple
J   2.14   In the temple he found those

J 2.14 *who were selling oxen and sheep and pigeons, and the money-changers at*
J 2.15 *their business. And making a whip*

M   21.12   and   drove out   all   who sold and   bought in the temple,
Mk 11.15   and began to drive out   those who sold and   those who bought in the temple,
L   19.45   and began to drive out   those who sold,
J   2.15   of cords, he drove them all, with the sheep and oxen, out   of the temple;

M   21.12   and he overturned the   tables of the money-changers and the seats of
Mk 11.15   and he overturned the   tables of the money-changers and the seats of
J   2.15   and he poured out the   coins of the money-changers

J 2.16 and   overturned *their* tables.   And   *he told*

M   21.12   those who sold   pigeons.
Mk 11.16   those who sold   pigeons; *and he would not allow any one to carry any-*
J   2.16   those who sold the pigeons,

M   21.13   He   said   to them, "It is
Mk 11.17   *thing through the temple. And* he taught, and said   to them, "Is it not
L   19.46   saying to them, "It is
J   2.16   "Take these

M   21.13   written, 'My house shall be called a house of prayer';
Mk 11.17   written, 'My house shall be called a house of prayer for all the nations'?
L   19.46   written, 'My house shall be   a house of prayer';
J   2.16   things away;

M   21.13   but you   make   it   a den   of robbers."
Mk 11.17   But you have   made   it   a den   of robbers."
L   19.46   but you have   made   it   a den   of robbers."
J   2.16   you shall not make my Father's house a house of trade."

J 2.17 *His disciples remembered that it was written, "Zeal for thy house will*
J 2.18 *consume me." The Jews then said to him, "What sign have you to show us*
J 2.19 *for doing this?" Jesus answered them, "Destroy this temple, and in three*
J 2.20 *days I will raise it up." The Jews then said, "It has taken forty-six*
J 2.21 *years to build this temple, and will you raise it up in three days?" But*
J 2.22 *he spoke of the temple of his body. When therefore he was raised from the*
J 2.22 *dead, his disciples remembered that he had said this; and they believed*
J 2.22 *the scripture and the word which Jesus had spoken.*

M   21.14   And the blind and the lame came to him in the temple, and he healed

```
M    21.15   them.  But when the chief priests and the scribes saw the wonderful
Mk   11.18          And           the chief priests and the scribes heard it and sought
L    19.39          And           some of the Pharisees in the multitude


M    21.15   things that he did, and the children crying out in the temple, "Hosanna
Mk   11.18   a way to destroy him; for they feared him, because all the multitude


M    21.16   to the Son of David!" they were indignant; and they said to him,
Mk   11.18   was astonished at his teaching.
L    19.39                                                          said to him,


M    21.16   "Do you hear what these are saying?"  And Jesus said to them, "Yes;
L    19.40   "Teacher, rebuke your disciples."       He    answered, "I tell you,


M    21.16   have you never read,
L    19.40   if these were silent, the very stones would cry out."


M    21.16            'Out of the mouth of babes and sucklings
M    21.16            thou hast brought perfect praise'?"


M    21.17   And leaving them,                                            he
Mk   11.19   And                                    when evening came they
L    21.37   And every day he was teaching in the temple, but at night   he


M    21.17   went out of the city to Bethany and lodged there.
Mk   11.19   went out of the city.
L    21.37   went out                    and lodged on the mount called Olivet.


  L  21.38   And early in the morning all the people came to him in the temple to
  L  21.38   hear him.
```

57. THE WITHERED FIG TREE

Matthew 21.18-22

```
M    21.18   In the morning,        as  he was returning to the city,  he was hungry.
Mk   11.12   On the following day, when they     came     from Bethany, he was hungry.
  L  13.6                                                                  And he told


M    21.19   And seeing                   a fig tree by the wayside he went
Mk   11.13   And seeing in the distance a fig tree in leaf,     he went to see if
  L  13.6    this parable:  "A man had a fig tree planted in his vineyard;


M    21.19                                            to it,              and
Mk   11.13   he could find anything on it. When he came to it,            he
  L  13.6                               and he came seeking fruit on it and


M    21.19   found nothing on it but leaves only.
Mk   11.13   found nothing       but leaves, for it was not the season for figs.
  L  13.6    found none.


M    21.19   And he said to it,          "May no
Mk   11.14   And he said to it,          "May no one ever
  L  13.7    And he said to the vinedresser, 'Lo, these three years I have come
```

126

```
M    21.19                fruit ever come from you again!"
Mk   11.14    eat         fruit              from you again."  And his disciples heard it.
 L   13.7     seeking fruit on this fig tree, and I find none.  Cut it down; why


M    21.19    And                                    the fig tree withered at
Mk   11.20    As they passed by in the morning, they saw the fig tree withered away
 L   13.8     should it use up the ground?'  And he answered him, 'Let it alone, sir,


M    21.20    once.   When the disciples saw it they marveled, saying,
Mk   11.21    to its roots.  And Peter      remembered      and said to him, "Master,
 L   13.9     this year also, till I dig about it and put on manure.  And if it bears


M    21.21    "How did the fig tree              wither at once?"  And
Mk   11.22    look!  The fig tree which you cursed has withered."           And
 L   13.9     fruit next year, well and good; but if not, you can cut it down.'"
 L   17.6                                                                  And the


M    21.21    Jesus answered them,                                    "Truly, I
Mk   11.23a   Jesus answered them,            "Have faith in God.  Truly, I
 M   17.20    He     said  to them, "Because of your little faith.   For truly, I
 L   17.6     Lord  said,


M    21.21    say to you, if you have faith and        never doubt, you will not only
Mk   11.23c   say to you,                    |and does not   doubt in his heart, but
 M   17.20    say to you, if you have faith as a grain of mustard seed,
 L   17.6                 "If you had  faith as a grain of mustard seed,


M    21.21    do what has been done to the fig tree, but even if you      say  to
Mk   11.23b   believes that what he says will come to pass,    |whoever  says  to
 M   17.20                                                       you will  say  to
 L   17.6                                                        you could say  to


M    21.21    this mountain,       'Be taken  up  and   cast   into the sea,'
Mk   11.23b   this mountain,       'Be taken  up  and   cast   into the sea,'
 M   17.20    this mountain,       'Move from here            to there,'
 L   17.6     this sycamine tree,  'Be rooted up, and be planted in  the sea,'
 J   16.23                                              In that day you


M    21.22         it will be done.         And            whatever you ask
Mk   11.23d,24    |it will be done for him.  Therefore I tell you, whatever you ask
 M   17.20    and it will    move; and nothing will be impossible to you."
 L   17.6     and it would   obey    you.
 J   14.13                                              Whatever you ask
 J   14.14                                              if       you ask
 J   16.23    will ask nothing of me.  Truly, truly, I say to you, if     you ask
 J   16.24             Hitherto you have asked nothing in my name; ask,


M    21.22         in    prayer,          you will receive,  if    you
Mk   11.24         in    prayer, believe that you have received it, and   it
 J   14.13         in my name,          I   will do    it, that the
 J   14.14    anything in my name,      I   will do    it.
 J   16.23    anything of the Father,      he  will give  it  to  you
 J   16.24          and you will receive,      that your joy


M    21.22    have faith."
Mk   11.25    will be yours.  And whenever you stand praying, forgive, if you have
 J   14.13    Father may be glorified in the Son;
 J   16.23    in my name.
 J   16.24    may be full.
```

Mk 11.25   *anything against any one; so that your Father also who is in heaven may*
Mk 11.25   *forgive you your trespasses."*

58. CONTROVERSIES IN JERUSALEM

Matthew 21.23-22.46

a. The Authority of Jesus

Matthew 21.23-27

M	21.23		And when he entered
Mk	11.27	And they came again to Jerusalem.	And as he was walking
L	20.1		One day, as he was teaching the people

M	21.23	the temple,	the chief priests
Mk	11.27	in the temple,	the chief priests and the scribes
L	20.1	in the temple and preaching the gospel,	the chief priests and the scribes

M	21.23	and the elders of the people came up to him as he was teaching, and
Mk	11.28	and the elders came to him, and they
L	20.2	with the elders came up and

M	21.23	said, "By what authority are you doing these things, and
Mk	11.28	said to him, "By what authority are you doing these things, or
L	20.2	said to him, "Tell us by what authority you do these things, or

M	21.24	who gave you this authority?" Jesus answered them,
Mk	11.29	who gave you this authority to do them?" Jesus said to them,
L	20.3	who it is that gave you this authority." He answered them,

M	21.24	"I also will ask you a question; and if you tell me the answer, then I
Mk	11.29	"I will ask you a question; answer me, and I
L	20.3	"I also will ask you a question; now tell me,

M	21.25	also will tell you by what authority I do these things. The baptism
Mk	11.30	will tell you by what authority I do these things. Was the baptism
L	20.4	Was the baptism

M	21.25	of John, whence was it? From heaven or from men?" And they
Mk	11.31	of John from heaven or from men? Answer me." And they
L	20.5	of John from heaven or from men?" And they

M	21.25	argued with one another, "If we say, 'From heaven,' he will
Mk	11.31	argued with one another, "If we say, 'From heaven,' he will
L	20.5	discussed it with one another, saying, "If we say, 'From heaven,' he will

M	21.26	say to us, 'Why then did you not believe him?' But if we say, 'From
Mk	11.32	say, 'Why then did you not believe him?' But shall we say, 'From
L	20.6	say, 'Why did you not believe him?' But if we say, 'From

M	21.26	men,' we are afraid of the multitude; for all hold
Mk	11.32	men'?"--they were afraid of the people, for all held
L	20.6	men,' all the people will stone us; for they are convinced

M	21.27	that John was a _____ prophet." So they answered Jesus, "We do not know."
Mk	11.33	that John was a real prophet. So they answered Jesus, "We do not know."
L	20.7	that John was a _____ prophet." So they answered that they did not know

M	21.27	And he ____ said to them, "Neither will I tell you by what
Mk	11.33	And Jesus said to them, "Neither will I tell you by what
L	20.8	whence it was. And Jesus said to them, "Neither will I tell you by what

M	21.27	authority I do these things.
Mk	11.33	authority I do these things."
L	20.8	authority I do these things."

b. The Two Sons

Matthew 21.28-32

M	21.28	"What do you think? A man had two sons; and he went to the first and
M	21.29	said, 'Son, go and work in the vineyard today.' And he answered, 'I
M	21.30	will not'; but afterward he repented and went. And he went to the
M	21.30	second and said the same; and he answered, 'I go, sir,' but did not go.
M	21.31	Which of the two did the will of his father?" They said, "The first."

M	21.31	Jesus said to them, "Truly, I say to you, the tax collectors and the
L	*7.29*	*(When they heard this all the people and* the tax collectors

M	21.31	harlots go into the kingdom of God before you.
L	*7.29*	*justified* God, *having been baptized with the baptism*

M	21.32	For John came to you in the way of righteousness, and ____ you
L	*7.30*	*of* John; ____ *but the Pharisees and*

M	21.32	did not believe him, but the tax collectors and the harlots
L	*7.30*	*the lawyers rejected the purpose of God for themselves,*

M	21.32	believed him; and even when you saw it, you did not afterward repent and
L	*7.30*	not *having been baptized*

M	21.32	believe him.
L	*7.30*	*by* him.)

c. The Wicked Tenants

Matthew 21.33-46

M	21.33	"Hear ____ another parable. There was a householder
Mk	12.1	And he began to speak to them in parables. "A man
L	20.9	And he began to tell the people this parable: "A man

M	21.33	who planted a vineyard, and set a hedge around it, and dug a
Mk	12.1	planted a vineyard, and set a hedge around it, and dug a pit for the
L	20.9	planted a vineyard,

129

```
M    21.33   wine press in it, and built a tower, and let it out to tenants, and went
Mk   12.1    wine press,        and built a tower, and let it out to tenants, and went
L    20.9                                          and let it out to tenants, and went


M    21.34   into another country.                When the season of fruit drew
Mk   12.2    into another country.                When the time            came,
L    20.10   into another country for a long while. When the time          came,


M    21.34   near, he sent his servants to the tenants,          to get
Mk   12.2          he sent a    servant  to the tenants,         to get from them
L    20.10         he sent a    servant  to the tenants, that they should give    him


M    21.35         his fruit;              and the tenants took his servants and
Mk   12.3    some of the fruit of the vineyard. And     they    took    him      and
L    20.10   some of the fruit of the vineyard; but the tenants


M    21.35   beat one,
Mk   12.4    beat him, and sent him away empty-handed.  Again he sent to them another
L    20.11   beat him, and sent him away empty-handed.  And   he sent        another


M    21.35               killed another,           and stoned another.
Mk   12.4    servant, and      they wounded him in the head, and treated him shamefully.
L    20.11   servant; him also they beat                and treated      shamefully,


M    21.36                             Again he sent   other servants, more than
Mk   12.5                              And   he sent another, and him        they
L    20.12   and sent him away empty-handed. And   he sent yet a third; this one they


M    21.36   the first;                    and they did the same to them.
Mk   12.6    killed; and so with many others, some they beat and some they killed.  He
L    20.13   wounded and cast out.       Then the  owner of the vineyard said, 'What


M    21.37        Afterward he sent his       son                  to them,
Mk   12.6    had still one other,     a beloved son; finally he sent him to them,
L    20.13   shall I do? I will send my beloved son;                       it


M    21.38   saying, 'They will respect my son.'  But when the   tenants saw the son,
Mk   12.7    saying, 'They will respect my son.'  But       those tenants
L    20.14   may be  they will respect    him.'  But when the   tenants saw    him,


M    21.38   they said to themselves,  'This is the heir; come, let us kill him  and
Mk   12.7         said to one another, 'This is the heir; come, let us kill him, and
L    20.14   they said to themselves,  'This is the heir;       let us kill him, that


M    21.39   have his inheritance.'       And they took him
Mk   12.8         the inheritance will be ours.' And they took him and killed him,
L    20.15         the inheritance may  be ours.' And they


M    21.40   and cast him out of the vineyard, and killed him.  When therefore the
Mk   12.8    and cast him out of the vineyard.
L    20.15        cast him out of the vineyard and killed him.


M    21.40   owner of the vineyard comes, what   will    he              do
Mk   12.9                                 What   will the owner of the vineyard do?
L    20.15                                 What then will the owner of the vineyard do
```

130

M	21.41	to those tenants?" They said to him, "He will put those
Mk	12.9	He will come and destroy the
L	20.16	to them? He will come and destroy those

M	21.41	wretches to a miserable death, and let out the vineyard to other tenants
Mk	12.9	tenants, and give the vineyard to others,
L	20.16	tenants, and give the vineyard to others." When

M	21.41	who will give him the fruits in their seasons."
L	20.16	they heard this, they said, "God forbid!"

M	21.42	Jesus said to them, "Have you never read in the
Mk	12.10	Have you not read this
L	20.17	But he looked at them and said, "What then is this that is

M	21.42	scriptures:
Mk	12.10	scripture:
L	20.17	written:

M	21.42	'The very stone which the builders rejected
Mk	12.10	'The very stone which the builders rejected
L	20.17	'The very stone which the builders rejected

M	21.42	has become the head of the corner;
Mk	12.10	has become the head of the corner;
L	20.17	has become the head of the corner'?

M	21.42	this was the Lord's doing,
Mk	12.11	this was the Lord's doing,

M	21.42	and it is marvelous in our eyes'?
Mk	12.11	and it is marvelous in our eyes'?"

M	21.43	Therefore I tell you, the kingdom of God will be taken away from you
M	21.43	and given to a nation producing the fruits of it."

M	21.44	*"And he* *who falls on this stone will be broken to pieces; but*
L	20.18	Every one who falls on that stone will be broken to pieces; but

M	21.44	*when it falls on any one, it will crush him."*
L	20.18	when it falls on any one it will crush him."

M	21.45	When the chief priests and the Pharisees heard his parables, they
Mk	12.12b	for they
L	20.19b	for they

M	21.46	perceived that he was speaking about them. But when they
Mk	12.12a	perceived that he had told the parable against them; And they
L	20.19a	perceived that he had told this parable against them. The scribes

M	21.46	tried to arrest him,
Mk	12.12a	tried to arrest him, but
L	20.19a	and the chief priests tried to lay hands on him at that very hour, but

131

M	21.46	<u>they feared the multitudes</u>, <u>because they held him to be a prophet.</u>
Mk	12.12c	<u>feared the</u> multitude, $\lvert$ so <u>they</u> left <u>him</u> and went away.
L	20.19a	<u>they feared the</u> people;

d. The Marriage Feast

Matthew 22.1-14

L	*14.15*	*When one of those who sat at table with him heard this, he said to him,*
L	*14.15*	*"Blessed is he who shall eat bread in the kingdom of God!"*

M	22.1,2	<u>And again Jesus spoke to them in parables</u>, <u>saying</u>, $\lvert$<u>"The kingdom of</u>
L	14.16	But he said <u>to</u> him,

M	22.2	<u>heaven may be compared to a king who gave a marriage feast</u> for his son,
L	14.16	"A man once <u>gave a</u> great banquet, and invited

M	22.3	$\lvert$and <u>sent his servants to call</u>
L	14.17	many; <u>and</u> at the time for the banquet he <u>sent his</u> servant <u>to</u> say to

M	22.3	<u>those who</u> <u>were invited to the marriage feast</u>; <u>but they</u>
L	14.18	<u>those who</u> had been <u>invited</u>, 'Come; for all is now ready.' <u>But they</u>

M	22.4	<u>would not come.</u> <u>Again he sent other servants</u>, <u>saying</u>,
L	14.18	all alike began to make excuses. The first said to him, 'I have bought

M	22.4	<u>'Tell those who are invited, Behold, I have made ready my dinner</u>, <u>my</u>
L	14.18	a field, and I must go out and see it; I pray you, have me excused.'

M	22.4	<u>oxen and my fat calves are killed</u>, <u>and everything is ready</u>; <u>come to the</u>
L	14.19	And another said, 'I have bought five yoke of oxen, and I go to examine

M	22.5	<u>marriage feast.'</u> <u>But they made light of it and went off</u>, <u>one to his</u>
L	14.20	them; I pray you, have me excused.' And another said, 'I have married

M	22.6	<u>farm, another to his business,</u> $\lvert$<u>while the rest seized his servants,</u>
L	14.21	a wife, and therefore I cannot come.' So the servant came and

M	22.7	<u>treated them shamefully</u>, <u>and killed them.</u> <u>The king</u> was angry,
L	14.21	reported this to his master. Then the householder in anger

M	22.7	<u>and he sent his troops and destroyed those murderers and burned their</u>

M	22.8	<u>city.</u> <u>Then he said to his servants</u>, <u>'The wedding is ready</u>, <u>but those</u>
L	14.21	<u>said to his</u> servant,

M	22.9	<u>invited were not worthy.</u> <u>Go therefore</u> <u>to the thoroughfares,</u>
L	14.21	'<u>Go</u> out quickly <u>to the</u> streets and lanes of the

M	22.10	<u>and invite to the marriage feast as many as you find.'</u> <u>And those</u>
L	14.22	city, <u>and</u> bring in the poor and maimed and blind and lame.' <u>And the</u>

M	22.10	servants
L	14.22	servant said, 'Sir, what you commanded has been done, and still there

M	22.10	went out into the
L	14.23	is room.' And the master said to the servant, 'Go out to the

M	22.10	streets and gathered all whom they found, both bad and good;
L	14.23	highways and hedges, and compel people to come in,

M	22.10	so the wedding hall was filled with guests.
L	14.24	that my house may be filled. For I tell you, none of those men

L	*14.24*	*who were invited shall taste my banquet.'"*

M	22.11	"But when the king came in to look at the guests, he saw there a man
M	22.12	who had no wedding garment; and he said to him, 'Friend, how did you get
M	22.13	in here without a wedding garment?' And he was speechless. |Then the

M	22.13	king said to the attendants, 'Bind him hand and foot,
L	*13.28b*	*when you see Abraham and Isaac and Jacob and all the prophets in the*

M	22.13	and	cast
M	*8.12*	*while the sons of the kingdom will be* thrown
M	*13.42*	and	*throw*
M	*13.50*	and	*throw*
M	*24.51b*	and	*put*
M	*25.30*	And	cast *the worthless*
L	*13.28b*	*kingdom of God* and *you yourselves*	*thrust out.*

M	22.13	him	into the outer darkness; there men will weep and gnash their
M	*8.12*		into the outer darkness; there men will weep and gnash their
M	*13.42*	*them*	into the *furnace of fire;* there men will weep and gnash their
M	*13.50*	*them*	into the *furnace of fire;* there men will weep and gnash their
M	*24.51b*	*him*	*with the hypocrites;* there men will weep and gnash their
M	*25.30*	*servant*	into the outer darkness; there men will weep and gnash their
L	*13.28a*		There *you* will weep and gnash *your*

M	22.14	teeth.' For many are called, but few are chosen."
M	*8.12*	teeth."
M	*13.42*	teeth.
M	*13.50*	teeth.
M	*24.51b*	teeth.'
M	*25.30*	teeth.'
L	*13.28a*	teeth,

e. Render to God

Matthew 22.15-22

M	22.15	Then the Pharisees went and took counsel
L	20.20	So they watched him, and sent spies, who pretended to be sincere,

M	22.15	how to entangle him in his talk.
Mk	12.13b	to entrap him in his talk.
L	20.20	that they might take hold of what he said, so as to deliver him up to

```
M    22.16                                                            And they sent
Mk   12.13a                                                           And they sent to him some
L    20.21       the authority and jurisdiction of the governor.  They


M    22.16          their disciples to him, along with the Herodians,
Mk   12.14    of the     Pharisees        and some of the Herodians, |And they came and


M    22.16    saying,        "Teacher, we know that you are true, and teach the way of
Mk   12.14    said to him, "Teacher, we know that you are true,
L    20.21    asked    him, "Teacher, we know that you speak      and teach


M    22.16    God truthfully, and care for no man; for you do not regard the position
Mk   12.14                   and care for no man; for you do not regard the position
L    20.21         rightly,     and show     no partiality,


M    22.17    of men. |Tell us, then, what you think.  Is it lawful       to pay
Mk   12.14    of men, but truly teach the way of God.  Is it lawful       to pay
L    20.22            but truly teach the way of God.  Is it lawful for us to give


M    22.18    taxes   to Caesar, or not?"                                        But
Mk   12.15    taxes   to Caesar, or not? |Should we pay them, or should we not?"  But
L    20.23    tribute to Caesar, or not?"                                        But


M    22.18    Jesus, aware of  their malice,       said,       "Why put me to the
Mk   12.15           knowing   their hypocrisy,  he said to them, "Why put me to the
L    20.23    he    perceived their craftiness, and said to them,


M    22.19    test, you hypocrites? |Show  me the money for the tax."        And
Mk   12.16    test?                  Bring me a   coin, and let me look at it." |And
L    20.24                          |"Show  me a   coin.


M    22.20    they brought him a coin.  And Jesus said to them, "Whose likeness and
Mk   12.16    they brought       one.  And he     said to them, "Whose likeness and
L    20.24                                                      Whose likeness and


M    22.21    inscription is  this?" |They said,      "Caesar's." Then he    said
Mk   12.17    inscription is  this?"  They said to him, "Caesar's."  |Jesus said
L    20.25    inscription has it?"    They said,      "Caesar's."  |He    said


M    22.21    to them,    "Render therefore to Caesar the things that are Caesar's,
Mk   12.17    to them,    "Render             to Caesar the things that are Caesar's,
L    20.25    to them, "Then render            to Caesar the things that are Caesar's,


M    22.22    and to God the things that are God's."  When they heard it,
Mk   12.17    and to God the things that are God's."  And
L    20.26    and to God the things that are God's."  And  they were not able in the


M    22.22                                             they       marveled;
Mk   12.17                                             they were amazed     at
L    20.26    presence of the people to catch him by what he said; but marveling at


M    22.22            and they left him and went away.
Mk   12.12b   him.   so  they left him and went away.
L    20.26    his answer they were silent.
```

134

f. The God of the Living

Matthew 22.23-33

M	22.23	The same day Sadducees came to him, who say that there is no
Mk	12.18	And Sadducees came to him, who say that there is no
L	20.27	There came to him some Sadducees, those who say that there is no

M	22.24	resurrection; and they asked him a question, ⎪saying, "Teacher, Moses
Mk	12.19	resurrection; and they asked him a question, saying, ⎪"Teacher, Moses
L	20.28	resurrection, ⎪and they asked him a question, saying, "Teacher, Moses

M	22.24	said, 'If a man dies, having
Mk	12.19	wrote for us that if a man's brother dies and leaves a wife, but leaves
L	20.28	wrote for us that if a man's brother dies, having a wife but

M	22.24	no children, his brother must marry the widow, and raise up children
Mk	12.19	no child, the man must take the wife, and raise up children
L	20.28	no children, the man must take the wife and raise up children

M	22.25	for his brother.' Now there were seven brothers among us; the first
Mk	12.20	for his brother. There were seven brothers; the first
L	20.29	for his brother. Now there were seven brothers; - the first

M	22.25	married, and died, and having no children left his wife to
Mk	12.20	took a wife, and when he died left no children;
L	20.29	took a wife, and died without children;

M	22.26	his brother. So too the second
Mk	12.21	⎪and the second took her, and died, leaving no children;
L	20.30	and the second

M	22.26	and third, down to the seventh.
Mk	12.22	and the third likewise; ⎪and the seven left no children.
L	20.31	⎪and the third took her, and likewise all seven left no children and

M	22.27,28	After them all, the woman died. In the resurrection,
Mk	12.23	Last of all the woman also died. ⎪In the resurrection
L	20.32,33	died. Afterward the woman also died. In the resurrection,

M	22.28	therefore, to which of the seven will she be wife? For they all
Mk	12.23	whose wife will she be? For the seven
L	20.33	therefore, whose wife will the woman be? For the seven

M	22.28	had her."
Mk	12.23	had her as wife."
L	20.33	had her as wife."

M	22.29	But Jesus answered them, "You are wrong,
Mk	12.24	Jesus said to them, "Is not this why you are wrong,
L	20.34	And Jesus said to them, "The sons of this age marry and are given in

M	22.30	because you know neither the scriptures nor the power of God. For
Mk	12.25	that you know neither the scriptures nor the power of God? For
L	20.35	marriage; but those who are accounted worthy to attain to that age and

135

```
M    22.30    in    the    resurrection              they neither marry nor are given
Mk   12.25    when they rise          from the dead, they neither marry nor are given
L    20.35    to    the    resurrection from the dead        neither marry nor are given


M    22.30    in marriage,                              but          are like
Mk   12.25    in marriage,                              but          are like
L    20.36    in marriage, |for they cannot die any more, because they are equal to


M    22.31    angels in heaven.                                    And as for
Mk   12.26    angels in heaven.                                    And as for
L    20.37    angels and are sons of God, being sons of the resurrection.  But that


M    22.31    the resurrection of the dead, have you not read
Mk   12.26    the dead          being raised, have you not read in the book of Moses,
L    20.37    the dead          are    raised,                      even Moses showed,


M    22.32                              what was said to you by God, |'I am the
Mk   12.26    in the passage about the bush, how  God said to him,      'I am the
L    20.37    in the passage about the bush, where he calls      the Lord      the


M    22.32    God of Abraham, and the God of Isaac, and the God of Jacob'?    He is
Mk   12.27    God of Abraham, and the God of Isaac, and the God of Jacob'?    He is
L    20.38    God of Abraham  and the God of Isaac  and the God of Jacob.  Now he is


M    22.33    not God of the dead, but of the living."              And when
Mk   12.27    not God of the dead, but of the living; you are quite wrong."
L    20.39    not God of the dead, but of the living; for all live to him."  And some


M    22.33      the crowd heard it,                                they were
L    20.40    of the scribes answered, "Teacher, you have spoken well."  For they no


M    22.33    astonished at his teaching.
L    20.40    longer dared to ask him any question.
```

g. The Great Commandment

Matthew 22.34-40

```
M    22.34    But when    the Pharisees          heard
Mk   12.28    And one of the scribes came up and heard them disputing with one another,


M    22.35              that he had silenced the Sadducees, they came together.  And
Mk   12.28    and seeing that he       answered    them well,
L    10.25                                                                        And


M    22.36    one of them, a lawyer, asked him a question, to    test him.    "Teacher,
Mk   12.28                           asked him,
L    10.25    behold,     a lawyer stood up to put him   to the test, saying, "Teacher,


M    22.36    which is the great commandment
Mk   12.28    "Which          commandment is the first of all?"
L    10.26    what shall I do to inherit eternal life?"  He said to him, "What is
```

136

M	22.37	in the law?" And he said to him,
Mk	12.29	Jesus answered, "The first is,
L	10.27	written in the law? How do you read?" And he answered,

M	22.37	"You shall love
Mk	12.30	'Hear, O Israel: The Lord our God, the Lord is one; |and you shall love
L	10.27	"You shall love

M	22.37	the Lord your God with all your heart, and with all your soul, and with
Mk	12.30	the Lord your God with all your heart, and with all your soul, and with
L	10.27	the Lord your God with all your heart, and with all your soul, and with

M	22.38,39	all your mind. This is the great and first commandment. And a second
Mk	12.31	all your mind, and with all your strength.' The second
L	10.27	all your strength, and with all your mind; and
M	19.19b	and,

M	22.40	is like it, You shall love your neighbor as yourself. On these two
Mk	12.31	is this, 'You shall love your neighbor as yourself.' There is no other
L	10.28	your neighbor as yourself." And he said to
M	19.19b	You shall love your neighbor as yourself."

M	22.40	commandments depend all the law and the prophets."
Mk	12.32	commandment greater than these." *And the scribe said to him, "You are*
L	10.28	him, "You have answered right; do this, and you will live."

Mk	12.32	*right, Teacher; you have truly said that he is one, and there is no other*
Mk	12.33	*but he; and to love him with all the heart, and with all the understanding,*
Mk	12.33	*and with all the strength, and to love one's neighbor as oneself, is much*
Mk	12.34	*more than all whole burnt offerings and sacrifices." And when Jesus saw*
Mk	12.34	*that he answered wisely, he said to him, "You are not far from the kingdom*
Mk	12.34	*of God." And after that no one dared to ask him any question.*

h. The Son of David

Matthew 22.41-46

M	22.41	Now while the Pharisees were gathered together, Jesus asked them a
Mk	12.35	And as Jesus taught in the
L	20.41	But he
J	7.40	*When they heard these words, some of the people said, "This is really*

M	22.42	question, |saying, "What do you think of the Christ?
Mk	12.35	temple, he said, "How can the scribes say that the Christ
L	20.41	said to them, "How can they say that the Christ
J	7.41	*the prophet." Others said, "This is the Christ."*

J	7.41	*But some said, "Is the Christ*
J	7.42	*to come from Galilee? Has not the scripture said that the Christ*

M	22.43	Whose son is he?" They said to him, "The son of David." |He said to
Mk	12.35	is the son of David?
L	20.41	is David's son?
J	7.42	*is descended from David, and comes from*

137

```
M    22.43    them,    "How is it then that David,              inspired by the           Spirit,
Mk   12.36                                    David himself, inspired by the Holy Spirit,
L    20.42                          For  David himself
 J    7.42    Bethlehem, the village where David was?"


M    22.43    calls him Lord, saying,
Mk   12.36                        declared,
L    20.42                        says in the Book of Psalms,


M    22.44              'The Lord said to my Lord,
Mk   12.36              'The Lord said to my Lord,
L    20.42              'The Lord said to my Lord,


M    22.44              Sit at my right hand,
Mk   12.36              Sit at my right hand,
L    20.42              Sit at my right hand,


M    22.44              till I put  thy enemies          under thy feet'?
Mk   12.36              till I put  thy enemies          under thy feet.'
L    20.43              till I make thy enemies a stool for   thy feet.'


M    22.45,46  If David thus    calls him Lord,    how is he his son?"  And
Mk   12.37      |David himself calls him Lord; so how is he his son?"  And
L    20.44       David thus    calls him Lord; so how is he his son?"
 Mk  12.34b                                                            And  after that
 L   20.40                                                             For
 J    7.43                                                             So   there was


M    22.46    no one was able to answer him a word, nor from that day did any one
Mk   12.37    the great throng heard him gladly.
 Mk  12.34b   no one
 L   20.40    they no longer
 J    7.44    a division among the people over him.  Some of them wanted to arrest him,


M    22.46    dare  to ask him any more questions.
 Mk  12.34b   dared to ask him any     question.
 L   20.40    dared to ask him any     question.
 J    7.44    but no one laid hands on him.
```

59. WOES AGAINST SCRIBES AND PHARISEES

Matthhew 23.1-36

```
 L   11.45    One of the lawyers answered him, "Teacher, in saying this you reproach
 L   11.45    us also."


M    23.1     Then                               said Jesus to the crowds and to
Mk   12.38a   And in his teaching           he said,
L    11.46    And                           he said,
L    20.45    And in the hearing of all the people he said                     to


M    23.2     his disciples,          |"The scribes and the Pharisees sit on Moses' seat;
Mk   12.38a                  "Beware of the scribes,
L    11.46               "Woe  to you lawyers also!
L    20.46a   his disciples, |"Beware of the scribes,
```

138

```
M    23.3      so practice and observe whatever they tell you, but not what they do;


M    23.4      for they preach, but do not practice.  They bind    heavy burdens, hard
L    11.46                                       for you  load men with  burdens  hard


M    23.4      to bear, and lay them on men's shoulders; but they themselves will not
L    11.46      to bear,                                 and you  yourselves do     not


M    23.5      move       them    with        their finger.  They do all       their deeds
L    11.46      touch the burdens  with one of your   fingers.
  M   6.1                                               "Beware of practicing your   piety


M    23.5                         to be seen by men;  for they make their phylacteries
Mk   12.38a                                            who   like to go about
L    20.46a                                            who   like to go about
  M   6.1       before men in order to be seen by them; for then you will have no reward


M    23.6      broad and their fringes long,       |and they love the place  of honor
Mk   12.39b                        in long robes,  |and          the places of honor
L    11.43               Woe to you Pharisees!      |for you  love
L    20.46d                     In long robes,      |and          the places of honor
  M   6.1       from your Father who is in heaven.


M    23.7      at feasts    and the best seats in the synagogues,  |and
Mk   12.39a,38b at feasts,  |and the best seats in the synagogues  |and to have
L    11.43                   the best seat  in the synagogues       |and
L    20.46c,b  at feasts,   |and the best seats in the synagogues   |and     love


M    23.8      salutations in the market places, and being called rabbi by men.  But
Mk   12.38b    salutations in the market places
L    11.43     salutations in the market places.
L    20.45b    salutations in the market places


M    23.8      you are not to be called rabbi, for you have one teacher, and you are
  J   13.13                                     You call me   Teacher  and Lord; and


M    23.9      all brethren.  And call no man your father on earth, for you have one
  J   13.13     you are right, for so I am.


M    23.10     Father, who is in heaven.  Neither be called masters, for you have one


M    23.11     master, the Christ.                    He  who      is       greatest
  M  20.26      It shall not be so among you; but whoever would be       great
  Mk  9.35b                                     "If any one would be       first,
  Mk 10.43     But it shall not be so among you; but whoever would be    great
  L   9.48b                                     for he  who      is       least
  L  22.26     But        not    so with  you; rather         let the greatest
  J  13.16      Truly, truly, I say to you,   a servant    is not  greater


M    23.11     among you                          shall be              your
  M  20.26     among you                          must  be              your
  Mk  9.35b                                 he must  be last of all and
  Mk 10.43     among you                          must  be              your
  L   9.48b    among you all                            is the  one who is
  L  22.26     among you become as the youngest, and the leader as  one who
  J  13.16      than his master; nor is he who is sent greater than   he  who
```

```
M    23.12      servant;  whoever exalts himself will be humbled, and whoever humbles
L    14.11      For every one who exalts himself will be humbled, and he  who humbles
L    18.14b     for every one who exalts himself will be humbled, but he  who humbles
  M   20.26     servant,
  Mk  9.35b     servant of all."
  Mk 10.43      servant,
  L   9.48b     great."
  L  22.26      serves.
  J  13.16      sent him.


M    23.12      himself will be exalted.
L    14.11      himself will be exalted."
L    18.14b     himself will be exalted."


M    23.13       "But woe to you, scribes and Pharisees, hypocrites! because you
L    11.52           Woe to you  lawyers!                         for      you have


M    23.13      shut      the kingdom of heaven against men; for you neither enter
L    11.52      taken away the key      of knowledge;           you did not enter


M    23.14      yourselves, nor     allow    those who would enter to go in.  Woe to you,
L    11.52      yourselves, and you hindered those who were  entering."


M    23.14      scribes and Pharisees, hypocrites! for you devour widows' houses and
Mk   12.40                               who devour widows' houses and
L    20.47                               who devour widows' houses and


M    23.14      for a pretense you make long prayers; therefore you  will receive the
Mk   12.40      for a pretense     make long prayers.        They will receive the
L    20.47      for a pretense     make long prayers.        They will receive the


M    23.15      greater condemnation.  Woe to you, scribes and Pharisees, hypocrites!
Mk   12.40      greater condemnation."
L    20.47      greater condemnation."


M    23.15      for you traverse sea and land to make a single proselyte, and when he
M    23.15      becomes a proselyte, you make him twice as much a child of hell as
M    23.15      yourselves.

M    23.16       "Woe to you, blind guides, who say, 'If any one swears by the temple,
M    23.16      it is nothing; but if any one swears by the gold of the temple, he is
M    23.17      bound by his oath.'  You blind fools!  For which is greater, the gold
M    23.18      or the temple that has made the gold sacred?  And you say, 'If any one
M    23.18      swears by the altar, it is nothing; but if any one swears by the gift
M    23.19      that is on the altar, he is bound by his oath.'  You blind men!  For
M    23.19      which is greater, the gift or the altar that makes the gift sacred?


M    23.20               So he who swears by the altar, swears by it and by everything
  M   5.33     "Again you have heard that it was said to the men of old, 'You shall not


M    23.21      on it; and he who swears by the temple, swears by it and by him who
  M   5.33     swear falsely, but shall perform to the Lord what you have sworn.'


M    23.22      dwells in it; and he who swears            by heaven, swears by the
  M   5.34     But I say to you, Do not swear at all, either by heaven, for it is the


M    23.22      throne of God and by him who sits upon it.
  M   5.35     throne of God, |or by the earth, for it is his footstool, or by Jerusalem,
```

M 5.35   *for it is the city of the great King.*

M 23.23   "Woe to you, scribes and Pharisees, hypocrites! for you tithe mint
L 11.42   "But woe to you   Pharisees!   for you tithe mint

M 23.23   and dill and   cummin, and have neglected the weightier matters of the
L 11.42   and rue and every herb, and   neglect

M 23.23   law, justice and   mercy and faith; these you ought to have done,
L 11.42   justice and the love of God;   these you ought to have done,

M 23.24   without neglecting the others.   You blind guides, straining out a gnat
L 11.42   without neglecting the others.

M 23.24   and swallowing a camel!

L 11.37   *While he was speaking, a Pharisee asked him to dine with him; so he*
L 11.38   *went in and sat at table. The Pharisee was astonished to see that he*
L 11.38   *did not first wash before dinner.*

M 23.25   "Woe to you, scribes   and Pharisees, hypocrites! for you
L 11.39   And the Lord said to him, "Now you Pharisees
Mk 7.3   (For   the Pharisees, and all the Jews, do

M 23.25   cleanse the outside of the cup and of the plate, but inside they are
L 11.39   cleanse the outside of the cup and of the dish, but inside you are
Mk 7.3   not eat unless they wash their hands, observing the tradition of the

M 23.26   full of extortion and rapacity.   You blind Pharisee! first cleanse
L 11.40   full of extortion and wickedness. You   fools! Did not he who made
Mk 7.4   elders; and when they come from the market place, they do not eat unless

M 23.26   the inside of the cup and of the plate,   that
L 11.41   the outside make the inside also? But give for alms those things which
Mk 7.4   they purify themselves; and there are many other traditions which they

M 23.26   the outside also   may be clean.
L 11.41   are within; and behold, everything is clean for you.
Mk 7.4   observe, the washing of cups and pots and vessels of bronze.)

M 23.27   "Woe to you, scribes and Pharisees, hypocrites! for you are like
L 11.44   Woe to you!   for you are like

M 23.27   whitewashed tombs, which outwardly appear beautiful, but within they
L 11.44   graves which are not seen, and men walk over them without

M 23.28   are full of dead men's bones and all uncleanness.   So you also outwardly
L 11.44   knowing it."

M 23.28   appear righteous to men, but within you are full of hypocrisy and
M 23.28   iniquity.

M	23.29	"Woe to you, scribes and Pharisees, hypocrites! for you build the tombs
L	11.47	Woe to you! for you build the tombs

M	23.30	of the prophets and adorn the monuments of the righteous, |saying, 'If
L	11.48	of the prophets whom your fathers killed. So

M	23.30	we had lived in the days of our fathers, we would
L	11.48	you are witnesses and consent to the deeds of your fathers; for they

M	23.30	not have taken part with them in shedding the blood of the prophets.'
L	11.48	killed them, and you build their tombs.

M	23.31	Thus you witness against yourselves, that you are sons of those who
M	23.32	murdered the prophets. Fill up, then, the measure of your fathers.
M	23.33	You serpents, you brood of vipers, how are you to escape being sentenced

M	23.34	to hell? Therefore I send you
L	11.49	Therefore also the Wisdom of God said, 'I will send them

M	23.34	prophets and wise men and scribes, some of whom you will kill and
L	11.49	prophets and apostles, some of whom they will kill
M	*10.17*	*Beware of men; for they will deliver you up to councils,*

M	23.34	crucify, and some you will scourge in your synagogues and persecute
L	11.49	and persecute,'
M	*10.17*	*and flog you in their synagogues,*

M	23.35	from town to town, |that upon you may come all the righteous blood
L	11.50	|that the blood of

M	23.35	shed on earth,
L	11.50	all the prophets, shed from the foundation of the world, may be required

M	23.35	from the blood of innocent Abel to the blood of
L	11.51	of this generation, |from the blood of Abel to the blood of

M	23.35	Zechariah the son of Barachiah, whom you murdered between the sanctuary
L	11.51	Zechariah, who perished between the altar

M	23.36	and the altar. Truly, I say to you, all this will come upon
L	11.51	and the sanctuary. Yes, I tell you, it shall be required of

M	23.36	this generation.
L	11.51	this generation.

60. LAMENT OVER JERUSALEM

Matthew 23.37-39

L	*13.31*	*At that very hour some Pharisees came, and said to him, "Get away*
L	*13.32*	*from here, for Herod wants to kill you." And he said to them, "Go*
L	*13.32*	*and tell that fox, 'Behold, I cast out demons and perform cures today*

L	13.33	*and tomorrow, and the third day I finish my course. Nevertheless I*
L	13.33	*must go on my way today and tomorrow and the day following; for it*
L	13.33	*cannot be that a prophet should perish away from Jerusalem.'*

M	23.37	"O Jerusalem, Jerusalem, killing the prophets and stoning those who
L	13.34	O Jerusalem, Jerusalem, killing the prophets and stoning those who

M	23.37	are sent to you! How often would I have gathered your children together
L	13.34	are sent to you! How often would I have gathered your children together

M	23.38	as a hen gathers her brood under her wings, and you would not! Behold,
L	13.35	as a hen gathers her brood under her wings, and you would not! Behold,

M	23.39	your house·is forsaken and desolate. For I tell you, you will not see
L	13.35	your house is forsaken. And I tell you, you will not see

M	23.39	me again, until you say, 'Blessed is he who comes in the name of the
L	13.35	me until you say, 'Blessed is he who comes in the name of the

M	23.39	Lord.'"
L	13.35	Lord!'"

61. FIFTH DISCOURSE: THE END OF THE AGE

Matthew 24.1-26.2

a. Setting: Destruction of the Temple

Matthew 24.1-2

M	24.1	Jesus left the temple and was going away, when his
Mk	13.1	And as he came out of the temple, one of his
L	21.5	And as

M	24.1	disciples came to point out to him
Mk	13.1	disciples said to him, "Look, Teacher, what wonderful
L	21.5	some spoke

M	24.1	the buildings of the temple.
Mk	13.1	stones and what wonderful buildings!"
L	21.5	of the temple, how it was adorned

M	24.2	But he answered them, "You see all
Mk	13.2	And Jesus said to him, "Do you see
L	21.6	with noble stones and offerings, he said, |"As for

M	24.2	these, do you not? Truly, I say to you, there will not be
Mk	13.2	these great buildings? There will not be
L	21.6	these things which you see, the days will come when there shall not be

M	24.2	left here one stone upon another, that will not be thrown down."
Mk	13.2	left here one stone upon another, that will not be thrown down."
L	21.6	left here one stone upon another that will not be thrown down."

Matthew 24.3-44

M	24.3	As he sat on the Mount of Olives, the disciples
Mk	13.3	And as he sat on the Mount of Olives opposite the temple, Peter and
L	21.7	And they

M	24.3	came to him privately, saying, "Tell us, when
Mk	13.4	James and John and Andrew asked him privately, |"Tell us, when
L	21.7	asked him, "Teacher, when

M	24.3	will this be, and what will be the sign of your coming and of the close
Mk	13.4	will this be, and what will be the sign when these things are all to
L	21.7	will this be, and what will be the sign when this is about to

M	24.4	of the age?" And Jesus answered them, "Take heed that no
Mk	13.5	be accomplished?" And Jesus began to say to them, "Take heed that no
L	21.8	take place?" And he said, "Take heed that you

M	24.5	one leads you astray. For many will come in my name, saying, 'I am
Mk	13.6	one leads you astray. Many will come in my name, saying, 'I am
L	21.8	are not led astray; for many will come in my name, saying, 'I am

M	24.6	the Christ,' and they will lead many astray. And
Mk	13.7	he!' and they will lead many astray. And
L	21.9	he!' and,'The time is at hand!' Do not go after them. |And

M	24.6	you will hear of wars and rumors of wars; see that you are not
Mk	13.7	when you hear of wars and rumors of wars, do not be
L	21.9	when you hear of wars and tumults, do not be

M	24.6	alarmed; for this must take place, but the end is not
Mk	13.7	alarmed; this must take place, but the end is not
L	21.9	terrified; for this must first take place, but the end will not be at

M	24.7	yet. For nation will rise against nation, and
Mk	13.8	yet. For nation will rise against nation, and
L	21.10	once." Then he said to them, "Nation will rise against nation, and

M	24.7	kingdom against kingdom, and there will be famines and earthquakes
Mk	13.8	kingdom against kingdom; there will be earthquakes
L	21.11	kingdom against kingdom; there will be great earthquakes, and

M	24.8	in various places: all this is but the beginning of
Mk	13.8	in various places, there will be famines; this is but the beginning of
L	21.11	in various places famines and pestilences; and there

M	24.8	the birth-pangs.
Mk	13.8	the birth-pangs.
L	21.11	will be terrors and great signs from heaven.

M	24.9	"Then they will
Mk	13.9	"But take heed to yourselves; for they will
L	21.12	But before all this they will lay their
M	10.17	*Beware of men;* for they will
J	16.2	They will

144

```
M   24.9                                          deliver    you up  to        tribulation,
Mk  13.9                                          deliver    you up  to        councils;
L   21.12     hands on you and persecute you, delivering you up  to the synagogues and
  M  10.17                                        deliver    you up  to        councils,
  J  16.2                                          put        you out of the synagogues;
```

```
Mk 13.9     and you will be beaten      in         synagogues; and you will      stand
 L 21.12    prisons,                                            and you will be brought
 M 10.17    and                  flog you in their synagogues,
 J 16.2     indeed, the hour is coming when whoever kills you will think he is
```

```
Mk 13.9     before governors and kings for my          sake,
 L 21.13    before kings and governors for my name's sake.  This will be a time for
 J 16.2     offering service to God.
```

```
Mk 13.9            to bear testimony before them.
 L 21.14    you to bear testimony.  Settle it therefore in your minds, not to meditate
```

```
 L 21.15    beforehand how to answer; for I will give you a mouth and wisdom, which
 L 21.16    none of your adversaries will be able to withstand or contradict.  You
 L 21.16    will be delivered up even by parents and brothers and kinsmen and friends,
```

```
M   24.9    and                          put you to death;
L   21.16   and some of you they will put      to death;
```

```
M   24.10      and you will be hated by all nations for my name's sake.  And then many
Mk  13.13      and you will be hated by all         for my name's sake.
L   21.17,18       you will be hated by all         for my name's sake.  But not a hair
  M 10.22      and you will be hated by all         for my name's sake.
  J 15.18      "If the world     hates you, know that it has hated me before it hated you.
  J 15.21      But all this they will do to you      on  my account, because they do not
```

```
M   24.11   will fall away, and betray one another, and hate one another.  And many
L   21.18   of your head will perish.
  J 15.21   know him who sent me.
```

```
M   24.12   false prophets will arise and lead many astray.  And because wickedness
M   24.12   is multiplied, most men's love will grow cold.
```

```
M   24.13,14   But he who endures to the end will be saved.  And this gospel of the
Mk  13.13,10   But he who endures to the end will be saved.  And the gospel
L   21.19      By   your   endurance      you will    gain your lives.
  M 10.22      But he who endures to the end will be saved.
```

```
M   24.14   kingdom will          be preached throughout the whole world, as a testimony
Mk  13.10          must first be preached
L   21.13                          This will be a time for you to bear testimony.
```

```
M   24.14   to all nations; and then the end will come.
Mk  13.11   to all nations.  And when they bring you to trial and deliver you up, do
```

```
Mk 13.11   not be anxious beforehand what you are to say; but say whatever is given
Mk 13.12   you in that hour, for it is not you who speak, but the Holy Spirit.  And
Mk 13.12   brother will deliver up brother to death, and the father his child, and
Mk 13.12   children will rise against parents and have them put to death;
```

M	24.15	"So <u>when you see</u> <u>the</u>
Mk	13.14	"But <u>when you see</u> <u>the</u>
L	21.20	"But <u>when you see</u> Jerusalem surrounded by armies, then know that its

M	24.15	desolating sacrilege spoken of by the prophet Daniel, <u>standing in the</u>
Mk	13.14	<u>desolating sacrilege</u> set up where
L	21.20	desolation has come near.

M	24.16	holy place (let the reader understand), │<u>then let those who are</u>
Mk	13.14	it ought not to be (let the reader understand), <u>then let those who are</u>
L	21.21	Then let those who are

M	24.17	<u>in Judea flee to the mountains;</u> <u>let him</u> <u>who is</u> on the housetop
Mk	13.15	<u>in Judea flee to the mountains;</u> <u>let him</u> <u>who is</u> on the housetop
L	17.31	On that day, <u>let him</u> <u>who is</u> on the housetop ,
L	21.21	<u>in Judea flee to the mountains,</u> and <u>let</u> those <u>who</u> are inside the city

M	24.17	<u>not go</u> <u>down</u> <u>to take</u>
Mk	13.15	<u>not go</u> <u>down</u>, nor enter his house, <u>to take</u>
L	17.31	with his goods in the house, <u>not</u> come <u>down</u> <u>to take</u>
L	21.21	depart, and let not those who are out

M	24.18	<u>what is in his house;</u> <u>and</u> <u>let him who is in the field not turn</u>
Mk	13.16	anything away; <u>and</u> <u>let him who is in the field not turn</u>
L	17.31	them away; <u>and</u> likewise <u>let him who is in the field not turn</u>
L	21.22	in the country enter it; for these are days of vengeance, to fulfil all

M	24.19	<u>back to take his mantle.</u> <u>And alas for those who are with child and for</u>
Mk	13.17	<u>back to take his mantle.</u> <u>And alas for those who are with child and for</u>
L	17.31	<u>back.</u>
L	21.23	that is written. <u>Alas for those who are with child and for</u>

M	24.20	<u>those who give suck in those days!</u> <u>Pray that your flight may not be</u>
Mk	13.18	<u>those who give suck in those days!</u> <u>Pray that</u> it <u>may not</u> happen
L	21.23	<u>those who give suck in those days!</u>

M	24.21	<u>in winter or on a sabbath.</u> <u>For</u> <u>then there will be great</u>
Mk	13.19	<u>in winter.</u> <u>For</u> in those days <u>there will be</u> such
L	21.23	<u>For</u> <u>great</u>

M	24.21	<u>tribulation, such as has not been from the beginning of the world</u>
Mk	13.19	<u>tribulation</u> <u>as has not been from the beginning of the</u> creation
L	21.24	distress shall be upon the earth and wrath upon this people; *they will*

L	21.24	*fall by the edge of the sword, and be led captive among all nations;*
L	21.24	*and Jerusalem will be trodden down by the Gentiles, until the times*
L	21.24	*of the Gentiles are fulfilled.*

M	24.22	<u>until now, no,</u> <u>and never will be.</u> <u>And if those days</u>
Mk	13.20	which God created <u>until now,</u> <u>and never will be.</u> <u>And if</u> the Lord

M	24.22	<u>had not been shortened,</u> <u>no human being would be saved;</u> <u>but for</u>
Mk	13.20	<u>had not</u> <u>shortened</u> the days, <u>no human being would be saved;</u> <u>but for</u>

M	24.22	<u>the sake of the elect</u> those days will be shortened.
Mk	13.20	<u>the sake of the elect,</u> whom he chose, he <u>shortened</u> the days.

L 17.20 *Being asked by the Pharisees when the kingdom of God was coming,*
L 17.20 *he answered them, "The kingdom of God is not coming with signs to be*
L 17.20 *observed;*

L 17.22 *And he said to the disciples, "The days are coming when you will desire*
L 17.22 *to see one of the days of the Son of man, and you will not see it.*

M   24.23   Then if any one   says to you, 'Lo,   here   is the Christ!' or
Mk 13.21 And then if any one says to you, 'Look, here   is the Christ!' or
L   17.21 nor will   they   say,   'Lo, here it is!'   or
L   17.23 And   they will say to you, 'Lo, there!'   or

M   24.24   'There he is!' do not believe it. For false Christs and false
Mk 13.22 'Look, there he is!' do not believe it.   False Christs and false
L   17.21   'There!' for behold, the kingdom of God is in the midst of you."
L   17.23 'Lo,   here!'

M   24.24 prophets will arise and show great signs and wonders, so as to lead
Mk 13.22 prophets will arise and show   signs and wonders,   to lead

M   24.25 astray, if possible, even the elect.   Lo,   I have told you
Mk 13.23 astray, if possible,   the elect. But take heed; I have told you all

M   24.26   beforehand. So, if they say to you, 'Lo, he is in the wilderness,'
Mk 13.23 things beforehand.

M   24.26 do not go out; if they say, 'Lo, he is in the inner rooms,' do not believe
L   17.23 Do not go,   do not follow

M   24.27 it. For as the lightning comes from the east and shines as far as the
L   17.24 them. For as the lightning flashes   and lights up the sky

M   24.27 west,   so will be the coming of the Son of man.
L   17.24 from one side to the other, so will   the Son of man be in

L 17.25 *his day. But first he must suffer many things and be rejected by this*
L 17.25 *generation.*

M   24.28   Wherever the body is, there the eagles will be gathered
L   17.37b He said to them, "Where the body is, there the eagles will be gathered

M   24.28   together.
L   17.37b together."

M   24.29 "Immediately   after the tribulation of those days the sun will
Mk 13.24 "But in those days, after that tribulation,   the sun will
L   21.25 "And   there will be signs in sun

M   24.29 be darkened, and the moon will not give its light, and the stars will
Mk 13.25 be darkened, and the moon will not give its light, |and the stars will
L   21.25   and   moon   and   stars, and

M   24.29 fall   from heaven,
Mk 13.25 be falling from heaven,
L   21.25 upon the earth distress of nations in perplexity at the roaring of the

M   24.29   and the powers of the heavens will be shaken;
Mk   13.25   and the powers in the heavens will be shaken.
L   21.26   *is coming on the world;* for the powers of the heavens will be shaken.

M   24.30   then will appear the sign of the Son of man in heaven, and then all the

M   24.30   tribes of the earth will mourn, and   they will see the Son of man
Mk   13.26   And then they will see the Son of man
L   21.27   And then they will see the Son of man

M   24.31   coming on the clouds of heaven with   power and great glory;   and
Mk   13.27   coming in   clouds   with great power and   glory.   And
L   21.28   coming in a   cloud   with   power and great glory.   Now

M   24.31   he will send out his angels with a loud trumpet call, and they will
Mk   13.27   then he will send out the angels,   and
L   21.28   when these things begin to take place, look up and raise your heads,

M   24.31   gather his elect from the four winds, from one end
Mk   13.27   gather his elect from the four winds, from the ends of the earth to the
L   21.28   because your redemption is drawing near."

M   24.31   of heaven to the other.
Mk   13.27   ends of heaven.

M   24.32   "From   the fig tree   learn its lesson:
Mk   13.28   "From   the fig tree   learn its lesson:
L   21.29   And he told them a parable: "Look at the fig tree, and all the trees;

M   24.32   as soon as its branch becomes tender and puts forth its leaves, you
Mk   13.28   as soon as its branch becomes tender and puts forth its leaves, you
L   21.30   as soon as   they   come out   in   leaf,   you see

M   24.33   know that   summer is   near. So also, when
Mk   13.29   know that   summer is   near. So also, when
L   21.31   for yourselves and know that the summer is already near. So also, when

M   24.33   you see all these things,   you know that   he
Mk   13.29   you see   these things taking place, you know that   he
L   21.31   you see   these things taking place, you know that the kingdom of God

M   24.34   is near, at the very gates. Truly, I say to you, this generation will
Mk   13.30   is near, at the very gates. Truly, I say to you, this generation will
L   21.32   is near.   Truly, I say to you, this generation will

M   24.35   not pass away till   all these things take   place. Heaven and earth will
Mk   13.31   not pass away before all these things take   place. Heaven and earth will
L   21.33   not pass away till   all   has taken place. Heaven and earth will
    M   5.18   *For truly, I say to you, till* heaven and earth
    L   16.17   *But it is easier for* heaven and earth *to*

M	24.35	pass away, but my words	will not pass away.
Mk	13.31	pass away, but my words	will not pass away.
L	21.33	pass away, but my words	will not pass away.
M	*5.18*	pass away, *not an iota, not a dot,* will pass *from the law until all*
L	*16.17*	pass away, *than for one dot* *of the law to become*

M	*5.18*	*is accomplished.*
L	*16.17*	*void.*

M	24.36	"But of that day and hour no one knows, not even the angels of
Mk	13.32	"But of that day or that hour no one knows, not even the angels in

M	24.37	heaven, nor the Son, but the Father only. As were the days
Mk	13.32	heaven, nor the Son, but only the Father.
L	17.26	As it was in the days

M	24.38	of Noah, so will be the coming of the Son of man. For as in
L	17.26	of Noah, so will it be in the days of the Son of man.

M	24.38	those days before the flood they were eating and drinking, marrying
L	17.27	They ate, they drank, they married,

M	24.38	and giving in marriage, until the day when Noah entered the ark,
L	17.27	they were given in marriage, until the day when Noah entered the ark,

M	24.39	|and they did not know until the flood came and swept them all away,
L	17.27	and the flood came and destroyed them all.

M	24.39	so will be the coming of the Son of man.

L	*17.28*	*Likewise as it was in the days of Lot--they ate, they drank, they bought,*
L	*17.29*	*they sold, they planted, they built, |but on the day when Lot went out*
L	*17.29*	*from Sodom fire and sulphur rained from heaven and destroyed them all--*
L	*17.30,31*	*|so will it be on the day when the Son of man is revealed. On that day,*
L	*17.31*	*let him who is on the housetop, with his goods in the house, not come .*
L	*17.31*	*down to take them away; and likewise let him who is in the field not turn*
L	*17.32,33*	*back. Remember Lot's wife. Whoever seeks to gain his life will lose it,*
L	*17.33*	*but whoever loses his life will preserve it.*

M	24.40	Then two men will be in the field; one
L	17.34	I tell you, in that night there will be two in one bed; one
L	17.36	*"Two men will be in the field; one*

M	24.41	is taken and one is left. Two women will be
L	17.35	will be taken and the other left. There will be two women
L	17.36	*will be taken and the other left."*

M	24.41	grinding at the mill; one is taken and one is left.
L	17.35,37	grinding together; one will be taken and the other left." *And they*

L	*17.37*	*said to him, "Where, Lord?" He said to them, "Where the body is, there*
L	*17.37*	*the eagles will be gathered together."*

149

<pre>
L 21.34   "But take heed to yourselves lest your hearts be weighed down with
L 21.34   dissipation and drunkenness and cares of this life, and that day come
L 21.35   upon you suddenly like a snare; for it will come upon all who dwell
L 21.35   upon the face of the whole earth.
</pre>

<pre>
M   24.42   Watch therefore, for you do not know on   what day your Lord
Mk   13.33   Take heed, watch;   for you do not know   when   the time
Mk   13.35   Watch therefore--for you do not know   when   the master
L   21.36   But watch at all times, praying that you may have strength to escape
  M 25.13   Watch therefore, for you   know neither the day nor the
</pre>

<pre>
M   24.42   is   coming.
Mk   13.34   will come. It is like a man going on a journey, when he
Mk   13.35   of the house will come, in the evening, or at midnight, or at cockcrow,
L   21.36   all these things that will take place, and to stand before the Son of man."
  M 25.13   hour.
</pre>

<pre>
Mk 13.34   leaves home and puts his servants in charge, each with his work, and
Mk 13.34   commands the doorkeeper to be on the watch.
</pre>

<pre>
Mk 13.36,37   or in the morning--|lest he come suddenly and find you asleep. And what
Mk 13.37   I say to you I say to all: Watch."
</pre>

<pre>
M   24.43   But know this, that if the householder had known in what part of the night
L   12.39   But know this, that if the householder had known at what   hour
</pre>

<pre>
M   24.43   the thief was coming, he would have watched and would not have let his
L   12.39   the thief was coming, he   would not have left his
</pre>

<pre>
M   24.44   house   be broken into. Therefore you also must be ready; for the Son
L   12.40   house to be broken into.   You also must be ready; for the Son
</pre>

<pre>
M   24.44   of man is coming at an   hour you do not expect.
L   12.40   of man is coming at an unexpected hour."
</pre>

c. The Faithful and Wise Servant

Matthew 24.45-51

<pre>
L 12.41   Peter said, "Lord, are you telling this parable for us or for all?"
</pre>

<pre>
M   24.45   "Who then is the faithful and wise servant, whom his
L   12.42   And the Lord said, "Who then is the faithful and wise steward, whom his
</pre>

<pre>
M   24.45   master has set over his household, to give them their   food
L   12.42   master will set over his household, to give them their portion of food
</pre>

<pre>
M   24.46   at the proper time? Blessed is that servant whom his master when he
L   12.43   at the proper time? Blessed is that servant whom his master when he
</pre>

<pre>
M   24.47   comes will find so doing. Truly, I say to you, he will set him over
L   12.44   comes will find so doing. Truly I say to you, he will set him over
</pre>

M	24.48	all his possessions. But if that wicked servant says to himself, 'My
L	12.45	all his possessions. But if that servant says to himself, 'My

M	24.49	master is delayed,' |and begins to beat his fellow servants,
L	12.45	master is delayed in coming,' and begins to beat the menservants and the

M	24.50	and eats and drinks with the drunken, |the master of
L	12.46	maidservants, and to eat and drink and get drunk, |the master of

M	24.50	that servant will come on a day when he does not expect him and at an
L	12.46	that servant will come on a day when he does not expect him and at an
M	*22.13*	*Then the king said*
L	*13.28b*	*when you see Abraham and Isaac and Jacob*

M	24.51	hour he does not know, |and will punish him, and put
L	12.46	hour he does not know, and will punish him, and put
M	*8.12*	*while the sons of the kingdom will be* *thrown*
M	*13.42*	and *throw*
M	*13.50*	and *throw*
M	*22.13*	*to the attendants, 'Bind him hand and foot,* and *cast*
M	*25.30*	And *cast the*
L	*13.28b*	*and all the prophets in the kingdom of God* and *you yourselves thrust*

M	24.51	him with the hypocrites; there men will weep and gnash
L	12.47	*him with the unfaithful. And that servant who knew his*
M	*8.12*	*into the outer darkness;* there men will weep and gnash
M	*13.42*	*them into the furnace of fire;* there men will weep and gnash
M	*13.50*	*them into the furnace of fire;* there men will weep and gnash
M	*22.13*	*him into the outer darkness;* there men will weep and gnash
M	*25.30*	*worthless servant into the outer darkness;* there men will weep and gnash
L	*13.28a*	*out.* There *you* will weep and gnash

M	24.51	their teeth.
L	12.47	*master's will, but did not make ready or act according to his will, shall*
M	*8.12*	their teeth."
M	*13.42*	their teeth.
M	*13.50*	their teeth.
M	*22.13*	their teeth.'
M	*25.30*	their teeth.'
L	*13.28a*	*your* teeth,

L	*12.48*	*receive a severe beating. But he who did not know, and did what deserved*
L	*12.48*	*a beating, shall receive a light beating. Every one to whom much is given,*
L	*12.48*	*of him will much be required; and of him to whom men commit much they*
L	*12.48*	*will demand the more.*

d. The Ten Maidens

Matthew 25.1-13

M	25.1	"Then the kingdom of heaven shall be compared to ten maidens who took
M	25.2	their lamps and went to meet the bridegroom. Five of them were foolish,
M	25.3	and five were wise. For when the foolish took their lamps, they took no
M	25.4,5	oil with them; but the wise took flasks of oil with their lamps. As the
M	25.6	bridegroom was delayed, they all slumbered and slept. But at midnight
M	25.7	there was a cry, 'Behold, the bridegroom! Come out to meet him.' Then

151

```
M    25.8     all those maidens rose and trimmed their lamps.  And the foolish said to
M    25.9     the wise, 'Give us some of your oil, for our lamps are going out.' But
M    25.9     the wise replied, 'Perhaps there will not be enough for us and for you;
M    25.9     go rather to the dealers and buy for yourselves.'


M    25.10    And while they went to buy, the bridegroom came, and those who were ready
 L   13.25    When once                      the householder has risen up


M    25.11    went in with him to the marriage feast; and the door was shut.  Afterward
 L   13.25                                              and       shut the door, you will


M    25.11    the other maidens came also,                          saying,      'Lord, lord,
  M   7.21                                        "Not every one who says to me, 'Lord, Lord,'
  L  13.25     begin to stand outside and to knock at the door, saying,      'Lord,


M    25.12    open to us.'  But       he      replied, 'Truly, I say to you, I do not
  M   7.21    shall enter the kingdom of heaven, but he who does the will of my Father
  M   7.23                  And then will I declare to them,                  'I      never
  L  13.25    open to us.'            He will answer     you,                 'I do not
  L  13.27                 But       he will say,                    'I tell   you, I do not


M    25.13    know       you.'                     Watch therefore, for you          know
  M   7.21    who is in heaven.
  M   7.23    knew       you; depart from me, you evildoers.'
  M  24.42                                    Watch therefore, for you do not know
 Mk 13.33                        Take heed, watch;           for you do not know
 Mk 13.35                                    Watch therefore--for you do not know
  L  13.25    know where you come from.'
  L  13.27    know where you come from; depart from me, all you workers of iniquity!'
  L  21.36                       But watch at all times, praying that you


M    25.13    neither the  day nor the hour.
  M  24.42    on      what day your Lord     is    coming.
 Mk 13.33    when    the  time           will come.
 Mk 13.35    when    the master of the house will come, in the evening, or at midnight,
  L  21.36    may have strength to escape all these things that will take place, and to


 Mk 13.35    or at cockcrow, or in the morning--
  L  21.36    stand before the Son of man."
```

e. The Talents

Matthew 25.14-30

```
  L  19.11    As they heard these things, he proceeded to tell a parable, because
  L  19.11    he was near to Jerusalem, and because they supposed that the kingdom of
  L  19.11    God was to appear immediately.


M    25.14    "For it will be as when a man      going on   a journey
L    19.12    He said therefore,    "A nobleman went  into a far country to receive
 Mk 13.34        It      is like    a man      going on   a journey, when he leaves


M    25.14                                    called        his servants and entrusted
L    19.13    a kingdom and then return.  Calling ten of his servants,
 Mk 13.34    home      and                 puts         his servants in charge,
```

152

M	25.15	to them his property; to one he gave five talents, to another two,
L	19.13	he gave them ten pounds,

M	25.15	to another one, to each according to his ability. Then he went away.
L	19.13	and said to them, 'Trade with these till I come.'
Mk	13.34	*each with his work, and commands the doorkeeper to*

M	25.16	He who had received the five talents went at once and traded with them;
L	19.14	But his citizens hated him and sent an embassy after him, saying, 'We
Mk	13.34	*be on the watch.*

M	25.17	and he made five talents more. So also, he who had the two talents
L	19.14	do not want this man to reign over us.'

M	25.18	made two talents more. But he who had received the one talent went and
M	25.18	dug in the ground and hid his master's money.

M	25.19	Now after a long time the master of those servants came
L	19.15	When he returned, having received

L	19.15	*the kingdom, he commanded these servants, to whom he had given the money,*
L	19.15	*to be called to him, that he might know what they*

M	25.20	and settled accounts with them. And he who had received the five talents
L	19.16	had gained by trading. The first

M	25.20	came forward, bringing five talents more, saying, 'Master, you delivered
L	19.16	came before him, saying, 'Lord,

M	25.21	to me five talents; here I have made five talents more.' His master said
L	19.17	your pound has made ten pounds more.' And he said

M	25.21	to him, 'Well done, good and faithful servant; you have been
L	19.17	to him, 'Well done, good servant! Because you have been
L	16.10	*"He who is*

M	25.21	faithful over a little, I will set you over much; enter
L	19.17	faithful in a very little, you shall have authority over ten cities.'
L	16.10	*faithful in a very little is faithful also in much; and he*

M	25.22	into the joy of your master.' And he also who had the two talents came
L	19.18	And the second came,
L	16.10	*who is dishonest in a very little is dishonest also in much.*

M	25.22	forward, saying, 'Master, you delivered to me two talents; here I have
L	19.18	saying, 'Lord, your pound has

M	25.23	made two talents more.' His master said to him, 'Well done, good and
L	19.19	made five pounds.' And he said to him,

M	25.23	faithful servant; you have been faithful over a little, I will set you
L	19.19	'And you

153

```
M    25.24                      over much; enter into the joy of your master.'  He also who
L    19.20a       are to be over five cities.'                                  Then another


M    25.24       had received the one talent came forward, saying, 'Master, I knew  you
L    19.21b                                    came,        saying, 'Lord, |because you


M    25.24       to be  a hard   man,      reaping where you did not sow,   and gathering
L    19.21d,c      are a severe man; |and reap    what  you did not sow.' |you take up


M    25.25       where you did not winnow;   so  I was afraid,        and   I went and
L    19.21a,20c  what  you did not lay down, |for I was afraid of you, |which I


M    25.26       hid your talent in the ground. Here you have what is yours.' |But his
L    19.20b      kept laid away  in a   napkin; |here              is your pound,


M    25.26       master answered him,                                'You wicked
L    19.22a      He      said  to him, 'I will condemn you out of your own mouth, you wicked


M    25.26       and slothful servant! You knew that I                 reap    where
L    19.22c                   servant! You knew that I was a severe man, |and reaping what


M    25.27       I have now sowed, and gather   where I have not winnowed?    Then
L    19.22b,23   I did  not sow?        |taking up what  I did  not lay down |Why then


M    25.27          you ought to have invested my money with the bankers, and at my coming
L    19.23       did you          not put     my money into the bank,    and at my coming


M    25.27       I should have received what was my own with interest.
L    19.24       I should have collected it            with interest?'  And he said to


M    25.28                 So take the talent from him, and give it to him who
L    19.24       those who stood by, 'Take the pound  from him, and give it to him who


M    25.28       has the ten talents.
L    19.25       has the ten pounds.'  (And they said to him, 'Lord, he has ten pounds!')


M    25.29                          For to every one who has will more be given,
L    19.26              'I tell you, that to every one who has will more be given;
 M  13.12                        For to him    who has will more be given,
 Mk  4.25                        For to him    who has will more be given;
  L  8.18   Take heed then how you hear; for to him    who has will more be given,


M    25.29       and he will have abundance; but from him who has not, even what he
L    19.26                                   but from him who has not, even what he
 M  13.12        and he will have abundance; but from him who has not, even what he
 Mk  4.25                                    and from him who has not, even what he
  L  8.18                                    and from him who has not, even what he thinks


M    25.29              has will be taken away.
L    19.26              has will be taken away.
 M   8.12                                                           while the
 M  13.12              has will be taken away.
 M  22.13                     Then the king said to the attendants, 'Bind him hand
 Mk  4.25              has will be taken away."
  L  8.18   that he has will be taken away."
  L 13.28b  when you see Abraham and Isaac and Jacob and all the prophets in the kingd
```

154

M	25.30		And				cast the worthless servant	into
L	19.27		But as for these enemies of mine, who did not want
M	8.12	*sons of the kingdom will be*			*thrown*			into
M	13.42		and		*throw*		them	into
M	13.50		and		*throw*		them	into
M	22.13	*and foot,*	and		cast		him	into
M	24.51	*and will punish him,*	and		put		him	with
L	13.28b	*of God*	and *you yourselves thrust out.*

M	25.30	the outer darkness;	there men will weep and gnash their teeth.'
L	19.27	me to reign over them,	bring them here and slay them before me.'"
M	8.12	the outer darkness;	there men will weep and gnash their teeth."
M	13.42	*the furnace of fire;*	there men will weep and gnash their teeth.
M	13.50	*the furnace of fire;*	there men will weep and gnash their teeth.
M	22.13	the outer darkness;	there men will weep and gnash their teeth.'
M	24.51	*the hypocrites;*	there men will weep and gnash their teeth.
L	13.28a		There *you* will weep and gnash *your* teeth,

f. The Last Judgment

Matthew 25.31–46

M	25.31	"When the Son of man comes in his glory, and all the angels with him,
M	25.32	then he will sit on his glorious throne. Before him will be gathered
M	25.32	all the nations, and he will separate them one from another as a shepherd
M	25.33	separates the sheep from the goats, |and he will place the sheep at his
M	25.34	right hand, but the goats at the left. Then the King will say to those
M	25.34	at his right hand, 'Come, O blessed of my Father, inherit the kingdom
M	25.35	prepared for you from the foundation of the world; for I was hungry and
M	25.35	you gave me food, I was thirsty and you gave me drink, I was a stranger
M	25.36	and you welcomed me, |I was naked and you clothed me, I was sick and
M	25.37	you visited me, I was in prison and you came to me.' Then the righteous
M	25.37	will answer him, 'Lord, when did we see thee hungry and feed thee, or
M	25.38	thirsty and give thee drink? And when did we see thee a stranger and
M	25.39	welcome thee, or naked and clothe thee? And when did we see thee sick
M	25.40	or in prison and visit thee?' And the King will answer them, 'Truly, I
M	25.40	say to you, as you did it to one of the least of these my brethren, you
M	25.41	did it to me.' Then he will say to those at his left hand, 'Depart from
M	25.41	me, you cursed, into the eternal fire prepared for the devil and his
M	25.42	angels; for I was hungry and you gave me no food, I was thirsty and you
M	25.43	gave me no drink, |I was a stranger and you did not welcome me, naked
M	25.43	and you did not clothe me, sick and in prison and you did not visit me.'
M	25.44	Then they also will answer, 'Lord, when did we see thee hungry or thirsty
M	25.44	or a stranger or naked or sick or in prison, and did not minister to

M	25.45	thee?' Then he will answer them, 'Truly, I say to you, as you did it
J	5.28	*Do not marvel at this; for the hour is*

M	25.46	not to one of the least of these, you did it not to me.' And they will
J	5.29	*coming when all who are in the tombs will hear his voice* |*and*

M	25.46	go away			into	eternal punishment,	but
J	5.29	*come forth,*	*those who have done good,*	*to the resurrection of life,*			*and*

M	25.46	the righteous	into	eternal life."
J	5.29	*those who have done evil,*	*to the resurrection of judgment.*

g. Summary

Matthew 26.1-2

M	26.1	When Jesus had finished all these sayings, he said to his disciples,
Mk	14.1a	It was now
L	22.1	Now the feast of Unleavened

M	26.2	"You know that after two days the Passover is coming, and the
Mk	14.1a	two days before the Passover and the feast of
L	22.1	Bread drew near, which is called the Passover.

M	26.2	Son of man will be delivered up to be crucified."
Mk	14.1a	Unleavened Bread.

62. THE PLOT TO KILL JESUS

Matthew 26.3-5

J 11.45   Many of the Jews therefore, who had come with Mary and had seen what
J 11.46   he did, believed in him; but some of them went to the Pharisees and
J 11.46   told them what Jesus had done.

M	26.3	Then the chief priests and the elders of the people gathered in the
Mk	14.1b	And the chief priests and the scribes
L	22.2	And the chief priests and the scribes
J	11.47	So the chief priests and the Pharisees gathered the

M	26.3	palace of the high priest,
J	11.47	council, and said, "What are we to do? For this man performs many signs.

J 11.48   If we let him go on thus, every one will believe in him, and the Romans
J 11.48   will come and destroy both our holy place and our nation."

M	26.3	who was called Caiaphas,
J	11.49	But one of them, Caiaphas, who was high priest that year, said to them,

J 11.50   "You know nothing at all; you do not understand that it is expedient
J 11.50   for you that one man should die for the people, and that the whole nation
J 11.51   should not perish." He did not say this of his own accord, but being
J 11.51   high priest that year he prophesied that Jesus should die for the nation,
J 11.52 |and not for the nation only, but to gather into one the children of God
J 11.53   who are scattered abroad. So from that day on

M	26.4	|and took counsel together in order to arrest Jesus by stealth and
Mk	14.1b	were seeking how to arrest him by stealth, and
L	22.2	were seeking how to
J	11.53	they took counsel how to

M	26.5	kill him. But they said, "Not during the feast, lest there be a tumult
Mk	14.2	kill him; for they said, "Not during the feast, lest there be a tumult
L	22.2	put him to death; for they feared
J	11.53	put him to death.

M	26.5	among the people."
Mk	14.2	of the people."
L	22.2	the people.

156

63. JESUS ANOINTED FOR BURIAL

Matthew 26.6-13

M	26.6	Now when		Jesus was at
Mk	14.3a	And while		he was at
L	7.36a	One of the Pharisees asked him to eat with him, and		he went
J	12.1	Six days before the Passover,		Jesus came to

M	26.6	Bethany in the	house of Simon the leper,
Mk	14.3a	Bethany in the	house of Simon the leper,
L	7.37	into the Pharisee's	house, And behold,
J	12.2	Bethany, where Lazarus was, whom Jesus had raised from the dead. *There*

> *J 12.2*   *they made him a supper; Martha served, and Lazarus was one of those at*
> *J 12.2*   *table with him.*

M	26.7	a woman	
Mk	14.3c	a woman	
L	7.37	a woman of the city, who was a sinner, when she learned that he was at
J	12.3	Mary	

M	26.7		came up to him with an alabaster flask
Mk	14.3c		came with an alabaster flask
L	7.37	table in the Pharisee's house, brought	an alabaster flask
J	12.3		took a pound

M	26.7	of very expensive ointment,	
Mk	14.3c	of	ointment of pure nard, very costly,
L	7.38	of	ointment, and standing behind him at his feet, weeping,
J	12.3	of costly	ointment of pure nard

> *L 7.38*   *she began to wet his feet with her tears, and wiped them with the hair*

M	26.7		and she poured it on	his head,
Mk	14.3c	and she broke the flask and	poured it over	his head.
L	7.38	of her head, and kissed his feet, and	anointed	them
J	12.3		and anointed	the feet of

> *J 12.3*   *Jesus and wiped his feet with her hair; and the house was filled*

M	26.7		as he sat	at table.
Mk	14.3b		as he sat	at table.
L	7.36b	with	the ointment. and took his place	at table.
J	12.3	with the fragrance of the ointment.		
J	*12.2b*		*Martha served, and Lazarus was one of those*	*at table with*

M	26.8	But when	the disciples	saw it, they
Mk	14.4	But there were	some who	
L	7.39	Now when	the Pharisee who had invited him	saw it, he
J	12.4	But Judas Iscariot, one of his	disciples (he who was to betray him),	
J	*12.2b*	*him.*		

M	26.8	were	indignant, saying, "Why	this waste?
Mk	14.4	said to themselves indignantly,	"Why was the ointment thus wasted?
L	7.39	said to himself, "If this man were a prophet, he would have known who
J	12.5		said, "Why was

L	7.39	*and what sort of woman this is who is touching him, for she is a sinner."*
L	7.40	*And Jesus answering said to him, "Simon, I have something to say to you."*
L	7.41	*And he answered, "What is it, Teacher?" "A certain creditor had two*

M	26.9	<u>For this ointment might have been sold for</u> <u>a large sum,</u>
Mk	14.5	<u>For this ointment might have been sold for</u> more than three hundred denarii,
L	7.41	debtors; one owed five hundred denarii,
J	12.5	<u>this ointment</u> not <u>sold for</u> three hundred denarii

M	26.9	<u>and given to the poor."</u>
Mk	14.5	<u>and given to the poor."</u> And they reproached her.
L	7.42	and the other fifty. When they could not pay, he forgave them both. Now
J	12.6	<u>and given to the poor?"</u> *This he said, not that he cared for the poor*

J	12.6	*but because he was a thief, and as he had the money box he used to take*
J	12.6	*what was put into it.*

M	26.10	But Jesus, <u>aware of this</u>, <u>said</u> to them,
Mk	14.6	<u>But Jesus</u> <u>said</u>, "Let her alone;
L	7.43	which of them will love him more?" Simon answered, "The one, I suppose,
J	12.7a	<u>Jesus</u> <u>said</u>, "Let her alone,

L	7.43	*to whom he forgave more." And he said to him, "You have judged rightly."*
L	7.44	*Then turning toward the woman he said to Simon,*

M	26.10	"Why do you trouble the woman? <u>For she has done a beautiful thing to me.</u>
Mk	14.6	<u>why do you trouble</u> her? <u>She has done a beautiful thing to me.</u>
L	7.44	"<u>Do you</u> see this <u>woman</u>? I entered your house, you gave me no water

L	7.44	*for my feet, but she has wet my feet with her tears and wiped them with*
L	7.45	*her hair. You gave me no kiss, but from the time I came in she has not*

M	26.11	<u>For you always have the poor with you,</u>
Mk	14.7	<u>For you always have the poor with you,</u> and whenever you will, you can do
L	7.45	ceased to kiss my feet.
J	12.8	The poor you always have <u>with you,</u>

M	26.11	<u>but you will not always have me.</u>
Mk	14.8	good to them; <u>but you will not always have me.</u> She has done what she
L	7.46	<u>You</u> did <u>not</u> anoint my head with oil, but she has
J	12.8	<u>but you</u> do <u>not always have me."</u>

M	26.12	<u>In pouring this ointment on my body she has done it to prepare</u>
Mk	14.8	could; she has anointed <u>my body</u> beforehand
L	7.47	anointed my feet with <u>ointment</u>. Therefore I tell you, her sins, which
J	12.7b	let her keep <u>it</u> for the day of

M	26.13	me for burial. <u>Truly</u>, <u>I say to you</u>, <u>wherever this gospel is</u>
Mk	14.9	<u>for</u> burying. And <u>truly</u>, <u>I say to you</u>, <u>wherever</u> the <u>gospel is</u>
L	7.47	are many, are forgiven, for she loved much; but he who is forgiven
J	12.7b	my <u>burial.</u>

M	26.13	<u>preached in the whole world, what she has done will be told in memory</u>
Mk	14.9	<u>preached in the whole world, what she has done will be told in memory</u>
L	7.48	little, loves little." And he said to her, "Your sins are forgiven."

M	26.13	of her."
Mk	14.9	of her."
L	7.49	Then those who were at table with him began to say among themselves,

L	7.50	*"Who is this, who even forgives sins?" And he said to the woman,*
L	7.50	*"Your faith has saved you; go in peace."*

64. JUDAS PLANS THE BETRAYAL

Matthew 26.14-16

M	26.14	Then one of the twelve, who was called
Mk	14.10	Then
L	22.3	Then Satan entered into
J	6.70	*Jesus answered them, "Did I not choose you, the twelve, and one of you*
J	13.2	*And during supper, when the devil had already put it into the heart*
J	13.27	*Then after the morsel, Satan entered into*

M	26.14	Judas Iscariot,
Mk	14.10	Judas Iscariot, who was
L	22.3	Judas called Iscariot, who was of the
J	6.71	*is a devil?" He spoke of Judas the son of Simon Iscariot, for he,*
J	13.2	*of Judas Iscariot, Simon's son,*
J	13.27	*him. Jesus said to him, "What you are going to*

M	26.14	went to the chief priests
Mk	14.10	one of the twelve, went to the chief priests
L	22.4	number of the twelve; he went away and conferred with the chief priests
J	6.71	*one of the twelve,*
J	13.27	*do, do quickly."*

M	26.15	and said, "What will you give me if I deliver him to you?" And
Mk	14.11	in order to betray him to them. And
L	22.5	and officers how he might betray him to them. And

M	26.15	they paid him thirty pieces
Mk	14.11	when they heard it they were glad, and promised to give him
L	22.5	they were glad, and engaged to give him

M	26.16	of silver. And from that moment he sought an opportunity
Mk	14.11	money. And he sought an opportunity
L	22.6	money. So he agreed, and sought an opportunity
J	6.71	*was*

M	26.16	to betray him.
Mk	14.11	to betray him.
L	22.6	to betray him to them in the absence of the multitude.
J	6.71	*to betray him.*
J	13.2	*to betray him,*

65. THE PASSOVER MEAL

Matthew 26.17-29

M	26.17	Now on the first day of Unleavened Bread
Mk	14.12	And on the first day of Unleavened Bread, when they sacrificed the
L	22.7	Then came the day of Unleavened Bread, on which the

```
Mk 14.12      passover lamb,
L  22.8       passover lamb had to be sacrificed.  So Jesus sent Peter and John, saying,


L  22.8       "Go and prepare the passover for us, that we may eat it."


M  26.17      the disciples came to Jesus, saying,      "Where will you have us
Mk 14.12      his disciples              said to him, "Where will you have us go and
L  22.9            They                  said to him, "Where will you have us


M  26.18      prepare for you to eat the passover?"      He
Mk 14.13      prepare for you to eat the passover?"  And he sent two of his disciples,
L  22.10      prepare                it?"              He


M  26.18       said,                        "Go into the city  to  a certain
Mk 14.13      and said to them,             "Go into the city, and a
L  22.10       said to them, "Behold, when you have entered the city,      a


M  26.18      one,
Mk 14.14      man carrying a jar of water will meet you; follow him, |and wherever
L  22.10      man carrying a jar of water will meet you; follow him into the house which


M  26.18                  and say to      him,    'The Teacher says,      My time
Mk 14.14      he enters,      say to the householder, 'The Teacher says,      Where
L  22.11      he enters, |and tell  the householder, 'The Teacher says to you, Where


M  26.18      is at hand;        I will  keep the passover at your house with my
Mk 14.14      is my  guest room, where I am to eat  the passover        with my
L  22.11      is the guest room, where I am to eat  the passover        with my


M  26.18      disciples.'"
Mk 14.15      disciples?'  And he will show you a large upper room furnished and ready;
L  22.12      disciples?'  And he will show you a large upper room furnished;


M  26.19                          And the disciples
Mk 14.16      there prepare for us."  And the disciples set out and went to the city,
L  22.13      there make ready."      And      they              went,


M  26.19       did      as Jesus had directed them, and they prepared the passover.
Mk 14.16      and found it as he    had told   them; and they prepared the passover.
L  22.13      and found it as he    had told   them; and they prepared the passover.


M  26.20            When it was evening,      he sat at table  with the twelve
Mk 14.17      And when it was evening       he came       with the twelve.
L  22.14      And when the hour came,       he sat at table, and  the apostles
J  13.21          When Jesus had thus spoken, he was troubled in spirit,


M  26.21      disciples; and as they were           eating, he     said, "Truly,
Mk 14.18               And as they were at table eating, Jesus said, "Truly,
L  22.21      with him.  But                                      behold
J  13.21               and                        testified, "Truly, truly,


M  26.21      I say to you, one of you will betray  me."
Mk 14.18      I say to you, one of you will betray  me, one who is eating with me."
L  22.21      the hand of   him   who     betrays me            is       with me on
J  13.21      I say to you, one of you will betray  me."
```

160

M   26.22   <u>And they</u>   <u>were very sorrowful, and began to say to</u>

Mk   14.19   <u>They</u> began to be   <u>sorrowful, and</u>   to say to

L   22.23   the table. <u>And they</u> began to question

J   13.22   The disciples looked at   one another, uncertain of whom he

J   13.23   spoke. One of his disciples, whom Jesus loved, was lying close to the

J   13.24   breast of Jesus; so Simon Peter beckoned to him and said, "Tell us who

J   13.25   it is of whom he speaks." So lying thus, close to the breast of Jesus,

M   26.23   <u>him one after another</u>, "Is it I,   Lord?" He   <u>answered</u>,

Mk   14.20   <u>him one after another</u>, "Is it I?"   He   said to them, "It is

L   22.23   <u>one</u>   <u>another</u>, which of them it was that would do this.

J   13.26   he said to him,   "Lord, who is it?" Jesus <u>answered</u>,   "It is

M   26.23   "He   <u>who</u> has dipped   his   hand in   the dish with

Mk   14.20   one of the twelve, one   <u>who</u> is dipping   bread into <u>the dish with</u>

J   13.26   <u>he</u> to whom I shall give this morsel when I have dipped

J   13.26   it."   So when <u>he</u>   had <u>dipped</u>   the morsel, he gave it to

J   13.27   Judas, the son of Simon Iscariot. Then after the morsel, Satan entered into

J   13.28   him. Jesus said to him, "What you are going to do, do quickly." |Now

J   13.29   no one at the table knew why he said this to him. Some thought that,

J   13.29   because Judas had the money box, Jesus was telling him, "Buy what we

J   13.29   need for the feast"; or, that he should give something to the poor.

M   26.24   <u>me, will betray me. The Son of man goes as it is written of him,</u>   but

Mk   14.21   <u>me.</u>   For <u>the Son of man goes as it is written of him,</u>   but

L   22.22   For <u>the Son of man goes as it</u> has been determined; but

M   26.24   <u>woe to that man by whom the Son of man is betrayed!</u>   It would have been

Mk   14.21   <u>woe to that man by whom the Son of man is betrayed!</u>   It would have been

L   22.22   <u>woe to that man by whom</u>   he   is betrayed!"

M   26.25   <u>better for that man if he had not been born."</u>   Judas, <u>who betrayed him,</u>

Mk   14.21   <u>better for that man if he had not been born."</u>

J   13.30   So, after receiving the morsel, he immediately went out;

M   26.25   <u>said, "Is it I, Master?"</u> He said to him, <u>"You have said so."</u>

J   13.30   and it was night.

M   26.26   Now <u>as they were eating,</u>

Mk   14.22   And <u>as they were eating,</u>

L   22.19   And

1 C   11.23   For I received from the Lord what I also delivered to you, that the

M   26.26   <u>Jesus</u>   took bread,   and

Mk   14.22   he   took bread,   and

L   22.19   he   took bread,   and when he

1 C   11.24   Lord <u>Jesus</u> on the night when he was betrayed took bread, |and when he

J   6.48   I am the <u>bread</u> of life.

J   6.49   Your fathers ate the manna in the wilderness, and they died.

J   6.50   This is the <u>bread</u> which comes

J   6.51   down from heaven, that a man may eat of it and not die. I am the

J   6.51   living bread which came down from heaven; if any one eats of this

```
M    26.26           blessed,     and broke it, and gave it to the disciples and said,
Mk   14.22           blessed,     and broke it, and gave it to      them,      and said,
L    22.19      had given thanks he broke it   and gave it to      them,      saying,
1 C  11.24      had given thanks, he broke it,                                 and said,
   J  6.51      bread, he will live for ever; and the bread which I shall give for the


M    26.26      "Take, eat; this is my body."
Mk   14.22      "Take;      this is my body."
L    22.19           "This is my body which is given for you.  Do this in
1 C  11.24           "This is my body which is      for you.  Do this in
   J  6.52      life of the world is my flesh."  The Jews then disputed among themselves,


   J  6.53      saying, "How can this man give us his flesh to eat?"  So Jesus said to
   J  6.53      them, "Truly, truly, I say to you, unless you eat the flesh of the Son
   J  6.53      of man


M    26.27                         And he took        a   cup, and when he had given
Mk   14.23                         And he took        a   cup, and when he had given
L    22.17                         And he took        a   cup, and when he had given
L    22.20a     remembrance of me." And likewise      the cup  after supper,
1 C  11.25      remembrance of me." In the same way also the cup, after supper,


M    26.27      thanks he gave it to them, saying,      "Drink of it, all of you;
Mk   14.24      thanks he gave it to them, and they all drank of it.  And he said to
L    22.17      thanks he                  said,        "Take this, and divide it among
L    22.20a                                saying,
1 C  11.25                                 saying,
   J  6.53                                    and drink his blood, you have no


   J  6.54      life in you; he who eats my flesh and drinks my blood has eternal life,
   J  6.55      and I will raise him up at the last day.  For my flesh is food indeed,
   J  6.56      and my blood is drink indeed.  He who eats my flesh and drinks my blood
   J  6.57      abides in me, and I in him.  As the living Father sent me, and I live
   J  6.58      because of the Father, so he who eats me will live because of me.  This
   J  6.58      is the bread which came down from heaven, not such as the fathers ate
   J  6.59      and died; he who eats this bread will live for ever."  This he said in
   J  6.59      the synagogue, as he taught at Capernaum.


M    26.28      for   this     is my blood of the     covenant,            which
Mk   14.24      them, "This    is my blood of the     covenant,            which
L    22.17      yourselves;
L    22.20c,b        "This cup |is            the new covenant in my blood. |which
1 C  11.25           "This cup  is            the new covenant in my blood.  Do this,


M    26.28      is poured out for many for the forgiveness of sins.
Mk   14.24      is poured out for many.
L    22.15      is poured out for you   |And he said to them, "I have earnestly desired
1 C  11.25      as often as you drink it, in remembrance of me."


   L  22.16     to eat this passover with you before I suffer; for I tell you I shall
   L  22.16     not eat it until it is fulfilled in the kingdom of God."


M    26.29          I tell  you            I shall not drink again of this
Mk   14.25      Truly, I say to you,       I shall not drink again of the
L    22.18      for   I tell you that from now on I shall not drink     of the
1 C  11.26      For as often as you eat this bread and drink the cup, you proclaim
```

```
M    26.29   fruit of the vine until that day when I drink it new with you in my
Mk   14.25   fruit of the vine until that day when I drink it new         in the
L    22.18   fruit of the vine until                                          the
1 C  11.27   the Lord's death until he comes.  Whoever, therefore, eats the bread


M    26.29   Father's kingdom."
Mk   14.25             kingdom of God."
L    22.18             kingdom of God comes."
1 C  11.27   or drinks the cup of the Lord in an unworthy manner will be guilty of


1 C 11.28    profaning the body and blood of the Lord.  Let a man examine himself,
1 C 11.29    and so eat of the bread and drink of the cup.  For any one who eats
1 C 11.29    and drinks without discerning the body eats and drinks judgment upon
1 C 11.30    himself.  That is why many of you are weak and ill, and some have died.
1 C 11.31,32 But if we judged ourselves truly, we should not be judged.  But when
1 C 11.32    we are judged by the Lord, we are chastened so that we may not be con-
1 C 11.32    demned along with the world.
```

66. PETER'S DENIAL FORETOLD

Matthew 26.30-35

```
M    26.30   And when they had sung a hymn,          they went out
Mk   14.26   And when they had sung a hymn,          they went out
L    22.39   And       he  came out,              and went, as was his custom,
J    18.1              When Jesus had spoken these words, he  went forth with his


M    26.31           to    the Mount of Olives.  Then Jesus said to them,
Mk   14.27           to    the Mount of Olives.  And  Jesus said to them,
L    22.39           to    the Mount of Olives; and the disciples followed him.
J    18.1    disciples across the Kidron valley, where there was a garden, which he


M    26.31   "You will all fall away because of me this night; for it is written, 'I
Mk   14.27   "You will all fall away;                          for it is written, 'I
L    22.31   "Simon, Simon, behold, Satan demanded to have you, that he might sift
J    18.1     and his disciples entered.


M    26.31   will strike the shepherd, and the sheep of the flock will be scattered.'
Mk   14.27   will strike the shepherd, and the sheep         will be scattered.'
L    22.32   you like wheat, |but I have prayed for you that your faith may not fail;
   J 16.32   The hour is coming,    indeed it has come,   when you will be scattered,


   J 16.32   every man to his home, and will leave me alone; yet I am not alone,
   J 16.32   for the Father is with me.


M    26.32,33  But after I am raised up, I will go before you to Galilee."    Peter
Mk   14.28,29  But after I am raised up, I will go before you to Galilee."    Peter
L    22.33     and when you have turned again, strengthen your brethren."  And he
   J 13.37                                                                   Peter


M    26.33   declared to him,      "Though they all fall away because of you, I will
Mk   14.29   said      to him, "Even though they all fall away,                I will
L    22.33   said      to him, "Lord,                                          I am
   J 13.37   said      to him, "Lord, why cannot I follow you now?            I will
```

163

```
M    26.34    never fall away."                                          Jesus said to him,
Mk   14.30    not."                                              And    Jesus said to him,
L    22.34    ready to go with you to prison and to death."      He      said,
J    13.38    lay down my life for you."                                 Jesus answered, "Will you


M    26.34                                        "Truly,         I say to you, this very night,
Mk   14.30                                        "Truly,         I say to you, this very night,
L    22.34                                                       "I tell   you, Peter,
J    13.38    lay down your life for me? Truly, truly, I say to you,


M    26.34    before the cock              crows,                    you will           deny
Mk   14.30    before the cock              crows twice,             you will           deny
L    22.34             the cock will not crow  this day, until you three times deny that
J    13.38             the cock will not crow,            till you have            denied


M    26.35              me three times."     Peter said to him, "Even if I must die
Mk   14.31              me three times."  But he      said vehemently, "If I must die
L    22.34    you know me."
J    13.38              me three times.


M    26.35    with you, I will not deny you."  And so         said all the disciples.
Mk   14.31    with you, I will not deny you."  And they all said      the same.
```

67. GETHSEMANE

Matthew 26.36-46

```
L    22.39    And he came out, and went, as was his custom, to the Mount of Olives;
L    22.39    and the disciples followed him.


M    26.36    Then      Jesus                        went       with       them
Mk   14.32    And       they                         went
L    22.40a   And when he                            came
J    18.1              When Jesus had spoken these words, he went forth with his disciples


M    26.36    to a   place           called Gethsemane,           and   he said to
Mk   14.32    to a   place which was called Gethsemane;           and   he said to
L    22.40a   to the place
J    18.1     across the Kidron valley, where there was a garden, which he       and


M    26.37    his disciples, "Sit here, while I go yonder and pray."  And      taking
Mk   14.33    his disciples, "Sit here, while I            pray."  And he took
J    18.1     his disciples entered.


M    26.37    with him Peter and the two sons of Zebedee, he began to be
Mk   14.33    with him Peter and      James and John, and    began to be greatly


M    26.38    sorrowful  and troubled.  Then he said to them, "My soul is very
Mk   14.34    distressed and troubled.  And  he said to them, "My soul is very
J    12.27                                           "Now is my soul


M    26.39    sorrowful, even to death; remain here, and watch with me."  And
Mk   14.35    sorrowful, even to death; remain here, and watch."          And
L    22.41                                                                And he
J    12.27    troubled.
```

```
M   26.39   going                      a little farther   he fell on his face    and
Mk  14.35   going                      a little farther,  he fell on the ground  and
L   22.41   withdrew from them about a stone's throw, and knelt down             and


M   26.39   prayed,
Mk  14.36   prayed that, if it were possible, the hour might pass from him.  And he
L   22.41   prayed,
J   12.27                                                        And what shall I


M   26.39            "My    Father, if   it    be  possible,         let    this cup
Mk  14.36   said, "Abba, Father, all things are possible to thee; remove this cup
L   22.42            |"Father, if   thou   art willing,             remove this cup
J   6.38                                                                    For I
J   12.27   say?         'Father, save me from this hour'?


M   26.39   pass from me; nevertheless, not as   I     will, but as        thou
Mk  14.36        from me; yet           not what I     will, but what      thou
L   22.42        from me; nevertheless  not       my   will, but           thine,
J   6.38    have come down from heaven, not to do my own will, but the will of him
J   12.27                               No, for this purpose I have come to this hour.


M   26.40     wilt."  And                    he came to the disciples and
Mk  14.37     wilt."  And                    he came                    and
L   22.45   be done."  And when he rose from prayer,  he came to the disciples and
J   6.38    who sent me;


M   26.40   found them sleeping;       and he said to Peter, "So,
Mk  14.37   found them sleeping,       and he said to Peter, "Simon, are you
L   22.40b  found them sleeping for sorrow, |he said to them,


M   26.41          could you not watch with me one hour?  Watch and pray that you
Mk  14.38   asleep?  Could you not watch        one hour? |Watch and pray that you
L   22.40b                                                 "Pray that you


M   26.41   may not enter into temptation; the spirit indeed is willing, but the
Mk  14.38   may not enter into temptation; the spirit indeed is willing, but the
L   22.40b  may not enter into temptation."


M   26.42   flesh is weak."      Again, for the second time, he went away and prayed,
Mk  14.39   flesh is weak."  And again                       he went away and prayed,
L   22.44               And being in an agony               he           prayed


M   26.42   "My Father, if this cannot pass unless I drink it, thy  will be done."
Mk  14.39    saying the same words.
L   22.44   more earnestly; and his sweat became like great drops of blood falling


M   26.43   And again he came and found them sleeping, for their eyes were
Mk  14.40   And again he came and found them sleeping, for their eyes were very
L   22.44   down upon the ground.


M   26.44   heavy.  So, leaving them again, he went away and prayed for the third
Mk  14.40   heavy;  and they did not know what to answer him.


M   26.45   time, saying the same words.  Then he came to the disciples and     said
Mk  14.41                                 And  he came the third time,   and     said
L   22.46                                                               and he said
```

```
M   26.45    to them, "Are    you still sleeping and taking your rest? Behold,
Mk  14.41    to them, "Are    you still sleeping and taking your rest? It is enough;
L   22.46    to them, "Why do you         sleep?   Rise and pray that you may not


M   26.45    the hour is at hand, and the Son of man is betrayed into the hands of
Mk  14.41    the hour has   come;        the Son of man is betrayed into the hands of
L   22.46    enter into temptation."


M   26.46    sinners. Rise, let us be going; see, my betrayer is at hand."
Mk  14.42    sinners. Rise, let us be going; see, my betrayer is at hand."
J   14.31b            Rise, let us    go hence.
```

68. JESUS ARRESTED

Matthew 26.47-56

```
J   18.2    Now Judas, who betrayed him, also knew the place; for Jesus often met
J   18.2    there with his disciples.


M   26.47                          While he was still speaking,
Mk  14.43    And immediately, while he was still speaking,
L   22.47                          While he was still speaking, there came a crowd, and
J   18.3                           So


M   26.47                Judas                          came, one of the twelve, and
Mk  14.43                Judas                          came, one of the twelve, and
L   22.47    the man called Judas,                            one of the twelve, was
J   18.3                    Judas, procuring a band of soldiers and some officers from


M   26.47                          with him a great crowd with swords
Mk  14.43                          with him a         crowd with swords
L   22.47    leading them.
J   18.3     the chief priests and the Pharisees, went there with lanterns and torches


M   26.47    and clubs, from the chief priests            and the elders of the
Mk  14.43    and clubs, from the chief priests and the scribes and the elders.
J   18.4     and weapons.  Then Jesus, knowing all that was to befall him, came forward


M   26.48    people.  Now the betrayer had given them a sign, saying, "The one I shall
Mk  14.44             Now the betrayer had given them a sign, saying, "The one I shall
J   18.5     and said to them, "Whom do you seek?"  They answered him, "Jesus of


M   26.49    kiss is the man; seize him."                            And
Mk  14.45    kiss is the man; seize him and lead him away under guard."  And when
J   18.5     Nazareth."  Jesus said to them, "I am he."


M   26.49    he came         up to Jesus at once  and said, "Hail, Master!"  And he
Mk  14.45    he came, he went up to him   at once, and said,        "Master!"  And he
L   22.47    He drew near        to Jesus
J   18.5     Judas, who betrayed him, was standing with them.                    to


M   26.50    kissed him.   |Jesus said to him,  "Friend, why are you here?"  Then
Mk  14.46    kissed him.                                                      And
L   22.48    kiss    him; but Jesus said to him,  "Judas,  would you betray the Son
J   18.6                  When he    said to them, "I am he," they drew back and fell
```

M	26.50	they came up and laid hands on Jesus and seized him.
Mk	14.46	they laid hands on him and seized him.
L	22.49	of man with a kiss?" *And when those who were about him saw what would*
J	18.6	to the ground.

| L | 22.49 | *follow, they said, "Lord, shall we strike with the sword?"* |

M	26.51	And behold, one of those who were with Jesus stretched out his hand and
Mk	14.47	But one of those who stood by
L	22.50	And one of them
J	18.10	Then Simon Peter, having a sword,

M	26.51	drew his sword, and struck the slave of the high priest,
Mk	14.47	drew his sword, and struck the slave of the high priest
L	22.50	struck the slave of the high priest
J	18.10	drew it and struck the high priest's slave

M	26.52	and cut off his ear. Then Jesus said
Mk	14.47	and cut off his ear.
L	22.51	and cut off his right ear. But Jesus said,
J	18.11	and cut off his right ear. The slave's name was Malchus. Jesus said

M	26.52	to him, "Put your sword back into its place; for all who take the
L	22.51	"No more of this!" And he touched his ear and healed him.
J	18.11	to Peter, "Put your sword into its sheath; shall I not drink the

| M | 26.53 | sword will perish by the sword. Do you think that I cannot appeal to |
| J | 18.11 | cup which the Father has given me?" |

| M | 26.53 | my Father, and he will at once send me more than twelve legions of angels? |
| M | 26.54 | But how then should the scriptures be fulfilled, that it must be so?" |

M	26.55	At that hour Jesus said to the crowds,
Mk	14.48	And Jesus said to them,
L	22.52	Then Jesus said to the chief priests and officers of the temple
J	18.7	Again he asked them,

M	26.55	"Have you come out as against
Mk	14.48	"Have you come out as against
L	22.52	and elders, who had come out against him, "Have you come out as against
J	18.7	"Whom do you seek?" And they

M	26.55	a robber, with swords and clubs to capture me? Day after day I
Mk	14.49	a robber, with swords and clubs to capture me? Day after day I
L	22.53	a robber, with swords and clubs? When I was with you day after day
J	18.8	said, "Jesus of Nazareth." Jesus answered, "I told you that I am he;

M	26.55	sat in the temple teaching, and you did not seize me.
Mk	14.49	was with you in the temple teaching, and you did not seize me.
L	22.53	in the temple, you did not lay hands on me.
J	18.8	so, if you seek me, let these men go."

M	26.56	But all this has taken place, that the scriptures of the prophets might
Mk	14.49	But let the scriptures
L	22.53	But this is your hour, and the power of darkness."
J	18.9	This was to fulfil the word which he had spoken, "Of

```
M   26.56    be fulfilled."  Then all the disciples forsook him  and fled.
Mk  14.50    be fulfilled."  And          they all  forsook him, and fled.
J   18.9                those whom thou gavest me I lost not one."
```

69. BEFORE THE HIGH PRIEST

Matthew 26.57-68

```
M   26.57    Then    those who had
Mk  14.53    And     they
L   22.54    Then    they
J   18.12    So the band of soldiers and their captain and the officers of the Jews


M   26.57    seized Jesus                              led him
Mk  14.53                                              led Jesus
L   22.54    seized him    and                         led him away, bringing him
J   18.13    seized Jesus and bound him.  First they led him to Annas; for he was the
J   18.24                                               Annas then sent him


M   26.57               to Caiaphas     the high priest, where   the scribes
Mk  14.53                   to          the high priest; and all the chief priests
L   22.54              into            the high priest's house.
J   18.14    father-in-law of Caiaphas, who was high priest that year.  It was Caiaphas
J   18.24    bound       to Caiaphas    the high priest.


J   18.14    who had given counsel to the Jews that it was expedient that one man
J   18.14    should die for the people.


M   26.58    and the elders                 had  gathered.  But Peter      followed
Mk  14.54    and the elders and the scribes were assembled.  And Peter had followed
L   22.54                                                        Peter      followed
J   18.15                                                 Simon Peter      followed


M   26.58    him at a distance,
Mk  14.54    him at a distance,
L   22.55       at a distance;                            and when they had kindled
J   18.15    Jesus, and so did another disciple.  As this disciple was known to the


M   26.58               as far as  the courtyard of the high priest, and going
Mk  14.54               right into the courtyard of the high priest;
L   22.55    a fire in the middle of  the courtyard              and sat down
J   18.15    high priest, he entered the court      of the high priest  along with


M   26.58    inside      he   sat   with the guards  to see the end.
Mk  14.54            and he was sitting with the guards, and warming himself at
L   22.66    together,    Peter sat   among   them.  When day came, the assembly
J   18.16    Jesus, |while Peter  stood outside at the door.  So the other disciple,


J   18.16    who was known to the high priest, went out and spoke to the maid who kept
J   18.17    the door, and brought Peter in.  The maid who kept the door said to
J   18.17    Peter, "Are not you also one of this man's disciples?"  He said, "I am
J   18.18    not."  Now the servants and officers had made a charcoal fire, because
J   18.18    it was cold, and they were standing and warming themselves; Peter also
J   18.18    was with them, standing and warming himself.


M   26.59                                       Now the chief priests
Mk  14.55    the fire.                          Now the chief priests
L   22.66    of the elders of the people gathered together, both chief priests and
J   18.19                                         The high  priest then
```

```
M    26.59              and                    the whole council sought false testimony
Mk   14.55              and                    the whole council sought         testimony
L    22.66    scribes; and they led him away to their council,
J    18.20    questioned Jesus about his disciples and his teaching.  Jesus answered


M    26.60    against Jesus that they might put him to death, |but they found none,
Mk   14.55    against Jesus             to put him to death;  but they found none.
J    18.20    him, "I have spoken openly to the world; I have always taught in


M    26.60    though many       false witnesses came forward.
Mk   14.56    For   many bore false witness against him, and their witness did not
J    18.20    synagogues and in the temple, where all Jews come together; I have said


M    26.61        At last two  came forward |and
Mk   14.57    agree.  And some stood up     and bore false witness against him,
J    18.21    nothing secretly.  Why do you ask me? Ask those who have heard me,


M    26.61    said,   "This    fellow said, 'I am able to destroy the  temple of
Mk   14.58    saying, |"We heard him    say,  'I   will   destroy this temple that
J    2.19                      Jesus answered them,      "Destroy this temple,
J    18.21    what I said to them; they know what I said."


M    26.61    God,          and to build it in three days.'"
Mk   14.58    is made with hands, and           in three days I will build another,
J    2.19                         and           in three days I will raise it up."


    Mk 14.59    not made with hands.'"  Yet not even so did their testimony agree.


M    26.62    And the high priest stood up             and said,       "Have you no
Mk   14.60    And the high priest stood up in the midst, and asked Jesus, "Have you no


M    26.63    answer to make? What is it that these men testify against you?" |But
Mk   14.61    answer to make? What is it that these men testify against you?" |But


M    26.63    Jesus was silent.              And  the high priest  said to
Mk   14.61    he    was silent and made no answer. Again the high priest  asked
L    22.66                                   and            they   said,
L    22.70                                   And            they all said,


M    26.63    him, "I adjure you by the living God, tell us if you are the Christ, the
Mk   14.61    him,                                          "Are you the Christ, the
L    22.67                                               |"If you are the Christ, tell
L    22.70                                                "Are you            the


M    26.64    Son of      God."      Jesus said to him, "You have said so.
Mk   14.62    Son of the Blessed?"  And Jesus said,        "I am;
L    22.67    us."                  But he    said to them, "If I tell you, you will
L    22.70    Son of      God, then?" And he    said to them, "You    say that I am."


M    26.64                                                  But I tell you,
Mk   14.62                                                  and
L    22.68,69 not believe; and if I ask you, you will not answer.  But


M    26.64    hereafter you will see the Son of man         seated at the right hand
Mk   14.62              you will see the Son of man         seated at the right hand
L    22.69    from now on           the Son of man shall be seated at the right hand
```

```
M    26.65    of     Power, and coming on   the clouds of heaven."  Then the high priest
Mk   14.63    of     Power, and coming with the clouds of heaven."  And  the high priest
L    22.71    of the power  of God."                                And           they


M    26.65    tore his robes,    and said,   "He has uttered blasphemy.  Why do we
Mk   14.63    tore his garments, and said,                               "Why do we
L    22.71                       said,                                    "What


M    26.66    still need witnesses?            You have now heard his blasphemy.  |What
Mk   14.64    still need witnesses?           |You have     heard his blasphemy.   What
L    22.71    further    testimony do we need? We  have     heard it ourselves from his


M    26.66    is your judgment?"    They      answered, "He    deserves  death."
Mk   14.64    is your decision?" And they all condemned  him as deserving death.
L    22.71    own lips."
J    18.22                                               When he had said


M    26.67    Then    they          spat in his face,                        and
Mk   14.65    And     some began to spit on       him, and to cover his face, and to
L    22.63    Now the men who were holding Jesus mocked him                  and
J    18.22    this,   one of the officers standing by


M    26.68    struck him; and some slapped him,            |saying,      "Prophesy to
Mk   14.65    strike him,                                   saying to him, "Prophesy!"
L    22.64    beat   him; they also blindfolded him and asked    him, "Prophesy!
J    18.22    struck Jesus with his hand,                   saying,      "Is that how


M    26.68    us, you Christ! Who is it that struck you?"
Mk   14.65    And the guards received him with blows.
L    22.65                   Who is it that struck you?"  And they spoke many other
J    18.23    you answer the high priest?"  Jesus answered him, "If I have spoken


L    22.65    words against him, reviling him.
J    18.23    wrongly, bear witness to the wrong; but if I have spoken rightly, why


J    18.23    do you strike me?"
```

70. PETER'S DENIAL

Matthew 26.69-75

```
M    26.69     Now    Peter was sitting outside in the courtyard.
Mk   14.66     And as Peter was           below   in the courtyard,
L    22.55b           Peter     sat       among them.
J    18.16     while  Peter     stood     outside at the door.  So the other disciple,


J    18.16     who was known to the high priest, went out and spoke to the maid who
J    18.16     kept the door, and brought Peter in.


M    26.69     And     a    maid            came up to him,
Mk   14.67     one of the maids of the high priest came; and seeing Peter  warming
L    22.56     Then    a    maid,                           seeing him as he sat in
J    18.17             The maid who kept the door
```

```
M   26.69                               and said,              "You also were
Mk  14.67   himself,  she looked at him, and said,             "You also were
L   22.56   the light and gazing at him,    said,          "This man also was
J   18.17                               said to Peter, "Are not you also one


M   26.70   with Jesus the Galilean."      But he denied it before them all,
Mk  14.68   with         the Nazarene, Jesus."  But he denied it,
L   22.57   with him."                     But he denied it,
J   18.17   of   this man's disciples?"          He


M   26.71   saying,        "I do not   know                 what you mean."   And
Mk  14.68   saying,        "I   neither know nor understand what you mean."   And
L   22.58   saying, "Woman, I do not   know                 him."             And
J   18.25   said,          "I am not."                                        Now


M   26.71   when he went out to   the porch,     another maid    saw him, and she
Mk  14.69          he went out into the gateway. And the maid   saw him, and began
L   22.58   a little later                   some one else saw him  and
J   18.25   Simon Peter was standing and warming himself.               They


M   26.71           said to the bystanders, "This man    was with Jesus of
Mk  14.69   again to say  to the bystanders, "This man    is    one   of
L   22.58           said,                    "You also are      one   of
J   18.25           said to him,         "Are not you also      one   of


M   26.72   Nazareth."  And again he    denied it with an oath, "I do not know the
Mk  14.70   them."      But again he    denied it.
L   22.58   them."      But        Peter said,          "Man,  I am not."
J   18.26   his disciples?"       He    denied it and said,    "I am not."  |One of


M   26.73   man."  After a little while              the bystanders came up and
Mk  14.70      And after a little while        again the bystanders
L   22.59      And after an interval of about an hour still another insisted,
J   18.26   the servants of the high priest, a kinsman of the man whose ear Peter


M   26.73              said to Peter, "Certainly    you     are also one of
Mk  14.70              said to Peter, "Certainly    you     are       one of
L   22.59              saying,        "Certainly this man also was         with
J   18.26   had cut off, asked,       "Did I not see you in the garden     with


M   26.74   them, for your accent betrays you."  Then he began to invoke a curse on
Mk  14.71   them; for you  are a Galilean."      But  he began to invoke a curse on
L   22.60   him;  for he   is  a Galilean."      But  Peter
J   18.27   him?"                                Peter again


M   26.74   himself and to swear,     "I do not know the  man."
Mk  14.71   himself and to swear,     "I do not know this man of whom you      speak."
L   22.60              said, "Man, I do not know what              you are saying."
J   18.27              denied it;


M   26.74   And immediately                      the cock crowed.
Mk  14.72   And immediately                      the cock crowed a second
L   22.61   And immediately, while he was still speaking, the cock crowed.  And the
J   18.27   and at once                          the cock crowed.


M   26.75                             And Peter remembered the saying of
Mk  14.72   time.                     And Peter remembered
L   22.61   Lord turned and looked at Peter.  And Peter remembered the word  of the
```

171

M	26.75	Jesus,	"Before the cock crows,		you will
Mk	14.72	how Jesus had said to him,	"Before the cock crows twice,	you will
L	22.61	Lord, how he had said to him,	"Before the cock crows today, you will

M	26.75	deny me three times." And he went out and wept bitterly.
Mk	14.72	deny me three times." And he broke down and wept.
L	22.62	deny me three times." And he went out and wept bitterly.

71. JESUS BROUGHT BEFORE PILATE

Matthew 27.1-2

M	27.1	When	morning came,	all the chief priests	and	the
Mk	15.1	And as soon as it was	morning	the chief priests,	with	the
L	22.66a	When	day came,	the assembly	of	the

M	27.1	elders of the people
Mk	15.1	elders and scribes,
L	22.66a	elders of the people gathered together, both chief priests and scribes;

M	27.1		took counsel against Jesus to
Mk	15.1	and the whole council held a consultation;
L	22.66a	and they led him away to their council,

M	27.2	put him to death; and	they bound him	and led	him
Mk	15.1	and	they bound Jesus	and led	him
L	23.1	Then the whole company of them arose, and brought	him
J	18.28	Then	they	led	Jesus

M	27.2	away and delivered him	to	Pilate the governor.
Mk	15.1	away and delivered him	to	Pilate.
L	23.1		before	Pilate.
J	18.28	from the house of Caiaphas	to	the praetorium. *It was early. They them-*

J	18.28	*selves did not enter the praetorium, so that they might not be defiled,*
J	18.29	*but might eat the passover. So Pilate went out to them and said, "What*
J	18.30	*accusation do you bring against this man?" They answered him, "If this*
J	18.31	*man were not an evildoer, we would not have handed him over." Pilate*
J	18.31	*said to them, "Take him yourselves and judge him by your own law." The*
J	18.31	*Jews said to him, "It is not lawful for us to put any man to death."*
J	18.32	*This was to fulfil the word which Jesus had spoken to show by what*
J	18.32	*death he was to die.*

72. DEATH OF THE BETRAYER

Matthew 27.3-10

M	27.3	When Judas, his betrayer, saw that he was condemned, he repented and
M	27.3	brought back the thirty pieces of silver to the chief priests and the
M	27.4	elders, saying, "I have sinned in betraying innocent blood." They
M	27.5	said, "What is that to us? See to it yourself." And throwing down the

M	27.5	pieces of silver in the temple, he departed; and he went and hanged
A	1.18b	*and falling*

M	27.6	himself. But the chief priests, taking the pieces of silver, said, "It
A	1.18b	*headlong he burst open in the middle and all his bowels gushed out.*

M	27.6	is not lawful to put them into the treasury, since they are blood money."

M	27.7	So they took counsel, and bought with them the potter's field,
A	1.18a	*(Now this man* *bought* *a* *field*

A	1.19	*with the reward of his wickedness; And it became known to all the*

M	27.8	to bury strangers in. Therefore that field has been called
A	1.19	*inhabitants of Jerusalem, so that the* field *was* called *in their*

M	27.9	the Field of Blood to this day. Then was
A	1.19	*language Akeldama, that is,* Field of Blood.*)*

M	27.9	fulfilled what had been spoken by the prophet Jeremiah, saying, "And
M	27.9	they took the thirty pieces of silver, the price of him on whom a price
M	27.10	had been set by some of the sons of Israel, ⎸and they gave them for the
M	27.10	potter's field, as the Lord directed me."

73. THE TRIAL BEFORE PILATE

Matthew 27.11-26

M	27.11	Now Jesus stood before the governor;
J	18.33	Pilate entered the praetorium again and

M	27.11	and the governor asked him, "Are you the King of the
Mk	15.2	And Pilate asked him, "Are you the King of the
L	23.3	And Pilate asked him, "Are you the King of the
J	18.33	called Jesus, and said to him, "Are you the King of the

M	27.11	Jews?" Jesus said, "You have said so."
Mk	15.2	Jews?" And he answered him, "You have said so."
L	23.4	Jews?" And he answered him, "You have said so." *And Pilate said to*
J	18.34	Jews?" Jesus answered, "Do you say this

L	23.4	*the chief priests and the multitudes, "I find no crime in this man."*

M	27.12	But when he was accused by the chief priests and elders, he made no
Mk	15.3	And the chief priests accused him of many things.
L	23.5	But they were urgent, saying, "He stirs
J	18.35	of your own accord, or did others say it to you about me?" *Pilate*

L	23.5	*up the people, teaching throughout all Judea, from Galilee even to this*
L	23.5	*place."*
L	23.6,7	*When Pilate heard this, he asked whether the man was a Galilean. And*
L	23.7	*when he learned that he belonged to Herod's jurisdiction, he sent him*
L	23.8	*over to Herod, who was himself in Jerusalem at that time. When Herod*
L	23.8	*saw Jesus, he was very glad, for he had long desired to see him, because*
L	23.8	*he had heard about him, and he was hoping to see some sign done by him.*

J	18.35	*answered, "Am I a Jew? Your own nation and the chief priests have handed*
J	18.36	*you over to me; what have you done?" Jesus answered, "My kingship is not*
J	18.36	*of this world; if my kingship were of this world, my servants would fight,*

J	18.36	*that I might not be handed over to the Jews; but my kingship is not from*
J	18.37	*the world."* |*Pilate said to him, "So you are a king?" Jesus answered,*
J	18.37	*"You say that I am a king. For this I was born, and for this I have*
J	18.37	*come into the world, to bear witness to the truth. Every one who is of*
J	18.38	*the truth hears my voice." Pilate said to him, "What is truth?"*
J	18.38	*After he had said this, he went out to the Jews again, and told them,*
J	18.38	*"I find no crime in him."*

M	27.13	answer. Then Pilate said to him, "Do you not
Mk	15.4	And Pilate again asked him, "Have you no answer to make?
L	23.9	So he questioned him at some length;
J	19.8,9	When Pilate heard these words, he was the more afraid; he

M	27.13	hear how many things they testify against you?"
Mk	15.4	See how many charges they bring against you."
J	19.9	entered the praetorium again and said to Jesus, "Where are you from?"

M	27.14	But he gave him no answer, not even to a single charge; so
Mk	15.5	But Jesus made no further answer, so
L	23.10	but he made no answer. The chief priests and the scribes
J	19.9	But Jesus gave no answer.

M	27.14	that the governor wondered greatly.
Mk	15.5	that Pilate wondered.
L	23.11	stood by, vehemently accusing him. *And Herod with his soldiers treated*

L	23.11	*him with contempt and mocked him; then, arraying him in gorgeous apparel,*
L	23.12	*he sent him back to Pilate. And Herod and Pilate became friends with*
L	23.12	*each other that very day, for before this they had been at enmity with*
L	23.12	*each other.*
L	23.13	*Pilate then called together the chief priests and the rulers and the*
L	23.14	*people,* |*and said to them, "You brought me this man as one who was*
L	23.14	*perverting the people; and after examining him before you, behold, I*
L	23.15	*did not find this man guilty of any of your charges against him; neither*
L	23.15	*did Herod, for he sent him back to us. Behold, nothing deserving death*
L	23.16	*has been done by him; I will therefore chastise him and release him."*

J	19.10	*Pilate therefore said to him, "You will not speak to me? Do you not*
J	19.11	*know that I have power to release you, and power to crucify you?" Jesus*
J	19.11	*answered him, "You would have no power over me unless it had been given*
J	19.11	*you from above; therefore he who delivered me to you has the greater*
J	19.11	*sin."*
J	19.12	*Upon this Pilate sought to release him, but the Jews cried out, "If*
J	19.12	*you release this man, you are not Caesar's friend; every one who makes*
J	19.13	*himself a king sets himself against Caesar." when Pilate heard these*
J	19.13	*words, he brought Jesus out and sat down on the judgment seat at a*
J	19.14	*place called The Pavement, and in Hebrew, Gabbatha. Now it was the*
J	19.14	*day of Preparation of the Passover; it was about the sixth hour. He*
J	19.14	*said to the Jews, "Behold your King!"*

M	27.15	Now at the feast the governor was accustomed to release for
Mk	15.6	Now at the feast he used to release for
L	23.17	*Now* he *was obliged* to release
J	18.39a	But you have a custom that I should release

M	27.16	the crowd any one prisoner whom they wanted. And they had
Mk	15.7	them one prisoner for whom they asked. And among the
L	23.19	*one man* to *them at the festival.* |a man who
J	18.40b	one man for you at the Passover; Now

174

```
M   27.16    then      a notorious prisoner,
Mk  15.7     rebels           in    prison, who had committed murder    in the insur-
L   23.19    had been thrown into prison  for an insurrection started in the city,


M   27.17                                      called Barabbas.  So when they had gathered,
Mk  15.8     rection, there was a man called Barabbas.  And the crowd came up and
L   23.19    and for murder.
J   18.40b                                     Barabbas was a robber.


M   27.17                                                               Pilate
Mk  15.9     began to ask Pilate to do as he was wont to do for them.  And he


M   27.17    said  to them, "Whom do  you want me to release for you, Barabbas or
Mk  15.9     answered them,      "Do  you want me to release for you
J   18.39b                       will you have me     release for you


M   27.18    Jesus who is called Christ?"  For he knew    that it was out of envy
Mk  15.10        the King of the Jews?"  For he perceived that it was out of envy
J   18.39b       the King of the Jews?"


M   27.19    that         they     had delivered him up.  Besides, while he was
Mk  15.10    that the chief priests had delivered him up.


M   27.19    sitting on the judgment seat, his wife sent word to him, "Have nothing
M   27.19    to do with that righteous man, for I have suffered much over him today


M   27.20    in a dream."  Now  the chief priests and the elders persuaded  the
Mk  15.11                  But  the chief priests               stirred up the
L   23.18                  But           they all         cried out together,
J   19.6                   When the chief priests and the officers saw him,


M   27.20    people       to       ask   for    Barabbas and destroy Jesus.
Mk  15.11    crowd        to have him release for them Barabbas instead.
L   23.18    "Away with this man, and release to us   Barabbas"--


M   27.21    The governor again said   to them, "Which of the two do you want me to
L   23.20        Pilate         addressed them once more,            desiring to


M   27.21    release for you?"  And they said,                          "Barabbas."
L   23.20    release Jesus;                                             "Barabbas."
J   18.40a                      They cried out again, "Not this man, but Barabbas!"


M   27.22    Pilate     said to them, "Then what shall I do with Jesus    who
Mk  15.12    And Pilate again said to them, "Then what shall I do with the man whom


M   27.22    is called   Christ?"              They all said, "Let him be
Mk  15.13    you call the King of the Jews?"  And they    cried   out again,
L   23.21                        but they    shouted out,
J   19.6                             they    cried   out,


M   27.23    crucified."          And      he    said,
Mk  15.14    "Crucify him."       And      Pilate said to them,
L   23.22    "Crucify,    crucify him!"  A third time he    said to them,
J   19.6     "Crucify him, crucify him!"            Pilate said to them, "Take him


                                175
```

```
M    27.23                                    "Why,    what evil has he done?"
Mk   15.14                                    "Why,    what evil has he done?"
L    23.22                                    "Why,    what evil has he done?  I have found
J    19.7        yourselves and crucify him, for I find no crime in him."  The Jews


  L  23.22       in him no crime deserving death; I will therefore chastise him and
  J  19.7        answered him, "We have a law, and by that law he ought to die, because


M    27.23                      But they shouted all the more,              "Let him
Mk   15.14                      But they shouted all the more,
L    23.23       release him."  But they were urgent, demanding with loud cries that he
J    19.7        he has made himself the Son of God."
J    19.15                      They cried out,            "Away with him, away


M    27.23          be crucified."
Mk   15.14           "Crucify him."
L    23.23       should be crucified.  And their voices prevailed.
J    19.15       with him, crucify him!"  Pilate said to them, "Shall I crucify your King?"


  J  19.15       The chief priests answered, "We have no king but Caesar."


M    27.24       So when Pilate saw that he was gaining nothing, but rather that a riot
Mk   15.15       So      Pilate, wishing to satisfy the crowd,
L    23.24       So      Pilate gave sentence that their demand should be granted.


M    27.24       was beginning, he took water and washed his hands before the crowd,
M    27.25       saying, "I am innocent of this man's blood; see to it yourselves."  And
M    27.25       all the people answered, "His blood be on us and on our children!"


M    27.26       Then he released for them Barabbas,
Mk   15.15              released for them Barabbas;
L    23.25            He released      the man who had been thrown into prison for insur-
J    19.1        Then Pilate


M    27.26                               and having scourged Jesus,    delivered him
Mk   15.15                               and having scourged Jesus, he delivered him
L    23.25       rection and murder, whom they asked for; but Jesus  he delivered up
J    19.1                        took Jesus and        scourged him.
J    19.16                                               Then he handed       him


M    27.26                   to be crucified.
Mk   15.15                   to be crucified.
L    23.25                   to their    will.
J    19.16       over to them to be crucified.



                    74.  CRUCIFIXION AND DEATH

                       Matthew 27.27-56


M    27.27       Then the soldiers of the governor took Jesus    into
Mk   15.16       And   the soldiers              led   him away inside the palace (that
J    19.2a       And   the soldiers


M    27.27         the praetorium,  and they gathered     the whole battalion before
Mk   15.16       is, the praetorium); and they called together the whole battalion.
```

176

```
M   27.28     him.  And they stripped him and put          a scarlet  robe upon him,
Mk  15.17           And they                  clothed  him in a purple   cloak,
L   23.11b          then,                     arraying him in   gorgeous apparel,
J   19.2c           and                       arrayed  him in a purple    robe;
```

```
M   27.29     |and plaiting a crown of thorns  they put it on his head, and put a reed
Mk  15.17      and plaiting a crown of thorns  they put it on him.
J   19.2b      |plaited  a crown of thorns, and  put it on his head,
```

```
M   27.29     in his right hand.  And       kneeling  before          him
Mk  15.19c                        and they knelt down in homage    to him.
L   23.11a                        And Herod with his soldiers treated him with contempt
```

```
M   27.29         they        mocked    him, saying, "Hail, King of the Jews!"
Mk  15.18     And they began to salute   him,          "Hail, King of the Jews!"
L   23.11a    and           mocked    him;
J   19.3          they        came up to him, saying, "Hail, King of the Jews!"
```

```
M   27.30     And they spat upon him, and took the reed and      struck him on the
Mk  15.19b,a  and         spat upon him,                 And they struck          his
J   19.3                                                 and      struck him
```

```
M   27.31     head.                   And when they had mocked him, they stripped him
Mk  15.20     head with a     reed,  |And when they had mocked him, they stripped him
J   19.4           with their hands.  Pilate went out again, and said to them, "See,
```

```
J   19.4     I am bringing him out to you, that you may know that I find no crime in
J   19.5     him." So Jesus came out, wearing the crown of thorns and the purple
J   19.5     robe.  Pilate said to them, "Behold the man!"
```

```
M   27.31     of the        robe,  and put his own clothes on him,  and      led  him
Mk  15.20     of the purple cloak, and put his own clothes on him.  And they led  him
L   23.11c                                                          he      sent him
```

```
M   27.31     away to crucify him.
Mk  15.20     out  to crucify him.
L   23.11c    back to Pilate.
```

```
M   27.32         As they                    went out,  they came upon a man
Mk  15.21     And                                       they compelled a passer-by,
L   23.26     And as they led   him               away, they seized      one
J   19.17         So they took Jesus, and he went out,
```

```
M   27.32         of Cyrene, Simon by name;           this man they compelled
Mk  15.21     Simon of Cyrene, who was coming in from the country, the father of
L   23.26     Simon of Cyrene, who was coming in from the country, and laid
```

```
M   27.32                         to carry  his    cross.
Mk  15.21     Alexander and Rufus, to carry  his    cross.
L   23.27        on him the cross, to carry       it behind Jesus.  And there
J   19.17                        bearing his own cross,
```

```
L   23.27     followed him a great multitude of the people, and of women who bewailed
L   23.28     and lamented him.  But Jesus turning to them said, "Daughters of
```

177

```
L   23.28    Jerusalem, do not weep for me, but weep for yourselves and for your
L   23.29    children.  For behold, the days are coming when they will say, 'Blessed
L   23.29    are the barren, and the wombs that never bore, and the breasts that
L   23.30    never gave suck!'  Then they will begin to say to the mountains, 'Fall
L   23.31    on us'; and to the hills, 'Cover us.'  For if they do this when the wood
L   23.31    is green, what will happen when it is dry?"


M   27.33    And when they came        to a   place           called Golgotha (which
Mk  15.22    And        they brought him to the place           called Golgotha (which
L   23.33a   And when they came        to the place which is called
J   19.17                              to the place           called


M   27.34    means the place of a    skull),   |they offered him wine to drink,
Mk  15.23    means the place of a    skull).  And they offered him wine
L   23.33a                  The Skull,
J   19.17       the place of a    skull, which is called in Hebrew Golgotha.


M   27.35    mingled with gall;  but when he tasted it, he would not drink it.  And
Mk  15.24    mingled with myrrh;  but                  he did   not take  it.  And


M   27.35    when      they    had crucified him,
Mk  15.24              they        crucified him,
L   23.34    there     they        crucified him,  |And Jesus said, "Father, forgive
J   19.18a   There     they        crucified him,
J   19.23    When the soldiers had crucified Jesus


M   27.35                                              they          divided
Mk  15.24                                         and               divided
L   23.34    them; for they know not what they do."  And they cast lots to divide
J   19.23                                              they          took


M   27.35    his garments
Mk  15.24    his garments
L   23.34    his garments.
J   19.23    his garments and made four parts, one for each soldier; also his tunic.


J   19.24    But the tunic was without seam, woven from top to bottom;  |so they said


M   27.35                              among them by casting lots;
Mk  15.24                              among them,   casting lots for them, to decide
J   19.24    to one another, "Let us not tear it, but cast   lots for it    to see


Mk 15.24    what each should take.
J  19.24    whose it shall be."  This was to fulfil the scripture, "They parted my


J  19.24    garments among them, and for my clothing they cast lots."


M   27.36,37    then they sat down and kept watch over him there.   And over his head
Mk  15.25,26   And it was the third hour, when they crucified him.  And          the
L   23.38                                                            There was also an
J   19.25a,19  So the soldiers did this.  |Pilate also wrote a title and


M   27.37    they put    the charge against him, which read, "This is Jesus
Mk  15.26    inscription of the charge against him        read,
L   23.38    inscription                  over   him,           "This is
J   19.19        put         it on the cross;   it   read,          "Jesus of
```

178

M	27.37	the King of the Jews."
Mk	15.26	"The King of the Jews."
L	23.38	the King of the Jews."
J	19.20	Nazareth, the King of the Jews." *Many of the Jews read this title, for*

J	19.20	*the place where Jesus was crucified was near the city; and it was written*
J	19.21	*in Hebrew, in Latin, and in Greek. The chief priests of the Jews then*
J	19.21	*said to Pilate, "Do not write, 'The King of the Jews,' but, 'This man said,*
J	19.22	*I am King of the Jews.'" Pilate answered, "What I have written I have*
J	19.22	*written."*

M	27.38	Then two robbers were
Mk	15.27	And with him they
L	23.32	Two others also, who were criminals, were led away to be
L	23.33b	and the criminals,
J	19.18b	and with him two others,

M	27.39	crucified with him, one on the right and one on the left. And those
Mk	15.29	crucified two robbers, one on his right and one on his left. And those
L	23.32	put to death with him.
L	23.35	one on the right and one on the left. And the
J	19.18b	one on either side, and Jesus between them.

M	27.40	who passed by derided him, wagging their heads |and saying, "You
Mk	15.29	who passed by derided him, wagging their heads, and saying, "Aha! You
L	23.35	people stood by, watching;

M	27.40	who would destroy the temple and build it in three days, save yourself!
Mk	15.30	who would destroy the temple and build it in three days, |save yourself,

M	27.41	If you are the Son of God, come down from the cross." So also the chief
Mk	15.31	and come down from the cross!" So also the chief
L	23.35	but the

M	27.41	priests, with the scribes and elders, mocked him,
Mk	15.31	priests mocked him to one another with
L	23.35	rulers scoffed at him,

M	27.42	saying, |"He saved others; he cannot save himself.
Mk	15.31	the scribes, saying, "He saved others; he cannot save himself.
L	23.35	saying, "He saved others; let him save himself, if

M	27.42	He is the King of Israel; let him come down now from the cross,
Mk	15.32	Let the Christ, the King of Israel, come down now from the cross,
L	23.35	he is the Christ of God, his Chosen One!"

M	27.43	and we will believe in him. He trusts in God; let God deliver
Mk	15.32	that we may see and believe."

M	27.44	him now, if he desires him; for he said, 'I am the Son of God.'" And
L	23.39	One of

M	27.44	the robbers who were crucified with him also reviled him in the same
Mk	15.32	Those who were crucified with him also reviled him.
L	23.39	the criminals who were hanged railed at him, saying,

M	27.44	way.
L	23.40	*"Are you not the Christ? Save yourself and us!" But the other rebuked*

L	23.40	*him, saying, "Do you not fear God, since you are under the same sentence*
L	23.41	*of condemnation? And we indeed justly; for we are receiving the due*
L	23.42	*reward of our deeds; but this man has done nothing wrong." And he said,*
L	23.43	*"Jesus, remember me when you come into your kingdom." And he said to*
L	23.43	*him, "Truly, I say to you, today you will be with me in Paradise."*

M	27.45	Now from the sixth hour there was darkness over all
Mk	15.33	And when the sixth hour had come, there was darkness over
L	23.44	It was now about the sixth hour, and there was darkness over

M	27.46	the land until the ninth hour. And about the ninth hour Jesus
Mk	15.34	the whole land until the ninth hour. And at the ninth hour Jesus
L	23.45a	the whole land until the ninth hour, |while the sun's light failed;
J	19.28	After this Jesus,

M	27.46	cried with a loud voice, "Eli, Eli, lama sabachthani?" that is,
Mk	15.34	cried with a loud voice, "Eloi, Eloi, lama sabachthani?" which means,
J	19.28	knowing that all was now finished, said (to fulfil the scripture),

M	27.47	"My God, my God, why hast thou forsaken me?" And some of the bystanders
Mk	15.35	"My God, my God, why hast thou forsaken me?" And some of the bystanders
J	19.28	"I thirst."

M	27.48	hearing it said, "This man is calling Elijah." And one of them at
Mk	15.36	hearing it said, "Behold, he is calling Elijah." And one
L	23.36	The soldiers also
J	19.29	A bowl full of vinegar stood there; so they

M	27.48	once ran and took a sponge, filled it with vinegar, and put it on
Mk	15.36	ran and, filling a sponge full of vinegar, put it on
L	23.36	mocked him, coming up and offering him vinegar,
J	19.29	put a sponge full of the vinegar on

M	27.49	a reed, and gave it to him to drink. But the others said, "Wait,
Mk	15.36	a reed and gave it to him to drink, saying, "Wait,
L	23.37	|and saying, "If you
J	19.30	hyssop and held it to his mouth. When Jesus had received the

M	27.50	let us see whether Elijah will come to save him." And Jesus
Mk	15.37	let us see whether Elijah will come to take him down." And Jesus
L	23.46	are the King of the Jews, save yourself!" Then Jesus,
J	19.30	vinegar, he said, "It is finished"; and he

M	27.50	cried again with a loud voice
Mk	15.37	uttered a loud cry,
L	23.46	crying with a loud voice, said, "Father, into thy hands I commit
J	19.30	bowed his head

M	27.50	and yielded up his spirit.
Mk	15.37	and breathed his last.
L	23.46	my spirit!" And having said this he breathed his last.
J	19.30	and gave up his spirit.

M	27.51	And behold, the curtain of the temple was torn in two, from top to
Mk	15.38	And the curtain of the temple was torn in two, from top to
L	23.45b	and the curtain of the temple was torn in two.

M	27.52	bottom; and the earth shook, and the rocks were split; the tombs also
Mk	15.38	bottom.

M	27.52	were opened, and many bodies of the saints who had fallen asleep were
M	27.53	raised, and coming out of the tombs after his resurrection they went
M	27.53	into the holy city and appeared to many.

M	27.54	When the centurion and those who were with him, keeping watch over
Mk	15.39	And when the centurion, who stood facing him,
L	23.47	Now when the centurion

M	27.54	Jesus, saw the earthquake and what took place, they were filled
Mk	15.39	saw that he thus breathed his last,
L	23.47	saw what had taken place, he praised God,

M	27.54	with awe, and said, "Truly this was the Son of God!"
Mk	15.39	he said, "Truly this man was the Son of God!"
L	23.47	and said, "Certainly this man was innocent!"

M	27.55	There were also many women there, looking on from afar,
Mk	15.40a	There were also women looking on from afar,
L	23.49	And all his acquaintances and the women
J	19.25b	But standing by the cross of Jesus were his mother, and his mother's

M	27.55	who had followed Jesus from Galilee, ministering to
Mk	15.41	who, when he was in Galilee, followed him, and ministered to
L	23.49	who had followed him from Galilee stood at a distance and saw these
J	19.25b	sister, Mary the wife of Clopas,

M	27.56	him; among whom were Mary Magdalene, and Mary the mother of James
Mk	15.40b	among whom were Mary Magdalene, and Mary the mother of James the
Mk	15.41	him; and also many other women who came up with him to Jerusalem.
L	23.48	things. And all the multitudes who assembled to see the sight, when
J	19.26	and Mary Magdalene. When Jesus saw his mother, and

M	27.56	and Joseph, and the mother of the sons of Zebedee.
Mk	15.40b	younger and of Joses, and Salome,
L	23.48	they saw what had taken place, returned home beating their breasts.
J	19.26	*the disciple whom he loved standing near, he said to his mother, "Woman,*

J	19.27	*behold, your son!" Then he said to the disciple, "Behold, your mother!"*
J	19.27	*And from that hour the disciple took her to his own home.*

75. THE BURIAL

Matthew 27.57-61

M	27.57	When it was evening,
Mk	15.42	And when evening had come, since it was the day of
L	23.54	It was the day of
J	19.42a	So because of the Jewish day of

```
Mk 15.42    Preparation, that is, the day before the sabbath,
 L  23.50    Preparation,                       and the sabbath was beginning.   Now
 J  19.42a   Preparation,


M   27.57    there came a rich man                    from                      Arimathea,
Mk  15.43                    |Joseph               of                           Arimathea,
L   23.50    there was  a       man named Joseph from the Jewish town of Arimathea.
J   19.38    After this       Joseph               of                           Arimathea,


M   27.57    named Joseph,
Mk  15.43           a respected member of the council,
L   23.50    He was a            member of the council, a good and righteous man,


M   27.57                                                          who also was
Mk  15.43                                                          who was also
L   23.51    |who had not consented to their purpose and deed, and he      was
J   19.38                                                          who       was


M   27.58    a disciple of Jesus.                          He   went to Pilate
Mk  15.43    himself looking for the kingdom of God, took courage and went to Pilate,
L   23.52              looking for the kingdom of God.        This man went to Pilate
J   19.38    a disciple of Jesus, but secretly, for fear of the Jews, asked    Pilate


M   27.58    and asked for                    the body of Jesus.  Then Pilate
Mk  15.44    and asked for                    the body of Jesus.  And  Pilate wondered
L   23.52    and asked for                    the body of Jesus.
J   19.38             that he might take away the body of Jesus,  and  Pilate


Mk 15.44     if he were already dead; and summoning the centurion, he asked him whether
Mk 15.45     he was already dead.  And when he learned from the centurion that he was


M   27.59             ordered    it to be given to him.     And  Joseph
Mk  15.46    dead, he granted the body        to Joseph.    And  he bought a linen
L   23.53                                                   Then he
J   19.38             gave                him leave.  So    he came and took


 J  19.39    away his body.  Nicodemus also, who had at first come to him by night,
 J  19.39    came bringing a mixture of myrrh and aloes, about a hundred pounds'


M   27.59             took    the body,        and wrapped it  in a clean linen
Mk  15.46    shroud,   and taking   him down,     wrapped him in the       linen
L   23.53             took      it  down     and wrapped it  in a          linen
J   19.40    weight.  They took  the body of Jesus, and bound  it  in          linen


M   27.59    shroud,
Mk  15.46    shroud,
L   23.53    shroud,
J   19.41    cloths with the spices, as is the burial custom of the Jews.  Now in the


M   27.60                                              |and laid it   in    his
Mk  15.46                                              and laid him in    a
L   23.53                                              and laid him in    a
J   19.41    place where he was crucified there was a garden, and in the garden a
```

M	27.60	own new	tomb, which he had	hewn in	the rock; and he rolled a
Mk	15.46		tomb which	had been hewn out of	the rock; and he rolled a
L	23.53	rock-hewn tomb, where no one had ever yet been laid.			
J	19.42	new tomb where no one had ever		been laid. So because of the	

M	27.61	great stone to	the door of the tomb, and departed.	Mary Magdalene
M	15.47	stone against	the door of the tomb.	Mary Magdalene
L	23.55			The women who
J	19.42	Jewish day of Preparation, as the tomb was close at hand, they laid		

M	27.61	and the other Mary were there,			sitting opposite
Mk	15.47	and	Mary the mother of Joses	saw	where he
L	23.55	had come with him from Galilee followed, and saw the tomb, and how his body			
J	19.42	Jesus there.			

M	27.61	the sepulchre.
Mk	15.47	was laid.
L	23.56	was laid; *then they returned, and prepared spices and ointments.*

L	23.56	*On the sabbath they rested according to the commandment.*

76. THE GUARD POSTED AT THE TOMB

Matthew 27.62-66

M	27.62	Next day, that is, after the day of Preparation, the chief priests and
M	27.63	the Pharisees gathered before Pilate |and said, "Sir, we remember how
M	27.63	that impostor said, while he was still alive, 'After three days I will
M	27.64	rise again.' Therefore order the sepulchre to be made secure until the
M	27.64	third day, lest his disciples go and steal him away, and tell the people,
M	27.64	'He has risen from the dead,' and the last fraud will be worse than the
M	27.65	first." Pilate said to them, "You have a guard of soldiers; go, make it
M	27.66	as secure as you can." So they went and made the sepulchre secure by
M	27.66	sealing the stone and setting a guard.

77. THE EMPTY TOMB

Matthew 28.1-10

M	28.1	Now after the sabbath,	toward the dawn of the first day of
Mk	16.1a,2a	And when the sabbath was past, |And very early	on the first day of
L	24.1a	But	on the first day of
J	20.1a	Now	on the first day of

M	28.1	the week,	Mary Magdalene	and the
Mk	16.1b	the week	|Mary Magdalene	and
L	24.10a	the week, at early dawn, |Now it was Mary Magdalene and Joanna and		
J	20.1a	the week	Mary Magdalene	

M	28.1	other Mary		
Mk	16.1b	Mary the mother of James, and Salome,		bought
L	24.1c	Mary the mother of James and the other women with them	taking	

M	28.1		went to see the
Mk	16.2b	spices, so that they might go and anoint him. |they	went to the
L	24.1b	the spices which they had prepared. |they	went to the
J	20.1a		came to the

```
M    28.1    sepulchre.
Mk   16.3    tomb             when the sun had risen.  And they were saying to one another,
L    24.1b   tomb,
J    20.1a   tomb early, while it was still dark,


   Mk 16.3    "Who will roll away the stone for us from the door of the tomb?"


M    28.2    And behold, there was a great earthquake;
Mk   16.4a   And looking up,
L    24.2a   And
J    20.1a   and saw


   J 20.11    But Mary stood weeping outside the tomb, and as she wept she stooped


M    28.2                                                                    for an
Mk   16.5a                     And entering the tomb, they saw                 a
L    24.4a                     While they were perplexed about this, behold, two
J    20.12a  to look into the tomb; and                        she   saw       two


M    28.2           angel of the Lord descended from heaven and came and rolled back
Mk   16.4b   young man                                         |they saw that
L    24.2b       men                                           |they found
J    20.1b       angels                                                |that


M    28.2    the stone,
Mk   16.4b   the stone     was   rolled back---it was very large.
L    24.3    the stone           rolled away from the tomb, |but when they went in they
J    20.1b   the stone had been taken  away from the tomb.


M    28.3                         and sat    upon it.  His appearance was like
Mk   16.5b                        |sitting on the right side,
L    24.4b   did not find the body. |stood  by them
J    20.12c                        sitting where the body of Jesus had lain,


M    28.4    lightning, and his raiment      white as snow.  And for fear of him
Mk   16.5b                     dressed in a white  robe;     and     they were
L    24.5                             in dazzling apparel;   and as they were
J    20.12b,d                      |in  white, |one at the head and one at


M    28.5    the guards trembled and became like dead men.  But the angel said to
Mk   16.6a   amazed.                                        And    he    said to
L    24.5    frightened and bowed their faces to the ground,  the men  said to
J    20.13   the feet.                                        They   said to


M    28.5    the women, "Do not be afraid;
Mk   16.6a      them,  "Do not be amazed;
L    24.5       them,
J    20.13      her,   "Woman, why are you weeping?"  She said to them, "Because


   J 20.13    they have taken away my Lord, and I do not know where they have laid
   J 20.14    him."  Saying this, she turned round and saw Jesus standing, but she
   J 20.15    did not know that it was Jesus.  Jesus said to her, "Woman, why are you


M    28.5    for I know that   you seek Jesus           who was crucified.
Mk   16.6a                     you seek Jesus of Nazareth, who was crucified.
L    24.5             "Why  do you seek the living among the dead?
J    20.15   weeping?  Whom do you seek?"  Supposing him to be the gardener, she


                                     184
```

```
J   20.15    said to him, "Sir, if you have carried him away, tell me where you have
J   20.16    laid him, and I will take him away." Jesus said to her, "Mary." She
J   20.16    turned and said to him in Hebrew, "Rabboni!" (which means Teacher).


M   28.6     He is not here; for he has risen, as he said. Come, see the place where
Mk  16.6c,b,d |he is not here;  |He has risen,                    |see the place where
L   24.7                                             that the Son of man must be


M   28.7     he  lay.    |Then go quickly and tell his disciples        that he
Mk  16.7     they laid him. But  go,            tell his disciples and Peter  that
L   24.7     delivered into the hands of sinful men, and be crucified, and on the third


M   28.7     has risen from the dead,       and behold, he is  going before you to
Mk  16.7                                              he is  going before you to
L   24.6     day rise." Remember how he told you, while he was still            in


M   28.8     Galilee; there you will see him.  Lo, I have told you."  |So  they
Mk  16.8     Galilee; there you will see him,  as  he      told you."  And they
L   24.8,9   Galilee,                And they remembered his words,  |and
J   20.18                                                              Mary


M   28.8            departed quickly  from the tomb  with fear      and great joy,
Mk  16.8            went out and fled  from the tomb; for  trembling and astonishment
L   24.9            returning          from the tomb
J   20.18    Magdalene went


M   28.9            and ran to tell            his disciples.  And
Mk  16.8     had come upon them; and they  said nothing  to    any one, for they
L   24.9               they     told all this to the eleven    and to
J   20.18            and        said          to the disciples, "I have


M   28.9     behold, Jesus met them and said, "Hail!"  And they came up      and took
Mk  16.8     were afraid.
L   24.9     all the rest.
J   20.17                                        Jesus said to her, "Do not
J   20.18    seen the Lord";     and she told them that


M   28.10    hold of his feet and worshiped him.  Then Jesus  said
L   24.10    Now it was Mary Magdalene and Joanna and Mary the mother of James and
J   20.17    hold      me, for I have not yet ascended to the Father; but go to my
J   20.18                                    he had said these things


M   28.10    to them, "Do not be afraid; go and tell      my  brethren  to go to
L   24.11    the other women with them      who told this to the apostles; but these
J   20.17    brethren and say to them, I am ascending to my Father and your Father,
J   20.18    to her.


M   28.10    Galilee, and there they will see me."
L   24.11    words seemed to them an idle tale, and they did not believe them.
J   20.17    to my God and your God."
```

78. BRIBING THE GUARD

Matthew 28.11-15

```
M   28.11    While they were going, behold, some of the guard went into the city
```

185

M	28.12	and told the chief priests all that had taken place. And when they had
M	28.12	assembled with the elders and taken counsel, they gave a sum of money to
M	28.13	the soldiers |and said, "Tell people, 'His disciples came by night and
M	28.14	stole him away while we were asleep.' And if this comes to the governor's
M	28.15	ears, we will satisfy him and keep you out of trouble." So they took the
M	28.15	money and did as they were directed; and this story has been spread among
M	28.15	the Jews to this day.

79. GO AND MAKE DISCIPLES

Matthew 28.16-20

| M | 28.16 | Now the eleven disciples went to Galilee, to the mountain to which |
| M | 28.17 | Jesus had directed them. And when they saw him they worshiped him; |

L	24.44	*Then he said to them, "These are my words which I spoke to you, while*
L	24.44	*I was still with you, that everything written about me in the law of*
L	24.45	*Moses and the prophets and the psalms must be fulfilled." Then he*
L	24.45	*opened their minds to understand the scriptures,*

M	28.18	but some doubted. And Jesus came and said to them, "All authority in
Mk	16.15	*And he* *said to them,*
L	24.46	|and *said to them,* "Thus it is written,

| L | 24.46 | *that the Christ should suffer and on the third day rise from the dead,* |

M	28.19	heaven and on earth has been given to me. Go therefore and
Mk	16.15	*"Go into all the world and*
L	24.47	|and that repentance and forgiveness of sins should be

M	28.19	make disciples of all nations,
Mk	16.16	*preach the gospel to the whole creation. He who believes and is*
L	24.47	preached in his name to all nations, beginning from Jerusalem.

M	28.19	baptizing them in the name of the Father and of the Son and of the Holy
Mk	16.16	*baptized will be saved; but he who does not believe will be condemned.*
L	24.48	You are witnesses of these things.

| M | 28.20 | Spirit, |teaching them to observe all that I have commanded you; and |
| L | 24.49 | And |

| M | 28.20 | lo,   I am   with you always, to the close |
| L | 24.49 | behold, I send the promise of my Father upon you; but stay in the city, |

| M | 28.20 | of the age." |
| L | 24.49 | until you are clothed with power from on high." |

186

PART II

THE GOSPEL ACCORDING TO MARK

CONTENTS AND CROSS REFERENCES: MARK

			Parallel Sections in		
		Page	Matthew	Luke	John
1. The Prologue	1.1	193	1	11	42
2. John the Baptist	1.2–8	193	4	9	2
3. The Baptism of Jesus	1.9–11	196	5	10	
4. The Temptation	1.12–13	197	6	12	
5. Jesus Announces the Kingdom of God	1.14–15	198	7	13	
6. The First Disciples	1.16–20	199	8	17	3
7. Healings at Capernaum	1.21–34	201	13	15	
8. The Mission to Galilee	1.35–39	203	9	16	
9. A Leper Cleansed	1.40–45	204	11	18	
10. A Paralytic Healed	2.1–12	205	17	19	10
11. Levi the Tax Collector	2.13–17	207	18	20	
12. Questions of Fasting and Sabbath Observance	2.18–28	208	19,25	21	
13. A Withered Hand	3.1–6	210	26	22,65	
14. Healing by the Sea	3.7–12	212	9	24	
15. The Twelve	3.13–19	213	22a	23	
16. How Can Satan Cast Out Satan?	3.20–30	214	27	52	
17. His Mother and Brothers	3.31–35	216	29	33	
18. Parable of the Soils	4.1–20	217	30b	31	
19. The Lamp and the Measure	4.21–25	221	10c	32,54	
20. The Seed Growing Secretly	4.26–29	223	30c		
21. The Mustard Seed	4.30–32	223	30d	62	
22. Summary of Teaching by Parable	4.33–34	224	30e		
23. The Storm at Sea	4.35–41	224	15	34	
24. The Demon 'Legion'	5.1–20	225	16	35	
25. Jairus' Daughter and a Woman with a Hemorrhage	5.21–43	228	20	36	
26. Jesus Rejected by His Own	6.1–6a	231	31	14	17
27. Mission of the Twelve	6.6b–13	232	22c	37,47	
28. Death of John the Baptist	6.14–29	235	32	9	

			Page	Matthew	Luke	John
29. The Five Thousand Fed		6.30–44	236	33	38	12
30. Walking on the Water		6.45–52	240	34		13
31. Healing at Gennesaret		6.53–56	241	35		
32. A Question of Defilement		7.1–23	242	36	55	
33. The Syrophoenician Woman		7.24–30	244	37		
34. The Deaf Mute		7.31–37	245	38		
35. The Four Thousand Fed		8.1–10	246	39		
36. Pharisees Seek a Sign and a Warning		8.1–21	250	40,28	53	
37. The Blind Man of Bethsaida		8.22–26	252			20
38. Peter's Confession and the First Pre- diction of the Passion		8.27–33	252	41	39	15
39. Cost of Discipleship		8.34–9.1	254	42	40	26
40. The Transfiguration		9.2–13	255	43	41	
41. The Epileptic Boy		9.14–29	257	44	42	
42. Second Prediction of the Passion		9.30–32	259	45	43	
43. True Greatness and Causes of Sin		9.33–50	260	47b	44,73	
44. Marriage and Divorce		10.1–12	263	48	71	
45. Let the Children Come		10.13–16	265	49	78	
46. The Peril of Riches		10.17–31	265	50	79	
47. Third Prediction of the Passion		10.32–34	268	52	80	
48. The Sons of Zebedee		10.35–45	269	53	93	27
49. Blind Bartimaeus		10.46–52	271	54	81	
50. Jesus Enters Jerusalem		11.1–11	272	55	84	25
51. The Barren Fig Tree		11.12–14	274	57	60	
52. Cleansing the Temple		11.15–19	275	56	85	5
53. The Withered Fig Tree		11.20–26	276	57	60	
54. Controversies in Jerusalem		11.27–12.37	278			
a. The Authority of Jesus	11.27–33		278	58a	86a	
b. The Wicked Tenants	12.1–12		279	58c	86b	
c. Render to God	12.13–17		281	58e	86c	
d. The God of the Living	12.18–27		282	58f	86d	
e. The Great Commandment	12.28–34		284	58g	49	
f. The Son of David	12.35–37		285	58h	86e	17

		Page	Matthew	Luke	John
55. Beware of the Scribes	12.38-40	286	59	87	
56. The Widow's Penny	12.41-44	287		88	
57. The End of the Age	13.1-37	287			
a. Destruction of the Temple 13.1-2		287	61a	89a	
b. The Signs of the End 13.3-37		288	61b	89b	
58. The Plot to Kill Jesus	14.1-2	294	62	91	23
59. Jesus Anointed for Burial	14.3-9	296	63	29	24
60. Judas Plans the Betrayal	14.10-11	298	64	91	15
61. The Passover Meal	14.12-25	298	65	92	28,14
62. Peter's Denial Foretold	14.26-31	302	66	94	29
63. Gethsemane	14.32-42	303	67	96	
64. Jesus Arrested	14.43-52	305	68	97	35
65. Before the High Priest	14.53-65	307	69	98	36
66. Peter's Denial	14.66-72	309	70	98	36
67. Trial before Pilate	15.1-15	311	73	99,101	37
68. Crucifixion and Death	15.16-41	315	74	102	38
69. The Burial	15.42-47	320	75	103	39
70. The Empty Tomb	16.1-8	321	77	104	40
71. The Longer Ending of Mark	16.9-20	324	79		
72. The Shorter Ending of Mark		326			

1. THE PROLOGUE

Mark 1.1

Mk	1.1	The beginning of the gospel	of Jesus	Christ,
M	1.1	The book of the genealogy	of Jesus	Christ,
L	3.23		Jesus, when he began
J	20.31	*but these are written that you may believe that* Jesus *is the* Christ,

Mk	1.1		the Son
M	1.1		the son
L	3.23	his ministry, was about thirty years of age, being the son (as was
J	20.31		the Son

Mk	1.1	of God.
M	1.1	of David, the son of Abraham.
L	3.23	supposed) of Joseph, the son of Heli,
J	20.31	of God, *and that believing you may have life in his name.*

2. JOHN THE BAPTIST

Mark 1.2-8

Mk	1.2	As it	is written in
M	3.3a	For this is he who	was spoken of by
L	3.4a	As it	is written in the book of the words of
J	1.23b	as	
M	11.10	*This is he of whom it* is written,
L	7.27	*This is he of whom it* is written,

Mk	1.2	Isaiah the prophet,
M	3.3	the prophet Isaiah when he said,
L	3.4	Isaiah the prophet,
J	1.23a	the prophet Isaiah said." He said, "I am

Mk	1.2	"Behold, I send my messenger before thy face,
M	11.10	'Behold, I send my messenger before thy face,
L	7.27	'Behold, I send my messenger before thy face,

Mk	1.2	who shall prepare thy way;
M	11.10	who shall prepare thy way *before thee.'*
L	7.27	who shall prepare thy way *before thee.'*

Mk	1.3	the voice of one crying in the wilderness:
M	3.3	"The voice of one crying in the wilderness:
L	3.4	"The voice of one crying in the wilderness:
J	1.23a	the voice of one crying in the wilderness,

Mk	1.3	Prepare the way of the Lord,
M	3.3	Prepare the way of the Lord,
L	3.4	Prepare the way of the Lord,
J	1.23a	'Make straight the way of the Lord,'

Mk	1.3	make his paths straight--"
M	3.3	make his paths straight."
L	3.4	make his paths straight.

```
L    3.5         Every valley shall be filled,
L    3.5         and every mountain and hill shall be brought low,
L    3.5         and the crooked shall be made straight,
L    3.5         and the rough ways shall be made smooth;
L    3.6         and all flesh shall see the salvation of God."


M    3.1     In    those        days
L    3.1     In    the fifteenth year of the reign of Tiberius Caesar, Pontius Pilate
M    4.17    From that          time


L    3.1     being governor of Judea, and Herod being tetrarch of Galilee, and his
L    3.1     brother Philip tetrarch of the region of Ituraea and Trachonitis, and
L    3.2     Lysanias tetrarch of Abilene, |in the high-priesthood of Annas and


Mk   1.4                                                          John the baptizer
M    3.1                                        came             John the Baptist,
L    3.2     Caiaphas, the word of God came                   to John the son of
M    4.17                                                         Jesus began to
J    1.6,7       There was a man sent from God, whose name was John.  He came
J    1.19        And this is the testimony                       of John, when the


Mk   1.4     appeared  in the wilderness,
M    3.1     preaching in the wilderness                                    of
L    3.3     Zechariah in the wilderness; and he went into all the region about the
J    1.7         for testimony, to bear witness to the light, that all might believe
J    1.19        Jews sent priests and Levites from Jerusalem to ask him, "Who are you?"


Mk   1.4                 preaching a baptism of repentance for the forgiveness of sins.
M    3.2     Judea,                                      |"Repent,    for the kingdom of heaven is
L    3.3     Jordan,   preaching a baptism of repentance for the forgiveness of sins.
M    4.17              preach, saying,            "Repent,    for the kingdom of heaven is
J    1.7     through him.


M    3.2     at hand."
M    4.17    at hand."


Mk   1.5     And there went out to him          all the country of Judea, and all
M    3.5     Then        went out to him Jerusalem and all            Judea  and all
J    1.24    Now they had been sent from the Pharisees.


Mk   1.5     the people of      Jerusalem; and they were baptized by him in the river
M    3.6     the region about the Jordan, |and they were baptized by him in the river
J    1.25             They asked him, "Then why are  you baptizing, if you are neither


Mk   1.6     Jordan, confessing their sins.  Now John was  clothed with camel's hair,
M    3.4     Jordan, confessing their sins.* Now John wore a garment of camel's hair,
J    1.25    the Christ, nor Elijah, nor the prophet?"


Mk   1.6     and had a leather girdle around his waist, and     ate      locusts and
M    3.4     and      a leather girdle around his waist; and his food was locusts and


Mk   1.7     wild honey.  And he    preached,              saying,
M    3.4     wild honey.
L    3.16a                      John answered them all,
J    1.15                  (John bore witness to him, and cried, "This was he of whom
J    1.26a,c               John answered them, |but among you stands one whom you do
```

Mk	1.7	"After me comes he who is mightier than I, the thong
M	3.11b	but he who is coming after me is mightier than I,
L	3.16c	|but he who is mightier than I is coming, the thong
J	1.15	I said, 'He who comes after me ranks before me, for he was
J	1.27	not know, |even he who comes after me, the thong

Mk	1.8	of whose sandals I am not worthy to stoop down and untie. I have
M	3.11a	whose sandals I am not worthy to carry; |"I
L	3.16b	of whose sandals I am not worthy to untie; |"I
J	1.15	before me.'")
J	1.26b	of whose sandal I am not worthy to untie."|"I
J	1.33	I myself did not know him; but he who sent me to

Mk	1.8	baptized you with water;
M	3.11a	baptize you with water for repentance,
L	3.16b	baptize you with water;
J	1.26b	baptize with water;
J	1.33	baptize with water said to me, 'He on whom you see the Spirit

Mk	1.8	but he will baptize you with the Holy Spirit."
M	3.11c	he will baptize you with the Holy Spirit
L	3.16d	he will baptize you with the Holy Spirit
J	1.33	descend and remain, this is he who baptizes with the Holy Spirit.'

M	3.12	*and with fire. His winnowing fork is in his hand, and he will clear*
L	3.17	*and with fire. His winnowing fork is in his hand, to clear*

M	3.12	*his threshing floor and gather his wheat into the granary, but the*
L	3.17	*his threshing floor, and to gather the wheat into his granary, but the*

M	3.12	*chaff he will burn with unquenchable fire."*
L	3.17	*chaff he will burn with unquenchable fire."*

*M	3.7	*But when he saw many of the Pharisees and Sadducees coming for*
*L	3.7	*He said therefore to the multitudes that came out to be*

*M	3.7	*baptism, he said to them, "You brood of vipers! Who warned you to flee*
*L	3.7	*baptized by him, "You brood of vipers! Who warned you to flee*

*M	3.8,9	*from the wrath to come? Bear fruit that befits repentance, |and do not*
*L	3.8	*from the wrath to come? Bear fruits that befit repentance, and do not*

*M	3.9	*presume to say to yourselves, 'We have Abraham as our father'; for I tell*
*L	3.8	*begin to say to yourselves, 'We have Abraham as our father'; for I tell*

*M	3.9	*you, God is able from these stones to raise up children to Abraham.*
*L	3.8	*you, God is able from these stones to raise up children to Abraham.*

*M	3.10	*Even now the axe is laid to the root of the trees; every tree therefore*
*L	3.9	*Even now the axe is laid to the root of the trees; every tree therefore*

*M	3.10	*that does not bear good fruit is cut down and thrown into the fire.*
*L	3.9	*that does not bear good fruit is cut down and thrown into the fire."*

```
*L   3.10,11   And the multitudes asked him, "What then shall we do?" And he answered
*L   3.11      them, "He who has two coats, let him share with him who has none; and he
*L   3.12      who has food, let him do likewise." Tax collectors also came to be bap-
*L   3.13      tized, and said to him, "Teacher, what shall we do?" And he said to them,
*L   3.14      "Collect no more than is appointed you." Soldiers also asked him, "And
*L   3.14      we, what shall we do?" And he said to them, "Rob no one by violence or
*L   3.14      by false accusation, and be content with your wages."

*L   3.15         As the people were in expectation, and all men questioned in their
*L   3.15      hearts concerning John, whether perhaps he were the Christ,
```

3. THE BAPTISM OF JESUS

Mark 1.9-11

```
Mk   1.9      In those days Jesus came from Nazareth of Galilee
M    3.13     Then            Jesus came from            Galilee to the Jordan to
```

```
M    3.14     John, to be baptized by him. John would have prevented him, saying, "I
M    3.15     need to be baptized by you, and do you come to me?" But Jesus answered
M    3.15     him, "Let it be so now; for thus it is fitting for us to fulfil all
```

```
                                                          and                 was
Mk   1.9      righteousness." Then he consented. |And when Jesus              was
M    3.16
L    3.21     Now when all the people were baptized, and when Jesus also had been
J    1.33         I myself did not know him; but he who sent me to
```

```
Mk   1.10     baptized by John in the Jordan. And when he came up out of the water,
M    3.16     baptized,                        he went up immediately from
L    3.21     baptized                    and        was praying,
J    1.33     baptize with water said to me,
```

```
Mk   1.10     immediately  he saw the heavens      opened   and         the
M    3.16     the water, and behold, the heavens were opened    and he saw the
L    3.22                  the heaven was  opened, |and         the Holy
J    1.32              And John bore witness, "I    saw the
J    1.33              'He on whom  you see the
```

```
Mk   1.10     Spirit           descending upon him          like a dove;
M    3.16     Spirit of God descending                      like a dove,
L    3.22     Spirit           descended  upon him in bodily form, as a dove,
J    1.32     Spirit           descend                  as a dove from heaven,
J    1.33     Spirit           descend
M   17.5              He was still speaking, when lo, a bright cloud
Mk   9.7                                       And      a      cloud
L    9.34             As he        said this,        a      cloud came
```

```
M    3.16     and    alighting on him;
J    1.32     and it remained  on him.
J    1.33     and    remain,
J   12.28                                        Father, glorify thy name."
M   17.5             overshadowed them,
Mk   9.7             overshadowed them,
L    9.34     and    overshadowed them; and they were afraid as they entered the cloud.
```

196

```
Mk   1.11       and      a voice came from        heaven,              "Thou art my beloved
M    3.17       and lo, a voice      from          heaven, saying,      "This is  my beloved
L    3.22       and      a voice came from          heaven,              "Thou art my beloved
  J  1.33                                                                this is   he who
  J  1.34       And I have seen     and have borne witness that this is  the
  J  12.28      Then     a voice came from          heaven,             "I have glorified it,
  M  17.5       and      a voice      from    the cloud  said,          "This is  my beloved
  Mk 9.7        and      a voice came out of the cloud,                 "This is  my beloved
  L  9.35       And      a voice came out of the cloud, saying,         "This is  my
```

```
Mk   1.11       Son; with thee I am well pleased."
M    3.17       Son, with whom I am well pleased."
L    3.22       Son; with thee I am well pleased."
  J  1.33       baptizes with the Holy Spirit.'
  J  1.34       Son of God."
  J  12.28      and I will glorify it again."
  M  17.5       Son, with whom I am well pleased; listen to him."
  Mk 9.7        Son;                             listen to him."
  L  9.35       Son, my Chosen;                  listen to him!"
```

4. THE TEMPTATION

Mark 1.12-13

```
M    4.1        Then Jesus                                                              was
L    4.1        And Jesus, full of the Holy Spirit, returned from the Jordan, and was
```

```
Mk   1.12,13            The Spirit immediately drove him out into the wilderness.  And
M    4.1        led up by the Spirit                          into the wilderness
L    4.2        led    by the Spirit       |for forty days in   the wilderness,
```

```
Mk   1.13       he was in the wilderness forty days, tempted by      Satan;
M    4.2                                      to be tempted by the devil.  And he*
L    4.2                                            tempted by the devil.  And he*
```

```
Mk   1.13                                     and he was with the wild beasts; and
M    4.11       Then the devil                               left        him, and
L    4.13       And when the devil had ended every temptation, he departed from him until
  J  1.51       And he said to him, "Truly, truly, I say to you, you will see heaven
```

```
Mk   1.13              the angels        ministered to him.
M    4.11       behold,    angels came and ministered to him.
L    4.13       an opportune time.
  J  1.51       opened, and the angels of God ascending and descending upon the Son of
  J  1.51       man."
```

```
*M   4.2        fasted        forty days and forty nights, and afterward
*L   4.2        ate nothing in those days;          and when they were ended,
```

```
*M   4.3        he was hungry.  And the tempter came and said to him. "If you are the
*L   4.3        he was hungry.      The devil          said to him, "If you are the
```

```
*M   4.4        Son of God, command these stones to become loaves of bread."  But he
*L   4.4        Son of God, command this  stone  to become          bread."  And Jesus
```

```
*M   4.4        answered,     "It is written,
*L   4.4        answered him, "It is written,
```

197

*M	4.4	'Man shall not live by bread alone,
*L	4.4	'Man shall not live by bread alone.'"

*M	4.4	but by every word that proceeds from the mouth of God.'"

*M	4.5	Then the devil took him to the holy city, and set him on the pinnacle of
*L	4.9	And he took him to Jerusalem, and set him on the pinnacle of

*M	4.6	the temple, |and said to him, "If you are the Son of God, throw yourself
*L	4.9	the temple, and said to him, "If you are the Son of God, throw yourself

*M	4.6	down; for it is written,
*L	4.10	down from here; for it is written,

*M	4.6	'He will give his angels charge of you,'
*L	4.10	'He will give his angels charge of you, to guard you,'

*M	4.6	and
*L	4.11	|and

*M	4.6	'On their hands they will bear you up,
*L	4.11	'On their hands they will bear you up,

*M	4.6	lest you strike your foot against a stone.'"
*L	4.11	lest you strike your foot against a stone.'"

*M	4.7	Jesus said to him, "Again it is written, 'You shall not tempt the
*L	4.12	And Jesus answered him, "It is said, 'You shall not tempt the

*M	4.8	Lord your God.'" Again, the devil took him to a very high mountain, and
*L	4.5	Lord your God.'" And the devil took him up, and

*M	4.9	showed him all the kingdoms of the world and the glory of them; and he
*L	4.6	showed him all the kingdoms of the world in a moment of time, |and

*M	4.9	said to him, "All these I will give you,
*L	4.6	said to him, "To you I will give all this authority and their glory;

*M	4.9	if you
*L	4.7	for it has been delivered to me, and I give it to whom I will. If you,

*M	4.10	will fall down and worship me." Then Jesus
*L	4.8	then, will worship me, it shall all be yours." And Jesus

*M	4.10	said to him, "Begone, Satan! for it is written,
*L	4.8	answered him, "It is written,

*M	4.10	'You shall worship the Lord your God
*L	4.8	'You shall worship the Lord your God,

*M	4.10	and him only shall you serve.'"
*L	4.8	and him only shall you serve.'"

5. JESUS ANNOUNCES THE KINGDOM OF GOD

Mark 1.14-15

Mk	1.14	Now after
M	4.12	Now when he heard that
L	4.14	And
J	1.43a	The next day
M	14.3	For Herod
L	3.19	But Herod the tetrarch, who had been reproved by him for Herodias, his
J	4.43	After the two days

198

| L | 3.20 | *brother's wife, and for all the evil things that Herod had done,* |*added* |

Mk	1.14	John <u>was</u> <u>arrested,</u> <u>Jesus</u>
M	4.12	<u>John</u> had been <u>arrested,</u> he
L	4.14	<u>Jesus</u>
J	1.43a	<u>Jesus</u> decided
M	*14.3*	*had seized* <u>John</u> *and bound him and put him in*
L	*3.20*	*this to them all, that he shut up* <u>John</u> *in*
J	*4.3*	*he left Judea*
J	*4.43*	*he*

Mk	1.14	<u>came</u> <u>into Galilee,</u>
M	4.13	<u>withdrew</u> <u>into Galilee;</u> and leaving Nazareth
L	4.14	<u>returned</u> in the power of the Spirit <u>into Galilee,</u>
J	1.43a	to <u>go</u> to <u>Galilee.</u>
M	*14.3*	*prison, for the sake of Herodias, his brother* <u>*Philip*</u>*'s wife;*
L	*3.20*	*prison.*
J	*4.3*	*and departed again* to <u>Galilee.</u>
J	*4.43*	*departed* to <u>Galilee.</u>

M	*4.13*	*he went and dwelt in Capernaum by the sea, in the territory of Zebulun*
M	*4.14*	*and Naphtali,* |*that what was spoken by the prophet Isaiah might be*
M	*4.14*	*fulfilled:*
M	*4.15*	*"The land of Zebulun and the land of Naphtali,*
M	*4.15*	*toward the sea, across the Jordan,*
M	*4.15*	*Galilee of the Gentiles—*
M	*4.16*	*the people who sat in darkness*
M	*4.16*	*have seen a great light,*
M	*4.16*	*and for those who sat in the region*
M	*4.16*	*and shadow of death*
M	*4.16*	*light has dawned."*

Mk	1.14	<u>preaching the gospel of God,</u>
M	4.17	From that time Jesus began to <u>preach,</u>
L	4.14	and a report concerning him went out through all the surrounding
M	*3.1*	*In those days came John the Baptist,* <u>preaching</u> *in the wilderness*
M	*10.7*	*And* preach *as you go,*
L	*4.43*	*but* *he said to them, "I must* preach *the good news*

Mk	1.15		and saying, <u>"The time is fulfilled, and the kingdom of God</u> <u>is at</u>
M	4.17	<u>saying,</u> "Repent, <u>for the kingdom of</u> heaven <u>is at</u>
L	4.15	country. And he taught in their synagogues, being glorified by all.
M	*3.2*	*of Judea,* *"Repent,* <u>*for the kingdom of*</u> *heaven* <u>*is at*</u>
M	*10.7*	<u>*saying,*</u> '<u>The kingdom of</u> *heaven* <u>is at</u>
L	*4.43*	*of* <u>the kingdom of God</u> *to the*

Mk	1.15	<u>hand; repent, and believe in the gospel."</u>
M	4.17	<u>hand."</u>
M	*3.2*	<u>hand."</u>
M	*10.7*	<u>hand.</u>'
L	*4.43*	*other cities also; for I was sent for this purpose."*

6. THE FIRST DISCIPLES

Mark 1.16-20

Mk	1.16	<u>And</u>
M	4.18	<u>As</u> he
L	5.1	While the people pressed upon him to hear the word of God, he was

199

Mk	1.16	passing along by the Sea of Galilee,		he saw
M	4.18	walked by the Sea of Galilee,		he saw two brothers,
L	5.2	standing by the lake of Gennesaret. And he saw two boats by the		
J	1.41		He first found his brother	

Mk	1.16	Simon
M	4.18	Simon who is called
L	5.2	lake;
J	1.41	Simon, and said to him, "We have found the Messiah" (which means Christ).

J	1.42	He brought him to Jesus. Jesus looked at him, and said, "So you are
J	1.42	Simon the son of John? You shall be called Cephas" (which means

Mk	1.16	and Andrew
M	4.18	Peter and Andrew
L	5.2	but the fishermen
J	1.40	Peter). One of the two who heard John speak, and followed him, was Andrew,

Mk	1.16	the brother of Simon casting a net in the sea; for they
M	4.18	his brother, casting a net into the sea; for they
L	5.3	had gone out of them and were washing their nets. Getting into one of
J	1.40	Simon Peter's brother.

Mk	1.16	were fishermen.
M	4.18	were fishermen.
L	5.3	the boats, which was Simon's, he asked him to put out a little from the

L	5.4	land. And he sat down and taught the people from the boat. |And when he
L	5.4	had ceased speaking, he said to Simon, "Put out into the deep and let down
L	5.5	your nets for a catch." And Simon answered, "Master, we toiled all night
L	5.6	and took nothing! But at your word I will let down the nets." |And when
L	5.6	they had done this, they enclosed a great shoal of fish; and as their nets
L	5.7	were breaking, |they beckoned to their partners in the other boat to come
L	5.7	and help them. And they came and filled both the boats, so that they be-
L	5.8	gan to sink. But when Simon Peter saw it, he fell down at Jesus' knees,
L	5.9	saying, "Depart from me, for I am a sinful man, O Lord." For he was as-
L	5.9	tonished, and all that were with him, at the catch of fish which they had

Mk	1.17	And Jesus said to them, "Follow me and I will make you become
M	4.19	And he said to them, "Follow me, and I will make you
L	5.10b	taken; And Jesus said to Simon, "Do not be afraid; henceforth you will be

Mk	1.18	fishers of men." And immediately they left their nets and followed him.
M	4.20	fishers of men." Immediately they left their nets and followed him.
L	5.10b	catching men."

Mk	1.19	And going on a little farther, he saw James the
M	4.21	And going on from there he saw two other brothers, James the
L	5.10a	and so also were James and John,

Mk	1.19	son of Zebedee and John his brother, who were in their boat
M	4.21	son of Zebedee and John his brother, in the boat with Zebedee
L	5.10a	sons of Zebedee, who were partners with Simon.

Mk	1.20	mending the nets. And immediately he called them;
M	4.21	their father, mending their nets, and he called them.
L	5.11	And when they had brought their

Mk	1.20	<u>and</u>	<u>they left</u>		<u>their father Zebedee in the boat</u>
M	4.22	<u>Immediately</u>	<u>they left</u> the boat and	<u>their father,</u>
L	5.11	boats to land,	<u>they left</u> everything	

Mk	1.20	<u>with the hired servants,</u> <u>and followed him.</u>
M	4.22	<u>and followed him.</u>
L	5.11	<u>and followed him.</u>

7. HEALINGS AT CAPERNAUM

Mark 1.21-34

Mk	1.21	<u>And</u>		<u>they went</u>		<u>into Capernaum;</u>
M	4.13	<u>and</u> leaving Nazareth he		<u>went</u> and dwelt in	<u>Capernaum</u> by the sea, in
L	4.31	<u>And</u>	he	<u>went</u> down	to <u>Capernaum,</u> a city of
J	2.12	*After this*	*he*	*went down*	*to* <u>Capernaum,</u> *with his mother*

Mk	1.21		<u>and immediately</u>	<u>on the sabbath he entered the synagogue</u>
M	4.13	the territory of Zebulun and Naphtali,
L	4.31	Galilee. <u>And</u> he was teaching them <u>on the sabbath;</u>
J	2.12	*and his brothers and his disciples; and there they stayed for a few days.*

Mk	1.22	<u>and taught.</u> And			<u>they</u> <u>were</u>
M	7.28		<u>And</u> when Jesus finished these sayings, the crowds <u>were</u>
L	4.32		<u>and</u>		<u>they</u> <u>were</u>
J	7.46				*The officers*

Mk	1.22	<u>astonished at his teaching,</u>	<u>for he taught them as one who had authority,</u>
M	7.29	<u>astonished at his teaching,</u>	<u>for he taught them as one who had authority,</u>
L	4.32	<u>astonished at his teaching,</u>	<u>for his word</u> <u>was with authority.</u>
J	7.46	*answered, "No man ever spoke like this man!"*

Mk	1.23	<u>and not as the</u> <u>scribes.</u> <u>And immediately there was in their synagogue</u>
M	7.29	<u>and not as their</u> <u>scribes.</u>
L	4.33	<u>And</u> <u>in</u> the <u>synagogue</u>

Mk	1.24	<u>a man with</u>	<u>an unclean spirit;</u> <u>and he cried out,</u>
L	4.33	there was <u>a man</u> who had the spirit of <u>an unclean</u> demon; <u>and he cried out</u>
J	2.4	*And Jesus said*
J	6.68	*Simon Peter answered*

Mk	1.24	<u>"What have you to do with us,</u> <u>Jesus of Nazareth?</u>
L	4.34	with a loud voice, |"Ah! <u>What have you to do with us,</u> <u>Jesus of Nazareth?</u>
J	2.4	*to her,* *"O woman,* <u>what have you</u> to do with *me? My hour has not*
J	6.69	*him, "Lord, to whom shall we go? You have the words of eternal life; and*

Mk	1.24	<u>Have you come to destroy us?</u> <u>I know</u> <u>who</u> <u>you are,</u>
L	4.34	<u>Have you come to destroy us?</u> <u>I know</u> <u>who</u> <u>you are,</u>
J	2.4	*yet come."*
J	6.69	*we have believed, and* <u>have</u> <u>come to</u> <u>know,</u> *that* <u>you are</u>

Mk	1.25	<u>the Holy One of God."</u> <u>But Jesus rebuked him,</u> <u>saying,</u> <u>"Be silent, and</u>
L	4.35	<u>the Holy One of God."</u> <u>But Jesus rebuked him,</u> <u>saying,</u> <u>"Be silent, and</u>
J	6.69	<u>the Holy One of God."</u>

| Mk | 1.26 | <u>come out of him!"</u> <u>And</u> <u>the unclean spirit,</u> <u>convulsing him and crying</u> |
| L | 4.35 | <u>come out of him!"</u> <u>And</u> when <u>the</u> demon had thrown <u>him</u> down in the |

```
Mk   1.27    with a loud voice, came out of him.                      And they
L    4.36    midst,            he came out of him, having done him no harm.  And they


Mk   1.27    were all amazed, so that they questioned among themselves, saying, "What
L    4.36    were all amazed      and        said       to one another,        "What


Mk   1.27    is this? A new teaching!  With authority       he commands even the
L    4.36    is this         word? For with authority and power he commands      the


Mk   1.28    unclean spirits, and they obey him."  And at once his fame
L    4.37    unclean spirits, and they come out."  And           reports of him


Mk   1.28    spread everywhere throughout all the surrounding region of Galilee.
L    4.37    went out into every place in     the surrounding region.


Mk   1.29    And immediately he              left the synagogue, and entered the house
M    8.14    And when      Jesus                          entered    Peter's
L    4.38    And           he arose and left the synagogue, and entered    Simon's


Mk   1.30    of Simon and Andrew, with James and John.  Now Simon's mother-in-law
M    8.14        house,                         he saw his      mother-in-law
L    4.38        house.                          Now Simon's mother-in-law


Mk   1.30    lay   sick with a     fever, and immediately they told    him of  her.
M    8.14    lying sick with a     fever;
L    4.38    was   ill  with a high fever, and           they besought him for her.


Mk   1.31    And he came and took   her by the hand and lifted her up,    and the
M    8.15        he           touched her        hand,                    and the
L    4.39    And he stood     over    her              and rebuked the fever, and


Mk   1.31    fever left her; and         she          served them.
M    8.15    fever left her, and         she rose and served him.
L    4.39    it    left her; and immediately she rose and served them.


Mk   1.32    That evening, at sundown,              they
M    8.16a   That evening                           they
L    4.40    Now      when the sun was setting, all those who had any that were sick
  M  4.24    So his fame spread throughout all Syria, and they


Mk   1.32                           brought    to him all  who were sick         or
M    8.16a                          brought    to him many who were
L    4.40    with various diseases brought them to him;
  M  4.24                           brought    him all  the        sick, those


Mk   1.33    possessed with                       demons.  And the whole city
M    8.16a   possessed with                       demons;
L    4.40                                                   and he
  M  4.24    afflicted with various diseases and pains, demoniacs, epileptics, and


Mk   1.34    was gathered together about the door.  And he       healed many
M    8.16c                                          and         healed all
L    4.40    laid his hands on every one of them    and         healed them.
  M  4.24    paralytics,                             and he      healed them.
  M  12.15b            And many followed him,        and he      healed them all,
  Mk 3.10                                            for he had healed many, so that
```

202

Mk	1.34	who were sick with various diseases,	and	cast out
M	8.16b	who were sick.	and he	cast out
L	4.41		And	
Mk	*3.11*	*all who had diseases pressed upon him to touch him.*	*And whenever*	

Mk	1.34	many demons;		
M	8.16b	the spirits with a word,		
L	4.41	demons also came out of many,	crying,	
Mk	*3.11*	*the unclean spirits beheld him, they fell down before him and cried out,*		

Mk	1.34		and he	would
L	4.41	"You are the Son of God!" But he rebuked them,	and	would
M	*12.16*		and	ordered
Mk	*3.12*	*"You are the Son of God."*	And he strictly ordered	

Mk	1.34	not permit the demons to speak, because they knew	him.	
L	4.41	not allow them to speak, because they knew	that he was the	
M	*12.16*	*them not to make him known.*		
Mk	*3.12*	*them not to make him known.*		

L	*4.41*	*Christ.*

8. THE MISSION TO GALILEE

Mark 1.35-39

Mk	1.35	And in the morning, a great while before day, he rose	and went out	
L	4.42	And when it was day he departed	and went	
L	*5.16*	*But he*	*withdrew*	

Mk	1.36	to a lonely place, and there he prayed.	And Simon and those who were	
L	4.42	into a lonely place.	And the people	
L	*5.16*	*to the wilderness and prayed.*		
J	*6.24*		*So when the people saw*	

Mk	1.37	with him pursued him,	and they found him and said	
L	4.42	sought him	and came to him, and would	
J	*6.24*	*that Jesus was not there, nor his disciples, they themselves got into*		

Mk	1.38	to him, "Every one is searching for you."	And he said to	
L	4.43	have kept him from leaving them;	but he said to	
J	*6.24*	*the boats and went to Capernaum, seeking Jesus.*		

Mk	1.38	them, "Let us go on to the next towns, that I may preach
L	4.43	them, "I must preach the good news

Mk	1.38	there also; for that is why I	
L	4.43	of the kingdom of God to the other cities also; for I was	

Mk	1.39	came out."	And he	went	throughout all Galilee,
M	4.23		And he	went	about all Galilee,
L	4.44	sent for this purpose."	And he	was	
M	*9.35*		*And Jesus*	*went*	*about all the cities*
Mk	*6.6b*		*And he*	*went*	*about among the*
L	*8.1a*	*Soon afterward he*		*went on*	*through cities*

Mk	1.39	preaching in their synagogues
M	4.23	teaching in their synagogues and preaching the gospel
L	4.44	preaching in the synagogues of Judea.
M	*9.35*	*and villages, teaching in their synagogues and preaching the gospel*
Mk	*6.6b*	*villages teaching.*
L	*8.1a*	*and villages, preaching and bringing the good news*

Mk	1.39	and casting out demons.
M	4.23	of the kingdom and healing every disease and every infirmity among the
M	*9.35*	*of the kingdom, and healing every disease and every infirmity.*
L	*8.1a*	*of the kingdom of God.*

M	4.23	people.

9. A LEPER CLEANSED

Mark 1.40-45

M	*8.1*	*When he came down from the mountain, great crowds followed him;*

Mk	1.40	And a leper came to
M	8.2	and behold, a leper came to
L	5.12	While he was in one of the cities, there came a man full of
L	*17.12*	*And as he entered a village, he was met by ten lepers, who*

Mk	1.40	him beseeching him,
M	8.2	him
L	5.12	leprosy; and when he saw Jesus, he fell on his face and besought him,
L	*17.13*	*stood at a distance |and lifted up their*

Mk	1.40	and kneeling said to him, "If you will, you can make me clean."
M	8.2	and knelt before him, saying, "Lord, if you will, you can make me clean."
L	5.12	"Lord, if you will, you can make me clean."
L	*17.13*	*voices and said, "Jesus, Master, have mercy on us."*

Mk	1.41	Moved with pity, he stretched out his hand and touched him, and said to
M	8.3	And he stretched out his hand and touched him, saying,
L	5.13	And he stretched out his hand, and touched him, saying,

Mk	1.42	him, "I will; be clean." And immediately the leprosy left him, and he was
M	8.3	"I will; be clean." And immediately his leprosy was cleansed.
L	5.13	"I will; be clean." And immediately the leprosy left him.
L	*17.14b*	*And as they went they were cleansed.*

Mk	1.43,44	made clean. And he sternly charged him, and sent him away at once, |and
M	8.4	And
L	5.14	And he charged him
L	*17.14a*	*When he saw them*

Mk	1.44	said to him, "See that you say nothing to any one; but go, show
M	8.4	Jesus said to him, "See that you say nothing to any one; but go, show
L	5.14	to tell no one; but "go and show
L	*17.14a*	*he said to them, "Go and show*

Mk	1.44	<u>yourself</u> <u>to the priest, and</u> <u>offer</u> <u>for your cleansing what</u>
M	8.4	<u>yourself</u> <u>to the priest, and</u> <u>offer</u> the gift that
L	5.14	<u>yourself</u> <u>to the priest, and</u> make an offering <u>for your cleansing,</u> as
L	17.14a	yourselves <u>to the</u> priests."

Mk	1.45	<u>Moses commanded, for a proof to the people.</u>" <u>But he went out and began</u>
M	8.4	<u>Moses commanded, for a proof to the people.</u>"
L	5.15a	<u>Moses commanded, for a proof to the people.</u>" <u>But</u> so much the more the

Mk	1.45	<u>to talk freely about it, and to spread the news,</u> so that Jesus could no
L	5.15a	report went abroad concerning him;

Mk	1.45	<u>longer openly enter a town, but</u> was out in the country;
L	5.16	<u>But</u> he withdrew to the wilderness and prayed.

Mk	1.45	<u>and</u> <u>people</u> <u>came</u> <u>to him from every</u> quarter.
L	5.15b	|<u>and</u> great multitudes gathered <u>to</u> hear and to be healed of their

L	5.15b	*infirmities.*

10. A PARALYTIC HEALED

Mark 2.1-12

Mk	2.1	And <u>when he</u> <u>returned</u>
M	9.1	<u>And getting into a boat</u> <u>he</u> crossed over and
J	5.1	After this there was a feast of the Jews, and Jesus went up

Mk	2.1	<u>to</u> Capernaum after some days, <u>it was reported that he was at</u>
M	9.1	came <u>to</u> his own city.
L	5.17	On one of those <u>days,</u> as he was teaching,
J	5.2	<u>to</u> Jerusalem. Now there is in Jerusalem by the Sheep Gate a

Mk	2.2	<u>home. And many</u> <u>were</u> <u>gathered together,</u>
L	5.17	there <u>were</u> Pharisees and teachers of the law sitting by, who
J	5.2	pool, in Hebrew called Bethzatha, which has five porticoes.

Mk	2.2	<u>so that there was no longer room for them, not even about the door; and</u>
L	5.17	had come from every village of Galilee and Judea and from Jerusalem; and

Mk	2.3	<u>he was preaching the word to them.</u> And they came,
M	9.2	And behold, <u>they</u>
L	5.18	the power of the Lord was with him to heal. And behold, men were
J	5.3	In these lay a multitude

Mk	2.3	<u>bringing to him</u> <u>a</u> <u>paralytic</u> carried by four men.
M	9.2	brought <u>to him</u> <u>a</u> <u>paralytic,</u> lying on his bed;
L	5.18	<u>bringing</u> on a bed <u>a</u> man who was paralyzed, and they sought to bring him
J	5.5	of invalids, blind, lame, paralyzed. One man was there, who had

Mk	2.4	<u>And when they could not get near him because</u>
L	5.19	in and lay him before Jesus; but finding no way to bring him in, <u>because</u>
L	5.5	been ill for thirty-eight years.

205

Mk	2.4	of the crowd, they removed the roof above him; and when they had made
L	5.19	of the crowd, they went up on the roof and

Mk	2.4	an opening, they let down the pallet on which the paralytic lay.
L	5.19	let him down with his bed through the tiles into the midst

Mk	2.5	And when Jesus saw their faith,
M	9.2	and when Jesus saw their faith
L	5.20	before Jesus. And when he saw their faith
J	5.6	When Jesus saw him and knew that he had been lying there

Mk	2.5	he said to the paralytic, "My son, your sins are
M	9.2	he said to the paralytic, "Take heart, my son; your sins are
L	5.20	he said, "Man, your sins are
J	5.6	a long time, he said to him, "Do you want to be

Mk	2.6	forgiven." Now some of the scribes were sitting there,
M	9.3	forgiven." And behold, some of the scribes
L	5.21	forgiven you." And the scribes and the Pharisees began to
J	5.7	healed?" *The sick man answered him, "Sir, I have no man to put me into th*
J	10.33	*The Jews*

Mk	2.7	questioning in their hearts, |"Why does this man speak thus? It is
M	9.3	said to themselves, "This man is
L	5.21	question, saying, "Who is this that speaks
J	5.7	*pool when the water is troubled, and while I am going another steps down*
J	10.33	*answered him, "It is not for a good work that we stone you but*

Mk	2.8	blasphemy! Who can forgive sins but God alone?" And immediately
M	9.4	blaspheming." But
L	5.22	blasphemies? Who can forgive sins but God only?" When
J	5.7	*before me."*
J	2.24	*but*
J	10.33	*for blasphemy; because you, being a man, make yourself God."*

Mk	2.8	Jesus, perceiving in his spirit that they thus questioned within themselv
M	9.4	Jesus, knowing their thoughts,
L	5.22	Jesus perceived their questionings,
J	2.25	Jesus *did not trust himself to them, |because he knew all men and needed*

Mk	2.9	said to them, "Why do you question thus in your hearts? Which is
M	9.5	said, "Why do you think evil in your hearts? For which is
L	5.23	answered them, "Why do you question in your hearts? Which is
J	2.25	*no one to bear witness of man; for he himself knew what was in man.*

Mk	2.9	easier, to say to the paralytic, 'Your sins are forgiven,' or to say
M	9.5	easier, to say, 'Your sins are forgiven,' or to say
L	5.23	easier, to say, 'Your sins are forgiven you,' or to say

Mk	2.10	'Rise, take up your pallet and walk'? But that you may know that the So
M	9.6	'Rise and walk'? But that you may know that the So
L	5.24	'Rise and walk'? But that you may know that the So

Mk	2.10	of man has authority on earth to forgive sins"--he said to the
M	9.6	of man has authority on earth to forgive sins"--he then said to the
L	5.24	of man has authority on earth to forgive sins"--he said to the man
J	5.8	Jesus said to

Mk	2.11		paralytic--|"I say to you, rise, take up your pallet and go
M	9.6		paralytic-- "Rise, take up your bed and go
L	5.24	who was	paralyzed-- "I say to you, rise, take up your bed and go
J	5.8		him, "Rise, take up your pallet, and walk."

Mk	2.12	home." And he rose, and immediately took up the
M	9.7	home." And he rose
L	5.25	home." And immediately he rose before them, and took up that
J	5.9	And at once the man was healed, and he took up his

Mk	2.12	pallet and went out before them all; so that
M	9.8	and went home. When the crowds saw it,
L	5.26	on which he lay, and went home, glorifying God. And
J	5.9	pallet and walked.

Mk	2.12	they were all amazed and glorified God,
M	9.8	they were afraid, and they glorified God,
L	5.26	amazement seized them all, and they glorified God and were

Mk	2.12	saying, "We never saw anything like this!"
M	9.8	who had given such authority to men.
L	5.26	filled with awe, saying, "We have seen strange things today."

11. LEVI THE TAX COLLECTOR

Mark 2.13-17

Mk	2.13	He went out again beside the sea; and all the crowd gathered
L	5.27	After this he went out,

Mk	2.14	about him, and he taught them. And as he passed on, he saw
M	9.9	As Jesus passed on from there, he saw
L	5.27	and saw

Mk	2.14	Levi the son of Alphaeus sitting at the tax office,
M	9.9	a man called Matthew sitting at the tax office;
L	5.27	a tax collector, named Levi, sitting at the tax office;

Mk	2.14	and he said to him, "Follow me." And he rose and
M	9.9	and he said to him, "Follow me." And he rose and
L	5.28	and he said to him, "Follow me." And he left everything, and rose and

Mk	2.14	followed him.
M	9.9	followed him.
L	5.28	followed him.

Mk	2.15	And as he sat at table in his house,
M	9.10	And as he sat at table in the house, behold,
L	5.29	And Levi made him a great feast in his house; and there was a large

Mk	2.15	many tax collectors and sinners were sitting with
M	9.10	many tax collectors and sinners came and sat down with
L	5.29	company of tax collectors and others sitting at table with
L	15.1	Now the tax collectors and sinners were all drawing near to hear

M	2.16	Jesus and his disciples; for there were many who followed him. And the
M	9.11	Jesus and his disciples. And when
L	5.30	them. And
L	*15.2*	*him.* And
L	*19.7*	And *when*

Mk	2.16	scribes of the Pharisees, when they saw that he was eating with sinners
M	9.11	the Pharisees saw this,
L	5.30	the Pharisees and their scribes
L	*15.2*	the Pharisees *and the* scribes
L	*19.7*	*they* saw *it*

Mk	2.16	and tax collectors, said to his disciples, "Why does
M	9.11	they said to his disciples, "Why does your
L	5.30	murmured against his disciples, saying, "Why do
L	*15.2*	*murmured,* saying, *"This*
L	*19.7*	*they all murmured,* "He has gone in

Mk	2.17	he eat with tax collectors and sinners?" And when
M	9.12	teacher eat with tax collectors and sinners?" But when
L	5.31	you eat and drink with tax collectors and sinners?" And
L	*15.2*	*man receives* sinners *and eats with*
L	*19.7*	*to be the guest of a man who is a sinner."*

Mk	2.17	Jesus heard it, he said to them, "Those who are well have no need of
M	9.12	he heard it, he said, "Those who are well have no need of
L	5.31	Jesus answered them, "Those who are well have no need of
L	*15.2*	them."

Mk	2.17	a physician, but those who are sick;
M	9.13	a physician, but those who are sick. *Go and learn what this means, 'I*
L	5.31	a physician, but those who are sick;

Mk	2.17	I came not to call the
M	9.13	*desire mercy, and not sacrifice.' For* I came not to call the
L	5.32	I have not come to call the

Mk	2.17	righteous, but sinners."
M	9.13	righteous, but sinners."
L	5.32	righteous, but sinners to repentance."

12. QUESTIONS OF FASTING AND SABBATH OBSERVANCE

Mark 2.18-28

Mk	2.18	Now John's disciples and the Pharisees were fasting; and people
M	9.14	Then the disciples of John
L	5.33	And they

Mk	2.18	came and said to him, "Why do John's disciples
M	9.14	came to him, saying, "Why do we
L	5.33	said to him, "The disciples of John fast often and

Mk	2.18	and the disciples of the Pharisees fast, but your
M	9.14	and the Pharisees fast, but your
L	5.33	offer prayers, and so do the disciples of the Pharisees, but yours

```
Mk   2.19   disciples do not fast?"   And Jesus said to them, "Can      the wedding
M    9.15   disciples do not fast?"   And Jesus said to them, "Can      the wedding
L    5.34                eat and drink."  And Jesus said to them, "Can you make wedding


Mk   2.19   guests fast  while       the bridegroom is with them?  As long as they
M    9.15   guests mourn as long as  the bridegroom is with them?
L    5.34   guests fast  while       the bridegroom is with them?
  J  3.29   He who has the bride is  the bridegroom;


Mk   2.20   have the bridegroom with them, they cannot fast.  The days will come,
M    9.15                                                     The days will come,
L    5.35                                                     The days will come,
  J  3.29                                                        the friend


Mk   2.20   when the bridegroom is taken away from them, and then they will fast in
M    9.15   when the bridegroom is taken away from them, and then they will fast.
L    5.35   when the bridegroom is taken away from them, and then they will fast in
  J  3.29   of   the bridegroom, who stands and hears him, rejoices greatly at the


Mk   2.21   that  day.                              No one sews  a piece of
M    9.16                                  And  no one puts  a piece of
L    5.36   those days."  He told them a parable also:  "No one tears a piece from
  J  3.29   bridegroom's voice; therefore this joy of mine is now full.


Mk   2.21   unshrunk cloth           on an old garment; if he does,  the patch
M    9.16   unshrunk cloth           on an old garment, for          the patch
L    5.36   a new  garment and puts it upon an old garment; if he does,  he will


Mk   2.21   tears away from      it,                    the new         from  the
M    9.16   tears away from the garment,
L    5.36   tear                the new, and the piece from the new will not match the


Mk   2.22   old, and a worse tear is made.  And no one puts new wine   into old
M    9.17        and a worse tear is made.  Neither   is   new wine put into old
L    5.37   old.                            And no one puts new wine      into old


Mk   2.22   wineskins; if he does, the     wine will burst the skins,  and the wine
M    9.17   wineskins; if it is,                      the skins burst, and the wine
L    5.37   wineskins; if he does, the new wine will burst the skins   and     it


Mk   2.22      is lost,    and so are the skins;              but new wine
M    9.17      is spilled, and       the skins  are destroyed; but new wine
L    5.38   will be spilled, and     the skins will be  destroyed.  But new wine


Mk   2.22      is    for  fresh   skins."
M    9.17      is put into fresh wineskins,  and so both are preserved."
L    5.39   must be put into fresh wineskins.  And no one after drinking old wine


  L  5.39   desires new; for he says, 'The old is good.'"


Mk   2.23   One  sabbath      he was going through the grainfields; and as they
M   12.1    At that time      Jesus  went  through the grainfields on the sabbath;
L    6.1    On a sabbath, while he was going through the grainfields,
```

209

Mk	2.23	made their way his disciples began to pluck
M	12.1	his disciples were hungry, and they began to pluck
L	6.1	his disciples plucked and

Mk	2.24	heads of grain. And the
M	12.2	heads of grain and to eat. But when the
L	6.2	ate some heads of grain, rubbing them in their hands. But some of the

Mk	2.24	Pharisees said to him, "Look, why are they doing
M	12.2	Pharisees saw it, they said to him, "Look, your disciples are doing
L	6.2	Pharisees said, "Why are you doing

Mk	2.25	what is not lawful on the sabbath?" And he said to them, "Have
M	12.3	what is not lawful to do on the sabbath." He said to them, "Have
L	6.3	waht is not lawful to do on the sabbath?" And Jesus answered, "Have

Mk	2.25	you never read what David did, when he was in need and was hungry, he
M	12.3	you not read what David did, when he was hungry,
L	6.3	you not read what David did when he was hungry, he

Mk	2.26	and those who were with him: how he entered the house of God, when
M	12.4	and those who were with him: how he entered the house of God
L	6.4	and those who were with him: how he entered the house of God,

Mk	2.26	Abiathar was high priest, and ate the bread of the Presence, which it
M	12.4	and ate the bread of the Presence, which it
L	6.4	and took and ate the bread of the Presence, which it

Mk	2.26	is not lawful for any but the priests to eat, and also gave it to
M	12.4	was not lawful for him to eat nor for
L	6.4	is not lawful for any but the priests to eat, and also gave it to

Mk	2.26	those who were with him?"
M	12.5	those who were with him, but only for the priests? Or have you not
L	6.4	those with him?"

M	12.5	*read in the law how on the sabbath the priests in the temple profane*
M	12.6	*the sabbath, and are guiltless? I tell you, something greater than the*
M	12.7	*temple is here. And if you had known what this means,*

Mk	2.27	And he said to them, "The sabbath was made for man, not man for the
M	12.7	'I desire mercy, and not sacrifice,' you would not have condemned the
L	6.5	And he said to them,

Mk	2.28	sabbath; so the Son of man is lord even of the sabbath."
M	12.8	guiltless. For the Son of man is lord of the sabbath."
L	6.5	"The Son of man is lord of the sabbath."

13. A WITHERED HAND

Mark 3.1-6

Mk	3.1	Again he entered the synagogue,
M	12.9	And he went on from there, and entered their synagogue.
L	6.6	On another sabbath, when he entered the synagogue
L	14.1	*One sabbath when he went to dine at the house of a*

Mk	3.1	and
M	12.10	And behold,
L	6.6	and taught,
L	*14.2*	*ruler who belonged to the Pharisees, they were watching him.* And behold,

Mk	3.2	a man was there who had a withered hand. And
M	12.10	there was a man with a withered hand. And
L	6.7	a man was there whose right hand was withered. And the
L	*14.3*	*there was a man before him who had dropsy.* And *Jesus spoke to the*

Mk	3.2	they watched him, to see whether he would heal him
M	12.10	they asked him, "Is it lawful to heal
L	6.7	scribes and the Pharisees watched him, to see whether he would heal
L	*14.3*	*lawyers and Pharisees, saying, "Is it lawful to heal*

Mk	3.2	on the sabbath, so that they might accuse him.
M	12.10	on the sabbath?" so that they might accuse him.
L	6.8	on the sabbath, so that they might find an accusation against him. But
L	*14.3*	*on the sabbath, or not?"*

Mk	3.3	And he said to the man who had the withered hand,
L	6.8	he knew their thoughts, and he said to the man who had the withered hand,

Mk	3.4	"Come here." And he said to
M	12.11	He said to
L	6.9	"Come and stand here." And he rose and stood there. And Jesus said to
L	*14.5*	And he said to

Mk	3.4	them,
M	12.11	them, "What man of you, if he has one sheep and it falls
L	6.9	them,
L	*14.5*	*them, "Which of you, having a son or an ox that has fallen*

M	12.11	*into a pit on the sabbath, will not lay hold of it and lift it out?*
L	*14.5*	*into a well, will not immediately pull him out*

Mk	3.4	"Is it lawful on the sab-
M	12.12	Of how much more value is a man than a sheep! So it is lawful to do good
L	6.9	"I ask you, is it lawful on the sab-

Mk	3.4	bath to do good or to do harm, to save life or to kill?" But they were
M	12.12	on the sabbath."
L	6.9	bath to do good or to do harm, to save life or to destroy it?" But they were
L	*14.6,4*	*on a sabbath day?" And they could not reply to this.* But they were

Mk	3.5	silent. And he looked around at them with anger, grieved at their hard-
M	12.13	Then he
L	6.10	And he looked around on them all,
L	*14.4*	*silent. Then he took him*

Mk	3.5	ness of heart, and said to the man, "Stretch out your hand." He
M	12.13	said to the man, "Stretch out your hand." And the man
L	6.10	and said to him, "Stretch out your hand." And he

Mk	3.5	stretched it out, and his hand was restored.
M	12.14	stretched it out, and it was restored, whole like the other. But
L	6.11	did so, and his hand was restored. But
L	*14.4*	and healed him, and let him go.*

```
Mk    3.6     The Pharisees went out,        and immediately held counsel with the
M    12.14    the Pharisees went out         and                took counsel
L     6.11          they were filled with fury and                discussed   with one


Mk    3.6     Herodians against him,  how      to destroy  him.
M    12.14             against him,  how      to destroy  him.
L     6.11    another               what they might do to Jesus.
```

14. HEALING BY THE SEA

Mark 3.7-12

```
Mk    3.7         Jesus                  withdrew  with his disciples  to the sea,
M    12.15        Jesus, aware of this, withdrew                      from there.
L     6.17    And he                    came down with them and stood on a level place,


Mk    3.7                                     and a great multitude from Galilee
M    12.15                                    And           many
L     6.17    with a great crowd of his disciples and a great multitude of people


Mk    3.8     followed; also from     Judea |and Jerusalem and Idumea and from beyond
M    12.15    followed him,
L     6.17              from all Judea   and Jerusalem


Mk    3.8     the Jordan and from about    Tyre and Sidon a great multitude, hearing
L     6.17            and the seacoast of Tyre and Sidon, who came       to hear


Mk    3.9     all that he did, came to him.  And he told his disciples to have a boat
L     6.17                         him


Mk    3.9     ready for him because of the crowd, lest they should crush him;


Mk    3.10    for he had healed many, so that all who had diseases pressed upon him
M    12.15    and he       healed them        all,
L     6.17    and   to be healed            of their diseases;


Mk    3.11    to touch him.  And whenever            the unclean spirits beheld
L     6.18               and those who were troubled with unclean spirits were


Mk    3.11    him, they fell down before him and cried out, "You are the Son of God."
L     6.19    cured.  And all the crowd sought to touch him,


Mk    3.12    And he strictly ordered them not to make him known.
M    12.16    |and              ordered them not to make him known.
L     6.19    for power came forth from him and healed them all.
```

```
M    12.17    This was to fulfil what was spoken by the prophet Isaiah:
M    12.18          "Behold, my servant whom I have chosen,
M    12.18            my beloved with whom my soul is well pleased.
M    12.18    I will put my Spirit upon him,
M    12.18          and he shall proclaim justice to the Gentiles.
M    12.19    He will not wrangle or cry aloud,
M    12.19          nor will any one hear his voice in the streets;
```

```
M    12.20                   he will not break a bruised reed
M    12.20                     or quench a smoldering wick,
M    12.20                   till he brings justice to victory;
M    12.21                   and in his name will the Gentiles hope."
```

15. THE TWELVE

Mark 3.13-19a

```
L     6.12      In these days he went out to the mountain to pray; and all night he
L     6.12      continued in prayer to God.


Mk    3.13      And                           he went up on the mountain, and called to him those
M    10.1       And                           he                              called to him
L     6.13      And when it was day,          he                              called
  Mk  6.7       And                           he                              called to him
  L   9.1       And                           he                              called
  L  10.1       After this            the Lord


Mk    3.14      whom he desired; and they came to him.  And he appointed     twelve, to
M    10.1                                                            his  twelve
L     6.13                                                           his
  Mk  6.7                                                            the  twelve,
  L   9.1                                                            the  twelve
  L  10.1                                                     appointed     seventy


Mk    3.15      be with him, and        to be sent        out to preach            |and
M    10.1       disciples                                                           and
L     6.13      disciples,     and chose from them twelve,
  Mk  6.7                       and began to      send them out            two by two, and
  L   9.1       together                                                               and
  L  10.1       others,        and              sent them on ahead of him, two by two, into


Mk    3.15      have          authority                        to cast
M    10.1       gave them     authority over    unclean spirits, to cast them
  Mk  6.7       gave them     authority over the unclean spirits.
  L   9.1       gave them power and authority over
  L  10.1       every town and place where he himself was about to come.


Mk    3.15      out demons:
M    10.2       out,        and to heal every disease and every infirmity.  The      names of
L     6.13                                                            whom he named
  L   9.1       all demons and to cure        diseases,
  J   1.42                                        He brought him to Jesus.  Jesus
  A   1.13                          and when they had entered, they went up to the


Mk    3.16                                      Simon              whom
M    10.2       the twelve apostles are these:  first, Simon,      who
L     6.14                 apostles;            Simon,             whom
  J   1.40                          One of the two who heard John speak,
  J   1.41          He first found his brother Simon, and said to him, "We have
  J   1.42      looked at him,  and said,  "So you are Simon the son of John?  You shall
  A   1.13      upper room, where they were staying,


Mk    3.16      he surnamed                    Peter;
M    10.2         is called                    Peter, and Andrew  his brother;
L     6.14      he     named                   Peter, and Andrew  his brother, and
  J   1.40      and followed  him, was Andrew, Simon Peter's              brother.
  J   1.41      found the Messiah" (which means Christ).
  J   1.42        be called Cephas"    (which means Peter).
  A   1.13                                      Peter                              and
```

Mk	3.17	James the son of Zebedee and John the brother of James, whom he surnamed
M	10.2	James the son of Zebedee, and John his brother;
L	6.14	James and John,
A	*1.13*	*John* *and James*

Mk	3.18	Boanerges, that is, sons of thunder; |Andrew, and Philip, and
M	10.3	Philip and
L	6.14	and Philip, and
J	*1.43*	*The next day Jesus decided to go to Galilee.* And he found Philip *and*
J	*1.44*	*Now* Philip *was*
A	*1.13*	*and Andrew,* Philip and

Mk	3.18	Bartholomew, and Matthew, and Thomas, and James the
M	10.3	Bartholomew; Thomas and Matthew the tax collector; James the
L	6.15	Bartholomew, |and Matthew, and Thomas, and James the
J	*1.43*	*said to him, "Follow me."*
J	*1.44*	*from Bethsaida, the city of Andrew and Peter.*
A	*1.13*	*Thomas,* *Bartholomew and Matthew,* James the

Mk	3.18	son of Alphaeus, and Thaddaeus, and Simon the
M	10.4	son of Alphaeus, and Thaddaeus; |Simon the
L	6.16	son of Alphaeus, and Simon who was called the Zealot, |and Judas the
A	*1.13*	son of Alphaeus and *Simon* *the Zealot* and *Judas the*

Mk	3.19a	Cananaean, |and Judas Iscariot, who betrayed him.
M	10.4	Cananaean, and Judas Iscariot, who betrayed him.
L	6.16	son of James, and Judas Iscariot, who became a traitor.
A	*1.13*	*son of James.*

16. HOW CAN SATAN CAST OUT SATAN?

Mark. 3.19b-30

Mk	3.19b,20	Then he went home; and the crowd came together again, so that they
M	12.22	Then
L	11.14	Now he was casting out

Mk	3.21	could not even eat. And when his family heard it, they went out to
M	12.22	a blind and dumb demoniac was brought to him, and he healed him, so
L	11.14	a demon that was dumb; when the demon had gone out,

Mk	3.21	seize him, for people were saying, "He is beside himself."
M	12.23	that the dumb man spoke and saw. And all the people were amazed, and
L	11.14	the dumb man spoke, and the people marveled.

Mk	3.22	And the scribes who came
M	12.24	said, "Can this be the Son of David?" But when the Pharisees heard it
L	11.15	But some of them
M	*9.34*	*But* *the Pharisees*
J	*7.20*	*The people*
J	*8.48*	*The Jews*
J	*8.49*	*Jesus*
J	*8.52*	*The Jews*
J	*10.20*	*Many of them*
J	*10.21*	*Others*

```
Mk   3.22    down from Jerusalem said,          "He is possessed    by Beelzebul,
M   12.24    they                said,          "It is only         by Beelzebul,
L   11.15                         said,          "He casts out demons by Beelzebul,
  M  9.34                         said,          "He casts out demons by
  J  7.20                         answered,      "You
  J  8.48                         answered him,  "Are we not right in saying that you are a
  J  8.49                         answered,      "I
  J  8.52                         said   to him, "Now we know that you
  J 10.20                         said,          "He
  J 10.21                         said,          "These are not the sayings of one


Mk   3.22         and by the prince of demons              he  casts out the demons."
M   12.24                the prince of demons, that this man casts out      demons."
L   11.16                the prince of demons"; while others, to test him, sought from
  M  9.34                the prince of demons."
  J  7.20             have     a demon! Who is seeking to kill you?"
  J  8.48   Samaritan and have     a demon?"
  J  8.49             have not a demon;  but I honor my Father, and you dishonor me.
  J  8.52             have     a demon.  Abraham died, as did the prophets; and you
  J 10.20             has      a demon, and he is mad; why listen to him?"
  J 10.21   who       has      a demon.  Can a demon open the eyes of the blind?"


Mk   3.23                                          And he called them to him, and said to them
M   12.25                                Knowing their thoughts,      he said to them,
L   11.17   him a sign from heaven.  But he, knowing their thoughts,     said to them,
  J  8 52   say, 'If any one keeps my word, he will never taste death.'


Mk   3.24   in parables, "How can Satan cast out Satan? If a  kingdom is divided against
M   12.25                                       "Every kingdom      divided against
L   11.17                                       "Every kingdom      divided against


Mk   3.25   itself, that kingdom cannot stand. And if      a house  is divided against
M   12.25   itself  is laid waste,             and no city or house     divided against
L   11.17   itself  is laid waste,             and          a divided household


Mk   3.26   itself, that house will not be able to stand.  And if Satan has risen up
M   12.26   itself            will                stand; and if Satan casts out
L   11.18                                          falls. And if Satan also


Mk   3.26   against himself and is divided,                           he cannot
M   12.26   Satan,            he is divided against himself; how then will his kingdom
L   12.26            is divided against himself, how     will his kingdom


Mk   3.26   stand, but is coming to an end.
M   12.26   stand?
L   11.18   stand?  For you say that I cast out demons by Beelzebul.


  M 12.27   And if I cast out demons by Beelzebul, by whom do your sons cast them out?
  L 11.19   And if I cast out demons by Beelzebul, by whom do your sons cast them out?

  M 12.28   Therefore they shall be your judges. |But if it is by the Spirit of God
  L 11.20   Therefore they shall be your judges. |But if it is by the finger of God

  M 12.28   that I cast out demons, then the kingdom of God has come upon you.
  L 11.20   that I cast out demons, then the kingdom of God has come upon you.


Mk   3.27   But no one can enter a strong man's                         house
M   12.29   Or how can one enter a strong man's                         house
L   11.21   When                     a strong man, fully armed, guards his own palace,
```

Mk	3.27	and plunder his goods,	unless he first
M	12.29	and plunder his goods,	unless he first
L	11.22	his goods are in peace; but when one stronger than he	

Mk	3.27	binds the strong man; then
M	12.29	binds the strong man? Then
L	11.22	assails him and overcomes him, he takes away his armor in which he

Mk	3.27	indeed he may plunder his house.
M	12.30	indeed he may plunder his house. *He who is not with me is against me,*
L	11.23	trusted, and divides his spoil. *He who is not with me is against me,*

M	*12.30*	*and he who does not gather with me scatters.*
L	*11.23*	*and he who does not gather with me scatters.*

L	*12.8*	*"And I tell you, every one who acknowledges me before men, the Son of man*
L	*12.9*	*also will acknowledge before the angels of God; but he who denies me*
L	*12.9*	*before men will be denied before the angels of God.*

Mk	3.28	"Truly, I say to you, all sins will be forgiven
M	12.31	Therefore I tell you, every sin and blasphemy will be forgiven
M	12.32	And whoever says a word against the Son of man will be forgiven;
L	12.10	And every one who speaks a word against the Son of man will be forgiven;

Mk	3.29	the sons of men, and whatever blasphemies they utter; but whoever blasphemes
M	12.31	men, but the blasphemy
M	12.32	but whoever speaks
L	12.10	but he who blasphemes

Mk	3.29	against the Holy Spirit never has forgiveness, but is guilty of an
M	12.31	against the Spirit will not be forgiven.
M	12.32	against the Holy Spirit will not be forgiven, either in this age or
L	12.11	against the Holy Spirit will not be forgiven. And when they bring you

Mk	3.30	eternal sin"--|for they had said, "He has an unclean spirit."
L	12.11	before the synagogues and the rulers and the authorities, do not be anxious

L	*12.12*	*how or what your are to answer or what you are to say; for the Holy Spirit*
L	*12.12*	*will teach you in that very hour what you ought to say."*

17. HIS MOTHER AND BROTHERS

Mark 3.31-35

Mk	3.31	And his mother and his
M	12.46	While he was still speaking to the people, behold, his mother and his
L	8.19	Then his mother and his

Mk	3.31	brothers came; and standing outside they sent to him and called him.
M	12.46	brothers stood outside, asking to speak to him.
L	8.19	brothers came to him, but they could not reach him

216

```
Mk   3.32    And a    crowd was sitting about him; and they     said to him, "Your
M   12.47                                        Some one told      him, "Your
L    8.20    for the crowd.                       And he     was told,        "Your


Mk   3.32    mother and your brothers are              outside, asking         for
M   12.47    mother and your brothers are standing outside, asking   to speak to
L    8.20    mother and your brothers are standing outside, desiring to see


Mk   3.33    you." .And he replied,                    "Who are my mother   and
M   12.48    you." But he replied to the man who told him, "Who is  my mother, and
L    8.20    you."


Mk   3.34              my brothers?"  And looking around    on those who sat about him,
M   12.49    who are my brothers?"  And stretching out his hand toward his disciples,
L    8.21                            But


Mk   3.35    he said, "Here are my mother and my brothers!          Whoever
M   12.50    he said, "Here are my mother and my brothers!      For whoever
L    8.21    he said to them,  "My mother and my brothers are those who hear the
  M  7.21    "Not every one who says to me, 'Lord, Lord,' shall enter the kingdom of


Mk   3.35                does the will of    God             is my
M   12.50                does the will of my Father      in heaven is my
L    8.21    word of God    and do   it."
  M  7.21    heaven, but he who does the will of my Father who is in heaven.


Mk   3.35    brother, and sister, and mother."
M   12.50    brother, and sister, and mother."
```

18. PARABLE OF THE SOILS

Mark 4.1-20

```
Mk   4.1     Again        he                     began to teach    beside the sea.
M   13.1     That same day Jesus went out of the house and sat     beside the sea.
  Mk 2.13    He      went out again                            beside the sea;
  L  5.1b    he                           was standing by      the lake


Mk   4.1                  And      a very large crowd  gathered
M   13.2                  And           great crowds  gathered
L    8.4                  And when a     great crowd   came together and people
  Mk 2.13                 and  all the         crowd   gathered
  L  5.1a    of Gennesaret. While   the         people pressed


Mk   4.1                       about him,
M   13.2                       about him,
L    8.4     from town after town came to   him,
  Mk 2.13                      about him,
  L  5.2                      upon  him to hear the word of God, |And he saw


  L  5.2     two boats by the lake; but the fishermen had gone out of them and were


Mk   4.1              so that he got    into      a  boat and    sat in it on
M   13.2              so that he got    into      a  boat and    sat there;
  L  5.3     washing their nets. Getting into one of the boats, which was Simon's,

  L  5.3     he asked him to put out a little from the land.    And he sat down
```

217

```
Mk    4.2      the sea; and the whole crowd was beside the sea on the land.    And he
M     13.3              and the whole crowd stood                on the beach.    And he
L     8.4                                                                            he
  Mk  2.13                                                                        and he
  L   5.3                                                                         and


Mk    4.2      taught      them    many things in   parables, and in his teaching he said
M     13.3     told        them    many things in   parables,                         saying:
L     8.4      said                         in a parable:
  Mk  2.13     taught      them.
  L   5.3      taught  the people from the boat.


Mk    4.3,4    to them: "Listen!  A sower went out to sow.      And as he sowed,  some
M     13.4              "A sower went out to sow.               And as he sowed,  some
L     8.5              "A sower went out to sow his seed; and as he sowed,  some


Mk    4.4      seed  fell along the path,                      and the birds came
M     13.4     seeds fell along the path,                      and the birds came
L     8.5            fell along the path, and was trodden under foot, and the birds of the


Mk    4.5      and devoured it.    Other seed  fell on    rocky ground, where it    had
M     13.5     and devoured them.  Other seeds fell on    rocky ground, where they  had
L     8.6      air devoured it.  And some      fell on the rock;


Mk    4.5      not much soil, and immediately it   sprang up,                since
M     13.5     not much soil, and immediately they sprang up,                since
L     8.6                     and as          it   grew  up, it withered away, because


Mk    4.6      it   had no depth of soil;  and when the sun rose it   was  scorched, and
M     13.6     they had no depth of soil, |but when the sun rose they were scorched; and
L     8.6      it   had no moisture.


Mk    4.7      since it   had no root it   withered away.  Other seed  fell among thorns
M     13.7     since they had no root they withered away.  Other seeds fell upon  thorns,
L     8.7                               And some          fell among thorns;


Mk    4.8      and the thorns grew up      and choked it, and it yielded no grain.   And
M     13.7     and the thorns grew up      and choked them.
L     8.8      and the thorns grew with it and choked it.                            And


Mk    4.8      other seeds fell into good soil and brought forth grain, growing up and
M     13.8     Other seeds fell on   good soil and brought forth grain,
L     8.8      some        fell into good soil and                      grew,


Mk    4.8      increasing and yielding   thirtyfold   and  sixtyfold and a hundredfold."
M     13.8                 some a hundredfold, some sixty,   some thirty.
L     8.8              and yielded  a hundredfold."


Mk    4.9      And he said,             "He  who has ears to hear, let him hear."
M     13.9                               He  who has ears,         let him hear."
L     8.8      As  he said this, he called out, "He  who has ears to hear, let him hear."
  M   11.15                               He  who has ears to hear, let him hear.
  M   13.43b                              He  who has ears,         let him hear.
  Mk  4.23                           If any man has ears to hear, let him hear."
  Mk  7.16                          "If any man has ears to hear, let him hear."
  L   14.35b                              He  who has ears to hear, let him hear."
```

218

```
Mk   4.10      And when he was alone, those who were about him with the twelve
M    13.10     Then                                                  the disciples came
L    8.9       And when                                              his disciples


Mk   4.11          asked     him              concerning the parables.  And he said  to
M    13.11     and said to  him, "Why do you speak to them in parables?"  And he answered
L    8.10          asked     him    what              this parable meant, |he said,


Mk   4.11      them, "To you     has been given           the secret  of the kingdom of
M    13.11     them, "To you it has been given  to know the secrets of the kingdom of
L    8.10            "To you it has been given  to know the secrets of the kingdom of


Mk   4.11      God,     but for those outside
M    13.12     heaven, but to  them it has not been given.  For to him who has will more
L    8.10      God;    but for others


M    13.12     be given, and he will have abundance; but from him who has not, even what
M    13.13     he has will be taken away.  This is why I


Mk   4.12      everything is  in parables;  so that they may indeed see     but      not
M    13.13     speak to them  in parables,  because              seeing they do  not
L    8.10      they      are  in parables,  so that              seeing they may not
  Mk 8.18                                                  Having eyes   do you   not
  J  9.39      Jesus said, "For judgment I came into this world, that those who do  not


Mk   4.12      perceive,   and may indeed              hear but not
M    13.13     see,        and        hearing they do not  hear,    nor do they
L    8.10      see,        and                              hearing          they
  Mk 8.17b                              Do you not yet perceive or
  Mk 8.18      see,        and having ears  do you not   hear?  And do you
  J  9.39      see may see, and that those  who see may become blind."


Mk   4.12               understand;
M    13.14               understand.  With them indeed  is fulfilled the prophecy of
L    8.10      may not  understand.
  Mk 8.17b               understand?  Are your hearts hardened?
  Mk 8.18            not remember?
  J  12.38                            it was that the word spoken by the prophet


  M  13.14     Isaiah which says:
  J  12.38     Isaiah might be fulfilled:


  J  12.38             "Lord, who has believed our report,
  J  12.38               and to whom has the arm of the Lord been revealed?"
  J  12.39     Therefore they could not believe.  For Isaiah again said,


  M  13.14             'You shall indeed hear but never understand,


  M  13.14               and you shall indeed see but never perceive.
  J  12.40             "He has blinded their eyes


  M  13.15         For this people's  heart has grown dull,
  J  12.40           and hardened their heart,


  M  13.15               and their ears are heavy of hearing,
  M  13.15               and their eyes they have closed,


Mk   4.12               lest they should
M    13.15              lest they should perceive with their eyes,
  J  12.40              lest they should see      with their eyes
```

M 13.15   *and hear with their ears,*

M 13.15   *and understand with their heart,*
J 12.40   *and perceive   with their heart,*

Mk 4.12   turn again, and be forgiven."
M 13.15   and turn for me   to heal them.'
J 12.40   *and* turn *for me   to heal them."*

M 13.16   *But blessed are your eyes,*
L 10.23   *Then turning to the disciples he said privately, "Blessed are the eyes*
J 12.41   *Isaiah said this*

M 13.17   *for   they see, and your ears, for they hear. Truly, I say to you,*
L 10.24   *which   see what you see!   For   I tell   you that*
J 8.56   *because he   saw his glory and spoke of him.*

M 13.17   *many prophets and righteous men longed   to see what you see, and did not*
L 10.24   *many prophets and kings   desired   to see what you see, and did not*
J 8.56   *Your father Abraham rejoiced that he was to see my day;   he*

M 13.17   *see it, and to hear what you hear, and did not hear it.*
L 10.24   *see it, and to hear what you hear, and did not hear it."*
J 8.56   *saw it and was glad."*

Mk 4.13   And he said to them, "Do you not understand this parable? How then will
M 13.18   "Hear then the parable
L 8.11   Now   the parable is this:

Mk 4.14,15   you understand all the parables? The sower sows the word. And these are
M 13.19b   of the sower.   this is
L 8.11   The seed is   the word of God.

Mk 4.15   the ones   along the path, where the word is sown; when they
M 13.19a   what was sown along the path.   When any one
L 8.12   The ones   along the path   are   those who have

Mk 4.15   hear,   Satan
M 13.19a   hears the word of the kingdom and does not understand it, the evil one
L 8.12   heard;   then the devil

Mk 4.15   immediately comes and takes   away the word which is sown in
M 13.19a   comes and snatches away   what is sown in   his
L 8.12   comes and takes   away the word   from their

Mk 4.16   them.   And these in like manner
M 13.20   heart;   As for
L 8.13   hearts, that they may not believe and be saved. And

Mk 4.16   are the ones   sown upon   rocky ground,   who, when they hear
M 13.20   what was sown on   rocky ground, this is he who   hears
L 8.13   the ones   on the rock   are   those who, when they hear

Mk 4.17   the word,   immediately receive it with joy; and they have no root in
M 13.21   the word and immediately receives it with joy; yet he   has no root in
L 8.13   the word,   receive it with joy; but these have no root,

```
Mk   4.17    themselves, but        endure for a while; then, when    tribulation or
M    13.21   himself,    but        endures for a while, and  when    tribulation or
L    8.13                      they believe for a while and in time of temptation


Mk   4.17    persecution arises on account of the word, immediately they fall  away.
M    13.21   persecution arises on account of the word, immediately he   falls away.
L    8.13                                                              fall  away.


Mk   4.18    And others are the ones    sown among      thorns; they are those who
M    13.22       As for        what was sown among      thorns, this is he    who
L    8.14    And as for        what     fell among the  thorns, they are those who


Mk   4.19    hear  the word, |but                                       the cares
M    13.22   hears the word, but                                        the cares
L    8.14    hear,           but as they go on their way they are choked by the cares


Mk   4.19    of the world, and the delight in riches, and the desire for other things,
M    13.22   of the world  and the delight in riches
L    8.14                  and                riches and     pleasures of life,


Mk   4.20    enter in and choke the word, and it  proves   unfruitful. But those
M    13.23           choke the word, and it  proves   unfruitful.    As for
L    8.15                    and their fruit does not mature. And as for


Mk   4.20    that were sown upon the good soil    are the ones who hear    the
M    13.23   what was  sown on     good soil, this is he    who hears   the
L    8.15    that          in  the good soil, they are those who, hearing the


Mk   4.20    word and accept    it                          and
M    13.23   word and understands it;                           he indeed
L    8.15    word,     hold     it fast in an honest and good heart, and


Mk   4.20    bear    fruit,                        thirtyfold  and
M    13.23   bears   fruit, and yields, in one case a hundredfold, in another
L    8.15    bring forth fruit  with patience.


Mk   4.20    sixtyfold and    a      hundredfold."
M    13.23   sixty,    and in another thirty."
```

19. THE LAMP AND THE MEASURE

Mark 4.21-25

M   5.14   *"You are the light of the world. A city set on a hill cannot be hid.*

```
Mk   4.21        And he said to them,  "Is a lamp brought in to be put
M    5.15        Nor do men      light    a lamp          and put     it
L    8.16        "No    one after lighting a lamp             covers it
L    11.33       "No    one after lighting a lamp             puts  it in a cellar


Mk   4.21        under a bushel, or        under a bed, and not    on a stand?
M    5.15        under a bushel,                         but       on a stand, and
L    8.16        with  a vessel, or puts it under a bed, but puts it on a stand, that
L    11.33   or under a bushel,                          but       on a stand, that
```

```
M    5.16    it gives light to all in the house.  Let your light so shine before men,
L    8.16    those who enter may see the light.
L   11.34    those who enter may see the light.   Your eye is the lamp of your body;

M    5.16    that they may see your good works and give glory to your Father who is
L   11.34    when your eye is sound, your whole body is full of light; but when it is

M    5.16    in heaven.
L   11.35    not sound, your body is full of darkness.  Therefore be careful lest the

L   11.36    light in you be darkness.  If then your whole body is full of light,
L   11.36    having no part dark, it will be wholly bright, as when a lamp with its
L   11.36    rays gives you light."


Mk   4.22                             For there is nothing hid,        except to
L    8.17                                  For   nothing is hid         that shall not
 M  10.26    "So have no fear of them; for      nothing is covered      that will   not
 L  12.2                                        Nothing is covered up that will   not


Mk   4.22    be made manifest; nor is anything secret,
L    8.17    be made manifest, nor     anything secret that shall not be known
 M  10.26    be      revealed, or              hidden that will  not be known.
 L  12.2     be      revealed, or              hidden that will  not be known.


Mk   4.22                                                    except to come   to
L    8.17                                                      and      come   to
 M  10.27          What      I       tell you in the dark,          utter in the
 L  12.3     Therefore whatever you have said     in the dark shall be heard in the


Mk   4.22    light.
L    8.17    light.
 M  10.27    light; and what you hear whispered,                    proclaim
 L  12.3     light, and what you have whispered in private rooms shall be proclaimed


Mk   4.23                            If any man has ears to hear, let him hear."
 M  10.27    upon the housetops.
 L  12.3     upon the housetops.
 M  11.15                             He  who has ears to hear, let him hear."
 M  13.9                              He  who has ears,         let him hear."
 M  13.43b                            He  who has ears,         let him hear.
 Mk  4.9     And he said,           "He  who has ears to hear, let him hear."
 Mk  7.16                     "If any man has ears to hear, let him hear."
 L   8.8b    As  he said this, he called out, "He  who has ears to hear, let him hear."
 L  14.35b                           He  who has ears to hear, let him hear."


Mk   4.24    And he said to them, "Take heed what you hear;        the measure
M    7.2     For with the judgment you pronounce you will be judged, and the measure
L    6.38b                                                     For the measure


Mk   4.24    you give will be the measure you get, and still more will be given you.
M    7.2     you give will be the measure you get.
L    6.38b   you give will be the measure you get back."


Mk   4.25                            For to him      who has will more be given;
L    8.18    Take heed then how you hear; for to him who has will more be given,
 M  13.12                            For to him      who has will more be given,
 M  25.29                            For to every one who has will more be given,
 L  19.26              'I tell you, that to every one who has will more be given;
```

222

Mk	4.25	and from him who has not, even what he
L	8.18	and from him who has not, even what he thinks
M	13.12	and he will have abundance; but from him who has not, even what he
M	25.29	and he will have abundance; but from him who has not, even what he
L	19.26	but from him who has not, even what he

Mk	4.25	has will be taken away."
L	8.18	that he has will be taken away."
M	13.12	has will be taken away.
M	25.29	has will be taken away.
L	19.26	has will be taken away.

20. THE SEED GROWING SECRETLY

Mark 4.26-29

Mk	4.26	And he said, "The kingdom of God
M	13.24	Another parable he put before them, saying, "The kingdom of heaven

Mk	4.27	is as if a man should scatter seed upon the ground, |and
M	13.25	may be compared to a man who sowed good seed in his field; but while

Mk	4.27	should sleep and rise night and day,
M	13.25	men were sleeping, his enemy came and sowed weeds among the wheat,

Mk	4.27	and the seed should sprout and grow, he knows
M	13.26	and went away. So when the plants came up and bore grain, then the

Mk	4.28	not how. The earth produces of itself, first the blade, then the ear,
M	13.27	weeds appeared also. And the servants of the householder came and said

Mk	4.28	then the full grain in the ear.
M	13.27	to him, 'Sir, did you not sow good seed in your field? How then has it

M	13.28	weeds?' He said to them, 'An enemy has done this.' The servants said
M	13.29	to him, 'Then do you want us to go and gather them?' But he said, 'No;
M	13.29	lest in gathering the weeds you root up the wheat along with them.

Mk	4.29	But when the grain is ripe,
M	13.30	Let both grow together until the harvest; and at harvest time

Mk	4.29	at once he puts in the sickle, because the harvest has come."
M	13.30	I will tell the reapers, Gather the weeds first and bind them in bundles

M	13.30	to be burned, but gather the wheat into my barn.'"

21. THE MUSTARD SEED

Mk 4.30-32

Mk	4.30	And he said, "With what can we
M	13.31	Another parable he put before them, saying,
L	13.18	He said therefore, "What

```
Mk   4.30   compare the kingdom of God,        or    what parable shall we use
M    13.31         "The kingdom of heaven
L    13.18   is      the kingdom of God like?  And to what        shall I  compare


Mk   4.31   for it?  It is like a grain of mustard seed, which,        when sown
M    13.31              is like a grain of mustard seed  which a man took and sowed
L    13.19       it?  It is like a grain of mustard seed  which a man took and sowed


Mk   4.32   upon the ground,   is the smallest of all the seeds on earth;  yet when
M    13.32   in   his field; it is the smallest of all      seeds,       but when
L    13.19   in   his garden;                                             and


Mk   4.32   it is sown it    grows up and becomes the greatest of all shrubs,  and
M    13.32             it has grown      it is    the greatest of      shrubs  and
L    13.19             it       grew                                           and


Mk   4.32   puts forth large branches,  so that the birds of the air       can make
M    13.32   becomes       a tree,      so that the birds of tha air  come and make
L    13.19   became        a tree,      and      the birds of the air           made


Mk   4.32   nests in its shade."
M    13.32   nests in its branches."
L    13.19   nests in its branches."
```

22. SUMMARY OF TEACHING BY PARABLE

Mark 4.33-34

```
Mk   4.33   With many such parables he   spoke the word to    them,  as they were
M    13.34   All this              Jesus said              to the crowds in parables;


Mk   4.34   able to hear it; he did not speak to them without a parable,  but
M    13.35            indeed he said  nothing to them without a parable.  This


Mk   4.34   privately to his own disciples he explained everything.
M    13.35   was to fulfil what was spoken by the prophet:
```

```
M  13.35               "I will open my mouth in parables,
M  13.35                I will utter what has been hidden since the foundation
M  13.35                   of the world."
```

23. THE STORM AT SEA

Mark 4.35-41

```
Mk   4.35   On that day, when evening had come,              he said to them,
M    8.18   Now when Jesus saw great crowds around him,      he gave orders
L    8.22   One    day he got into a boat with his disciples, and he said to them,


Mk   4.35   "Let us go across to the other side."
M    8.18          to go over   to the other side.
L    8.22   "Let us go across to the other side of the lake."  So they set out,
```

Mk	4.36	And leaving the crowd, they took him with them in the boat, just as he
M	8.23	And when he got into the boat,

Mk	4.37	was. And other boats were with him. │And a great
M	8.24	his disciples followed him. │And behold, there arose a great
L	8.23b	│And a

Mk	4.37	storm of wind arose, and the waves beat into the boat, so that the boat
M	8.24	storm on the sea, so that the boat
L	8.23b	storm of wind came down on the lake, and they

Mk	4.38	was already filling. But
M	8.24	was being swamped by the waves; but
L	8.23a	were filling with water, and were in danger. │and as they sailed

Mk	4.38	he was in the stern, asleep on the cushion; and they woke him
M	8.25	he was asleep. And they went and woke him,
L	8.24	he fell asleep. And they went and woke him,

Mk	4.39	and said to him, "Teacher, do you not care if we perish?" And
M	8.26b	saying, "Save, Lord; we are perishing." Then
L	8.24	saying, "Master, Master, we are perishing!" And

Mk	4.39	he awoke and rebuked the wind, and said to the sea, "Peace! Be
M	8.26b	he rose and rebuked the winds and the sea;
L	8.24	he awoke and rebuked the wind and the raging waves;

Mk	4.40	still!" And the wind ceased, and there was a great calm. He said
M	8.26a	and there was a great calm. And he said
L	8.25	and they ceased, and there was a calm. He said

Mk	4.41	to them, "Why are you afraid? Have you no faith?" And they were
M	8.27	to them, "Why are you afraid, O men of little faith?" And
L	8.25	to them, "Where is your faith?" And they were

Mk	4.41	filled with awe, and said to one another, "Who then is
M	8.27	the men marveled, saying, "What sort of man is
L	8.25	afraid, and they marveled, saying to one another, "Who then is

Mk	4.41	this, that even wind and sea obey him?"
M	8.27	this, that even winds and sea obey him?"
L	8.25	this, that he commands even wind and water, and they obey him?"

24. THE DEMON 'LEGION'

Mark 5.1-20

Mk	5.1	They came to the other side of the sea, to the country of the
M	8.28	And when he came to the other side, to the country of the
L	8.26	Then they arrived at the country of the

Mk	5.2	Gerasenes. And when he had come out of the
M	8.28	Gadarenes,
L	8.27	Gerasenes, which is opposite Galilee. And as he stepped out on

Mk	5.2	boat, there met him
M	8.28	two demoniacs met him,
L	8.27	land, there met him a man from the city who had demons; for a long

Mk	5.2	out of the
M	8.28	coming out of the
L	8.27	time he had worn no clothes, and he lived not in a house but among the

Mk	5.3	tombs a man with an unclean spirit, |who lived among the tombs; and no
M	8.28	tombs, so fierce that no one could pass that way.
L	8.27	tombs.

Mk	5.4	one could bind him any more, even with a chain; for he had often been
Mk	5.4	bound with fetters and chains, but the chains he wrenched apart, and the
Mk	5.4	fetters he broke in pieces; and no one had the strength to subdue him.
Mk	5.5	Night and day among the tombs and on the mountains he was always crying
Mk	5.6	out, and bruising himself with stones. And

Mk	5.7	when he saw Jesus from afar, he ran and worshiped him; |and
M	8.29	And behold, they
L	8.28	When he saw Jesus, he

Mk	5.7	crying out with a loud voice, he said,
M	8.29	cried out,
L	8.28	cried out and fell down before him, and said with a loud voice,

Mk	5.7	"What have you to do with me, Jesus, Son of the Most High God? I
M	8.29	"What have you to do with us, O Son of God?
L	8.28	"What have you to do with me, Jesus, Son of the Most High God? I

Mk	5.8	adjure you by God, do not torment me." For he had said to
M	8.29	Have you come here to torment us before the time?"
L	8.29	beseech you, do not torment me." For he had commanded the unclean

Mk	5.8	him, "Come out of the man, you unclean spirit!"
L	8.29	spirit to come out of the man. (For many a time it had seized him; he was

L	*8.29*	*kept under guard, and bound with chains and fetters, but he broke the*

Mk	5.9	And Jesus asked
L	8.30	*bonds and was driven by the demon into the desert.)* Jesus then asked

Mk	5.9	him, "What is your name?" He replied, "My name is Legion; for we
L	8.30	him, "What is your name?" And he said, "Legion"; for

Mk	5.10	are many." And he begged him eagerly not to
L	8.31	many demons had entered him. And they begged him not to

Mk	5.11	send them out of the country. Now a great herd of swine
M	8.30	Now a herd of many swine
L	8.32	command them to depart into the abyss. Now a large herd of swine

Mk	5.12	was feeding there on the hillside; and they begged him,
M	8.31	was feeding at some distance from them. And the demons begged him, "If
L	8.32	was feeding there on the hillside; and they begged him

```
Mk   5.12                        "Send us         to the          swine, let us    enter
M    8.31        you cast us out, send us away into the herd of swine."
L    8.32                                         to              let them enter


Mk   5.13        them."  So  he gave      them leave.  And  the unclean spirits came out,
M    8.32                And he said to them, "Go."  So                 they    came out
L    8.33        these.  So  he gave      them leave.  Then the              demons  came out of


Mk   5.13                  and entered   the swine; and          the        herd, numbering
M    8.32                  and went into the swine; and behold, the whole herd
L    8.33        the man and entered   the swine, and          the        herd


Mk   5.13        about two thousand, rushed down the steep bank into the sea, and were
M    8.32                            rushed down the steep bank into the sea, and
L    8.33                            rushed down the steep bank into the lake and were


Mk   5.14        drowned  in the sea.   The herdsmen                          fled,
M    8.33        perished in the waters. The herdsmen                         fled,
L    8.34        drowned.              When the herdsmen saw what had happened, they fled,


Mk   5.14        and told it in  the city and in the country.  And  people came       to
M    8.33        and going  into the city they told everything, and
L    8.35        and told it in  the city and in the country.  Then people went out to


Mk   5.15        see what it was that had happened.              And       they
M    8.34            what             had happened to the demoniacs.  And behold, all the
L    8.35        see what             had happened,              and       they


Mk   5.15            came    to     Jesus, and          saw   the demoniac
M    8.34        city came out to meet Jesus; and when they saw      him,
L    8.35            came    to     Jesus, and          found the man from whom the


Mk   5.15                           sitting there,          clothed and in his right
L    8.35        demons had gone, sitting at the feet of Jesus, clothed and in his right


Mk   5.16        mind, the man who had had the legion; and they were afraid.  And those
L    8.36        mind;                                  and they were afraid.  And those


Mk   5.16        who had seen it told    what       had happened to the    demoniac
L    8.36        who had seen it told them how he who had been possessed with demons


Mk   5.17        and to the swine.  And        they began
M    8.34                                      they
L    8.37        was healed.       Then all the people of the surrounding country of the


Mk   5.17              to beg   Jesus to depart from their neighborhood.
M    8.34                       begged him  to leave      their neighborhood.
L    8.37        Gerasenes asked  him  to depart from them; for they were seized with


Mk   5.18              And as he was getting into the boat,            the man
L    8.37        great fear; so he     got     into the boat and returned.  The man from


Mk   5.18        who had been possessed with demons          begged him that he might be
L    8.38        whom                     the demons had gone begged       that he might be
```

227

Mk	5.19	with him. But he refused, and said to him, "Go home to
L	8.39	with him; but he sent him away, saying, |"Return to your home,

Mk	5.19	your friends, and tell them how much the Lord has done for you, and how
L	8.39	and declare how much God has done for you."

Mk	5.20	he has had mercy on you." And he went away and began to proclaim
L	8.39	And he went away, proclaiming

Mk	5.20	in the Decapolis how much Jesus had done for him; and all men
L	8.39	throughout the whole city how much Jesus had done for him.

Mk	5.20	marveled.

25. JAIRUS' DAUGHTER AND A WOMAN WITH A HEMORRHAGE

Mark 5.21-43

Mk	5.21	And when Jesus had crossed again in the boat to the other side, a
L	8.40	Now when Jesus returned, the

Mk	5.22	great crowd gathered about him; and he was beside the sea. Then
M	9.18	While
L	8.41	crowd welcomed him, for they were all waiting for him. And

Mk	5.22	came one of the rulers of the synagogue,
M	9.18	he was thus speaking to them, behold, a ruler
L	8.41	there came a man named Jairus, who was a ruler of the synagogue;

Mk	5.23	Jairus by name; and seeing him, he fell at his feet, |and besought
M	9.18	came in and knelt before him,
L	8.41	and falling at Jesus' feet he besought

Mk	5.23	him, saying, "My little daughter
M	9.18	saying, "My daughter
L	8.42	him to come to his house, |for he had an only daughter, about twelve

Mk	5.23	is at the point of death. Come and lay your
M	9.18	has just died; but come and lay your
L	8.42	years of age, and she was dying.

Mk	5.24	hands on her, so that she may be made well, and live." And he
M	9.19	hand on her, and she will live." And Jesus rose
L	8.42	As he

Mk	5.24	went with him.
L	8.42	went,

Mk	5.25	And a great crowd followed him and thronged about him. |And there was
M	9.20	and followed him, with his disciples. And behold,
L	8.43	the people pressed round him. And

Mk	5.26	a woman who had had	a flow of blood for twelve years,	and
M	9.20	a woman who had suffered from a hemorrhage	for twelve years
L	8.43	a woman who had had	a flow of blood for ·twelve years	and

| Mk | 5.26 | who had suffered much under many physicians, and had spent all that |
| L | 8.43 | could not be healed by | any one, |

| Mk | 5.27 | she had, and was no better but rather grew worse. She had heard the |
| Mk | 6.56 | And wherever he came, in villages, cities, or country, they laid the |

Mk	5.27	reports about Jesus, and came up behind him in the crowd and
M	9.20	came up behind him	and
L	8.44	came up behind him,	and
M	14.36	and besought him that they might only
Mk	3.10	for he had healed many, so that all who had diseases pressed upon him to
Mk	6.56	sick in the market places, and besought him that they might
L	6.19	And	all the crowd	sought	to

Mk	5.28	touched	his garment. For she said,	"If I
M	9.21	touched	the fringe of his garment;	for she said to herself, "If I
L	8.44	touched	the fringe of his garment;
M	14.36	touch	the fringe of his garment;
Mk	3.10	touch	him.
Mk	6.56	touch even the fringe of his garment;
L	6.19	touch	him,

Mk	5.29	touch even his garments, I shall be made well."	And immediately the
M	9.22b	only touch	his garment, I shall be made well."	And instantly the
L	8.44	and immediately her
M	14.36	and as many as
Mk	6.56	and as many as
Mk	10.52b	And immediately
L	6.19	for power came

Mk	5.29	hemorrhage	ceased; and she felt in her body that she was healed of
M	9.22b	woman	was	made well.
L	8.44	flow of blood	ceased.
M	14.36	touched it were made well.
Mk	6.56	touched it were made well.
Mk	10.52b	he	received his sight and followed him on the way.
L	6.19	forth from him and healed them all.

Mk	5.30	her disease. And Jesus, perceiving in himself that power had gone forth
M	9.22a	Jesus
L	8.45	And Jesus

Mk	5.30	from him, immediately turned about in the crowd, and said, "Who
M	9.22a	turned,
L	8.45	said, "Who was it

| Mk | 5.31 | touched my garments?" And | his disciples said to him, |
| L | 8.45 | that touched me?" | When all denied it, Peter | said, |

| Mk | 5.31 | "You see the crowd | pressing around you, and yet |
| L | 8.46 | "Master, the multitudes surround you and press | upon | you!" But |

Mk	5.32	you	say, 'Who	touched me?'" And he looked around to see	who
M	9.22a	and	seeing her
L	8.46	Jesus said, "Some one touched me;	for I	perceive that power has gone

Mk	5.33	had done it.	But	the woman, knowing what had been done to her,
L	8.47	forth from me."	And when the woman saw	that she was not hidden, she

Mk	5.33	came in fear and trembling and fell down before him, and told him the
L	8.47	came trembling, and falling down before him declared in

L	8.48	the presence of all the people why she had touched him, and how she had

Mk	5.34	whole truth. And he said to her,
M	9.22a	he said, "Take heart,
L	8.48	been immediately healed. And he said to her,
Mk	10.52a	And Jesus said to him, "Go
L	7.50	And he said to the woman,
L	17.19	And he said to him, "Rise and go
L	18.42	And Jesus said to him, "Receive your

Mk	5.34	"Daughter, your faith has made you well; go in peace, and be healed of
M	9.22a	daughter; your faith has made you well."
L	8.48	"Daughter, your faith has made you well; go in peace."
Mk	10.52a	your way; your faith has made you well."
L	7.50	"Your faith has saved you; go in peace."
L	17.19	your way; your faith has made you well."
L	18.42	sight; your faith has made you well."

Mk	5.34	your disease."

Mk	5.35	While he was still speaking, there came from the ruler's house some who
L	8.49	While he was still speaking, a man from the ruler's house came and

Mk	5.35	said, "Your daughter is dead. Why trouble the Teacher any further?"
L	8.49	said, "Your daughter is dead; do not trouble the Teacher any more."

Mk	5.36	But ignoring what they said, Jesus said to the ruler of the
L	8.50	But Jesus on hearing this answered him,

Mk	5.37	synagogue, "Do not fear, only believe." And he allowed no one to follow
L	8.50	"Do not fear; only believe, and she shall be well."

Mk	5.37	him except Peter and James and John the brother of James.

Mk	5.38	When they came to the house of the ruler of the synagogue, he saw
M	9.23	And when Jesus came to the ruler's house, and saw
L	8.51	And when he came to the house, he permitted no one to enter with him,

Mk	5.38	a tumult,
M	9.23	the flute players,
L	8.51	except Peter and John and James, and the father and mother of the child.

Mk	5.39	and people weeping and wailing loudly. And when he had entered,
M	9.23	and the crowd making a tumult,
L	8.52	And all were weeping and bewailing her; but

Mk	5.39	he said to them, "Why do you make a tumult and weep? The child is not
M	9.24	he said, "Depart; for the girl is not
L	8.52	he said, "Do not weep; for she is not

230

Mk	5.40	dead but sleeping." |And they laughed at him. But · he
M	9.25	dead but sleeping." And they laughed at him. |But when the crowd had
L	8.53	dead but sleeping." And they laughed at him, knowing that she was dead.

Mk	5.40	put them all outside, and took the child's father and mother and
M	9.25	been put outside,

Mk	5.41	those who were with him, and went in where the child was. Taking her
M	9.25	he went in and took her
L	8.54	But taking her

Mk	5.41	by the hand he said to her, "Talitha cumi"; which means, "Little
M	9.25	by the hand,
L	8.54	by the hand he called, saying,

Mk	5.42	girl, I say to you, arise." And immediately
M	9.25	and
L	8.55	"Child, arise." And her spirit returned, and

Mk	5.42	the girl got up and walked (she was twelve years of age),
M	9.25	the girl arose.
L	8.55	she got up at once; and he directed that something should be given

Mk	5.42	and they were immediately overcome with amazement.
M	9.26	And the report of this went through all that district.
L	8.56	her to eat. And her parents were amazed;

Mk	5.43	And he strictly charged them that no one should know this, and told
L	8.56	but he charged them to tell no one what had happened.

Mk	5.43	them to give her something to eat.

26. JESUS REJECTED BY HIS OWN

Mark 6.1-6a

Mk	6.1	He went away from there
M	13.53	And when Jesus had finished these parables, he went away from there,

Mk	6.2	and came to his own country; and his disciples followed him. And
M	13.54	and coming to his own country
L	4.16a	And he came to Nazareth, where he had been brought up; and

Mk	6.2	on the sabbath he began to teach in the synagogue;
M	13.54	he taught them in their synagogue,
L	4.16a	he went to the synagogue, as his custom

Mk	6.2	and many who heard him were astonished,
M	13.54	so that they were astonished, and
L	4.22	was, on the sabbath day. And all spoke well of him, and wondered at the
J	6.42	They
J	7.15	The Jews marveled at it,

231

Mk	6.2	saying, "Where did <u>this man get all this</u>? <u>What is the wisdom given</u>
M	13.54	said, "Where did <u>this man get</u> <u>this</u> <u>wisdom</u>
L	4.22	*gracious words which proceeded out of his mouth;*
J	6.42	said,
J	7.15	*saying, "How is it that* <u>this man</u> *has learning, when he has never studied?"*

Mk	6.3	<u>to him? What mighty works are wrought by his hands!</u> <u>Is not this</u>
M	13.55	and these <u>mighty works?</u> <u>Is not this</u>
L	4.22	*and they said,* "<u>Is not this</u>
J	6.42	"<u>Is not this</u> *Jesus,*

Mk	6.3	<u>the carpenter,</u> <u>the son of Mary</u> <u>and</u>
M	13.55	<u>the carpenter</u>'s son? Is not his mother called <u>Mary</u>? <u>And</u> are not
L	4.22	*Joseph's son?"*
J	6.42	*the son of Joseph, whose father and mother we know? How does he now*

Mk	6.3	<u>brother of James and Joses</u> <u>and Judas and Simon,</u> <u>and are not</u>
M	13.56	his <u>brothers</u> <u>James and</u> Joseph <u>and Simon and</u> Judas? <u>And are not</u> all
J	6.42	*say, 'I have come down from heaven'?"*

Mk	6.3	<u>his sisters here with us?"</u> <u>And</u>
M	13.57	<u>his sisters</u> <u>with us?</u> Where then did this man get all this?" <u>And</u>
L	4.28	*When they heard this,*

Mk	6.4	<u>they</u> <u>took offense</u> <u>at him.</u> And Jesus <u>said to</u>
M	13.57	<u>they</u> <u>took offense</u> <u>at him.</u> But Jesus <u>said to</u>
L	4.24	*all in the synagogue were filled with wrath. And he* *said,*
J	4.44	*For* <u>Jesus</u> *himself testified*

Mk	6.4	<u>them,</u> "A <u>prophet is</u> <u>not without honor,</u> <u>except in his</u>
M	13.57	<u>them,</u> "A <u>prophet is</u> <u>not without honor</u> <u>except in his</u>
L	4.24	*"Truly, I say to you, no* <u>prophet is</u> *acceptable* <u>in his</u>
J	4.44	*that* <u>a</u> <u>prophet</u> *has no* <u>honor</u> <u>in his</u>

Mk	6.5	<u>own country, and among his own kin,</u> <u>and in his own house."</u> <u>And he could</u>
M	13.58	<u>own country</u> <u>and in his own house."</u> <u>And he did</u>
L	4.24	<u>own country.</u>
J	4.44	<u>own country.</u>

Mk	6.5	<u>do no</u> <u>mighty work</u> <u>there,</u> except that he laid his hands upon a
M	13.58	not do many <u>mighty</u> works <u>there,</u>

Mk	6.6a	<u>few sick people and healed them.</u> And he marveled <u>because of their</u>
M	13.58	<u>because of their</u>

Mk	6.6a	<u>unbelief.</u>
M	13.58	<u>unbelief.</u>

27. MISSION OF THE TWELVE

Mark 6b-13

Mk	6.6b	<u>And</u> <u>he</u> <u>went about</u> among <u>the</u> <u>villages</u>
M	9.35	<u>And</u> Jesus <u>went about</u> all <u>the</u> cities and <u>villages,</u>
L	8.1	Soon afterward <u>he</u> <u>went</u> on through cities and <u>villages,</u>

```
Mk    6.6b    teaching.
M     9.35    teaching in their synagogues and preaching the gospel     of the kingdom,
L     8.1a    preaching                      and bringing  the good news of the kingdom


  M   9.35    and healing every disease and every infirmity.
  L   8.1a    of God.


Mk    6.7     And he called to him        the twelve,
M     10.5    These                       twelve
L     9.1     And he called               the twelve together and gave them power and
  L   10.1    After this the Lord appointed seventy others,


Mk    6.7                                                      and began to send them
M     10.5                                                     Jesus sent
L     9.2     authority over all demons and to cure diseases, |and    he   sent them
  L   10.1                                                      and        sent them


Mk    6.7     out              two by two, and gave them authority over the unclean
M     10.5    out,
L     9.2     out
  L   10.1    on ahead of him, two by two.


Mk    6.8     spirits.  He charged  them
M     10.5               charging  them, "Go nowere among the Gentiles, and enter no
L     9.3            And he said   to them,
  L   10.1                                                               into every


  M   10.6    town of the Samaritans, |but go rather to the lost sheep of the house of
  L   10.2    town and place where he himself was about to come.  And he said to them,

  M   10.7    Israel.  And preach as you go, saying, 'The kingdom of heaven is at hand.'
  L   0.9              to preach              the kingdom of God          and to
  L   10.2    "The harvest is plentiful, but the laborers are few; pray therefore the

  M   10.8    Heal the sick, raise the dead, cleanse lepers, cast out demons.  You
  L   9.2     heal.
  L   10.3    Lord of the harvest to send out laborers into his harvest.  Go your way;


Mk    6.8                                                          to take nothing
M     10.9    received without paying, give without pay.            Take
L     9.3                                                          "Take nothing
  L   10.4    behold, I send you out as lambs in the midst of wolves.  Carry


Mk    6.8     for their journey except a staff; no  bread, no  bag, no  money
M     10.9                                                          no  gold, nor
L     9.3     for your  journey,      no staff, nor bag, nor bread, nor money;
  L   10.4                                                          no  purse,


Mk    6.9                       in their belts;                      but to wear
M     10.10   silver, nor copper in your  belts, |no bag for your journey, nor    two
L     9.3                                                    and do not have two
  L   10.4                              no bag                        no


Mk    6.9     sandals and not put on two tunics.
M     10.10   tunics,      nor           sandals, nor a staff;
L     9.3     tunics.
  L   10.5    sandals; and salute no one on the road.  Whatever house you enter, first
```

233

```
L  10.6       say, 'Peace be to this house!' And if a son of peace is there, your peace
L  10.7       shall rest upon him; but if not, it shall return to you.  And remain in
L  10.7       the same house, eating and drinking what they provide,


M  10.11      for the laborer deserves his food.                              And
L  10.7       for the laboerer deserves his wages; do not go from house to house.


M  10.11      whatever              town or village you enter, find out who is worthy in
L  10.8       whenever you enter a town and they receive you, eat what is set before you;


Mk  6.10      And he said to them, "Where    you enter a    house,              stay
M   10.12,11b it,            |As           you enter the house, salute it.  |and stay
L   9.4       And                whatever house you     enter,              stay
L   10.9      heal the sick in it and say to them, 'The kingdom of God has come near to


Mk  6.10      there     until you leave the place.
M   10.13     with him  until you depart.  And if the house is worthy, let your peace
L   9.4       there, and from there depart.
L   10.9      you.'


M   10.13     come upon it; but if it is not worthy, let your peace return to you.
L   10.10                              But whenever you enter a town


Mk  6.11      And if      any place will not receive you and they refuse to hear
M   10.14     And if      any one   will not receive you or         listen to
L   9.5       And wherever they     do   not receive you,
L   10.10     and          they     do   not receive you,


Mk  6.11      you,       when you leave,           shake off the dust       that
M   10.14     your words,                          shake off the dust       from
L   9.5                  when you leave that town  shake off the dust       from
L   10.11                go into its streets and say, |'Even the dust of your town that


Mk  6.12      is     on your feet  for a testimony against them."  So  they
M   10.14             your feet    as you leave that house or town.
L   9.6                your feet   as  a testimony against them."  And they departed and
L   10.11     clings to our  feet, we wipe off      against you; nevertheless know this,


Mk  6.13      went out               and preached that men should repent.  And they
M   10.15                            Truly, I say to you, it shall be more
L   9.6        went through the villages, preaching the gospel
L   10.12      that the kingdom of God has come near.'  I tell   you, it shall be more


Mk  6.13      cast out many demons, and anointed with oil many that were sick and
M   10.15     tolerable on the  day of judgment for the land of Sodom and Gomorrah than
L   9.6                                                                  and
L   10.12     tolerable on that day              for       Sodom               than


Mk  6.13      healed  them.
M   10.15     for that town.
L   9.6       healing everywhere.
L   10.12     for that town.
```

Mark 6.14-29

Mk	6.14	King Herod heard of it; for Jesus' name
M	14.1	At that time Herod the tetrarch heard about the fame of Jesus;
L	9.7	Now Herod the tetrarch heard of all that was done, and he was

Mk	6.14	had become known. Some said, "John the
M	14.2	and he said to his servants, "This is John the
L	9.7	perplexed, because it was said by some that John

Mk	6.14	baptizer has been raised from the dead; that is why these powers are
M	14.2	Baptist, he has been raised from the dead; that is why these powers are
L	9.7	had been raised from the dead,

Mk	6.15	at work in him." But others said, "It is Elijah." And
M	14.2	at work in him."
L	9.8	|by some that Elijah had appeared, and by

Mk	6.15	others said, "It is a prophet, like one of the prophets of old."
L	9.8	others that one of the old prophets had risen.

Mk	6.16	But when Herod heard of it he said, "John, whom I beheaded, has been
L	9.9	Herod said, "John I beheaded; but who is

Mk	6.16	raised."
L	9.9	this about whom I hear such things?" And he sought to see him.

Mk	6.17	For Herod had sent and seized John, and bound him in prison
M	14.3	For Herod had seized John and bound him and put him in prison,
L	*3.19*	*But Herod the tetrarch, who had been reproved by him*

Mk	6.17	for the sake of Herodias, his brother Philip's wife; because he had married
M	14.3	for the sake of Herodias, his brother Philip's wife;
L	*3.19*	*for Herodias, his brother's wife, and for all the evil*

Mk	6.18	her. For John said to Herod, "It is not lawful for you to have your
M	14.4	because John said to him, "It is not lawful for you to have
L	*3.20*	*things that Herod had done, |added this to them all, that he shut up John*

Mk	6.19	brother's wife." And Herodias had a grudge against him, and wanted
M	14.5	her." And though he wanted
L	*3.20*	*in prison.*

Mk	6.20	to kill him. But she could not, |for Herod feared John, knowing that he
M	14.5	to put him to death, he feared the people, because

Mk	6.20	was a righteous and holy man, and kept him safe. When he heard him, he
M	14.5	they held him to be a prophet.

Mk	6.21	was much perplexed; and yet he heard him gladly. But an opportunity came
M	14.6	But

```
Mk    6.21    when Herod on his birthday gave a banquet for his courtiers and officers
M     14.6    when Herod's      birthday came,


Mk    6.22    and the leading men of Galilee.  For when Herodias'    daughter came in and
M     14.6                                                      the daughter of Herodias


Mk    6.22    danced,                          she pleased Herod and his guests;  and the king
M     14.7    danced before the company, and pleased Herod,              |so that he


Mk    6.22    said to the girl,     "Ask me for whatever you      wish, and I will grant
M     14.7    promised with an oath to give her whatever she might ask.


Mk    6.23    it."  And he vowed to her, "Whatever you ask me, I will give you, even half


Mk    6.24    of my kingdom."  And she went out, and said to her mother, "What shall I
M     14.8                                                 Prompted by her mother,


Mk    6.25    ask?"  And she said,        "The head of John the baptizer."  And she came
M     14.8              she said, "Give me the head of John the Baptist here


Mk    6.25    in immediately with haste to the king, and asked, saying, "I want you to


Mk    6.26    give me at once the head of John the Baptist on a platter."  And the king
M     14.9                                          on a platter."  And the king


Mk    6.26    was exceedingly sorry; but because of his oaths and his guests he did not
M     14.9    was             sorry; but because of his oaths and his guests


Mk    6.27    want to break his word to her.  And immediately the king sent a soldier of
M     14.9                                                           he


Mk    6.27    the guard and gave orders to bring his head.  He went and        beheaded
M     14.10              commanded      it to be given;  he sent and had John beheaded


Mk    6.28    him in the prison, |and brought      his head on a platter, and gave it to
M     14.11       in the prison, |and his head was brought on a platter and given   to


Mk    6.29    the girl; and the girl gave  it to her mother.  When his disciples heard
M     14.12    the girl, and    she brought it to her mother.  And  his disciples


Mk    6.29    of it, they came and took his body, and laid  it  in a tomb.
M     14.12          came and took the body  and buried it; and they went and told


M     14.12   Jesus.
```

29. THE FIVE THOUSAND FED

Mark 6.30-44

```
Mk    6.30                   The apostles returned to Jesus, and told him all that
M     14.13   Now when                            Jesus       heard this,
L     9.10    On their return the apostles                    told him     what
```

```
Mk   6.31    they had done and taught.  And he said to them, "Come away by yourselves
L    9.10    they had done.


Mk   6.31    to a lonely place, and rest a while."  For many were coming and going,
Mk   6.31    and they had no leisure even to eat.


Mk   6.32    And           they           went     away      in the boat to a    lonely
M   14.13                  he                      withdrew from there in a    boat to a    lonely
L    9.10    And           he took them and withdrew apart                 to a    city
J    6.1     After this Jesus            went                             to the other


Mk   6.33    place by themselves.                                         Now
M   14.13    place     apart.                                             But
L    9.10    called Bethsaida.
J    6.2     side of the Sea of Galilee, which is the Sea of Tiberias.  And
  Mk  8.1                                                                 In those days,


Mk   6.33                          many saw them going, and knew them, and they ran there
M   14.13    when         the      crowds heard   it,                    they followed
L    9.11    When         the      crowds learned it,                    they followed
J    6.2                  a        multitude                             followed
  Mk  8.1    when again a great crowd  had                               gathered,


Mk   6.34         on foot from all the towns, and got there ahead of them.  As he
M   14.14    him on foot from      the towns.                               As he
L    9.11    him;
J    6.2     him,
  M   9.36                                                              When
  M  15.32                                             Then Jesus called his
  Mk  8.1     and they had nothing to eat,              he     called his


Mk   6.34    went ashore he saw a great throng, and he had  compassion on      them,
M   14.14    went ashore he saw a great throng; and he had  compassion on      them,
L    9.11                                       and he      welcomed           them
  M   9.36               he saw the      crowds,     he had  compassion for     them,
  M  15.32    disciples to him   and said,       "I have compassion on the crowd,
  Mk  8.2     disciples to him,  and said to them, "I have compassion on the crowd,


Mk   6.34    because they were                          like sheep without a shepherd;
M   14.14                                               and healed their sick.
L    9.11    and spoke to them of the kingdom of God, and cured  those who had need
  M   9.36    because they were harassed and helpless, like sheep without a shepherd.
  M  15.32    because they have been with me now three days, and have nothing to eat;
  Mk  8.2     because they have been with me now three days, and have nothing to eat;


  J   6.3     Jesus went up on the mountain, and there sat down with his disciples.
  J   6.4     Now the Passover, the feast of the Jews, was at hand.


Mk   6.35    and he began to teach them many things.  And when it grew        late,
M   14.15                                             When it was          evening,
L    9.12a   of healing.                              Now the day began to wear away;
J    6.5                            Lifting up his eyes, then, and seeing


Mk   6.35        his disciples     came    to him  and   said,      "This   is
M   14.15        the disciples     came    to him  and   said,      "This   is
L    9.12c   and the twelve        came            and   said to him, |for we are
J    6.5     that a  multitude was coming to him, Jesus said to Philip,
```

```
Mk   6.36                  a lonely place, and the hour is now late; send      them    away,
M   14.15                  a lonely place, and the day   is now over; send the crowds  away
L    9.12b    here in a lonely place."                            |"Send the crowd   away,
  M  15.32                              and   I am unwilling to   send      them    away
  Mk  8.3                               and if I                  send      them    away


Mk   6.36     to go into the country and villages                     round about
M   14.15     to go into the             villages
L    9.12b    to go into the             villages and country round about, to lodge
  M  15.32    hungry,          lest they      faint on the way."
  Mk  8.3     hungry to their homes, they will faint on the way; and some of them have


Mk   6.36                                                                      and buy
M   14.15                                                                      and buy
L    9.12b                                                                     and get
J    6.5                                                     "How    are we to buy
  M  15.33             And the disciples said  to him, "Where are we to get
  Mk  8.4    come a long way." And his disciples answered him, "How   can one feed


Mk   6.37                          themselves something to eat." But  he     answered
M   14.16                food for themselves."                        Jesus said,
L    9.13a               provisions;                                  But  he    said  to
J    6.6                 bread, so that these people  may eat?" This he    said
  M  15.33               bread enough in the desert to feed so great a crowd?"
  Mk  8.4    these men with bread here   in the desert?"


Mk   6.37     them,              "You give them something to eat."  And they
M   14.16     "They need not go away; you give them something to eat."
L    9.13a    them,              "You give them something to eat."
J    6.7      to test him, for he himself knew what he would do.          Philip


Mk   6.37     said  to him, "Shall  we      go and buy two hundred denarii
L    9.13c                 |unless we are to go and buy
J    6.7      answered him,                           "Two hundred denarii would not


Mk   6.38         worth of bread, and give it to them to eat?"      And he     said to
L    9.13c              food   for all these people."
J    6.7      buy enough    bread for each of    them to get a little."
  M  15.34                                                 And Jesus said to
  Mk  8.5                                                  And he    asked


Mk   6.38     them, "How many loaves have you? Go and see."  And when they had found
  M  15.34    them, "How many loaves have you?"
  Mk  8.5     them, "How many loaves have you?"


Mk   6.38     out, they                                    said,
M   14.17          They                                    said to him,
L    9.13b         They                                    said,
J    6.8      One of his disciples, Andrew, Simon Peter's brother, said to him,
  M  15.34         They                                    said,
  Mk  8.5           They                                    said,


Mk   6.38                            "Five,              and        two
M   14.17     "We    have only        five    loaves here and        two
L    9.13b    "We    have no more than five    loaves    and        two
J    6.9      |"There is a lad here who has five barley loaves and        two
  M  15.34                            "Seven,             and        a few
  Mk  8.7a                            "Seven."            And they had a few
```

238

```
Mk    6.39           fish."                                              Then he      commanded
M     14.18,19       fish."  And he said, "Bring them here to me."       Then he      ordered
L     9.14b          fish---                                            |And  he      said to his
J     6.10a          fish;  but what are they among so many?"               Jesus said,
  M   15.35    small fish."                                              And          commanding
  Mk  8.6      small fish;                                               And  he      commanded


Mk    6.39                                   them all to sit down by companies upon the green
M     14.19                         the crowds   to sit down              on the
L     9.14b    disciples, "Make     them         sit down in companies, about fifty
J     6.10a              "Make the people        sit down."         Now there was much
  M   15.35                     the crowd     to sit down                 on the
  Mk  8.6                       the crowd     to sit down                 on the


Mk    6.40     grass.           So     they                              sat down in
M     14.19    grass;
L     9.15     each."           And    they did so, and made them all sit down.
J     6.10a    grass in the place; so the men                               sat down,
  M   15.35    ground,
  Mk  8.6      ground;


Mk    6.41     groups, by hundreds and by fifties.  And    taking the five  loaves  and
M     14.19                                          and    taking the five  loaves  and
L     9.16                                           And    taking the five  loaves  and
J     6.11                             Jesus then    took        the         loaves,
  M   15.36                                          |he took     the seven   loaves  and
  Mk  8.6                                            and he took  the seven   loaves,


Mk    6.41     the two fish he looked up to heaven, and                  blessed,
M     14.19    the two fish he looked up to heaven, and                  blessed,
L     9.16     the two fish he looked up to heaven, and                  blessed
J     6.11                                           and when he had  given thanks,
  M   15.36    the      fish,                        and        having given thanks
  Mk  8.6                                             and        having given thanks


Mk    6.41     and broke          the loaves, and gave      them to the disciples
M     14.19    and broke and gave the loaves                   to the disciples, and
L     9.16     and broke          them,       and gave     them to the disciples
J     6.11     he                             distributed them to
  M   15.36    he broke           them        and gave     them to the disciples, and
  Mk  8.6      he broke           them        and gave     them to his disciples


Mk    6.41              to set       before the people; and he divided the two fish
M     14.19    the disciples gave them to      the crowds.
L     9.16              to set       before the crowd.
J     6.11                      those who  were seated; so also       the      fish,
  M   15.36    the disciples gave them to      the crowds.
  Mk  8.6               to set       before the people; and they set them before the


  Mk  8.7      crowd.  And they had a few small fish; and having blessed them, he
  Mk  8.7      commanded that these also should be set before them.


Mk    6.42     among them all.      And     they all ate   and were satisfied.
M     14.20                         And     they all ate   and were satisfied.
L     9.17                          And          all ate   and were satisfied.
J     6.12     as much as they wanted.  And when they had eaten their    fill, he told
  M   15.37                         And     they all ate   and were satisfied;
  Mk  8.8                            And     they     ate,  and were satisfied;
```

239

J   6.12   *his disciples, "Gather up the fragments left over, that nothing may be*

Mk	6.43		And they took	up			twelve
M	14.20		And they took	up			twelve
L	9.17		And they took	up what		was left over,	twelve
J	6.13	*lost."*	So they gathered them up and filled				twelve
M	*15.37*		*and they took*	*up*			*seven*
Mk	*8.8*		*and they took*	*up the broken pieces left over,*			*seven*

Mk	6.43	baskets full of	broken pieces and of the fish.
M	14.20	baskets full of the broken pieces	left over.
L	9.17	baskets of broken pieces.	
J	6.13	baskets with fragments from the five barley loaves, left	
M	*15.37*	*baskets full of the broken pieces*	*left over.*
Mk	*8.8*	baskets full.	

Mk	6.44	And those who	ate the loaves were	five thousand men.	
M	14.21	And those who	ate	were about five thousand men,	besides
L	9.14a	For there		were about five thousand men.	
J	6.10b	by those who had eaten.	|in number about five thousand.		
M	*15.38*	*Those who*	*ate*	*were four thousand men,*	*besides*
Mk	*8.9*	And *there*		*were about four thousand people.*	

M	*14.21*	*women and children.*
J	*6.14*	*When the people saw the sign which he had done, they said, "This is*
M	*15.39*	*women and children. And sending away the crowds, he got into*
Mk	*8.10*	*And he sent them away; and immediately he got into*

J	*6.14*	*indeed the prophet who is to come into the world!"*
M	*15.39*	*the boat and went to the region of Magadan.*
Mk	*8.10*	*the boat with his disciples, and went to the district of Dalmanutha.*

30. WALKING ON THE WATER

Mark 6.45-52

Mk	6.45	Immediately he made his disciples	get into
M	14.22	Then he made the disciples	get into
J	6.16b,17a	his disciples went down to the sea,	|got into

Mk	6.45	the boat	and go before him to the other side, to Bethsaida,	while he
M	14.22	the boat	and go before him to the other side,	while he
J	6.15	a boat, and started	across the sea to Capernaum.	Perceiving

Mk	6.46	dismissed the crowd.	And after he had taken leave of them,
M	14.23a	dismissed the crowds.	And after he had dismissed the crowds,
J	6.15	then that they were about to come	and take him by force to make him king,
L	*6.12*		*In these days*

Mk	6.47	he	went up	on the mountain	to pray. And when
M	14.23a	he	went up	on the mountain by himself	to pray. When
J	6.16a	Jesus	withdrew again	to the mountain by himself.	When
L	*6.12*	*he*	*went out*	*to the mountain*	*to pray; and all*

Mk	6.47	evening came,	the boat	was	out on
M	14.24a	evening came,	|but the boat by this time	was many furlongs	distant from
J	6.16a	evening came,			
L	*6.12*	*night he continued in prayer to God.*			

```
Mk   6.48     the sea, and he was          alone on the land.  And he saw that they were
M    14.23b   the land,    |he was there alone,
```

```
Mk   6.48         making headway painfully, for the      wind was against them.  And about
M    14.24b,25    beaten by the waves;        for the     wind was against them.  And in
J    6.18                   The sea rose because a strong wind was blowing.
```

```
Mk   6.48     the fourth watch of the night      he              came to them, walking
M    14.25    the fourth watch of the night      he              came to them, walking
J    6.17b              It was now dark, and Jesus had not yet come to them.
```

```
Mk   6.49     on the sea.  He meant to pass by them, |but when      they       saw him
M    14.26a   on the sea.                             But when the disciples  saw him
J    6.19              When they had rowed about three or four miles, they       saw Jesus
```

```
Mk   6.49     walking on the sea  they thought  it was a ghost,   and       cried out;
M    14.26c   walking on the sea,     |saying, "It is  a ghost!"  And they cried out
J    6.19     walking on the sea and drawing near to the boat.
```

```
Mk   6.50            |for they all saw him, and       were terrified.   But immediately
M    14.26b,27 for fear.                         |they were terrified,   But immediately
J    6.20                          They were frightened,  |But
```

```
Mk   6.50     he spoke to them and said,   "Take heart, it is I; have no      fear."
M    14.27    he spoke to them,      saying, "Take heart, it is I; have no      fear."
J    6.20     he said   to them,                        "It is I; do    not be afraid."
```

```
 M   14.28      And Peter answered him, "Lord, if it is you, bid me come to you on the
 M   14.29      water." He said, "Come." So Peter got out of the boat and walked on
 M   14.30      the water and came to Jesus; but when he saw the wind, he was afraid,
 M   14.31      and beginning to sink he cried out, "Lord, save me." Jesus immediately
 M   14.31      reached out his hand and caught him, saying to him, "O man of little
 M   14.31      faith, why did you doubt?"
```

```
Mk   6.51     And       he              got      into the boat with them and
M    14.32    And when they             got      into the boat,
J    6.21              Then they were glad to take him into the boat,           and
```

```
Mk   6.52                     the wind ceased.  And they were utterly astounded,  |for they
M    14.33                    the wind ceased.  And those in the boat worshiped him,
J    6.21     immediately the boat was at the land to which they were going.
```

```
Mk   6.52     did not understand about the loaves, but their hearts were hardened.
M    14.33    saying, "Truly you are the Son of God."
```

31. HEALING AT GENNESARET

Mark 6.53-56

```
Mk   6.53     And when they had crossed over, they came to land at Gennesaret, and
M    14.34    And when they had crossed over, they came to land at Gennesaret.
```

```
Mk   6.54     moored to the shore.  And when they got out of the boat, immediately
M    14.35                           And when
```

```
Mk   6.55   the people                  recognized him, |and ran  about the whole
M    14.35  the men of that place recognized him,  they sent round      to all


Mk   6.55   neighborhood and began to bring                       sick people on
M    14.35  that region   and            brought to him all that were sick,


Mk   6.56   their pallets to any place where they heard he was.  And wherever he came,
Mk   6.56   in villages, cities, or country, they laid the sick in the market places,


Mk   6.56   and besought him that they might     touch even the fringe of his
M    14.36  |and besought him that they might only touch        the fringe of his


Mk   6.56   garment; and as many as touched it were made well.
M    14.36  garment; and as many as touched it were made well.
```

32. A QUESTION OF DEFILEMENT

Mark 7.1-23

```
Mk   7.1    Now when                the Pharisees gathered together to him, with some
M    15.1   Then                    Pharisees
L    11.37  While he was speaking, a Pharisee asked him to dine with him; so he


Mk   7.2    of  the scribes, who had come        from Jerusalem, |they saw that
M    15.1   and      scribes          came to Jesus from Jerusalem
L    11.37  went in and sat at table.


Mk   7.3    some of his disciples ate with hands defiled, that is, unwashed.  (For
Mk   7.3    the Pharisees, and all the Jews, do not eat unless they wash their hands,
Mk   7.4    observing the tradition of the elders; and when they come from the
Mk   7.4    market place, they do not eat unless they purify themselves; and there
Mk   7.4    are many other traditions which they observe, the washing of cups and
Mk   7.4    pots and vessels of bronze.)


Mk   7.5    And the Pharisees and the scribes asked him, "Why do your disciples
M    15.2   and                            said,      |"Why do your disciples
L    11.38      The Pharisee           was astonished to see


Mk   7.5    not live according to the tradition of the elders,  but
M    15.2   transgress            the tradition of the elders?  For they do  not
L    11.38                                                      that he  did not


Mk   7.6        eat  with  hands       defiled?"  And he said to them, "Well did
M    15.7        wash their hands when they eat."      You hypocrites!  Well did
L    11.38  first wash            before dinner.


Mk   7.6    Isaiah prophesy of you hypocrites, as it is written,
M    15.7   Isaiah prophesy of you,            when  he said:


Mk   7.6                'This people honors me with their lips,
M    15.8                'This people honors me with their lips,


Mk   7.6                but their heart is far from me;
M    15.8                but their heart is far from me;
```

Mk	7.7	in vain do they worship me,
M	15.9	in vain do they worship me,

Mk	7.7	teaching as doctrines the precepts of men.'
M	15.9	teaching as doctrines the precepts of men.'"

Mk	7.8	You leave the commandment of God, and hold fast the tradition of men."

Mk	7.9	And he said to them, "You have a fine way of rejecting
M	15.3	He answered them, "And why do you transgress
L	11.39	And the Lord said to him, "Now you Pharisees cleanse the

Mk	7.10	the commandment of God, in order to keep your tradition! For Moses
M	15.4	the commandment of God for the sake of your tradition? For God
L	11.39	outside of the cup and of the dish, but inside you are full of extortion

Mk	7.10	said, 'Honor your father and your mother'; and, 'He who speaks evil
M	15.4	commanded, 'Honor your father and your mother,' and, 'He who speaks evil
L	11.39	and wickedness.

Mk	7.11	of father and mother, let him surely die'; but you say, 'If a man tells
M	15.5	of father and mother, let him surely die.' But you say, 'If any one tells

Mk	7.11	his father or his mother, What you would have gained from me is Corban'
M	15.5	his father or his mother, What you would have gained from me is

Mk	7.12	(that is, given to God)--|then you no longer permit him to do anything
M	15.5	given to God, he need not honor

Mk	7.13	for his father or mother, |thus making
M	15.6	his father.' So, for the sake of your tradition, you have made

Mk	7.13	void the word of God through your tradition which you hand on. And many
M	15.6	void the word of God.

Mk	7.13	such things you do."

Mk	7.14	And he called the people to him again, and said to them, "Hear me, all
M	15.10	And he called the people to him and said to them, "Hear

Mk	7.15	of you, and understand: there is nothing outside a man which by going
M	15.11	and understand: not what goes

Mk	7.15	into him can defile him; but the things which come out of a
M	15.11	into the mouth defiles a man, but what comes out of the

Mk	7.16	man are what defile him." "*If any man has ears to hear, let him hear.*"
M	15.11	mouth, this defiles a man."
M	*11.15*	He who has ears to hear, let him hear.
M	*13.9*	He who has ears let him hear."
M	*13.43b*	He who has ears, let him hear.
Mk	*4.9*	*And he said,* "He who has ears to hear, let him hear."
Mk	*4.23*	If any man has ears to hear, let him hear."
L	*8.8b*	*As he said this, he called out,* "He who has ears to hear, let him hear."
L	*14.35b*	He who has ears to hear, let him hear."

| Mk | 7.17 | And when he had entered the house, and left the people, his disciples |
| M | 15.12 | Then   the disciples |

| Mk | 7.17 | asked   him |
| M | 15.12 | came and said to him, "Do you know that the Pharisees were offended when |

M	15.13	*they heard this saying?" He answered, "Every plant which my heavenly*
M	15.14	*Father has not planted will be rooted up. |Let them alone; they are blind*
M	15.14	*guides. And if a blind man leads a blind man, both will fall into a pit."*

| Mk | 7.18 | about   the parable.   And he said to them, |
| M | 15.15,16 | But Peter said to him, "Explain the parable to us." And he said, |

| Mk | 7.18 | "Then are you also   without understanding? Do you not see that |
| M | 15.17 | "Are you also still without understanding? Do you not see that |

| Mk | 7.19 | whatever goes into a   man from outside cannot defile him, |since it |
| M | 15.17 | whatever goes into the mouth |

| Mk | 7.19 | enters, not his heart but his stomach, and so passes on?" (Thus he |
| M | 15.17 | passes   into the stomach, and so passes on? |

| Mk | 7.20 | declared all foods clean.) And he said, "What comes out of a   man |
| M | 15.18 | But what comes out of the mouth |

| Mk | 7.21 | is what defiles a man. For from within, out of |
| M | 15.19 | proceeds from the heart, and this defiles a man. For   out of |

| Mk | 7.21 | the heart of man, come evil thoughts,   fornication, theft, |
| M | 15.19 | the heart   come evil thoughts, murder, adultery, fornication, theft, |

| Mk | 7.22 | murder, adultery, |coveting, wickedness, deceit, licentiousness, envy, |
| M | 15.19 | false witness, |

| Mk | 7.23 | slander, pride, foolishness. All these evil things come from within, and |
| M | 15.20 | slander.   These are |

| Mk | 7.23 | they defile a man." |
| M | 15.20 | what defile a man; but to eat with unwashed hands does not defile a man." |

33. THE SYROPHOENICIAN WOMAN

Mark 7.24-30

| Mk | 7.24 | And from there he arose and went away   to the |
| M | 15.21 | And   Jesus   went away from there and withdrew to the |

| Mk | 7.24 | region   of Tyre and Sidon. And he entered a house, and would not have |
| M | 15.21 | district of Tyre and Sidon. |

| Mk | 7.25 | any one know it; yet he could not be hid. But immediately a |
| M | 15.22 | And behold,   a Canaanite |

Mk	7.25	woman,
M	15.22	woman from that region came out and cried, "Have mercy on me, O Lord, Son

Mk	7.25	whose little daughter was possessed by an unclean spirit,
M	15.22	of David; my daughter is severely possessed by a demon."

M	15.23	*But he did not answer her a word. And his disciples came and begged him,*
M	15.24	*saying, "Send her away, for she is crying after us." He answered, "I was*
M	15.24	*sent only to the lost sheep of the house of Israel."*

Mk	7.26	heard of him, and came and fell down at his feet. Now the woman was a
M	15.25	But she came and knelt before him,

Mk	7.26	Greek, a Syrophoenician by birth. And she begged him to cast the demon out
M	15.25	saying, "Lord, help me."

Mk	7.27	of her daughter. And he said to her, "Let the children first be fed, for it
M	15.26	And he answered, "It

Mk	7.28	is not right to take the children's bread and throw it to the dogs." But
M	15.26	is not fair to take the children's bread and throw it to the dogs."
M	7.6	*"Do not give dogs what is*

Mk	7.28	she answered him, "Yes, Lord; yet even the dogs under the table eat the
M	15.27	She said, "Yes, Lord, yet even the dogs eat the
M	7.6	*holy; and do not throw your pearls before swine, lest they trample them*

Mk	7.29	children's crumbs." And he
M	15.28	crumbs that fall from their masters' table." Then Jesus
M	7.6	*under foot and turn to attack you.*

Mk	7.29	said to her, "For this saying you may go your way; the demon has left
M	15.28	answered her, "O woman, great is your faith! Be it done for you

Mk	7.30	your daughter." And she went home, and found the
M	15.28	as you desire." And her
L	7.10	*And when those who had been sent returned to the house, they found the*

Mk	7.30	child lying in bed, and the demon gone.
M	15.28	daughter was healed instantly.
L	7.10	*slave well.*

34. THE DEAF MUTE

Mark 7.31-37

Mk	7.31	Then he returned from the region of Tyre, and went through Sidon to
M	15.29	*And Jesus went on from there and passed along*

Mk	7.31	the Sea of Galilee, through the region of the Decapolis.
M	15.29	*the Sea of Galilee. And he went up on the mountain, and sat down there.*

Mk	7.32	And they brought to him a man who was
M	15.30	*And great crowds came to him, bringing with them the lame, the maimed,*

245

Mk	7.32	deaf and had an impediment in his speech; and they besought him to lay
M	15.30	*the blind, the dumb, and many others,* and they *put* them at

Mk	7.33	his hand upon him. And taking him aside from the multitude privately, he
M	15.30	his *feet,*

Mk	7.34	put his fingers into his ears, and he spat and touched his tongue; and
Mk	7.34	looking up to heaven, he sighed, and said to him, "Ephphatha," that is,

Mk	7.35	"Be opened." And his ears were opened, his tongue was released, and he
M	15.30	and *he healed them,*

Mk	7.36	spoke plainly. And he charged them to tell no one; but the more he
Mk	7.36	charged them, the more zealously they proclaimed it.

Mk	7.37	And they were astonished beyond measure, saying, "He has done
M	15.31	*so that the throng wondered,*

Mk	7.37	all things well; he even makes the deaf hear and the dumb speak."
M	15.31	*when they saw* the dumb *speaking, the*

M	15.31	*maimed whole, the lame walking, and the blind seeing; and they glorified*
M	15.31	*the God of Israel.*

35. THE FOUR THOUSAND FED

Mark 8.1-10

Mk	8.1	In those days, when again a great crowd had gathered, and they had
M	15.32	Then

Mk	8.1	nothing to eat, he called his disciples to him, and said to them,
M	15.32	Jesus called his disciples to him and said,
M	9.36	*When he saw the crowds,*
M	14.14	*As he went ashore* he *saw a great throng;* and
Mk	6.34	*As he went ashore* he *saw a great throng,* and
L	9.11	*When the crowds learned it, they followed* him; and
J	6.2	*And a multitude followed him,*

Mk	8.2	"I have compassion on the crowd, because they have been with me now
M	15.32	"I have compassion on the crowd, because they have been with me now
M	9.36	*he* had compassion *for* *them,* because they *were harassed and help-*
M	14.14	*he* had compassion on *them,*
Mk	6.34	*he* had compassion on *them,* because they *were*
L	9.11	*he welcomed them and spoke to them of the kingdom of*
J	6.2	because they *saw the signs which he*

Mk	8.2	three days, and have nothing to eat;
M	15.32	three days, and have nothing to eat;
M	9.36	*less, like sheep without a shepherd.*
M	14.14	*and healed their sick.*
Mk	6.34	*like sheep without a shepherd; and he began to teach them many things*
L	9.11	*God, and cured those who had need of healing.*
J	6.3	*did on those who were diseased. Jesus went up on the mountain, and there*

```
J    6.4        sat down with his disciples.  Now the Passover, the feast of the Jews, was


M   14.15                              When it was          evening,      the disciples
Mk   6.35                       And when it grew            late,         his disciples
L    9.12a                      Now the day began to wear away; and the twelve
J    6.5        at hand.  Lifting up his eyes, then, and seeing that a   multitude was


M   14.15       came    to him  and    said,          "This  is          a lonely place,
Mk   6.35       came    to him  and    said,          "This  is          a lonely place,
L    9.12c      came            and    said to him,  |for we are here in a lonely place."
J    6.5        coming to him,  Jesus  said to Philip,


Mk   8.3              and if I                send     them   away hungry to their homes,
M   15.32       and     I am unwilling to     send     them   away hungry,
M   14.15       and the day  is now over;     send the crowds away  to go into the
Mk   6.36       and the hour is now late;     send     them   away,  to go into the country
L    9.12b                             "Send the crowd  away,  to go into the


Mk   8.3                they will faint on the way; and some of them have come a long way."
M   15.32       lest they        faint on the way."
M  14.15              villages
Mk  6.36        and villages                round about
L   9.12b             villages and country round about, to lodge


Mk   8.4        And his disciples answered him, "How  can one      feed these men with
M   15.33       And the disciples said  to him, "Where are we  to  get
M  14.15                                                    and buy
Mk  6.36                                                    and buy
L   9.12b                                                   and get
J   6.5                                   "How  are we  to  buy


Mk   8.4        bread here   in the desert?"
M   15.33       bread enough in the desert to feed so great a crowd?"
M  14.16        food for themselves."                      Jesus said,   "They need
Mk  6.37                  themselves something to eat." But  he    answered them,
L   9.13a       provisions;                             But  he    said  to them,
J   6.6         bread, so that these people may eat?"  This he    said  to test him,


M  14.16        not go away; you give them something to eat."
Mk  6.37                    "You give them something to eat." And they   said  to him,
L   9.13a                   "You give them something to eat."
J   6.7         for he himself knew what he would do.          Philip answered him,


Mk  6.37        "Shall  we        go and buy two hundred denarii             worth of
L   9.13d       unless we are to go and buy
J   6.7                              "Two hundred denarii would not buy enough


Mk   8.5                                          And he     asked    them,  "How
M   15.34a                                        And Jesus said to  them,  "How
Mk  6.38a       bread, and give it to them to eat?"      And he     said to them,  "How
L   9.13d       food  for all these people."
J   6.7         bread for each of them to get a little."


Mk   8.5        many loaves have you?"                                        They
M   15.34a      many loaves have you?"                                        They
M  14.17a                                                                     They
Mk  6.38a       many loaves have you? Go and see." And when they had found out, they
L   9.13b                                                                     They
J   6.8                                                                       One of
```

```
Mk    8.5                                                      said,
M    15.34a                                                    said,
  M   14.17a                                                   said to him,   "We      have
  Mk   6.38a                                                   said,
  L    9.13b                                                   said,         "We      have
  J    6.9a        his disciples, Andrew, Simon Peter's brother, said to him, |"There is a


Mk    8.6                            "Seven."              And   he      commanded
M    15.35                           "Seven,              |And           commanding
  M   14.19        only          five          loaves here  Then  he      ordered
  Mk   6.39                          "Five,                 Then  he      commanded
  L    9.14b       no more than    five         loaves     |And   he      said to his disciples,
  J    6.10a       lad here who has five barley loaves      |Jesus said,


Mk    8.6              the crowd    to sit down              on the       ground;
M    15.35             the crowd    to sit down              on the       ground,
  M   14.19            the crowds   to sit down              on the       grass;
  Mk   6.39                them all to sit down by companies upon the green grass.
  L    9.14b   "Make    them         sit down in companies, about fifty each."
  J    6.10a   "Make the people      sit down."         Now there was much grass in the


  Mk   6.40              So     they                     sat down in groups, by
  L    9.15              And    they did so, and made them all sit down.
  J    6.10a   place; so the men                        sat down,


Mk    8.6                              and he took    the seven loaves,
M    15.35                             he took    the seven loaves  and the
  M   14.19                            and    taking the five  loaves  and the two
  Mk   6.41     hundreds and by fifties. And    taking the five  loaves  and the two
  L    9.16                             And    taking the five  loaves  and the two
  J    6.11             Jesus then    took    the       loaves,


Mk    8.6                            and         having given thanks   he broke
M    15.36     fish,                 and         having given thanks   he broke
  M   14.19    fish he looked up to heaven, and                blessed, and broke
  Mk   6.41    fish he looked up to heaven, and                blessed, and broke
  L    9.16    fish he looked up to heaven, and                blessed and broke
  J    6.11                           and when he had    given thanks,


Mk    8.6             them     and gave them to his disciples to set before
M    15.36            them     and gave them to the disciples,
  M   14.19   and gave the loaves               to the disciples,
  Mk   6.41        the loaves, and gave them to the disciples to set before
  L    9.16          them,     and gave them to the disciples to set before


Mk    8.6     the people; and    they    set     them before the crowd.
M    15.36                and the disciples gave them to   the crowds.
  M   14.19               and the disciples gave them to   the crowds.
  Mk   6.41   the people;                                       and he
  L    9.16   the crowd.
  J    6.11               he        distributed them to those who were seated;


Mk    8.7                                      And they had a few small
M    15.34b                                    and          a few small
  M   14.17b                                   and          two
  Mk   6.38b   divided the two fish among them all.   and   two
  L    9.13c                                    and         two
  J    6.9b    so also the      fish, as much as they wanted. and   two
```

248

```
Mk    8.7      fish; and having blessed them, he commanded that these also should be set
M     15.34b   fish."
  M   14.18    fish."   And he said, "Bring them here to me."
  Mk  6.38b    fish."
  L   9.13c    fish--
  J   6.9b     fish;


Mk    8.8      before them.  And        they      ate,   and were satisfied;
M     15.37                  And        they all ate     and were satisfied;
  M   14.20                  And        they all ate      and were satisfied.
  Mk  6.42                   And        they all ate      and were satisfied.
  L   9.17                   And             all ate      and were satisfied.
  J   6.12                   And when they had eaten their fill, he told his disciples,


Mk    8.8                                                                    and they
M     15.37                                                                  and they
  M   14.20                                                                  And they
  Mk  6.43                                                                   And they
  L   9.17                                                                   And they
  J   6.13     "Gather up the fragments left over, that nothing may be lost." So  they


Mk    8.8      took           up the broken pieces left over,  seven  baskets full.
M     15.37    took           up                                seven  baskets full of the
  M   14.20    took           up                                twelve baskets full of the
  Mk  6.43     took           up                                twelve baskets full of
  L   9.17     took           up what           was left over, twelve baskets      of
  J   6.13     gathered them  up and filled                    twelve baskets      with


Mk    8.9                                                     And there
M     15.38    broken pieces                     left over.       Those who       ate
  M   14.21    broken pieces                     left over.  And those who       ate
  Mk  6.44     broken pieces and of the fish.                And those who       ate
  L   9.14a    broken pieces.                                For there
  J   6.13     fragments from the five barley loaves, left       by  those who had eaten.


Mk    8.9                 were     about four thousand people.
M     15.38               were           four thousand men, besides women and children.
  M   14.21               were     about five thousand men, besides women and children.
  Mk  6.44     the loaves were           five thousand men.
  L   9.14a               were     about five thousand men.
  J   6.10b,14 |in number         about five thousand.  When the people saw the sign


Mk    8.10     And he sent them away; and immediately he got into the boat with his
M     15.39    And     sending   away the crowds,        he got into the boat
  J   6.14     which he had done, they said, "This is indeed the prophet who is to come


Mk    8.10     disciples, and went to the district of Dalmanutha.
M     15.39               and went to the region  of Magadan.
  J   6.14     into the world!"
```

Mark 8.11-21

Mk	8.11			The Pharisees		came and began
M	16.1	And		the Pharisees and Sadducees came, and		
M	12.38	*Then some of the scribes and* Pharisees				
L	11.16	*while*		*others,*		
L	11.29	*When*		*the crowds*	*were increasing,*	
J	2.18			*The Jews*	*then*	

Mk	8.11	to argue with him,	seeking from him			
M	16.1	to test	him they asked	him		to show them
M	12.38		*said*	*to*	*him,*	*"Teacher, we wish to see*
L	11.16	to test	*him,*	*sought*	from him	
J	2.18		*said*	*to*	*him,*	*"What*
J	6.30	*So they said*	*to*	*him,*	*"Then what*

Mk	8.12	a sign from heaven, to test him.	And he sighed deeply in his spirit,		
M	16.2	a sign from heaven.	He		
M	12.39	a sign from *you."*	But he		
L	11.16	a sign from heaven.			
L	11.29		he *began*		
L	12.54		He *also*		
J	2.18	sign *have you to show us for doing this?"*			
J	6.30	sign *do you do, that we may see, and believe you? What work do you*			

Mk	8.12	and said,		
M	16.2	answered them,	"When it is evening,	
M	12.39	*answered them,*		
L	11.29	*to* say,		
L	12.54	said *to the multitudes, "When you see a cloud rising in the west,*		
J	6.30	*perform?*		

M	16.3	*you say,*	*'It will be fair weather; for the sky is red.' And*
L	12.55	*you say at once, 'A shower is coming'; and so it happens. And*	

M	16.3	*in the morning,*	*'It will be stormy*
L	12.55	*when you see the south wind blowing, you say, 'There will be scorching*	

M	16.3	*today, for the sky is red and threatening.' You know how to interpret*	
L	12.56	*heat';and it happens. You hypocrites! You know how to interpret*	

M	16.3	*the appearance of the sky, but you cannot*	
L	12.56	*the appearance of earth and sky; but why do you not know how to*	

Mk	8.12		"Why does this	generation
M	16.4	interpret the signs of the times.	An evil and adulterous	generation
M	12.39		*"An evil and adulterous*	generation
L	11.29		*"This generation is an evil*	generation;
L	12.56	*interpret the present time?*		

Mk	8.12	seek	a sign?	Truly, I say to you,	no sign shall be given to
M	16.4	seeks for	a sign,	but	no sign shall be given to
M	12.39	seeks *for*	a sign;	*but*	no sign shall be given to
L	11.29	*it* seeks	a sign,	*but*	no sign shall be given to

Mk	8.13	this generation."		And he left them, and
M	16.4	it except the sign of	Jonah."	So he left them and
M	12.39	*it except the sign of the prophet Jonah.*		
L	11.29	*it except the sign of*	*Jonah.*	

Mk	8.13	getting into the boat again he departed to the other side.
M	16.4	departed.

Mk	8.14	Now _____ they had forgotten to bring
M	16.5	When the disciples reached the other side, they had forgotten to bring
L	12.1	In the meantime, when so many thousands of the

Mk	8.15	bread; and they had only one loaf with them in the boat. And he
M	16.6	any bread. Jesus
L	12.1	multitude had gathered together that they trod upon one another, he

Mk	8.15	cautioned them, saying, "Take heed, beware of the leaven
M	16.6	said to them, "Take heed and beware of the leaven
L	12.1	began to say to his disciples first, "Beware of the leaven

Mk	8.16	of the Pharisees and the leaven of Herod." And they discussed it
M	16.7	of the Pharisees and Sadducees." And they discussed it
L	12.1	of the Pharisees, which is hypocrisy.

Mk	8.17	with one another, saying, "We have no bread." And being aware of
M	16.8	among themselves, saying, "We brought no bread." But Jesus, aware of

Mk	8.17	it, Jesus said to them, "Why do you discuss
M	16.8	this, said, "O men of little faith, why do you discuss among your-

Mk	8.17	the fact that you have no bread? Do you not yet perceive or
M	16.9	selves the fact that you have no bread? Do you not yet perceive?

Mk	8.18	understand? Are your hearts hardened? |Having eyes do you not see,

Mk	8.19	and having ears do you not hear? And do you not remember? |When I
M	16.9	Do you not remember

Mk	8.19	broke the five loaves for the five thousand, how many baskets full
M	16.9	the five loaves of the five thousand, and how many baskets

Mk	8.20	of broken pieces did you take up?" They said to him, "Twelve." "And the
M	16.10	you gathered? Or the

Mk	8.20	seven for the four thousand, how many baskets full of broken
M	16.10	seven loaves of the four thousand, and how many baskets

Mk	8.21	pieces did you take up?" And they said to him, "Seven." |And he said
M	16.10	you gathered?

Mk	8.21	to them, "Do you not yet understand?"
M	16.11	How is it that you fail to perceive that I did not speak about bread?

M	16.12	*Beware of the leaven of the Pharisees and Sadducees." Then they*
M	16.12	*understood that he did not tell them to beware of the leaven of bread,*
M	16.12	*but of the teaching of the Pharisees and Sadducees.*

37. THE BLIND MAN OF BETHSAIDA

Mark 8.22-26

Mk 8.22   And they came to Bethsaida.   And some people brought to him a blind man,
J 9.1   *As he passed by,*   *he saw a man blind*

Mk 8.23   and begged him to touch him.   And he took the blind man by the hand,
J 9.6   *from his birth.*   *As he said this,*

Mk 8.23   and led him out of the village; and when he had spit
J 9.6   *he*   *spat on the ground and*

Mk 8.23   on his   eyes and laid his hands
J 9.6   *made clay of the spittle and anointed the man's eyes with the clay,*

Mk 8.24   upon him, he asked him, "Do you see anything?"   And he looked up and
Mk 8.25   said, "I see men; but they look like trees, walking."   Then again he

Mk 8.25   laid his hands upon his eyes; and he looked intently and was restored,
J 9.7 |*saying to him, "Go, wash*

Mk 8.26   and saw everything clearly.   And he sent him away to his home, saying,
J 9.7   *in the pool of Siloam" (which means* Sent).   *So he went and washed and*

Mk 8.26   "Do not even enter the village."
J 9.7   *came back seeing.*

38. PETER'S CONFESSION AND FIRST PREDICTION OF THE PASSION

Mark 8.27-33

Mk 8.27   And   Jesus went on with his disciples, to the villages
M 16.13   Now when   Jesus came   into the district
L 9.18   Now it happened that as he was praying alone the disciples were
J 6.66   *After this many of his disciples drew back and no longer went about*

Mk 8.27   of Caesarea Philippi; and on the way he asked   his disciples, "Who do
M 16.13   of Caesarea Philippi,   he asked   his disciples, "Who do
L 9.18   with him;   and   he asked   them,   "Who do
J 6.67   *with him.*   *Jesus said to the twelve,*   "Do

Mk 8.28   men   say that   I   am?"   And they told him,   "John
M 16.14   men   say that the Son of man is?"   And they said, "Some say John
L 9.19   the people say that   I   am?"   And they answered,   "John
J 6.67   *you also wish to go away?"*

Mk 8.28   the Baptist; and others say, Elijah; and others   one of the
M 16.14   the Baptist,   others say   Elijah, and others Jeremiah or one of the
L 9.19   the Baptist; but others say, Elijah; and others,   that one of the

Mk 8.29   prophets."   And he asked   them, "But who do you say that
M 16.15   prophets."   He said to them, "But who do you say that
L 9.20   old prophets has risen."   And he said to them, "But who do you say that

```
Mk    8.29    I am?"        Peter answered him,
M    16.16    I am?"  Simon Peter replied,
L     9.20    I am?"  And   Peter answered,
 J    1.49              Nathanael  answered him,      "Rabbi,
 J    6.68              Simon Peter answered him,      "Lord, to whom shall we go?  You
 J   11.27              She          said  to him, "Yes, Lord; I believe


 J    6.69    have the words of eternal life; and we have believed, and have come to


Mk    8.29                        "You are the Christ."
M    16.17                        "You are the Christ, the Son of the living God."  And Jesus
L     9.20                         "The Christ        of         God."
 J    1.49                  you are        the Son of      God!  You are the
 J    6.69    know, that you are the Holy One       of       God."
 J   11.27            that you are the Christ, the Son of      God, he who is


M    16.17    answered him, "Blessed are you, Simon Bar-Jona!  For flesh and blood has
 J    1.49    King of Israel!"
 J   11.27    coming into the world."


M    16.18    not revealed this to you, but my Father who is in heaven.  And I tell
M    16.18    you, you are Peter, and on this rock I will build my church, and the
M    16.19    powers of death shall not prevail against it.  I will give you the keys
M    16.19    of the kingdom of heaven, and whatever you bind on earth shall be bound
M    16.19    in heaven, and whatever you loose on earth shall be loosed in heaven."


Mk    8.30    And   he          charged            them   to tell        no one
M    16.20    Then  he strictly charged        the disciples to tell        no one
L     9.21    But   he          charged and commanded them   to tell this to no one,


Mk    8.30    about him.
M    16.20    that  he was the Christ.


Mk    8.31    And            he     began to teach   them      that the Son of man
M    16.21    From that time Jesus began to show his disciples that      he
L     9.22                                                     |saying, "The Son of man


Mk    8.31    must                        suffer many things, and be rejected by   the
M    16.21    must go to Jerusalem and    suffer many things              from the
L     9.22    must                        suffer many things, and be rejected by   the


Mk    8.31    elders and the chief priests and the scribes, and be killed, and after
M    16.21    elders and     chief priests and     scribes, and be killed, and on the
L     9.22    elders and     chief priests and     scribes, and be killed, and on the


Mk    8.32    three days rise again. |And he said this plainly.  And Peter took him,
M    16.22    third day  be raised.                              And Peter took him,
L     9.22    third day  be raised."


Mk    8.32    and began to rebuke him.
M    16.22    and began to rebuke him, saying, "God forbid, Lord!  This shall never


Mk    8.33                    But    turning and seeing his disciples, he rebuked
M    16.23    happen to you." But he turned                            and said to
```

```
Mk   8.33    Peter, and said, "Get behind me, Satan!                                    For
M   16.23    Peter,           "Get behind me, Satan!  You are a hindrance to me; for


Mk   8.33    you are not on the side of God, but of men."
M   16.23    you are not on the side of God, but of men."
```

39. COST OF DISCIPLESHIP

Mark 8.34-9.1

```
Mk   8.34    And  he     called to him the multitude with his disciples, and said to
M   16.24    Then Jesus told                              his disciples,
L    9.23    And  he                                                              said to


Mk   8.34    them, "If any man would come after me, let him deny himself and take up
M   16.24          "If any man would come after me, let him deny himself and take up
L    9.23    all,  "If any man would come after me, let him deny himself and take up
   M 10.38                                             and he who  does  not take
   L 14.27                                             Whoever does not bear


Mk   8.35    his      cross       and follow   me.                  For whoever
M   16.25    his      cross       and follow   me.                  For whoever
L    9.24    his      cross daily and follow   me.                  For whoever
   M 10.39    his      cross       and follow   me is not worthy of me.    He  who
   L 14.27    his own cross        and come after me, cannot be my disciple.
   L 17.33                                                           Whoever
   J 12.25                                                           He  who


Mk   8.35    would    save  his life will lose  it; and whoever loses his life for
M   16.25    would    save  his life will lose  it; and whoever loses his life for
L    9.24    would    save  his life will lose  it; and whoever loses his life for
   M 10.39             finds his life will lose  it, and he  who loses his life for
   L 17.33    seeks to gain  his life will lose  it, but whoever loses his life
   J 12.25             loves his life        loses it, and he  who hates his life in


Mk   8.36    my sake and the gospel's will save   it.  For what does it profit a
M   16.26    my sake                  will find   it.  For what will it profit a
L    9.25    my sake, he              will save   it.  For what does it profit a
   M 10.39    my sake                  will find   it.
   L 17.33                             will preserve it.
   J 12.26    this world               will keep   it for eternal life.  If any one


Mk   8.37    man,    to gain  the whole world and      forfeit  his life?  For
M   16.26    man, if he gains the whole world and      forfeits his life?  Or
L    9.25    man  if he gains the whole world and loses or forfeits himself?
   J 12.26    serves me, he must follow me; and where I am, there shall my servant


Mk   8.38    what can   a man give in return for his life?  For whoever is ashamed
M   16.27    what shall a man give in return for his life?  For
L    9.26                                                    For whoever is ashamed
   J 12.26    be also; if any one serves me, the Father will honor him.


Mk   8.38    of me and of my words in this adulterous and sinful generation, of him
L    9.26    of me and of my words,                                          of him
```

```
Mk   8.38    will the Son of man also be ashamed, when he comes                        in
M   16.27         the Son of man                    is to come with his angels in
L    9.26    will the Son of man         be ashamed  when he comes                     in


Mk   8.38              the glory of his Father     with the holy angels."
M   16.27              the glory of his Father, and then he will repay every man
L    9.26    his glory and the glory of the Father  and of the holy angels.


Mk   9.1     And he said  to them, "Truly, I say to you,
M   16.28    for what he has done.  Truly, I say to you,
L    9.27                    But     I tell   you truly,
  J  8.51                   Truly, truly, I say to you,
  J  8.52     The Jews said to him, "Now we know that you have a demon.  Abraham died,


Mk   9.1                              there are some standing here who will
M   16.28                             there are some standing here who will
L    9.27                             there are some standing here who will
  J  8.51                             if any one     keeps my word, he will
  J  8.52     as did the prophets; and you say,  'If any one     keeps my word, he will


Mk   9.1     not   taste death before they see that the
M   16.28    not   taste death before they see        the Son of man coming in his
L    9.27    not   taste death before they see        the
  J  8.51    never see   death."
  J  8.52    never taste death.'


Mk   9.1     kingdom of God has come with power."
M   16.28    kingdom."
L    9.27    kingdom of God."
```

40. THE TRANSFIGURATION

Mark 9.2-13

```
Mk   9.2     And after six  days                Jesus took with him Peter and
M   17.1     And after six  days                Jesus took with him Peter and
L    9.28    Now about eight days after these sayings he took with him Peter and


Mk   9.2     James and John,           and led them up    a high mountain apart
M   17.1     James and John his brother, and led them up    a high mountain apart.
L    9.28    John  and James,          and went    up on the    mountain to pray.


Mk   9.2     by themselves; and    he was transfigured before them,
M   17.2                    And    he was transfigured before them, and his face shone
L    9.29               And as he was praying, the appearance   of his countenance


Mk   9.3            |and his garments became glistening, intensely white, as
M   17.2     like the sun, and his garments became              white  as
L    9.29    was altered, and his raiment  became dazzling       white.


Mk   9.4     no fuller on earth could bleach them.  And      there    appeared to
M   17.3     light.                                 And behold, there    appeared to
L    9.30                                           And behold, two men talked with
```

Mk	9.4	them Elijah with Moses;		and they were talking
M	17.3	them Moses and Elijah,		talking
L	9.31	him, Moses and Elijah, |who appeared in glory and		spoke

Mk	9.4	to Jesus.
M	17.3	with him.
L	9.32	of his departure, which he was to accomplish at Jerusalem. *Now Peter*

L 9.32 and those who were with him were heavy with sleep, and when they wakened
L 9.32 they saw his glory and the two men who stood with him.

Mk	9.5	And		Peter said to Jesus, "Master, it
M	17.4	And		Peter said to Jesus, "Lord, it
L	9.33	And as the men were parting from him,	Peter said to Jesus, "Master, it

Mk	9.5	is well that we are here;		let us	make three booths,
M	17.4	is well that we are here; if you wish, I will	make three booths here,
L	9.33	is well that we are here;		let us	make three booths,

Mk	9.6	one for you and one for Moses and one for Elijah."	For he did not
M	17.5	one for you and one for Moses and one for Elijah."	He was
L	9.33	one for you and one for Moses and one for Elijah"--	not

Mk	9.7	know	what to say, for they were exceedingly afraid.	And a
M	17.5		still speaking, when lo,	a bright
L	9.34	knowing what he said.	As he said this,	a
J	12.27	*"Now is my soul troubled. And what shall I say? 'Father, save me from*

Mk	9.7	cloud	overshadowed them,
M	17.5	cloud	overshadowed them,
L	9.34	cloud came and overshadowed them; and they were afraid as they entered
J	12.28	*this hour'? No, for this purpose I have come to this hour. Father,*

Mk	9.7		and	a voice came out of the cloud,
M	17.5		and	a voice	from	the cloud	said,
L	9.35	the cloud.	And	a voice came out of the cloud,	saying,
J	12.28	*glorify thy name."*	*Then*	a voice came *from*	*heaven,*	*saying,*
M	3.17		and *lo,*	a voice	*from*	*heaven, saying,*
Mk	1.11		and	a voice came *from*	*heaven,*
L	3.22b		and	a voice came *from*	*heaven,*

Mk	9.7	"This is my beloved Son;		listen to him."
M	17.5	"This is my beloved Son, with whom I am well pleased;	listen to him."
L	9.35	"This is my Son, my Chosen;		listen to him!"
J	12.28	*"I have glorified it, and I will glorify it again."*
M	3.17	*"This is* my beloved Son, *with whom I am well pleased."*
Mk	1.11	*"Thou art* my beloved Son; *with thee I am well pleased."*
L	3.22a	*"Thou art* my beloved Son; *with thee I am well pleased."*

M 17.6 When the disciples heard this, they fell on their faces, and
J 12.29 The crowd standing by heard it and said that it had thundered.

M 17.7 were filled with awe. But Jesus came and touched them,
J 12.30 Others said, "An angel has spoken to him." |Jesus

Mk	9.8	
M	17.8	saying, "Rise, and have no fear."
L	9.36	
J	12.30	answered, "This voice has come for your sake, not for mine."

And suddenly looking around
And when they lifted up their eyes,
And when the voice had spoken,

Mk	9.8	they no longer saw any one with them but Jesus only.
M	17.8	they saw no one but Jesus only.
L	9.36	Jesus was found alone.

Lk	9.9	And as they were coming down the mountain, he
M	17.9	And as they were coming down the mountain, Jesus
L	9.36	And they kept silence
L	9.37	On the next day, when they had come down from the mountain, a great

Mk	9.9	charged them to tell no one what they had
M	17.9	commanded them, "Tell no one the vision,
L	9.36	and told no one in those days anything of what they had
L	9.37	crowd met him.

Mk	9.10	seen, until the Son of man should have risen from the dead. So they
M	17.9	until the Son of man is raised from the dead."
L	9.36	seen.

Mk	9.10	kept the matter to themselves, questioning what the rising from the dead

Mk	9.11	meant. And they asked him, "Why do the scribes say that
M	17.10	And the disciples asked him, "Then why do the scribes say that

Mk	9.12	first Elijah must come?" And he said to them, "Elijah does come first
M	17.11	first Elijah must come?" He replied, "Elijah does come, and he

Mk	9.12	to restore all things; and how is it written of the Son of man, that
M	17.12b	is to restore all things; So also the Son of man
M	11.13	For all the prophets

Mk	9.13	he should suffer many things and be treated with contempt? But I tell
M	17.12a	will suffer at their hands." but I tell
M	11.14	and the law aprophesied until John; and if you are willing to accept it,

Mk	9.13	you that Elijah has come, and they did to
M	17.12a	you that Elijah has already come, and they did not know him, but did to
M	11.13	he is Elijah who is to come.

Mk	9.13	him whatever they pleased, as it is written of him."
M	17.13	him whatever they pleased. Then the disciples understood that he was

M	17.13	speaking to them of John the Baptist.

41. THE EPILEPTIC BOY

Mark 9.14-29

Mk	9.14	And when they came to the disciples, they saw a great
M	17.14	And when they came to the
L	9.37	On the next day, when they had come down from the mountain, a great

257

```
Mk    9.15     crowd about them, and scribes arguing with them.  And immediately all
M     17.14    crowd,
L     9.37     crowd


Mk    9.15     the crowd, when they saw him, were greatly amazed, and ran up to him and
L     9.37                                                           met        him.


Mk    9.16     greeted him.  And he asked them, "What are you discussing with them?"


Mk    9.17     And           one of   the crowd                        answered him,
M     17.14                  a man came up to him and kneeling before him said,
L     9.38     And behold, a man from the crowd                        cried,


Mk    9.17     "Teacher, I brought          my son to you, for he has
M     17.15a   |"Lord,    have mercy    on my son,        for he is
L     9.38     "Teacher, I beg you to look upon my son,     for he is  my only child;


Mk    9.18                    a dumb spirit; and wherever it seizes him,
M     17.15a                  an  epileptic
L     9.39     and behold, a      spirit              seizes him, and he suddenly


Mk    9.18          it dashes    him down; and  he foams  and grinds his teeth and
M     17.15a                               and  he suffers terribly;
L     9.39     cries out; it convulses him till he foams, and shatters him,     and


Mk    9.18     becomes rigid;       and I asked      your disciples to cast it
M     17.16                         And I brought him to your disciples,
L     9.40     will hardly leave him.  And I begged     your disciples to cast it


Mk    9.19     out, and they were  not able."   And he    answered them, "O faithless
M     17.17         and they could not heal him." And Jesus answered,      "O faithless
L     9.41     out, but they could not."          Jesus answered,      "O faithless
  J   14.9                                        Jesus said to him,   "Have I been


Mk    9.19                    generation, how long am I to be with you?  How long am I to
M     17.17    and perverse generation, how long am I to be with you?  How long am I to
L     9.41     and perverse generation, how long am I to be with you            and
  J   14.9     with you              so long, and yet you do not know me, Philip?


Mk    9.20     bear with you?  Bring     him    to me."  And they brought the boy
M     17.17    bear with you?  Bring     him here to me."
L     9.41     bear with you?  Bring your son here."
  J   14.9     He who has seen me has seen the Father; how can you say, 'Show us the


Mk    9.20     to him; and when        the spirit saw him, immediately it convulsed
L     9.42            While he was coming, the demon tore him        and convulsed
  J   14.9     Father'?


Mk    9.20     the boy, and he fell on the ground and rolled about, foaming at the mouth.
L     9.42         him.


Mk    9.21     And Jesus asked his father, "How long has he had this?"  And he said,


Mk    9.22     "From childhood.  And it has often    cast him into the fire  and
M     17.15b                     for       often he falls    into the fire, and often
```

Mk	9.22	into the water, to destroy him; but if you can do anything, have pity
M	17.15b	into the water.

Mk	9.23	on us and help us." And Jesus said to him, "If you can! All things are
Mk	9.24	possible to him who believes." Immediately the father of the child cried
Mk	9.24	out and said, "I believe; help my unbelief!"

Mk	9.25	And when Jesus saw that a crowd came running together, he rebuked the
M	17.18	And Jesus rebuked
L	9.42	But Jesus rebuked the

Mk	9.25	unclean spirit, saying to it, "You dumb and deaf spirit, I command you,
M	17.18	him,
L	9.42	unclean spirit,

Mk	9.26	come out of him, and never enter him again." And after crying out and
M	17.18	and

Mk	9.26	convulsing him terribly, it came out, and the boy was like a corpse;
M	17.18	the demon came out of him,

Mk	9.27	so that most of them said, "He is dead." But Jesus took him by the hand

Mk	9.27	and lifted him up, and he arose.
M	17.18	and the boy was cured instantly.
L	9.42	and healed the boy, and gave him back to his father.

Mk	9.28	And when he had entered the house, his disciples asked him privately,
M	17.19	Then the disciples came to Jesus privately
L	9.43a	And all were astonished at the majesty of God.

Mk	9.29	"Why could we not cast it out?" And he said to them,
M	17.20	and said, "Why could we not cast it out?" He said to them, "Because

M	17.20	*of your little faith. For truly, I say to you, if you have faith as a*
M	17.20	*grain of mustard seed, you will say to this mountain, 'Move from here to*
M	17.20	*there,' and it will move; and nothing will be impossible to you."*

Mk	9.29	"This kind cannot be driven out by anything but prayer."
M	17.21	*"But this kind never comes out except by prayer and*

M	17.21	*fasting."*

42. SECOND PREDICTION OF THE PASSION

Mark 9.30-32

Mk	9.30	They went on from there and passed through Galilee. And he
M	17.22	As they were gathering in Galilee,
L	9.43b	But while they were all marveling at everything he did,
J	7.1	*After this Jesus went about in Galilee; he*

```
Mk    9.31    would not have any one know it; for he was teaching his disciples,
M     17.22                                                   Jesus
L     9.43b                                                   he
  J   7.1     would not go about in Judea, because the Jews sought to kill him.


Mk    9.31    saying to    them,                                         "The
M     17.22   said   to    them,                                         "The
L     9.44    said   to his disciples, |"Let these words sink into your ears; for the


Mk    9.31    Son of man will  be delivered into the hands of men,  and they will kill
M     17.23   Son of man is to be delivered into the hands of men,  |and they will kill
L     9.44    Son of man is to be delivered into the hands of men."


Mk    9.31    him; and when he is killed, after three days he will      rise."
M     17.23   him, and      he                                     will be raised on the
  J   16.6                                                          But because


Mk    9.32                       But they did not       understand the  saying,
M     17.23   third day." And they were greatly distressed.
L     9.45                       But they did not       understand this saying, and it was
  J   16.6     I have said these things to you,    sorrow has filled your hearts.


Mk    9.32                                                            and they were
L     9.45    concealed from them, that they should not perceive it; and they were


Mk    9.32    afraid to ask him.
L     9.45    afraid to ask him about this saying.
```

43. TRUE GREATNESS AND CAUSES OF SIN

Mark 9.33-50

```
Mk    9.33    And                  they       came to Capernaum; and when he was in the
M     18.1    At that time the disciples came to Jesus,


Mk    9.34    house he asked them, "What were you discussing on the way?"  But they


Mk    9.34    were silent; for on the way they had discussed with one another who
M     18.1                                              saying,              "Who
L     9.46             And                        an argument arose  among them as to which


Mk    9.35                 was the greatest.  And he sat down and called the twelve; and
M     18.1                 is  the greatest in the kingdom of heaven?"
L     9.46    of them was the greatest.


Mk    9.35    he said to them, "If any one would be first, he must be last of all and


Mk    9.36    servant of all."  And
M     18.2                      · And
L     9.47                      But when Jesus perceived the thought of their hearts,


Mk    9.36    he took            a child, and  put him in the midst of them;
M     18.2           calling to him a child,    he put him in the midst of them,
L     9.47    he took            a child and   put him by his side,
```

260

```
Mk    9.36    and taking him in his arms, he              said to them,
M     18.3    and                                         said,              "Truly, I
L     9.48    and                                         said to them,
  J   12.44   And                         Jesus cried out and  said,
  J   13.20   Truly, truly,               I                say to you,


  M   18.3    say to you, unless you turn and become like children, you will never enter
  M   18.4    the kingdom of heaven.  Whoever humbles himself like this child, he is the
  M   18.4    greatest in the kingdom of heaven.


Mk    9.37    "Whoever receives one such child in my name receives me;
M     18.5    "Whoever receives one such child in my name receives me;
L     9.48    "Whoever receives       this child in my name receives me,
  M   10.40   "He who   receives         you          receives me,
  L   10.16   "He who   hears           you          hears  me, and he who rejects
  J   12.44   "He who   believes              in               me,
  J   13.20    he who   receives any one  whom I send     receives me;


Mk    9.37                and whoever receives me, receives not      me but      him who
L     9.48                and whoever receives me  receives                       him who
  M   10.40               and he who   receives me  receives                       him who
  L   10.16   you rejects me,  and he who   rejects  me  rejects                    him who
  J   12.44                                      believes not in me but in  him who
  J   12.45               And he who   sees     me  sees                      him who
  J   13.20               and he who   receives me  receives                  him who


Mk    9.37    sent me."
L     9.48    sent me; for he who is least among you all is the one who is great."
  M   10.40   sent me.
  L   10.16   sent me."
  J   12.44   sent me.
  J   12.45   sent me.
  J   13.20   sent me."


Mk    9.38    John said to him, "Teacher, we saw a man casting out demons in your name,
L     9.49    John answered,    "Master,  we saw a man casting out demons in your name,


Mk    9.39    and we forbade him, because he was  not following   us."  But Jesus said,
L     9.50    and we forbade him, because he does not follow with us."  But Jesus said


Mk    9.39              "Do not forbid him; for no one who does a mighty work in my name
L     9.50    to him, "Do not forbid him;


Mk    9.40    will be able soon after to speak evil of me.  For he that is not against
M     12.30                                                 He who   is not with
L     9.50                                                 for he that is not against
L     11.23                                                 He who  is not with


Mk    9.41    us  is for      us.  For truly, I say to you, whoever gives      you
M     10.42                        And                      whoever gives to one of these
M     12.30   me  is against me, and he who does not gather with me scatters.
L     9.50    you is for     you."
L     11.23   me  is against me, and he who does not gather with me scatters.


Mk    9.41                    a cup of      water to drink because you bear the name
M     10.42   little ones even a cup of cold water       because he is   a disciple,
```

261

```
Mk    9.41    of Christ,              will by no means lose his reward.
M    10.42    truly, I say to you, he shall    not      lose his reward."


 L   17.1         And he said to his disciples, "Temptations to sin are sure to come; but
 L   17.1         woe to him by whom they come!


Mk    9.42        "Whoever     causes one of these little ones who believe in me
M    18.6     but  whoever     causes one of these little ones who believe in me
L    17.2b    than that he should cause  one of these little ones


Mk    9.42    to sin,  it would be better for him if      a great millstone were hung
M    18.6     to sin,  it would be better for him to have a great millstone fastened
L    17.2a    to sin.  It would be better for him if      a     millstone were hung


Mk    9.42    round his neck and he were thrown  into          the sea.
M    18.6     round his neck and to be    drowned in the depth of the sea.
L    17.2a    round his neck and he were cast    into          the sea,


 M  18.7          "Woe to the world for temptations to sin! For it is necessary that
 M  18.7          temptations come, but woe to the man by whom the temptation comes!


Mk    9.43    And if your      hand            causes you to sin, cut it off;
M    18.8     And if your          hand or your foot causes you to sin, cut it off and
L    17.3     Take heed to yourselves; if your brother sins, rebuke him, and if he
 M   5.30     And if your right hand            causes you to sin, cut it off and


Mk    9.43                it is better for  you to enter life maimed          than
M    18.8     throw it away; it is better for  you to enter life maimed or lame than
L    17.4     repents, forgive him; and if he sins against you seven times in the day,
 M   5.30     throw it away; it is better that you lose one of your members      than


Mk    9.43    with two hands          to     go     to hell, to the unquenchable
M    18.8     with two hands or two feet to be thrown into          the eternal
L    17.4     and turns to you seven times, and says, 'I repent,' you must forgive him."
 M   5.30     that your whole body            go     into hell.


Mk    9.44    fire, where their worm does not die, and the fire is not quenched.
M    18.8     fire.


Mk    9.45    And if            your foot causes you to sin, cut it off;
M    18.8     And if your hand or your foot causes you to sin, cut it off and throw it


Mk    9.45        it is better for you to enter life       lame than with
M    18.8     away; it is better for you to enter life maimed or lame than with two hands


Mk    9.46        two feet to be thrown into          hell, where their worm does
M    18.8     or two feet to be thrown into the eternal fire.


Mk    9.47    not die, and the fire is not quenched.  And if your      eye causes you
M    18.9                                            And if your      eye causes you
 M   5.29                                            If your right eye causes you


Mk    9.47    to sin, pluck it out;                 it is better for  you to enter
M    18.9     to sin, pluck it out and throw it away; it is better for  you to enter
 M   5.29     to sin, pluck it out and throw it away; it is better that you lose one
```

```
Mk    9.47   the kingdom of God with one eye than with two eyes     to be thrown into
M    18.9              life            with one eye than with two eyes     to be thrown into
  M   5.29   of your members                    than that your whole body  be thrown into


Mk    9.48              hell, |where their worm does not die, and the fire is not quenched.
M    18.9   the hell                                                       of fire.
  M   5.29              hell.


Mk  9.49,50  For every one will be      salted with fire.  Salt is good;  but if the
M    5.13            "You          are the salt  of the earth;            but if
L    14.34                                          "Salt is good;  but if


Mk    9.50   salt has lost its saltness, how will  you season it?         Have
M    5.13    salt has lost its taste,    how shall its saltness be restored?  It is
L    14.35   salt has lost its taste,    how shall its saltness be restored?  It is


Mk    9.50   salt in yourselves, and be at peace with one another."
M    5.13    no longer good for anything              except to be thrown out and
L    14.35        fit neither for the land nor for the dunghill; men throw  it away.


  M   5.13   trodden under foot by men.
  L  14.35   He who has ears to hear, let him hear."
```

44. MARRIAGE AND DIVORCE

Mark 10.1-12

```
Mk   10.1    And                                        he left there and went
M    19.1    Now when Jesus had finished these sayings, he              went away


Mk   10.1                       to the region of Judea and beyond the Jordan, and
M    19.2    from Galilee and entered the region of Judea     beyond the Jordan; and


Mk   10.1         crowds gathered to him again; and again, as his custom was, he
M    19.2    large crowds followed     him,         and                       he


Mk   10.1    taught them.
M    19.2    healed them there.


Mk   10.2    And Pharisees came up          and in order to test  him    asked,  "Is
M    19.3    And Pharisees came up to him and               tested him by asking, "Is


Mk   10.3    it lawful for a man to divorce his   wife?"          He answered
M    19.4a   it lawful         to divorce one's  wife for any cause?"  He answered,


Mk   10.4    them, "What did Moses command you?"  They said,              "Moses
M    19.7                                          They said to him, "Why then did Moses
  M   5.31                          "It was also said,      'Whoever divorces


Mk   10.4    allowed    a man to write   a certificate of divorce, and to put her
M    19.7    command      one to give    a certificate of divorce, and to put her
  M   5.31   his wife, let him    give her a certificate of divorce.'
```

Mk	10.5	away." But Jesus said to them, "For your hardness of heart he wrote
M	19.8	away?" He said to them, "For your hardness of heart Moses allowed

Mk	10.5	you this commandment.
M	19.4b	you to divorce your wives, but from the beginning it was not so. |"Have

Mk	10.6	But from the beginning of creation, 'God
M	19.4b	you not read that he who made them from the beginning

Mk	10.7	made them male and female.' 'For this reason a man shall leave
M	19.5	made them male and female, |and said, 'For this reason a man shall leave

Mk	10.8	his father and mother and be joined to his wife, |and the two shall become
M	19.5	his father and mother and be joined to his wife, and the two shall become

Mk	10.9	one flesh.' So they are no longer two but one flesh. |What therefore
M	19.6	one flesh'? |So they are no longer two but one flesh. What therefore

Mk	10.9	God has joined together, let not man put asunder."
M	19.6	God has joined together, let not man put asunder."

Mk	10.10	And in the house the disciples asked him again about this matter.

Mk	10.11	And he said to them, "Whoever divorces his wife
M	19.9	And I say to you: whoever divorces his wife, except for
L	16.18	"Every one who divorces his wife
M	5.32	*But I say to you that every one who* divorces his wife, *except on the*

Mk	10.11	and marries another, commits adultery against
M	19.9	unchastity, and marries another, commits adultery."
L	16.18	and marries another commits adultery,
M	5.32	*ground of unchastity,* *makes her an* adulteress;

Mk	10.12	her; and if she divorces her husband and marries
L	16.18	and he who marries a woman divorced from her husband
M	5.32	*and whoever marries a divorced woman*

Mk	10.12	another, she commits adultery."
L	16.18	commits adultery.
M	5.32	commits adultery.

M	19.10	*The disciples said to him, "If such is the case of a man with his wife,*
M	19.11	*it is not expedient to marry." But he said to them, "Not all men can*
M	19.12	*receive this saying, but only those to whom it is given. For there are*
M	19.12	*eunuchs who have been so from birth, and there are eunuchs who have been*
M	19.12	*made eunuchs by men, and there are eunuchs who have made themselves*
M	19.12	*eunuchs for the sake of the kingdom of heaven. He who is able to receive*
M	19.12	*this, let him receive it."*

264

45. LET THE CHILDREN COME

Mark 10.13-16

Mk	10.13	And they	were bringing		children to him,	that he might touch
M	19.13	Then children	were brought		to him	that he might lay
L	18.15	Now they	were bringing	even infants	to him	that he might touch

Mk	10.13		them; and	the disciples	rebuked
M	19.13	his hands on	them and pray.	The disciples	rebuked the
L	18.15		them; and when	the disciples saw it, they	rebuked

Mk	10.14	them. But when Jesus saw it he was indignant, and said to them,	"Let
M	19.14	people; but Jesus	said, "Let
L	18.16	them. But Jesus called them to him,	saying, "Let

Mk	10.14	the children come to me,	do not hinder them; for to such belongs the
M	19.14	the children come to me, and	do not hinder them; for to such belongs the
L	18.16	the children come to me, and	do not hinder them; for to such belongs the

Mk	10.15	kingdom of God. Truly, I say to you, whoever does not receive the kingdom
M	19.14	kingdom of heaven."
L	18.17	kingdom of God. Truly, I say to you, whoever does not receive the kingdom

Mk	10.16	of God like a child shall not enter it." And he took them in his arms and
M	19.15	And he
L	18.17	of God like a child shall not enter it."

Mk	10.16	blessed them, laying his hands upon them.
M	19.15	laid his hands on them and went away.

46. THE PERIL OF RICHES

Mark 10.17-31

Mk	10.17	And as he was setting out on his journey,	a man	ran	up and knelt
M	19.16	And behold,		one	came up
L	18.18	And		a ruler	
L	10.25	And behold,		a lawyer stood up	to put

Mk	10.17	before him,	and asked him,	"Good Teacher, what	must
M	19.16	to him,	saying,	"Teacher, what good deed	must
L	18.18		asked him,	"Good Teacher, what	shall
L	10.25	him to the test,	saying,	"Teacher, what	shall

Mk	10.18	I do to inherit eternal life?"	And Jesus said to him,	"Why do you call
M	19.17	I do, to have eternal life?"	And he said to him,	"Why do you ask
L	18.19	I do to inherit eternal life?"	And Jesus said to him,	"Why do you call
L	10.26	I do to inherit eternal life?"	He said to him,	

Mk	10.19	me	good? No one	is good but God alone.	|You
M	19.17	me about what is good?	One there is who	is good.	If you
L	18.20	me	good? No one	is good but God alone.	|You
L	10.26				"What is written

```
Mk  10.19                        know the commandments:
M   19.18    would enter life, keep the commandments."                He said to him,
L   18.20                        know the commandments:
  L  10.27                          in the law? How do you read?"  And he answered,


Mk  10.19                                          'Do   not kill,        Do   not
M   19.18    "Which?"  And Jesus said, "You shall not kill,      You shall not
L   18.20                                          'Do   not commit adultery, Do   not
  L  10.27                      "You shall love the Lord your God with all


Mk  10.19    commit adultery,    Do   not steal,    Do   not bear false witness,
M   19.18    commit adultery, You shall not steal, You shall not bear false witness,
L   18.20    kill,               Do   not steal,    Do   not bear false witness,
  L  10.27    your heart, and with all your soul, and with all your strength, and


Mk  10.19    Do not defraud, Honor your father and mother.'"
M   19.19                    |Honor your father and mother, and, You shall love your
L   18.20                     Honor your father and mother.'"
  L  10.27    with all your mind;                          and            your


Mk  10.20                                  And      he  said to him, "Teacher, all these
M   19.20    neighbor as yourself."  The young man said to him,      "All these
L   18.21                                  And      he  said,        "All these
  L  10.28    neighbor as yourself."  And      he  said to him,      "You have


Mk  10.21    I have observed  from my youth."  And        Jesus looking upon him loved
M   19.21    I have observed; what do I still lack?"    Jesus
L   18.22    I have observed  from my youth."  And when Jesus heard it,
  L  10.28    answered right; do this, and you will live."


Mk  10.21    him, and said to him,            "You      lack one thing; go, sell
M   19.21             said to him, "If      you would be perfect,    go, sell
L   18.22         he said to him, "One thing you still lack.             Sell all


Mk  10.21    what you have,    and give       to the poor, and you will have treasure
M   19.21    what you possess and give       to the poor, and you will have treasure
L   18.22    that you have    and distribute to the poor, and you will have treasure


Mk  10.22    in heaven; and come, follow me."  At that saying his countenance fell,
M   19.22    in heaven; and come, follow me."      When the young man heard this
L   18.23    in heaven; and come, follow me."  But when          he  heard this


Mk  10.22    and he went away sorrowful; for he had great possessions.
M   19.22        he went away sorrowful; for he had great possessions.
L   18.23        he became    sad,       for he  was very  rich.


Mk  10.23    And Jesus looked  around and said to his disciples,
M   19.23    And Jesus                  said to his disciples, "Truly, I say to
L   18.24        Jesus looking at him   said,


Mk  10.23    "How      hard it will be for those who have riches  to enter
M   19.23    you, it will be hard           for         a rich man to enter
L   18.24    "How      hard it      is for those who have riches  to enter
```

Mk	10.24	the kingdom of God!" ⎮And the disciples were amazed at his words. But
M	19.23	the kingdom of heaven.
L	18.24	the kingdom of God!

Mk	10.24	Jesus said to them again, "Children, how hard it is to enter the kingdom
M	19.24	Again I tell you,

Mk	10.25	of God! It is easier for a camel to go through the eye of a needle than
M	19.24	it is easier for a camel to go through the eye of a needle than
L	18.25	For it is easier for a camel to go through the eye of a needle than

Mk	10.26	for a rich man to enter the kingdom of God." And
M	19.25	for a rich man to enter the kingdom of God." When the disciples heard
L	18.26	for a rich man to enter the kingdom of God." Those who heard

Mk	10.26	they were exceedingly astonished, and said to him, "Then who can
M	19.25	this they were greatly astonished, saying, "Who then can
L	18.26	it said, "Then who can

Mk	10.27	be saved?" Jesus looked at them and said, "With men it
M	19.26	be saved?" But Jesus looked at them and said to them, "With men this
L	18.27	be saved?" But he said, "What

Mk	10.27	is impossible, but not with God; for all things are possible with God."
M	19.26	is impossible, but with God all things are possible."
L	18.27	is impossible with men is possible with God."

Mk	10.28	Peter began to say to him, "Lo, we have left everything and
M	19.27	Then Peter said in reply, "Lo, we have left everything and
L	18.28	And Peter said, "Lo, we have left our homes and

Mk	10.29	followed you." Jesus said, "Truly, I
M	19.28	followed you. What then shall we have?" Jesus said to them, "Truly, I
L	18.29	followed you." And he said to them, "Truly, I

Mk	10.29	say to you,
M	19.28	say to you, in the new world, when the Son of man shall sit on his
L	18.29	say to you,

M	19.28	*glorious throne, you who have followed me will also sit on twelve thrones,*
M	19.28	*judging the twelve tribes of Israel.*

Mk	10.29	there is no one who has left house or brothers or sisters or
M	19.29	And every one who has left houses or brothers or sisters or
L	18.29	there is no man who has left house or wife or brothers or
L	14.26	*"If any one comes to me and does not hate his own*

Mk	10.29	mother or father or children or lands, for my sake
M	19.29	father or mother or children or lands, for my name's sake,
L	18.29	parents or children, for the sake
L	14.26	*father and mother and wife and children and brothers and sisters, yes,*

Mk	10.30	and for the gospel,	who will not receive a hundredfold now in
M	19.29		will receive a hundredfold,
L	18.30	of the kingdom of God,	who will not receive manifold more in
L	14.26	and even his own life, he cannot be my disciple.	

Mk	10.30	this time, houses and brothers and sisters and mothers and children and
L	18.30	this time,

Mk	10.30	lands, with persecutions, and in the age to come eternal life.
M	19.29	and inherit eternal life.
L	18.30	and in the age to come eternal life."
Mk	9.35	And he sat down and called the twelve; and he said to them,

Mk	10.31	But	many that	are first	will be last, and	the last
M	19.30	But	many that	are first	will be last, and	the last
M	20.16	So		the last	will be first, and	the first
Mk	9.35	"If	any one would be	first,	he must be last of all and servant
L	13.30	And behold, some		are last	who will be first, and some are first

Mk	10.31	first."
M	19.30	first.
M	20.16	last."
Mk	9.35	of all."
L	13.30	who will be last."

47. THIRD PREDICTION OF THE PASSION

Mark 10.32-34

Mk	10.32	And they were on the road, going up to Jerusalem, and Jesus was
M	20.17	And as Jesus was going up to Jerusalem,

Mk	10.32	walking ahead of them; and they were amazed, and those who followed

Mk	10.32	were afraid. And taking the twelve again, he
M	20.17	he took the twelve disciples aside, and on the way he
L	18.31	And taking the twelve, he

Mk	10.33	began to tell them what was to happen to him,	saying, "Behold, we
M	20.18	said to them,	"Behold, we
L	18.31	said to them,	"Behold, we

Mk	10.33	are going up to Jerusalem; and the Son of
M	20.18	are going up to Jerusalem; and the Son of
L	18.31	are going up to Jerusalem, and everything that is written of the Son of

Mk	10.33	man will be delivered to the chief priests and the
M	20.18	man will be delivered to the chief priests and
L	18.31	man by the prophets will be accomplished.

Mk	10.33	scribes, and they will condemn him to death, and deliver
M	20.19	scribes, and they will condemn him to death,	and deliver
L	18.32	For he will be delivered

Mk	10.34	him to the Gentiles; and they will mock him, and
M	20.19	him to the Gentiles to be mocked
L	18.32	to the Gentiles, and will be mocked and shamefully treated and

Mk	10.34	spit upon him, and scourge him, and kill him; and after three days
M	20.19	and scourged and crucified, and
L	18.33	spit upon; they will scourge him and kill him, and on the third day

Mk	10.34	he will rise."
M	20.19	he will be raised on the third day."
L	18.34	he will rise." But they understood none of these things; this saying

L   18.34   was hid from them, and they did not grasp what was said.

48. THE SONS OF ZEBEDEE

Mark 10.35-45

Mk	10.35	And James and John, the sons of Zebedee, came forward to him, and
M	20.20	Then the mother of the sons of Zebedee came up to him, with

Mk	10.35	said to him, "Teacher, we want you to do for us whatever we
M	20.20	her sons, and kneeling before him she

Mk	10.36	ask of you." And he said to them, "What do you want me to
M	20.21	asked him for something. And he said to her, "What do you want?"

Mk	10.37	do for you?" And they said to him, "Grant us
M	20.21	She said to him, "Command that these two sons of

Mk	10.37	to sit, one at your right hand and one at your left, in your
M	20.21	mine may sit, one at your right hand and one at your left, in your

Mk	10.38	glory." But Jesus said to them, "You do not know what you are asking.
M	20.22	kingdom." But Jesus answered, "You do not know what you are asking.

Mk	10.38	Are you able to drink the cup that I drink, or to be baptized
M	20.22	Are you able to drink the cup that I am to drink?"

Mk	10.39	with the baptism with which I am baptized?" And they said to him, "We
M	20.22	They said to him, "We

Mk	10.39	are able." And Jesus said to them, "The cup that I drink you will drink;
M	20.23	are able." He said to them, "You will drink

Mk	10.40	and with the baptism with which I am baptized, you will be baptized; but
M	20.23	my cup, but

Mk	10.40	to sit at my right hand or at my left is not mine to grant, but it is
M	20.23	to sit at my right hand and at my left is not mine to grant, but it is

```
Mk   10.41    for those for whom it has been prepared."              And when the
M    20.24    for those for whom it has been prepared by my Father."  And when the
L    22.24                                            A dispute also arose


Mk   10.42    ten heard it, they began to be   indignant at James and John.   And
M    20.25    ten heard it, they        were  indignant at the two brothers.  But
L    22.25    among them, which of them was to be regarded as the greatest.    And


Mk   10.42    Jesus called them to him and said to them,  "You know that those who are
M    20.25    Jesus called them to him and said,          "You know that
L    22.25    he                             said to them,


Mk   10.42    supposed to rule over the Gentiles       lord it   over them, and
M    20.25                the rulers of the Gentiles    lord it   over them, and
L    22.25          "The kings  of the Gentiles exercise lordship over them; and


Mk   10.42    their great men exercise authority over them.
M    20.25    their great men exercise authority over them.
L    22.25             those in    authority over them are called benefactors.


Mk   10.43    But it shall not be so among you; but whoever would be      great
M    20.26       It shall not be so among you; but whoever would be      great
L    22.26    But          not    so with  you; rather      let the greatest
  M  23.11                                   He  who     is       greatest
  J  13.16         Truly, truly, I say to you,  a servant    is not  greater


Mk   10.43    among you                                 must  be your servant,
M    20.26    among you                                 must  be your servant,
L    22.26    among you become as the youngest, and the leader as one who serves.
  M  23.11    among you                          shall  be your servant;
  J  13.16    than his master; nor is he who is sent greater than he who sent him.


  Mk  9.35    And he sat down and called the twelve; and he said to them,
  L   9.48b   "Whoever receives this child in my name receives me, and whoever receives


Mk   10.44                         and whoever would be first  among you must
M    20.27                         and whoever would be first  among you must
  Mk  9.35                         "If any one would be first,    he  must
  L   9.48b   me receives him who sent me; for he  who    is least among you all


Mk   10.45    be              slave  of all.  For    the Son of man also came
M    20.28    be          your slave;         even as the Son of man       came
L    22.27                               For  which is the greater, one who
  Mk  9.35    be last of all and servant of all."
  L   9.48b   is the one who is  great."
  J  13.15                            For        I           have


Mk   10.45    not to be served  but to serve, and to give his life as a ransom for
M    20.28    not to be served  but to serve, and to give his life as a ransom for
L    22.27    sits at table, or one who serves?  Is it not the one who sits at table?
  J  13.15    given you an example, that you also should do as I have done to you.


Mk   10.45    many."
M    20.28    many."
L    22.27    But I am among you as one who serves.
```

49. BLIND BARTIMAEUS

Mark 10.46-52

Mk	10.46	And they came to Jericho; and as he was leaving Jericho
M	20.29	And as they went out of Jericho,
L	18.35	As he drew near to Jericho,
M	*9.27*	*And as Jesus passed on from there,*

Mk	10.46	with his disciples and a great multitude, Bartimaeus, a
M	20.30	a great crowd followed him. And behold, two
L	18.35	a
M	*9.27*	*two*

Mk	10.46	blind beggar, the son of Timaeus, was sitting by the roadside.
M	20.30	blind men sitting by the roadside,
L	18.35	blind man was sitting by the roadside begging;
M	*9.27*	blind *men* *followed him,*

Mk	10.47	And when he heard
M	20.30	when they heard
L	18.36	and hearing a multitude going by, he inquired what this meant.

Mk	10.47	that it was Jesus of Nazareth, he began to
M	20.30	that Jesus was passing by,
L	18.37,38	They told him, "Jesus of Nazareth is passing by." And he

Mk	10.47	cry out and say, "Jesus, Son of David, have mercy on me!"
M	20.30	cried out, "Have mercy on us, Son of
L	18.38	cried, "Jesus, Son of David, have mercy on me!"
M	*9.27*	*crying aloud,* "Have mercy on *us,* Son *of*

Mk	10.48	And many rebuked him, telling him to be
M	20.31	David!" The crowd rebuked them, telling them to be
L	18.39	And those who were in front rebuked him, telling him to be
M	*9.28*	*David." When he entered the house,*

Mk	10.48	silent; but he cried out all the more, "Son of David, have mercy on
M	20.31	silent; but they cried out the more, "Lord, have mercy on
L	18.39	silent; but he cried out all the more, "Son of David, have mercy on
M	*9.28*	*the blind men came to him;*

Mk	10.49	me!" And Jesus stopped and said, "Call him." And
M	20.32	us, Son of David!" And Jesus stopped and called them,
L	18.40	me!" And Jesus stopped, and commanded him to be

Mk	10.49	they called the blind man, saying to him, "Take heart; rise, he is calling
Mk	10.50	you." And throwing off his mantle he sprang up and came to Jesus.

Mk	10.51	And Jesus said to him, "What do you
M	20.32	saying, "What do you
L	18.41	brought to him; and when he came near, he asked him, "What do you
M	*9.28*	*said to them,* "Do you

Mk	10.51	want me to do for you?" And the blind man said to him, "Master,
M	20.33	want me to do for you?" They said to him, "Lord,
L	18.41	want me to do for you?" He said, "Lord,
M	*9.28*	*believe that I am able to do this?"* *They* said to him, *"Yes, Lord."*

Mk	10.52	let me receive my sight." And Jesus said to him, "Go your way;
M	20.34	let our eyes be opened." And Jesus in pity touched their eyes,
L	18.42	let me receive my sight." And Jesus said to him, "Receive your sight;
M	*9.29*	*Then he* *touched their eyes, saying,*

Mk	10.52	your faith has made you well." And immediately he
M	20.34	and immediately they
L	18.43	your faith has made you well." And immediately he
M	*9.30*	*"According to* your faith *be it done to you."* And *their eyes*

Mk	10.52	received his sight and followed him on the way.
M	20.34	received their sight and followed him.
L	18.43	received his sight and followed him, glorifying God; and all the people,
M	*9.30*	*were opened. And Jesus sternly charged them, "See that no one knows it."*

L	*18.43*	*when they saw it, gave praise to God.*
M	*9.31*	*But they went away and spread his fame through all that district.*

50. JESUS ENTERS JERUSALEM

Mark 11.1-11

L	*19.28*	*And when he had said this, he went on ahead, going up to Jerusalem.*

Mk	11.1	And when they
M	21.1	And when they
L	19.29	When he
J	12.12	The next day a great crowd who had come to the feast heard that Jesus

Mk	11.1	drew near to Jerusalem, to Bethphage and Bethany, at the Mount
M	21.1	drew near to Jerusalem and came to Bethphage, to the Mount
L	19.29	drew near to Bethphage and Bethany, at the mount
J	12.12	was coming to Jerusalem.

Mk	11.2	of Olives, he sent two of his disciples, |and said
M	21.2	of Olives, then Jesus sent two disciples, |saying
L	19.30	that is called Olivet, he sent two of the disciples, |saying,

Mk	11.2	to them, "Go into the village opposite you, and immediately as you
M	21.2	to them, "Go into the village opposite you, and immediately
L	19.30	"Go into the village opposite, where on

Mk	11.2	enter it you will find a colt tied, on which no one has ever sat;
M	21.2	you will find an ass tied, and a colt with her;
L	19.30	entering you will find a colt tied, on which no one has ever yet sat;

Mk	11.3	untie it and bring it. If any one says to you, 'Why
M	21.3	untie them and bring them to me. If any one says anything to you,
L	19.31	untie it and bring it here. If any one asks you, 'Why

272

Mk	11.3	are you doing this?' say, 'The Lord has need of it
M	21.3	you shall say, 'The Lord has need of them,'
L	19.31	are you untying it?' you shall say this, 'The Lord has need of it.'"

Mk	11.3	and will send it back here immediately.'"
M	21.4	and he will send them immediately." This took place to fulfil

M	21.4	*what was spoken by the prophet, saying,*
J	12.14b	*as it is written,*

M	21.5	*"Tell the daughter of Zion,*
J	12.15	*"Fear not, daughter of Zion;*

M	21.5	*Behold, your king is coming to you,*
J	12.15	*behold, your king is coming,*

M	21.5	*humble, and mounted on an ass,*
J	12.15	*sitting on an ass's*

M	21.5	*and on a colt, the foal of an ass."*
J	12.15	*colt!"*

Mk	11.4	And they went away, and found a colt tied at the door out
M	21.6	The disciples went and did as Jesus had
L	19.32	So those who were sent went away and found it as he had

Mk	11.5	in the open street; and they untied it. And
M	21.6	directed them;
L	19.33	told them. And as they were untying the

Mk	11.5	those who stood there said to them, "What are you doing, untying
L	19.33	colt, its owners said to them, "Why are you untying

Mk	11.6	the colt?" And they told them what Jesus had said; and they let them go.
L	19.34	the colt?" And they said, "The Lord has need of it."

Mk	11.7	And they brought the colt to Jesus, and threw their
M	21.7	they brought the ass and the colt, and put their
L	19.35	And they brought it to Jesus, and throwing their
J	12.14a	And Jesus found a young ass

Mk	11.8	garments on it; and he sat upon it. And many
M	21.8	garments on them, and he sat thereon. Most of the
L	19.36	garments on the colt they set Jesus upon it. And as he rode along,
J	12.14a	and sat upon it;

Mk	11.8	spread their garments on the road, and others spread leafy branches
M	21.8	crowd spread their garments on the road, and others cut branches
L	19.37	they spread their garments on the road. As he was now drawing near, at
J	12.13	So they took branches

Mk	11.9	which they had cut from the fields. And those who
M	21.9	from the trees and spread them on the road. And the crowds that
L	19.37	the descent of the Mount of Olives, the whole multitude of the
J	12.13	of palm trees and

Mk	11.9	went before	and those who followed	cried out, "Hosanna!
M	21.9	went before	him and that	followed him shouted, "Hosanna to
L	19.37	disciples began to rejoice and praise God with a loud voice for all the
J	12.13	went out to meet him,	crying, "Hosanna!

Mk	11.9		Blessed is he who comes
M	21.9	the Son of David!	Blessed is he who comes
L	19.38	mighty works that they had seen, |saying, "Blessed is the King who comes
J	12.13		Blessed is he who comes

Mk	11.10	in the name of the Lord! Blessed is the kingdom of our father David
M	21.9	in the name of the Lord!
L	19.38	in the name of the Lord! Peace in
J	12.13	in the name of the Lord, even the King of Israel!"

Mk	11.11	that is coming! Hosanna in the highest!" And he entered Jerusalem,
M	21.10	Hosanna in the highest!" And when he entered Jerusalem,
L	19.39	heaven and glory in the highest!" And some of the Pharisees in
J	12.16	His disciples did not under-

Mk	11.11	and went into the temple; and when he had looked round at everything,
M	21.11	all the city was stirred, saying, "Who is this?" And the crowds said,
L	19.40	the multitude said to him, "Teacher, rebuke your disciples." He answered,
J	12.16	stand this at first; but when Jesus was glorified, then they remembered

Mk	11.11	as it was already late, he went out to Bethany with the twelve.
M	21.11	"This is the prophet Jesus from Nazareth of Galilee."
L	19.40	"I tell you, if these were silent, the very stones would cry out."
J	12.17	that this had been written of him and had been done to him. *The crowd*

J	12.17	*that had been with him when he called Lazarus out of the tomb and raised*
J	12.18	*him from the dead bore witness. The reason why the crowd went to meet*
J	12.19	*him was that they heard he had done this sign. The Pharisees then said*
J	12.19	*to one another, "You see that you can do nothing; look, the world has*
J	12.19	*gone after him."*

51. THE BARREN FIG TREE

Mark 11.12-14

Mk	11.12	On the following day, when they came from Bethany, he was hungry.
M	21.18	In the morning, as he was returning to the city, he was hungry.
L	*13.6*	*And he told*

Mk	11.13	And seeing in the distance a fig tree in leaf, he went to see if
M	21.19a	And seeing a fig tree by the wayside he went
L	*13.6*	*this parable: "A man had a fig tree planted in his vineyard;*

Mk	11.13	he could find anything on it. When he came to it, he
M	21.19a	to it, and
L	*13.6*	*and he came seeking fruit on it and*

Mk	11.13	found nothing but leaves, for it was not the season for figs.
M	21.19a	found nothing on it but leaves only.
L	*13.6*	*found none.*

```
Mk   11.14      And he said to it,              "May no one ever
M    21.19a     And he said to it,              "May no
  L  13.7       And he said to the vinedresser, 'Lo, these three years I have come


Mk   11.14      eat     fruit            from you again." And his disciples heard it.
M    21.19a              fruit ever come from you again!"
  L  13.7       seeking fruit on this fig tree, and I find none. Cut it down; why should


  L  13.8       it use up the ground?' And he answered him, 'Let it alone, sir, this year
  L  13.9       also, till I dig about it and put on manure. And if it bears fruit next
  L  13.9       year, well and good; but if not, you can cut it down.'"
```

52. CLEANSING THE TEMPLE

Mark 11.15-19

```
  J  2.13       The Passover of the Jews was at hand, and Jesus went up to Jerusalem.


Mk   11.15      And they came to Jerusalem. And he     entered the temple
M    21.12                                  And Jesus entered the temple of God
L    19.45                                  And he     entered the temple
J    2.14                                             In the temple he found those


  J  2.14       who were selling oxen and sheep and pigeons, and the money-changers at
  J  2.15       their business. And making a whip


Mk   11.15      and began to drive out  those who sold and those who bought in the temple,
M    21.12      and             drove out all    who sold and            bought in the temple,
L    19.45      and began to drive out  those who sold,
J    2.15       of cords, he drove them all, with the sheep and oxen, out  of the temple;


Mk   11.15      and he overturned the  tables of the money-changers and the seats of
M    21.12      and he overturned the  tables of the money-changers and the seats of
J    2.15       and he poured out the  coins  of the money-changers


  J  2.16       and     overturned their tables.                      And     he told


Mk   11.16      those who sold       pigeons; and he would not allow any one to carry any-
M    21.12      those who sold       pigeons.
J    2.16       those who sold the pigeons,


Mk   11.17      thing through the temple. And he taught, and said  to them, "Is it not
M    21.13                                He              said  to them, "It is
L    19.46                                              saying to them, "It is
J    2.16                                                                "Take these


Mk   11.17      written, 'My house shall be called a house of prayer for all the nations'?
M    21.13      written, 'My house shall be called a house of prayer';
L    19.46      written, 'My house shall be        a house of prayer';
J    2.16       things away;


Mk   11.17      But you have      made           it   a den   of robbers."
M    21.13      but you          make           it   a den   of robbers."
L    19.46      but you have      made           it   a den   of robbers."
J    2.16           you shall not make my Father's house a house of trade."
```

J	2.17	*His disciples remembered that it was written, "Zeal for thy house will*
J	2.18	*consume me." The Jews then said to him, "What sign have you to show us*
J	2.19	*for doing this?" Jesus answered them, "Destroy this temple, and in three*
J	2.20	*days I will raise it up." The Jews then said, "It has taken forty-six*
J	2.21	*years to build this temple, and will you raise it up in three days?" But*
J	2.22	*he spoke of the temple of his body. When therefore he was raised from the*
J	2.22	*dead, his disciples remembered that he had said this; and they believed*
J	2.22	*the scripture and the word which Jesus had spoken.*

M 21.14   *And the blind and the lame came to him in the temple, and he healed*

Mk	11.18	<u>And</u> <u>the chief priests and the scribes heard it and sought</u>
M	21.15	them. But when <u>the chief priests and the scribes</u> saw the wonderful
L	19.39	<u>And</u> some of the Pharisees in the multitude

Mk	11.18	<u>a way to destroy him; for they feared him,</u> <u>because all the multitude</u>
M	21.15	things that he did, and the children crying out in the temple, "Hosanna

Mk	11.18	<u>was astonished at his teaching.</u>
M	21.16	to the Son of David!" they were indignant; and they said to him,
L	19.39	said to him,

M	21.16	*"Do you hear what these are saying?" And Jesus said to them, "Yes;*
L	19.40	*"Teacher, rebuke your disciples."* *He* *answered, "I tell you,*

M	21.16	*have you never read,*
L	19.40	*if these were silent, the very stones would cry out."*

M	21.16	*'Out of the mouth of babes and sucklings*
M	21.16	*thou hast brought perfect praise'?"*

Mk	11.19	<u>And</u> <u>when evening came they</u>
M	21.17	<u>And</u> leaving them, he
L	21.37	<u>And</u> every day he was teaching in the temple, but at night he

Mk	11.19	<u>went out of the city</u>.
M	21.17	<u>went out of the city</u> to Bethany and lodged there.
L	21.37	<u>went out</u> and lodged on the mount called Olivet.

L	21.38	*And early in the morning all the people came to him in the temple to*
L	21.38	*hear him.*

53. THE WITHERED FIG TREE

Mark 11.20-26

Mk	11.20	<u>As they passed by in the morning,</u> <u>they saw the fig tree withered away</u>
M	21.19b	And <u>the fig tree withered</u> at

Mk	11.21	<u>to its roots.</u> And Peter remembered <u>and</u> <u>said to him,</u> "Master,
M	21.20	once. When the disciples saw it they marveled, saying,

Mk	11.22	look! <u>The fig tree which you cursed has withered."</u> <u>And</u>
M	21.21a	"How did <u>the fig tree</u> wither at once?" <u>And</u>
L	17.6a	<u>And</u> *the*

```
Mk   11.23      Jesus answered them,                        "Have faith in God.  Truly, I
M    21.21a     Jesus answered them,                                             "Truly, I
  M  17.20a     He   said   to  them, "Because of your little faith.    For truly, I
  L  17.6a      Lord  said,


Mk   11.23      say to you,                       whoever   says to this mountain,      'Be
M    21.21c     say to you, |but even if you      say   to this mountain,               'Be
  M  17.20c     say to you,              |you will say   to this mountain,              'Move
  L  17.6c                               |you could say  to this sycamine tree,         'Be


Mk   11.23      taken   up   and     cast    into the sea,'          |          and does
M    21.21b     taken   up   and     cast    into the sea,'          |if you have faith and
  M  17.20b     from here    to      there,'                         |if you have faith as a
  L  17.6b      rooted  up,  and be planted in    the sea,'          |"If you had   faith as a


Mk   11.23      not    doubt in his heart,  but believes that what he says will come to
M    21.21b     never  doubt, you will not  only do what has been done to the fig tree,
  M  17.20b     grain of mustard seed,
  L  17.6b      grain of mustard seed,
  J  16.23                                                           In that day you


Mk   11.24      pass, it will be done for him.   Therefore I tell you, whatever you ask
M    21.21d,22        |it will be done.          And                 whatever you ask
  M  17.20d      |and it will    move; and nothing will be impossible to you."
  L  17.6d       |and it would   obey    you.
  J  14.13                                                           Whatever you ask
  J  14.14                                                           if          you ask
  J  16.23       will ask nothing of me. Truly, truly, I say to you,  if          you ask
  J  16.24                               Hitherto you have asked nothing in my name; ask,


Mk   11.24              in     prayer, believe that you have received it, and  it
M    21.22              in     prayer,              you will receive,      if   you
  J  14.13              in my  name,                I   will do    it, that the
  J  14.14      anything in my name,                I   will do    it.
  J  16.23      anything of the Father,             he  will give  it  to   you
  J  16.24                                  and  you will receive,     that your joy


Mk   11.25      will be yours.  And whenever you stand praying, forgive, if you have
M     6.14                           For if    you                forgive men their
M    21.22      have faith."
  J  14.13      Father may be glorified in the Son;
  J  16.23      in my name.
  J  16.24      may be full.


Mk   11.25      anything against any one; so that your        Father also who is in
M     6.14      trespasses,                      your heavenly Father also
  M  18.35                           So also my     heavenly Father


Mk   11.26      heaven may  forgive          you your trespasses."  "But if you do not
M     6.15              will forgive         you;                    but if you do not
  M  18.35            will do to every one of you,                       if you do not


Mk   11.26      forgive,                      neither will your Father who is in
M     6.15      forgive      men their trespasses, neither will your Father
  M  18.35      forgive your brother from your heart."


Mk   11.26      heaven forgive your trespasses."
M     6.15              forgive your trespasses.
```

54. CONTROVERSIES IN JERUSALEM

Mark 11.27-12.37

a. The Authority of Jesus

Mark 11.27-33

Mk	11.27	And they came again to Jerusalem. And as he was walking
M	21.23	And when he entered
L	20.1	One day, as he was teaching the people

Mk	11.27	in the temple, the chief priests and the scribes
M	21.23	the temple, the chief priests
L	20.1	in the temple and preaching the gospel, the chief priests and the scribes

Mk	11.28	and the elders came to him, |and they
M	21.23	and the elders of the people came up to him as he was teaching, and
L	20.2	with the elders came up |and

Mk	11.28	said to him, "By what authority are you doing these things, or
M	21.23	said, "By what authority are you doing these things, and
L	20.2	said to him, "Tell us by what authority you do these things, or

Mk	11.29	who gave you this authority to do them?" Jesus said to them,
M	21.24	who gave you this authority?" Jesus answered them,
L	20.3	who it is that gave you this authority." He answered them,

Mk	11.29	"I will ask you a question; answer me, and I
M	21.24	"I also will ask you a question; and if you tell me the answer, then I
L	20.3	"I also will ask you a question; now tell me,

Mk	11.30	will tell you by what authority I do these things. Was the baptism
M	21.25	also will tell you by what authority I do these things. The baptism
L	20.4	Was the baptism

Mk	11.31	of John from heaven or from men? Answer me." And they
M	21.25	of John, whence was it? From heaven or from men?" And they
L	20.5	of John from heaven or from men?" And they

Mk	11.31	argued with one another, "If we say, 'From heaven,' he will
M	21.25	argued with one another, "If we say, 'From heaven,' he will
L	20.5	discussed it with one another, saying, "If we say, 'From heaven,' he will

Mk	11.32	say, 'Why then did you not believe him?' But shall we say, 'From
M	21.26	say to us, 'Why then did you not believe him?' But if we say, 'From
L	20.6	say, 'Why did you not believe him?' But if we say, 'From

Mk	11.32	men'?"--they were afraid of the people, for all held
M	21.26	men,' we are afraid of the multitude; for all hold
L	20.6	men,' all the people will stone us; for they are convince

Mk	11.33	that John was a real prophet. So they answered Jesus, "We do not know."
M	21.27	that John was a prophet." So they answered Jesus, "We do not know."
L	20.7	that John was a prophet." So they answered that they did not know

Mk	11.33	And Jesus said to them, "Neither will I tell you by what
M	21.27	And he said to them, "Neither will I tell you by what
L	20.8	whence it was. And Jesus said to them, "Neither will I tell you by what

Mk	11.33	authority I do these things."
M	21.27	authority I do these things.
L	20.8	authority I do these things."

b. The Wicked Tenants

Mark 12.1-12

Mk	12.1	And he began to speak to them in parables. "A man
M	21.33	"Hear another parable. There was a householder
L	20.9	And he began to tell the people this parable: "A man

Mk	12.1	planted a vineyard, and set a hedge around it, and dug a pit for the
M	21.33	who planted a vineyard, and set a hedge around it, and dug a
L	20.9	planted a vineyard,

Mk	12.1	wine press, and built a tower, and let it out to tenants, and went
M	21.33	wine press in it, and built a tower, and let it out to tenants, and went
L	20.9	and let it out to tenants, and went

Mk	12.2	into another country. When the time came,
M	21.34	into another country. When the season of fruit drew
L	20.10	into another country for a long while. When the time came,

Mk	12.2	he sent a servant to the tenants, to get from them
M	21.34	near, he sent his servants to the tenants, to get
L	20.10	he sent a servant to the tenants, that they should give him

Mk	12.3	some of the fruit of the vineyard. And they took him and
M	21.35	his fruit; and the tenants took his servants and
L	20.10	some of the fruit of the vineyard; but the tenants

Mk	12.4	beat him, and sent him away empty-handed. Again he sent to them another
M	21.35	beat one,
L	20.11	beat him, and sent him away empty-handed. And he sent another

Mk	12.4	servant, and they wounded him in the head, and treated him shamefully.
M	21.35	killed another, and stoned another.
L	20.11	servant; him also they beat and treated shamefully,

Mk	12.5	And he sent another, and him they
M	21.36	Again he sent other servants, more than
L	20.12	and sent him away empty-handed. And he sent yet a third; this one they

Mk	12.6	killed; and so with many others, some they beat and some they killed. He
M	21.36	the first; and they did the same to them.
L	20.13	wounded and cast out. Then the owner of the vineyard said, 'What

Mk	12.6	had still one other, a beloved son; finally he sent him to them,
M	21.37	Afterward he sent his son to them,
L	20.13	shall I do? I will send my beloved son; it

Mk	12.7	saying, 'They will respect my son.'	But	those tenants
M	21.38	saying, 'They will respect my son.'	But when the	tenants saw the son,
L	20.14	may be they will respect him.'	But when the	tenants saw him,

Mk	12.7	said to one another, 'This is the heir; come, let us kill him, and
M	21.38	they said to themselves, 'This is the heir; come, let us kill him and
L	20.14	they said to themselves, 'This is the heir; let us kill him, that

Mk	12.8	the inheritance will be ours. And they took him and killed him,
M	21.39	have his inheritance.' And they took him
L	20.15	the inheritance may be ours.' And they

Mk	12.8	and cast him out of the vineyard.
M	21.40	and cast him out of the vineyard, and killed him. When therefore the
L	20.15	cast him out of the vineyard and killed him.

Mk	12.9	What will the owner of the vineyard do?
M	21.40	owner of the vineyard comes, what will he do
L	20.15	What then will the owner of the vineyard do

Mk	12.9	He will come and destroy the
M	21.41	to those tenants?" They said to him, "He will put those
L	20.16	to them? He will come and destroy those

Mk	12.9	tenants, and give the vineyard to others.
M	21.41	wretches to a miserable death, and let out the vineyard to other tenants
L	20.16	tenants, and give the vineyard to others." When

M	21.41	*who will give him the fruits in their seasons."*
L	20.16	*they heard this, they said, "God forbid!"*

Mk	12.10	Have you not read this
M	21.41	Jesus said to them, "Have you never read in the
L	20.17	But he looked at them and said, "What then is this that is

Mk	12.10	scripture:
M	21.42	scriptures:
L	20.17	written:

Mk	12.10	'The very stone which the builders rejected
M	21.42	'The very stone which the builders rejected
L	20.17	'The very stone which the builders rejected

Mk	12.10	has become the head of the corner;
M	21.42	has become the head of the corner;
L	20.17	has become the head of the corner'?

Mk	12.11	this was the Lord's doing,
M	21.42	this was the Lord's doing,

Mk	12.11	and it is marvelous in our eyes'?"
M	21.42	and it is marvelous in our eyes'?

M	21.43	*Therefore I tell you, the kingdom of God will be taken away from you*
M	21.43	*and given to a nation producing the fruits of it."*

```
M   21.44    "And he          who falls on this stone will be broken to pieces; but
L   20.18                    Every one who falls on that stone will be broken to pieces; but


M   21.44    when it falls on any one, it will crush him."
L   20.18    when it falls on any one  it will crush him."


Mk  12.12    And      they                            tried to arrest         him,
M   21.46    But when they                            tried to arrest         him,
L   20.19            The   scribes and the chief priests tried to lay hands on him at that


Mk  12.12            but        feared the multitude,
M   21.46                   they feared the multitudes, because they held him to be a
L   20.19    very hour, but they feared the people;


Mk  12.12                                                                        for
M   21.45    prophet. When the chief priests and the Pharisees heard his parables,
L   20.19                                                                        for


Mk  12.12    they perceived that he had told the  parable against them; so they left
M   21.45    they perceived that he was speaking          about     them.
L   20.19    they perceived that he had told this parable against them.


Mk  12.12    him and went away.
```

c. Render to God

Mark 12.13-17

```
Mk  12.13    And they                    sent to him some of the  Pharisees
M   22.16a   And they                    sent             their disciples to him,
L   20.20    So  they watched him, and sent                  spies, who
    J  3.1   Now there was a man                     of the   Pharisees, named


Mk  12.13    and some of the Herodians,
M   22.15    along  with the Herodians, |Then the Pharisees went and took counsel
L   20.20    pretended to be sincere,
    J  3.1   Nicodemus, a ruler of the Jews.


Mk  12.13              to entrap    him in his talk.
M   22.15    how       to entangle  him in his talk.
L   20.20    that they might take hold of what he said, so as to deliver him up to


Mk  12.14                                        And they came
L   20.21    the authority and jurisdiction of the governor.  They
    J  3.2                                      This man came to Jesus by


Mk  12.14          and said to him, "Teacher, we know that you are
M   22.16b         |saying,        "Teacher, we know that you are
L   20.21          asked    him, "Teacher, we know that you speak and teach
    J  3.2   night and said to him, "Rabbi,   we know that you are a teacher come


Mk  12.14    true,     and care for no man; for you do not regard the position of men,
M   22.16d   true,    |and care for no man; for you do not regard the position of men.
L   20.21    rightly, and show     no partiality,
    J  3.2   from God; for no one can do these signs that you do, unless God is with
```

281

```
Mk   12.14        but truly teach the way of God.
M    22.16c,17   |and         teach the way of God truthfully, |Tell us, then, what you
L    20.21        but truly teach the way of God.
  J   3.2         him."


Mk   12.15                   Is it lawful          to pay taxes  to Caesar, or not?  |Should
M    22.17       think.      Is it lawful          to pay taxes  to Caesar, or not?"
L    20.22                   Is it lawful for us to give tribute to Caesar,  or not?"


Mk   12.15       we pay them, or should we not?"  But          knowing   their hypocrisy,
M    22.18                                        But Jesus, aware of   their malice,
L    20.23                                        But he        perceived their craftiness,


Mk   12.15       he  said to them, "Why put me to the test?                 Bring me a
M    22.19           said,          "Why put me to the test, you hypocrites? |Show  me the
L    20.24       and said to them,                                          |"Show  me a


Mk   12.16       coin, and let me look at it."  |And they brought      one.  And he
M    22.20       money for the tax."             And they brought him a coin. |And Jesus
L    20.24       coin.


Mk   12.16       said to them, "Whose likeness and inscription is  this?"  They said to
M    22.21       said to them, "Whose likeness and inscription is  this?"  |They said,
L    20.24                     Whose likeness and inscription has it?"      They said,


Mk   12.17       him, "Caesar's."    |Jesus said to them,       "Render         to
M    22.21            "Caesar's." Then he      said to them,    "Render therefore to
L    20.25            "Caesar's."    |He       said to them, "Then render        to


Mk   12.17       Caesar the things that are Caesar's, and to God the things that are God's."
M    22.21       Caesar the things that are Caesar's, and to God the things that are God's."
L    20.25       Caesar the things that are Caesar's, and to God the things that are God's."


Mk   12.17       And
M    22.22       When they heard it,
L    20.26       And  they were not able in the presence of the people to catch him by what


Mk   12.17          they were amazed    at him.
M    22.22          they      marveled;         and they left him and went away.
L    20.26       he said; but marveling at his answer they were silent.


                     d. The God of the Living

                       Mark 12.18-27


Mk   12.18       And              Sadducees came to him, who say that there is no
M    22.23       The same day     Sadducees came to him, who say that there is no
L    20.27       There came to him some Sadducees,    those  who say that there is no


Mk   12.19       resurrection;  and they asked him a question,  saying, |"Teacher, Moses
M    22.24       resurrection;  and they asked him a question, |saying,  "Teacher, Moses
L    20.28       resurrection, |and they asked him a question,  saying,  "Teacher, Moses


Mk   12.19       wrote for us that  if a man's brother dies and leaves a wife, but leaves
M    22.24       said,              'If a man        dies,                    having
L    20.28       wrote for us that  if a man's brother dies,    having a wife but
```

```
Mk  12.19    no child,   the man     must take  the wife,  and raise up children
M   22.24    no children, his brother must marry the widow, and raise up children
L   20.28    no children, the man     must take  the wife   and raise up children


Mk  12.20    for his brother.      There were seven brothers;        the first
M   22.25    for his brother.' Now there were seven brothers among us; the first
L   20.29    for his brother.  Now there were seven brothers;         the first


Mk  12.20    took a wife, and when he died       left   no children;
M   22.25    married,     and          died, and having no children left his wife to
L   20.29    took a wife, and          died           without children;


Mk  12.21                      |and    the second took her, and died, leaving no children;
M   22.26    his brother.  So too the second
L   20.30                      and     the second


Mk  12.22    and the third likewise; |and          the seven left no children.
M   22.26    and       third,            down to the seventh.
L   20.31    |and the third took her,   and likewise all seven left no children and


Mk  12.23            Last of   all  the woman also died. |In the resurrection
M   22.27,28         After them all, the woman      died. In the resurrection,
L   20.32,33 died. Afterward       the woman also died.  In the resurrection,


Mk  12.23                    whose wife      will      she   be?       For the seven
M   22.28    therefore, to which of the seven will      she   be wife? For they all
L   20.33    therefore,   whose wife          will the woman be?       For the seven


Mk  12.23    had her as wife."
M   22.28    had her."
L   20.33    had her as wife."


Mk  12.24            Jesus said  to them, "Is not this why you are wrong,
M   22.29    But Jesus answered them,                "You are wrong,
L   20.34    And Jesus said  to them, "The sons of this age marry and are given in


Mk  12.25    that    you know neither the scriptures nor the power of God?     For
M   22.30    because you know neither the scriptures nor the power of God.     For
L   20.35    marriage; but those who are accounted worthy to attain to that age and


Mk  12.25    when they rise      from the dead, they neither marry nor are given
M   22.30    in   the   resurrection           they neither marry nor are given
L   20.35    to   the   resurrection from the dead   neither marry nor are given


Mk  12.25    in marriage,                    but      are like
M   22.30    in marriage,                    but      are like
L   20.36    in marriage, |for they cannot die any more, because they are equal to


Mk  12.26    angels in heaven.                                   And as for
M   22.31    angels in heaven.                                   And as for
L   20.37    angels and are sons of God, being sons of the resurrection.  But that


Mk  12.26    the dead       being raised, have you not read in the book of Moses,
M   22.31    the resurrection of the dead, have you not read
L   20.37    the dead       are   raised,                      even Moses showed,
```

Mk	12.26	in the passage about the bush, how God said to him, 'I am the
M	22.32	what was said to you by God, |'I am the
L	20.37	in the passage about the bush, where he calls the Lord the

Mk	12.27	God of Abraham, and the God of Isaac, and the God of Jacob'? He is
M	22.32	God of Abraham, and the God of Isaac, and the God of Jacob'? He is
L	20.38	God of Abraham and the God of Isaac and the God of Jacob. Now he is

Mk	12.27	not God of the dead, but of the living; you are quite wrong."
M	22.33	not God of the dead, but of the living." And when
L	20.39	not God of the dead, but of the living; for all live to him." And some

M	22.33	*the crowd heard it,* *they were*
L	20.40	*of the scribes answered, "Teacher, you have spoken well." For they no*

M	22.33	*astonished at his teaching.*
L	20.40	*longer dared to ask him any question.*

e. The Great Commandment

Mark 12.28-34

Mk	12.28	And one of the scribes came up and heard them disputing with one another,
M	22.34	But when the Pharisees heard

Mk	12.28	and seeing that he answered them well,
M	22.35	that he had silenced the Sadducees, they came together. And
L	10.25	And

Mk	12.28	asked him,
M	22.36	one of them, a lawyer, asked him a question, to test him. "Teacher,
L	10.25	behold, a lawyer stood up to put him to the test, saying, "Teacher,

Mk	12.28	"Which commandment is the first of all?"
M	22.36	which is the great commandment
L	10.26	what shall I do to inherit eternal life?" He said to him, "What is

Mk	12.29	Jesus answered, "The first is,
M	22.37	in the law?" And he said to him,
L	10.27	written in the law? How do you read?" And he answered,

Mk	12.30	'Hear, O Israel: The Lord our God, the Lord is one; |and you shall love
M	22.37	"You shall love
L	10.27	"You shall love

Mk	12.30	the Lord your God with all your heart, and with all your soul, and with
M	22.37	the Lord your God with all your heart, and with all your soul, and with
L	10.27	the Lord your God with all your heart, and with all your soul, and with

Mk	12.31	all your mind, and with all your strength.' The second
M	22.38,39	all your mind. This is the great and first commandment. And a second
L	10.27	all your strength, and with all your mind; and
M	*19.19b*	and,

Mk	12.31	is this, 'You shall love your neighbor as yourself.' There is no other
M	22.40	is like it, You shall love your neighbor as yourself. On these two
L	10.28	your neighbor as yourself." And he said to
M	*19.19b*	You shall love your neighbor as yourself."

Mk	12.32	commandment greater than these." And the scribe said to him, "You are
M	22.40	commandments depend all the law and the prophets."
L	10.28	him, "You have answered right; do this, and you will live."

Mk	12.32	right, Teacher; you have truly said that he is one, and there is no other
Mk	12.33	but he; and to love him with all the heart, and with all the understanding,
Mk	12.33	and with all the strength, and to love one's neighbor as oneself, is much
Mk	12.34	more than all whole burnt offerings and sacrifices." And when Jesus saw
Mk	12.34	that he answered wisely, he said to him, "You are not far from the kingdom
Mk	12.34	of God." And after that no one dared to ask him any question.

f. The Son of David

Mark 12.35-37

Mk	12.35	And as Jesus taught in the
M	22.41	Now while the Pharisees were gathered together, Jesus asked them a
L	20.41	But he
J	*7.40*	*When they heard these words, some of the people said, "This is really*

Mk	12.35	temple, he said, "How can the scribes say that the Christ
M	22.42	question, |saying, "What do you think of the Christ?
L	20.41	said to them, "How can they say that the Christ
J	*7.41*	*the prophet."* *Others said, "This is the Christ."*

J	*7.41*	*But some said, "Is the Christ*
J	*7.42*	*to come from Galilee? Has not the scripture said that the Christ*

Mk	12.35	is the son of David?
M	22.43	Whose son is he?" They said to him, "The son of David." |He said to
L	20.41	is David's son?
J	*7.42*	*is descended from David, and comes from*

Mk	12.36	David himself, inspired by the Holy Spirit,
M	22.43	them, "How is it then that David, inspired by the Spirit,
L	20.42	For David himself
J	*7.42*	*Bethlehem, the village where David was?"*

Mk	12.36	declared,
M	22.43	calls him Lord, saying,
L	20.42	says in the Book of Psalms,

Mk	12.36	'The Lord said to my Lord,
M	22.44	'The Lord said to my Lord,
L	20.42	'The Lord said to my Lord,

Mk	12.36	Sit at my right hand,
M	22.44	Sit at my right hand,
L	20.42	Sit at my right hand,

Mk	12.36		till I put	thy enemies	under thy feet.'	
M	22.44		till I put	thy enemies	under thy feet'?	
L	20.43		till I make	thy enemies	a stool for thy feet.'	

Mk 12.37 |David himself calls him Lord; so how is he his son?" And the great
M 22.45,46   If David thus   calls him Lord,   how is he his son?" And no one was
L 20.44   David thus   calls him Lord; so how is he his son?"

Mk 12.37   throng heard him gladly.
M 22.46   able to answer him a word, nor from that day did any one dare to ask him

M 22.46   any more questions.

55. BEWARE OF THE SCRIBES

Mark 12.38-40

Mk 12.38   And in his teaching   he   said,
M 23.1   Then   said Jesus to the crowds and to
L 20.45   And in the hearing of all the people he   said   to

Mk 12.38   "Beware of the scribes,
M 23.2   his disciples, |"The scribes and the Pharisees sit on Moses'
L 20.46   his disciples, |"Beware of the scribes,

M 23.3   seat; so practice and observe whatever they tell you, but not what they
M 23.4   do; for they preach, but do not practice. They bind heavy burdens, hard
M 23.4   to bear, and lay them on men's shoulders; but they themselves will not
M 23.5   move them with their finger. They do all their deeds to be seen by men;

Mk 12.38   who like to go about in long robes,   and to
M 23.7   for they make their phylacteries broad and their fringes long, |and
L 20.46   who like to go about in long robes,   and

Mk 12.38   have salutations in the market places
M 23.7   salutations in the market places, and being called rabbi by men.
L 20.46   love salutations in the market places

Mk 12.39 |and the best seats in the synagogues   and   the places of honor
M 23.6b,a |and the best seats in the synagogues, |and they love the place of honor
L 20.46   and the best seats in the synagogues   and   the places of honor

Mk 12.39   at feasts,
M 23.8   at feasts   *But you are not to be called rabbi, for you have one teacher,*
L 20.46   at feasts,

M 23.9   and you are all brethren. And call no man your father on earth, for you
M 23.10   have one Father, who is in heaven. Neither be called masters, for you
M 23.11   have one master, the Christ. He who is greatest among you shall be your
M 23.12   servant; whoever exalts himself will be humbled, and whoever humbles
M 23.12   himself will be exalted.

M 23.13   "But woe to you, scribes and Pharisees, hypocrites! because you shut
M 23.13   the kingdom of heaven against men; for you neither enter yourselves, nor
M 23.14   allow those who would enter to go in. Woe to you, scribes and Pharisees,

Mk	12.40	who devour widows' houses and for a pretense make
M	23.14	*hypocrites! for* you *devour widows' houses and for a pretense* you *make*
L	20.47	who devour widows' houses and for a pretense make

Mk	12.40	long prayers. They will receive the greater condemnation."
M	23.14	*long prayers; therefore* you *will receive the greater condemnation.*
L	20.47	long prayers. They will receive the greater condemnation."

M	23.15	*Woe to you, scribes and Pharisees, hypocrites! for you traverse sea and*
M	23.15	*land to make a single proselyte, and when he becomes a proselyte, you*
M	23.15	*make him twice as much a child of hell as yourselves.*

56. THE WIDOW'S PENNY

Mark 12.41-44

| Mk | 12.41 | And he sat down opposite the treasury, and watched the multitude |
| L | 21.1 | He looked up   and saw   the rich |

| Mk | 12.41 | putting   money into the treasury. Many rich people put in large |
| L | 21.1 | putting their gifts into the treasury; |

| Mk | 12.42 | sums. And   a poor widow came, and put in two copper coins, which |
| L | 21.2 | and he saw a poor widow   put in two copper coins. |

| Mk | 12.43 | make a penny. And he called his disciples to him, and   said to them, |
| L | 21.3 | And he said, |

| Mk | 12.43 | "Truly, I say to you, this poor widow has put in more than all   those |
| L | 21.3 | "Truly I tell you, this poor widow has put in more than all of them; |

| Mk | 12.44 | who are contributing to the treasury. For they all contributed out of |
| L | 21.4 | for they all contributed out of |

| Mk | 12.44 | their abundance; but she out of her poverty has put in everything |
| L | 21.4 | their abundance, but she out of her poverty   put in all the living |

| Mk | 12.44 | she had, her whole living." |
| L | 21.4 | that she had." |

57. THE END OF THE AGE

Mark 13.1-37

a. Destruction of the Temple

Mark 13.1-2

Mk	13.1	And as he came out of the temple, one of his
M	24.1	Jesus left the temple and was going away, when his
L	21.5	And as

```
Mk   13.1    disciples said                        to him, "Look, Teacher, what wonderful
M    24.1    disciples came to point out to him
L    21.5    some      spoke


Mk   13.1    stones and what wonderful buildings!"
M    24.1                  the              buildings of the temple.
L    21.5                                   of the temple, how it was adorned


Mk   13.2                                 And Jesus said  to him, "Do you see
M    24.2                                 But he          answered them,  "You see all
L    21.6    with noble stones and offerings, he      said,        |"As         for


Mk   13.2    these  great buildings?                          There will  not be
M    24.2    these, do you not?        Truly, I say to you, there will  not be
L    21.6    these things which you see, the days will come when there shall not be


Mk   13.2    left here one stone upon another, that will not be thrown down."
M    24.2    left here one stone upon another, that will not be thrown down."
L    21.6    left here one stone upon another  that will not be thrown down."
```

b. The Signs of the End

Mark 13.3-37

```
Mk   13.3    And as he sat on the Mount of Olives opposite the temple, Peter and
M    24.3          As he sat on the Mount of Olives,              the disciples
L    21.7    And                                                  they


Mk   13.4    James and John and Andrew asked   him privately,     |"Tell us, when
M    24.3                         came to him privately, saying, "Tell us, when
L    21.7                  asked   him,                    "Teacher, when


Mk   13.4    will this be, and what will be the sign when these things are all  to
M    24.3    will this be, and what will be the sign of your coming and of the close
L    21.7    will this be, and what will be the sign when this      is about to


Mk   13.5    be accomplished?"  And Jesus began to say to them, "Take heed that no
M    24.4    of the age?"     And Jesus      answered    them,. "Take heed that no
L    21.8      take place?"    And he          said,         "Take heed that you


Mk   13.6    one    leads you astray.    Many will come in my name, saying, 'I am
M    24.5    one    leads you astray.  For many will come in my name, saying, 'I am
L    21.8    are not led       astray;  for many will come in my name, saying, 'I am


Mk   13.7        he!'   and they will lead many astray.            And
M    24.6    the Christ,' and they will lead many astray.          And
L    21.9        he!'   and, 'The time is at hand!' Do not go after them. |And


Mk   13.7    when you    hear of wars and rumors of wars, do       not be
M    24.6        you will hear of wars and rumors of wars; see that you are not
L    21.9    when you    hear of wars and tumults,      do         not be


Mk   13.7    alarmed;    this must     take place, but the end   is not
M    24.6    alarmed;  for this must     take place, but the end   is not
L    21.9    terrified; for this must first take place, but the end will not be
```

```
Mk   13.8     yet.                                      For nation will rise against nation, and
M    24.7     yet.                                      For nation will rise against nation, and
L    21.10    at once."  Then he said to them, "Nation will rise against nation, and


Mk   13.8     kingdom against kingdom;      there will be                    earthquakes
M    24.7     kingdom against kingdom, and there will be famines and earthquakes
L    21.11    kingdom against kingdom;      there will be          great earthquakes, and


Mk   13.8     in various places, there will be famines; this is but the beginning of
M    24.8     in various places;                         all this is but the beginning of
L    21.11    in various places              famines and pestilences; and there


Mk   13.8     the birth-pangs.
M    24.8     the birth-pangs.
L    21.11    will be terrors and great signs from heaven.


Mk   13.9        "But take heed to yourselves; for                     they will
M    24.9a                                       "Then                  they will
L    21.12                                       But before all this they will lay their
  M  10.17      Beware of men;                   for                    they will
  J  16.2a                                                              They will


Mk   13.9                                  deliver    you up  to      councils;
M    24.9a                                 deliver    you up  to      tribulation,
L    21.12    hands on you and persecute you, delivering you up  to
  M  10.17                                 deliver    you up  to      councils,
  J  16.2a                                 put        you out of


Mk   13.9     and        you will be beaten    in        synagogues;           and
M    24.9a    and                      put  you to        death;
L    21.12                                      the  synagogues and prisons, and
  M  10.18    and                 flog you in  their synagogues,          |and
  L  12.11    And when they      bring you before the  synagogues              and
  J  16.2a                                      the  synagogues;


Mk   13.9     you will    stand   before      governors and    kings    for my
L    21.12    you will be brought before      kings     and    governors for my name's
  M  10.18    you will be dragged before      governors and    kings    for my
  L  12.11                            the rulers   and the authorities,


Mk   13.10    sake,                                    to bear testimony before them.  And the
M    24.14                                                                              And this
L    21.13    sake.  This will be a time for you to bear testimony.
  M  10.18    sake,                                    to bear testimony before them    and the


Mk   13.10    gospel              must first be preached
M    24.14    gospel of the kingdom will       be preached throughout the whole world,
  M  10.18    Gentiles.


Mk   13.11                 to all nations.  And when they bring you to trial and
M    24.14    as a testimony to all nations;  and then the end will come.
L    21.14                                    Settle it therefore
  M  10.19                                    When they


Mk   13.11    deliver you up, do not be anxious  beforehand
L    21.14    in your minds,     not to meditate beforehand how              to
  M  10.19    deliver you up, do not be anxious              how      you are to
  L  12.11                     do not be anxious             how or what you are to
```

289

```
Mk   13.11                    what you are to say; but say whatever                    is given
L    21.15        answer;                              for                    I will    give
  M  10.19        speak  or  what you are to say;  for      what you are to say will be given
  L  12.11        answer or  what you are to say;


Mk   13.11            you in that hour,  for it is not you who speak, but
L    21.15            you a mouth and wisdom, which none of your adversaries will be able
  M  10.20        to you in that hour; |for it is not you who speak, but
  L  12.12                                                            for
  J  14.26                                                         But the Counselor,


Mk   13.12        the Holy Spirit.                              And brother will
L    21.16        to withstand or contradict.             You       will be
  M  10.21        the       Spirit of  your Father speaking through you.   Brother will
  L  12.12        the Holy Spirit will teach you in that very hour what you ought to say."
  J  14.26        the Holy Spirit, whom the Father will send in my name, he will teach you
  J  16.2b                                                               indeed, the hour is


Mk   13.12        deliver   up                          brother to death, and the father his
L    21.16        delivered up even by parents and brothers and kinsmen and friends,
  M  10.21        deliver   up                          brother to death, and the father his
  J  14.26        all things, and bring to your remembrance all that I have said to you.
  J  16.2b        coming when whoever kills you will think he is offering service to God.


Mk   13.12        child, and children will rise against parents and have        them
L    21.16                                                      and some of you they will
  M  10.21        child, and children will rise against parents and have        them


Mk   13.13        put to death; and you will be   hated by all
M    24.9b                       and you will be   hated by all nations
L    21.17        put to death;      you will be   hated by all
  M  10.22        put to death; and you will be   hated by all
  L   6.22            "Blessed are you when men hate  you, and when they exclude you and
  J  15.18                        "If the world  hates you, know  that it has hated me


  J  15.19                         before it hated you.  If you were of the world, the
  J  15.19        world would love its own; but because you are not of the world, but I
  J  15.19        chose you out of the world,
  J  15.19            therefore the world hates you.


Mk   13.13                                                  for         my name's sake.
M    24.9b                                                  for         my name's sake.
L    21.17                                                  for         my name's sake.
  M  10.22                                                  for         my name's sake.
  L   6.22        revile you, and cast out your name as evil, on account of the Son of man!


  M  24.10        And then many will fall away, and betray one another, and hate one another.
  M  24.11,12     And many false prophets will arise and lead many astray.  And because
  M  24.12        wickedness is multiplied, most men's love will grow cold.

  L  21.18        But not a hair of your head will perish.


Mk   13.13        But he who endures to the end will be       saved.
M    24.13        But he who endures to the end will be       saved.
L    21.19        By   your   endurance     you will gain your lives.
  M  10.22        But he who endures to the end will be       saved.
  J  16.1         "I have said all this to you to keep you from falling away.
```

Mk	13.14	"But when you see the
M	24.15	"So when you see the
L	21.20	"But when you see Jerusalem surrounded by armies, then know that its

Mk	13.14	desolating sacrilege set up where
M	24.15	desolating sacrilege spoken of by the prophet Daniel, standing in the
L	21.20	desolation has come near.

Mk	13.14	it ought not to be (let the reader understand), then let those who are
M	24.16	holy place (let the reader understand), |then let those who are
L	21.21	Then let those who are

Mk	13.15	in Judea flee to the mountains; let him who is on the housetop
M	24.17	in Judea flee to the mountains; let him who is on the housetop
L	17.31	On that day, let him who is on the housetop,
L	21.21	in Judea flee to the mountains, and let those who are inside the city

Mk	13.15	not go down, nor enter his house, to take
M	24.17	not go down to take
L	17.31	with his goods in the house, not come down to take
L	21.21	depart, and let not those who are out

Mk	13.16	anything away; and let him who is in the field not turn
M	24.18	what is in his house; and let him who is in the field not turn
L	17.31	them away; and likewise let him who is in the field not turn
L	21.22	in the country enter it; for these are days of vengeance, to fulfil all

Mk	13.17	back to take his mantle. And alas for those who are with child and for
M	24.19	back to take his mantle. And alas for those who are with child and for
L	17.31	back.
L	21.23	that is written. Alas for those who are with child and for

Mk	13.18	those who give suck in those days! Pray that it may not happen
M	24.20	those who give suck in those days! Pray that your flight may not be
L	21.23	those who give suck in those days!

Mk	13.19	in winter. For in those days there will be such
M	24.21	in winter or on a sabbath. For then there will be great
L	21.23	For great

Mk	13.19	tribulation as has not been from the beginning of the creation
M	24.21	tribulation, such as has not been from the beginning of the world
L	21.24	distress shall be upon the earth and wrath upon this people; *they will*

L	21.24	*fall by the edge of the sword, and be led captive among all nations;*
L	21.24	*and Jerusalem will be trodden down by the Gentiles, until the times*
L	21.24	*of the Gentiles are fulfilled.*

Mk	13.20	which God created until now, and never will be. And if the Lord
M	24.22	until now, no, and never will be. And if those days

Mk	13.20	had not shortened the days, no human being would be saved; but for
M	24.22	had not been shortened, no human being would be saved; but for

Mk	13.20	the sake of the elect, whom he chose, he shortened the days.
M	24.22	the sake of the elect those days will be shortened.

L	17.20	*Being asked by the Pharisees when the kingdom of God was coming,*
L	17.20	*he answered them, "The kingdom of God is not coming with signs to be*
L	17.20	*observed;*

Mk	13.21	And then if any one says to you, 'Look, here is the Christ!' or
M	24.23	Then if any one says to you, 'Lo, here is the Christ!' or
L	17.21	nor will they say, 'Lo, here it is!' or
L	17.23	And they will say to you, 'Lo, there!' or

Mk	13.22	'Look, there he is!' do not believe it. False Christs and false
M	24.24	'There he is!' do not believe it. For false Christs and false
L	17.21	'There!' for behold, the kingdom of God is in the midst of you."
L	17.23	'Lo, here!'

L	17.22	*And he said to the disciples, "The days are coming when you will desire*
L	17.22	*to see one of the days of the Son of man, and you will not see it.*

Mk	13.22	prophets will arise and show signs and wonders, to lead
M	24.24	prophets will arise and show great signs and wonders, so as to lead

Mk	13.23	astray, if possible, the elect. But take heed; I have told you all
M	24.25	astray, if possible, even the elect. Lo, I have told you

Mk	13.23	things beforehand.
M	24.26	beforehand. *So, if they say to you, 'Lo, he is in the wilderness,'*

M	24.26	*do not go out; if they say, 'Lo, he is in the inner rooms,' do not believe*
L	17.23	*Do not go, do not follow*

M	24.27	*it. For as the lightning comes from the east and shines as far as the*
L	17.24	*them. For as the lightning flashes and lights up the sky*

M	24.27	*west, so will be the coming of the Son of man.*
L	17.24	*from one side to the other, so will the Son of man be in*

L	17.25	*his day. But first he must suffer many things and be rejected by this*
L	17.25	*generation.*

M	24.28	*Wherever the body is, there the eagles will be gathered together.*

Mk	13.24	"But in those days, after that tribulation, the sun will
M	24.29	"Immediately after the tribulation of those days the sun will
L	21.25	"And there will be signs in sun

Mk	13.25	be darkened, and the moon will not give its light, |and the stars will
M	24.29	be darkened, and the moon will not give its light, and the stars will
L	21.25	and moon and stars, and

Mk	13.25	be falling from heaven,
M	24.29	fall from heaven,
L	21.25	upon the earth distress of nations in perplexity at the roaring of the

L	21.26	*sea and the waves, |men fainting with fear and with foreboding of what*

Mk	13.25	and the powers in the heavens will be shaken.
M	24.29	and the powers of the heavens will be shaken;
L	21.26	*is coming on the world;* for the powers of the heavens will be shaken.

then will appear the sign of the Son of man in heaven, and then all the

Mk   13.26   And then they will see the Son of man
M   24.30   *tribes of the earth will mourn,* and   they will see the Son of man
L   21.27   And then they will see the Son of man

Mk   13.27   coming in   clouds   with great power and   glory.   And
M   24.31   coming on the clouds of heaven with   power and great glory;   and
L   21.28   coming in a   cloud   with   power and great glory.   Now

Mk   13.27   then he will send out the angels,   and
M   24.31   he will send out his angels with a loud trumpet call, and they will
L   21.28   when these things begin to take place, look up and raise your heads,

Mk   13.27   gather his elect from the four winds, from the ends of the earth to the
M   24.31   gather his elect from the four winds, from one end
L   21.28   because your redemption is drawing near."

Mk   13.27   ends of heaven.
M   24.31   of heaven to the other.

Mk   13.28   "From   the fig tree learn its lesson:
M   24.32   "From   the fig tree learn its lesson:
L   21.29   And he told them a parable: "Look at the fig tree, and all the trees;

Mk   13.28   as soon as its branch becomes tender and puts forth its leaves, you
M   24.32   as soon as its branch becomes tender and puts forth its leaves, you
L   21.30   as soon as   they   come out   in leaf,   you see

Mk   13.29   know that   summer is   near. So also, when
M   24.33   know that   summer is   near. So also, when
L   21.31   for yourselves and know that the summer is already near. So also, when

Mk   13.29   you see   these things taking place, you know that   he
M   24.33   you see all these things,   you know that   he
L   21.31   you see   these things taking place, you know that the kingdom of God

Mk   13.30   is near, at the very gates. Truly, I say to you, this generation will
M   24.34   is near, at the very gates. Truly, I say to you, this generation will
L   21.32   is near.   Truly, I say to you, this generation will

Mk   13.31   not pass away before all these things take place. Heaven and earth will
M   24.35   not pass away till   all these things take place. Heaven and earth will
L   21.33   not pass away till   all   has taken place. Heaven and earth will
  M   5.18   *For truly, I say to you, till* heaven and earth
  L   16.17   *But it is easier for* heaven and earth *to*

Mk   13.31   pass away, but my words   will not pass away.
M   24.35   pass away, but my words   will not pass away.
L   21.33   pass away, but my words   will not pass away.
  M   5.18   pass away, *not an iota, not a   dot,* will   *pass from the law until all*
  L   16.17   pass away, *than for   one dot*   *of   the law to become*

  M   5.18   *is accomplished.*
  L   16.17   *void.*

Mk	13.32	"But of that day or that hour no one knows, not even the angels in
M	24.36	"But of that day and hour no one knows, not even the angels of

Mk	13.33	heaven, nor the Son, but only the Father. Take heed, watch;
M	24.42	heaven, nor the Son, but the Father only. Watch therefore,
L	21.36	But watch at all times,
M	*25.13*	Watch *therefore,*

Mk	13.33	for you do not know when the time will come.
M	24.42	For you do not know on what day your Lord is coming.
L	21.36	praying that you may have strength to escape all these things that will
M	*25.13*	for you know *neither the day nor the hour.*

Mk	13.34	It is like a man going on a journey, when he leaves
L	21.36	take place, and to stand before the Son of man."
M	*25.14*	*"For* it *will be as when* a man going on a journey
L	*19.12*	*He said therefore,* *"A nobleman went into a far country to receive a*

Mk	13.34	home and puts his servants in charge,
M	*25.14*	called his servants *and entrusted to them*
L	*19.1*	*kingdom* and *then return. Calling ten of* his servants,

Mk	13.34	each with his work, and commands the doorkeeper to be on
M	*25.15*	*his property; to one he gave* vive *talents, to another two, to another*
L	*19.13*	*he gave them ten pounds,*

Mk	13.35	the watch. Watch therefore
M	24.42	Watch therefore,
L	21.36	But watch at all
M	*25.13*	*one, to each according to his ability. Then he went away.* Watch *therefore,*
L	*19.13*	*and said to them,* *'Trade with these till I come.'*

Mk	13.35	--for you do not know when the master of the house will
M	24.42	for you do not know on what day your Lord is
L	21.36	times, praying that you may have strength to escape all these things
M	*25.13*	for you know *neither the day nor the hour.*
L	*12.38*	*If* he

Mk	13.35	come, in the evening, or at midnight, or at cockcrow, or in the
M	24.42	coming.
L	21.36	that will take place, and to stand before the Son of man."
L	*12.38*	*comes* in the *second watch,* or *in the third,*

Mk	13.36,37	morning--⎮lest he come suddenly and find you asleep. And what I say to
L	*12.38*	*and* finds *them so, blessed are those*

Mk	13.37	you I say to all: Watch."
L	*12.38*	*servants!*

58. THE PLOT TO KILL JESUS

Mark 14.1-2

M	*26.1*	*When Jesus had finished all these sayings, he said to his disciples,*

J	11.45	Many of the Jews therefore, who had come with Mary and had seen what
J	11.46	he did, believed in him; but some of them went to the Pharisees and
J	11.46	told them what Jesus had done.

Mk	14.1	It was now two days before
M	26.2	"You know that after two days
L	22.1	Now the feast of Unleavened Bread drew near, which is called
J	11.55	Now

Mk	14.1	the Passover and the feast of Unleavened Bread.
M	26.2	the Passover is coming, and the Son of man will be delivered up to be
L	22.1	the Passover.
J	11.55	the Passover of the Jews was at hand, and many went up from the country

M	26.2	*crucified."*
J	11.56	*to Jerusalem before the Passover, to purify themselves. They were looking*

J	11.56	*for Jesus and saying to one another as they stood in the temple, "What*
J	11.56	*do you think? That he will not come to the feast?"*

Mk	14.1	And the chief priests and the scribes
M	26.3	Then the chief priests and the elders of the people gathered in the
L	22.2	And the chief priests and the scribes
J	11.47	So the chief priests and the Pharisees gathered the
J	11.53	So from that day on they
J	11.57	Now the chief priests and the Pharisees had given orders that if

Mk	14.1	were seeking
M	26.4	palace of the high priest, who was called Caiaphas, |and took counsel
L	22.2	were seeking
J	11.47	council, and said, "What are we to do? For this man performs many signs.
J	11.53	took counsel
J	11.57	any one knew where he was, he should let them know,

Mk	14.1	how to arrest him by stealth, and kill him;
M	26.4	together in order to arrest Jesus by stealth and kill him.
L	22.2	how to put him to death;
J	11.53	how to put him to death.
J	11.57	so that they might arrest him.

J	11.48	*If we let him go on thus, every one will believe in him, and the Romans*
J	11.49	*will come and destroy both our holy place and our nation." But one of*
J	11.49	*them, Caiaphas, who was high priest that year, said to them, "You know*
J	11.50	*nothing at all; you do not understand that it is expedient for you that*
J	11.50	*one man should die for the people, and that the whole nation should not*
J	11.51	*perish." He did not say this of his own accord, but being high priest*
J	11.52	*that year he prophesied that Jesus should die for the nation, |and not*
J	11.52	*for the nation only, but to gather into one the children of God who are*
J	11.52	*scattered abroad.*

J	11.54	*Jesus therefore no longer went about openly among the Jews, but went*
J	11.54	*from there to the country near the wilderness, to a town called Ephraim;*
J	11.54	*and there he stayed with the disciples.*

Mk	14.2	for they said, "Not during the feast, lest there be a tumult of the
M	26.5	But they said, "Not during the feast, lest there be a tumult among the
L	22.2	for they feared the

Mk	14.2	people."
M	26.5	people."
L	22.2	people.

Mark 14.3-9

Mk	14.3	And while	he was at
M	26.6	Now when	Jesus was at
L	7.36	One of the Pharisees asked him to eat with him, and he	went
J	12.1	Six days before the Passover,	Jesus came to

Mk	14.3	Bethany in the house of Simon the leper,	as he sat
M	26.7b	Bethany in the house of Simon the leper,	|as he sat
L	7.36	into the Pharisee's house,	and took his place
J	12.2	Bethany, where Lazarus was, whom Jesus had raised from the dead.	*There*

J 12.2 they made him a supper; Martha served, and Lazarus was one of those

Mk	14.3	at table,	a woman came
M	26.7a	at table.	|a woman came up
L	7.37	at table. And behold, a woman of the city, who was a sinner, when she
J	12.3	at table with him. Mary

L 7.37 learned that he was sitting at table in the Pharisees's house,

Mk	14.3	with an alabaster flask of	ointment of pure nard,
M	26.7a	to him with an alabaster flask of very expensive ointment,
L	7.38	brought an alabaster flask of	ointment, |and standing
J	12.3	took a pound of costly	ointment of pure nard

L 7.38 behind him at his feet, weeping, she began to wet his feet with her tears,
L 7.38 and wiped them with the hair of her head, and kissed his feet,

Mk	14.3	very costly, and she broke the flask and poured it over his head.
M	26.7a	and she poured it on his head,
L	7.38	and anointed them with
J	12.3	and anointed the feet of Jesus

J 12.3 and wiped his feet with her hair; and the house was filled with the

Mk	14.4	But there were some who
M	26.8	But when the disciples
L	7.39	the ointment. Now when the Pharisee who had invited him
J	12.4	fragrance of the ointment. But Judas Iscariot, one of his disciples (he

Mk	14.4	said to themselves indignantly, "Why was
M	26.8	saw it, they were indignant, saying, "Why
L	7.39	saw it, he said to himself, "If this man were a prophet, he
J	12.5	who was to betray him), said, |"Why was

Mk	14.5	the ointment thus wasted? For this ointment might have been sold for
M	26.9	this waste? For this ointment might have been sold for
L	7.39	would have known who and what sort of woman this is who is touching him,
J	12.5	this ointment not sold for

L 7.40 for she is a sinner." And Jesus answering said to him, "Simon, I have
L 7.41 something to say to you." And he answered, "What is it, Teacher?" \|"A

```
Mk   14.5                                       more than three hundred denarii, and
M    26.9                                               a large    sum,            and
L     7.41   certain creditor had two debtors; one owed five  hundred denarii, and
J    12.5                                               three hundred denarii  and


M    14.5    given to the poor."  And they reproached her.
M    26.9    given to the poor."
L     7.42   the other fifty.  When they could not pay, he forgave them both.  Now
J    12.6    given to the poor?"  This he said, not that he cared for the poor but


   J 12.6    because he was a thief, and as he had the money box he used to take what
   J 12.6    was put into it.


Mk   14.6    But Jesus                   said, "Let her alone;
M    26.10   But Jesus, aware of this, said to them,
L     7.43   which of them will love him more?"  Simon answered, "The one, I suppose,
J    12.7a       Jesus                   said, "Let her alone,


   L 7.43    to whom he forgave more."  And he said to him, "You have judged rightly."
   L 7.44    Then turning toward the woman he said to Simon,


Mk   14.6    why do you trouble    her?       She has done a beautiful thing to me.
M    26.10   "Why do you trouble the woman?  For she has done a beautiful thing to me.
L     7.44         "Do you see    this woman?  I entered your house, you gave me no water


   L 7.44    for my feet, but she has wet my feet with her tears and wiped them with
   L 7.45    her hair.  You gave me no kiss, but from the time I came in she has not


Mk   14.7    For you always have the poor with you, and whenever you will, you can do
M    26.11   For you always have the poor with you,
L     7.45   ceased to kiss my feet.
J    12.8        The poor you always have with you,


Mk   14.8    good to them; but you will not always have me.  She has done what she
M    26.11                 but you will not always have me.
L     7.46             You did  not anoint my head with oil,
J    12.8        but you do  not always have me."


Mk   14.8    could;  she has anointed    my body               beforehand     for
M    26.12   In pouring this ointment on my body she has done it to prepare me for
L     7.46       but she has anointed    my feet with ointment.
J    12.7b                               let her    keep it for the day of my


Mk   14.9    burying.  And truly, I say to you, wherever the  gospel is preached in
M    26.13   burial.       Truly, I say to you, wherever this gospel is preached in
L     7.47        Therefore  I tell   you, her sins, which are many, are forgiven,


Mk   14.9    the whole world, what she has done will be told in memory of her."
M    26.13   the whole world, what she has done will be told in memory of her."
L     7.47   for she loved much; but he who is forgiven little, loves little."


   L 7.48    And he said to her, "Your sins are forgiven."
   L 7.49                       Then those who were at table with him
```

297

L	7.49	*began to say among themselves, "Who is this, who even forgives sins?"*
L	7.50	*And he said to the woman, "Your faith has saved you; go in peace."*

60. JUDAS PLANS THE BETRAYAL

Mark 14.10-11

Mk	14.10	Then
M	26.14	Then one of the twelve, who was called
L	22.3	Then Satan entered into
J	6.70	*Jesus answered them, "Did I not choose you, the twelve, and one of you*
J	13.2	*And during supper, when the devil had already put it into the heart*
J	13.27	*Then after the morsel,* Satan entered into

Mk	14.10	Judas Iscariot, who was
M	26.14	Judas Iscariot,
L	22.3	Judas called Iscariot, who was of the
J	6.71	*is a devil?" He spoke of* Judas *the son of Simon* Iscariot, *for he,*
J	13.2	*of* Judas Iscariot, *Simon's son,*
J	13.27	*him. Jesus said to him, "What you are going to*

Mk	14.10	one of the twelve, went to the chief priests
M	26.14	went to the chief priests
L	22.4	number of the twelve; he went away and conferred with the chief priests
J	6.71	one of the twelve,
J	13.27	*do, do quickly."*

Mk	14.11	in order to betray him to them. And
M	26.15	|and said, "What will you give me if I deliver him to you?" And
L	22.5	and officers how he might betray him to them. And

Mk	14.11	when they heard it they were glad, and promised to give him
M	26.15	they paid him thirty pieces
L	22.5	they were glad, and engaged to give him

Mk	14.11	money. And he sought an opportunity
M	26.16	of silver. And from that moment he sought an opportunity
L	22.6	money. So he agreed, and sought an opportunity
J	6.71	*was*

Mk	14.11	to betray him.
M	26.16	to betray him.
L	22.6	to betray him to them in the absence of the multitude.
J	6.71	to betray him.
J	13.2	to betray him,

61. THE PASSOVER MEAL

Mark 14.12-25

Mk	14.12	And on the first day of Unleavened Bread, when they sacrificed the
M	26.17	Now on the first day of Unleavened Bread
L	22.7	Then came the day of Unleavened Bread, on which the

Mk	14.12	passover lamb,
L	22.8	passover lamb had to be sacrificed. So Jesus sent Peter and John, saying,

"Go and prepare the passover for us, that we may eat it."

Mk	14.12	his disciples said to him, "Where will you have us go and
M	26.17	the disciples came to Jesus, saying, "Where will you have us
L	22.9	They said to him, "Where will you have us

Mk	14.13	prepare for you to eat the passover?" And he sent two of his disciples,
M	26.18	prepare for you to eat the passover?" He
L	22.10	prepare it?" He

Mk	14.13	and said to them, "Go into the city, and a
M	26.18	said, "Go into the city to a certain
L	22.10	said to them, "Behold, when you have entered the city, a

Mk	14.14	man carrying a jar of water will meet you; follow him, ǀand wherever
M	26.18	one,
L	22.10	man carrying a jar of water will meet you; follow him into the house which

Mk	14.14	he enters, say to the householder, 'The Teacher says, Where
M	26.18	and say to him, 'The Teacher says, My time
L	22.11	he enters, ǀand tell the householder, 'The Teacher says to you, Where

Mk	14.14	is my guest room, where I am to eat the passover with my
M	26.18	is at hand; I will keep the passover at your house with my
L	22.11	is the guest room, where I am to eat the passover with my

Mk	14.15	disciples?' And he will show you a large upper room furnished and ready;
M	26.18	disciples.'"
L	22.12	disciples?' And he will show you a large upper room furnished;

Mk	14.16	there prepare for us." And the disciples set out and went to the city,
M	26.19	And the disciples
L	22.13	there make ready." And they went,

Mk	14.16	and found it as he had told them; and they prepared the passover.
M	26.19	did as Jesus had directed them, and they prepared the passover.
L	22.13	and found it as he had told them; and they prepared the passover.

Mk	14.17	And when it was evening he came with the twelve.
M	26.20	When it was evening, he sat at table with the twelve
L	22.14	And when the hour came, he sat at table, and the apostles
J	13.21	When Jesus had thus spoken, he was troubled in spirit,

Mk	14.18	And as they were at table eating, Jesus said, "Truly,
M	26.21	disciples; and as they were eating, he said, "Truly,
L	22.21	with him. But behold
J	13.21	and testified, "Truly, truly,

Mk	14.18	I say to you, one of you will betray me, one who is eating with me."
M	26.21	I say to you, one of you will betray me."
L	22.21	the hand of him who betrays me is with me on
J	13.21	I say to you, one of you will betray me."

Mk	14.19		They began to be		sorrowful, and		to say to
M	26.22		And they	were very	sorrowful, and	began	to say to
L	22.23	the table.	And they began to	question			
J	13.22		The disciples looked at one another, uncertain of whom he				

J 13.23 spoke. One of his disciples, whom Jesus loved, was lying close to the
J 13.24 breast of Jesus; so Simon Peter beckoned to him and said, "Tell us who
J 13.25 it is of whom he speaks." So lying thus, close to the breast of Jesus,

Mk	14.20	him one after another, "Is it I?"		He	said to them, "It is
M	26.23	him one after another, "Is it I,	Lord?"	He	answered,
L	22.23	one another,	which of them it was that would do this.		
J	13.26	he said to him,	"Lord, who is it?"	Jesus answered,	"It is

Mk	14.20	one of the twelve, one	who	is	dipping	bread into the dish with
M	26.23		"He	who	has dipped	his	hand in	the dish with
J	13.26			he to whom I shall give this morsel when I have dipped

J 13.26 it." So when he had dipped the morsel, he gave it to
J 13.27 Judas, the son of Simon Iscariot. Then after the morsel, Satan entered
J 13.27 into him. Jesus said to him, "What you are going to do, do quickly."
J 13.28,29 Now no one at the table knew why he said this to him. Some thought that,
J 13.29 because Judas had the money box, Jesus was telling him, "Buy what we
J 13.29 need for the feast"; or, that he should give something to the poor.

Mk	14.21	me.	For the Son of man goes as it is written of him,	but
M	26.24	me, will betray me.	The Son of man goes as it is written of him,	but
L	22.22		For the Son of man goes as it	has been determined;	but

Mk	14.21	woe to that man by whom the Son of man is betrayed!	It would have been
M	26.24	woe to that man by whom the Son of man is betrayed!	It would have been
L	22.22	woe to that man by whom	he	is betrayed!"

Mk	14.21	better for that man if he had not been born."
M	26.25	better for that man if he had not been born."	Judas, who betrayed him,
J	13.30	So, after receiving the morsel, he immediately went out;

M 26.25 said, "Is it I, Master?" He said to him, "You have said so."
J 13.30 and it was night.

Mk	14.22	And as they were eating,
M	26.26	Now as they were eating,
L	22.19	And
1 C	11.23	For I received from the Lord what I also delivered to you, that the

Mk	14.22	he	took bread, and
M	26.26	Jesus	took bread, and
L	22.19	he	took bread, and when he
1 C	11.24	Lord Jesus on the night when he was betrayed took bread,	and when he
J	6.48	I am the bread of life.

J 6.49 Your fathers ate the manna in the wilderness, and they died.
J 6.50 This is the bread which comes
J 6.51 down from heaven, that a man may eat of it and not die. I am the
J 6.51 living bread which came down from heaven; if any one eats of this

Mk	14.22		blessed,	and broke it,	and gave it to	them,	and said,
M	26.26		blessed,	and broke it,	and gave it to	the disciples	and said,
L	22.19	had given thanks	he broke it	and gave it to	them,	saying,
1 C	11.24	had given thanks,	he broke it,			and said,
J	6.51	*bread, he will live for ever; and the bread which I shall give for the*

Mk	14.22	"Take;	this is my body."
M	26.26	"Take, eat;	this is my body."
L	22.19		"This is my body which is given for you. Do this in
1 C	11.24		"This is my body which is for you. Do this in
J	6.52	*life of the world is my flesh." The Jews then disputed among themselves,*

J	6.53	*saying, "How can this man give us his flesh to eat?" So Jesus said to*
J	6.53	*them, "Truly, truly, I say to you, unless you eat the flesh of the Son*
J	6.53	*of man*

Mk	14.23		And he took	a	cup, and when he had given
M	26.27		And he took	a	cup, and when he had given
L	22.17		And he took	a	cup, and when he had given
L	22.20a	remembrance of me."	And likewise	the cup	after supper,
1 C	11.25	remembrance of me."	In the same way also	the cup,	after supper,

Mk	14.24	thanks he gave it to them,	and they all drank of it. And he said to
M	26.27	thanks he gave it to them,	saying,	"Drink of it, all of you;
L	22.17	thanks he	said,	"Take this, and divide it among
L	22.20a		saying,
1 C	11.25		saying,
J	6.53			*and drink his blood, you have no*

J	6.54	*life in you; he who eats my flesh and drinks my blood has eternal life,*
J	6.55	*and I will raise him up at the last day. For my flesh is food indeed,*
J	6.56	*and my blood is drink indeed. He who eats my flesh and drinks my blood*
J	6.57	*abides in me, and I in him. As the living Father sent me, and I live*
J	6.58	*because of the Father, so he who eats me will live because of me. This*
J	6.58	*is the bread which came down from heaven, not such as the fathers ate*
J	6.59	*and died; he who eats this bread will live forever." This he said in*
J	6.59	*the synagogue, as he taught at Capernaum.*

Mk	14.24	them, "This	is my blood of the	covenant,	which
M	26.28	for this	is my blood of the	covenant,	which
L	22.17	yourselves;
L	22.20c,b	"This cup	is	the new covenant in my blood.	which
1 C	11.25	"This cup	is	the new covenant in my blood. Do this,

Mk	14.24	is poured out for many.
M	26.28	is poured out for many for the forgiveness of sins.
L	22.15	is poured out for you |And he said to them, "I have earnestly desired
1 C	11.25	as often as you drink it, in remembrance of me."

L	22.16	*to eat this passover with you before I suffer; for I tell you I shall*
L	22.16	*not eat it until it is fulfilled in the kingdom of God."*

Mk	14.25	Truly, I say to you,	I shall not drink again of the
M	26.29	I tell you	I shall not drink again of this
L	22.18	for I tell you that from now on I shall not drink	of the
1 C	11.26	For as often as you eat this bread and drink the cup, you proclaim

301

```
Mk    14.25    fruit of the vine until that day when I drink it new          in the
M     26.29    fruit of the vine until that day when I drink it new with you in my
L     22.18    fruit of the vine until                                         the
1 C   11.27    the Lord's death until he comes.  Whoever, therefore, eats the bread


Mk    14.25              kingdom of God."
M     26.29    Father's  kingdom."
L     22.18              kingdom of God comes."
1 C   11.27    or drinks the cup of the Lord in an unworthy manner will be guilty of
```

1 C 11.28   *profaning the body and blood of the Lord. Let a man examine himself,*
1 C 11.29   *and so eat of the bread and drink of the cup. For any one who eats*
1 C 11.29   *and drinks without discerning the body eats and drinks judgment upon*
1 C 11.30   *himself. That is why many of you are weak and ill, and some have died.*
1 C 11.31,32 *But if we judged ourselves truly, we should not be judged. But when*
1 C 11.32   *we are judged by the Lord, we are chastened so that we may not be*
1 C 11.32   *condemned along with the world.*

62. PETER'S DENIAL FORETOLD

Mark 14.26-31

```
Mk    14.26    And when they  had sung a hymn,          they went out
M     26.30    And when they  had sung a hymn,          they went out
L     22.39    And       he   came out,                and went, as was his custom,
J     18.1         When Jesus had spoken these words, he  went forth with his


Mk    14.27              to    the Mount of Olives.  And  Jesus said to them,
M     26.31              to    the Mount of Olives.  Then Jesus said to them,
L     22.39              to    the Mount of Olives;  and the disciples followed him.
J     18.1     disciples across the Kidron valley, where there was a garden, which he


Mk    14.27    "You will all fall away;                           for it is written, 'I
M     26.31    "You will all fall away because of me this night; for it is written, 'I
L     22.31    "Simon, Simon, behold, Satan demanded to have you, that he might sift
J     18.1     and his disciples entered.


Mk    14.27    will strike the shepherd, and the sheep          will be scattered.'
M     26.31    will strike the shepherd, and the sheep of the flock will be scattered.'
L     22.32    you like wheat, |but I have prayed for you that your faith may not fail;
```
J   16.32   *The hour is coming,   indeed it has come,   when you will be scattered,*

J   16.32   *every man to his home, and will leave me alone; yet I am not alone,*
J   16.32   *for the Father is with me.*


```
Mk    14.28,29  But after I am raised up, I will go before you to Galilee."      Peter
M     26.32,33  But after I am raised up, I will go before you to Galilee."      Peter
L     22.33     and when you have turned again, strengthen your brethren."  And he
```
J   13.37   Peter


```
Mk    14.29    said      to him,  "Even though they all fall away,         I will
M     26.33    declared  to him,     "Though they all fall away because of you, I will
L     22.33    said      to him,  "Lord,                                    I am
```
J   13.37   said   to him, *"Lord, why cannot I follow you now?*   I will

Mk	14.30	not."	And Jesus said to him,
M	26.34	never fall away."	Jesus said to him,
L	22.34	ready to go with you to prison and to death."	He said,
J	13.38	lay down my life for you."	Jesus answered, "Will you

Mk	14.30		"Truly,	I say to you, this very night,
M	26.34		"Truly,	I say to you, this very night,
L	22.34			"I tell you, Peter,
J	13.38	lay down your life for me? Truly, truly, I say to you,		

Mk	14.30	before the cock	crows twice,	you will	deny
M	26.34	before the cock	crows,	you will	deny
L	22.34	the cock will not crow this day, until	you three times deny that		
J	13.38	the cock will not crow,	till you have	denied	

Mk	14.31	me three times." But he	said vehemently, "If I must die
M	26.35	me three times." Peter	said to him, "Even if I must die
L	22.34	you know me."	
J	13.38	me three times.	

Mk	14.31	with you, I will not deny you." And they all said the same.
M	26.35	with you, I will not deny you." And so said all the disciples.

63. GETHSEMANE

Mark 14.32-42

L	22.39	*And he came out, and went, as was his custom, to the Mount of Olives;*
L	22.39	*and the disciples followed him.*

Mk	14.32	And they	went
M	26.36	Then Jesus	went with them
L	27.40a	And when he	came
J	18.1	When Jesus had spoken these words, he	went forth with his disciples

Mk	14.32	to a place which was called Gethsemane;	and he said to
M	26.36	to a place called Gethsemane,	and he said to
L	22.40a	to the place	
J	18.1	across the Kidron valley, where there was a garden, which he and	

Mk	14.33	his disciples, "Sit here, while I pray." And he took
M	26.37	his disciples, "Sit here, while I go yonder and pray." And taking
J	18.1	his disciples entered.

Mk	14.33	with him Peter and James and John, and began to be greatly
M	26.37	with him Peter and the two sons of Zebedee, he began to be

Mk	14.34	distressed and troubled. And he said to them, "My soul is very
M	26.38	sorrowful and troubled. Then he said to them, "My soul is very
J	12.27	"Now is my soul

Mk	14.35	sorrowful, even to death; remain here, and watch." And
M	26.39	sorrowful, even to death; remain here, and watch with me." And
L	22.41	And he
J	12.27	troubled.

303

Mk	14.35	going	a little farther, he fell on the ground and
M	26.39	going	a little farther he fell on his face and
L	22.41	withdrew from them about	a stone's throw, and knelt down and

Mk	14.36	prayed that, if it were possible, the hour might pass from him. And he
M	26.39	prayed,
L	22.41	prayed,
J	12.27	And what shall I

Mk	14.36	said, "Abba, Father, all things are possible to thee; remove this cup
M	26.39	"My Father, if it be possible, let this cup
L	22.42	|"Father, if thou art willing, remove this cup
J	6.38	For I
J	12.27	say? 'Father, save me from this hour'?

Mk	14.36	from me; yet not what I will, but what thou
M	26.39	pass from me; nevertheless, not as I will, but as thou
L	22.42	from me; nevertheless not my will, but thine,
J	6.38	have come down from heaven, not to do my own will, but the will of him
J	12.27	No, for this purpose I have come to this hour.

Mk	14.37	wilt." And he came and
M	26.40	wilt." And he came to the disciples and
L	22.45	be done." And when he rose from prayer, he came to the disciples and
J	6.38	who sent me;

Mk	14.37	found them sleeping, and he said to Peter, "Simon, are you
M	26.40	found them sleeping; and he said to Peter, "So,
L	22.40b	found them sleeping for sorrow, |he said to them,

Mk	14.38	asleep? Could you not watch one hour? |Watch and pray that you
M	26.41	could you not watch with me one hour? Watch and pray that you
L	22.40b	"Pray that you

Mk	14.38	may not enter into temptation; the spirit indeed is willing, but the
M	26.41	may not enter into temptation; the spirit indeed is willing, but the
L	22.40b	may not enter into temptation."

Mk	14.39	flesh is weak." And again he went away and prayed,
M	26.42	flesh is weak." Again, for the second time, he went away and prayed,
L	22.44	*And being in an agony* he *prayed*

Mk	14.39	saying the same words.
M	26.42	"My Father, if this cannot pass unless I drink it, thy will be done."
L	22.44	*more earnestly; and his sweat became like great drops of blood falling*

Mk	14.40	And again he came and found them sleeping, for their eyes were very
M	26.43	And again he came and found them sleeping, for their eyes were
L	22.44	*down upon the ground.*

| Mk | 14.40 | heavy; and they did not know what to answer him. |
| M | 26.44 | heavy. So, leaving them again, he went away and prayed for the third |

Mk	14.41	And he came the third time, and said
M	26.45	time, saying the same words. Then he came to the disciples and said
L	22.46	and he said

304

Mk	14.41	to them, "Are <u>you still sleeping and taking your rest? It is enough;</u>
M	26.45	to them, "Are <u>you still sleeping and taking your rest?</u> Behold,
L	22.46	to them, "Why do <u>you</u> sleep? Rise and pray that you may not

Mk	14.41	<u>the hour has</u> come; <u>the Son of man is betrayed into the hands of</u>
M	26.45	<u>the hour</u> is at hand, and <u>the Son of man is betrayed into the hands of</u>
L	22.46	enter into temptation."

Mk	14.42	<u>sinners.</u> <u>Rise, let us be going;</u> <u>see, my betrayer is at hand."</u>
M	26.46	<u>sinners.</u> <u>Rise, let us be going; see, my betrayer is at hand."</u>
J	14.31b	<u>Rise, let us</u> go hence.

64. JESUS ARRESTED

Mark 14.43-52

J	18.2	*Now Judas, who betrayed him, also knew the place; for Jesus often met*
J	18.2	*there with his disciples.*

Mk	14.43	<u>And immediately,</u> <u>while he was still speaking</u>,
M	26.47	<u>While he was still speaking,</u>
L	22.47	<u>While he was still speaking</u>, there came a crowd, and
J	18.3	So

Mk	14.43	Judas came, <u>one of the twelve,</u> and
M	26.47	Judas came, <u>one of the twelve,</u> and
L	22.47	the man called Judas, , <u>one of the twelve,</u> was
J	18.3	<u>Judas,</u> procuring a band of soldiers and some officers from

Mk	14.43	<u>with him a</u> <u>crowd with swords</u>
M	26.47	<u>with him a</u> great <u>crowd with swords</u>
L	22.47	leading them.
J	18.3	the chief priests and the Pharisees, went there with lanterns and torches

Mk	14.43	<u>and clubs, from the chief priests and the scribes and the elders.</u>
M	26.47	<u>and clubs, from the chief priests</u> and the elders of the
J	18.4	<u>and</u> weapons. Then Jesus, knowing all that was to befall him, came forward

Mk	14.44	<u>Now the betrayer had given them a sign, saying, "The one I shall</u>
M	26.48	people. <u>Now the betrayer had given them a sign, saying, "The one I shall</u>
J	18.5	and said to them, "Whom do you seek?" They answered him, "Jesus of

Mk	14.45	<u>kiss is the man; seize him and lead him away under guard."</u> <u>And when</u>
M	26.49	<u>kiss is the man; seize him."</u> <u>And</u>
J	18.5	Nazareth." Jesus said to them, "I am he."

Mk	14.45	<u>he came, he went up to him</u> at once, <u>and said,</u> "Master!" And he
M	26.49	<u>he came</u> up to Jesus at once <u>and said,</u> "Hail, <u>Master!</u>" And he
L	22.47	He drew near to Jesus to
J	18.5	Judas, who betrayed him, was standing with them.

Mk	14.46	<u>kissed him.</u> And
M	26.50	<u>kissed him.</u> |Jesus said to him, "Friend, why are you here?" Then
L	22.48	<u>kiss</u> <u>him;</u> but Jesus said to him, "Judas, would you betray the Son
J	18.6	When he said to them, "I am he," they drew back and fell

Mk	14.46	they_____laid hands on him__and seized him.
M	26.50	they came up and laid hands on Jesus and seized him.
L	22.49	of man with a kiss?" *And when those who were about him saw what would*
J	18.6	to the ground.

L	22.49	*follow, they said, "Lord, shall we strike with the sword?"*

Mk	14.47	But_____one of those who stood by
M	26.51	And behold, one of those who were with Jesus stretched out his hand and
L	22.50	And_____one of them
J	18.10	Then_____Simon Peter,_____having a sword,

Mk	14.47	drew his sword, and struck the_____slave of the high priest
M	26.51	drew his sword, and struck the_____slave of the high priest,
L	22.50	_____struck the_____slave of the high priest
J	18.10	drew____it____and struck the high priest's slave

Mk	14.47	and cut off his_____ear.
M	26.52	and cut off his_____ear._____Then Jesus said
L	22.51	and cut off his right ear._____But Jesus said,
J	18.11	and cut off his right ear. The slave's name was Malchus. Jesus said

M	26.52	to him,___"Put your sword back into its place; for all who take the
L	22.51	_____"No more of this!" And he touched his ear and healed him.
J	18.11	to Peter,___"Put your sword___into its sheath; shall I not drink the

M	26.53	sword will perish by the sword. Do you think that I cannot appeal to
J	18.11	cup which the Father has given me?"

M	26.53	my Father, and he will at once send me more than twelve legions of angels?
M	26.54	But how then should the scriptures be fulfilled, that it must be so?"

Mk	14.48	And_____Jesus said to___them,
M	26.55	At that hour Jesus said to the crowds,
L	22.52	Then_____Jesus said to the chief priests and officers of the temple
J	18.7	Again___he___asked___them,

Mk	14.48	_____"Have you come out as against
M	26.55	_____"Have you come out as against
L	22.52	and elders, who had come out against him, "Have you come out as against
J	18.7	_____"Whom do you seek?" And they

Mk	14.49	a robber, with swords and clubs to capture me?___Day after day I
M	26.55	a robber, with swords and clubs to capture me?___Day after day I
L	22.53	a robber, with swords and clubs? When I was with you day after day
J	18.8	said, "Jesus of Nazareth." Jesus answered, "I told you that I am he;

Mk	14.49	was with you in the temple teaching, and you did not seize___me.
M	26.55	sat___in the temple teaching, and you did not seize___me.
L	22.53	___in the temple,_____you did not lay hands on me.
J	18.8	so, if you seek me, let these men go."

Mk	14.49	But_____let___the scriptures
M	26.56	But all this has taken place, that the scriptures of the prophets might
L	22.53	But___this is your hour, and the power of darkness."
J	18.9	___This was to fulfil_____the word which he had spoken, "Of

Mk	14.50	be fulfilled." <u>And</u> <u>they all</u> <u>forsook him</u>, <u>and fled</u>.
M	26.56	be fulfilled." Then all the disciples <u>forsook him</u> <u>and fled</u>.
J	18.9	those whom thou gavest me I lost not one."

Mk	14.51	<u>And a young man followed him</u>, <u>with nothing but a linen cloth about his</u>
Mk	14.52	<u>body</u>; <u>and they seized him,</u> │<u>but he left the linen cloth and ran away</u>
Mk	14.52	<u>naked</u>.

65. BEFORE THE HIGH PRIEST

Mark 14.53-65

Mk	14.53	<u>And</u> <u>they</u>
M	26.57	Then those who had
L	22.54	Then <u>they</u>
J	18.12	So the band of soldiers and their captain and the officers of the Jews

Mk	14.53	<u>led Jesus</u>
M	26.57	seized Jesus <u>led</u> him
L	22.54	seized him and <u>led</u> him away, bringing him
J	18.13	seized Jesus and bound him. First they <u>led</u> him to Annas; for he was the
J	18.24	Annas then sent him

Mk	14.53	<u>to</u> <u>the high priest</u>; <u>and all the chief priests</u>
M	26.57	<u>to</u> Caiaphas <u>the high priest</u>, where the scribes
L	22.54	into <u>the high</u> priest's house.
J	18.14	father-in-law of Caiaphas, who was <u>high priest</u> that year. *It was Caiaphas*
J	18.24	bound <u>to</u> Caiaphas <u>the high priest</u>.

J	18.14	*who had given counsel to the Jews that it was expedient that one man*
J	18.14	*should die for the people.*

Mk	14.54	<u>and the elders and the scribes were assembled</u>. <u>And Peter had followed</u>
M	26.58	<u>and the elders</u> had gathered. But <u>Peter</u> <u>followed</u>
L	22.54	<u>Peter</u> <u>followed</u>
J	18.15	Simon <u>Peter</u> <u>followed</u>

Mk	14.54	<u>him at a distance</u>,
M	26.58	<u>him at a distance</u>,
L	22.55	<u>at a distance</u>; and when they had kindled
J	18.15	Jesus, and so did another disciple. As this disciple was known to the

Mk	14.54	<u>right into the courtyard of the high priest</u>;
M	26.58	as far as <u>the courtyard of the high priest</u>, and going
L	22.55	a fire in the middle of <u>the courtyard</u> and sat down
J	18.15	high priest, he entered <u>the</u> court of <u>the high priest</u> along with

Mk	14.54	<u>and</u> <u>he was sitting with the guards</u>, <u>and warming himself at</u>
M	26.58	inside <u>he</u> sat <u>with the guards</u> to see the end.
L	22.66	together, Peter sat among them. When day came, the assembly
J	18.16	Jesus, │while Peter stood outside at the door. *So the other disciple,*

J	18.16	*who was known to the high priest, went out and spoke to the maid who kept*
J	18.17	*the door, and brought Peter in. The maid who kept the door said to*
J	18.17	*Peter, "Are not you also one of this man's disciples?" He said, "I am*
J	18.18	*not." Now the servants and officers had made a charcoal fire, because*
J	18.18	*it was cold, and they were standing and warming themselves; Peter also*
J	18.18	*was with them, standing and warming himself.*

```
Mk   14.55   the fire.                                              Now the chief priests
M    26.59                                                          Now the chief priests
L    22.66   of the elders of the people gathered together, both chief priests and
J    18.19                                                          The high  priest then


Mk   14.55             and                  the whole council sought        testimony
M    26.59             and                  the whole council sought false testimony
L    22.66   scribes; and they led him away to their council,
J    18.20   questioned Jesus about his disciples and his teaching.  Jesus answered


Mk   14.55   against Jesus              to put him to death;  but they found none.
M    26.60   against Jesus that they might put him to death,  |but they found none,
J    18.20   him, "I have spoken openly to the world; I have always taught in


Mk   14.56   For   many bore false witness against him, and their witness did not
M    26.60   though many      false witnesses came forward.
J    18.20   synagogues and in the temple, where all Jews come together; I have said


Mk   14.57   agree.  And some stood up      and bore false witness against him,
M    26.61        At last two  came forward |and
J    18.21   nothing secretly.  Why do you ask me? Ask those who have heard me,


Mk   14.58   saying, |"We heard him    say, 'I   will   destroy this temple that
M    26.61   said,      "This    fellow said, 'I am able to destroy the  temple of
J    2.19                              Jesus answered them,    "Destroy this temple,
J    18.21   what I said to them; they know what I said."


Mk   14.58   is made with hands, and              in three days I will build another,
M    26.61   God,                   and to build it in three days.'"
J    2.19                           and           in three days I will raise it up."


Mk   14.59   not made with hands.'"  Yet not even so did their testimony agree.


Mk   14.60   And the high priest stood up in the midst, and asked Jesus, "Have you no
M    26.62   And the high priest stood up              and said,      "Have you no


Mk   14.61   answer to make? What is it that these men testify against you?"  |But
M    26.63   answer to make? What is it that these men testify against you?"  |But


Mk   14.61   he   was silent and made no answer.  Again the high priest    asked
M    26.63   Jesus was silent.                    And   the high priest    said to
L    22.66                                        and           they    said,
L    22.70                                        And           they all said,


Mk   14.61   him,                                        "Are you the Christ, the
M    26.63   him, "I adjure you by the living God, tell us if you are the Christ, the
L    22.67                                             |"If you are the Christ, tell
L    22.70                                              "Are you              the


Mk   14.62   Son of the Blessed?"  And Jesus said,      "I am;
M    26.64   Son of    God."        Jesus said to him, "You have said so.
L    22.67   us."                   But he   said to them, "If I tell you, you will
L    22.70   Son of    God, then?"  And he   said to them, "You     say that I am."
```

308

```
Mk   14.62                                                            and
M    26.64                                                            But I tell you,
L    22.68,69  not believe; and if I ask you, you will not answer.    But


Mk   14.62                 you will see the Son of man          seated at the right hand
M    26.64     hereafter   you will see the Son of man          seated at the right hand
L    22.69     from now on            the Son of man shall be   seated at the right hand


Mk   14.63     of     Power, and coming with the clouds of heaven."   And   the high priest
M    26.65     of     Power, and coming on   the clouds of heaven."   Then  the high priest
L    22.71     of the power   of God."


Mk   14.63     tore his garments, and said,                          "Why do we
M    26.65     tore his robes,    and said, "He has uttered blasphemy. Why do we
L    22.71                        said,                               "What


Mk   14.64     still need witnesses?           |You have     heard his blasphemy.   What
M    26.66     still need witnesses?            You have now heard his blasphemy.  |What
L    22.71     further     testimony do we need? We have     heard it ourselves from his


Mk   14.64     is your decision?"  And they all condemned   him as deserving death.
M    26.66     is your judgment?"         They     answered, "He      deserves  death."
L    22.71     own lips."
J    18.22                                                   When he had said


Mk   14.65     And     some began to spit on       him, and to cover his face, and to
M    26.67     Then    they              spat in his face,                       and
L    22.63     Now the men who were holding Jesus mocked him              and
J    18.22     this,    one of the officers standing by


Mk   14.65     strike him,                            saying to him, "Prophesy!"
M    26.68     struck him; and some slapped him,     |saying,        "Prophesy to
L    22.64     beat   him; they also blindfolded him and asked    him, "Prophesy!
J    18.22     struck Jesus with his hand,            saying,        "Is that how


Mk   14.65     And the guards received him with blows.
M    26.68     us, you Christ! Who is it that struck you?"
L    22.65                     Who is it that struck you?"  And they spoke many other
J    18.23     you answer the high priest?"  Jesus answered him, "If I have spoken


  L   22.65    words against him, reviling him.
  J   18.23    wrongly, bear witness to the wrong; but if I have spoken rightly, why

  J   18.23    do you strike me?"
```

66. PETER'S DENIAL

Mark 14.66-72

```
Mk   14.66     And as Peter was            below   in the courtyard,
M    26.69     Now    Peter was sitting outside in the courtyard.
L    22.55b            Peter     sat      among them.
J    18.16     while  Peter     stood    outside at the door.  So the other disciple


  J   18.16    who was known to the high priest, went out and spoke to the maid who
  J   18.16    kept the door, and brought Peter in.
```

309

```
Mk   14.67    one of the maids of the high priest came; and seeing Peter   warming
M    26.69    And     a    maid                    came up to him,
L    22.56    Then    a    maid,                              seeing him as he sat in
J    18.17            The maid who kept the door


Mk   14.67    himself,  she looked at him, and said,                  "You also were
M    26.69                                 and said,                  "You also were
L    22.56    the light and gazing at him,     said,         "This man also was
J    18.17                                 said to Peter, "Are not you also one


Mk   14.68    with        the Nazarene, Jesus."   But he denied it,
M    26.70    with Jesus the Galilean."           But he denied it before them all,
L    22.57    with him."                           But he denied it,
J    18.17    of    this man's disciples?"         He


Mk   14.68    saying,        "I   neither know nor understand what you mean."   And
M    26.71    saying,        "I do not    know              what you mean."   And
L    22.58    saying, "Woman, I do not    know              him."           And
J    18.25    said,          "I am not."                                      Now


Mk   14.69            he went out into the gateway.   And the maid    saw him, and began
M    26.71    when he went out  to the porch,    another maid    saw him, and she
L    22.58    a little later                    some one else saw him  and
J    18.25    Simon Peter was standing and warming himself.                     They


Mk   14.69    again to say  to the bystanders, "This man    is       one  of
M    26.71           said to the bystanders, "This man    was with Jesus of
L    22.58           said,                    "You also are      one  of
J    18.25           said to him,          "Are not you also      one  of


Mk   14.70    them."      But again he    denied it.
M    26.72    Nazareth."  And again he    denied it with an oath, "I do not know the
L    22.58    them."      But     Peter said,            "Man,  I am not."
J    18.26    his disciples?"    He    denied it and said,   "I am not."   |One of


Mk   14.70        And after a little while        again the bystanders
M    26.73    man."  After a little while              the bystanders came up and
L    22.59        And after an interval of about an hour still another insisted,
J    18.26    the servants of the high priest, a kinsman of the man whose ear Peter


Mk   14.70             said to Peter, "Certainly    you     are     one of
M    26.73             said to Peter, "Certainly    you     are also one of
L    22.59             saying,     "Certainly this man also was       with
J    18.26    had cut off, asked,    "Did I not see you in the garden   with


Mk   14.71    them; for you  are a Galilean."   But  he began to invoke a curse on
M    26.74    them, for your accent betrays you." Then he began to invoke a curse on
L    22.60    him;  for he   is  a Galilean."   But  Peter
J    18.27    him?"                                  Peter again


Mk   14.71    himself and to swear,    "I do not know this man of whom you      speak."
M    26.74    himself and to swear,    "I do not know the   man."
L    22.60             said, "Man, I do not know what        you are saying."
J    18.27             denied it;
```

310

```
Mk  14.72   And immediately                                    the cock crowed a second
M   26.74   And immediately                                    the cock crowed.
L   22.61   And immediately, while he was still speaking, the cock crowed.  And the
J   18.27   and at once                                        the cock crowed.


Mk  14.72   time.                                  And Peter remembered
M   26.75                                          And Peter remembered the saying of
L   22.61   Lord turned and looked at Peter.  And Peter remembered the word   of the


Mk  14.72           how Jesus had said to him, "Before the cock crows twice, you will
M   26.75              Jesus,                    "Before the cock crows,        you will
L   22.61   Lord, how he      had said to him, "Before the cock crows today, you will


Mk  14.72   deny me three times."  And he broke down and wept.
M   26.75   deny me three times."  And he went   out  and wept bitterly.
L   22.62   deny me three times."  And he went   out  and wept bitterly.
```

67. TRIAL BEFORE PILATE

Mark 15.1-15

```
Mk  15.1    And as soon as it was morning              the chief priests, with the
M   27.1    When                   morning came, all the chief priests  and   the
L   22.66a  When                   day    came,      the assembly        of    the


Mk  15.1    elders                                                  and scribes,
M   27.1    elders of the people
L   22.66a  elders of the people gathered together, both chief priests and scribes;


Mk  15.1    and                    the whole council held a consultation;
M   27.1                                       took   counsel against Jesus to
L   22.66a  and they led him away to their council,


Mk  15.1                       and         they bound Jesus   and led       him
M   27.2    put him to death; and         they bound him     and led       him
L   23.1                       Then the whole company of them arose, and brought him
J   18.28                      Then         they                      led    Jesus


Mk  15.1    away and delivered him    to      Pilate.
M   27.2    away and delivered him    to      Pilate the governor.
L   23.1                            before  Pilate.
J   18.28   from the house of Caiaphas to the praetorium.  It was early.  They them-
```

```
J   18.28   selves did not enter the praetorium, so that they might not be defiled,
J   18.29   but might eat the passover.  So Pilate went out to them and said, "What
J   18.30   accusation do you bring against this man?"  They answered him, "If this
J   18.31   man were not an evildoer, we would not have handed him over."  Pilate
J   18.31   said to them, "Take him yourselves and judge him by your own law."  The
J   18.31   Jews said to him, "It is not lawful for us to put any man to death."
J   18.32   This was to fulfil the word which Jesus had spoken to show by what
J   18.32   death he was to die.

M   27.11      Now Jesus stood before the governor;
J   18.33                              Pilate entered the praetorium again and
```

```
Mk  15.2                        And      Pilate    asked    him,  "Are you the King of the
M   27.11                       and the governor   asked    him,  "Are you the King of the
L   23.3                        And      Pilate    asked    him,  "Are you the King of the
J   18.33   called Jesus, and                      said to  him,  "Are you the King of the


Mk  15.2    Jews?"  And he     answered him,  "You have said so."
M   27.11   Jews?"      Jesus said,          "You have said so."
L   23.4    Jews?"  And he     answered him,  "You have said so."   And Pilate said to
J   18.34   Jews?"      Jesus answered,  "Do  you       say this
```

L   23.4   *the chief priests and the multitudes, "I find no crime in this man."*

```
Mk  15.3    And           the chief priests        accused him of many things.
M   27.12   But when he was accused by the chief priests and elders, he made no
L   23.5    But                they were urgent,    saying, "He stirs up the people,
J   18.35   of your own accord, or did others say it to you about me?"  Pilate
```

L   23.5   *teaching throughout all Judea, from Galilee even to this place."*
L   23.6,7   *When Pilate heard this, he asked whether the man was a Galilean. And*
L   23.7   *when he learned that he belonged to Herod's jurisdiction, he sent him*
L   23.8   *over to Herod, who was himself in Jerusalem at that time. When Herod*
L   23.8   *saw Jesus, he was very glad, for he had long desired to see him, because*
L   23.8   *he had heard about him, and he was hoping to see some sign done by him.*

J   18.35   *answered, "Am I a Jew? Your own nation and the chief priests have handed*
J   18.36   *you over to me; what have you done?" Jesus answered, "My kingship is not*
J   18.36   *of this world; if my kingship were of this world, my servants would fight,*
J   18.36   *that I might not be handed over to the Jews; but my kingship is not from*
J   18.37   *the world." |Pilate said to him, "So you are a king?" Jesus answered,*
J   18.37   *"You say that I am a king. For this I was born, and for this I have*
J   18.37   *come into the world, to bear witness to the truth. Every one who is of*
J   18.38   *the truth hears my voice." Pilate said to him, "What is truth?"*
J   18.38   *After he had said this, he went out to the Jews again, and told them,*
J   18.38   *"I find no crime in him.*

```
Mk  15.4                   And  Pilate again      asked        him,  "Have you no answer to make?
M   27.13   answer.  Then  Pilate            said     to him,  "Do   you not
L   23.9                   So   he                questioned him   at some length;
J   19.8,9                 When Pilate heard these words, he was the more afraid; he


Mk  15.4    See  how many charges they bring    against you."
M   27.13   hear how many things    they testify against you?"
J   19.9    entered the praetorium again and said to Jesus, "Where are you from?"


Mk  15.5    But Jesus made    no further answer,                                      so
M   27.14   But he    gave him no         answer, not even to a single charge; so
L   23.10   but he    made    no          answer.  The chief priests and the scribes
J   19.9    But Jesus gave    no          answer.


Mk  15.5    that    Pilate  wondered.
M   27.14   that the governor wondered greatly.
L   23.11   stood by, vehemently accusing him.  And Herod with his soldiers treated
```

L   23.11   *him with contempt and mocked him; then, arraying him in gorgeous apparel,*
L   23.12   *he sent him back to Pilate. And Herod and Pilate became friends with*
L   23.12   *each other that very day, for before this they had been at enmity with*
L   23.12   *each other.*

L 23.13   *Pilate then called together the chief priests and the rulers and the*
L 23.14   *people, |and said to them, "You brought me this man as one who was*
L 23.14   *perverting the people; and after examining him before you, behold, I*
L 23.15   *did not find this man guilty of any of your charges against him; neither*
L 23.15   *did Herod, for he sent him back to us. Behold, nothing deserving death*
L 23.16   *has been done by him; I will therefore chastise him and release him."*

J 19.10   *Pilate therefore said to him, "You will not speak to me? Do you not*
J 19.11   *know that I have power to release you, and power to crucify you?" Jesus*
J 19.11   *answered him, "You would have no power over me unless it had been given*
J 19.11   *you from above; therefore he who delivered me to you has the greater*
J 19.11   *sin."*
J 19.12   *Upon this Pilate sought to release him, but the Jews cried out, "If*
J 19.12   *you release this man, you are not Caesar's friend; every one who makes*
J 19.13   *himself a king sets himself against Caesar." When Pilate heard these*
J 19.13   *words, he brought Jesus out and sat down on the judgment seat at a*
J 19.14   *place called The Pavement, and in Hebrew, Gabbatha. Now it was the*
J 19.14   *day of Preparation of the Passover; it was about the sixth hour. He*
J 19.14   *said to the Jews, "Behold your King!"*

Mk	15.6	Now at the feast		he		used	to release for
M	27.15	Now at the feast	the	governor	was	accustomed	to release for
L	23.17	*Now*		*he*		*was obliged*	*to release*
J	18.39a	But		you		have a custom that I should	release

Mk	15.7		them	one prisoner for whom they asked.		And among the
M	27.16	the crowd any	one prisoner	whom they wanted.		And they had
L	23.19		*one man*	*to*	*them at the festival.*	|a man who
J	18.40b		one man	*for* you	at the Passover;	Now

Mk	15.7	rebels	in	prison, who had committed murder	in the
M	27.16	then	a notorious	prisoner,	
L	23.19	had been thrown into	prison		for an

Mk	15.8	insurrection, there was a man called Barabbas.	And the crowd came up and
M	27.17	called Barabbas.	So when they had gathered,
L	23.19	insurrection started in the city, and for murder.	
J	18.40b	Barabbas was a robber.	

Mk	15.9	began to ask Pilate to do as he was wont to do for them. And he
M	27.17	Pilate

Mk	15.9	answered them, "Do you want me to release for you
M	27.17	said to them, "Whom do you want me to release for you, Barabbas or
J	18.39b	will you have me release for you

Mk	15.10	the King of the Jews?" For he perceived that it was out of envy
M	27.18	Jesus who is called Christ?" For he knew that it was out of envy
J	18.39b	the King of the Jews?"

Mk	15.10	that the chief priests had delivered him up.
M	27.19	that they had delivered him up. Besides, while he was

M 27.19   *sitting on the judgment seat, his wife sent word to him, "Have nothing*
M 27.19   *to do with that righteous man, for I have suffered much over him today*

```
Mk   15.11                     But   the chief priests                    stirred up the
M    27.20   in a dream."  Now   the chief priests and the elders persuaded  the
L    23.18                     But             they all            cried out together,
J    19.6                    When  the chief priests and the officers saw him,


Mk   15.11   crowd         to have him release for them Barabbas instead.
M    27.20   people        to         ask      for      Barabbas and destroy Jesus.
L    23.18   "Away with this man, and release to  us   Barabbas"--


  M  27.21   The governor again said    to them, "Which of the two do you want me to
  L  23.20       Pilate           addressed them once more,             desiring to

  M  27.21   release for you?"  And they said,                        "Barabbas."
  L  23.20   release Jesus;
  J  18.40a                           They cried out again, "Not this man, but Barabbas!"


Mk   15.12   And Pilate again said to them, "Then what shall I do with the man whom
M    27.22       Pilate       said to them, "Then what shall I do with  Jesus   who


Mk   15.13   you call the King of the Jews?"  And they    cried   out again,
M    27.22   is   called   Christ?"               They all said, "Let him be
L    23.21                                    but they        shouted out,
J    19.6                                         they        cried   out,


Mk   15.14   "Crucify him."                And            Pilate said to them,
M    27.23   crucified."                   And            he   said,
L    23.22   "Crucify,      crucify him!"  A third time he     said to them,
J    19.6    "Crucify him, crucify him!"                  Pilate said to them, "Take him


Mk   15.14                            "Why,   what evil has he done?"
M    27.23                            "Why,   what evil has he done?"
L    23.22                            "Why,   what evil has he done?  I have found
J    19.7    yourselves and crucify him, for I find no crime in him."  The Jews


  L  23.22   in him no crime deserving death; I will therefore chastise him and
  J  19.7    answered him, "We have a law, and by that law he ought to die, because


Mk   15.14                        But they shouted all the more,
M    27.23                        But they shouted all the more,            "Let him
L    23.23   release him."  But they were urgent, demanding with loud cries that he
J    19.7    he has made himself the Son of God."
J    19.15                        They cried out,            "Away with him, away


Mk   15.14          "Crucify him."
M    27.23          be crucified."
L    23.23   should be crucified.  And their voices prevailed.
J    19.15   with him, crucify him!"  Pilate said to them, "Shall I crucify your King?"


  J  19.15   The chief priests answered, "We have no king but Caesar."


Mk   15.15   So      Pilate, wishing to satisfy the crowd,
M    27.24   So when Pilate saw that he was gaining nothing, but rather that a riot
L    23.24   So      Pilate gave sentence that their demand should be granted.


  M  27.24   was beginning, he took water and washed his hands before the crowd,
  M  27.25   saying, "I am innocent of this man's blood; see to it yourselves." And
  M  27.25   all the people answered, "His blood be on us and on our children!"
```

```
Mk   15.15                        released for them Barabbas;
M    27.26     Then he released for them Barabbas,
L    23.25            He released      the man who had been thrown into prison for insur-
J    19.1      Then Pilate


Mk   15.15                              and having scourged Jesus, he delivered him
M    27.26                              and having scourged Jesus,      delivered him
L    23.25     rection and murder, whom they asked for; but Jesus he delivered up
J    19.1                      took Jesus and           scourged him.
J    19.16                                         Then he handed         him


Mk   15.15                   to be crucified.
M    27.26                   to be crucified.
L    23.25                   to their    will.
J    19.16     over to them to be crucified.
```

68. CRUCIFIXION AND DEATH

Mark 15.16-41

```
Mk   15.16     And  the soldiers                     led  him away inside the palace (that
M    27.27     Then the soldiers of the governor took Jesus     into
J    19.2a     And  the soldiers


Mk   15.16     is, the praetorium); and they called together the whole battalion.
M    27.27         the praetorium,  and they gathered       the whole battalion before


Mk   15.17          And they              clothed  him in a purple   cloak,
M    27.28     him. And they stripped him and put       a scarlet   robe upon him,
L    23.11c         then,               arraying him in   gorgeous apparel,
J    19.2c          and                 arrayed  him in a purple    robe;


Mk   15.17     and plaiting a crown of thorns  they put it on him.
M    27.29a    |and plaiting a crown of thorns  they put it on his head, and put a reed
J    19.2b      |plaited   a crown of thorns,  and  put it on his head,


Mk   15.18                        And they began to salute     him,        "Hail,
M    27.29c    in his right hand.       |they         mocked    him, saying, "Hail,
L    23.11b                        and              mocked    him;
J    19.3                           they          came up to him, saying, "Hail,


Mk   15.19     King of the Jews!"                    And they struck         his head
M    27.30b    King of the Jews!" |and took the reed and     struck him on the head.
J    19.3      King of the Jews!"                    and     struck him


Mk   15.19     with a     reed, and     spat upon him,  and they knelt down in homage
M    27.30a,29b                 And they spat upon him,  |And       kneeling    before
L    23.11a                                             And Herod with his soldiers
J    19.4      with their hands. Pilate went out again, and said to them, "See, I am


Mk   15.20          to him.           And when they had mocked him, they stripped him
M    27.31           him |And when they had mocked him, they stripped him
L    23.11a    treated him with contempt


 J   19.4      bringing him out to you, that you may know that I find no crime in him."
 J   19.5      So Jesus came out, wearing the crown of thorns and the purple robe.
 J   19.5      Pilate said to them, "Behold the man!"
```

315

Mk	15.20	of the purple cloak, and put his own clothes on him. And they led him
M	27.31	of the robe, and put his own clothes on him, and led him
L	23.11d	he sent him

Mk	15.20	out to crucify him.
M	27.31	away to crucify him.
L	23.11d	back to Pilate.

Mk	15.21	And they compelled a passer-by,
M	27.32	As they went out, they came upon a man
L	23.26	And as they led him away, they seized one
J	19.17	So they took Jesus, and he went out,

Mk	15.21	Simon of Cyrene, who was coming in from the country, the father of
M	27.32	of Cyrene, Simon by name; this man they compelled
L	23.26	Simon of Cyrene, who was coming in from the country, and laid

Mk	15.21	Alexander and Rufus, to carry his cross.
M	27.32	to carry his cross.
L	23.27	on him the cross, to carry it behind Jesus. *And there*
J	19.17	bearing his own cross,

L 23.27 followed him a great multitude of the people, and of women who bewailed
L 23.28 and lamented him. But Jesus turning to them said, "Daughters of
L 23.28 Jerusalem, do not weep for me, but weep for yourselves and for your
L 23.29 children. For behold, the days are coming when they will say, 'Blessed
L 23.29 are the barren, and the wombs that never bore, and the breasts that
L 23.30 never gave suck!' Then they will begin to say to the mountains, 'Fall
L 23.31 on us'; and to the hills, 'Cover us.' For if they do this when the wood
L 23.31 is green, what will happen when it is dry?"

Mk	15.22	And they brought him to the place called Golgotha (which
M	27.33	And when they came to a place called Golgotha (which
L	23.33a	And when they came to the place which is called
J	19.17	to the place called

Mk	15.23	means the place of a skull). And they offered him wine
M	27.34	means the place of a skull), |they offered him wine to drink,
L	23.33a	The Skull,
J	19.17	the place of a skull, which is called in Hebrew Golgotha.

Mk	15.24	mingled with myrrh; but he did not take it. And
M	27.35	mingled with gall; but when he tasted it, he would not drink it. And

Mk	15.24	they crucified him,
M	27.35	when they had crucified him,
L	23.34	there they crucified him, |*And Jesus said, "Father, forgive*
J	19.18a	There they crucified him,
J	19.23	When the soldiers had crucified Jesus

Mk	15.24	and divided
M	27.35	they divided
L	23.34	*them; for they know not what they do."* And they cast lots to divide
J	19.23	they took

```
Mk   15.24        his garments
M    27.35        his garments
L    23.34        his garments.
J    19.23        his garments and made four parts, one for each soldier; also his tunic.


  J  19.24        But the tunic was without seam, woven from top to bottom; |so they said


Mk   15.24                              among them,   casting lots for them, to decide
M    27.35                              among them by casting lots;
J    19.24        to one another, "Let us not tear it, but cast    lots for it    to see


Mk   15.24        what each should take.
J    19.24        whose it  shall  be."  This was to fulfil the scripture, "They parted my


  J  19.24        garments among them, and for my clothing they cast lots."


Mk   15.25,26  And it was the third hour, when they crucified him.   And           the
M    27.36,37  then they sat down and kept watch over him there.     And over his head
L    23.38                                                           There was also an
J    19.25a,19 So the soldiers did this. |Pilate also wrote a title and


Mk   15.26     inscription of the charge against him        read,
M    27.37     they put        the charge against him, which read, "This is Jesus
L    23.38     inscription              over      him,                "This is
J    19.19         put         it on the cross;    it     read,           "Jesus of


Mk   15.26              "The King of the Jews."
M    27.37               the King of the Jews."
L    23.38               the King of the Jews."
J    19.20     Nazareth, the King of the Jews."  Many of the Jews read this title, for


  J  19.20     the place where Jesus was crucified was near the city; and it was written
  J  19.21     in Hebrew, in Latin, and in Greek.  The chief priests of the Jews then
  J  19.21     said to Pilate, "Do not write, 'The King of the Jews,' but, 'This man said,
  J  19.22     I am King of the Jews.'"  Pilate answered, "What I have written I have
  J  19.22     written."


Mk   15.27     And with him they
M    27.38     Then        two                          robbers     were
L    23.32                 Two others also, who were criminals, were led away to be
L    23.33b    and                                  the criminals,
J    19.18b    and with him two others,


Mk   15.29     crucified two robbers, one on his right and one on his left.  And those
M    27.39     crucified    with him, one on the right and one on the left.  And those
L    23.32     put to death with him.
L    23.35                            one on the right and one on the left.  And the
J    19.18b                           one on either side, and Jesus between them.


Mk   15.29     who    passed by derided him, wagging their heads, and saying, "Aha! You
M    27.40     who    passed by derided him, wagging their heads |and saying,      "You
L    23.35     people stood by, watching;


Mk   15.30     who would destroy the temple and build it in three days, |save yourself,
M    27.40     who would destroy the temple and build it in three days,  save yourself!
```

```
Mk   15.31                                    and come down from the cross!"  So also the chief
M    27.41      If you are the Son of God, come down from the cross."  So also the chief
L    23.35                                                             but       the


Mk   15.31      priests                              mocked       him to one another with
M    27.41      priests, with the scribes and elders, mocked       him,
L    23.35      rulers                               scoffed at him,


Mk   15.31      the scribes, saying, "He saved others;     he cannot save himself.
M    27.42                   saying, |"He saved others;     he cannot save himself.
L    23.35                   saying,  "He saved others; let him        save himself, if


Mk   15.32      Let   the Christ, the King of Israel,        come down now from the cross,
M    27.42      He is              the King of Israel; let him come down now from the cross,
L    23.35      he is the Christ of God, his Chosen One!"


Mk   15.32      that we may see and believe."
M    27.43      and  we will           believe in him.  He trusts in God; let God deliver


M    27.44      him now, if he desires him; for he said, 'I am the Son of God.'"  And
L    23.39                                                                          One of


Mk   15.32          Those   who were crucified with him also reviled  him.
M    27.44      the robbers who were crucified with him also reviled  him in the same
L    23.39      the criminals who were hanged                  railed at him, saying,


M    27.44      way.
L    23.40      "Are you not the Christ?  Save yourself and us!"  But the other rebuked


L    23.40      him, saying, "Do you not fear God, since you are under the same sentence
L    23.41      of condemnation?  And we indeed justly; for we are receiving the due
L    23.42      reward of our deeds; but this man has done nothing wrong."  And he said,
L    23.43      "Jesus, remember me when you come into your kingdom."  And he said to
L    23.43      him, "Truly, I say to you, today you will be with me in Paradise."


Mk   15.33          And when  the sixth hour had come, there was darkness over
M    27.45          Now from  the sixth hour            there was darkness over all
L    23.44      It was now about the sixth hour,      and there was darkness over


Mk   15.34      the whole land until the ninth hour.  And at     the ninth hour Jesus
M    27.46      the       land until the ninth hour.  And about the ninth hour Jesus
L    23.45a     the whole land until the ninth hour, |while the sun's light failed;
J    19.28                                            After this            Jesus,


Mk   15.34      cried with a loud voice, "Eloi, Eloi, lama sabachthani?" which means,
M    27.46      cried with a loud voice, "Eli,  Eli,  lama sabachthani?" that  is,
J    19.28      knowing that all was now finished, said (to fulfil  the scripture),


Mk   15.35      "My God, my God, why hast thou forsaken me?"  And some of the bystanders
M    27.47      "My God, my God, why hast thou forsaken me?"  And some of the bystanders
J    19.28      "I thirst."


Mk   15.36      hearing it said, "Behold, he is calling Elijah."  And one
M    27.48      hearing it said, "This   man is calling Elijah."  And one of them at
L    23.36                                                         The soldiers also
J    19.29                       A bowl full of vinegar stood there; so        they
```

318

Mk	15.36	<u>ran and, filling a sponge</u> <u>full</u> of <u>vinegar,</u> <u>put it on</u>
M	27.48	once <u>ran and</u> took <u>a sponge</u>, filled it with <u>vinegar,</u> and <u>put it on</u>
L	23.36	mocked him, coming up and offering him <u>vinegar,</u>
J	19.29	put <u>a sponge</u> <u>full</u> of the <u>vinegar</u> on

Mk	15.36	<u>a reed</u> <u>and gave it to him to drink,</u> <u>saying,</u> "Wait,
M	27.49	<u>a reed</u>, <u>and gave it to him to drink</u>. But the others <u>said,</u> "Wait,
L	23.37	|and <u>saying,</u> "If you
J	19.30	hyssop <u>and</u> held <u>it to</u> his mouth. When Jesus had received the

Mk	15.37	<u>let us see whether Elijah will come to take him down.</u>" And Jesus
M	27.50	<u>let us see whether Elijah will come to</u> save <u>him.</u>" And Jesus
L	23.46	are the King of the Jews, save yourself!" Then <u>Jesus,</u>
J	19.30	vinegar, he said, "It is finished"; <u>and</u> he

Mk	15.37	uttered <u>a loud</u> cry,
M	27.50	cried again with <u>a loud</u> voice
L	23.46	crying with <u>a loud</u> voice, said, "Father, <u>into</u> thy hands I commit
J	19.30	bowed his head

Mk	15.37	<u>and</u> <u>breathed</u> <u>his last.</u>
M	27.50	<u>and</u> yielded up <u>his</u> spirit.
L	23.46	my spirit!" <u>And</u> having said this he <u>breathed</u> <u>his last.</u>
J	19.30	<u>and</u> gave up <u>his</u> spirit.

Mk	15.38	<u>And</u> <u>the curtain of the temple was torn in two</u>, <u>from top to</u>
M	27.51	<u>And</u> behold, <u>the curtain of the temple was torn in two</u>, <u>from top to</u>
L	23.45b	<u>and</u> <u>the curtain of the temple was torn in two.</u>

Mk	15.38	bottom.
M	27.52	<u>bottom</u>; and the earth shook, and the rocks were split; |*the tombs also*

M	27.52	*were opened, and many bodies of the saints who had fallen asleep were*
M	27.53	*raised,* |*and coming out of the tombs after his resurrection they went*
M	27.53	*into the holy city and appeared to many.*

Mk	15.39	<u>And when the centurion</u>, <u>who stood facing him,</u>
M	27.54	<u>When the centurion</u> and those who were with him, keeping watch over
L	23.47	Now <u>when the centurion</u>

Mk	15.39	<u>saw that he thus breathed his last,</u>
M	27.54	Jesus, <u>saw</u> the earthquake and what took place, they were filled
L	23.47	<u>saw</u> what had taken place, he praised God,

Mk	15.39	he <u>said,</u> "Truly <u>this</u> man <u>was the Son of God!</u>"
M	27.54	with awe, and <u>said,</u> "Truly <u>this</u> <u>was the Son of God!</u>"
L	23.47	and <u>said,</u> "Certainly <u>this man was</u> innocent!"

Mk	15.40	<u>There were also</u> <u>women</u> <u>looking on from afar,</u>
M	27.55a	<u>There were also</u> many <u>women</u> there, <u>looking on from afar,</u>
L	23.49a	And all his acquaintances and the <u>women</u>
J	19.25b	But standing by the cross of Jesus were his mother, and his mother's

319

Mk	15.40	among whom were Mary Magdalene, and Mary the mother
M	27.56	among whom were Mary Magdalene, and Mary the mother
L	23.48	And all the multitudes who assembled to see the sight, when they saw what
J	19.26	sister, Mary the wife of Clopas, and Mary Magdalene. *When Jesus saw his*

Mk	15.40	of James the younger and of Joses, and Salome,
M	27.56	of James and Joseph, and the mother of the sons of Zebedee.
L	23.48	had taken place, returned home beating their breasts.
J	19.26	*mother, and the disciple whom he loved standing near, he said to his*

Mk	15.41	who, when he was in Galilee, followed him, and ministered to
M	27.55b	who had followed Jesus from Galilee, ministering to
L	23.49b	who had followed him from Galilee stood at a distance and saw these
J	19.27	*mother, "Woman, behold, your son!" Then he said to the disciple, "Behold,*

Mk	15.41	him; and also many other women who came up with him to Jerusalem.
M	27.55b	him;
L	23.49b	things.
J	19.27	*your mother!" And from that hour the disciple took her to his own home.*

69. THE BURIAL

Mark 15.42-47

Mk	15.42	And when evening had come, since it was the day of
M	27.57	When it was evening,
L	23.54	It was the day of
J	19.42a	So because of the Jewish day of

Mk	15.42	Preparation, that is, the day before the sabbath,
L	23.50	Preparation, and the sabbath was beginning. Now
J	19.42a	Preparation,

Mk	15.43	Joseph of Arimathea,
M	27.57	there came a rich man from Arimathea,
L	23.50	there was a man named Joseph from the Jewish town of Arimathea.
J	19.38	After this Joseph of Arimathea,

Mk	15.43	a respected member of the council,
M	27.57	named Joseph,
L	23.50	He was a member of the council, a good and righteous man,

Mk	15.43	who was also
M	27.57	who also was
L	23.51	who had not consented to their purpose and deed, and he was
J	19.38	who was

Mk	15.43	himself looking for the kingdom of God, took courage and went to Pilate,
M	27.58	a disciple of Jesus. He went to Pilate
L	23.52	looking for the kingdom of God. This man went to Pilate
J	19.38	a disciple of Jesus, but secretly, for fear of the Jews, asked Pilate

Mk	15.44	and asked for the body of Jesus. And Pilate wondered
M	27.58	and asked for the body of Jesus. Then Pilate
L	23.52	and asked for the body of Jesus.
J	19.38	that he might take away the body of Jesus, and Pilate

| Mk | 15.44 | if he were already dead; and summoning the centurion, he asked him whether |
| Mk | 15.45 | he was already dead. And when he learned from the centurion that he was |

Mk	15.46	dead, he granted the body	to Joseph.	And	he bought a linen
M	27.59	ordered	it to be given to him.	And	Joseph
L	23.53			Then	he
J	19.38	gave	him leave. So	he came and took

| J | 19.39 | *away his body. Nicodemus also, who had at first come to him by night,* |
| J | 19.30 | *came bringing a mixture of myrrh and aloes, about a hundred pounds'* |

Mk	15.46	shroud,	and taking	him down,	wrapped him in the	linen
M	27.59	took	the body,	and wrapped it	in a clean linen
L	23.53	took	it down	and wrapped it	in a	linen
J	19.40	weight. They took	the body of Jesus, and bound	it	in	linen

Mk	15.46	shroud,
M	27.59	shroud,
L	23.53	shroud,
J	19.41	cloths with the spices, as is the burial custom of the Jews. Now in the

Mk	15.46	and laid him in	a
M	27.60	and laid it in	his
L	23.53	and laid him in	a
J	19.41	place where he was crucified there was a garden, and in the garden a

Mk	15.46	tomb	which	had been hewn out of the rock; and he rolled a
M	27.60	own new	tomb, which he had	hewn in	the rock; and he rolled a
L	23.53	rock-hewn	tomb, where no one had ever yet been laid.
J	19.42	new	tomb where no one had ever	been laid. So because of the

Mk	15.47	stone against the door of the tomb.	Mary Magdalene
M	27.61	great stone to	the door of the tomb, and departed.	Mary Magdalene
L	23.55		The women who
J	19.42	Jewish day of Preparation, as the tomb was close at hand, they laid

Mk	15.47	and	Mary the mother of Joses	saw	where	he
M	27.61	and the other Mary were there,		sitting opposite
L	23.55	had come with him from Galilee followed, and saw the tomb, and how his body
J	19.42	Jesus there.

Mk	15.47	was laid.
M	27.61	the sepulchre.
L	23.56	was laid; *then they returned, and prepared spices and ointments.*

| L | 23.56 | *On the sabbath they rested according to the commandment.* |

70. THE EMPTY TOMB

Mark 16.1-8

Mk	16.1	And when the sabbath was past, Mary Magdalene,	and
M	28.1a,c	Now after the sabbath,	Mary Magdalene	and the other
L	24.10	Now it was	Mary Magdalene and Joanna and

```
Mk  16.1    Mary the mother of James, and Salome, bought    spices, so that they
M   28.1c   Mary
L   24.1b                                        |taking the spices  which    they
L   24.10   Mary the mother of James  and the other women with them who told this


Mk  16.2    might go and anoint him.  And very early  on the first day of the week
M   28.1b                             |toward the dawn of the first day of the week,
L   24.1a   had prepared.             But           on the first day of the week,
L   24.10   to the apostles;
J   20.1                               Now          on the first day of the week


Mk  16.2                   they           went to    the tomb         when the sun
M   28.1d                              |went to see the sepulchre.
L   24.1a   at early dawn, they           went to    the tomb,
J   20.1               Mary Magdalene came to        the tomb early, while it was


Mk  16.3    had risen.  And they were saying to one another, "Who will roll away the
J   20.1    still dark,


Mk  16.4    stone for us from the door of the tomb?"  And looking up, they saw that
M   28.2a                                             And behold, there was a great
L   24.2                                              And           they found
J   20.1                                              and           saw that


Mk  16.5    the stone           was rolled back--it was very large.  And
M   28.2c   earthquake;  |and came and rolled back the stone, and sat upon it.
L   24.3    the stone           rolled away from the tomb,    |but when they
J   20.1    the stone     had been taken  away from the tomb.
J   20.11                                             But Mary stood weeping


Mk  16.5    entering the tomb,
L   24.4    went in they did not find the body.  While they were perplexed about this,
J   20.11   outside  the tomb, and as she wept she stooped to look into the tomb;


Mk  16.5          they saw a young man     sitting
M   28.2b   |for           an     angel of the Lord descended from heaven
L   24.4    behold,        two    men      stood   by them
J   20.12a,c  and she  saw two    angels |sitting where the body of Jesus had lain,


Mk  16.5         on the right side,              dressed in a white
M   28.3    |His appearance was like lightning, and his raiment    white as snow.
L   24.4                                                    in    dazzling
J   20.12b  one at the head and one at the feet.  |in   white,


Mk  16.5    robe;   and                    they were amazed.
M   28.4            And for fear of him the guards    trembled   and became like
L   24.5    apparel; and as               they were frightened and bowed their


Mk  16.6               And    he    said to   them,  "Do not be amazed;
M   28.5    dead men.    But the angel said to the women, "Do not be afraid;
L   24.5    faces to the ground, the men   said to   them,  "Why do
J   20.13                         They    said to   her,   "Woman, why are you


J   20.13   weeping?"  She said to them, "Because they have taken away my Lord, and
J   20.14   I do not know where they have laid him."  Saying this, she turned round
J   20.15   and saw Jesus standing, but she did not know that it was Jesus.  Jesus
J   20.15   said to her, "Woman, why are you
```

Mk	16.6	<u>you seek Jesus of Nazareth</u>, <u>who was crucified</u>.
M	28.5	for I know that <u>you seek Jesus</u> <u>who was crucified</u>.
L	24.5	<u>you seek</u> the living among the dead?
J	20.15	weeping? Whom do <u>you seek</u>?" Supposing him to be the gardener, she said

J	20.15	*to him, "Sir, if you have carried him away, tell me where you have laid*
J	20.16	*him, and I will take him away." Jesus said to her, "Mary." She turned*
J	20.16	*and said to him in Hebrew, "Rabboni!" (which means Teacher).*

Mk	16.6	<u>He has risen,</u> <u>he is not here;</u> <u>see the place where</u>
M	28.6b,a,c	|for <u>he has risen</u>, as he said. |<u>He is not here;</u> |Come, <u>see the place where</u>
L	24.7	that the Son of man must be

Mk	16.7	<u>they laid him</u>. But <u>go</u>, <u>tell his disciples and Peter that</u>
M	28.7	he lay. Then <u>go</u> quickly and <u>tell his disciples</u> <u>that</u> he
L	24.7	delivered into the hands of sinful men, and be crucified, and on the third

Mk	16.7	<u>he is</u> <u>going before you to</u>
M	28.7	has risen from the dead, and behold, <u>he is</u> <u>going before</u> you <u>to</u>
L	24.6	day rise." Remember how <u>he</u> told you, while <u>he</u> was still in

Mk	16.8	<u>Galilee</u>; <u>there you will see him</u>, <u>as</u> <u>he</u> <u>told you</u>." <u>And they</u>
M	28.8	<u>Galilee</u>; <u>there you will see him</u>. Lo, I have <u>told you</u>." |So <u>they</u>
L	24.8,9	<u>Galilee,</u> And they remembered his words, |and
J	20.18	Mary

Mk	16.8	<u>went out and fled from the tomb</u>; <u>for</u> <u>trembling and astonishment</u>
M	28.8	departed quickly <u>from the tomb</u> with fear <u>and</u> great joy,
L	24.9	returning <u>from the tomb</u>
J	20.18	Magdalene <u>went</u>

Mk	16.8	<u>had come upon them</u>; <u>and they</u> <u>said nothing</u> <u>to</u> <u>any one, for they</u>
M	28.9	<u>and</u> ran to tell his <u>disciples</u>. And
L	24.9	<u>they</u> told all this <u>to</u> the eleven and to
J	20.18	<u>and</u> <u>said</u> <u>to</u> the disciples, "I have

Mk	16.8	<u>were afraid</u>.
M	28.9	behold, Jesus met them and said, "Hail!" *And they came up and took*
L	24.9	all the rest.
J	20.17	*Jesus said to her, "Do not*
J	20.18	seen the Lord"; and she told them that

M	28.10	*hold of his feet and worshiped him. Then Jesus said*
L	24.10	*Now it was Mary Magdalene and Joanna and Mary the mother of James and*
J	20.17	*hold me, for I have not yet ascended to the Father; but go to my*
J	20.18	*he had said these things*

M	28.10	*to them, "Do not be afraid; go and tell my brethren to go to*
L	24.11	*the other women with them who told this to the apostles; but these*
J	20.17	*brethren and say to them, I am ascending to my Father and your Father,*
J	20.18	*to her.*

M	28.10	*Galilee, and there they will see me."*
L	24.11	*words seemed to them an idle tale, and they did not believe them.*
J	20.17	*to my God and your God."*

Mark 16.9-20

Mk	16.9	<u>Now when he rose early on the first day of the week, he appeared first</u>
L	8.2	and also some women who had been healed of evil spirits and infirmities:
L	24.10	<u>Now</u> it was

Mk	16.9	<u>to Mary</u>	<u>Magdalene, from whom he had cast out seven demons.</u>
L	8.2	Mary, called	Magdalene, from whom seven demons had
L	24.10	Mary	Magdalene and Joanna and Mary the mother of James and
J	20.18a	Mary	Magdalene

Mk	16.10	<u>She went and told those who had been with him</u>, <u>as they</u>
L	8.2	gone out,
L	24.10	the other women with them who <u>told</u> this to the apostles;
J	20.18a	<u>went and</u> said to the disciples,
J	20.18b	and <u>she</u> told them that he had said these things

Mk	16.11	<u>mourned and wept.</u> <u>But when they heard that he was alive and had been</u>
L	24.11	<u>but</u> these words seemed to them an idle tale,
J	20.18a	"I have
J	20.18b	to her.

Mk	16.11	<u>seen by her, they would not believe it.</u>
L	24.11	and <u>they</u> did <u>not believe</u> them.
J	20.18a	<u>seen</u> the Lord";

Mk	16.12	<u>After this he appeared in another form to two of them</u>, <u>as they were</u>
L	24.13	That very day two of them were

Mk	16.12	<u>walking into the country.</u>
L	24.13	going to a village named Emmaus, about seven miles from Jerusalem,

L	24.14	*|and talking with each other about all these things that had happened.*
L	24.15	*While they were talking and discussing together, Jesus himself drew near*
L	24.15	*and went with them.*

Mk	16.13	<u>And they</u> <u>went back</u>
L	24.33	<u>And they</u> rose that same hour and <u>returned</u> to Jerusalem; and they found

L	24.34	*the eleven gathered together and those who were with them, |who said,*
L	24.34	*"The Lord has risen indeed, and has appeared to Simon!"*

Mk	16.13	<u>and</u> <u>told the rest</u>, <u>but they did not believe them.</u>
L	24.35	Then they <u>told</u> what had happened on the road, and how he was known to

L	24.35	*them in the breaking of the bread.*

Mk	16.14	<u>Afterward</u> <u>he</u> <u>appeared to the eleven</u>
M	28.16	Now <u>the eleven</u>
L	24.36	As they were saying this, Jesus himself stood among them.

Mk	16.14	themselves as they sat at table;
M	28.16	disciples went to Galilee, to the mountain to which Jesus had directed
L	24.37	But they were startled and frightened, and supposed that they saw a spirit.

Mk	16.14	and he upbraided them for their unbelief and hardness of heart, because
M	28.17	them. And when they saw him they worshiped him;
L	24.38	And he said to them, "Why are you troubled, and why do questionings rise

Mk	16.15	they had not believed those who saw him after he had risen. And he
M	28.18	but some doubted. And Jesus came
L	24.38	in your hearts?
L	24.46	and

Mk	16.15	said to them,
M	28.18	and said to them, "All authority in heaven and on earth has been given to
L	24.46	said to them, "Thus it is written, that the Christ should suffer and

Mk	16.15	"Go into all the world and
M	28.19a	me. Go therefore and make disciples of all nations,
L	24.47	on the third day rise from the dead, |and that repentance and forgiveness

Mk	16.15	preach the gospel to the whole creation.
M	28.20	|teaching them to observe all that I have commanded you;
L	24.47	of sins should be preached in his name to all nations, beginning

M	28.20	*and lo, I am with you always, to the close of the age."*
L	24.47	*from Jerusalem.*
J	14.12	*"Truly, truly, I say to you,*

Mk	16.16	He who believes and is baptized will be saved; but he who does not
M	28.19b	|baptizing them in the name of the Father and of
J	3.18	He who believes *in him* *is not condemned;* he who does not
J	14.12	he who believes *in me*

Mk	16.17	believe will be condemned. And these signs will accompany those who
M	28.19b	the Son and of the Holy Spirit,
M	10.1	*And he called to him his twelve disciples and*
L	9.1	*And he called the twelve together and*
L	10.17	*The seventy*
J	3.18	believe *is* condemned *already, because he has not*
J	14.12	*will also do the works that I do; and greater*

Mk	16.17	believe: in my name they will cast out demons; they will speak in
M	10.1	*gave them authority over unclean spirits, to cast them out,*
L	9.1	*gave them power and authority over all* demons
L	10.17	*returned with joy, saying, "Lord, even the* demons *are subject to us in*
J	3.18	believed *in* the name *of the only Son of God.*
J	14.12	*works than these will he do, because I go to the Father.*

Mk	16.17	new tongues;
M	10.1	*and to heal every disease and every infirmity.*
L	9.1	*and to cure diseases,*
L	10.18	*your name!" And he said to them, "I saw Satan fall like lightning from*

Mk	16.18	they will pick up serpents,
L	10.19	*heaven. Behold, I have given you authority to tread upon* serpents *and*

325

| Mk | 16.18 | and if they drink any deadly thing, it will not | hurt |
| L | 10.19 | *scorpions, and over all the power of the enemy; and nothing shall* | hurt |

| Mk | 16.18 | them; they will lay their hands on the sick, and they will recover." |
| L | 10.19 | *you.* |

| Mk | 16.19 | So then the Lord Jesus, after he had spoken to them, |
| L | 24.50 | Then   he led them out as far as Bethany, and lifting up his |

| L | 24.51 | *hands he blessed them. While he blessed them, he parted from them, and* |

| Mk | 16.20 | was taken   up into heaven, and sat down at the right hand of God.   And |
| L | 24.52 | was carried up into heaven.   And |

| Mk | 16.20 | they went forth and preached everywhere, while the Lord worked with them |
| L | 24.53 | they returned to Jerusalem with great joy, ⎸and were continually in the |

| Mk | 16.20 | and confirmed the message by the signs that attended it.   Amen. |
| L | 24.53 | temple blessing God. |

72. THE SHORTER ENDING OF MARK

But they reported briefly to Peter and those with him all that they had been told.
And after this, Jesus himself sent out by means of them, from east to west, the sacred
and imperishable proclamation of eternal salvation.

PART III

THE GOSPEL ACCORDING TO LUKE

		Page	Parallel Sections in		
			Matthew	Mark	John
1. The Prologue	1.1–4	333			
2. The Annunciation to Zechariah	1.5–25	333			
3. The Annunciation to Mary	1.26–38	334			
4. Mary Visits Elizabeth	1.39–56	335			
5. The Birth of John	1.57–80	335			
6. The Birth of Jesus	2.1–20	336	2		
7. Circumcision and Presentation	2.21–40	337			
8. A Visit to the Temple	2.41–52	338			
9. John the Baptist	3.1–20	338	4	2	2
10. The Baptism of Jesus	3.21–22	341	5	3	
11. The Genealogy of Jesus	3.23–38	342	1		
12. The Temptation	4.1–13	344	6	4	
13. Preaching in Galilee	4.14–15	346	7	5	
14. Jesus Rejected by His Own	4.16–30	347	31	26	17
15. Healings at Capernaum	4.31–41	349	13	7	
16. The Mission to Judea	4.42–44	351	9	8	
17. The First Disciples	5.1–11	352	8	6	3,44
18. A Leper Cleansed	5.12–16	354	11	9	
19. A Paralytic Healed	5.17–26	355	17	10	10
20. Levi the Tax Collector	5.27–32	357	18	11	
21. Questions of Fasting and Sabbath Observance	5.33–6.5	358	19,25	12	
22. A Withered Hand	6.6–11	360	26	13	
23. The Twelve	6.12–16	362	22a	15	3
24. Healing on the Plain	6.17–19	363	9	8	
25. The Sermon on the Plain	6.20–49	364			
a. Beatitudes and Woes	6.20–26	364	10b		
b. Love for Enemies	6.27–38	365	10d		
c. Parable on Blindness	6.39–42	367			
d. The Good Tree	6.43–46	368	10e		
e. The Two Houses	6.47–49	368	10f		

		Page	Matthew	Mark	John
26. The Centurion's Slave	7.1-10	369	12		9
27. A Dead Man Raised at Nain	7.11-17	371			
28. John the Baptist and the 'Coming One'	7.18-35	371	23		
29. The Anointing of Jesus	7.36-50	373	63	59	24
30. The Women Minister to Jesus	8.1-3	376			
31. Parable of the Soils	8.4-15	376	30b	18	
32. The Lamp and the Measure	8.16-18	380	10c	19	
33. His Mother and Brothers	8.19-21	381	29	17	
34. The Storm at Sea	8.22-25	382	15	23	
35. The Demon 'Legion'	8.26-39	383	16	24	
36. Jairus' Daughter and a Woman with a Hemorrhage	8.40-56	386	20	25	
37. Mission of the Twelve	9.1-9	389	22c	27	
38. The Five Thousand Fed	9.10-17	392	33	29	
39. Peter's Confession and First Prediction of the Passion	9.18-22	395	41	38	15
40. Conditions of Discipleship	9.23-27	397	42	39	
41. The Transfiguration	9.28-36	398	43	40	
42. The Epileptic Boy	9.37-43a	400	44	41	
43. Second Prediction of the Passion	9.43b-45	402	45	42	
44. True Greatness	9.46-50	403	47b	42	
45. Rejected by the Samaritans	9.51-56	404			
46. The Demands of Discipleship	9.57-62	405	14		
47. The Mission of the Seventy	10.1-12	405	22c	27	
48. Woes and Thanksgiving	10.13-24	408	24		
49. The Great Commandment and the Good Samaritan	10.25-37	410	58g	54e	
50. The Home of Martha and Mary	10.38-42	412			22,24
51. Prayer	11.1-13	412	10e		
52. How Can Satan Cast Out Satan?	11.14-28	414	27	16	
53. An Evil Generation Seeks a Sign	11.29-32	417	40,28	36	
54. The Lamp	11.33-36	418	10c	19	
55. Woes upon Pharisees and Lawyers	11.37-54	419	36	32	

		Page	Parallel Sections in		
			Matthew	Mark	John
56. Instruction of the Twelve	12.1–12	422	22d		
57. The Rich Fool	12.13–21	425			
58. Trust and Faithfulness	12.22–48	425	10e,61c	57b	
59. Fire on the Earth	12.49–59	429			
60. A Call to Repentance	13.1–9	431	57	51,53	
61. A Woman Freed from an Infirmity	13.10–17	432			
62. The Mustard Seed and the Leaven	13.18–21	432	30d	21	
63. The Saved are Few	13.22–30	433	10e		
64. Lament over Jerusalem	13.31–35	435	60		
65. A Man with Dropsy	14.1–6	435	26	13	10
66. Teaching on Humility	14.7–14	437			
67. The Marriage Feast	14.15–24	437	58d		
68. The Cost of Discipleship	14.25–35	438	42	39	26
69. The Lost Sheep, the Lost Coin, and and the Lost Son	15.1–32	440	47c		
70. The Dishonest Steward	16.1–15	442			
71. The Law and the Prophets	16.16–18	442	23,48	44	
72. The Rich Man and Lazarus	16.19–31	444			
73. Causes of Sin, Forgiveness, and Duty	17.1–10	444	47b	43	
74. The Ten Lepers	17.11–19	447	11	9	
75. The Kingdom of God and the Son of Man	17.20–37	448	61b		
76. The Unjust Judge	18.1–8	450			
77. The Pharisee and the Tax Collector	18.9–14	451			
78. Let the Children Come	18.15–17	451	49	45	
79. The Peril of Riches	18.18–30	452	50	46	
80. Third Prediction of the Passion	18.31–34	454	52	47	
81. A Blind Man at Jericho	18.35–43	455	54	49	
82. Zacchaeus	19.1–10	457			
83. The Pounds	19.11–28	457	61e		
84. Jesus Approaches Jerusalem	19.29–44	459	55	50	25
85. Cleansing the Temple	19.45–48	462	56	52	5

		Page	Parallel Sections in Matthew	Mark	John
86. Controversies in Jerusalem	20.1–45	463			
a. The Authority of Jesus	20.1–8	463	58a	54a	
b. The Wicked Tenants	20.9–19	464	58c	54b	
c. Render to God	20.20–26	467	58e	54c	
d. The God of the Living	20.27–40	468	58f	54d	
e. The Son of David	20.41–45	470	58h	54f	17
87. Beware of the Scribes	20.46–47	471	59	55	
88. The Widow's Copper Coins	21.1–4	472		56	
89. The End of the Age	21.5–6	472			
a. The Destruction of the Temple	21.5–6	472	61a	58a	
b. Signs of the End	21.7–36	473	61b	58b	
90. Daily Teaching in the Temple	21.37–38	478			
91. The Plot to Kill Jesus	22.1–6	479	62	58	23
92. The Passover Meal	22.7–23	480	65	61	28,14
93. A Dispute about Greatness	22.24–30	484	53	48	27
94. Peter's Denial Foretold	22.31–34	486	66	62	29
95. The Two Swords	22.35–38	487			
96. The Mount of Olives	22.39–46	487	67	63	
97. Jesus Arrested	22.47–53	489	68	64	35
98. Before the High Priest and Peter's Denial	22.54–71	491	69,70	65,66	36
99. Trial before Pilate	23.1–5	495	73	67	37
100. Jesus before Herod	23.6–12	496			
101. Condemned by Pilate	23.13–25	497	73	67	37
102. Crucifixion and Death	23.26–49	500	74	68	38
103. The Burial	23.50–56	504	75	69	39
104. The Empty Tomb	24.1–12	505	77	70	40
105. Two Travelers to Emmaus	24.13–35	508			
106. Appearances in Jerusalem and Ascension	24.36–53	509			41,42

1. THE PROLOGUE

Luke 1.1-4

L	1.1	Inasmuch as many have undertaken to compile a narrative of the things
L	1.2	which have been accomplished among us, |just as they were delivered to
L	1.2	us by those who from the beginning were eyewitnesses and ministers of the
L	1.3	word, |it seemed good to me also, having followed all things closely for
L	1.3	some time past, to write an orderly account for you, most excellent The-
L	1.4	ophilus, |that you may know the truth concerning the things of which you
L	1.4	have been informed.

2. THE ANNUNCIATION TO ZECHARIAH

Luke 1.5-25

L	1.5	In the days of Herod, king of Judea, there was a priest named Zechariah,
L	1.5	of the division of Abijah; and he had a wife of the daughters of Aaron,
L	1.6	and her name was Elizabeth. And they were both righteous before God,
L	1.7	walking in all the commandments and ordinances of the Lord blameless. But
L	1.7	they had no child, because Elizabeth was barren, and both were advanced in
L	1.7	years.

L	1.8	Now while he was serving as priest before God when his division was on
L	1.9	duty, |according to the custom of the priesthood, it fell to him by lot
L	1.10	to enter the temple of the Lord and burn incense. And the whole multitude
L	1.11	of the people were praying outside at the hour of incense. And there
L	1.11	appeared to him an angel of the Lord standing on the right side of the
L	1.12	altar of incense. And Zechariah was troubled when he saw him, and fear
L	1.13	fell upon him. But the angel said to him, "Do not be afraid, Zechariah,
L	1.13	for your prayer is heard, and your wife Elizabeth will bear you a son,
L	1.13	and you shall call his name John.

L	1.14	And you will have joy and gladness,
L	1.14	and many will rejoice at his birth;
L	1.15	for he will be great before the Lord,
L	1.15	and he shall drink no wine nor strong drink,
L	1.15	and he will be filled with the Holy Spirit,
L	1.15	even from his mother's womb.
L	1.16	And he will turn many of the sons of Israel
L	1.16	to the Lord their God,
L	1.17	and he will go before him in the spirit
L	1.17	and power of Elijah,
L	1.17	to turn the hearts of the fathers to the children,
L	1.17	and the disobedient to the wisdom of the just,
L	1.17	to make ready for the Lord a people prepared."

L	1.18	And Zechariah said to the angel, "How shall I know this? For I am an
L	1.19	old man, and my wife is advanced in years." And the angel answered him,
L	1.19	"I am Gabriel, who stand in the presence of God; and I was sent to speak
L	1.20	to you, and to bring you this good news. And behold, you will be silent
L	1.20	and unable to speak until the day that these things come to pass, because
L	1.20	you did not believe my words, which will be fulfilled in their time."
L	1.21	And the people were waiting for Zechariah, and they wondered at his delay
L	1.22	in the temple. And when he came out, he could not speak to them, and
L	1.22	they perceived that he had seen a vision in the temple; and he made signs
L	1.23	to them and remained dumb. And when his time of service was ended, he
L	1.23	went to his home.

L	1.24	After these days his wife Elizabeth conceived, and for five months she
L	1.25	hid herself, saying, |"Thus the Lord has done to me in the days when he
L	1.25	looked on me, to take away my reproach among men."

3. THE ANNUNCIATION TO MARY

Luke 1.26-38

L	1.26	In the sixth month the angel Gabriel was sent from God to a city of
M	1.18	Now the birth of Jesus Christ took place in this way.

L	1.27	Galilee named Nazareth, |to a virgin betrothed to a man whose name
M	1.18	When his mother Mary had been betrothed to

L	1.28	was Joseph, of the house of David; and the virgin's name was Mary. And
M	1.18	Joseph, before they came together she was found to be with child of

L	1.28	he came to her and said, "Hail, O favored one, the Lord is with you!"
M	1.19	the Holy Spirit; and her husband Joseph, being a just man and unwilling

L	1.29	But she was greatly troubled at the saying, and considered
M	1.20	to put her to shame, resolved to divorce her quietly. But as he considered

L	1.30	in her mind what sort of greeting this might be. And the angel
M	1.20	this, behold, an angel of the

L	1.30	said to her, "Do not be
M	1.20	Lord appeared to him in a dream, saying, "Joseph, son of David, do not

L	1.31	afraid, Mary, for you have found favor with God. And behold, you
M	1.20	fear to take Mary your wife, for that which

L	1.31	will conceive in your womb and bear a son, and you
M	1.21	is conceived in her is of the Holy Spirit; she will bear a son, and you

L	1.31	shall call his name Jesus.
M	1.21	shall call his name Jesus, for he will save his people from their sins."

L	1.32	He will be great, and will be called
L	1.32	the Son of the Most High;
L	1.32	and the Lord God will give to him
L	1.32	the throne of his father David,
L	1.33	and he will reign over the house of Jacob for ever;
L	1.33	and of his kingdom there will be no end."
L	1.34	And Mary said to the angel, "How shall this be, since I have no husband?"
L	1.35	And the angel said to her,
L	1.35	"The Holy Spirit will come upon you,
L	1.35	and the power of the Most High will overshadow you;
L	1.35	therefore the child to be born will be called holy,
L	1.35	the Son of God.
L	1.36	And behold, your kinswoman Elizabeth in her old age has also conceived a
L	1.37	son; and this is the sixth month with her who was called barren. For
L	1.38	with God nothing will be impossible." And Mary said, "Behold, I am the
L	1.38	handmaid of the Lord; let it be to me according to your word." And the
L	1.38	angel departed from her.

4. MARY VISITS ELIZABETH

Luke 1.39-56

L	1.39	In those days Mary arose and went with haste into the hill country, to
L	1.40	a city of Judah, │and she entered the house of Zechariah and greeted
L	1.41	Elizabeth. And when Elizabeth heard the greeting of Mary, the babe leaped
L	1.42	in her womb; and Elizabeth was filled with the Holy Spirit │and she ex-
L	1.42	claimed with a loud cry, "Blessed are you among women, and blessed is the
L	1.43	fruit of your womb! And why is this granted me, that the mother of my Lord
L	1.44	should come to me? For behold, when the voice of your greeting came to my
L	1.45	ears, the babe in my womb leaped for joy. And blessed is she who believed
L	1.45	that there would be a fulfilment of what was spoken to her from the Lord."
L	1.46	And Mary said,
L	1.46	"My soul magnifies the Lord,
L	1.47	and my spirit rejoices in God my Savior,
L	1.48	for he has regarded the low estate of his handmaiden.
L	1.48	For behold, henceforth all generations will call me
L	1.48	blessed;
L	1.49	for he who is mighty has done great things for me,
L	1.49	and holy is his name.
L	1.50	And his mercy is on those who fear him
L	1.50	from generation to generation.
L	1.51	He has shown strength with his arm,
L	1.51	he has scattered the proud in the imagination of
L	1.51	their hearts,
L	1.52	he has put down the mighty from their thrones,
L	1.52	and exalted those of low degree;
L	1.53	he has filled the hungry with good things,
L	1.53	and the rich he has sent empty away.
L	1.54	He has helped his servant Israel,
L	1.54	in remembrance of his mercy,
L	1.55	as he spoke to our fathers,
L	1.55	to Abraham and to his posterity for ever."
L	1.56	And Mary remained with her about three months, and returned to her home.

5. THE BIRTH OF JOHN

Luke 1.57-80

L	1.57	Now the time came for Elizabeth to be delivered, and she gave birth to a
L	1.58	son. And her neighbors and kinsfolk heard that the Lord had shown great
L	1.59	mercy to her, and they rejoiced with her. And on the eighth day they came
L	1.59	to circumcise the child; and they would have named him Zechariah after his
L	1.60,61	father, │but his mother said, "Not so; he shall be called John." And they
L	1.62	said to her, "None of your kindred is called by this name." And they made
L	1.63	signs to his father, inquiring what he would have him called. And he
L	1.63	asked for a writing tablet, and wrote, "His name is John." And they all
L	1.64	marveled. And immediately his mouth was opened and his tongue loosed, and
L	1.65	he spoke, blessing God. │And fear came on all their neighbors. And all
L	1.66	these things were talked about through all the hill country of Judea; and
L	1.66	all who heard them laid them up in their hearts, saying, "What then will
L	1.66	this child be?" For the hand of the Lord was with him.
L	1.67	And his father Zechariah was filled with the Holy Spirit, and prophesied,
L	1.67	saying,
L	1.68	"Blessed be the Lord God of Israel,
L	1.68	for he has visited and redeemed his people,
L	1.69	and has raised up a horn of salvation for us
L	1.69	in the house of his servant David,
L	1.70	as he spoke by the mouth of his holy prophets
L	1.70	from of old,

L	1.71	that we should be saved from our enemies,
L	1.71	and from the hand of all who hate us;
L	1.72	to perform the mercy promised to our fathers,
L	1.72	and to remember his holy covenant,
L	1.73	the oath which he swore to our
L	1.74	father Abraham, |to grant us
L	1.74	that we, being delivered from the
L	1.74	hand of our enemies,
L	1.74	might serve him without fear,
L	1.75	in holiness and righteousness before him
L	1.75	all the days of our life.
L	1.76	And you, child, will be called the prophet
L	1.76	of the Most High;
L	1.76	for you will go before the Lord to prepare his ways,
L	1.77	to give knowledge of salvation to his people
L	1.77	in the forgiveness of their sins,
L	1.78	through the tender mercy of our God,
L	1.78	when the day shall dawn upon us from on high
L	1.79	to give light to those who sit in darkness
L	1.79	and in the shadow of death,
L	1.79	to guide our feet into the way of peace."
L	1.80	And the child grew and became strong in spirit, and he was in the
L	1.80	wilderness till the day of his manifestation to Israel.

6. THE BIRTH OF JESUS

Luke 2.1-20

L	2.1	In those days a decree went out from Caesar Augustus that all the world
L	2.2	should be enrolled. This was the first enrollment, when Quirinius was
L	2.3	governor of Syria. And all went to be enrolled, each to his own city.
L	2.4	And Joseph also went up from Galilee, from the city of Nazareth, to Judea,
L	2.4	to the city of David, which is called Bethlehem, because he was of the
L	2.5	house and lineage of David, |to be enrolled with Mary, his betrothed, who
L	2.6	was with child. And while they were there, the time came for her to be
L	2.7	delivered. And she gave birth to her first-born son and wrapped him in
L	2.7	swaddling cloths, and laid him in a manger, because there was no place
L	2.7	for them in the inn.

L	2.8	And in that region there were shepherds out in the field, keeping watch
L	2.9	over their flock by night. And an angel of the Lord appeared to them, and
L	2.9	the glory of the Lord shone around them, and they were filled with fear.
L	2.10	And the angel said to them, "Be not afraid; for behold, I bring you good

M	2.3	*When Herod the king heard this, he was troubled, and all Jerusalem with*
M	2.4	*him; and assembling all the chief priests and scribes of the people, he*

L	2.11	<u>news of a great joy which will come to all the people; for to you is born</u>
M	2.4	*inquired of them* *where the Christ was to be* <u>born.</u>

L	2.11	<u>this day</u> <u>in the city</u> of David a Savior, <u>who is Christ the Lord.</u>
M	2.5	*They told him, "In Bethlehem of Judea; for so it is written by the prophet*

L	2.12	And this will be a sign for you: you will find a babe wrapped in swaddlin
L	2.13	cloths and lying in a manger." And suddenly there was with the angel a
L	2.13	multitude of the heavenly host praising God and saying,

L	2.14	"Glory to God in the highest,
L	2.14	and on earth peace among men with whom
L	2.14	he is pleased!"

336

L	2.15	When the angels went away from them into heaven, the shepherds said to
L	2.15	one another, "Let us go over to Bethlehem and see this thing that has
L	2.16	happened, which the Lord has made known to us." And they went with haste,
L	2.17	and found Mary and Joseph, and the babe lying in a manger. And when they
L	2.17	saw it they made known the saying which had been told them concerning this
L	2.18,19	child; and all who heard it wondered at what the shepherds told them. But
L	2.20	Mary kept all these things, pondering them in her heart. And the shepherds
L	2.20	returned, glorifying and praising God for all they had heard and seen,
L	2.20	as it had been told them.

7. CIRCUMCISION AND PRESENTATION

Luke 2.21-40

L	2.21	And at the end of eight days, when he was circumcised, he was called
L	2.21	Jesus, the name given by the angel before he was conceived in the womb.

L	2.22	And when the time came for their purification according to the law of
L	2.23	Moses, they brought him up to Jerusalem to present him to the Lord |(as
L	2.23	it is written in the law of the Lord, "Every male that opens the womb shall
L	2.24	be called holy to the Lord") |and to offer a sacrifice according to what
L	2.24	is said in the law of the Lord, "a pair of turtledoves, or two young
L	2.25	pigeons." Now there was a man in Jerusalem, whose name was Simeon, and
L	2.25	this man was righteous and devout, looking for the consolation of Israel,
L	2.26	and the Holy Spirit was upon him. And it had been revealed to him by the
L	2.26	Holy Spirit that he should not see death before he had seen the Lord's
L	2.27	Christ. And inspired by the Spirit he came into the temple; and when the
L	2.27	parents brought in the child Jesus, to do for him according to the custom
L	2.28	of the law, |he took him up in his arms and blessed God and said,

L	2.29	"Lord, now lettest thou thy servant depart in peace,
L	2.29	according to thy word;
L	2.30	for mine eyes have seen thy salvation
L	2.31	which thou hast prepared in the presence of all peoples,
L	2.32	a light for revelation to the Gentiles,
L	2.32	and for glory to thy people Israel."

L	2.33	And his father and his mother marveled at what was said about him;
L	2.34	and Simeon blessed them and said to Mary his mother,

L	2.34	"Behold, this child is set for the fall
L	2.34	and rising of many in Israel,
L	2.34	and for a sign that is spoken against
L	2.35	(and a sword will pierce through your own soul also),
L	2.35	that thoughts out of many hearts may be revealed."

L	2.36	And there was a prophetess, Anna, the daughter of Phanuel, of the tribe
L	2.36	of Asher; she was of a great age, having lived with her husband seven
L	2.37	years from her virginity, |and as a widow till she was eighty-four. She
L	2.37	did not depart from the temple, worshiping with fasting and prayer night
L	2.38	and day. And coming up at that very hour she gave thanks to God, and
L	2.38	spoke of him to all who were looking for the redemption of Jerusalem.

L	2.39	And when they had performed everything according to the law of the Lord,
M	2.22	*But when he heard that Archelaus reigned over Judea in place of his*

M	2.22	*father Herod, he was afraid to go there, and being warned in a dream*

L	2.39	they returned into	Galilee,
M	2.23	*he withdrew to the district of*	Galilee. *And he went and dwelt*

337

L	2.40	to their own city, Nazareth. And the child grew and became strong,
M	2.23	*in a* *city called* Nazareth, *that what was spoken by the prophets*

L	2.40	filled with wisdom; and the favor of God was upon him.
M	2.23	*might be fulfilled, "He shall be called a Nazarene."*

8. A VISIT TO THE TEMPLE

Luke 2.41-52

L	2.41	Now his parents went to Jerusalem every year at the feast of the Passover.
L	2.42,43	And when he was twelve years old, they went up according to custom; and
L	2.43	when the feast was ended, as they were returning, the boy Jesus stayed
L	2.44	behind in Jerusalem. His parents did not know it, |but supposing him to
L	2.44	be in the company they went a day's journey, and they sought him among
L	2.45	their kinsfolk and acquaintances; and when they did not find him, they
L	2.46	returned to Jerusalem, seeking him. After three days they found him in
L	2.46	the temple, sitting among the teachers, listening to them and asking them
L	2.47	questions; and all who heard him were amazed at his understanding and his
L	2.48	answers. And when they saw him they were astonished; and his mother said
L	2.48	to him, "Son, why have you treated us so? Behold, your father and I have
L	2.49	been looking for you anxiously." And he said to them, "How is it that you
L	2.50	sought me? Did you not know that I must be in my Father's house?" And
L	2.51	they did not understand the saying which he spoke to them. And he went
L	2.51	down with them and came to Nazareth, and was obedient to them; and his
L	2.51	mother kept all these things in her heart.
L	2.52	And Jesus increased in wisdom and in stature, and in favor with God and
L	2.52	man.

9. JOHN THE BAPTIST

Luke 3.1-20

L	3.1	In the fifteenth year of the reign of Tiberius Caesar, Pontius Pilate
M	3.1	In those days
M	4.17	*From that* *time*

L	3.1	being governor of Judea, and Herod being tetrarch of Galilee, and his
L	3.1	brother Philip tetrarch of the region of Ituraea and Trachonitis, and
L	3.2	Lysanias tetrarch of Abilene, |in the high-priesthood of Annas and

L	3.2	Caiaphas, the word of God came to John the son of
M	3.1	came John the Baptist,
Mk	1.4	John the baptizer
M	4.17	*Jesus began to*
J	1.6	*There was a man sent from God, whose name was* John.
J	1.19	*And this is the testimony* *of* John, *when the*

L	3.3	Zechariah in the wilderness; and he went into all the region about the
M	3.1	preaching in the wilderness of
Mk	1.4	appeared in the wilderness,
J	1.19	*Jews sent priests and Levites from Jerusalem to ask him, "Who are you?"*

L	3.3	Jordan, preaching a baptism of repentance for the forgiveness of sins.
M	3.2	Judea, "Repent, for the kingdom of heaven is
Mk	1.4	preaching a baptism of repentance for the forgiveness of sins.
M	4.17	*preach,* *saying, "Repent,* *for the kingdom of heaven is*
M	10.7	*And preach as you go, saying,* *'The kingdom of heaven is*

L	3.4		As it is		written in the book of the words of	
M	3.3	at hand."	For this is he who was	spoken of		by
Mk	1.2		As it is		written	in
M	*4.17*	*at hand."*				
M	*10.7*	*at hand.'*				

L	3.4	Isaiah the prophet,
M	3.3	the prophet Isaiah when he said,
Mk	1.2	Isaiah the prophet,
J	1.23a	the prophet Isaiah said." He said, "I am

Mk	*1.2*	*"Behold, I send my messenger before thy face,*
Mk	*1.2*	*who shall prepare thy way;*

L	3.4	"The voice of one crying in the wilderness:
M	3.3	"The voice of one crying in the wilderness:
Mk	1.3	the voice of one crying in the wilderness:
J	1.23a	the voice of one crying in the wilderness,

L	3.4	Prepare	the way of the Lord,
M	3.3	Prepare	the way of the Lord,
Mk	1.3	Prepare	the way of the Lord,
J	1.23a	'Make straight	the way of the Lord,'

L	3.4	make his paths straight.
M	3.3	make his paths straight."
Mk	1.3	make his paths straight--"

L	3.5	Every valley shall be filled,
L	3.5	and every mountain and hill shall be brought low,
L	3.5	and the crooked shall be made straight,
L	3.5	and the rough ways shall be made smooth;
L	3.6	and all flesh shall see the salvation of God."

M	*3.4*	*Now John wore a garment of camel's hair, and a leather girdle around*
Mk	*1.6*	*Now John was clothed with camel's hair, and had a leather girdle around*
M	*3.5*	*his waist; and his food was locusts and wild honey. Then went out*
Mk	*1.5*	*his waist, and ate locusts and wild honey. And there went out*
M	*3.5*	*to him Jerusalem and all Judea and all the region about*
Mk	*1.5*	*to him all the country of Judea, and all the people of*
M	*3.6*	*the Jordan, |and they were baptized by him in the river Jordan, confessing*
Mk	*1.5*	*Jerusalem; and they were baptized by him in the river Jordan, confessing*
M	*3.6*	*their sins.*
Mk	*1.5*	*their sins.*

L	3.7	He said therefore to the multitudes that came out to be
M	3.7	But when he saw many of the Pharisees and Sadducees coming for
L	3.7	baptized by him, "You brood of vipers! Who warned you to flee
M	3.7	baptism, he said to them, "You brood of vipers! Who warned you to flee
L	3.8	from the wrath to come? Bear fruits that befit repentance, and do not
M	3.8,9	from the wrath to come? Bear fruit that befits repentance, |and do not

L	3.8	<u>begin</u> <u>to say to yourselves,</u> <u>'We have</u> Abraham as our
M	3.9	presume <u>to say to yourselves,</u> <u>'We have</u> Abraham as our
J	8.33	*They answered him, "We are descendants of* Abraham, *and have*
J	8.39	*They answered him,* "Abraham *is* <u>our</u>

L	3.8	<u>father'; for I tell you,</u> <u>God is able from these stones to raise up</u>
M	3.9	<u>father'; for I tell you,</u> <u>God is able from these stones to raise up</u>
J	8.33	*never been in bondage to any one. How is it that you say, 'You will*
J	8.39	<u>father."</u> *Jesus said to them, "If you were*

L	3.9	<u>children to Abraham.</u> <u>Even now the axe is laid to the root of the trees;</u>
M	3.10	<u>children to Abraham.</u> <u>Even now the axe is laid to the root of the trees;</u>
J	8.33	*be made free'?"*
J	8.39	<u>Abraham's children,</u> *you would do what Abraham did,*

L	3.9	<u>every tree therefore that does not bear good fruit is cut down and</u>
M	3.10	<u>every tree therefore that does not bear good fruit is cut down and</u>
M	7.19	<u>Every tree</u> <u>that does not bear good fruit is cut down and</u>

L	3.9	<u>thrown into the fire."</u>
M	3.10	<u>thrown into the fire.</u>
M	7.19	<u>thrown into the fire.</u>

L	3.10,11	And the multitudes asked him, "What then shall we do?" <u>And he answered</u>
L	3.11	<u>them, "He who has two coats, let him share with him who has none; and he</u>
L	3.12	<u>who has food, let him do likewise."</u> Tax collectors also came to be bap-
L	3.13	tized, and said to him, "Teacher, what shall we do?" And he said to them,
L	3.14	"Collect no more than is appointed you." Soldiers also asked him, "And
L	3.14	we, what shall we do?" And he said to them, "Rob no one by violence or
L	3.14	by false accusation, and be content with your wages."

L	3.15	As the people were in expectation, <u>and all men questioned in their</u>
L	3.15	<u>hearts concerning John,</u> whether perhaps he were the Christ,

L	3.16	John answered them all, "<u>I</u> <u>baptize</u> <u>you with water;</u>
M	3.11	"<u>I</u> <u>baptize</u> <u>you with water</u>
Mk	1.7a,8a	And he preached, saying, │<u>I</u> have baptized <u>you with water;</u>
J	1.26	John answered them, "<u>I</u> <u>baptize</u> <u>with water;</u>
J	1.33	I myself did not know him; but he who sent me to <u>baptize</u> <u>with water</u>

L	3.16	<u>but he</u>
M	3.11	for repentance, <u>but he</u>
Mk	1.7b	"After me comes <u>he</u>
J	1.15	(John bore witness to him, and cried, "This was he of whom I said, '<u>He</u>
J	1.27	but among you stands one whom you do not know, │even <u>he</u>
J	1.33	said to me, '<u>He</u> on

L	3.16	<u>who is mightier than I is coming,</u> <u>the thong of whose sandals</u>
M	3.11	<u>who is coming after me is mightier than I,</u> <u>whose sandals</u>
Mk	1.7b	<u>who is mightier than I,</u> <u>the thong of whose sandals</u>
J	1.15	<u>who</u> comes after me ranks before me, for he was
J	1.27	<u>who</u> comes after me, <u>the thong of whose</u> sandal
J	1.33	whom you see the Spirit descend and remain,

L	3.16	<u>I am not worthy to</u> <u>untie;</u> <u>he will baptize you with</u>
M	3.11	<u>I am not worthy to</u> <u>carry;</u> <u>he will baptize you with</u>
Mk	1.8b	<u>I am not worthy to</u> stoop down and <u>untie.</u> │but <u>he will baptize you with</u>
J	1.15	before me.'")
J	1.27	<u>I am not worthy to</u> <u>untie."</u>
J	1.33	this is <u>he</u> who baptizes <u>with</u>

L	3.17	the Holy Spirit and with fire. His winnowing fork is in his hand,
M	3.12	the Holy Spirit and with fire. His winnowing fork is in his hand, and
Mk	1.8b	the Holy Spirit."
J	1.33	the Holy Spirit.'

L	3.17	to clear his threshing floor, and to gather the wheat into his
M	3.12	he will clear his threshing floor and gather his wheat into the

L	3.17	granary, but the chaff he will burn with unquenchable fire."
M	3.12	granary, but the chaff he will burn with unquenchable fire."

L	3.18	So, with many other exhortations, he preached good news to the people.

L	3.19	But Herod the tetrarch, who had been reproved by him
M	14.3	*For Herod had seized John and bound him and put him in prison,*
Mk	6.17	*For Herod had sent and seized John, and bound him in prison*

L	3.19	for Herodias, his brother's wife, and for all the evil
M	14.3	*for the sake of Herodias, his brother Philip's wife;*
Mk	6.17	*for the sake of Herodias, his brother Philip's wife; because he had married*

L	3.20	things that Herod had done, ⎮added this to them all, that he shut up John
M	14.4	*because John said to him, "It is not lawful for you to have*
Mk	6.18	*her. For John said to Herod, "It is not lawful for you to have your*

L	3.20	in prison.
M	14.4	*her."*
Mk	6.18	*brother's wife."*

10. THE BAPTISM OF JESUS

Luke 3.21-22

M	3.13	*Then Jesus came from Galilee to the Jordan to*
Mk	1.9	*In those days Jesus came from Nazareth of Galilee*

M	3.14	*John, to be baptized by him. John would have prevented him, saying, "I*
M	3.15	*need to be baptized by you, and do you come to me?" But Jesus answered*
M	3.15	*him, "Let it be so now; for thus it is fitting for us to fulfil all*

L	3.21	Now when all the people were baptized, and when Jesus also had been
M	3.16	righteousness." Then he consented. ⎮And when Jesus was
Mk	1.9	and was
J	1.33	*I myself did not know him; but he who sent me to*

L	3.21	baptized and was praying,
M	3.16	baptized,
Mk	1.10	baptized by John in the Jordan. And when he came up out of the water,
J	1.33	baptize *with water said to me,*

L	3.22	the heaven was opened, ⎮and the Holy
M	3.16	the water, and behold, the heavens were opened and he saw the
Mk	1.10	immediately he saw the heavens opened and the
J	1.32	*And John bore witness, "I saw the*
J	1.33	*'He on whom you see the*

```
L    3.22   Spirit           descended  upon him in bodily form, as a dove,
M    3.16   Spirit of God descending                        like a dove,
Mk   1.10   Spirit           descending upon him            like a dove;
 J   1.32   Spirit           descend                        as a dove from heaven,
 J   1.33   Spirit           descend
 M  17.5                           He was still speaking, when lo, a bright cloud
Mk   9.7                                               And      a      cloud
 L   9.34                      As he         said this,        a      cloud came


 M   3.16   and     alighting on him;
 J   1.32   and it remained   on him.
 J   1.33   and     remain,
 J  12.28                                            Father, glorify thy name."
 M  17.5              overshadowed them,
Mk   9.7              overshadowed them,
 L   9.34   and      overshadowed them; and they were afraid as they entered the cloud.


L    3.22   and    a voice came from      heaven,            "Thou art my beloved
M    3.17   and lo, a voice        from     heaven, saying,   "This is my beloved
Mk   1.11   and    a voice came from      heaven,            "Thou art my beloved
 J   1.33                                                   this is he who
 J   1.34   And I have seen     and have borne witness that this is the
 J  12.28   Then   a voice came from      heaven,            "I have glorified it,
 M  17.5    and    a voice        from   the cloud  said,    "This is my beloved
Mk   9.7    and    a voice came out of the cloud,            "This is my beloved
 L   9.35   And    a voice came out of the cloud, saying,    "This is my


L    3.22   Son; with thee I am well pleased."
M    3.17   Son, with whom I am well pleased."
Mk   1.11   Son; with thee I am well pleased."
 J   1.33   baptizes with the Holy Spirit.'
 J   1.34   Son of God."
 J  12.28   and I will glorify it again."
 M  17.5    Son, with whom I am well pleased; listen to him."
Mk   9.7    Son;                             listen to him."
 L   9.35        my Chosen;                  listen to him!"
```

11. THE GENEALOGY OF JESUS

Luke 3.23-38

```
L    3.23                                          Jesus, when he began
M    1.1    The book        of the genealogy      of   Jesus
M    1.16b                                   of whom Jesus was born, who is
Mk   1.1    The beginning of the gospel           of   Jesus
 J  20.31a  but these are written that you may believe that Jesus is


L    3.23   his ministry, was about thirty years of age, being the son (as was
M    1.1              Christ,                              the son
M    1.16a  called Christ.                                     ⌐and Jacob
Mk   1.1              Christ,
 J  20.31a  the    Christ,


L    3.24   supposed) of Joseph, the son of Heli, |the son of Matthat, the son    of
M    1.1             of David,   the son of Abraham.
M    1.15c  the father of Joseph the husband of Mary,   |and Matthan the father of


L    3.24   Levi,            the son  of Melchi,          the son   of Jannai,
M    1.15b,a Jacob, |and Eleazar the father of Matthan, |and Eliud the father of Eleazar
```

```
L   3.25    the son of Joseph, the son    of Mattathias,       the son    of Amos,
M   1.14c,b,a           |and Achim the father of Eliud, |and Zadok the father of Achim, |and


L   3.25           the son    of Nahum,              the son    of Esli,
M   1.13c,b   Azor the father of Zadok, |and Eliakim the father of Azor, |and Abiud


L   3.26    the son    of Naggai,              |the son    of Maath, the son of
M   1.13a    the father of Eliakim, |and Zerubbabel the father of Abiud,


L   3.27    Mattathias, the son of Semein, the son of Josech, the son of Joda, |the


L   3.27    son of Joanan, the son of Rhesa,    the son    of Zerubbabel,
M   1.12b,a                 and Shealtiel the father of Zerubbabel, |And after


L   3.27                              the son    of Shealtiel,
M   1.11    the deportation to Babylon: Jechoniah was the father of Shealtiel, |and


L   3.27           the son    of Neri,
M   1.11    Josiah the father of Jechoniah and his brothers, at the time of the depor-


L   3.28                |the son    of Melchi,            the son
M   1.10c,b   tation to Babylon. |and Amos the father of Josiah, |and Manasseh the father


L   3.28    of Addi,           the son    of Cosam,           the son    of
M   1.10a,9c  of Amos, |and Hezekiah the father of Manasseh, |and Ahaz the father of


L   3.29    Elmadam,           the son    of Er,           |the son    of Joshua,
M   1.9b,a   Hezekiah, |and Jotham the father of Ahaz, |and Uzziah the father of Jotham,


L   3.29           the son    of Eliezer,            the son    of Jorim,
M   1.8c,b   |and Joram the father of Uzziah, |and Jehoshaphat the father of Joram,


L   3.29           the son    of Matthat,            the son    of Levi,
M   1.8a,7c  |and Asa the father of Jehoshaphat, |and Abijah the father of Asa,


L   3.30    |the son of Simeon, the son of Judah, the son of Joseph, the son of Jonam,
L   3.31     the son of Eliakim, |the son of Melea, the son of Menna,


L   3.31           the son    of Mattatha, the son of Nathan,
M   1.7b,a   |and Rehoboam the father of Abijah,        |and Solomon the father of


  M  1.6b,a    Rehoboam, |And David was the father of Solomon by the wife of Uriah, |and


L   3.32           the son    of David,            |the son    of Jesse,
M   1.5c,b   Jesse the father of David the king. |and Obed the father of Jesse, |and


L   3.32           the son    of Obed,            the son    of Boaz,
M   1.5a    Boaz the father of Obed by Ruth, |and Salmon the father of Boaz by Rahab,


L   3.32              the son    of Sala,            the son    of Nahshon,
M   1.4c,b   |and Nahshon the father of Salmon, |and Amminadab the father of Nahshon,
```

343

```
L    3.33              |the son    of Amminadab,              the son    of Admin, the
M    1.4a,3c  |and Ram the father of Amminadab, |and Hezron the father of Ram,


L    3.33     son of Arni,             the son    of Hezron,             the son    of
M    1.3b,a                 |and Perez the father of Hezron, |and Judah the father of


L    3.33     Perez,                         the son    of Judah,
M    1.2c      Perez and Zerah by Tamar, |and Jacob the father of Judah and his brothers,


L    3.34              |the son    of Jacob,              the son    of Isaac, the
M    1.2b,a,1c  |and Isaac the father of Jacob, |Abraham was the father of Isaac, |the


L    3.35     son of Abraham, the son of Terah, the son of Nahor, |the son of Serug,
M    1.1c      son of Abraham.


L    3.36     the son of Reu, the son of Peleg, the son of Eber, the son of Shelah, |the
L    3.36     son of Cainan, the son of Arphaxad, the son of Shem, the son of Noah, the
L    3.37     son of Lamech, |the son of Methuselah, the son of Enoch, the son of Jared,
L    3.38     the son of Mahalaleel, the son of Cainan, |the son of Enos, the son of


L    3.38     Seth, the son of Adam, the son of God.
Mk   1.1                             the Son of God.
 J   20.31a                          the Son of God,
```

```
M    1.17          So all the generations from Abraham to David were fourteen generations,
M    1.17          and from David to the deportation to Babylon fourteen generations, and
M    1.17          from the deportation to Babylon to the Christ fourteen generations.
```

12. THE TEMPTATION

Luke 4.1-13

```
L    4.1     And   Jesus, full of the Holy Spirit, returned from the Jordan, and was
M    4.1     Then  Jesus                                                          was


L    4.2     led   by the Spirit        |for forty days in   the wilderness,
M    4.1     led up by the Spirit                     into the wilderness
Mk   1,12,13        The Spirit immediately drove him out into the wilderness.   And


L    4.2                                        tempted by the devil.   And he
M    4.2                              to be     tempted by the devil.   And he
Mk   1.13    he was in the wilderness forty days, tempted by       Satan;


L    4.2     ate nothing in those days;              and when they were ended,
M    4.2     fasted          forty days and forty nights, and afterward


L    4.3     he was hungry.    The devil          said to him, "If you are the
M    4.3     he was hungry.  And the tempter came and said to him, "If you are the


L    4.4     Son of God, command this  stone  to become            bread."  And Jesus
M    4.4     Son of God, command these stones to become loaves of bread."  But he
```

344

```
L   4.4    answered him, "It is written,
M   4.4    answered,     "It is written,


L   4.4              'Man shall not live by bread alone.'"
M   4.4              'Man shall not live by bread alone,


  M  4.4                    but by every word that proceeds from the mouth of God.'"


L   4.5    And    the devil took him up,                      and showed him all
M   4.8    Again, the devil took him to a very high mountain, and showed him all
    J  18.36                                                  Jesus answered,


L   4.6         the kingdoms      of   the  world in a moment of time,  |and     said
M   4.9         the kingdoms      of   the  world and the glory of them; and he said
    J  18.36    "My kingship is not of    this world;


    J  18.36    if my kingship were   of   this world, my servants would fight, that I
    J  18.36    might not be handed over to the Jews;
    J  18.36    but my kingship is not from the   world."


L   4.6    to him, "To  you   I will give all this authority and their glory; for it
M   4.9    to him, "All these I will give you,


L   4.7    has been delivered to me, and I give it to whom I will.  If you, then,
M   4.9                                                             if you


L   4.8    will              worship me, it shall all be yours."  And  Jesus answered
M   4.10   will fall down and worship me."                        Then Jesus said  to


L   4.8    him,                       "It is written,
M   4.10   him, "Begone, Satan!  for it is written,


L   4.8             'You shall worship the Lord your God,
M   4.10            'You shall worship the Lord your God


L   4.8             and him only shall you serve.'"
M   4.10            and him only shall you serve.'"


L   4.9    And    he    took him to      Jerusalem, and set him on the pinnacle of
M   4.5    Then the devil took him to the holy city, and set him on the pinnacle of


L   4.9    the temple, and said to him, "If you are the Son of God, throw yourself
M   4.6    the temple, |and said to him, "If you are the Son of God, throw yourself


L   4.10   down from here; for it is written,
M   4.6    down;            for it is written,


L   4.10            'He will give his angels charge of you, to guard you,'
M   4.6             'He will give his angels charge of you,'


L   4.11   and
M   4.6    and
```

```
L    4.11                    'On their hands they will bear you up,
M    4.6                     'On their hands they will bear you up,


L    4.11                         lest you strike your foot against a stone.'"
M    4.6                          lest you strike your foot against a stone.'"


L    4.12       And Jesus answered him,        "It is said,     'You shall not tempt the
M    4.7               Jesus said  to him, "Again it is written, 'You shall not tempt the


L    4.13       Lord your God.'"  And when the devil had ended every temptation, he
M    4.11       Lord your God.'"      Then the devil
Mk   1.13                                                         and he was with
  J  1.51       And he said to him, "Truly, truly, I say to you, you will see heaven


L    4.13       departed from him until an opportune time.
M    4.11       left          him, and behold, angels came and ministered to him.
Mk   1.13       the wild beasts;    and      the angels        ministered to him.
  J  1.51       opened, and                   the angels of God ascending and descending


  J  1.51       upon the Son of man."
```

13. PREACHING IN GALILEE

Luke 4.14-15

```
L    4.14       And                                              Jesus
M    4.12       Now when he heard that John had been arrested, he
Mk   1.14       Now after          John       was   arrested, Jesus
J    1.43a      The next day                                     Jesus decided to
  M  4.23       And                                              he
  M  9.35       And                                              Jesus
  J  4.3                                                         he left Judea and
  J  4.43       After the two days                               he


L    4.14       returned in the power of the Spirit into Galilee,
M    4.13       withdrew                            into Galilee; and leaving Nazareth he
Mk   1.14       came                                into Galilee,
J    1.43a      go                              to Galilee.
  M  4.23       went about all                      Galilee,
  M  9.35       went about all                  the cities and villages,
  J  4.3        departed again                  to Galilee.
  J  4.43       departed                        to Galilee.


  M  4.13       went and dwelt in Capernaum by the sea, in the territory of Zebulun and
  M  4.14       Naphtali, |that what was spoken by the prophet Isaiah might be fulfilled:
  M  4.15       "The land of Zebulun and the land of Naphtali,
  M  4.15          toward the sea, across the Jordan,
  M  4.15          Galilee of the Gentiles--
  M  4.16          the people who sat in darkness
  M  4.16            have seen a great light,
  M  4.16            and for those who sat in the region
  M  4.16               and shadow  of death
  M  4.16            light has dawned."


L    4.14       and a   report concerning him went out through   all the surrounding
  M  4.24       So  his fame                  spread    throughout all
```

L	4.15	country. And he taught in their synagogues,
M	4.17	From that time Jesus began to preach,
Mk	1.15	preaching the gospel of God, |and
M	4.23	teaching in their synagogues *and*
M	4.24	*Syria, and they brought him all the sick, those afflicted with various*
M	9.35	teaching in their synagogues *and*

L	4.15	being glorified by all.
M	4.17	saying, "Repent, for the kingdom of heaven is at hand."
Mk	1.15	saying, "The time is fulfilled, and the kingdom of God is at hand;
M	4.23	*preaching the gospel of the kingdom and healing every disease and every*
M	4.24	*diseases and pains, demoniacs, epileptics, and paralytics, and he healed*
M	9.35	*preaching the gospel of the kingdom, and healing every disease and every*

Mk	1.15	*repent, and believe in the gospel."*
M	4.23	*infirmity among the people.*
M	4.24	*them.*
M	9.35	*infirmity.*

14. JESUS REJECTED BY HIS OWN

Luke 4.16-30

M	13.53	*And when Jesus had finished these parables, he went away from there,*
Mk	6.1	*He went away from there*

L	4.16	And he came to Nazareth, where he had been brought up; and
M	13.54	and coming to *his own country*
Mk	6.2	and came to *his own country; and his disciples followed him.* And

L	4.16	he went to the synagogue, as his custom
M	13.54	he *taught them in their* synagogue,
Mk	6.2	*on the sabbath* he *began to teach* in the synagogue;

L	4.17	was, on the sabbath day. And he stood up to read; |and there was given to
L	4.17	him the book of the prophet Isaiah. He opened the book and found the place
L	4.17	where it was written,
L	4.18	"The Spirit of the Lord is upon me,
L	4.18	because he has anointed me to preach good news to the poor.
L	4.18	He has sent me to proclaim release to the captives
L	4.18	and recovering of sight to the blind,
L	4.18	to set at liberty those who are oppressed,
L	4.19	to proclaim the acceptable year of the Lord."
L	4.20	And he closed the book, and gave it back to the attendant, and sat down;
L	4.21	and the eyes of all in the synagogue were fixed on him. And he began to
L	4.21	say to them, "Today this scripture has been fulfilled in your hearing."

L	4.22	And all spoke well of him, and wondered at the gracious words which
M	13.54	*so that they* *were astonished, and said,* "Where did
Mk	6.2	*and* *many who heard him were astonished,* *saying,* "Where did
J	6.42	*They* *said,*
J	7.15	*The Jews* *marveled at it, saying,* "How is it that

L	4.22	proceeded out of his mouth;
M	13.54	*this man get this wisdom and these mighty*
Mk	6.2	*this man get all this? What is the wisdom given to him? What mighty*
J	7.15	*this man has learning, when he has never studied?"*

347

```
L    4.22                        and they said, "Is not this          Joseph's    son?"
  M  13.55      works?                                Is not this      the carpenter's son?
  Mk 6.3a       works are wrought by his hands!  Is not this      the carpenter,
  J  6.42                                  "Is not this Jesus, the son  of   Joseph,


L    4.23       And he said to them, "Doubtless you will quote to me this proverb,
  M  13.55              Is not his mother called Mary? And are not his brothers    James and
  Mk 6.3a                      the son of Mary    and               brother of James and
  J  6.42       whose father and mother we know? How does he now say, 'I have come down


L    4.23       'Physician, heal yourself; what we have heard you did at Capernaum, do
  M  13.56      Joseph and Simon and Judas? And are not all his sisters       with us?
  Mk 6.3a       Joses  and Judas and Simon,  and are not     his sisters here with us?"
  J  6.42       from heaven'?"


L    4.24       here also in your own country.'"      And he            said, "Truly, I
  M  13.57b     Where then did this man get all this?" But Jesus        said to them,
  Mk 6.4                                               And Jesus        said to them,
  J  4.44                                              For Jesus himself testified that


L    4.24       say to you, no prophet is           acceptable   in his own country.
  M  13.57b              "A  prophet is  not without honor  except in his own country
  Mk 6.4                 "A  prophet is  not without honor, except in his own country,
  J  4.44                 a  prophet has no          honor      in his own country.


L    4.25       But in truth, I tell you, there were many widows in Israel in the days of
  M  13.57b                              and in his own house."
  Mk 6.4        and among his own kin, and in his own house."


L    4.25       Elijah, when the heaven was shut up three years and six months, when there
L    4.26       came a great famine over all the land; and Elijah was sent to none of them
L    4.26       but only to Zarephath, in the land of Sidon, to a woman who was a widow.
L    4.27       And there were many lepers in Israel in the time of the prophet Elisha;
L    4.27       and none of them was cleansed, but only Naaman the Syrian."


L    4.28,29    When they heard this, all in the synagogue were filled with wrath.  And
  M  13.57a,58 And  they                            took offense    at him.  And
  Mk 6.3b,5    And  they                            took offense    at him.  And


L    4.29       they rose up and put him out of the city, and led him to the brow of the
  M  13.58      he did    not do many mighty works there,
  Mk 6.5        he could do   no      mighty work  there, except that he laid his hands


L    4.29       hill on which their city was built, that they might throw him down
  M  13.58                                                         because of
  Mk 6.6a       upon a few sick people and healed them.  And he marveled because of


L    4.30       headlong.  But passing through the midst of them he went away.
  M  13.58      their unbelief.
  Mk 6.6a       their unbelief.
```

15. HEALINGS AT CAPERNAUM

Luke 4.31-41

L	4.31	And ___ he ___ went down ___ to Capernaum, a city of
M	4.13	and leaving Nazareth he ___ went and dwelt in ___ Capernaum by the sea, in
Mk	1.21	And ___ they went ___ into Capernaum;
J	2.12	*After this ___ he ___ went down ___ to Capernaum, with his mother*

L	4.31	Galilee. And he was teaching them on the sabbath;
M	4.13	the territory of Zebulun and Naphtali,
Mk	1.21	and immediately ___ on the sabbath he entered the synagogue
J	2.12	*and his brothers and his disciples; and there they stayed for a few days.*

L	4.32	and ___ they ___ were
M	7.28	And when Jesus finished these sayings, the crowds were
Mk	1.22	and taught. And ___ they ___ were
J	7.46	The officers

L	4.32	astonished at his teaching, for his word ___ was with authority.
M	7.29	astonished at his teaching, |for he taught them as one who had authority,
Mk	1.22	astonished at his teaching, for he taught them as one who had authority,
J	7.46	*answered, "No man ever spoke like this man!"*

L	4.33	And ___ in the ___ synagogue
M	7.29	and not as their scribes.
Mk	1.23	and not as the ___ scribes. And immediately there was in their synagogue

L	4.33	there was a man who had the spirit of an unclean demon; and he cried out
Mk	1.24	a man with ___ an unclean spirit; and he cried out,
J	2.4	*And Jesus said*
J	6.68	*Simon Peter answered*

L	4.34	with a loud voice, |"Ah! What have you to do with us, Jesus of Nazareth?
Mk	1.24	"What have you to do with us, Jesus of Nazareth?
J	2.4	*to her, "O woman, what have you to do with me? My hour has not*
J	6.69	*him, "Lord, to whom shall we go? You have the words of eternal life; and*

L	4.34	Have you come to destroy us? I know who you are,
Mk	1.24	Have you come to destroy us? I know who you are,
J	2.4	*yet come."*
J	6.69	*we have believed, and have ___ come to ___ know, that you are*

L	4.35	the Holy One of God." But Jesus rebuked him, saying, "Be silent, and
Mk	1.25	the Holy One of God." But Jesus rebuked him, saying, "Be silent, and
J	6.69	*the Holy One of God."*

L	4.35	come out of him!" And when the ___ demon ___ had thrown him down in the
Mk	1.26	come out of him!" And ___ the unclean spirit, convulsing him and crying

L	4.36	midst, ___ he came out of him, having done him no harm. And they
Mk	1.27	with a loud voice, came out of him. ___ And they

L	4.36	were all amazed ___ and ___ said ___ to one another, ___ "What
Mk	1.27	were all amazed, so that they questioned among themselves, saying, "What

L	4.36	<u>is this</u>	<u>word</u>? For with authority and power he commands		<u>the</u>
Mk	1.27	<u>is this</u>? A new teaching! <u>With authority</u>	<u>he commands</u> even <u>the</u>		

L   4.36   <u>is this</u>   <u>word</u>? For with authority and power he commands   <u>the</u>
Mk   1.27   <u>is this</u>? A new teaching! <u>With authority</u>   <u>he commands</u> even <u>the</u>

L   4.37   <u>unclean spirits, and they come out</u>." <u>And</u>   <u>reports of him</u>
Mk   1.28   <u>unclean spirits, and they</u> obey him." <u>And</u> at once his fame

L   4.37   <u>went out into every place in</u>   <u>the surrounding region</u>.
Mk   1.28   spread everywhere throughout all <u>the surrounding region</u> of Galilee.

L   4.38   <u>And</u>   <u>he arose and left the synagogue, and entered</u>   <u>Simon's</u>
M   8.14   <u>And</u> when   Jesus   <u>entered</u>   Peter's
Mk   1.29   <u>And</u> immediately <u>he</u>   <u>left the synagogue, and entered</u> the house

L   4.38   <u>house</u>.   <u>Now Simon's mother-in-law</u>
M   8.14   <u>house</u>,   he saw his   <u>mother-in-law</u>
Mk   1.30   of Simon and Andrew, with James and John. <u>Now Simon's mother-in-law</u>

L   4.38   <u>was</u>   <u>ill</u> <u>with a high fever, and</u>   <u>they besought him for her</u>.
M   8.14   lying sick <u>with a</u>   fever;
Mk   1.30   lay   sick <u>with a</u>   fever, <u>and</u> immediately <u>they</u> told   <u>him</u> of <u>her</u>.

L   4.39   <u>And he stood</u>   over   <u>her</u>   <u>and rebuked the fever, and</u>
M   8.15   <u>he</u>   touched <u>her</u>   hand,   <u>and</u> the
Mk   1.31   <u>And he</u> came and took   <u>her</u> by the hand <u>and</u> lifted her up,   <u>and</u> the

L   4.39   <u>it</u>   <u>left her; and</u> immediately <u>she rose and served them</u>.
M   8.15   fever <u>left her, and</u>   <u>she rose and served</u> him.
Mk   1.31   fever <u>left her; and</u>   <u>she</u>   <u>served them</u>.

L   4.40   <u>Now</u>   when the sun was setting,   all those who had any that were sick
M   8.16a   That evening   they
Mk   1.32   That evening, at sundown,   they
M   *4.24*   *So his fame spread throughout all Syria, and they*

L   4.40   <u>with various diseases brought them to him</u>;
M   8.16a   <u>brought</u>   <u>to him</u> many who were
Mk   1.32   <u>brought</u>   <u>to him</u> all   who were sick   or
M   *4.24*   <u>*brought*</u>   *him* *all*   *the*   *sick, those*

L   4.40   <u>and he</u>
M   8.16a   possessed with   demons;
Mk   1.33   possessed with   demons.   <u>And</u> the whole city
M   *4.24*   *afflicted with various diseases and pains, demoniacs, epileptics, and*

L   4.40   <u>laid his hands on every one of them</u>   <u>and</u>   <u>healed them</u>.
M   8.16c   <u>and</u>   <u>healed</u> all
Mk   1.34   was gathered together about the door. <u>And</u> he   <u>healed</u> many
M   *4.24*   *paralytics*,   <u>*and*</u> *he*   <u>*healed*</u> *them*.
M   *12.15b*   *And many followed him,*   <u>*and*</u> *he*   <u>*healed*</u> *them all,*
Mk   *3.10*   *for he had* <u>*healed*</u> *many, so that*

L   4.41   <u>And</u>
M   8.16b   who were sick. | <u>and</u> he cast out
Mk   1.34   who were sick with various diseases,   <u>and</u>   cast out
Mk   *3.11*   *all who had   diseases pressed upon him to touch him.* <u>And</u> *whenever*

```
L    4.41                    demons also came out of many,                         crying,
M    8.16b    the           spirits with a word,
Mk   1.34     many          demons;
 Mk   3.11    the unclean spirits beheld him, they fell down before him and cried out,


L    4.41     "You are the Son of God!" But he rebuked them, and            would
Mk   1.34                                                    and he         would
 M   12.16                                                   and            ordered
 Mk   3.12    "You are the Son of God."                      And he strictly ordered


L    4.41           not allow      them   to speak, because they knew that he was the
Mk   1.34           not permit the demons to speak, because they knew       him.
 M   12.16    them not to make him known.
 Mk   3.12    them not to make him known.


L    4.41     Christ.
```

16. THE MISSION TO JUDEA

Luke 4.42-44

```
L    4.42     And                           when it was day  he departed and went
Mk   1.35     And in the morning, a great while before day, he rose      and went out


L    4.42     into a lonely place.
Mk   1.36        to a lonely place, and there he prayed.  And Simon and those who were


L    4.42                             And                        the people
Mk   1.37     with him pursued him, |and they found him and said to him, "Every one
 J    6.24                                                   So when the people


 J    6.24    saw that Jesus was not there, nor his disciples, they themselves got into


L    4.42                               sought       him and came to him, and
Mk   1.37                           is searching for you."
 J    6.24    the boats and went to Capernaum, seeking    Jesus.


L    4.43     would have kept him from leaving them; but he said to them,
Mk   1.38                                         And he said to them, "Let us go on


L    4.43                     "I must preach    the good news of the kingdom of
Mk   1.38     to the next towns, that I may preach
 M    4.23b                         and preaching the gospel   of the kingdom and
 M    9.35b                         and preaching the gospel   of the kingdom, and


L    4.43     God to the other cities also; for        I was sent for this purpose."
Mk   1.38                       there also; for that is why I    came out."
 M    4.23b   healing every disease and every infirmity among the people.
 M    9.35b   healing every disease and every infirmity.


L    4.44     And he   was                            preaching in the
M    4.23a    And he   went about    all Galilee,     teaching  in their
Mk   1.39     And he   went throughout all Galilee,   preaching in their
 M    4.23a   And he   went about    all Galilee,     teaching  in their
 M    9.35a   And Jesus went about    all the cities and villages, teaching in their
```

351

L	4.44	synagogues of Judea.
M	4.23a	synagogues
Mk	1.39	synagogues and casting out demons.
M	*4.23a*	*synagogues*
M	*9.35a*	*synagogues*

17. THE FIRST DISCIPLES

Luke 5.1-11

L	5.1	While the people pressed upon him to hear the word of God, he was
M	*4.18*	*As he*
Mk	*1.16*	*And*
J	*21.1*	*After this Jesus revealed himself again to the disciples*

L	5.2	standing by the lake of Gennesaret. And he saw two boats by the
M	*4.18*	*walked by the Sea of Galilee, he saw two brothers,*
Mk	*1.16*	*passing along by the Sea of Galilee, he saw*
J	*1.41*	*He first found his brother*
J	*21.1*	*by the Sea of Tiberias; and he revealed himself in this way.*

L	5.2	lake;
M	*4.18*	*Simon who is called*
Mk	*1.16*	*Simon*
J	*1.41*	*Simon, and said to him, "We have found the Messiah" (which means Christ).*
J	*21.2*	*Simon*

J	*1.42*	*He brought him to Jesus. Jesus looked at him, and said, "So you are*
J	*1.42*	*Simon the son of John? You shall be called Cephas" (which means*

L	5.2	but the fishermen
M	*4.18*	*Peter and Andrew*
Mk	*1.16*	*and Andrew*
J	*1.40*	*Peter). One of the two who heard John speak, and followed him, was Andrew,*
J	*21.2*	*Peter, Thomas called the Twin, Nathanael of Cana in Galilee, the sons of*

L	5.2	had gone out of them and were washing their nets.
M	*4.18*	*his brother, casting a net into the sea; for they*
Mk	*1.16*	*the brother of Simon casting a net in the sea; for they*
J	*1.40*	*Simon Peter's brother.*
J	*21.3*	*Zebedee, and two others of his disciples were together. Simon Peter said*

J	*21.3*	*to them, "I am going fishing." They said to him, "We will go with you."*

L	5.3	Getting into one of the boats, which was Simon's, he aske
M	*4.18*	*were fishermen.*
Mk	*1.16*	*were fishermen.*
J	*21.3*	*They went out and got into the boat;*

L	5.3	him to put out a little from the land. And he sat down and taught the
L	5.4	people from the boat. And when he had ceased speaking, he said to Simon,
L	5.5	"Put out into the deep and let down your nets for a catch." And Simon

L	5.5	answered, "Master, we toiled all night and took nothing!
J	*21.3*	*but that night they caught nothing.*

J	21.4	*Just as day was breaking, Jesus stood on the beach; yet the disciples*
J	21.5	*did not know that it was Jesus. Jesus said to them, "Children, have you*
J	21.6	*any fish?" They answered him, "No."* |*He said to them,*

L	5.5	But at your word I will let down the nets."
J	21.6	*"Cast* the *net on the right side of the boat,*

L	5.6	And when they had done this, they
J	21.6	*and you will find some." So* they *cast it, and now* they *were not able*

L	5.6	enclosed a great shoal of fish; and as their nets were breaking,
J	21.6	*to haul it in, for the quantity* of fish.

L	5.7	|they beckoned to their partners in the other boat to come and help them.

L	5.8	And they came and filled both the boats, so that they began to sink. |But
J	21.7	*That disciple whom Jesus loved said to Peter, "It is the Lord!"*

L	5.8	when Simon Peter saw it, he fell down at Jesus' knees,
J	21.7	When Simon Peter *heard that* it *was the Lord,* he *put on his clothes, for he*

L	5.9	saying, "Depart from me, for I am a sinful man, O Lord." For he was
J	21.8	*was stripped for work, and sprang into the sea. But the other disciples*

J	21.8	*came in the boat, dragging the net full of fish, for they were not far from*

L	5.9	astonished, and all that were with him, at the catch of fish which they had
J	21.8	*the land, but about a hundred yards off.*

L	5.10	taken; and so also were James and John,
M	4.21a	*And going on from there* *he saw two other brothers,* James *the*
Mk	1.19	*And going on a little farther, he saw* James *the*

L	5.10	sons of Zebedee, who were partners with Simon.
M	4.21a	son of Zebedee *and John his brother,* *in the* *boat with Zebedee*
Mk	1.19	son of Zebedee *and John his brother, who were in their boat*

L	5.10	And Jesus said to Simon, "Do not be
M	4.19	*their father, mending their nets,* |*And he* said to *them,* *"Follow me,*
Mk	1.17	*mending the* *nets.* And Jesus said to *them,* *"Follow me*

L	5.10	afraid; henceforth you will be catching men."
M	4.20	*and I will make* you *fishers of* men." *Immediately they left*
Mk	1.18	*and I will make* you *become fishers of* men." *And immediately they left*

L	5.11	And when they had brought their boats to
M	4.21b,22	*their nets and followed him.* |*and* *he called them.* *Immediately*
Mk	1.20	*their nets and followed him.* And *immediately he called them;* *and*

L	5.11	land, they left everything
M	4.22	they left *the boat and their father,*
Mk	1.20	they left *their father Zebedee in the boat with the*

```
L     5.11                              and followed him.
  M   4.22                              and followed him.
  Mk  1.20        hired servants, and followed him.
```

18. A LEPER CLEANSED

Luke 5.12-16

```
L     5.12        While  he was in one of the cities,        there came
M     8.1,2       When   he came down from the mountain, great crowds followed him; and
Mk    1.40                                                                          And
  L   17.12       And as he entered      a   village,        he was met


L     5.12                a man full of leprosy; and when he saw Jesus,    he fell on his
M     8.2         behold, a             leper came to him            and knelt before
Mk    1.40                a             leper came to him beseeching him, and kneeling
  L   17.13       by       ten          lepers  who stood at a distance  |and lifted up their


L     5.12        face  and besought him, "Lord, if you will, you can make me clean."
M     8.2         him,       saying,        "Lord, if you will, you can make me clean."
Mk    1.41                 said  to him,        "If you will, you can make me clean."  Moved
  L   17.13       voices and said,        "Jesus, Master,   have mercy on us."


L     5.13               And he stretched out his hand, and touched him,    saying,
M     8.3                And he stretched out his hand  and touched him,    saying,
Mk    1.41        with pity, he stretched out his hand  and touched him, and said to him,


L     5.13        "I will; be clean."  And immediately the leprosy left him.
M     8.3         "I will; be clean."  And immediately his leprosy              was
Mk    1.42        "I will; be clean."  And immediately the leprosy left him, and he was made
  L   17.14b                           And as they went they                   were


L     5.14                And he       charged him
M     8.4         cleansed.                                              And Jesus
Mk    1.43,44     clean.  And he sternly charged him, and sent him away at once, |and
  L   17.14a      cleansed.                                   When he saw them he


L     5.14                          to tell         no one; but "go and show
M     8.4         said to him, "See that you say nothing to any one; but go,    show
Mk    1.44        said to him, "See that you say nothing to any one; but go,    show
  L   17.14a      said to them,                                    "Go and show


L     5.14        yourself   to the priest, and make an offering for your cleansing,   as
M     8.4         yourself   to the priest, and         offer       the  gift       that
Mk    1.44        yourself   to the priest, and         offer    for your cleansing what
  L   17.14a      yourselves to the priests."


L     5.15        Moses commanded, for a proof to the people."  But so much the more
M     8.4         Moses commanded, for a proof to the people."
Mk    1.45a       Moses commanded, for a proof to the people."  But he went out and began to


L     5.15                          the report went abroad concerning him;
Mk    1.45a       talk freely about it, and to spread the news, so that Jesus could no longe
```

354

```
L     5.15                                    and great multitudes gathered to hear and to be healed
Mk    1.45c    openly enter a town, |and        people       came      to him from every
   Mk 1.35                                                              And in the morning, a great while


L     5.16     of their infirmities. But he withdrew to the wilderness      and
Mk    1.45b    quarter.              |but     was  out in the country;
   Mk 1.35     before day, he rose   and     went out to a    lonely place, and there he


L     5.16     prayed.
   Mk 1.35     prayed.
```

19. A PARALYTIC HEALED

Luke 5.17-26

```
M    9.1     And getting into a boat                        he    crossed over and
Mk   2.1     And                                  when he   returned
J    5.1     After this there was a feast of the Jews, and Jesus went up


L    5.17                     On one of those days, as he was teaching,
M    9.1     came to his own city.
Mk   2.1        to     Capernaum after some  days, it was reported that he was at
J    5.1        to     Jerusalem.  Now there is in Jerusalem by the Sheep Gate a


L    5.17                  there were Pharisees and teachers of the law sitting by, who
Mk   2.2     home.  And many were                                gathered together,
J    5.2     pool, in Hebrew called Bethzatha, which has five porticoes.


L    5.17    had come from every village of Galilee and Judea and from Jerusalem; and
Mk   2.2     so that there was no longer room for them, not even about the door;  and


L    5.18    the power of the Lord was with him to heal.  And behold, men  were
M    9.2                                                  And behold, they
Mk   2.3     he was preaching the word to them.           And         they came,
J    5.3                                                  In these lay a multitude


L    5.18    bringing on a bed a man who was paralyzed, and they sought to bring him
M    9.2     brought   to him   a          paralytic, lying on his bed;
Mk   2.3     bringing to him    a          paralytic carried by four men.
J    5.5     of invalids,       blind, lame, paralyzed.  One man was there, who had


L    5.19    in and lay him before Jesus; but finding no way to bring him in,  because
Mk   2.4                             And when they could not get near him because
J    5.5     been ill for thirty-eight years.


L    5.19    of the crowd, they went up on the roof            and
Mk   2.4     of the crowd, they removed   the roof above him; and when they had made


L    5.19                  let him down with his bed through the tiles into the midst
Mk   2.4     an opening, they let    down     the pallet on which the paralytic lay.


L    5.20    before Jesus.  And when he    saw their faith
M    9.2                    and when Jesus saw their faith
Mk   2.5                    And when Jesus saw their faith,
J    5.6                    When Jesus saw him and knew that he had been lying there
```

L	5.20	he said, "Man, your sins are

```
L    5.20                     he said,                                      "Man, your sins are
M    9.2                      he said to the paralytic, "Take heart, my son; your sins are
Mk   2.5                      he said to the paralytic,                  "My son, your sins are
J    5.6      a long time, he said to      him,              "Do   you want to be


L    5.21      forgiven you."  And                        the scribes and the Pharisees began to
M    9.3       forgiven."      And behold, some of the scribes
Mk   2.6       forgiven."      Now          some of the scribes were sitting there,
J    5.7       healed?"  The sick man answered him, "Sir, I have no man to put me into the
   J  10.33                                              The Jews


L    5.21      question, saying,              "Who is    this that speaks
M    9.3                  said to themselves,          "This man                    is
Mk   2.7       questioning    in their hearts, |"Why does this man   speak thus? It is
J    5.7       pool when the water is troubled, and while I am going another steps down
   J  10.33                           answered him, "It is not for a good work that we stone you but


L    5.22         blasphemies? Who can forgive sins but God only?"  When
M    9.4          blaspheming."                                     But
Mk   2.8          blasphemy!   Who can forgive sins but God alone?" And immediately
J    5.7       before me."
   J   2.24                                                            but
   J  10.33     for blasphemy; because you, being a man, make yourself God."


L    5.22      Jesus  perceived                       their     questionings,              he
M    9.4       Jesus, knowing                          their     thoughts,
Mk   2.8       Jesus, perceiving in his spirit that they thus questioned within themselves,
   J   2.25    Jesus  did not trust himself to them, |because he knew all men and needed


L    5.23      answered them, "Why do you question    in your hearts?     Which is
M    9.5       said,           "Why do you think evil  in your hearts? For which is
Mk   2.9       said  to them, "Why do you question thus in your hearts?    Which is
   J   2.25    no one to bear witness of man; for he himself knew what was in man.


L    5.23      easier, to say,                     'Your sins are forgiven you,' or to say,
M    9.5       easier, to say,                     'Your sins are forgiven,'      or to say,
Mk   2.9       easier, to say to the paralytic, 'Your sins are forgiven,'      or to say,


L    5.24      'Rise                   and walk'? But that you may know that the Son
M    9.6       'Rise                   and walk'? But that you may know that the Son
Mk   2.10      'Rise, take up your pallet and walk'? But that you may know that the Son


L    5.24      of man has authority on earth to forgive sins"--he       said to the man
M    9.6       of man has authority on earth to forgive sins"--he then said to the
Mk   2.10      of man has authority on earth to forgive sins"--he       said to the
J    5.8                                                      Jesus  said to


L    5.24      who was paralyzed-- "I say to you, rise, take up your bed   and go
M    9.6                  paralytic--            "Rise, take up your bed   and go
Mk   2.11                paralytic--|"I say to you, rise, take up your pallet  and go
J    5.8                 him,             "Rise, take up your pallet, and walk


L    5.25      home."  And immediately he rose before them, and        took up that
M    9.7       home."  And              he rose
Mk   2.12      home."  And              he rose,      and immediately took up the
J    5.9                And at once the man was healed,  and he        took up his
```

```
L    5.26    on which he lay, and went home, glorifying God.  And
M    9.8                     and went home.                   When the crowds saw it,
Mk   2.12    pallet          and went out before them all;    so that
J    5.9     pallet          and walked.


L    5.26                    amazement seized them all, and they glorified God and were
M    9.8     they were       afraid,                    and they glorified God,
Mk   2.12    they were all amazed                        and       glorified God,


L    5.26    filled with awe, saying, "We have  seen strange things today."
M    9.8                      who had given such authority to men.
Mk   2.12                     saying, "We never saw anything like this!"
```

20. LEVI THE TAX COLLECTOR

Luke 5.27-32

```
L    5.27    After this he went out
Mk   2.13    He went out again beside the sea; and all the crowd gathered


L    5.27                                        and                          saw
M    9.9                                As Jesus passed on from there, he saw
Mk   2.14    about him, and he taught them.  And as he    passed on,       he saw
 J   1.43b                                   And                       he found


L    5.27    a tax collector, named  Levi,              sitting at the tax office;
M    9.9     a man            called Matthew            sitting at the tax office;
Mk   2.14                            Levi the son of Alphaeus sitting at the tax office,
 J   1.43b                          Philip


L    5.28    and he said to him, "Follow me."  And he left everything, and rose and
M    9.9     and he said to him, "Follow me."  And he                       rose and
Mk   2.14    and he said to him, "Follow me."  And he                       rose and
 J   1.43b   and     said to him, "Follow me."


L    5.28    followed him.
M    9.9     followed him.
Mk   2.14    followed him.


L    5.29    And Levi made him a great feast in his house; and there was a large
M    9.10    And as        he  sat at table in the house,            behold,
Mk   2.15    And as        he  sat at table in his house,


L    5.29    company of tax collectors and others       sitting at table with
M    9.10    many         tax collectors and sinners came and sat down    with
Mk   2.15    many         tax collectors and sinners were    sitting      with
 L   15.1    Now the      tax collectors and sinners were all drawing near to hear


L    5.30    them.                                                    And
M    9.11    Jesus and his disciples.                                 And when
Mk   2.16    Jesus and his disciples; for there were many who followed him.  And the
 L   15.2    him.                                                     And
 L   19.7                                                             And when
```

357

L	5.30	the Pharisees and their scribes
M	9.11	the Pharisees saw this,
Mk	2.16	scribes of the Pharisees, when they saw that he was eating with sinners
L	*15.2*	the Pharisees and *the* scribes
L	*19.7*	*they* *saw it*

L	5.30	murmured against his disciples, saying, "Why do
M	9.11	they said to his disciples, "Why does your
Mk	2.16	and tax collectors, said to his disciples, "Why does
L	*15.2*	murmured, saying, *"This*
L	*19.7*	*they all* murmured, *"He has gone in*

L	5.31	you eat and drink with tax collectors and sinners?" And
M	9.12	teacher eat with tax collectors and sinners?" But when
Mk	2.17	he eat with tax collectors and sinners?" And when
L	*15.2*	*man* *receives* sinners *and eats with*
L	*19.7*	*to be the guest* *of a man* *who is a* sinner."

L	5.31	Jesus answered them, "Those who are well have no need of
M	9.12	he heard it, he said, "Those who are well have no need of
Mk	2.17	Jesus heard it, he said to them, "Those who are well have no need of
L	*15.2*	*them."*

L	5.31	a physician, but those who are sick;
M	9.13	a physician, but those who are sick. *Go and learn what this means, 'I*
Mk	2.17	a physician, but those who are sick;

L	5.32	I have not come to call the
M	9.13	*desire mercy, and not sacrifice.'* For I came not to call the
Mk	2.17	I came not to call the

L	5.32	righteous, but sinners to repentance."
M	9.13	righteous, but sinners."
Mk	2.17	righteous, but sinners."

21. QUESTIONS OF FASTING AND SABBATH OBSERVANCE

Luke 5.33-6.5

L	5.33	And they
M	9.14	Then the disciples of John
Mk	2.18	Now John's disciples and the Pharisees were fasting; and people

L	5.33	said to him, "The disciples of John fast often and
M	9.14	came to him, saying, "Why do we
Mk	2.18	came and said to him, "Why do John's disciples

L	5.33	offer prayers, and so do the disciples of the Pharisees, but yours
M	9.14	and the Pharisees fast, but your
Mk	2.18	and the disciples of the Pharisees fast, but your

L	5.34	eat and drink." And Jesus said to them, "Can you make wedding
M	9.15	disciples do not fast?" And Jesus said to them, "Can the wedding
Mk	2.19	disciples do not fast?" And Jesus said to them, "Can the wedding

358

```
L    5.34    guests fast   while       the bridegroom is with them?
M    9.15    guests mourn as long as the bridegroom is with them?
Mk   2.19    guests fast   while       the bridegroom is with them?  As long as they
 J   3.29    He who has the bride is the bridegroom;


L    5.35                                              The days will come,
M    9.15                                              The days will come,
Mk   2.20    have the bridegroom with them, they cannot fast.  The days will come,
 J   3.29                                                          the friend


L    5.35    when the bridegroom is taken away from them, and then they will fast in
M    9.15    when the bridegroom is taken away from them, and then they will fast.
Mk   2.20    when the bridegroom is taken away from them, and then they will fast in
 J   3.29    of   the bridegroom, who stands and hears him, rejoices greatly at the


L    5.36    those days."  He told them a parable also:  "No one tears a piece from
M    9.16                                     And no one puts  a piece of
Mk   2.21    that  day.                          No one sews  a piece of
 J   3.29    bridegroom's voice; therefore this joy of mine is now full.


L    5.36    a new  garment and puts it upon an old garment; if he does,  he will
M    9.16    unshrunk cloth            on an old garment, for         the patch
Mk   2.21    unshrunk cloth            on an old garment; if he does, the patch


L    5.36    tear            the new, and the piece from the new will not match the
M    9.16    tears away from the garment,
Mk   2.21    tears away from     it,                     the new         from the


L    5.37    old.                      And no one puts new wine      into old
M    9.17          and a worse tear is made. Neither  is   new wine put into old
Mk   2.22    old, and a worse tear is made. And no one puts new wine      into old


L    5.37    wineskins; if he does, the new wine will burst the skins and      it
M    9.17    wineskins; if it is,                the skins burst, and the wine
Mk   2.22    wineskins; if he does, the    wine will burst the skins, and the wine


L    5.38    will be spilled, and      the skins will be destroyed.  But new wine
M    9.17         is spilled, and      the skins    are destroyed;  but new wine
Mk   2.22         is lost,     and so are the skins;                but new wine


L    5.39    must be put into fresh wineskins.  And no one after drinking old wine
M    9.17         is put into fresh wineskins,  and so both are preserved."
Mk   2.22         is    for fresh      skins."


L    5.39    desires new; for he says, 'The old is good.'"


L    6.1     On a sabbath, while he was going through the grainfields,
M    12.1    At that time        Jesus  went   through the grainfields on the sabbath;
Mk   2.23    One  sabbath           he was going through the grainfields; and as they


L    6.1                his disciples                          plucked and
M    12.1               his disciples were hungry, and they began to pluck
Mk   2.23    made their way his disciples                      began to pluck
```

359

L	6.2	ate some heads of grain, rubbing them in their hands. But some of the
M	12.2	heads of grain and to eat. But when the
Mk	2.24	heads of grain. And the

L	6.2	Pharisees said, "Why are you doing
M	12.2	Pharisees saw it, they said to him, "Look, your disciples are doing
Mk	2.24	Pharisees said to him, "Look, why are they doing

L	6.3	what is not lawful to do on the sabbath?" And Jesus answered, "Have
M	12.3	what is not lawful to do on the sabbath." He said to them, "Have
Mk	2.25	what is not lawful on the sabbath?" And he said to them, "Have

L	6.3	you not read what David did when he was hungry, he
M	12.3	you not read what David did, when he was hungry,
Mk	2.25	you never read what David did, when he was in need and was hungry, he

L	6.4	and those who were with him: how he entered the house of God,
M	12.4	and those who were with him: how he entered the house of God
Mk	2.26	and those who were with him: how he entered the house of God, when

L	6.4	and took and ate the bread of the Presence, which it
M	12.4	and ate the bread of the Presence, which it
Mk	2.26	Abiathar was high priest, and ate the bread of the Presence, which it

L	6.4	is not lawful for any but the priests to eat, and also gave it to
M	12.4	was not lawful for him to eat nor for
Mk	2.26	is not lawful for any but the priests to eat, and also gave it to

L	6.4	those with him?"
M	12.5	those who were with him, but only for the priests? Or have you not
Mk	2.26	those who were with him?"

M	12.5	*read in the law how on the sabbath the priests in the temple profane*
M	12.6	*the sabbath, and are guiltless? I tell you, something greater than the*
M	12.7	*temple is here. And if you had known what this means,*

L	6.5	And he said to them,
M	12.7	'I desire mercy, and not sacrifice,' you would not have condemned the
Mk	2.27	And he said to them, "The sabbath was made for man, not man for the

L	6.5	"The Son of man is lord of the sabbath."
M	12.8	guiltless. For the Son of man is lord of the sabbath."
Mk	2.28	sabbath; so the Son of man is lord even of the sabbath."

22. A WITHERED HAND

Luke 6.6-11

L	6.6	On another sabbath, when he entered the synagogue
M	12.9	And he went on from there, and entered their synagogue.
Mk	3.1	Again he entered the synagogue,
L	*14.1*	*One sabbath when he went to dine at the house of a*

```
L    6.6                                                            and taught,
M   12.10                                                           And behold,
Mk   3.1                                                            and
  L  14.2      ruler who belonged to the Pharisees, they were watching him.  And behold,


L    6.7      a man was there whose right hand was withered.  And              the
M   12.10     there was a man with        a withered  hand.  And
Mk   3.2      a man was there who had     a withered  hand.  And
  L  14.3      there was a man before him who had dropsy.      And Jesus spoke to the


L    6.7      scribes and the Pharisees  watched him,  to see whether he would heal
M   12.10     they                       asked    him, "Is it lawful      to heal
Mk   3.2      they                       watched him,  to see whether he would heal him
  L  14.3      lawyers and      Pharisees, saying,      "Is it lawful        to heal


L    6.8      on the sabbath,  so that they might find an accusation against him.  But
M   12.10     on the sabbath?" so that they might          accuse         him.
Mk   3.2      on the sabbath,  so that they might          accuse         him.
  L  14.3      on the sabbath,  or not?"


L    6.8      he knew their thoughts, and he said to the man who had the withered hand,
Mk   3.3                              And he said to the man who had the withered hand,


L    6.9      "Come and stand here."  And he rose and stood there. |And Jesus said to
M   12.11                                                          He      said to
Mk   3.4      "Come            here."                          And he     said to
  L  14.5                                                       And he     said to


L    6.9      them,
M   12.11     them, "What man of you, if he has    one sheep    and it        falls
Mk   3.4      them,
  L  14.5      them, "Which     of you,       having a    son or an ox that has fallen


M   12.11      into a pit on the sabbath, will not lay hold of it and lift it  out?
  L  14.5      into a well,               will not immediately      pull him out


L    6.9                                              "I ask you, is it lawful on the sab-
M   12.12     Of how much more value is a man than a sheep!  So it is lawful to do good
Mk   3.4                                                      "Is it lawful on the sab-


L    6.9      bath to do good or to do harm, to save life or to destroy it?"
M   12.12     on the sabbath."
Mk   3.4      bath to do good or to do harm, to save life or to kill?"  But they were
  L  14.6,4    on a    sabbath day?"  And they could not reply to this.   But they were


L    6.10                 And he looked around on them all,
M   12.13                 Then he
Mk   3.5      silent. And he looked around at them with anger, grieved at their hard-
  L  14.4      silent. Then he took him


L    6.10                and said to    him, "Stretch out your hand."  And      he
M   12.13                     said to the man, "Stretch out your hand."  And the man
Mk   3.5      ness of heart, and said to the man, "Stretch out your hand."        He


L    6.11     did so,       and his hand was restored.                        But
M   12.14     stretched it out, and      it   was restored, whole like the other.  But
Mk   3.5      stretched it out, and his hand was restored.
  L  14.4                     and             healed him, and let him go.
```

361

```
L    6.11         they were filled with fury and              discussed    with one
M    12.14   the Pharisees went out          and              took counsel
Mk   3.6     The Pharisees went out,         and immediately held counsel with the


L    6.11    another              what they might do to Jesus.
M    12.14            against him, how        to destroy  him.
Mk   3.6     Herodians against him, how       to destroy  him.
```

23. THE TWELVE

Luke 6.12-16

```
L    6.12         In these days he went out to the mountain to pray; and all night he
Mk   3.13    And            he went up  on the mountain,


L    6.13    continued in prayer to God.  And when it was day, he called
M    10.1                                 And              he called to him
Mk   3.13                                 and                  called to him those
Mk   6.7                                  And              he called to him
L    9.1                                  And              he called
L    10.1                                 After this       the Lord


L    6.13                                                          his
M    10.1                                                          his twelve
Mk   3.14    whom he desired; and they came to him.  And he appointed   twelve, to
Mk   6.7                                                      the twelve,
L    9.1                                                      the twelve
L    10.1                                        appointed         seventy


L    6.13    disciples,   and chose      from them twelve,
M    10.1    disciples                                                        and
Mk   3.15    be with him, and       to be sent      out to preach      |and
Mk   6.7                  and began to    send them out              two by two, and
L    9.1     together                                                           and
L    10.1    others,      and           sent them on ahead of him, two by two, into


M    10.1    gave them         authority over    unclean spirits, to cast them
Mk   3.15    have              authority                           to cast
Mk   6.7     gave them         authority over the unclean spirits.
L    9.1     gave them power and authority over
L    10.1    every town and place where he himself was about to come.


L    6.13                                                      whom he named
M    10.2    out,       and to heal every disease and every infirmity. The      names of
Mk   3.15    out demons:
L    9.1     all demons and to cure      diseases,
J    1.42                                          He brought him to Jesus.  Jesus
A    1.13                      and when they had entered, they went up to the


L    6.14              apostles;        Simon,              whom
M    10.2    the twelve apostles are these:  first, Simon,           who
Mk   3.16                               Simon                        whom
J    1.40                    One of the two who heard John speak,
J    1.41          He first found his brother Simon, and said to him, "We have
J    1.42    looked at him,  and said,  "So you are Simon the son of John? You shall
A    1.13    upper room, where they were staying,
```

L	6.14	he named	Peter, and Andrew his brother, and
M	10.2	is called	Peter, and Andrew his brother;
Mk	3.16	he surnamed	Peter;
J	1.40	*and followed him, was Andrew, Simon* Peter's	brother.
J	1.41	*found the Messiah" (which means Christ).*	
J	1.42	*be called Cephas" (which means* Peter*).*	
A	1.13	Peter	and

L	6.14	James	and John,
M	10.2	James the son of Zebedee,	and John his brother;
Mk	3.17	James the son of Zebedee	and John the brother of James, whom he surnamed
A	1.13	*John*	*and James*

L	6.14	and	Philip, and
M	10.3		Philip and
Mk	3.18	Boanerges, that is, sons of thunder; |Andrew, and	Philip, and
J	1.43	*The next day Jesus decided to go to Galilee.* And *he found* Philip	*and*
J	1.44	*Now*	Philip *was*
A	1.13	*and Andrew,*	Philip *and*

L	6.15	Bartholomew, |and Matthew,	and Thomas,	and James the
M	10.3	Bartholomew; Thomas	and Matthew the tax collector; James the
Mk	3.18	Bartholomew, and Matthew,	and Thomas,	and James the
J	1.43	*said to him, "Follow me."*	
J	1.44	*from Bethsaida, the city of Andrew and Peter.*	
A	1.13	*Thomas,* *Bartholomew* and *Matthew,*	James the

L	6.16	son of Alphaeus, and Simon who was called the Zealot, |and Judas the
M	10.4	son of Alphaeus, and Thaddaeus; |Simon the
Mk	3.18	son of Alphaeus, and Thaddaeus,	and Simon the
A	1.13	son of Alphaeus and Simon the Zealot and Judas the

L	6.16	son of James, and Judas Iscariot, who became a traitor.
M	10.4	Cananaean, and Judas Iscariot, who betrayed him.
Mk	3.19a	Cananaean, |and Judas Iscariot, who betrayed him.
A	1.13	son of James.

24. HEALING ON THE PLAIN

Luke 6.17-19

L	6.17	And he came down with them and stood on a level place,
M	12.15	Jesus, aware of this, withdrew from there.
Mk	3.7	Jesus withdrew with his disciples to the sea,

L	6.17	with a great crowd of his disciples and a great multitude of people
M	12.15	And many
Mk	3.7	and a great multitude from Galilee

L	6.17	from all Judea and Jerusalem
M	12.15	followed him,
Mk	3.8	followed; also from Judea |and Jerusalem and Idumea and from beyond

L	6.17	and the seacoast of Tyre and Sidon, who came to hear
Mk	3.8	the Jordan and from about Tyre and Sidon a great multitude, hearing

363

```
L    6.17                                    him
Mk   3.9      all that he did, came to him.  And he told his disciples to have a boat


     Mk  3.9      ready for him because of the crowd, lest they should crush him;


L    6.17     and  to be healed                      of their diseases;
M    12.15    and he      healed them            all,
Mk   3.10     for he had  healed many, so that all who had diseases pressed upon him


L    6.18                      and those who were troubled with unclean spirits were
Mk   3.11     to touch him.  And whenever                 the unclean spirits beheld


L    6.19     cured.  And all the crowd sought to touch him,
Mk   3.11     him, they fell down before him and cried out, "You are the Son of God."


L    6.19    ⌐ for power came forth from him and healed them all.
M    12.16   |and            ordered them not to make him known.
Mk   3.12     And he strictly ordered them not to make him known.


     M  12.17    This was to fulfil what was spoken by the prophet Isaiah:
     M  12.18           "Behold, my servant whom I have chosen,
     M  12.18              my beloved with whom my soul is well pleased.
     M  12.18           I will put my Spirit upon him,
     M  12.18              and he shall proclaim justice to the Gentiles.
     M  12.19           He will not wrangle or cry aloud,
     M  12.19              nor will any one hear his voice in the streets;
     M  12.20           he will not break a bruised reed
     M  12.20              or quench a smoldering wick,
     M  12.20           till he brings justice to victory;
     M  12.21              and in his name will the Gentiles hope."
```

25. THE SERMON ON THE PLAIN

Luke 6.20-49

a. Beatitudes and Woes

Luke 6.20-26

```
     M  5.1      Seeing the crowds, he went up on the mountain, and when he sat down his
     M  5.1      disciples came to him.


L    6.20     And he lifted up his eyes on his disciples, and said:
M    5.2      And he opened    his mouth and taught them,     saying:


L    6.20     "Blessed are you poor,                for yours  is the kingdom of God.
M    5.3      "Blessed are the poor in spirit, for theirs  is the kingdom of heaven.


L    6.21     "Blessed are you    that hunger now,                         for you
M    5.6      "Blessed are those who    hunger and thirst for righteousness, for they


L    6.21     shall be satisfied.
M    5.6      shall be satisfied.
```

L	6.21	"Blessed are you ___ that weep now, for you ___ shall laugh.
M	5.4	"Blessed are those who ___ mourn, ___ for they shall be comforted.

M	5.5	"Blessed are the meek, for they shall inherit the earth.

L	6.22	"Blessed are you when men hate you, and when they exclude you and
M	5.11	"Blessed are you when men

L	6.22	revile you, ___ and cast out your name as evil,
M	5.11	revile you and persecute you and utter ___ all kinds of evil against you

L	6.23	___ on ___ account of the Son of man! Rejoice in that day, and leap
M	5.12	falsely on my account. ___ Rejoice ___ and be

L	6.23	for joy, for behold, your reward is great in heaven; for so their fathers
M	5.12	glad, for ___ your reward is great in heaven, for so ___ men

L	6.23	did to ___ the prophets.
M	5.12	persecuted the prophets who were before you.

L	6.24	"But woe to you that are rich, for you have received your consolation.
M	5.7	"Blessed are the merciful, for they shall obtain mercy.

L	6.25	"Woe to you that are full now, for you shall hunger.
M	5.8	"Blessed are the pure in heart, for they shall see God.

L	6.25	"Woe to you that laugh now, ___ for you shall mourn and weep.
M	5.9	"Blessed are the peacemakers, for they shall be called sons of God.

L	6.26	"Woe to you, when all men speak well of you,
M	5.10	"Blessed are those who are persecuted for righteousness' sake,

L	6.26	for so their fathers did to the false prophets.
M	5.10	for theirs is the kingdom of heaven.

b. Love for Enemies

Luke 6.27-38

M	5.43	"You have heard that it was said, 'You shall love your neighbor and hate
M	5.43	your enemy.'

L	6.27	"But I say to you that hear, Love your enemies, do good to those who
M	5.44	But I say to you, ___ Love your enemies

L	6.28	hate you, │bless those who curse you, pray for those who abuse ___ you.
M	5.44	___ and pray for those who persecute you,

M	5.38	"You have heard that it was said, 'An eye for an eye and a tooth for
M	5.39	a tooth.' But I say to you, Do not resist one who is evil. But

365

L	6.29	To him who strikes you on the <u>cheek</u>, <u>offer</u> the other also;
M	5.39	if any one <u>strikes you on the</u> right <u>cheek</u>, turn to him <u>the other also</u>;

L	6.29	<u>and from him who</u> <u>takes away your coat</u> <u>do not withhold</u>
M	5.40	<u>and</u> if any one would sue you and take <u>your coat</u>, let him have

L	6.29	<u>even your shirt</u>.
M	5.41	<u>your</u> cloak as well; *and if any one forces you to go one mile, go*

L	6.30	<u>Give to every one who begs from you; and</u>
M	5.42	*with him two miles.* <u>Give to</u> him who begs from you, <u>and</u> do not

L	6.30	<u>of him who</u> <u>takes away your goods do not ask them again.</u>
M	5.42	refuse <u>him who</u> would borrow from you.

L	6.31	<u>And as</u> <u>you wish that men would do to you</u>, <u>do so to them</u>.
M	7.12	So whatever <u>you wish that men would do to you</u>, <u>do so to them</u>; for this is

M	7.12	*the law and the prophets.*

L	6.32	"<u>If you love those who love you</u>, <u>what</u> credit is that to you? <u>For</u>
M	5.46	For <u>if you love those who love you</u>, <u>what</u> reward have you? Do not

L	6.33	<u>even</u> <u>sinners</u> <u>love those who love them</u>. And if you do good to
M	5.47	<u>even</u> the tax collectors do the same? And if you salute only

L	6.33	those who do good to you, <u>what</u> credit is that to you? <u>For</u>
M	5.47	your brethren, <u>what</u> more are you doing than others? Do not

L	6.34	<u>even</u> <u>sinners</u> <u>do the same</u>. And if you lend to those from whom you
M	5.47	<u>even</u> the Gentiles <u>do the same</u>? And if you salute only your brethren,

L	6.34	hope to receive, <u>what credit is</u> that to you? <u>Even</u>
M	5.47	<u>what</u> more are you doing than others? Do not <u>even</u> the

L	6.35	sinners <u>lend to sinners, to receive as much again</u>. <u>But</u>
M	5.44	Gentiles do the same? <u>But</u> I say to you,

L	6.35	<u>love your enemies</u>, <u>and do good</u>, <u>and lend</u>, <u>expecting nothing in return</u>;
M	5.44	<u>Love your enemies</u> and pray for those who persecute you,

L	6.35	<u>and your reward will be great</u>, <u>and</u> <u>you will be sons of the</u> Most High
M	5.45	|so that <u>you</u> may <u>be sons of</u> your Father who

L	6.35	<u>for he is kind</u> to the ungrateful and the
M	5.45	is in heaven; <u>for he</u> makes his sun rise on the evil <u>and</u> on the

L	6.35	selfish.
M	5.48	good, and sends rain on the just and on the unjust. You, therefore, must

L	6.36	<u>Be merciful</u>, <u>even as your</u> <u>Father is merciful</u>.
M	5.48	<u>be</u> perfect, <u>as your</u> heavenly <u>Father is</u> perfect.

L	6.37	"Judge not, and you will not be judged; condemn not, and you will not
M	7.1	"Judge not, that you be not judged.

L	6.38	be condemned; forgive, and you will be forgiven; |give, and it will be
L	6.38	given to you; good measure, pressed down, shaken together, running over,

L	6.38	will be put into your lap. For the measure
M	7.2	For with the judgment you pronounce you will be judged, and the measure
Mk	4.24	And he said to them, "Take heed what you hear; the measure

L	6.38	you give will be the measure you get back."
M	7.2	you give will be the measure you get.
Mk	4.24	you give will be the measure you get, and still more will be given you.

Mk	4.25	*For to him who has will more be given; and from him who has not, even*
Mk	4.25	*what he has will be taken away."*

c. Parable on Blindness

Luke 6.39-42

L	6.39	He also told them a parable: "Can a blind man lead a
M	15.14	Let them alone; they are blind guides. And if a blind man leads a

L	6.40	blind man? Will they not both fall into a pit? |A disciple is not above
M	10.24	"A disciple is not above
M	15.14	blind man, both will fall into a pit."

L	6.40	his teacher, but every one when he is
M	10.25	his teacher, nor a servant above his master; it is enough for the

L	6.40	fully taught will be like his teacher.
M	10.25	disciple to be like his teacher, and the servant like his master.

M	10.25	*If they have called the master of the house Beelzebul, how much more will*
M	10.25	*they malign those of his household.*

L	6.41	Why do you see the speck that is in your brother's eye, but do not notice
M	7.3	Why do you see the speck that is in your brother's eye, but do not notice

L	6.42	the log that is in your own eye? Or how can you say to your brother,
M	7.4	the log that is in your own eye? Or how can you say to your brother,

L	6.42	'Brother, let me take out the speck that is in your eye,' when you yourself
M	7.4	'Let me take the speck out of your eye,' when

L	6.42	do not see the log that is in your own eye? You hypocrite, first take the
M	7.5	there is the log in your own eye? You hypocrite, first take the

L	6.42	log out of your own eye, and then you will see clearly to take out the speck
M	7.5	log out of your own eye, and then you will see clearly to take the speck out

L	6.42	<u>that is in your brother's eye</u>.
M	7.5	of <u>your brother's eye</u>.

d. The Good Tree

Luke 6.43-46

M	*7.15*	*"Beware of false prophets, who come to you in sheep's clothing but*
M	*7.15*	*inwardly are ravenous wolves.*

L	6.43	<u>"For no good tree</u> <u>bears bad fruit, nor again does a</u>
M	7.17	So, every sound <u>tree</u> <u>bears good fruit</u>, but the
M	7.18	A sound <u>tree</u> cannot bear evil <u>fruit</u>, <u>nor</u> can <u>a</u>
M	*12.33*	*"Either make the <u>tree</u> good, and its fruit good; or make* the

L	6.44	<u>bad tree</u> bear <u>good fruit</u>; <u>for each tree is known</u> <u>by its own fruit</u>.
M	7.16	<u>You will know them by their</u> fruits
M	7.17	<u>bad tree</u> bears evil <u>fruit</u>.
M	7.18	<u>bad tree</u> bear <u>good fruit</u>.
M	*12.33*	*tree bad, and its fruit bad; <u>for</u> the <u>tree is known</u>* <u>by its</u> <u>fruit</u>.

L	6.44	<u>For figs are not gathered from thorns, nor are grapes picked from a</u>
M	7.16	Are grapes <u>gathered from thorns</u>, or figs <u>from</u>

L	6.45	<u>bramble bush.</u> <u>The good man out of the good treasure of his heart produces</u>
M	7.16	thistles?

L	6.45	<u>good, and the evil man out of his evil treasure produces evil; for out of</u>
L	6.45	<u>the abundance of the heart his mouth speaks</u>.

M	*7.19*	*Every tree that does not bear good fruit is cut down and thrown into the*
M	*7.20*	*fire. Thus you will know them by their fruits.*

L	6.46	<u>"Why do</u> <u>you</u> <u>call</u> <u>me</u> <u>'Lord, Lord,'</u>
M	7.21	"Not every one who says to <u>me</u>, <u>'Lord, Lord,'</u> shall enter the kingdom of

L	6.46	<u>and</u> <u>not do</u> <u>what I tell you?</u>
M	7.22	heaven, but he who does the will of my Father who is in heaven. *On that*

M	*7.22*	*day many will say to me, 'Lord, Lord, did we not prophesy in your name,*
M	*7.22*	*and cast out demons in your name, and do many mighty works in your name?'*
M	*7.23*	*And then will I declare to them, 'I never knew you; depart from me, you*
M	*7.23*	*evildoers.'*

e. The Two Houses

Luke 6.47-49

L	6.47	<u>Every one</u> <u>who comes to me and hears my</u> <u>words</u> <u>and does</u>
M	7.24	<u>"Every one</u> then <u>who</u> hears these <u>words</u> of mine <u>and does</u>

L	6.48	<u>them,</u> I will show you what he is like: he is like a man
M	7.24	<u>them</u> will be <u>like a</u> wise <u>man</u> who

| L | 6.48 | building a house, who dug deep, and laid the foundation upon rock; |
| M | 7.24 | built his house upon the rock; |

| L | 6.48 | and when a flood arose, the stream broke |
| M | 7.25 | and the rain fell, and the floods came, and the winds blew and beat |

| L | 6.48 | against that house, and could not shake it, because it had been well |
| M | 7.25 | upon that house, but it did not fall, because it had been founded |

| L | 6.49 | built. But he who hears and does not |
| M | 7.26 | on the rock. And every one who hears these words of mine and does not |

| L | 6.49 | do them is like a man who built a house on the ground |
| M | 7.26 | do them will be like a foolish man who built his house upon the sand; |

| L | 6.49 | without a foundation; against which the stream broke, |
| M | 7.27 | and the rain fell, and the floods came, and the winds blew |

| L | 6.49 | and immediately it fell, and the ruin of |
| M | 7.27 | and beat against that house, and it fell; and great |

| L | 6.49 | that house was great." |
| M | 7.27 | was the fall of it." |

26. THE CENTURION'S SLAVE

Luke 7.1-10

L	7.1	After he had ended all his sayings in the hearing of the people
M	7.28	And when Jesus finished these sayings, the crowds were astonished
Mk	1.22	And they were astonished

| M | 7.29 | *at his teaching,* |*for he taught them as one who had authority, and not* |
| Mk | 1.22 | *at his teaching,* *for he taught them as one who had authority, and not* |

| M | 7.29 | *as their scribes.* |
| Mk | 1.22 | *as the scribes.* |

L	7.2	he entered Capernaum. Now a centurion had
M	8.5	As he entered Capernaum, a centurion came forward to
Mk	2.1	And when he returned to Capernaum after some days, it was reported that
J	4.46b	And at Capernaum there was an official

L	7.2	a slave who was dear to him,
M	8.6	him, beseeching him |and saying, "Lord, my servant
Mk	2.1	he was at home.
J	4.46b	whose son

L	7.3	who was sick and at the point of death. When he heard of Jesus,
M	8.6	is lying paralyzed at home, in terrible distress."
J	4.47	was ill. When he heard that Jesus had come

| L | 7.3 | he sent to him elders of the Jews, asking him to |
| J | 4.47 | from Judea to Galilee, he went and begged him to |

369

```
L   7.4      come        and heal his slave.  And when they came to Jesus, they besought
J   4.47     come down   and heal his son, for he was at the point of death.


L   7.5      him earnestly, saying, "He is worthy to have you do this for him, |for
L   7.5      he loves our nation, and he built us our synagogue."


L   7.6      And Jesus            went with them.  When he was not far from the house,
M   8.7      And he               said to  him, "I will come and heal him."
J   4.48         Jesus therefore  said to  him, "Unless you see signs and wonders you


L   7.6                     the centurion sent friends to him, saying to him, "Lord,
M   8.8          But the centurion                          answered  him, "Lord,
J   4.49     will not believe."  The official               said  to him, "Sir,


L   7.6      do not trouble yourself, for I am not worthy to have you come under my
M   8.8                               I am not worthy to have you come under my


L   7.7      roof; |therefore I did not presume to come to you.  But      say the
M   8.8      roof;                                             but only say the


L   7.8      word, and let my servant    be healed.  For I am a man set under
M   8.9      word, and    my servant will be healed.  For I am a man     under
J   4.50b        come down before my child dies."  The man believed the word


L   7.8      authority, with soldiers under me:  and I say to one, 'Go,' and he goes;
M   8.9      authority, with soldiers under me; and I say to one, 'Go,' and he goes,
J   4.51     that Jesus spoke to him and went his way.  As he was  going down, his


L   7.8      and to another, 'Come,' and he comes; and to my slave, 'Do this,' and
M   8.9      and to another, 'Come,' and he comes, and to my slave, 'Do this,' and
J   4.52     servants met him and told him that his son was living.  So he asked


L   7.9      he does it."  When Jesus heard this he marveled at him, and turned and
M   8.10     he does it."  When Jesus heard him, he marveled,              and
J   4.52     them the hour when he began to mend, and they said to him, "Yesterday


L   7.9      said to the multitude that followed him,       "I tell   you, not even
M   8.10     said to      those   who followed him, "Truly, I say to you, not even
J   4.53     at the seventh hour the fever left him."  The father knew that was the


L   7.9      in Israel have I found such faith."
M   8.11     in Israel have I found such faith.  I tell you, many will come from east
J   4.53     hour when Jesus had said to him, "Your son will live"; and he himself


   M   8.11  and west and sit at table with Abraham, Isaac, and Jacob in the kingdom
   J   4.53  believed, and all his household.

   M   8.12  of heaven, |while the sons of the kingdom will be thrown into the outer
   M   8.12  darkness; there men will weep and gnash their teeth."


L   7.10     And when those who had been sent returned to the house,
M   8.13     And to the centurion Jesus said,        "Go; be it done for you as you
J   4.50a                        Jesus said to him, "Go;
```

370

L	7.10	they found the slave well.
M	8.13	have believed." And the servant was healed at that very moment.
J	4.50a	your son will live."

J 4.54   This was now the second sign that Jesus did when he had come from Judea
J 4.54   to Galilee.

27. A DEAD MAN RAISED AT NAIN

Luke 7.11-17

L	7.11	Soon afterward he went to a city called Nain, and his disciples and a
L	7.12	great crowd went with him. As he drew near to the gate of the city, behold,
L	7.12	a man who had died was being carried out, the only son of his mother, and
L	7.13	she was a widow; and a large crowd from the city was with her. And when
L	7.13	the Lord saw her, he had compassion on her and said to her, "Do not weep."
L	7.14	And he came and touched the bier, and the bearers stood still. And he
L	7.15	said, "Young man, I say to you, arise." And the dead man sat up, and began
L	7.16	to speak. And he gave him to his mother. |Fear seized them all; and they
L	7.16	glorified God, saying, "A great prophet has arisen among us!" and "God has
L	7.17	visited his people!" And this report concerning him spread through the
L	7.17	whole of Judea and all the surrounding country.

28. JOHN THE BAPTIST AND THE 'COMING ONE'

Luke 7.18-35

M 11.1   And when Jesus had finished instructing his twelve disciples, he went
M 11.1   on from there to teach and preach in their cities.

L	7.10,19	The disciples of John told him of all these things. And
M	11.2	Now when John heard in prison about the deeds of the Christ,

L	7.19	John, calling to him two of his disciples, sent them to the Lord,
M	11.2	he sent word by his disciples

L	7.19	saying, "Are you he who is to come, or shall we look for
M	11.3	|and said to him, "Are you he who is to come, or shall we look for

L	7.20	another?" And when the men had come to him, they said, "John the Baptist
M	11.3	another?"

L	7.20	has sent us to you, saying, 'Are you he who is to come, or shall we look
L	7.21	for another?'" In that hour he cured many of diseases and plagues and
L	7.21	evil spirits, and on many that were blind he bestowed sight.

L	7.22	And he answered them, "Go and tell John what you have seen and heard:
M	11.4	And Jesus answered them, "Go and tell John what you hear and see:

L	7.22	the blind receive their sight, the lame walk, lepers are cleansed,
M	11.5	the blind receive their sight and the lame walk, lepers are cleansed

L	7.22	and the deaf hear, the dead are raised up, the poor have good
M	11.5	and the deaf hear, and the dead are raised up, and the poor have good

L	7.23	news preached to them. And blessed is he who takes no offense at me."
M	11.6	news preached to them. And blessed is he who takes no offense at me."

L	7.24	When the messengers of John had gone, he began to speak to the
M	11.7	As they went away, Jesus began to speak to the

L	7.24	crowds concerning John: "What did you go out into the wilderness to
M	11.7	crowds concerning John: "What did you go out into the wilderness to

L	7.25	behold? A reed shaken by the wind? | What then did you go out to see?
M	11.8	behold? A reed shaken by the wind? | Why then did you go out? To see

L	7.25	A man clothed in soft clothing? Behold, those who are gorgeously
M	11.8	a man clothed in soft raiment? Behold, those who wear soft

L	7.26	appareled and live in luxury are in kings' courts. What then did you
M	11.9	raiment are in kings' houses. Why then did you

L	7.26	go out to see? A prophet? Yes, I tell you, and more than a prophet.
M	11.9	go out? To see a prophet? Yes, I tell you, and more than a prophet.

L	7.27	This is he of whom it is written,
M	11.10	This is he of whom it is written,
Mk	1.2	As it is written *in Isaiah the prophet,*

L	7.27	'Behold, I send my messenger before thy face,
M	11.10	'Behold, I send my messenger before thy face,
Mk	1.2	"Behold, I send my messenger before thy face,

L	7.27	who shall prepare thy way before thee.'
M	11.10	who shall prepare thy way before thee.'
Mk	1.2	who shall prepare thy way;

L	7.28	I tell you, among those born of women none is
M	11.11	Truly, I say to you, among those born of women there has risen no one

L	7.28	greater than John; yet he who is least in the kingdom of
M	11.11	greater than John the Baptist; yet he who is least in the kingdom of

L	7.29	God is greater than he." (When they heard this all the people and the
M	11.11	heaven is greater than he.

L	7.29	tax collectors justified God, having been baptized with the baptism of
L	7.30	John; but the Pharisees and the lawyers rejected the purpose of God for
L	7.30	themselves, not having been baptized by him.)

M	11.12	*From the days of John the Baptist until now the kingdom of heaven has*
M	11.13	*suffered violence, and men of violence take it by force. For all the*
M	11.14	*prophets and the law prophesied until John; and if you are willing to*
M	11.15	*accept it, he is Elijah who is to come. He who has ears to hear, let*
M	11.15	*him hear.*

L	7.31	"To what then shall I compare the men of this generation, and what
M	11.16	"But to what shall I compare this generation?

```
L    7.32   are they like?  They are like children sitting in the market place  and
M   11.16                   It    is    like children sitting in the market places and


L    7.32   calling to one another,
M   11.16   calling to their playmates,


L    7.32            'We piped to you, and you did not dance;
M   11.17            'We piped to you, and you did not dance;


L    7.32            we wailed, and you did not weep.'
M   11.17            we wailed, and you did not mourn.'


L    7.33   For John the Baptist has come        eating no bread and drinking no
M   11.18   For John                 came neither eating          nor drinking,


L    7.34   wine; and you say, 'He has a demon.'  The Son of man has come eating
M   11.19         and they say, 'He has a demon'; the Son of man     came eating


L    7.34   and drinking; and you say, 'Behold, a glutton and a drunkard, a friend
M   11.19   and drinking, and they say, 'Behold, a glutton and a drunkard, a friend


L    7.35   of tax collectors and sinners!' Yet wisdom is justified by all her
M   11.19   of tax collectors and sinners!' Yet wisdom is justified by     her


L    7.35   children."
M   11.19   deeds."
```

29. THE ANOINTING OF JESUS

Luke 7.36-50

```
L    7.36   One of the Pharisees asked him to eat with him, and he     went
M   26.6    Now when                                          Jesus was  at
Mk  14.3    And while                                         he    was  at
J   12.1    Six days before the Passover,                     Jesus came to


L    7.36            into the Pharisee's house,            and    took his place
M   26.7b   Bethany in    the          house of Simon the leper, |as he sat
Mk  14.3    Bethany in    the          house of Simon the leper, as he sat
J   12.2    Bethany, where Lazarus was, whom Jesus had raised from the dead.  There


J  12.2    they made him a supper; Martha served, and Lazarus was one of those


L    7.37   at table.  And behold, a woman of the city, who was a sinner, when she
M   26.7a   at table.              |a woman                                came up
Mk  14.3    at table,              a woman                                 came
J   12.3    at table with him.     Mary


L    7.37   learned that he was at table in the Pharisee's house,
```

L	7.38	brought	an alabaster flask of	ointment, |and standing
M	26.7a	to him with an alabaster flask of	very expensive	ointment,
Mk	14.3	with an alabaster flask of		ointment of pure nard,
J	12.3	took	a pound of	costly ointment of pure nard

L   7.38   behind him at his feet, weeping, she began to wet his feet with her tears,
L   7.38   and wiped them with the hair of her head, and kissed his feet,

L	7.38		and anointed	them with
M	26.7a	and she	poured it on	his head,
Mk	14.3	very costly, and she broke the flask	and poured it over	his head.
J	12.3		and anointed	the feet of Jesus

J   12.3   and wiped his feet with her hair; and the house was filled with the

L	7.39	the ointment. Now when the Pharisee who had invited him
M	26.8	But when the disciples
Mk	14.4	But there were some who
J	12.4	fragrance of the ointment. But Judas Iscariot, one of his disciples (he

L	7.39	saw it,	he	said to himself, "If this man were a prophet, he
M	26.8	saw it,	they were	indignant, saying, "Why
Mk	14.4			said to themselves indignantly, "Why was
J	12.5	who was to betray him),	said,	|"Why was

L	7.39	would have known who and what sort of woman this is who is touching him,
M	26.9	this waste? For this ointment might have been sold for
Mk	14.5	the ointment thus wasted? For this ointment might have been sold for
J	12.5	this ointment not sold for

L   7.40   for she is a sinner." And Jesus answering said to him, "Simon, I have
L   7.41   something to say to you." And he answered, "What is it, Teacher?" \|"A

L	7.41	certain creditor had two debtors; one owed five hundred denarii, and
M	26.9	a large sum, and
Mk	14.5	more than three hundred denarii, and
J	12.5	three hundred denarii and

L	7.42	the other fifty. When they could not pay, he forgave them both. Now
M	26.9	given to the poor."
Mk	14.5	given to the poor." And they reproached her.
J	12.6	given to the poor?" This he said, not that he cared for the poor but

J   12.6   because he was a thief, and as he had the money box he used to take what
J   12.6   was put into it.

L	7.43	which of them will love him more?" Simon answered, "The one, I suppose,
M	26.10	But Jesus, aware of this, said to them,
Mk	14.6	But Jesus said, "Let her alone;
J	12.7a	Jesus said, "Let her alone,

L   7.43   to whom he forgave more." And he said to him, "You have judged rightly."
L   7.44   Then turning toward the woman he said to Simon,

```
L     7.44        "Do you see    this woman? I entered your house, you gave me no water
M    26.10      "Why do you trouble the woman? For she has done a beautiful thing to me.
Mk   14.6        why do you trouble      her?        She has done a beautiful thing to me.


L     7.44        for my feet, but she has wet my feet with her tears and wiped them with
L     7.45        her hair.  You gave me no kiss, but from the time I came in she has not


L     7.45        ceased to kiss my feet.
M    26.11      For you always have the poor with you,
Mk   14.7       For you always have the poor with you, and whenever you will, you can do
J    12.8           The poor you always have with you,


L     7.46                        You did  not anoint my head with oil,
M    26.11                  but you will not always have me.
Mk   14.8       good to them; but you will not always have me.  She has done what she
J    12.8                   but you do   not always have me."


L     7.46            but she has anointed   my feet with ointment.
M    26.12      In pouring this ointment on my body she has done it to prepare me for
Mk   14.8       could;  she has anointed    my body              beforehand     for
J    12.7b                              let her      keep it for the day of my


L     7.47                Therefore I tell  you, her sins, which are many, are forgiven,
M    26.13      burial.          Truly, I say to you, wherever this gospel is
Mk   14.9       burying.  And truly, I say to you, wherever the  gospel is
J    12.7b      burial.


L     7.47        for she loved much; but he who is forgiven little, loves little."
M    26.13      preached in the whole world, what she has done will be told in memory
Mk   14.9       preached in the whole world, what she has done will be told in memory


L     7.48        And                          he said to her,
M    26.13      of her."
Mk   14.9       of her."
 M    9.2b       and when Jesus saw their faith  he said to the paralytic, "Take heart,
 Mk   2.5        And when Jesus saw their faith,  he said to the paralytic,
 L    5.20       And when he     saw their faith  he said,


L     7.49            "Your sins are forgiven."     Then those who were at table with
 M    9.2b       my son; your sins are forgiven."
 Mk   2.5        "My son, your sins are forgiven."
 L    5.21          "Man, your sins are forgiven you."  And the scribes and the Pharisees


L     7.49        him began to say among themselves, "Who is this,
 L    5.21            began to question, saying,      "Who is this that speaks blasphemies?


L     7.50        who even forgives sins?"             And          he    said to the
 M    9.22a                       Jesus turned, and seeing her he    said, "Take
 Mk   5.34                                          And          he    said to
 Mk  10.52a                                         And          Jesus said to
 L    5.21       Who can  forgive  sins but God only?"
 L    8.48                                           And          he    said to


L     7.50        woman,          "Your faith has saved you;      go in peace."
 M    9.22a       heart, daughter;  your faith has made you well."
 Mk   5.34        her, "Daughter,   your faith has made you well; go in peace, and be
 Mk  10.52a       him, "Go your way; your faith has made you well."
 L    8.48        her, "Daughter,   your faith has made you well; go in peace."


                                      375
```

30. THE WOMEN MINISTER TO JESUS

Luke 8.1-3

L	8.1	Soon afterward		he	went on through		cities
M	9.35	And		Jesus	went about	all the	cities
Mk	6.6b	And		he	went about among	the	

M   4.23   And   he   went about   all   Galilee,
Mk   1.14   Now after John was arrested, Jesus came into   Galilee,
Mk   1.39   And   he   went throughout all   Galilee,
L   4.44   And   he   was

L	8.1	and villages,		preaching and bringing
M	9.35	and villages, teaching in their synagogues and	preaching
Mk	6.6b	villages teaching.	

M   4.23   teaching in their synagogues and preaching
Mk   1.14   preaching
Mk   1.39   preaching in their
L   4.44   preaching in the

L	8.1	the good news of the kingdom of God. And the twelve were with him,
M	9.35	the gospel of the kingdom,

M   4.23   the gospel   of the kingdom
Mk   1.14   the gospel   of God,
Mk   1.39   synagogues
L   4.44   synagogues of Judea.

L	8.2	|and also some women who had been healed of evil spirits and
M	9.35	and healing every disease and every

M   4.23   and   healing every disease   and every
Mk   1.39   and   casting out   demons.
Mk 16.9   Now when he rose early on the first day of the week, he appeared

L	8.2	infirmities: Mary, called Magdalene, from whom seven
M	9.35	infirmity.

M   4.23   infirmity among the people.
Mk 16.9   first   to Mary   Magdalene, from whom he had cast out seven

L	8.3	demons had gone out, |and Joanna, the wife of Chuza, Herod's steward, and

Mk 16.9   demons.

L	8.3	Susanna, and many others, who provided for them out of their means.

31. PARABLE OF THE SOILS

Luke 8.4-15

M   13.1   That same day Jesus went out of the house and sat   beside the sea.
Mk   4.1   Again   he   began to teach beside the sea.
Mk   2.13   He   went out again   beside the sea;

L	8.4	And when a	great crowd	came together and people from town after
M	13.2	And	great crowds gathered	
Mk	4.1	And	a very large crowd	gathered

Mk   2.13   and   all   the crowd gathered

```
L    8.4    town came to    him,
M   13.2              about him, so that he got into a boat and sat there;
Mk   4.1              about him, so that he got into a boat and sat in it on the sea;
  Mk  2.13            about him,


L    8.4                                                              he said
M   13.3    and the whole crowd stood          on the beach. And he told    them
Mk   4.2    and the whole crowd was beside the sea on the land. And he taught them
  Mk  2.13                                                     and he taught them.


L    8.4              in a parable:
M   13.3    many things in   parables,                        saying:
Mk   4.2    many things in   parables, and in his teaching he said to them:


L    8.5              "A sower went out to sow his seed; and as he sowed, some
M   13.4              "A sower went out to sow.          |And as he sowed, some seeds
Mk   4.3,4  "Listen!  A sower went out to sow.          |And as he sowed, some seed


L    8.5    fell along the path, and was trodden under foot, and the birds of the air
M   13.4    fell along the path,                             and the birds came and
Mk   4.4    fell along the path,                             and the birds came and


L    8.6    devoured it.  And some         fell on the rock;
M   13.5    devoured them.    Other seeds fell on     rocky ground, where they had
Mk   4.5    devoured it.      Other seed  fell on     rocky ground, where it   had


L    8.6                    and as       it   grew  up, it withered away, because
M   13.5    not much soil, and immediately they sprang up,                   since
Mk   4.5    not much soil, and immediately it   sprang up,                   since


L    8.6    it   had no moisture.
M   13.6    they had no depth of soil, |but when the sun rose they were scorched; and
Mk   4.6    it   had no depth of soil;  and when the sun rose it   was scorched, and


L    8.7                                    And some        fell among thorns;
M   13.7    since they had no root they withered away. Other seeds fell upon  thorns,
Mk   4.7    since it   had no root it   withered away. Other seed  fell among thorns


L    8.8    and the thorns grew with it and choked it.                        And
M   13.7    and the thorns grew up     and choked them.
Mk   4.8    and the thorns grew up     and choked it, and it yielded no grain. And


L    8.8    some        fell into good soil and                grew,
M   13.8    Other seeds fell on   good soil and brought forth grain,
Mk   4.8    other seeds fell into good soil and brought forth grain, growing up and


L    8.8              and yielded                a hundredfold."
M   13.8                                some a hundredfold, some
Mk   4.8    increasing and yielding thirtyfold and sixtyfold and a hundredfold."


L    8.8    As  he said this, he called out, "He who has ears to hear, let him hear."
M   13.9    sixty, some thirty.              He who has ears,       let him hear."
Mk   4.9    And he said,                    "He who has ears to hear, let him hear."
  M  11.15                                   He who has ears to hear, let him hear.
  M  13.43b                                  He who has ears,       let him hear."
  Mk  4.23                          If any man has ears to hear, let him hear."
  Mk  7.16                         "If any man has ears to hear, let him hear."
  L  14.35b                         He who has ears to hear, let him hear."
```

377

```
L     8.9      And when                                                    his disciples
M     13.10    Then                                                        the disciples came
Mk    4.10     And when he was alone, those who were about him with the twelve


L     8.10       asked   him    what                       this parable meant, |he said,
M     13.11    and said to him, "Why do you speak to them in parables?" .And he answered
Mk    4.11       asked   him              concerning the parables.   And he said  to


L     8.10       "To you it has been given to know the secrets of the kingdom of
M     13.11    them, "To you it has been given to know the secrets of the kingdom of
Mk    4.11     them, "To you   has been given      the secret  of the kingdom of


L     8.10     God;    but for others
M     13.12    heaven, but to  them it has not been given.  For to him who has will more
Mk    4.11     God,    but for those outside


  M   13.12    be given, and he will have abundance; but from him who has not, even what
  M   13.13    he has will be taken away.  This is why I


L     8.10     they      are in parables, so that          seeing they may not
M     13.13    speak to them  in parables, because          seeing they do  not
Mk    4.12     everything is  in parables; so that they may indeed see    but    not
  Mk  8.18                                                     Having eyes   do  you not
  J   9.39     Jesus said, "For judgment I came into this world, that those who do  not


L     8.10     see,        and            hearing                                  they
M     13.13    see,        and            hearing they do not      hear, nor do they
Mk    4.12     perceive,   and may indeed hear                      but not
  Mk  8.17b                                       Do  you not yet perceive or
  Mk  8.18     see,        and     having ears   do  you not     hear? And do you
  J   9.39     see may see, and that those who see may become blind."


L     8.10     may not understand.
M     13.14              understand.  With them indeed is fulfilled the prophecy of Isaiah
Mk    4.12              understand;
  Mk  8.17b             understand?  Are your hearts hardened?
  Mk  8.18        not remember?


  M   13.14    which says:
  M   13.14                'You shall indeed hear but never understand,
  M   13.14                    and you shall indeed see but never perceive.
  M   13.15            For this people's heart has grown dull,
  M   13.15                and their ears are heavy of hearing,
  M   13.15                and their eyes they have closed,

  M   13.15                lest they should perceive with their eyes,
  Mk  4.12                 lest they should

  M   13.15                    and hear with their ears,
  M   13.15                and understand with their heart,

  M   13.15                    and turn for me       to heal them.'
  Mk  4.12                     turn again, and be forgiven."

  M   13.16    But blessed are your eyes, for they see, and your ears, for they hear.
  M   13.17    Truly, I say to you, many prophets and righteous men longed to see what
  M   13.17    you see, and did not see it, and to hear what you hear, and did not
  M   13.17    hear it.
```

378

```
L    8.11                                                     Now   the  parable is this:
M    13.18                                           "Hear then  the  parable
Mk   4.13        And he said to them, "Do you not understand this parable?  How then will


L    8.11                                         The seed  is   the word of God.
M    13.19b                            of the sower.                            |this
Mk   4.14,15  you understand all the parables?  The sower sows the word.  And these


L    8.12          The ones        along the path            are          those
M    13.19a   is  what was sown along the path.                   |When any one
Mk   4.15     are the ones         along the path, where the word is sown; when they


L    8.12     who have heard;                                            then the
M    13.19a            hears the word of the kingdom and does not understand it, the
Mk   4.15            hear,


L    8.12     devil         comes and takes    away the word           from their
M    13.19a   evil one      comes and snatches away           what  is sown in   his
Mk   4.15     Satan immediately comes and takes away the word which is sown in


L    8.13     hearts, that they may not believe and be saved. And
M    13.20    heart;                                          As for
Mk   4.16     them.                                           And these in like manner


L    8.13         the ones         on the rock        are  those who, when they hear
M    13.20        what was sown on     rocky ground, this is he  who          hears
Mk   4.16     are the ones        sown upon  rocky ground,       who, when they hear


L    8.13     the word,            receive it with joy; but these have no root,
M    13.21    the word and immediately receives it with joy; yet he   has  no root
Mk   4.17     the word,   immediately receive it with joy; and they have no root


L    8.13               they believe for a while  and in time of temptation
M    13.21    in himself,    but    endures for a while. and   when    tribulation
Mk   4.17     in themselves, but    endure  for a while; then,  when    tribulation


L    8.13                                                        fall  away.
M    13.21    or persecution arises on account of the word, immediately he  falls away.
Mk   4.17     or persecution arises on account of the word, immediately they fall away.


L    8.14     And as for      what     fell among the thorns, they are those who
M    13.22       As for       what was sown among    thorns, this is he    who
Mk   4.18     And others are the ones      sown among    thorns; they are those who


L    8.14     hear,        but as they go on their way they are choked by the cares
M    13.22    hears the word, but                                        the cares
Mk   4.19     hear  the word, |but                                       the cares


L    8.14             and          riches  and    pleasures of life,
M    13.22    of the world  and the delight in riches
Mk   4.19     of the world, and the delight in riches, and the desire for other things,


L    8.15                     and their fruit does not mature.  And as for
M    13.23         choke the word, and it   proves    unfruitful.    As for
Mk   4.20     enter in and choke the word, and it   proves    unfruitful.  But those
```

379

```
L    8.15    that            in    the good soil, they are those    who, hearing the
M   13.23    what was  sown on         good soil, this is he        who  hears      the
Mk   4.20    that were sown upon the good soil         are the ones who  hear       the


L    8.15    word,    hold        it fast in an honest and good heart, and
M   13.23    word and understands it;                                         he indeed
Mk   4.20    word and accept      it                                      and


L    8.15    bring forth fruit  with patience.
M   13.23    bears         fruit, and yields, in one case a hundredfold, in another
Mk   4.20    bear          fruit,                           thirtyfold  and
```

```
M  13.23    sixty,    and in another thirty."
Mk  4.20    sixtyfold and     a       hundredfold."
```

32. THE LAMP AND THE MEASURE

Luke 8.16-18

M   5.14   *"You are the light of the world. A city set on a hill cannot be hid.*

```
L    8.16    "No     one after lighting a lamp           covers it
M    5.15    Nor do men        light    a lamp       and put    it
Mk   4.21    And he said to them, "Is a lamp brought in to be put
L   11.33    "No     one after lighting a lamp               puts   it in a cellar


L    8.16    with  a vessel, or puts it under a bed, but puts it on a stand, that
M    5.15    under a bushel,                          but          on a stand, and
Mk   4.21    under a bushel, or           under a bed, and not     on a stand?
L   11.33    or under a bushel,                        but          on a stand, that


L    8.16    those who enter may see the light.
M    5.16    it gives light to all in the house.  *Let your light so shine before men,*
L   11.34    those who enter may see the light.   *Your eye is the lamp of your body;*
```

```
M   5.16    *that they may see your good works and give glory to your Father who is*
L  11.34    *when your eye is sound, your whole body is full of light; but when it is*

M   5.16    *in heaven.*
L  11.35    *not sound, your body is full of darkness. Therefore be careful lest the*

L  11.36    *light in you be darkness. If then your whole body is full of light,*
L  11.36    *having no part dark, it will be wholly bright, as when a lamp with its*
L  11.36    *rays gives you light."*
```

```
L    8.17                      For    nothing is hid         that shall not
Mk   4.22                      For there is nothing hid,      except to
M   10.26    "So have no fear of them; for  nothing is covered  that will    not
L   12.2                       Nothing is covered up that will  not
```

```
L    8.17    be made manifest, nor  anything secret that shall not be known
Mk   4.22    be made manifest; nor is anything secret,
M   10.26    be      revealed, or          hidden that will  not be known.
L   12.2     be      revealed, or          hidden that will  not be known.
```

```
L    8.17                                                        and      come  to
Mk   4.22                                                   except to come  to
  M  10.27              What      I        tell you in the dark,      utter in the
  L  12.3       Therefore whatever you have said     in the dark shall be heard in the


L    8.17     light.
Mk   4.23,24  light.  If any man has ears to hear, let him hear."  And he said to them,
  M  10.27    light; and what you hear whispered,                         proclaim
  L  12.3     light, and what you have whispered in private rooms shall be proclaimed


L    8.18     Take heed then how  you hear;
Mk   4.24     "Take heed       what  you hear; the measure you give will be the measure you
  M  10.27    upon the housetops.
  L  12.3     upon the housetops.


L    8.18                                               for to him      who has will
Mk   4.25     get, and still more will be given you.  For to him      who has will
  M  13.12                                             For to him      who has will
  M  25.29                                             For to every one who has will
  L  19.26                           'I tell you, that to every one who has will


L    0.18     more be given,                         and from him who has not, even
Mk   4.25     more be given;                         and from him who has not, even
  M  13.12    more be given, and he will have abundance; but from him who has not, even
  M  25.29    more be given, and he will have abundance; but from him who has not, even
  L  19.26    more be given;                           but from him who has not, even


L    8.18     what he thinks that he has will be taken away."
Mk   4.25     what he                has will be taken away."
  M  13.12    what he             has will be taken away.
  M  25.29    what he             has will be taken away.
  L  19.26    what he             has will be taken away.
```

33. HIS MOTHER AND BROTHERS

Luke 8.19-21

```
L    8.19     Then                                             his mother and his
M   12.46     While he was still speaking to the people, behold, his mother and his
Mk   3.31     And                                              his mother and his


L    8.19     brothers came to him, but they could not reach him for the crowd.
M   12.46     brothers        stood     outside,     asking      to speak to him.
Mk   3.31     brothers came; and standing outside they sent to him and called   him.


L    8.20                                 And he   was told,      "Your
M   12.47                               Some one told    him, "Your
Mk   3.32     And a crowd was sitting about him; and they    said to him, "Your


L    8.20     mother and your brothers are standing outside, desiring to see
M   12.47     mother and your brothers are standing outside, asking   to speak to
Mk   3.32     mother and your brothers are          outside, asking          for


L    8.20     you."
M   12.48     you."  But he replied to the man who told him, "Who is  my mother, and
Mk   3.33     you."  And he replied,                        "Who are my mother  and
```

381

```
L    8.21                            But
M   12.49   who are my brothers?"   And stretching out his hand toward his disciples,
Mk   3.34           my brothers?"   And looking around     on those who sat about him,


L    8.21   he said to them,  "My mother and my brothers are those who hear the
M   12.50   he said, "Here are my mother and my brothers!       For whoever
Mk   3.35   he said, "Here are my mother and my brothers!           Whoever
  M  7.21   "Not every one who says to me, 'Lord, Lord,' shall enter the kingdom of


L    8.21   word of God     and do   it."
M   12.50                        does the will of my Father      in heaven is my
Mk   3.35                        does the will of   God                     is my
  M  7.21   heaven, but he who does the will of my Father who is in heaven.


  M 12.50   brother, and sister, and mother."
  Mk 3.35   brother, and sister, and mother."
```

34 THE STORM AT SEA

Luke 8.22-25

```
L    8.22   One     day  he got into a boat with his disciples, and he said
M    8.18   Now     when Jesus saw great crowds around him,          he gave orders
Mk   4.35   On that day, when evening had come,                      he said


L    8.22   to them, "Let us go across to the other side of the lake."        So
M    8.23   to               go over   to the other side.    And
Mk   4.36   to them, "Let us go across to the other side."  And leaving the crowd,


L    8.22   they set out,
M    8.23               when he got into the boat,                 his disciples
Mk   4.36   they took him with them in   the boat, just as he was.  And other boats


L    8.23               and as they sailed he fell          asleep.
M   8.24b   followed   him. |but             he was          asleep.
Mk  4.38a   were with  him.  But             he was in the stern, asleep on the


L    8.23            And           a      storm of wind came down on the lake,
M   8.24a            And behold, there arose      a great storm    on the sea,
Mk   4.37   cushion; And             a great storm of wind arose,   and the waves


L    8.23                         and      they were      filling with water, and
M   8.24a                         so that the boat was being  swamped by the waves;
Mk   4.37   beat into the boat, so that the boat was already filling.


L    8.24   were in danger.  And they went and woke him,     saying, "Master, Master,
M    8.25                    And they went and woke him,     saying, "Save,   Lord;
Mk  4.38b                    and they           woke him and said to him,    "Teacher,


L    8.24                    we are perishing!"  And  he awoke and rebuked the wind
M   8.26b   do you not care if we are perishing."  Then he rose  and rebuked the winds
Mk   4.39   do you not care if we      perish?"   And  he awoke and rebuked the wind,
```

382

```
L    8.24    and            the raging waves;                    and       they ceased, and
M    8.26b   and            the        sea;                                              and
Mk   4.39    and said to the           sea, "Peace! Be still!" And the wind ceased, and


L    8.25    there was a        calm.      He said to them, "Where is  your
M    8.26a   there was a great  calm.  And he said to them, "Why    are you afraid, O men
Mk   8.40    there was a great  calm.      He said to them, "Why    are you afraid? Have


L    8.25             faith?" And they were afraid, and they marveled, saying to one
M    8.27    of little faith?" And                 the men   marveled, saying,
Mk   4.41    you no    faith?" And they were filled with awe,      and said  to one


L    8.25    another, "Who  then         is this, that he commands even wind  and water,
M    8.27             "What sort of man is this, that               even winds and sea
Mk   4.41    another, "Who  then         is this, that               even wind  and sea


L    8.25    and they obey him?"
M    8.27             obey him?"
Mk   4.41             obey him?"
```

35. THE DEMON 'LEGION'

Luke 8.26-39

```
L    8.26    Then      they arrived                              at the country of the
M    8.28    And when  he   came to the other side,             to the country of the
Mk   5.1                    They came to the other side of the sea, to the country of the


L    8.27    Gerasenes, which is opposite Galilee.  And as   he stepped  out on
M    8.28    Gadarenes,
Mk   5.2     Gerasenes.                             And when he had come out of the


L    8.27    land, there        met him a man from the city who had demons; for a long
M    8.28           two demoniacs met him,
Mk   5.2     boat, there        met him


L    8.27    time he had worn no clothes, and he lived not in a house but among  the
M    8.28                                                          coming out of the
Mk   5.2                                                                out of the


L    8.27    tombs.
M    8.28    tombs, so fierce that no one could pass that way.
Mk   5.3     tombs  a man with an unclean spirit, |who lived among the tombs; and no
```

```
Mk   5.4    one could bind him any more, even with a chain; for he had often been
Mk   5.4    bound with fetters and chains, but the chains he wrenched apart, and the
Mk   5.4    fetters he broke in pieces; and no one had the strength to subdue him.
Mk   5.5    Night and day among the tombs and on the mountains he was always crying
Mk   5.6    out, and bruising himself with stones.  And
```

```
L    8.28    When he saw Jesus,              he
M    8.29                                                       And behold, they
Mk   5.7     when he saw Jesus from afar, he ran and worshiped him; |and
```

```
L    8.28   cried out and fell down before him, and said with a loud voice,
M    8.29   cried out,
Mk   5.7    crying out                                        with a loud voice, he said,


L    8.28   "What have you to do with me, Jesus, Son of the Most High God?  I
M    8.29   "What have you to do with us,      O Son of            God?
Mk   5.7    "What have you to do with me, Jesus, Son of the Most High God?  I


L    8.29   beseech you,         do not torment me."  For he had commanded the unclean
M    8.29      Have you    come here to torment us before the time?"
Mk   5.8    adjure you by God, do not torment me."  For he had said    to


L    8.29   spirit to come out of the man.  (For many a time it had seized him; he was
Mk   5.8    him,     "Come out of the man, you unclean spirit!"


L    8.29   kept under guard, and bound with chains and fetters, but he broke the


L    8.30   bonds and was driven by the demon into the desert.)     Jesus then asked
Mk   5.9                                                   And Jesus      asked


L    8.30   him, "What is your name?"  And he said,              "Legion"; for
Mk   5.9    him, "What is your name?"      He replied, "My name is Legion;  for we


L    8.31      many demons had entered him.  And they begged him       not to
Mk   5.10   are many."                       And he  begged him eagerly not to


L    8.32   command them to depart into the abyss.   Now a large herd of     swine
M    8.30                                            Now a      herd of many swine
Mk   5.11   send    them      out of the country.  Now a great herd of     swine


L    8.32   was feeding there on the hillside;    and    they  begged him
M    8.31   was feeding at some distance from them.  And the demons begged him,  "If
Mk   5.12   was feeding there on the hillside;    and    they  begged him,


L    8.32                                         to         let them enter
M    8.31   you cast us out, send us away into the herd of swine."
Mk   5.12            "Send us    to the          swine, let us   enter


L    8.33   these.  So he gave    them leave. |Then the          demons came out of
M    8.32           |And he said to them, "Go." So             they   came out
Mk   5.13   them."  |So he gave    them leave.  And the unclean spirits came out,


L    8.33   the man and entered   the swine, and     the      herd
M    8.32           and went into the swine; and behold, the whole herd
Mk   5.13           and entered   the swine; and       the      herd, numbering


L    8.33                       rushed down the steep bank into the lake and were
M    8.32                       rushed down the steep bank into the sea, and
Mk   5.13   about two thousand, rushed down the steep bank into the sea, and were


L    8.34   drowned.          When the herdsmen saw what had happened, they fled,
M    8.33   perished in the waters.  The herdsmen                          fled,
Mk   5.14   drowned  in the sea.     The herdsmen                          fled,
```

L	8.35	and told it in the city and in the country. Then people went out to
M	8.33	and going into the city they told everything, and
Mk	5.14	and told it in the city and in the country. And people came to

L	8.35	see what had happened, and they
M	8.34	what had happened to the demoniacs. And behold, all the
Mk	5.15	see what it was that had happened. And they

L	8.35	came to Jesus, and found the man from whom the
M	8.34	city came out to meet Jesus; and when they saw him,
Mk	5.15	came to Jesus, and saw the demoniac

L	8.35	demons had gone, sitting at the feet of Jesus, clothed and in his right
Mk	5.15	sitting there, clothed and in his right

L	8.36	mind; and they were afraid. And those
Mk	5.16	mind, the man who had had the legion; and they were afraid. And those

L	8.36	who had seen it told them how he who had been possessed with demons
Mk	5.16	who had seen it told what had happened to the demoniac

L	8.37	was healed. Then all the people of the surrounding country of the
M	8.34	they
Mk	5.17	and to the swine. And they began

L	8.37	Gerasenes asked him to depart from them; for they were seized with
M	8.34	begged him to leave their neighborhood.
Mk	5.17	to beg Jesus to depart from their neighborhood.

L	8.38	great fear; so he got into the boat and returned. The man from
Mk	5.18	And as he was getting into the boat, the man

L	8.38	whom the demons had gone begged that he might be
Mk	5.18	who had been possessed with demons begged him that he might be

L	8.39	with him; but he sent him away, saying, |"Return to your home,
Mk	5.19	with him. But he refused, and said to him, "Go home to

L	8.39	and declare how much God has done for you."
Mk	5.19	your friends, and tell them how much the Lord has done for you, and how

L	8.39	And he went away, proclaiming
Mk	5.20	he has had mercy on you." And he went away and began to proclaim

L	8.39	throughout the whole city how much Jesus had done for him.
Mk	5.20	in the Decapolis how much Jesus had done for him; and all men

Mk	5.20	marveled.

385

Luke 8.40-56

L	8.40	Now when Jesus returned, the
Mk	5.21	And when Jesus had crossed again in the boat to the other side, a

L	8.41	crowd welcomed him, for they were all waiting for him. And
M	9.18	While
Mk	5.22	great crowd gathered about him; and he was beside the sea. Then

L	8.41	there came a man named Jairus, who was a ruler of the synagogue;
M	9.18	he was thus speaking to them, behold, a ruler
Mk	5.22	came one of the rulers of the synagogue,

L	8.41	and falling at Jesus' feet he besought
M	9.18	came in and knelt before him,
Mk	5.23	Jairus by name; and seeing him, he fell at his feet, |and besought

L	8.42	him to come to his house, |for he had an only daughter, about twelve
M	9.18	saying, "My daughter
Mk	5.23	him, saying, "My little daughter

L	8.42	years of age, and she was dying.
M	9.18	has just died; but come and lay your
Mk	5.23	is at the point of death. Come and lay your

M	*9.18*	*hand on her, and she will live."*
Mk	*5.23*	*hands on her, so that she may be made well, and live."*

L	8.42	As he went, the people
M	9.19	And Jesus rose and followed him, with his disciples.
Mk	5.24	And he went with him. And a great crowd followed him and

L	8.43	pressed round him. And a woman who had had a
M	9.20	And behold, a woman who had suffered from a
Mk	5.25	thronged about him. And there was a woman who had had a

L	8.43	flow of blood for twelve years and could not be healed by any one,
M	9.20	hemorrhage for twelve years
Mk	5.26	flow of blood for twelve years, |and who had suffered much under many

Mk	*5.26*	*physicians, and had spent all that she had, and was no better but rather*
Mk	*6.56*	* And wherever he came, in villages, cities, or*

L	8.44	|came up behind him,
M	9.20	came up behind him
Mk	5.27	*grew worse. She had heard the reports about Jesus,* and came up behind him
M	*14.36*	* and besought him*
Mk	*3.10*	*for he had healed many, so that all who had diseases pressed upon him*
Mk	*6.56*	*country, they laid the sick in the market places, and besought him*
L	*6.19*	* And all the crowd sought*

```
L    8.44                            and touched    the fringe of his garment;
M    9.21                            and touched    the fringe of his garment;  for she said to
Mk   5.28            in the crowd    and touched                his garment.  For she said
  M 14.36            that they might only touch     the fringe of his garment;
  Mk  3.10                              to touch                him.
  Mk  6.56            that they might     touch even the fringe of his garment;
  L   6.19                              to touch                him, for power came forth


  M   9.21            herself, "If I only touch      his garment,  I shall be made well."
  Mk  5.28                      "If I     touch even his garments, I shall be made well."
  L   6.19            from him and healed them all.


L    8.44            and immediately her flow of blood ceased.
M    9.22b           And instantly    the woman was      made well.
Mk   5.29            And immediately the hemorrhage      ceased; and she felt in her body that she
  M 14.36            and as many as touched it were      made well.
  Mk  6.56            and as many as touched it were      made well.
  Mk 10.52b          and immediately    he received his sight and followed him on the way.


L    8.45                                           And Jesus
M    9.22a                                            Jesus
Mk   5.30            was healed of her disease.  And Jesus, perceiving in himself that power


L    8.45                                                                        said,
M    9.22a                                                   turned
Mk   5.30            had gone forth from him, immediately turned about in the crowd, and said,


L    8.45            "Who was it that touched me?"          When all denied it, Peter
Mk   5.31            "Who             touched my garments?"  And             his disciples


L    8.45            said,        "Master, the multitudes surround you and press    upon    you!"
Mk   5.31            said to him, "You see the crowd                             pressing around you,


L    8.46            But      Jesus said, "Some one touched me; for I perceive that power has
M    9.22a                                                  and                          seeing
Mk   5.32            and yet you    say,  'Who       touched me?'"  And he looked around to see


L    8.47            gone forth from me."  And when the woman  saw    that she was not hidden,
M    9.22a           her
Mk   5.33            who had done it.      But       the woman, knowing what had been done to


L    8.47            she    came                 trembling, and falling down before him    declared
Mk   5.33            her,   came in fear and trembling  and fell    down before him, and told him


L    8.47            in the presence of all the people why she had touched him, and how she had
Mk   5.33            the whole truth.


L    8.48            been immediately healed.  And he    said to her,              "Daughter,
M    9.22a                                      he    said,           "Take heart, daughter;
Mk   5.34                                        And he    said to her,              "Daughter,
  Mk 10.52a                                      And Jesus said to him,      "Go your way;
  L   7.50                                        And he    said to the woman,
  L  17.19                                        And he    said to him,  "Rise and go your way;
  L  18.42                                        And Jesus said to him , "Receive your sight;
```

```
L      8.48    your faith has made  you well; go in peace."
M      9.22a   your faith has made  you well."
Mk     5.34    your faith has made  you well; go in peace, and be healed of your disease."
Mk 10.52       your faith has made  you well."
L    7.50      "Your faith has saved you;      go in peace."
L   17.19      your faith has made  you well."
L   18.42      your faith has made  you well."


L      8.49    While he was still speaking,      a man from the ruler's house came and
Mk     5.35    While he was still speaking, there came from the ruler's house some who


L      8.49    said, "Your daughter is dead,  do not trouble the Teacher any more."
Mk     5.35    said, "Your daughter is dead.  Why     trouble the Teacher any further?"


L      8.50    But Jesus on hearing  this              answered him,
Mk     5.36    But           ignoring what they said, Jesus said to the ruler of the


L      8.50            "Do not fear; only believe, and she shall be well."
Mk     5.37    synagogue, "Do not fear, only believe." And he allowed no one to follow


Mk   5.37      him except Peter and James and John the brother of James.


L      8.51    And when he    came to the              house, he permitted no one to enter
M      9.23    And when Jesus came to the ruler's     house,              and     saw the
Mk     5.38            When they came to the house of the ruler of the synagogue, he saw a


L      8.51    with him, except Peter and John and James, and the father and mother of
M      9.23    flute players,
Mk     5.38    tumult,


L      8.52    the child. And      all were weeping and bewailing her;
M      9.23               and the crowd    making          a tumult,
Mk     5.39               and     people  weeping and  wailing loudly.  And when he


L      8.52            but he said,          "Do              not weep; for
M      9.24            |he said,          "Depart;            for the
Mk     5.39    had entered, he said to them, "Why do you make a tumult and weep?    The


L      8.53    she   is not dead but sleeping."  And they laughed at him, knowing that
M      9.25    girl  is not dead but sleeping."  And they laughed at him.  But when the
Mk     5.40    child is not dead but sleeping."  |And they laughed at him.  But


L      8.53    she was dead.
M      9.25    crowd had been put          outside,
Mk     5.40    he            put them all outside, and took the child's father and mother


L      8.54                                             But taking her
M      9.25                              he went in     and took   her
Mk     5.41    and those who were with him, and went in where the child was.  Taking her


L      8.54    by the hand he called, saying,
M      9.25    by the hand,
Mk     5.41    by the hand he            said to her, "Talitha cumi"; which means, "Little
```

388

L	8.55	"Child, arise." And her spirit returned, and
M	9.25	and the
Mk	5.42a	girl, I say to you, arise." And immediately the

L	8.55	she got up at once; and he directed that
M	9.25	girl arose.
Mk	5.43b	girl got up and walked (she was twelve years of age), |and told them

L	8.56	something should be given her to eat. And her parents were
M	9.26	And the report of this
Mk	5.42b	to give her something to eat. |and they were

L	8.56	amazed; but he charged them to tell
M	9.26	went through all that district.
Mk	5.43a	immediately overcome with amazement. And he strictly charged them that

L	8.56	no one what had happened.
Mk	5.43a	no one should know this,

37 MISSION OF THE TWELVE

Luke 9.1-9

L	9.1	And he called the twelve together and gave them power and
M	10.5	These twelve
Mk	6.7	And he called to him the twelve,
L	*10.1*	*After this the Lord appointed seventy others,*

I,	9.2	authority over all demons and to cure diseases, |and he sent them
M	10.5	Jesus sent
Mk	6.7	and began to send them
L	*10.1*	and sent them

L	9.2	out
M	10.5	out,
Mk	6.8	out two by two, and gave them authority over the unclean spirits. He
L	*10.1*	*on ahead of him, two by two,*

M	*10.5*	*charging them, "Go nowhere among the Gentiles, and enter no town of the*
Mk	*6.8*	*charged them*
L	*10.1*	* into every town and place*

M	*10.6*	*Samaritans, |but go rather to the lost sheep of the house of Israel.*
L	*10.2*	*where he himself was about to come. And he said to them, "The harvest*

L	*10.2*	*is plentiful, but the laborers are few; pray therefore the Lord of the*
L	*10.3*	*harvest to send out laborers into his harvest. Go your way; behold, I*
L	*10.3*	*send you out as lambs in the midst of wolves.*

L	9.2	to preach
M	10.7	And preach as you
M	*3.1*	*In those days came John the Baptist, preaching in the*
M	*4.17*	*From that time Jesus began to preach,*
Mk	*1.14*	*Now after John was arrested, Jesus came into Galilee, preaching the*

```
L    9.2                                                          the kingdom of
M   10.7     go,                       saying,                   'The kingdom of
  M  3.2     wilderness of Judea,          |"Repent,        for  the kingdom of
  M  4.17                     saying, "Repent,               for  the kingdom of
  Mk 1.15    gospel of God, |and saying, "The time is fulfilled, and the kingdom of
  L  10.9b                   and say to them,                   'The kingdom of
  L  10.11b                  nevertheless know this,        that the kingdom of
```

```
L    9.2     God                     and to heal.
M   10.8     heaven is    at hand.'          Heal the sick, raise the dead, cleanse
  M  3.2     heaven is    at hand."
  M  4.17    heaven is    at hand."
  Mk 1.15    God     is   at hand; repent, and believe in the gospel."
  L  10.9a   God    has come near to you.' |heal the sick in it
  L  10.11b  God    has come near.'
```

```
L    9.3                                                  And he said to them,
M   10.8     lepers, cast out demons.  You received without paying, give without pay.
```

```
L    9.3     "Take nothing for your  journey,       no staff, nor bag, nor bread,
M   10.9      Take
Mk   6.8     to take nothing for their journey except a staff; no  bread, no  bag,
  L  10.4     Carry
```

```
L    9.3     nor money;
M   10.10    no  gold, nor silver, nor copper in your  belts, |no bag for your
Mk   6.8     no  money                      in their belts;
  L  10.4     no  purse,                                  no bag,
```

```
L    9.3               and do not have   two tunics.
M   10.10    journey,             nor    two tunics, nor sandals, nor a staff
Mk   6.9     but to wear sandals and    not put on two tunics.
  L  10.4                                        no  sandals; and salute
```

```
  L  10.5     no one on the road.  Whatever house you enter, first say, 'Peace be to thi
  L  10.6     house!'  And if a son of peace is there, your peace shall rest upon him;
  L  10.7     but if not, it shall return to you.  And remain in the same house, eating
  L  10.7     and drinking what they provide,
```

```
  M  10.11a   for the laborer deserves his food.                          And
  L  10.7     for the laborer deserves his wages; do not go from house to house.
```

```
  M  10.11a   whatever              town or village you enter, find out who is worthy in
  L  10.8     Whenever you enter a town and they receive you, eat what is set before you
```

```
L    9.4         And                  whatever house you    enter,                stay
M   10.12,11b it,            |As         you enter the house, salute it.  |and stay
Mk   6.10    And he said to them, "Where     you enter a    house,                stay
```

```
L    9.4     there, and from there depart.
M   10.13    with him   until you depart.  And if the house is worthy, let your peace
Mk   6.10    there      until you leave the place.
```

```
  M  10.13    come upon it; but if it is not worthy, let your peace return to you.
  L  10.10                          But whenever you enter a town
```

```
L    9.5      And wherever they      do   not receive you,
M    10.14    And if        any one  will not receive you or                        listen to
Mk   6.11     And if        any place will not receive you and they refuse to hear
  L  10.10    and           they     do   not receive you,


L    9.5                  when you leave that town   shake off the dust                    from
M    10.14    your words,                            shake' off the dust                   from
Mk   6.11     you,        when you leave,            shake off the dust                    that
  L  10.11a               go into its streets and say, |'Even the dust of your town that


L    9.6                      your feet  as  a testimony against them."  And they departed and
M    10.15                    your feet  as you leave that house or town.  Truly, I say to you,
Mk   6.12     is      on your feet  for a testimony against them."  So they
  L  10.11a   clings to our  feet,  we wipe off       against you;


L    9.6      went through the villages, preaching the gospel
M    10.15    it shall be more tolerable on the day of judgment for the land of Sodom and
Mk   6.13     went out                and preached that men should repent.  And they cast


L    9.6                                                                    and healing
M    10.15    Comorrah than for that town.
Mk   6.13     out many demons, and anointed with oil many that were sick and healed


L    9.6      everywhere.
Mk   6.13     them.


L    9.7      Now           Herod the tetrarch heard of all that was done, and he was
M    14.1      At that time Herod the tetrarch heard about the fame of Jesus;
Mk   6.14          King Herod            heard of it;          for Jesus' name


L    9.7      perplexed, because it was said by some that          John
M    14.2                 and       he     said to his servants, "This is John the
Mk   6.14     had become known.  Some  said,                      "John the


L    9.7                  had been raised from the dead,
M    14.2      Baptist, he has been raised from the dead; that is why these powers are
Mk   6.14     baptizer   has been raised from the dead; that is why these powers are


L    9.8                  |by  some    that          Elijah had appeared, and by
M    14.2      at work in him."
Mk   6.15     at work in him."  But others said, "It is Elijah."          And


L    9.8      others that                    one of the old prophets had risen.
Mk   6.15     others said, "It is a prophet, like one of the    prophets of old."


L    9.9               Herod          said, "John      I beheaded; but who is
Mk   6.16     But when Herod heard of it he said, "John, whom I beheaded, has been


L    9.9      this about whom I hear such things?"  And he sought to see him.
Mk   6.16     raised."
```

Luke 9.10-17

```
L      9.10      On their return the apostles                         told him      what
M     14.13      Now when                            Jesus            heard this,
Mk     6.30                      The apostles returned to Jesus, and told him all that


L      9.10      they had done.
Mk     6.31      they had done and taught.  And he said to them, "Come away by yourselves


  Mk   6.31      to a lonely place, and rest a while."  For many were coming and going,
  Mk   6.31      and they had no leisure even to eat.


L      9.10      And          he took them and withdrew apart                    to a     city
M     14.13                   he                        withdrew from there in a  boat to a  lonely
Mk     6.32      And          they                      went     away      in the boat to a  lonely
J      6.1       After this Jesus                       went                         to the other


L      9.10      called Bethsaida.
M     14.13      place       apart.                                            But
Mk     6.33      place by themselves.                                          Now
J      6.2       side of the Sea of Galilee, which is the Sea of Tiberias.  And
  Mk   8.1                                                                     In those days,


L      9.11      When        the      crowds learned it,                        they followed
M     14.13      when        the      crowds heard  it,                         they followed
Mk     6.33                           many saw them going, and knew them, and they ran there
J      6.2                     a      multitude                                    followed
  Mk   8.1       when again a great crowd  had                                  gathered,


L      9.11      him;
M     14.14      him on foot from     the towns.                                As he
Mk     6.34         on foot from all the towns, and got there ahead of them.  As he
J      6.2       him,
  M    9.36                                                                When
  M   15.32                                            Then Jesus called his
  Mk   8.1       and they had nothing to eat,                        he    called his


L      9.11                                           and he    welcomed          them
M     14.14      went ashore he saw a great throng; and he had  compassion on    them,
Mk     6.34      went ashore he saw a great throng, and he had  compassion on    them,
  M    9.36                  he saw the     crowds,      he had  compassion for   them,
  M   15.32      disciples to him    and said,      "I  have compassion on the crowd,
  Mk   8.2       disciples to him,   and said to them, |"I  have compassion on the crowd,


L      9.11      and spoke to them of the kingdom of God, and cured  those who had need
M     14.14                                                and healed their sick.
Mk     6.34      because they were               like sheep without a shepherd;
J      6.2       because they saw the signs which he did on those who were diseased.
  M    9.36      because they were harassed and helpless, like sheep without a shepherd.
  M   15.32      because they have been with me now three days, and have nothing to eat;
  Mk   8.2       because they have been with me now three days, and have nothing to eat;


  J    6.3       Jesus went up on the mountain, and there sat down with his disciples.
  J    6.4       Now the Passover, the feast of the Jews, was at hand.
```

392

```
L   9.12    of healing.                                   Now the day began to wear away;
M   14.15a                                                    When it was              evening,
Mk  6.35a   and he began to teach them many things.  And when it grew              late,
J   6.5                                                   Lifting up his eyes, then, and seeing


L   9.12    and the twelve     came           and  said to him, "Send the crowd
M   14.15c      the disciples  came   to him  and  said,          send the crowds
Mk  6.36        his disciples  came   to him  and  said,          send    them
J   6.5     that a  multitude was coming to him, Jesus said to Philip,
  M  15.32                              and    I am unwilling to send      them
  Mk 8.3                                and if I                  send      them


L   9.12    away, to go into the villages and country round about, to lodge
M   14.15c  away  to go into the villages
Mk  6.36    away, to go into the country and villages round about
  M  15.32  away  hungry,            lest they      faint on the way."
  Mk 8.3    away  hungry to their homes, they will faint on the way; and some of them


J   6.5                                                       "How   are we
M   15.33                       And the disciples said  to him, "Where are we
Mk  8.4     have come a long way." And his disciples answered him, "How   can one


L   9.12    and get               provisions;                     for we
M   14.15b  and buy          food for themselves."              "This
Mk  6.35b   and buy               themselves something to eat."  "This
J   6.5     to  buy          bread, so that these people  may eat?"
  M  15.33  to  get          bread enough in the desert to feed so great a
  Mk 8.4         feed these men with bread here   in the desert?"


L   9.13    are here in a lonely place."                        But  he    said  to
M   14.16   is            a lonely place, and the day  is now over;     Jesus said,
Mk  6.37a   is            a lonely place, and the hour is now late;  But  he    answered
J   6.6                                                          This he    said
  M  15.33  crowd?"


L   9.13    them,                   "You give them something to eat."
M   14.16   "They need not go away; you give them something to eat."
Mk  6.38b   them,                   "You give them something to eat."  And when they
J   6.6     to test him, for he himself knew what he would do.


L   9.13              They                                      said,
M   14.17             They                                      said
Mk  6.38b   had found out, they                                 said,
J   6.8               One of his disciples, Andrew, Simon Peter's brother, said
  M  15.34b           They                                      said,
  Mk 8.5b             They                                      said,


L   9.13    "We    have no more than    five        loaves    and
M   14.17   to him, "We  have only       five        loaves here and
Mk  6.38b                                "Five,                and
J   6.9     to him, |"There is a lad here who has five barley loaves  and
  M  15.34b                              "Seven,               and
  Mk 8.7a                                "Seven."                     And they had


L   9.13    two      fish---
M   14.18   two      fish."                         And he    said,
Mk  6.37b   two      fish."                         And they  said to him,
J   6.7     two      fish; but what are they among so many?" Philip answered him,
  M  15.34b a few small fish."
  Mk 8.7a   a few small fish;
```

393

```
L    9.13      unless we are to go and buy
M    14.18     "Bring them here to me."
Mk   6.37b     "Shall  we          go and buy two hundred denarii               worth of
J    6.7                            "Two hundred denarii would not buy enough


L    9.13      food   for all these people."
Mk   6.38a     bread, and give it to them to eat?"  And he      said to them, "How many
J    6.7       bread  for each of them to get a little."
  M  15.34a                                          And Jesus said to them, "How many
  Mk 8.5a                                            And he      asked   them,  "How many


L    9.14                                       For there                  were about
M    14.21                                      And those who ate          were about
Mk   6.44      loaves have you? Go and see."    And those who ate the loaves were
J    6.10b                                                         in number about
  M  15.38     loaves have you?"                Those who ate             were
  Mk 8.9       loaves have you?"                And there                 were about


L    9.14      five thousand men.                          And   he     said to his
M    14.21     five thousand men, besides women and children. Then he   ordered
Mk   6.39      five thousand men.                           Then he     commanded
J    6.10a     five thousand.                               Jesus said,
  M  15.35     four thousand men, besides women and children. And      commanding
  Mk 8.6       four thousand people.                         And  he    commanded


L    9.14      disciples, "Make    them      sit down in companies, about fifty
M    14.19                 the crowds   to sit down               on the
Mk   6.39                  them all to sit down by companies upon the green
J    6.10a     "Make the people     sit down."        Now there was much
  M  15.35             the crowd   to sit down               on the
  Mk 8.6               the crowd   to sit down               on the


L    9.15      each."          And    they did so, and made them all sit down.
M    14.19     grass;
Mk   6.40      grass.    So    they                        sat down in
J    6.10a     grass in the place; so the men             sat down,
  M  15.35     ground,
  Mk 8.6       ground;


L    9.16                                      And   taking the five  loaves  and
M    14.19                                     and   taking the five  loaves  and
Mk   6.41      groups, by hundreds and by fifties. And   taking the five  loaves  and
J    6.11                               Jesus then  took  the         loaves,
  M  15.36                                     he  took  the seven loaves  and
  Mk 8.6                                   and he  took  the seven loaves,


L    9.16      the two fish he looked up to heaven, and              blessed
M    14.19     the two fish he looked up to heaven, and              blessed,
Mk   6.41      the two fish he looked up to heaven, and              blessed,
J    6.11                                   and when he had   given thanks,
  M  15.36     the       fish,                     and     having given thanks
  Mk 8.6                                           and     having given thanks


L    9.16      and broke              them,   and gave      them to the disciples
M    14.19     and broke and gave the loaves              to the disciples, and
Mk   6.41      and broke         the loaves, and gave      them to the disciples
J    6.11      he                       distributed them to
  M  15.36     he broke           them   and gave      them to the disciples, and
  Mk 8.6       he broke           them   and gave      them to his disciples
```

394

```
L    9.16                    to set        before the crowd.
M   14.19   the disciples gave them to       the crowds.
Mk   6.41                    to set        before the people; and he divided the two fish
J    6.11                         those who were seated; so also        the      fish,
  M 15.16   the disciples gave them to       the crowds.
  Mk  8.6                    to set        before the people; and they set them before the
```

```
  Mk  8.7   crowd.  And they had a few small fish; and having blessed them, he
  Mk  8.7   commanded that these also should be set before them.
```

```
L    9.17                              And        all ate   and were satisfied.
M   14.20                              And    they all ate   and were satisfied.
Mk   6.42   among them all.            And    they all ate   and were satisfied.
J    6.12   as much as they wanted.    And when they had eaten their    fill, he told his
  M 15.37                              And    they all ate   and were satisfied;
  Mk  8.8                              And    they     ate,  and were satisfied;
```

```
  J   6.12   disciples, "Gather up the fragments left over, that nothing may be lost."
```

```
L    9.17   And they took        up what          was left over, twelve baskets
M   14.20   And they took        up                              twelve baskets full
Mk   6.43   And they took        up                              twelve baskets full
J    6.13   So  they gathered them up and filled                 twelve baskets
  M 15.37   and they took        up                              seven  baskets full
  Mk  8.8   and they took        up the broken pieces left over, seven  baskets full.
```

```
L    9.17   of      broken pieces.
M   14.20   of the  broken pieces                      left over.
Mk   6.43   of      broken pieces and of the fish.
J    6.13   with fragments from the five barley loaves, left by those who had eaten.
  M 15.37   of the  broken pieces                     left over.
```

```
  J   6.14   When the people saw the sign which he had done, they said, "This is
  M 15.39   And   sending  away the crowds,     he got into the boat
  Mk  8.10   And he sent them away; and immediately he got into the boat with his
```

```
  J   6.14   indeed the prophet who is to come into the world!"
  M 15.39                        and went to the region   of Magadan.
  Mk  8.10   disciples, and went to the district of Dalmanutha.
```

39. PETER'S CONFESSION AND FIRST PREDICTION OF THE PASSION

Luke 9.18-22

```
L    9.18   Now it happened that as he was praying alone the disciples were
M   16.13   Now when              Jesus  came                   into the district
Mk   8.27   And                   Jesus  went on  with his disciples, to the villages
  J  6.66   After this                        many of his disciples drew back
```

```
L    9.18                        with him; and       he asked       them,
M   16.13   of Caesarea Philippi,                    he asked       his disciples,
Mk   8.27   of Caesarea Philippi;              and on the way he asked  his disciples,
  J  6.67   and no longer went about with him.         Jesus said to the twelve,
```

```
L    9.19   "Who do the people say that      I         am?" And they answered,
M   16.14   "Who do     men   say that the Son of man is?" And they said, "Some say
Mk   8.28   "Who do     men   say that      I         am?" And they told him,
  J  6.67      "Do you also wish to go away?"
```

395

```
L    9.19    "John the Baptist; but others say, Elijah; and others,        that one of
M   16.14    John the Baptist,        others say  Elijah, and others Jeremiah or one of
Mk   8.28    "John the Baptist; and others say,  Elijah; and others              one of


L    9.20    the old prophets has risen."  And he said to them, "But who do you say
M   16.15    the        prophets."              He said to them, "But who do you say
Mk   8.29    the        prophets."         And he asked    them, "But who do you say


L    9.20    that I am?"  And    Peter answered,
M   16.16    that I am?"  Simon Peter replied,
Mk   8.29    that I am?"        Peter answered him,
 J   1.49            Nathanael    answered him,        "Rabbi,
 J   6.68            Simon Peter answered him,        "Lord, to whom shall we go?
 J  11.27                She    said  to him, "Yes, Lord; I believe


 J   6.69    You have the words of eternal life; and we have believed, and have come


L    9.20                        "The Christ      of        God."
M   16.17            "You are the Christ, the Son of the living God."  And Jesus
Mk   8.29            "You are the Christ."
 J   1.49               you are         the Son of        God! You are the
 J   6.69    to know, that you are the Holy One      of        God."
 J  11.27            that you are the Christ, the Son of        God, he who is


M   16.17    answered him, "Blessed are you, Simon Bar-Jona!  For flesh and blood has
 J   1.49    King of Israel!"
 J  11.27    coming into the world."


M   16.18    not revealed this to you, but my Father who is in heaven.  And I tell
M   16.18    you, you are Peter, and on this rock I will build my church, and the
M   16.19    powers of death shall not prevail against it.  I will give you the keys
M   16.19    of the kingdom of heaven, and whatever you bind on earth shall be bound
M   16.19    in heaven, and whatever you loose on earth shall be loosed in heaven."


L    9.21    But  he            charged and commanded them   to tell this to no one,
M   16.20    Then he strictly charged         the disciples to tell         no one
Mk   8.30    And  he            charged              them   to tell         no one


M   16.20    that  he was the Christ.
Mk   8.30    about him.


L    9.22                                    |saying, "The Son of man
M   16.21    From that time Jesus began to show his disciples that    he
Mk   8.31    And          he    began to teach    them    that the Son of man


L    9.22    must                      suffer many things, and be rejected by  the
M   16.21    must go to Jerusalem and suffer many things              from the
Mk   8.31    must                      suffer many things, and be rejected by  the


L    9.22    elders and   chief priests and    scribes, and be killed, and on the
M   16.21    elders and   chief priests and    scribes, and be killed, and on the
Mk   8.31    elders and the chief priests and the scribes, and be killed, and after


L    9.22    third day be raised."
M   16.22    third day be raised.                        And Peter took him
Mk   8.32    three days rise again.  |And he said this plainly.  And Peter took him,
```

M	16.22	*and began to rebuke him, saying, "God forbid, Lord! This shall never*
Mk	8.32	*and began to rebuke him.*

M	16.23	*happen to you." But he turned* *and said to*
Mk	8.33	*But turning and seeing his disciples, he rebuked*

M	16.23	*Peter,* *"Get behind me, Satan! You are a hindrance to me; for*
Mk	8.33	*Peter, and said, "Get behind me, Satan!* *For*

M	16.23	*you are not on the side of God, but of men."*
Mk	8.33	*you are not on the side of God, but of men."*

40. CONDITIONS OF DISCIPLESHIP

Luke 9.23-27

L	9.23	<u>And he</u> <u>said to</u>
M	16.24	Then Jesus told his disciples,
Mk	8.34	<u>And he</u> called to him the multitude with his disciples, and <u>said to</u>

L	9.23	all, <u>"If any man would come after</u> me, <u>let him deny himself and take up</u>
M	16.24	<u>"If any man would come after</u> me, <u>let him deny himself and take up</u>
Mk	8.34	them, <u>"If any man would come after</u> me, <u>let him deny himself and take up</u>
M	10.38	*and he who does not* <u>take</u>
L	14.27	*Whoever does not* <u>bear</u>

L	9.24	<u>his</u> cross daily and <u>follow</u> me. For whoever
M	16.25	<u>his</u> cross and <u>follow</u> me. For whoever
Mk	8.35	<u>his</u> cross and <u>follow</u> me. For whoever
M	10.39	<u>his</u> cross and <u>follow</u> me *is not worthy of me.* *He who*
L	14.27	<u>his</u> *own* cross and *come after* me, *cannot be my disciple.*
L	17.33	Whoever
J	12.25	*He who*

L	9.24	<u>would</u> save <u>his life will lose</u> it; and whoever loses his life for
M	16.25	<u>would</u> save <u>his life will lose</u> it; and whoever loses his life for
Mk	8.35	<u>would</u> save <u>his life will lose</u> it; and whoever loses his life for
M	10.39	*finds* <u>his life will lose</u> it, and *he who* loses his life for
L	17.33	*seeks to gain* <u>his life will lose</u> it, *but* whoever loses his life
J	12.25	*loves* <u>his life</u> loses it, and *he who* hates his life *in*

L	9.25	<u>my sake, he</u> <u>will save</u> it. For what does it profit a
M	16.26	<u>my sake</u> <u>will find</u> it. For what will it profit a
Mk	8.36	<u>my sake</u> and the gospel's <u>will save</u> it. For what does it profit a
M	10.39	<u>my sake</u> <u>will</u> *find* it.
L	17.33	<u>will</u> *preserve* it.
J	12.25	*this world* <u>will</u> *keep* it *for eternal life. If any one*

L	9.25	<u>man</u> if he gains the whole world and loses or forfeits himself?
M	16.26	<u>man,</u> if he gains the whole world and forfeits his life? Or
Mk	8.37	<u>man,</u> to gain the whole world and forfeit his life? For
J	12.26	*serves me, he must follow me; and where I am, there shall my servant*

L	9.26	<u>For whoever is ashamed</u>
M	16.27	what shall a man give in return for his life? <u>For</u>
Mk	8.38	what can a man give in return for his life? <u>For whoever is ashamed</u>
J	12.26	*be also; if any one serves me, the Father will honor him.*

L	9.26	of me and of my words, of him
Mk	8.38	of me and of my words in this adulterous and sinful generation, of him

L	9.26	will the Son of man be ashamed when he comes in
M	16.27	the Son of man is to come with his angels in
Mk	8.38	will the Son of man also be ashamed, when he comes in

L	9.26	his glory and the glory of the Father and of the holy angels.
M	16.27	the glory of his Father, and then he will repay every man
Mk	8.38	the glory of his Father with the holy angels."

L	9.27	But I tell you truly,
M	16.28	for what he has done. Truly, I say to you,
Mk	9.1	And he said to them, "Truly, I say to you,
J	*8.51*	*Truly, truly, I say to you,*
J	*8.52*	*The Jews said to him, "Now we know that you have a demon. Abraham died,*

L	9.27	there are some standing here who will
M	16.28	there are some standing here who will
Mk	9.1	there are some standing here who will
J	*8.51*	*if any one keeps my word, he* will
J	*8.52*	*as did the prophets; and you say, 'If any one keeps my word, he* will

L	9.27	not taste death before they see the
M	16.28	not taste death before they see the Son of man coming in his
Mk	9.1	not taste death before they see that the
J	*8.51*	*never see death."*
J	*8.52*	*never taste death.'*

L	9.27	kingdom of God."
M	16.28	kingdom."
Mk	9.1	kingdom of God has come with power."

41. THE TRANSFIGURATION

Luke 9.28-36

L	9.28	Now about eight days after these sayings he took with him Peter and
M	17.1	And after six days Jesus took with him Peter and
Mk	9.2	And after six days Jesus took with him Peter and

L	9.28	John and James, and went up on the mountain to pray.
M	17.1	James and John his brother, and led them up a high mountain apart.
Mk	9.2	James and John, and led them up a high mountain apart

L	9.29	And as he was praying, the appearance of his countenance
M	17.2	And he was transfigured before them, and his face shone
Mk	9.2	by themselves; and he was transfigured before them,

L	9.29	was altered, and his raiment became dazzling white.
M	17.2	like the sun, and his garments became white as
Mk	9.3		and his garments became glistening, intensely white, as

L	9.30	And behold, two men talked with
M	17.3	light. And behold, there appeared to
Mk	9.4	no fuller on earth could bleach them. And there appeared to

L	9.31	him, Moses and Elijah, |who appeared in glory and
M	17.3	them Moses and Elijah,
Mk	9.4	them Elijah with Moses;

spoke
talking
and they were talking

L	9.32	of his departure, which he was to accomplish at Jerusalem. Now Peter
M	17.3	with him.
Mk	9.4	to Jesus.

L	9.32	and those who were with him were heavy with sleep, and when they wakened
L	9.32	they saw his glory and the two men who stood with him.

L	9.33	And as the men were parting from him, Peter said to Jesus, "Master, it
M	17.4	And Peter said to Jesus, "Lord, it
Mk	9.5	And Peter said to Jesus, "Master, it

L	9.33	is well that we are here; let us make three booths,
M	17.4	is well that we are here; if you wish, I will make three booths here,
Mk	9.5	is well that we are here; let us make three booths,

L	9.33	one for you and one for Moses and one for Elijah"-- not
M	17.5	one for you and one for Moses and one for Elijah." He was
Mk	9.6	one for you and one for Moses and one for Elijah." For he did not

L	9.34	knowing what he said. As he said this, a
M	17.5	still speaking, when lo, a bright
Mk	9.7	know what to say, for they were exceedingly afraid. And a
J	12.27	*"Now is my soul troubled. And what shall I say? 'Father, save me from*

L	9.34	cloud came and overshadowed them; and they were afraid as they entered
M	17.5	cloud overshadowed them,
Mk	9.7	cloud overshadowed them,
J	12.28	*this hour'? No, for this purpose I have come to this hour. |Father,*

L	9.35	the cloud. And a voice came out of the cloud, saying,
M	17.5	and a voice from the cloud said,
Mk	9.7	and a voice came out of the cloud,
J	12.28	*glorify thy name." Then* a voice came *from* heaven,
M	3.17	and lo, a voice *from* heaven, saying,
Mk	1.11	and a voice came *from* heaven,
L	3.22b	and a voice came *from* heaven,

L	9.35	"This is my Son, my Chosen; listen to him!"
M	17.5	"This is my beloved Son, with whom I am well pleased; listen to him."
Mk	9.7	"This is my beloved Son; listen to him."
J	12.28	*"I have glorified it, and I will glorify it again."*
M	3.17	*"This is my beloved Son, with whom I am well pleased."*
Mk	1.11	*"Thou art my beloved Son; with thee I am well pleased."*
L	3.22b	*"Thou art my beloved Son; with thee I am well pleased."*

M	17.6	*When the disciples heard this, they fell on their faces, and were*
J	12.29	*The crowd standing by heard it and said that it had thundered. Others*

M	17.7	*filled with awe. But Jesus came and touched them, saying,*
J	12.30	*said, "An angel has spoken to him." Jesus answered,*

399

```
L    9.36                                   And when the  voice had spoken,
M    17.8    "Rise, and have no fear."      And when they lifted up their eyes, they
Mk   9.8                                    And suddenly looking around        they no
  J  12.30                                       "This voice has come for your sake,
```

```
L    9.36                             Jesus was found alone.  And    they kept
M    17.9        saw no  one    but Jesus          only.  And as they were
Mk   9.9     longer saw any one with them but Jesus          only.  And as they were
  J  12.30    not for mine.
```

```
L    9.36    silence                                      and told no one in those
M    17.9    coming down the mountain, Jesus commanded them,  "Tell no one
Mk   9.9     coming down the mountain, he       charged    them to tell no one
```

```
L    9.36    days anything of what they had seen.
M    17.9                        the vision,         until the Son of man        is
Mk   9.9                         what they had seen, until the Son of man should have
```

```
M   17.9    raised from the dead."
Mk   9.9    risen  from the dead.
```

42. THE EPILEPTIC BOY

Luke 9.37-43a

```
L    9.37    On the next day, when they had  come   down from the mountain,
M    17.9    And                as    they were coming down         the mountain, Jesus
Mk   9.9     And                as    they were coming down         the mountain, he
```

```
M   17.9    commanded them,  "Tell no one the vision,      until the Son of man
Mk   9.9    charged     them to tell no one what they had seen, until the Son of man
```

```
M   17.9           is   raised from the dead."
Mk   9.9    should have risen  from the dead.
```

```
                                             a great crowd met    him.
L    9.37                                        to the crowd,
M    17.14   And when they came
Mk   9.14    And when they came to the disciples, they saw a great crowd about them,
```

```
Mk   9.15    and scribes arguing with them.  And immediately all the crowd, when they
Mk   9.16    saw him, were greatly amazed, and ran up to him and greeted him.  And he
Mk   9.16    asked them, "What are you discussing with them?"
```

```
L    9.38    And behold, a man from the crowd              cried,
M    17.14               a man came up to him and kneeling before him said,
Mk   9.17    And         one of   the crowd                answered him,
```

```
L    9.38    "Teacher, I beg you to look upon my son,    for he is  my only child;
M    17.15   |"Lord,    have mercy    on my son,        for he is  an epileptic
Mk   9.17    "Teacher, I brought       my son to you, for he has a  dumb
```

```
L    9.39    and behold, a spirit              seizes him, and he suddenly cries
M    17.15   and                          he suffers terribly; for often
Mk   9.18              spirit; and wherever it seizes him,
```

400

```
L    9.39   out; it convulses him          till he foams, and shatters him,      and
M    17.15               he falls into the fire, and often into the water.
Mk   9.18               it dashes      him down;  and   he foams   and grinds his teeth and


L    9.40   will hardly leave him.  And I begged          your disciples to cast it
M    17.16                           And I brought him to your disciples,
Mk   9.18   becomes rigid;          and I asked          your disciples to cast it


L    9.41   out, but they could not."          Jesus answered,      "O faithless
M    17.17        and they could not heal him." And Jesus answered,      "O faithless
Mk   9.19   out, and they were  not able."     And he    answered them, "O faithless
   J 14.9                                       Jesus said to him,  "Have I been


L    9.41   and perverse generation, how long am I to be with you             and
M    17.17  and perverse generation, how long am I to be with you? How long am I to
Mk   9.19             generation, how long am I to be with you? How long am I to
   J 14.9   with you              so  long  and yet you do not know me, Philip?


L    9.41   bear with you? Bring your son here."
M    17.17  bear with you? Bring      him here to me."
Mk   9.20   bear with you? Bring      him      to me." And they brought the boy
   J 14.9   He who has seen me has seen the Father; how can you say, 'Show us the


L    9.42              While he was coming, the demon tore him         and convulsed
Mk   9.20   to him; and when          the spirit saw him, immediately it convulsed
   J 14.9   Father'?


L    9.42              him.
Mk   9.20   the boy, and he fell on the ground and rolled about, foaming at the mouth.


Mk  9.21    And Jesus asked his father, "How long has he had this?" And he said,
Mk  9.22    "From childhood. And it has often cast him into the fire and into the
Mk  9.22    water, to destroy him; but if you can do anything, have pity on us and
Mk  9.23    help us." And Jesus said to him, "If you can! All things are possible
Mk  9.24    to him who believes." Immediately the father of the child cried out
Mk  9.24    and said, "I believe; help my unbelief!"


L    9.42   But     Jesus                                         rebuked the
M    17.18  And     Jesus                                         rebuked
Mk   9.25   And when Jesus saw that a crowd came running together, he rebuked the


L    9.42   unclean spirit,
M    17.18          him,
Mk   9.25   unclean spirit, saying to it, "You dumb and deaf spirit, I command you,


M  17.18                                          and
Mk 9.26     come out of him, and never enter him again." And after crying out and


M  17.18                            the demon came out of him,
Mk 9.26     convulsing him terribly, it    came out, and the boy was like a corpse;


Mk 9.27     so that most of them said, "He is dead." But Jesus took him by the hand


L    9.42                and healed the boy, and gave him back to his father.
M    17.18               and           the boy was cured instantly.
Mk   9.27   and lifted him up, and          he      arose.
```

401

```
L    9.43a    And all were astonished at the majesty of God.
M    17.19    Then                               the disciples came to Jesus privately
Mk   9.28     And when he had entered the house, his disciples asked    him    privately,


M   17.20     and said, "Why could we not cast it out?"     He said to them, "Because
Mk  9.29                 "Why could we not cast it out?" And he said to them,


M   17.20     of your little faith. For truly, I say to you, if you have faith as a
M   17.20     grain of mustard seed, you will say to this mountain, 'Move from here to
M   17.21     there,' and it will move; and nothing will be impossible to you.   But


M   17.21      this kind   never    comes  out except by                prayer and fasting."
Mk  9.29      "This kind cannot be driven out          by anything but prayer."
```

43. SECOND PREDICTION OF THE PASSION

Luke 9.43b-45

```
L    9.43b    But while  they were all marveling at everything he did,
M    17.22    As           they were    gathering              in Galilee,
Mk   9.30                  They  went on from there and passed through Galilee.  And he
  J  7.1       After this Jesus went                 about in Galilee;           he


L    9.43b                                            he
M    17.22                                          Jesus
Mk   9.31     would not have any one know it; for he was teaching his disciples,
  J  7.1      would not go about in Judea, because the Jews sought to kill him.


L    9.44     said    to his disciples, |"Let these words sink into your ears; for the
M    17.22    said    to      them,                                              "The
Mk   9.31     saying to       them,                                             "The


L    9.44     Son of man is to be delivered into the hands of men."
M    17.23    Son of man is to be delivered into the hands of men, |and they will kill
Mk   9.31     Son of man will  be delivered into the hands of men,  and they will kill


M   17.23     him, and      he                              will be raised on the
Mk  9.31      him; and when he is killed, after three days he will   rise."
  J 16.6                                                             But because


L    9.45                  But they did not    understand this saying, and it was
M    17.23    third day." And they were greatly distressed.
Mk   9.32                  But they did not    understand the  saying,
  J  16.6     I have said these things to you,  sorrow has filled your hearts.


L    9.45     concealed from them, that they should not perceive it; and they were
Mk   9.32                                                              and they were


L    9.45     afraid to ask him about this saying.
Mk   9.32     afraid to ask him.
```

Luke 9.46-50

Mk	9.33	*And they came to Capernaum; and when he was in the house he asked them,*
Mk	9.34	*"What were you discussing on the way?" But they were silent;*

L	9.46	And an argument arose among them as
M	18.1	At that time the disciples came to Jesus, saying,
Mk	9.34	for on the way they had discussed with one another

L	9.46	to which of them was the greatest.
M	18.1	"Who is the greatest in the kingdom of heaven?"
Mk	9.35	who was the greatest. *And he sat down and called the twelve;*

Mk	9.35	*and he said to them, "If any one would be first, he must be last of all*

L	9.47	But when Jesus perceived the thought of their hearts,
M	18.2	And
Mk	9.36	*and servant of all."* And

L	9.48	he took a child and put him by his side, |and
M	18.3	calling to him a child, he put him in the midst of them, |and
Mk	9.36	he took a child, and put him in the midst of them; |and

L	9.48	said to them,
M	18.3	said, *"Truly, I say to you, unless you turn and*
Mk	9.36	taking him in his arms, he said to them,

M	18.4	*become like children, you will never enter the kingdom of heaven. Whoever*
M	18.4	*humbles himself like this child, he is the greatest in the kingdom of*

L	9.48	"Whoever receives
M	18.5	heaven. "Whoever receives one
Mk	9.37	"Whoever receives one
M	10.40	"He who receives
L	10.16	"He who hears
J	12.44	*And Jesus cried out and said,* "He who believes
J	13.20	*Truly, truly, I say to you,* he who receives any

L	9.48	this child in my name receives me, and
M	18.5	such child in my name receives me;
Mk	9.37	such child in my name receives me; and
M	10.40	you receives me, and
L	10.16	you hears me, *and he who rejects you rejects me,* and
J	12.44	in me,
J	12.45	And
J	13.20	one whom I send receives me; and

L	9.48	whoever receives me receives him who sent me; for he
Mk	9.37	whoever receives me, receives not me but him who sent me."
M	10.40	he who receives me receives him who sent me.
L	10.16	he who rejects me rejects him who sent me."
J	12.44	believes not in me but in him who sent me.
J	12.45	he who sees me sees him who sent me.
J	13.20	he who receives me receives him who sent me."

L   9.48   who is least among you all is the one who is great."
M 18.6   *but whoever causes one of these little ones who believe in me to sin, it*

M 18.6   *would be better for him to have a great millstone fastened round his neck*
M 18.6   *and to be drowned in the depth of the sea.*

L   9.49   John answered, "Master, we saw a man casting out demons in your name,
Mk 9.38   John said to him, "Teacher, we saw a man casting out demons in your name,

L   9.50   and we forbade him, because he does not follow with us." But Jesus said
Mk 9.39   and we forbade him, because he was not following   us." But Jesus said,

L   9.50   to him, "Do not forbid him;
Mk 9.39   "Do not forbid him; for no one who does a mighty work in my name

L   9.50   for he that is not against
M 12.30   He who is not with
Mk 9.40   will be able soon after to speak evil of me. For he that is not against
L 11.23   He who is not with

L   9.50   you is for   you."
M 12.30   me is against me, and he who does not gather with me scatters.
Mk 9.41   us is for   us. *For truly, I say to you, whoever gives you a cup of*
L 11.23   me is against me, and he who does not gather with me scatters.

Mk 9.41   *water to drink because you bear the name of Christ, will by no means lose*
Mk 9.41   *his reward.*

45. REJECTED BY THE SAMARITANS

Luke 9.51-56

L   9.51   When the days drew near for him to be received up, he set his face to
M 20.17   *And as   Jesus was*
Mk 10.32a   *And   they were on the road,*

L   9.52   go   to Jerusalem. And he sent messengers ahead of him, who went and
M 20.17   *going up* to Jerusalem,   *he took the twelve disciples aside, and on*
Mk 10.32a   *going up* to Jerusalem, and *Jesus was walking* ahead of *them;*   and

L   9.53   entered a village of the Samaritans, to make ready for him; but the people
M 20.17   *the way he said to them,*
Mk 10.32a   *they were amazed, and those who followed were afraid.*

L   9.54   would not receive him, because his face was set toward Jerusalem. And
L   9.54   when his disciples James and John saw it, they said, "Lord, do you want
L   9.55   us to bid fire come down from heaven and consume them?" But he turned
L   9.56   and rebuked them. And they went on to another village.

46. THE DEMANDS OF DISCIPLESHIP

Luke 9.57-62

M	8.18	*Now when Jesus saw great crowds around him, he gave orders to go over to*
M	8.18	*the other side.*

L	9.57	As they were going along the road, a man said to him,
M	8.19	And a scribe came up and said to him,

L	9.58	"I will follow you wherever you go." And Jesus said to him,
M	8.20	"Teacher, I will follow you wherever you go." And Jesus said to him,

L	9.58	"Foxes have holes, and birds of the air have nests; but the Son of man
M	8.20	"Foxes have holes, and birds of the air have nests; but the Son of man

L	9.59	has nowhere to lay his head." |To another he said, "Follow me." But he
M	8.21	has nowhere to lay his head." Another of the disciples

L	9.60	said, "Lord, let me first go and bury my father." But he said
M	8.22	said to him, "Lord, let me first go and bury my father." But Jesus said

L	9.60	to him, "Leave the dead to bury their own dead; but as for
M	8.22	to him, "Follow me, and leave the dead to bury their own dead."

L	9.61	you, go and proclaim the kingdom of God." Another said, "I will follow
L	9.62	you, Lord; but let me first say farewell to those at my home." Jesus said
L	9.62	to him, "No one who puts his hand to the plow and looks back is fit for
L	9.62	the kingdom of God."

47. THE MISSION OF THE SEVENTY

Luke 10.1-12

L	10.1	After this the Lord appointed seventy others,
M	10.5	*These twelve*
Mk	6.7	*And he called to him the twelve,*
L	9.1	*And he called the twelve together and gave them power and*

L	10.1	and sent them
M	10.5	*Jesus* sent
Mk	6.7	and *began to* send them
L	9.2a	*authority over all demons and to cure diseases,* |and *he* sent them

L	10.1	on ahead of him, two by two,
M	10.5	*out,*
Mk	6.7	*out* two by two, *and gave them authority over the unclean*
L	9.2a	*out*

L	10.1	into every
M	10.5	*charging them, "Go nowhere among the Gentiles, and enter no*
Mk	6.8	*spirits. He charged them*

```
L    10.2      town and place where he himself was about to come.  And  he said to
  M   9.37                                                               Then  he said to
  M  10.6      town of the Samaritans, |but go rather to the lost sheep of the house of
  J   4.35                              Do you not say, 'There are yet four months,


L    10.2          them,      "The harvest is plentiful, but the laborers are few; pray
  M   9.38      his disciples, "The harvest is plentiful, but the laborers are few; pray
  M  10.6       Israel.
  J   4.35      then comes      the harvest'?  I tell you, left up your eyes, and see how


L    10.2      therefore the Lord of the harvest to send out laborers into his harvest.
  M   9.38      therefore the Lord of the harvest to send out laborers into his harvest."
  J   4.35      the fields are already white                      for      harvest.


L    10.3      Go your way; behold, I send you out as lambs in the midst of wolves.
  M  10.16           "Behold, I send you out as sheep in the midst of wolves;


L    10.4                          Carry
  M  10.9                          Take
  Mk  6.8                    to take nothing for their journey except a staff;
  L   9.3       And he said to them, "Take nothing for your  journey,     no staff,


L    10.4      no  purse,
  M  10.9      no  gold, nor silver, nor copper in your  belts,
  Mk  6.8       no bread, no bag, no  money                in their belts;
  L   9.3       nor bag, nor bread, nor money;


L    10.4      no bag,                                   no          sandals;
  M  10.10a    |no bag for your journey, nor      two tunics,    nor      sandals,
  Mk  6.9                           but to wear sandals and not put on two tunics.
  L   9.3            and  do  not have two tunics.


L    10.5      and salute no one on the road.  Whatever       house you enter, first
  M  10.12     nor a staff;                    As     you enter the house,
  Mk  6.10             And he said to them, "Where you enter a  house,
  L   9.4              And                    whatever         house you enter,


L    10.6      say, 'Peace be to this house!'  And if a son of peace is there, your peace
  M  10.13         salute         it.          And if the house is worthy, let your peace


L    10.6      shall rest upon him; but if     not,          it shall return
  M  10.13         come upon it; but if it is not worthy, let your peace     return


L    10.7      to you.  And remain in the same house, eating and drinking what they
  M  10.11a    to you.  And whatever town or village you enter, find out who is worthy
  Mk  6.10                  stay there
  L   9.4                   stay there,


L    10.7      provide, for the laborer deserves his wages; do not go from house to
  M  10.10b,11b in it, |for the laborer deserves his food. |and stay with him until
  Mk  6.10                                                                      until
  L   9.4                                              and from there


L    10.8      house.  Whenever you enter a town and they receive you, eat what is set
  M  10.11b    you depart.
  Mk  6.13     you leave the place.  And they cast out many demons, and anointed with
  L   9.4           depart.
```

```
L   10.9     before you; heal the sick in it
  M  10.8                     Heal the sick, raise the dead, cleanse lepers, cast out demons.
  Mk  6.13   oil many     that were sick and healed them.


L   10.9                                                   and
  M   3.1                                                  In those days
  M   4.17                                                 From that time
  M  10.8,7  You received without paying, give without pay.  And
  Mk  1.14                                                 Now after John was arrested,


L   10.9                                say to them,
  M   3.1     came John the Baptist,   preaching in the wilderness of Judea,
  M   4.17    Jesus began        to preach,                      saying,
  M  10.7                        preach   as you go,             saying,
  Mk  1.15    Jesus came into Galilee, preaching the gospel of God,   |and saying,
  L   9.2b                       to preach


L   10.9                            'The kingdom of God    has come near to you.'
  M   3.2     |"Repent,        for  the kingdom of heaven is    at hand."
  M   4.17    "Repent,         for  the kingdom of heaven is    at hand."
  M  10.7                           'The kingdom of heaven is    at hand.'
  Mk  1.15    "The time is fulfilled, and the kingdom of God    is    at hand; repent
  L   9.2b                           the kingdom of God    and to heal.


L   10.10    But whenever you enter a town and they    do   not receive you,
  M  10.14    And if                          any one   will not receive you or
  Mk  1.15    and believe in the gospel."
  Mk  6.11    And if                          any place will not receive you and they
  L   9.5     And wherever                     they     do   not receive you,


L   10.11                              go into its streets and say,  |'Even the
  M  10.14                 listen to your words,              shake off the
  Mk  6.11    refuse to hear       you,        when you leave,       shake off the
  L   9.5                                       when you leave that town  shake off the


L   10.11    dust of your town that clings to our  feet, we wipe off     against you;
  M  10.14    dust              from        your feet  as you leave that house or town.
  Mk  6.11    dust              that is   on your feet  for a testimony against them."
  L   9.5     dust              from        your feet  as  a testimony against them."


L   10.11    nevertheless know this, that the kingdom of God has come near.'


L   10.12                I tell   you,      it shall be more tolerable on that day
  M  10.15        Truly, I say to you,      it shall be more tolerable on the  day
  M  11.24        But    I tell   you that  it shall be more tolerable on the  day
  Mk  6.12    So they           went out           and preached that men should
  L   9.6     And they departed and went through the villages, preaching the gospel


L   10.12               for        Sodom            than for that town.
  M  10.15    of judgment for the land of Sodom and Gomorrah than for that town.
  M  11.24    of judgment for the land of Sodom       than for    you."
  Mk  6.12    repent.
  L   9.6     and healing everywhere.
```

Luke 10.13-24

M	11.20	*Then he began to upbraid the cities where most of his mighty works had*
M	11.20	*been done, because they did not repent.*

L	10.13	"Woe to you, Chorazin! woe to you, Bethsaida! <u>for if the mighty works</u>
M	11.21	"Woe to you, Chorazin! woe to you, Bethsaida! <u>for if the mighty works</u>

L	10.13	done in you had been done in Tyre and Sidon, they would have repented long
M	11.21	done in you had been done in Tyre and Sidon, they would have repented long

L	10.14	ago, sitting in sackcloth and ashes. But it shall be more
M	11.22	ago in sackcloth and ashes. But I tell you, it shall be more

L	10.15	tolerable in the judgment for Tyre and Sidon than for you. And you,
M	11.23	tolerable on the day of judgment for Tyre and Sidon than for you. And you,

L	10.15	Capernaum, will you be exalted to heaven? You shall be brought down to
M	11.23	Capernaum, will you be exalted to heaven? You shall be brought down to

L	10.15	Hades.
M	11.23	Hades. For if the mighty works done in you had been done in Sodom, it

M	11.24	*would have remained until this day. But I tell you that it shall be more*
M	11.24	*tolerable on the day of judgment for the land of Sodom than for you."*

L	10.16	"He who hears
M	10.40	"He who *receives*
M	18.5	*"Whoever receives one such*
Mk	9.37	*"Whoever receives one such*
L	9.48	*and* *said to them,* "Whoever *receives* *this*
J	12.44	*And* *Jesus cried out and said,* "He who *believes*
J	13.20	*Truly, truly, I* *say* *to you,* he who *receives any one*

L	10.16	you hears me, and he who rejects you rejects me, and he
M	10.40	you *receives* me, and he
M	18.5	*child in my name receives* me;
Mk	9.37	*child in my name receives* me; and
L	9.48	*child in my name receives* me, and
J	12.44	*in* me,
J	12.45	And he
J	13.20	*whom I send* *receives* me; and he

L	10.16	who rejects me rejects him who sent me."
M	10.41	who *receives* me *receives* him who sent me. *He who*
Mk	9.37	*whoever receives* me *receives not* *me but* him who sent me."
L	9.48	*whoever receives* me *receives* him who sent me; *for he*
J	12.44	*believes not in me but in* him who sent me.
J	12.45	who *sees* me *sees* him who sent me.
J	13.20	who *receives* me *receives* him who sent me."

M	10.41	*receives a prophet because he is a prophet shall receive a prophet's*
L	9.48	*who is least among you all is the one who is great."*

```
M   10.41      reward, and he who receives a righteous man because he is a righteous
M   10.42      man shall receive a righteous man's reward.  And whoever gives to one of
M   10.42      these little ones even a cup of cold water because he is a disciple,
M   10.42      truly, I say to you, he shall not lose his reward."


L    10.17                      The seventy returned with joy, saying, "Lord, even
  Mk  6.30                      The apostles returned to Jesus, and told him all that
  Mk 16.17      And these signs will accompany those who believe:  in my name they
   L  9.10a                     On their    return the apostles    told him      what


L    10.18                  the demons are subject to us in your name!"  And he said to them,
  Mk  6.30      they had done and taught.
  Mk 16.17      will cast out demons; they will speak in new tongues;
   L  9.10a      they had done.
   J 12.31                                       Now is the judgment of this world, now


L    10.19      "I saw     Satan fall like lightning from heaven.  Behold, I have given
   J 12.31      shall the ruler of this world be cast out;


L    10.19      you authority to tread upon serpents and scorpions, and over all the power
  Mk 16.18                 they will pick up serpents, and if they drink any deadly thing,


L    10.20      of the enemy; and nothing shall hurt you.  Nevertheless do not rejoice in
  Mk 16.18                 it will not       hurt them; they will lay their hands on


L    10.20      this, that the spirits are subject to you; but rejoice that your names
  Mk 16.18      the sick, and they will recover."


L    10.20      are written in heaven."


L    10.21      In that same hour he rejoiced in the Holy Spirit and said,      "I thank
M    11.25      At that       time Jesus                              declared, "I thank


L    10.21      thee, Father, Lord of heaven and earth, that thou hast hidden these
M    11.25      thee, Father, Lord of heaven and earth, that thou hast hidden these


L    10.21      things from the wise and understanding and revealed them to babes; yea,
M    11.26      things from the wise and understanding and revealed them to babes; yea,
   J  3.35                                                                        the
   J 13.3                                               Jesus, knowing that the
   J 17.25                                                            O righteous


L    10.22      Father, for such was thy gracious will.  All things have been delivered
M    11.27      Father, for such was thy gracious will.  All things have been delivered
   J  3.35      Father loves the Son,   and has given   all things into his hand.
   J 10.14                      I am the good shepherd; I know my own and my own know
   J 13.3       Father                   had given     all things into his hands, and
   J 17.25      Father,


L    10.22      to me by my Father; and no one knows who the Son is except the Father,
M    11.27      to me by my Father; and no one knows     the Son    except the Father,
   J 10.15      me, |as the Father              knows       me
   J 13.3       that he had come from God and was going to God,
   J 17.25                    the world has not known thee, but I have known    thee;
```

409

```
L    10.22    or      who       the Father is except the Son and any one to whom the
M    11.27    and no one knows the Father       except the Son and any one to whom the
  J   7.29            I    know       him, for I come from him, and he          sent me."
  J  10.15    and    I    know   the Father; and I lay down my life for the sheep.
  J  17.25    and these   know                         that thou has sent me.


L    10.22    Son chooses to reveal him."
M    11.28    Son chooses to reveal him.  Come to me, all who labor and are heavy


  M  11.29    laden, and I will give you rest.  Take my yoke upon you, and learn from
  M  11.29    me; for I am gentle and lowly in heart, and you will find rest for your
  M  11.30    souls.  For my yoke is easy, and my burden is light."


L    10.23       Then turning to the disciples he said privately, "Blessed are the  eyes
M    13.16                                        But blessed are your eyes,


L    10.24    which     see  what you see!           For    I tell    you that
M    13.17    for they  see, and your ears, for they hear. Truly, I say to you,


L    10.24    many prophets and kings          desired  to see what you see, and did not
M    13.17    many prophets and righteous men longed     to see what you see, and did not
  J   8.56    Your father Abraham rejoiced that he was to see my day;               he


L    10.24    see it, and to hear what you hear, and did not hear it."
M    13.17    see it, and to hear what you hear, and did not hear it.
  J   8.56    saw it  and  was glad."
```

49. THE GREAT COMMANDMENT AND THE GOOD SAMARITAN

Luke 10.25-37

```
L    10.25    And behold,                            a   lawyer   stood up  to put
  M  19.16    And behold,                                one     came  up  to
  Mk 10.17    And as he was setting out on his journey, a   man     ran   up  and
  L  18.18    And                                    a   ruler
  M  22.35    And one of them,                       a   lawyer,
  Mk 12.28    And one of                             the scribes  came  up  and


  Mk 12.28    heard them disputing with one another, and seeing that he answered them


L    10.25                              him             to the test, saying,
  M  19.16                              him,                          saying,
  Mk 10.17    knelt before him, and asked him,                              "Good
  L  18.18                      asked him,                                  "Good
  M  22.35                      asked him a question, to      test him.
  Mk 12.28    well,            asked him,


L    10.26    "Teacher, what          shall I do  to inherit eternal life?"      He
  M  19.17    "Teacher, what good deed must  I do, to have    eternal life?" And he
  Mk 10.18    Teacher, what          must  I do  to inherit eternal life?" And Jesus
  L  18.19    Teacher, what          shall I do  to inherit eternal life?" And Jesus
  M  22.36,37 "Teacher, which is the great commandment in the law?"        And he
  Mk 12.29         "Which        commandment is the first of all?"        Jesus
```

410

```
L    10.26    said to him,
M    19.17    said to him,  "Why do you ask  me about what is good?    One there is who
Mk   10.18    said to him,  "Why do you call me                good? No one
L    18.19    said to him,  "Why do you call me                good? No one
M    22.37    said to him,
Mk   12.29    answered,
```

```
L    10.26              "What is written                    in the law? How do you
M    19.17    is good.            If you would enter life, keep the commandments."
Mk   10.19    is good but God alone. |You              know the commandments:
L    18.20    is good but God alone. |You              know the commandments;
Mk   12.29         "The first is, 'Hear, O Israel: The Lord our God, the Lord
```

```
L    10.27    read?"  And he answered,                        "You shall love the
M    19.18              He said to him, "Which?"  And Jesus said, "You shall not kill,
Mk   10.19                                                     'Do      not kill,
L    18.20                                                     'Do      not commit
M    22.37                                                "You shall love the
Mk   12.30    is one;                                     and you shall love the
```

```
L    10.27    Lord your God with all your heart, and with all your soul, and with all
M    19.18         You shall not commit adultery, You shall not steal, You shall not
Mk   10.19            Do    not commit adultery,    Do    not steal,   Do    not
L    18.20    adultery, Do   not kill,              Do    not steal,   Do    not
M    22.37    Lord your God with all your heart, and with all your soul,
Mk   12.30    Lord your God with all your heart, and with all your soul, and with all
```

```
L    10.27    your strength, and with all your mind;
M    19.19    bear false witness,              |Honor your father and mother,
Mk   10.19    bear false witness, Do not defraud, Honor your father and mother.'"
L    18.20    bear false witness,              Honor your father and mother.'"
M    22.38              and with all your mind.  This is the great and first
Mk   12.30    your mind,    and with all your  strength.'
```

```
L    10.27                    and                        your neighbor as
M    19.19                    and,                 You shall love your neighbor as
M    22.39    commandment.  And a    second is like it, You shall love your neighbor as
Mk   12.31          The second is this,   'You shall love your neighbor as
J    15.12         "This is my commandment, that you    love one another as
```

```
L    10.28    yourself."  And      he said to him,        "You have answered right;
M    19.20    yourself."  The young man said to him,      "All these I have observed;
Mk   10.20              And     he said to him, "Teacher, all these I have observed
L    18.21              And     he said,        "All these I have observed
M    22.40    yourself.  On these two commandments depend all the law and the prophets."
Mk   12.32    yourself.'  There is no other commandment greater than these."  And the
J    15.12    I have loved you.
```

```
M    19.21    what do I still lack?"          Jesus
Mk   10.21    from my youth."      And      Jesus looking upon him loved him, and
L    18.22    from my youth."        And when Jesus heard it,              he
Mk   12.32    scribe said to him, "You are right, Teacher; you have truly said that
```

```
Mk   12.33    he is one, and there is no other but he; and to love him with all the
Mk   12.33    heart, and with all the understanding, and with all the strength, and
Mk   12.33    to love one's neighbor as oneself, is much more than all whole burnt
Mk   12.34    offerings and sacrifices."  And when Jesus saw that he answered wisely,
Mk   12.34    he said to him, "You are not far from the kingdom of God."  And after
Mk   12.34    that no one dared to ask him any question.
```

```
L   10.28                                              do this,
M   19.21    said to him, "If        you would be    perfect, go, sell     what you
Mk  10.21    said to him,            "You        lack one thing; go, sell     what you
L   18.22    said to him, "One thing you still lack.           Sell all that you
```

```
L   10.28                                              and you will live."
M   19.21    possess and give         to the poor, and you will have treasure in heaven;
Mk  10.21    have,    and give         to the poor, and you will have treasure in heaven;
L   18.22    have     and distribute to the poor, and you will have treasure in heaven;
```

```
M   19.21    and come, follow me."
Mk  10.21    and come, follow me."
L   18.22    and come, follow me."
```

L   10.29   But he, desiring to justify himself, said to Jesus, "And who is my
L   10.30   neighbor?" Jesus replied, "A man was going down from Jerusalem to
L   10.30   Jericho, and he fell among robbers, who stripped him and beat him, and
L   10.31   departed, leaving him half dead. Now by chance a priest was going down
L   10.32   that road; and when he saw him he passed by on the other side. So like-
L   10.32   wise a Levite, when he came to the place and saw him, passed by on the
L   10.33   other side. But a Samaritan, as he journeyed, came to where he was;
L   10.34   and when he saw him, he had compassion, |and went to him and bound up
L   10.34   his wounds, pouring on oil and wine; then he set him on his own beast
L   10.35   and brought him to an inn, and took care of him. And the next day he
L   10.35   took out two denarii and gave them to the innkeeper, saying, 'Take care
L   10.35   of him; and whatever more you spend, I will repay you when I come back.'
L   10.36   Which of these three, do you think, proved neighbor to the man who fell
L   10.37   among the robbers?" He said, "The one who showed mercy on him." And
L   10.37   Jesus said to him, "Go and do likewise."

50. THE HOME OF MARTHA AND MARY

Luke 10.38-42

L   10.38   Now as they went on their way, he entered a village; and a woman named
L   10.39   Martha received him into her house. And she had a sister called Mary,
L   10.40   who sat at the Lord's feet and listened to his teaching. But Martha was
L   10.40   distracted with much serving; and she went to him and said, "Lord, do
L   10.40   you not care that my sister has left me to serve alone? Tell her then
L   10.41   to help me." But the Lord answered her, "Martha, Martha, you are anxious
L   10.42   and troubled about many things; |one thing is needful. Mary has chosen
L   10.42   the good portion, which shall not be taken away from her."

51. PRAYER

Luke 11.1-13

```
L   11.1    He was praying in a certain place, and when he ceased, one of his
L   11.1    disciples said to him, "Lord, teach us to pray, as John taught his
```

```
L   11.2    disciples." And he said to them, "When you pray, say:
M    6.9                                              Pray then like this:
```

```
L   11.2            "Father,
M    6.9      Our Father who art in heaven,
```

```
L   11.2              hallowed be thy name.
M    6.9              Hallowed be thy name.


L   11.2              Thy kingdom come.
M    6.10             Thy kingdom come.


  M   6.10            Thy will be done,
  M   6.10                On earth as it is in heaven.


L   11.3              Give us each day our daily bread;
M    6.11             Give us this day our daily bread;


L   11.4              and forgive us our sins,
M    6.12             And forgive us our debts,


L   11.4                 for we ourselves forgive every one who is indebted to us;
M    6.12                As  we also have forgiven              our debtors;


L   11.4              and lead us not into temptation."
M    6.13             And lead us not into temptation,


  M   6.13            But deliver us from evil.


L   11.5              And he said to them, "Which of you who has a friend will go to him at
L   11.6              midnight and say to him, 'Friend, lend me three loaves; for a friend of
L   11.6              mine has arrived on a journey, and I have nothing to set before him';
L   11.7              and he will answer from within, 'Do not bother me; the door is now shut,
L   11.7              and my children are with me in bed; I cannot get up and give you anything'?
L   11.8              I tell you, though he will not get up and give him anything because he is
L   11.8              his friend, yet because of his importunity he will rise and give him
L   11.8              whatever he needs.


L   11.9      And          I tell    you,
  M  18.19    Again        I say to  you,  if two of   you agree on earth about anything
  M  21.22    And                          whatever you
  Mk 11.24    Therefore    I tell    you,  whatever you
  J  14.13                                 Whatever you
  J  14.14                          if      you
  J  15.7                          If       you abide in me, and my words
  J  16.23b   Truly, truly, I say to you,  if       you
  J  16.24                          Hitherto you have asked nothing in my


L   11.9                 Ask, and                it will  be given    you;
M    7.7                 "Ask, and               it will  be given    you;
  M  18.19    they       ask,                    it will  be done   for them
  M  21.22               ask  in prayer,
  Mk 11.24              ask  in prayer, believe that
  J  14.13               ask          in my name,   I  will    do          it,
  J  14.14               ask  anything in my name,  I  will    do          it.
  J  15.7     abide in you, ask  whatever you will, and it shall be done  for you.
  J  16.23b             ask  anything of the Father, he will     give it to you
  J  16.24    name;      ask,


L   11.10    seek, and you will find; knock, and it will be opened to you.  For every
M    7.8     seek, and you will find; knock, and it will be opened to you.  For every
  M  18.19   by  my  Father in heaven.
  J  14.13   that the Father may be glorified in the Son;
  J  16.23b  in   my   name.
```

413

```
L    11.10    one who asks receives, and he who seeks finds, and to him who knocks it
M     7.8     one who asks receives, and he who seeks finds, and to him who knocks it
  M  21.22          you will receive     if you have faith."
  Mk 11.24          you have received it, and it will be yours.
  J  16.24    and you will receive,    that your joy may be full.


L    11.11    will be opened.   What father among you, if his son asks      for a
M     7.9     will be opened.   Or what man    of    you, if his son asks him for


L    11.12    fish,  will instead of a fish give him a serpent; or if he asks for an
M     7.10    bread, will                 give him a stone?   Or if he asks for a


L    11.13    egg,  will give him a scorpion?  If you then, who are evil, know how to
M     7.11    fish, will give him a serpent?   If you then, who are evil, know how to


L    11.13    give good gifts to your children, how much more will the   heavenly
M     7.11    give good gifts to your children, how much more will your Father who is


L    11.13        Father give the Holy Spirit to those who ask him!"
M     7.11    in heaven give     good things to those who ask him!
```

52. HOW CAN SATAN CAST OUT SATAN?

Luke 11.14-28

```
L    11.14      Now  he was casting out
M    12.22      Then
Mk   3.19b,20   Then he went home; and the crowd came together again, so that they
  M   9.32      As   they were going away, behold,


Mk   3.21    could not even eat. And when his family heard it, they went out to
Mk   3.21    seize him, for people were saying, "He is beside himself."


L    11.14    a           demon that was dumb;                  when the demon
M    12.22    a blind and dumb      demoniac was brought to him, and he
  M   9.33    a           dumb      demoniac was brought to him. And when the demon


L    11.14    had     gone out,      the dumb man spoke,      and
M    12.23            healed him, so that the dumb man spoke and saw. And all
  M   9.33    had been cast out,     the dumb man spoke;       and
  J   7.31                                                    Yet many of


L    11.14    the people     marveled.
M    12.23    the people were amazed,          and said,   "Can this be the Son of
  M   9.33    the crowds     marveled,           saying,   "Never was anything like
  J   7.31    the people     believed in him; they said,   "When the Christ appears,


L    11.15                                But      some  of them
M    12.24    David?"                     But when the Pharisees heard it              they
Mk   3.22                                 And      the scribes   who came down from Jerusalem
  M   9.34    this seen in Israel."  But      the Pharisees
  J   7.20                                     The people
  J   7.31    will he do more signs than this man has done?"
  J   8.48                                     The Jews
  J   8.49                                       Jesus
  J   8.52                                     The Jews
  J  10.20                                     Many  of them
  J  10.21                                     Others
```

414

```
L   11.15    said,           "He casts out demons by Beelzebul,              the
M   12.24    said,           "It is only         by Beelzebul,              the
Mk   3.22    said,           "He is possessed    by Beelzebul,      and by the
 M   9.34    said,           "He casts out demons by                       the
 J   7.20    answered,       "You
 J   8.48    answered him,   "Are we not right in saying that you are a Samaritan and
 J   8.49    answered,       "I
 J   8.52    said to him,    "Now we know that you
 J  10.20    said,           "He
 J  10.21    said,           "These are not the sayings of one          who


L   11.16    prince of demons"; while others, to test him, sought from him a sign
M   12.24    prince of demons, that this man casts out      demons."
Mk   3.22    prince of demons        he   casts out the demons."
 M   9.34    prince of demons."
 J   7.20    have    a demon!  Who is seeking to kill you?"
 J   8.48    have    a demon?"
 J   8.49    have not a demon;  but I honor my Father, and you dishonor me.
 J   8.52    have    a demon.  Abraham died, as did the prophets; and you say, 'If
 J  10.20    has     a demon, and he is mad; why listen to him?"
 J  10.21    has     a demon.  Can a demon open the eyes of the blind?"


L   11.17    from heaven.  But he, knowing their thoughts,         said to them,
M   12.25                         Knowing their thoughts,      he said to them,
Mk   3.23                     And he called them to him, and said to them in
 J   8.52    any one keeps my word, he will never taste death.'


L   11.17                                        "Every kingdom    divided against
M   12.25                                        "Every kingdom    divided against
Mk   3.24    parables, "How can Satan cast out Satan?  If a   kingdom is divided against


L   11.17    itself is laid waste,            and          a divided household
M   12.25    itself is laid waste,            and no city or house     divided
Mk   3.25    itself, that kingdom cannot stand.  And if     a house  is divided


L   11.18                                     falls.  And if Satan also
M   12.26    against itself             will        stand;  and if Satan casts
Mk   3.26    against itself, that house will not be able to stand.  And if Satan has


L   11.18                           is divided against himself, how      will
M   12.26    out Satan,        he is divided against himself; how then will
Mk   3.26    risen up against himself and is divided,


L   11.18    his kingdom stand?  For you say that I cast out demons by Beelzebul.
M   12.26    his kingdom stand?
Mk   3.26    he cannot    stand, but is coming to an end.


L   11.19    And if I cast out demons by Beelzebul, by whom do your sons cast them out?
M   12.27    And if I cast out demons by Beelzebul, by whom do your sons cast them out?


L   11.20    Therefore they shall be your judges. |But if it is by the finger of God
M   12.28    Therefore they shall be your judges. |But if it is by the Spirit of God


L   11.20    that I cast out demons, then the kingdom of God has come upon you.
M   12.28    that I cast out demons, then the kingdom of God has come upon you.
```

```
L    11.21   When                    a strong man, fully armed, guards his own palace,
M    12.29   Or how can one enter a strong man's                              house
Mk    3.27   But no one can enter a strong man's                              house


L    11.22                 his goods are in peace; but when one stronger than he
M    12.29   and plunder his goods,            unless  he first
Mk    3.27   and plunder his goods,            unless  he first


L    11.22   assails him and overcomes him, he takes away his armor in which he
M    12.29   binds the strong man?                              Then
Mk    3.27   binds the strong man;                              then


L    11.22   trusted, and divides his spoil.
M    12.29   indeed he may plunder his house.
Mk    3.27   indeed he may plunder his house.


Mk    9.38   John said to him, "Teacher, we saw a man casting out demons in your name,
L     9.49   John answered,   "Master, we saw a man casting out demons in your name,

Mk    9.39   and we forbade him, because he was  not following  us." But Jesus said,
L     9.50   and we forbade him, because he does not follow with us."  But Jesus said

Mk    9.39           "Do not forbid him; for no one who does a mighty work in my name
L     9.50   to him, "Do not forbid him;

Mk    9.39   will be able soon after to speak evil of me.


L    11.23       He who  is not with   me  is against me, and he who does not gather
M    12.30       He who  is not with   me  is against me, and he who does not gather
Mk    9.40,41 For he that is not against us  is for   us. For truly, I say to you,
L     9.50   for he that is not against you is for    you."


L    11.23   with me scatters.
M    12.31   with me scatters. Therefore I tell   you, every sin and blasphemy will
Mk    3.28                    "Truly,  I say to you, all  sins           will
Mk    9.41   whoever gives you a cup of water to drink because you bear the name of


M    12.31   be forgiven           men,                              but
Mk    3.29   be forgiven the sons of men, and whatever blasphemies they utter; but
Mk    9.41   Christ, will by no means lose his reward.

M    12.32       the blasphemy  against the     Spirit will not  be forgiven.  And
Mk    3.29   whoever blasphemes against the Holy Spirit      never has forgiveness,

M    12.32   whoever says a word against the Son of man will be forgiven; but whoever

M    12.32   speaks against the Holy Spirit will not be forgiven, either in this age
Mk    3.30   but is guilty of an eternal sin"--for they had said, "He has an unclean

M    12.32   or in the age to come.
Mk    3.30   spirit."


L    11.24   "When the unclean spirit has gone out of a man, he passes through
M    12.43   "When the unclean spirit has gone out of a man, he passes through


L    11.24   waterless places seeking rest; and    finding none     he says, 'I
M    12.44   waterless places seeking rest, but he finds    none. Then he says, 'I
```

416

L	11.25	will return to my house from which I came.'	And when he comes he finds
M	12.44	will return to my house from which I came.'	And when he comes he finds

L	11.26	it swept and put in order. Then he goes and brings
M	12.45	it empty, swept, and put in order. Then he goes and brings with him

L	11.26	seven other spirits more evil than himself, and they enter and dwell
M	12.45	seven other spirits more evil than himself, and they enter and dwell

L	11.26	there; and the last state of that man becomes worse than the first."
M	12.45	there; and the last state of that man becomes worse than the first. So

M	*12.45*	*shall it be also with this evil generation."*

L	11.27	As he said this, a woman in the crowd raised her voice and said to him,
L	11.27	"Blessed is the womb that bore you, and the breasts that you sucked!"
L	11.28	But he said, "Blessed rather are those who hear the word of God and keep
L	11.28	it!"

53. AN EVIL GENERATION SEEKS A SIGN

Luke 11.29-32

L	11.29	When the crowds were
M	12.38	Then some of the scribes and Pharisees
Mk	8.11	The Pharisees came and
M	*16.1*	*And the Pharisees and Sadducees came, and*

L	11.29	increasing,
M	12.38	said to him, "Teacher, we wish to
Mk	8.11	began to argue with him, seeking from him
M	*16.1*	*to test him they asked him to*

L	11.29	he began
M	12.39	see a sign from you." But he
Mk	8.12	a sign from heaven, to test him. And he sighed
M	*16.2*	*show them a sign from heaven.* He

L	11.29	to say,
M	12.39	answered them,
Mk	8.12	deeply in his spirit, and said,
M	*16.2*	*answered them, "When it is evening, you say,*

M	*16.3*	*'It will be fair weather; for the sky is red.' And in the morning, 'It*
M	*16.3*	*will be stormy today, for the sky is red and threatening.' You know how*
M	*16.3*	*to interpret the appearance of the sky, but you cannot interpret the signs*

L	11.29	"This generation is an evil generation; it seeks a
M	12.39	"An evil and adulterous generation seeks for a
Mk	8.12	"Why does this generation seek a
M	*16.4*	*of the times. An evil and adulterous generation seeks for a*

417

L	11.29	sign, but	no sign shall be given to	it except the
M	12.39	sign; but	no sign shall be given to	it except the
Mk	8.12	sign? Truly, I say to you,	no sign shall be given to this	generation."
M	*16.4*	sign, but	no sign shall be given to	it except the

L	11.30	sign of	Jonah.	For as Jonah became	a sign to the
M	12.40	sign of the prophet Jonah.	For as Jonah was	three days and
Mk	8.13		And he left them, and getting into the boat
M	*16.4*	sign of	Jonah." *So he left them and*

L	11.30	men of Nineveh,	so will the Son of man be to this
M	12.40	three nights in the belly of the whale,	so will the Son of man be three
Mk	8.13	again he departed to the other side.
M	*16.4*	*departed.*

L	11.31	generation.	The queen of the South
M	12.42	days and three nights in the heart of the earth.	The queen of the South

L	11.31	will arise at the judgment with the men of this generation and condemn
M	12.42	will arise at the judgment with this generation and condemn

L	11.31	them; for she came from the ends of the earth to hear the wisdom of Solomon,
M	12.42	it; for she came from the ends of the earth to hear the wisdom of Solomon,

L	11.32	and behold, something greater than Solomon is here.	The men of Nineveh
M	12.41	and behold, something greater than Solomon is here.	The men of Nineveh

L	11.32	will arise at the judgment with this generation and condemn it; for they
M	12.41	will arise at the judgment with this generation and condemn it; for they

L	11.32	repented at the preaching of Jonah, and behold, something greater than
M	12.41	repented at the preaching of Jonah, and behold, something greater than

L	11.32	Jonah is here.
M	12.41	Jonah is here.

54. THE LAMP

Luke 11.33-36

M	*5.14*	*"You are the light of the world. A city set on a hill cannot be hid.*

L	11.33	"No one after lighting a lamp	puts	it in a cellar
M	5.15	Nor do men light a lamp	and put	it
Mk	4.21	And he said to them, "Is a lamp brought in to be put
L	*8.16*	*"No one after lighting a lamp*	*covers it*

L	11.33	or under a bushel,	but	on a stand, that
M	5.15	under a bushel,	but	on a stand, and
Mk	4.21	under a bushel, or	under a bed, and not	on a stand?
L	*8.16*	*with a vessel, or puts it under a bed,*	*but puts it*	*on a stand, that*

418

L	11.33	those who enter may see the light.
M	5.16	it gives light to all in the house. *Let your light so shine before men,*
L	8.16	those who enter may see the light.

M	5.16	*that they may see your good works and give glory to your Father who is*
M	5.16	*in heaven.*

L	11.34	Your eye is the lamp of your body; when your eye is sound, your
M	6.22	"The eye is the lamp of the body. So, if your eye is sound, your

L	11.34	whole body is full of light; but when it is not sound, your
M	6.23	whole body will be full of light; but if your eye is not sound, your

L	11.35	body is full of darkness. Therefore be careful lest the
M	6.23	whole body will be full of darkness. If then the

L	11.36	light in you be darkness. If then your whole body is full of light,
M	6.23	light in you is darkness, how great is the darkness!

L	11.36	having no part dark, it will be wholly bright, as when a lamp with its
L	11.36	rays gives you light."

55. WOES UPON PHARISEES AND LAWYERS

Luke 11.37-54

L	11.37	he went in and sat at table.
M	15.1	scribes came to Jesus from Jerusalem
Mk	7.2	some of the scribes, who had come from Jerusalem, |*they saw that*
L	7.36	he went *into the Pharisee's house, and took his place at table.*

Mk	7.3	*some of his disciples ate with hands defiled, that is, unwashed. (For*
Mk	7.3	*the Pharisees, and all the Jews, do not eat unless they wash their hands,*
Mk	7.4	*observing the tradition of the elders; and when they come from the*
Mk	7.4	*market place, they do not eat unless they purify themselves; and there*
Mk	7.4	*are many other traditions which they observe, the washing of cups and*
Mk	7.4	*pots and vessels of bronze.)*

L	11.38	The Pharisee was astonished to see
M	15.2	and said, |"Why do your disciples
Mk	7.5	And the Pharisees and the scribes asked him, "Why do your disciples

L	11.38	that he did not
M	15.2	transgress the tradition of the elders? For they do not
Mk	7.5	not live according to the tradition of the elders, but

L	11.39	first wash before dinner. And the Lord said to him, "Now
M	15.2	wash their hands when they eat."
M	23.25	"Woe to you, scribes
Mk	7.5	eat with hands defiled?"

419

L	11.39	you Pharisees <u>cleanse the outside of the cup and of</u>
M	23.25	and <u>Pharisees</u>, hypocrites! for you <u>cleanse the outside of the cup and of</u>

L	11.40	<u>the dish, but inside you are full of extortion and</u> wickedness. <u>You</u>
M	23.26	<u>the plate, but inside</u> they <u>are full of extortion and</u> rapacity. <u>You</u> blind

L	11.41	<u>fools! Did not he who made the outside make the inside also?</u> <u>But give</u>
M	23.26	Pharisee! first cleanse <u>the inside</u> of the cup and

L	11.41	<u>for alms those things which are within; and behold, everything is clean</u>
M	23.26	of the plate, that the outside also may be <u>clean</u>.

L	11.41	<u>for you.</u>

L	11.42	"But <u>woe to you</u> <u>Pharisees</u>! <u>for you tithe mint</u>
M	23.23	"<u>Woe to you</u>, scribes and <u>Pharisees</u>, hypocrites! <u>for you tithe mint</u>

L	11.42	<u>and</u> rue <u>and every herb, and</u> neglect
M	23.23	<u>and</u> dill <u>and</u> cummin, <u>and</u> have neglected the weightier matters of the
J	5.42	*But I know*

L	11.42	<u>justice and the love of God</u>; <u>these you ought to have done</u>,
M	23.23	law, <u>justice and</u> mercy and faith; <u>these you ought to have done</u>,
J	5.42	*that you have not* <u>the love of God</u> *within you.*

L	11.42	<u>without neglecting the others.</u>
M	23.24	<u>without neglecting the others.</u> *You blind guides, straining out a gnat*

M	23.24	*and swallowing a camel!*

M	23.5	*They do all their deeds to be seen by men; for they make their phylacteries*
Mk	12.38b	*who like to go about*
L	20.46a	*who like to go about*

L	11.43	<u>Woe to you Pharisees</u>! <u>for you</u> <u>love</u>
M	23.6	*broad and their fringes long,* and they <u>love</u> the place of honor
Mk	12.39b	*in long robes,* and the places of honor
L	20.46d	*in long robes,* and *the places of honor*

L	11.43	<u>the best seat in the synagogues</u> and
M	23.7	at feasts and <u>the best seats in the synagogues</u>, and
Mk	12.39a,38c	*at feasts,* |and <u>the best seats in the synagogues</u> and to have
L	20.46c,b	*at feasts,* |*and* <u>the best seats in the synagogues</u> |and *love*

L	11.43	<u>salutations in the market places.</u>
M	23.8	<u>salutations in the market places</u>, and being called rabbi by men. *But you*
Mk	12.38c	<u>salutations in the market places</u>
L	20.46b	<u>salutations in the market places</u>

M	23.8	*are not to be called rabbi, for you have one teacher, and you are all*
M	23.9	*brethren. And call no man your father on earth, for you have one Father,*
M	23.10	*who is in heaven. Neither be called masters, for you have one master,*
M	23.11,12	*the Christ. He who is greatest among you shall be your servant; whoever*
M	23.12	*exalts himself will be humbled, and whoever humbles himself will be exalted*

L	11.44	Woe to you! <u>for you are like</u>
M	23.27	"<u>Woe to you</u>, scribes and Pharisees, hypocrites! <u>for you are like</u>

L	11.44	<u> graves which are not seen, and men walk over them without</u>
M	23.27	whitewashed tombs, <u>which</u> outwardly appear beautiful, but within they

L	11.44	<u>knowing it.</u>"
M	23.28	are full of dead men's bones and all uncleanness. *So you also outwardly*
M	*23.28*	*appear righteous to men, but within you are full of hypocrisy and*
M	*23.28*	*iniquity.*

L	11.45	<u>One of the lawyers answered him, "Teacher, in saying this you reproach</u>

L	11.46	<u>us also.</u>" And he said,
M	23.1	Then said Jesus to the crowds
Mk	12.38a	And in his teaching he said,
L	*20.45*	And *in the hearing of all the people* he said

L	11.46	"Woe to you lawyers also!
M	23.2	and to his disciples, ⌐"The scribes and the Pharisees sit on
Mk	12.38a	"Beware of the scribes,
L	*20.46a*	*to his disciples,* ⌐*"Beware of the scribes,*

M	*23.3*	*Moses' seat; so practice and observe whatever they tell you, but not what*
M	*23.3*	*they do; for they preach, but do not practice.*

L	11.46	<u>for you load men with burdens hard to bear,</u>
M	23.4	They bind heavy <u>burdens, hard to bear</u>, and lay them on men's

L	11.46	<u>and you yourselves do not touch the burdens with one of your</u>
M	23.4	shoulders; but they themselves will <u>not</u> move them <u>with</u> their

L	11.47	<u>fingers.</u> Woe to you! <u>for you build the</u>
M	23.29	<u>finger.</u> "Woe to you, scribes and Pharisees, hypocrites! <u>for you build the</u>

L	11.47	<u>tombs of the prophets whom your fathers killed.</u>
M	23.30	<u>tombs of the prophets</u> and adorn the monuments of the righteous, ⌐saying,

L	11.48	<u>So you are witnesses and consent to the deeds of your fathers; for they</u>
M	23.30	'If we had lived in the days <u>of</u> our <u>fathers,</u> we would

L	11.48	<u>killed them, and you build their tombs.</u>
M	23.30	not have taken part with them in shedding the blood of the prophets.'

M	*23.31*	*Thus you witness against yourselves, that you are sons of those who*
M	*23.32*	*murdered the prophets. Fill up, then, the measure of your fathers.*
M	*23.33*	*You serpents, you brood of vipers, how are you to escape being sentenced*

L	11.49	<u>Therefore also the Wisdom of God said,</u> '<u>I will send them</u>
M	23.34	*to hell?* <u>Therefore</u> <u>I</u> send you

L	11.49	prophets and apostles, some of whom they will kill
M	23.34	prophets and wise men and scribes, some of whom you will kill and

L	11.49	and persecute,'
M	23.34	crucify, and some you will scourge in your synagogues and persecute from

L	11.50	that the blood of all the
M	23.35	town to town, that upon you may come all the righteous blood

L	11.51	prophets, shed from the foundation of the world, may be required of this
M	23.35	shed on earth,

L	11.51	generation, from the blood of Abel to the blood of Zechariah,
M	23.35	from the blood of innocent Abel to the blood of Zechariah

L	11.51	who perished between the altar and the sanctuary.
M	23.35	the son of Barachiah, whom you murdered between the sanctuary and the altar.

L	11.51	Yes, I tell you, it shall be required of this generation.
M	23.36	Truly, I say to you, all this will come upon this generation.

L	11.52	Woe to you lawyers! for you have taken
M	23.13	"But woe to you, scribes and Pharisees, hypocrites! because you shut

L	11.52	away the key of knowledge; you did not enter yourselves,
M	23.13	the kingdom of heaven against men; for you neither enter yourselves,

L	11.52	and you hindered those who were entering."
M	23.13	nor allow those who would enter to go in.

L	11.53	As he went away from there, the scribes and the Pharisees began to
Mk	12.13	*And they sent to him some of the Pharisees and some of*

L	11.54	press him hard, and to provoke him to speak of many things, lying in
Mk	12.13	*the Herodians,*

L	11.54	wait for him, to catch at something he might say.
Mk	12.13	*to entrap him in his talk.*

56. INSTRUCTION OF THE TWELVE

Luke 12.1-12

L	12.1	In the meantime, when so many thousands of the
M	16.5	When the disciples reached the other side, they had forgotten to bring
Mk	8.14	Now they had forgotten to bring

L	12.1	multitude had gathered together that they trod upon one another, he
M	16.6	any bread. Jesus
Mk	8.15	bread; and they had only one loaf with them in the boat. And he

L	12.1	began	to say to his disciples first, "Beware of the leaven
M	16.6		said to them, "Take heed and beware of the leaven
Mk	8.15	cautioned them, saying, "Take heed, beware of the leaven

L	12.1	of the Pharisees, which is hypocrisy.
M	16.6	of the Pharisees and Sadducees."
Mk	8.15	of the Pharisees and the leaven of Herod."

L	12.2	Nothing is covered up that will
M	10.26	"So have no fear of them; for nothing is covered that will
Mk	4.22	For there is nothing hid, except to
L	8.17	For nothing is *hid* that *shall*

L	12.2	not be revealed, or hidden that will not be known.
M	10.26	not be revealed, or hidden that will not be known.
Mk	4.22	be made manifest; nor is anything secret
L	8.17	not be *made manifest, nor anything secret that shall* not be known

L	12.3	Therefore whatever you have said in the dark shall be heard in the
M	10.27	What I tell you in the dark, utter in the
Mk	4.22	except to come to
L	8.17	*and come to*

L	12.3	light, and what you have whispered in private rooms shall be proclaimed
M	10.27	light; and what you hear whispered proclaim
Mk	4.22	light.
L	8.17	light.

L	12.4	upon the housetops. "I tell you, my friends, do not fear those who kill
M	10.28	upon the housetops. And do not fear those who kill

L	12.5	the body, and after that have no more that they can do. But I will warn
M	10.28	the body but cannot kill the soul; rather

L	12.5	you whom to fear: fear him who, after he has killed, has power to cast
M	10.28	fear him who can destroy both soul and body

L	12.6	into hell; yes, I tell you, fear him! Are not five sparrows sold for two
M	10.29	in hell. Are not two sparrows sold for a

L	12.6	pennies? And not one of them is forgotten before God.
M	10.29	penny? And not one of them will fall to the ground without your Father's

L	12.7	Why, even the hairs of your head are all numbered. Fear not;
M	10.30,31	will. But even the hairs of your head are all numbered. Fear not,
L	21.18	*But not a hair of your head will perish.*

L	12.8	you are of more value than many sparrows. "And I tell you,
M	10.32	therefore; you are of more value than many sparrows. So

L	12.8	every one who acknowledges me before men, the Son of man also will
M	10.32	every one who acknowledges me before men, I also will

```
L    12.9    acknowledge before the angels of God;                              but he who
M    10.33   acknowledge before              my Father who is in heaven; but        whoever
  Mk  8.38                                                               For        whoever
  L   9.26                                                               For        whoever


L    12.9        denies    me     before men
M    10.33       denies    me     before men,
  Mk  8.38   is ashamed of me and of my words in this adulterous and sinful generation,
  L   9.26   is ashamed of me and of my words,


L    12.9                                      will be denied
M    10.33              I          also will     deny
  Mk  8.38   of him will the Son of man also      be ashamed, when he comes in the glory
  L   9.26   of him will the Son of man           be ashamed  when he comes in his glory


L    12.10            before the angels of  God.  And every one who speaks a word
M    10.33            before            my  Father who is in heaven.
M    12.32                                     And whoever      says   a word
  Mk  8.38               of              his Father with   the holy angels."
  L   9.27   and the glory of              the Father and of the holy angels.  But I


L    12.10   against the Son of man will be forgiven; but he who blasphemes against
M    12.32   against the Son of man will be forgiven; but whoever speaks      against
  L   9.27   tell you truly, there are some standing here who will not taste death


L    12.10   the Holy Spirit will not be forgiven.
M    12.32   the Holy Spirit will not be forgiven, either in this age or in the age to
  L   9.27   before they see the kingdom of God."


  M  10.16       "Behold, I send you out as sheep in the midst of wolves; so be wise as

  M  10.17   serpents and innocent as doves.  Beware of men; for they will deliver
  M  12.32   come.
  Mk 13.9                     "But take heed to yourselves; for they will deliver
  M  24.9                                 "Then they will deliver
  L  21.12               But before all this            they will lay their


L    12.11                     And when they        bring    you before the
M    10.17   you up to councils,    and             flog     you in        their
Mk   13.9    you up to councils;    and    you will be beaten    in
  M  24.9    you up to tribulation, and             put      you to
  L  21.12   hands on you and persecute you,        delivering you up to   the
  J  16.2a                     They will    put     you out of the


L    12.11   synagogues          and                      the rulers    and
M    10.18   synagogues,       | and you will be dragged before    governors and
Mk   13.9    synagogues;         and you will   stand  before    governors and
  M  24.9    death;              and you will be hated by all nations for my name's
  L  21.12   synagogues and prisons, and you will be brought before   kings    and
  J  16.2a   synagogues;


L    12.11   the authorities,
M    10.18         kings    for my     sake,                    to bear
Mk   13.9         kings    for my     sake,                    to bear
  M  24.9    sake.
  L  21.13        governors for my name's sake.  This will be a time for you to bear
```

```
M  10.18    testimony before them and the Gentiles.
Mk 13.10    testimony before them.  And the gospel must first be preached to all
L  21.13    testimony.


L  12.11                                                                  do not be
M  10.19                When they                   deliver you up, do not be
Mk 13.11    nations.  And when they bring you to trial and deliver you up, do not be
L  21.14                Settle it therefore in your minds,              not to


L  12.11    anxious              how or what you are to answer or what you are to say;
M  10.19    anxious              how          you are to speak  or what you are to say;
Mk 13.11    anxious  beforehand                                 what you are to say;
L  21.14    meditate beforehand how                  to answer;


M  10.20    for     what you are to say will be given to you in that hour; |for it is
Mk 13.11    but say whatever               is given    you in that hour,  for it is
L  21.15    for      I          will    give    you a mouth and wisdom, which


L  12.12                            for          the Holy Spirit
M  10.20    not you who speak, but          the      Spirit   of your Father
Mk 13.11    not you who speak, but          the Holy Spirit.
L  21.15    none of your adversaries will be able to withstand or contradict.
J  14.26                 But the Counselor, the Holy Spirit, whom the Father


L  12.12                            will teach you in that very hour
J  14.26    will send in my name, he will teach you all things, and bring to your


L  12.12                               what    you ought to say."
M  10.20                    speaking through you.
J  14.26    remembrance all that I have said    to     you.
```

57. THE RICH FOOL

Luke 12.13-21

```
L  12.13    One of the multitude said to him, "Teacher, bid my brother divide the
L  12.14    inheritance with me."  But he said to him, "Man, who made me a judge or
L  12.15    divider over you?"  And he said to them, "Take heed, and beware of all
L  12.15    covetousness; for a man's life does not consist in the abundance of his
L  12.16    possessions."  And he told them a parable, saying, "The land of a rich
L  12.17    man brought forth plentifully; and he thought to himself, 'What shall I
L  12.18    do, for I have nowhere to store my crops?'  And he said, 'I will do this:
L  12.18    I will pull down my barns, and build larger ones; and there I will store
L  12.19    all my grain and my goods.  And I will say to my soul, Soul, you have
L  12.19    ample goods laid up for many years; take your ease, eat, drink, be merry.'
L  12.20    But God said to him, 'Fool! This night your soul is required of you; and
L  12.21    the things you have prepared, whose will they be?'  So is he who lays
L  12.21    up treasure for himself, and is not rich toward God."
```

58. TRUST AND FAITHFULNESS

Luke 12.22-48

```
L  12.22    And he said to his disciples, "Therefore I tell you, do not be anxious
M   6.25                                  "Therefore I tell you, do not be anxious
```

```
L   12.22   about your life, what you shall eat,                              nor about
M    6.25   about your life, what you shall eat or what you shall drink, nor about


L   12.23   your body, what you shall put on.  For life is more than food, and the
M    6.25   your body, what you shall put on.  Is not life more than food, and the


L   12.24   body more than clothing.  Consider the ravens:        they neither sow
M    6.26   body more than clothing?  Look  at the birds of the air: they neither sow


L   12.24   nor reap, they have neither storehouse nor barn,  and yet
M    6.26   nor reap            nor      gather    into barns, and yet your heavenly


L   12.24   God     feeds them.                Of how much more value are you than the
M    6.26   Father feeds them.    Are you not of           more value         than
   M 10.31  Fear not, therefore; you are    of           more value         than many
   L 12.7b  Fear not;            you are    of           more value         than many


L   12.25   birds!  And which of you by being anxious can add a    cubit to his span
M    6.27   they?   And which of you by being anxious can add one cubit to his span
   M 10.31  sparrows.
   L 12.7b  sparrows.


L   12.26   of life?  If then you are not able to do as small a thing as that, why
M    6.28   of life?                                                   And why


L   12.27   are you anxious about the rest?  Consider the lilies,          how
M    6.28   are you anxious about clothing?  Consider the lilies of the field, how


L   12.27   they grow; they neither toil nor spin;  yet I tell you, even Solomon in
M    6.29   they grow; they neither toil nor spin; |yet I tell you, even Solomon in


L   12.28   all his glory was not arrayed like one of these.  But if God so clothes
M    6.30   all his glory was not arrayed like one of these.  But if God so clothes


L   12.28   the grass which is alive  in the field today and tomorrow is thrown into
M    6.30   the grass of the field, which today is alive and tomorrow is thrown into


L   12.28   the oven, how much more will he clothe you, O men of little faith!
M    6.30   the oven, will he not much more clothe you, O men of little faith?


L   12.29   And      do not seek              what you are to eat  and what
M    6.31   Therefore do not be anxious, saying, 'What shall   we eat?' or 'What


L   12.30   you are to drink, nor  be of anxious mind.  For all the nations of the
M    6.32   shall   we drink?' or 'What shall we wear?'  For      the Gentiles


L   12.30   world seek    these things; and your        Father knows that you
M    6.32         seek all these things; and your heavenly Father knows that you


L   12.31   need them.   Instead, seek      his kingdom,
M    6.33   need them all.  But      seek first his kingdom and his righteousness,
```

426

```
L    12.31     and      these things shall be yours as well.
M     6.33     and all these things shall be yours as well.


L    12.32     "Fear not, little flock, for it is your Father's good pleasure to give
  M   6.19     "Do not lay up for yourselves treasures on earth,
  L  22.29                              and I                                    assign


L    12.32     you                                    the kingdom.
  M   6.19                                              where moth and rust
  M  19.21                     Jesus                   said to him, "If you
  Mk 10.21      And    Jesus looking upon him loved him, and said to him, "You lack
  L  18.22      And when Jesus heard it,        he said to him, "One thing
  L  22.29      to you, as my Father assigned to me, a     kingdom,


L    12.33                          Sell        your possessions, and give
  M   6.19     consume and where thieves break in and steal,
  M  19.21     would be perfect, go, sell    what you  possess     and give      to
  Mk 10.21          one thing; go, sell    what you  have,       and give      to
  L  18.22     you still lack.      Sell all that you  have        and distribute to


L    12.33         alms; provide   yourselves with purses that do not grow old, with a
  M   6.30              but lay up for yourselves
  M  19.21     the poor,                                  and you will have
  Mk 10.21     the poor,                                  and you will have
  L  18.22     the poor,                                  and you will have


L    12.33     treasure  in the heavens that does not fail,              where
  M   6.20     treasures in    heaven, where neither moth nor rust consumes and where
  M  19.21     treasure  in    heaven; and come, follow me."
  Mk 10.21     treasure  in    heaven; and come, follow me."
  L  18.22     treasure  in    heaven; and come, follow me."


L    12.33     no     thief   approaches    and no    moth    destroys.
  M   6.20     neither moth nor rust consumes and where thieves do not break in and steal.


L    12.34     For where your treasure is, there will your heart be also.
  M   6.21     For where your treasure is, there will your heart be also.


L  12.35,36    "Let your loins be girded and your lamps burning, |and be like men who
L  12.36       are waiting for their master to come home from the marriage feast, so
L  12.37       that they may open to him at once when he comes and knocks.  Blessed are
L  12.37       those servants whom the master finds awake when he comes; truly, I say
L  12.37       to you, he will gird himself and have them sit at table, and he will


L  12.38       come and serve them.                    If        he
Mk 13.35       Watch therefore---for you do not know when the master of the house will


L  12.38       comes in the second watch, or in the third,
Mk 13.35       come, in the evening,      or at midnight, or at cockcrow, or in the


L  12.38                                  and finds them so, blessed are those
Mk 13.36,37    morning--|lest he come suddenly and find you asleep.  And what I say to


L  12.39       servants! But know this, that if the householder had known at what
M  24.43                 But know this, that if the householder had known in what part
Mk 13.37       you I say to all: Watch."
```

L	12.39	hour the thief was coming, he would not
M	24.43	of the night the thief was coming, he would have watched and would not

L	12.40	have left his house to be broken into. You also must be ready;
M	24.44	have let his house be broken into. Therefore you also must be ready;

L	12.40	for the Son of man is coming at an unexpected hour."
M	24.44	for the Son of man is coming at an hour you do not expect.

L	12.41	Peter said, "Lord, are you telling this parable for us or for all?"

L	12.42	/ And the Lord said, "Who then is the faithful and wise steward, whom his
M	24.45	"Who then is the faithful and wise servant, whom his

L	12.42	master will set over his household, to give them their portion of food
M	24.45	master has set over his household, to give them their food

L	12.43	at the proper time? Blessed is that servant whom his master when he
M	24.46	at the proper time? Blessed is that servant whom his master when he

L	12.44	comes will find so doing. Truly, I say to you, he will set him over
M	24.47	comes will find so doing. Truly, I say to you, he will set him over

L	12.45	all his possessions. But if that servant says to himself, 'My
M	24.48	all his possessions. But if that wicked servant says to himself, 'My

L	12.45	master is delayed in coming,' and begins to beat the menservants and the
M	24.49	master is delayed,' |and begins to beat his fellow servants,

L	12.46	maidservants, and to eat and drink and get drunk, the master of
M	24.50	and eats and drinks with the drunken, |the master of

L	12.46	that servant will come on a day when he does not expect him and at an
M	24.50	that servant will come on a day when he does not expect him and at an
M	22.13	*Then the king said*
L	13.28b	*when you see Abraham and Isaac and Jacob*

L	12.46	hour he does not know, and will punish him, and put
M	24.51	hour he does not know, |and will punish him, and put
M	8.12	*while the sons of the kingdom will be* *thrown*
M	13.42	*and* *throw*
M	13.50	*and* *throw*
M	22.13	*to the attendants, 'Bind him hand and foot,* and *cast*
M	25.30	And *cast the*
L	13.28l	*and all the prophets in the kingdom of God* and *you yourselves thrust*

L	12.47	him with the unfaithful. And that servant who knew his
M	24.51	him with the hypocrites; *there men will weep and gnash*
M	8.12	*into the outer darkness; there men will weep and gnash*
M	13.42	*them into the furnace of fire; there men will weep and gnash*
M	13.50	*them into the furnace of fire; there men will weep and gnash*
M	22.13	*him into the outer darkness; there men will weep and gnash*
M	25.30	*worthless servant into the outer darkness; there men will weep and gnash*
L	13.28a	*out. There you will weep and gnash*

L	12.47	master's will, <u>but did not make ready or act according to his will, shall</u>
M	24.51	*their teeth.*
M	8.12	*their teeth."*
M	13.42	*their teeth.*
M	13.50	*their teeth.*
M	22.13	*their teeth.'*
M	25.30	*their teeth.'*
L	13.28a	*your teeth,*

L	12.48	<u>receive a severe beating.</u> <u>But he who did not know, and did what deserved</u>
L	12.48	<u>a beating, shall receive a light beating.</u>

M	13.10	*Then the disciples came and said to him, "Why do you speak to them in*
M	13.11	*in parables?" And he answered them, "To you it has been given to know*
M	13.11	*the secrets of the kingdom of heaven, but to them it has not been given.*

L	12.48	<u>Every one to whom</u> <u>much is</u>
M	13.12	*For to* <u>him</u> *who has will more be*
M	25.29	*For to* <u>every one</u> *who has will more be*
Mk	4.25	*For to* <u>him</u> *who has will more be*
L	8.18	*Take heed then how you hear; for to him* *who has will more be*
L	19.26	*'I tell you, that to* <u>every one</u> *who has will more be*

L	12.48	<u>given</u>, <u>of him will</u> <u>much be required;</u> <u>and of</u> <u>him to whom men commit much</u>
M	13.12	<u>given</u>, *and he* <u>will</u> *have abundance;* *but from* <u>him</u> *who has not, even what*
M	25.29	<u>given</u>, *and he* <u>will</u> *have abundance;* *but from* <u>him</u> *who has not, even what*
Mk	4.25	<u>given</u>; *and from* <u>him</u> *who has not, even what*
L	8.18	<u>given</u>; *and from* <u>him</u> *who has not, even what*
L	19.26	<u>given</u>, *but from* <u>him</u> *who has not, even what*

L	12.48	<u>they will demand the more.</u>
M	13.13	*he* *has will be taken away.*
M	25.29	*he* *has will be taken away.*
Mk	4.25	*he* *has will be taken away."*
L	8.18	*he thinks that he has will be taken away."*
L	19.26	*he* *has will be taken away.*

59. FIRE ON THE EARTH

Luke 12.49-59

L	12.49	<u>"I came to cast fire upon the earth; and would that it were already</u>
Mk	10.38	*But Jesus said to them, "You do not know what you are asking. Are*

L	12.50	<u>kindled!</u> <u>I have a baptism to be baptized with; and</u>
Mk	10.38	*you able to drink the cup that* <u>I</u> *drink, or* <u>to be baptized with</u> *the*

L	12.51	<u>how I am constrained until it is accomplished!</u> <u>Do you think that I have</u>
M	10.34	<u>"Do not think that I have</u>
Mk	10.38	*baptism with which I am baptized?"*

L	12.51	<u>come to give</u> peace on earth? <u>No,</u> <u>I tell you,</u> <u>but</u>
M	10.34	<u>come to</u> bring <u>peace on earth;</u> <u>I</u> have not come to bring peace, <u>but</u>

L	12.52	<u>rather division; for henceforth in one house there will be five divided,</u>
M	10.34	a sword.

L	12.53	three against two and two against three; they will be divided, father
M	10.35	For I have come to set

L	12.53	against son and son against father, mother against daughter and
M	10.35	a man against his father, and a

L	12.53	daughter against her mother, mother-in-law against her daughter-in-law
M	10.35	daughter against her mother,

L	12.53	and _ daughter-in-law against her mother-in-law."
M	10.36	and a daughter-in-law against her mother-in-law; *and a man's foes will be*

M	10.37	*those of his own household. He who loves father or mother more than me is*
M	10.37	*not worthy of me; and he who loves son or daughter more than me is not*
M	10.38	*worthy of me; and he who does not take his cross and follow me is not worthy*
M	10.39	*of me. He who finds his life will lose it, and he who loses his life for*
M	10.39	*my sake will find it.*

M	16.1	*And the Pharisees and Sadducees came, and to test him they asked him to*
M	16.1	*show them a sign from heaven.*

L	12.54	He also said to the multitudes, "When you see a cloud rising in the west,
M	16.2	He answered them, "When it is evening,

L	12.55	you say at once, 'A shower is coming'; and so it happens. And when
M	16.3	you say, 'It will be fair weather; for the sky is red.' And in

L	12.55	you see the south wind blowing, you say, 'There will be scorching heat';
M	16.3	the morning, 'It will be stormy today,

L	12.56	and it happens. You hypocrites! You know how to interpret the
M	16.3	for the sky is red and threatening.' You know how to interpret the

L	12.56	appearance of earth and sky; but why do you not know how to interpret
M	16.3	appearance of the sky, but you cannot interpret

L	12.56	the present time?
M	16.4	the signs of the times. *An evil and adulterous generation seeks for a*

M	16.4	*sign, but no sign shall be given to it except the sign of Jonah." So he*
M	16.4	*left them and departed.*

M	5.21	*"You have heard that it was said to the men of old, 'You shall not kill;*
M	5.22	*and whoever kills shall be liable to judgment.' But I say to you that*
M	5.22	*every one who is angry with his brother shall be liable to judgment; who-*
M	5.22	*ever insults his brother shall be liable to the council, and whoever says,*
M	5.23	*'You fool!' shall be liable to the hell of fire. So if you are offering*
M	5.23	*your gift at the altar, and there remember that your brother has something*
M	5.24	*against you, |leave your gift there before the altar and go; first be*
M	5.24	*reconciled to your brother, and then come and offer your gift.*

L	12.57,58	"And why do you not judge for yourselves what is right? As you go
M	5.25	Make friends

L	12.58	<u>with your accuser</u> <u>before the</u>
M	5.25	quickly <u>with your accuser</u>, while you are going with him to

L 12.58   <u>magistrate, make an effort to settle with him on the way, lest</u>
M 5.25   court,   <u>lest</u> your

L 12.58   <u>he</u>   <u>drag you</u>   <u>to the judge, and the judge hand you over to the</u>
M 5.25   accuser hand <u>you</u> over <u>to the judge, and the judge</u>   <u>to the</u>

L 12.59   <u>officer, and the officer put</u>   <u>you in prison.</u>   <u>I tell</u>   <u>you, you</u>
M 5.26   guard,   <u>and</u>   you be put <u>in prison</u>; truly, <u>I</u> say to <u>you, you</u>

L 12.59   <u>will never get out till you have paid the very last copper."</u>
M 5.26   <u>will never get out till you have paid the</u>   <u>last</u> penny.

60. A CALL TO REPENTANCE

Luke 13.1-9

L 13.1   <u>There were some present at that very time who told him of the Galileans</u>
L 13.2   <u>whose blood Pilate had mingled with their sacrifices. And he answered</u>
L 13.2   <u>them, "Do you think that these Galileans were worse sinners than all the</u>
L 13.3   <u>other Galileans, because they suffered thus? I tell you, No; but unless</u>
L 13.4   <u>you repent you will all likewise perish. Or those eighteen upon whom</u>
L 13.4   <u>the tower in Siloam fell and killed them, do you think that they were</u>
L 13.5   <u>worse offenders than all the others who dwelt in Jerusalem? I tell you,</u>
L 13.5   <u>No; but unless you repent you will all likewise perish."</u>

L 13.6   <u>And he told</u>
M 21.18   *In the morning,*   *as*   *he was returning to the city,* *he was hungry.*
Mk 11.12   *On the following day, when they*   *came*   *from Bethany, he was hungry.*

L 13.6   <u>this parable:</u>   "A man had <u>a fig tree</u> planted in his vineyard;
M 21.19   *And seeing*   *a fig tree by the wayside he went*
Mk 11.13   *And seeing in the distance* <u>*a fig tree*</u> *in leaf,*   *he went to see if*

L 13.6   <u>and</u> <u>he came seeking fruit on it and</u>
M 21.19   *to it,*   *and*
Mk 11.13   *he could find anything on it. When* <u>*he came*</u> *to it,*   *he*

L 13.6   <u>found none.</u>
M 21.19   <u>found</u> *nothing on it but leaves only.*
Mk 11.13   <u>found</u> *nothing*   *but leaves, for it was not the season for figs.*

L 13.7   <u>And he said to the vinedresser,</u> 'Lo, these three years I have come
M 21.19   <u>And he said to</u> *it,*   *"May no*
Mk 11.14   <u>And he said to</u> *it,*   *"May no one ever*

L 13.7   <u>seeking fruit on this fig tree, and I find none. Cut it down; why</u>
M 21.19   <u>fruit</u> *ever come from you again!"*
Mk 11.14   *eat*   <u>fruit</u>   *from you again." And his disciples heard it.*

L 13.8   <u>should it use up the ground?'</u> And he answered him, 'Let it alone, sir,
M 21.19   *And*   *the fig tree withered at*
Mk 11.20   *As they passed by in the morning, they saw the fig tree withered away*

431

```
L    13.9     this year also, till I dig about it and put on manure.  And if it bears
M    21.20    once.        When the disciples saw it they marveled, saying,
Mk   11.21    to its roots.  And Peter       remembered        and  said to him, "Master,


L    13.9     fruit next year, well and good; but if not, you can cut it down.'"
M    21.20    "How did the fig tree                     wither at once?"
Mk   11.21    look!  The fig tree which you cursed has withered."
```

61. A WOMAN FREED FROM AN INFIRMITY

Luke 13.10-17

```
L    13.10,11  Now he was teaching in one of the synagogues on the sabbath.  And there
L    13.11     was a woman who had had a spirit of infirmity for eighteen years; she was
L    13.12     bent over and could not fully straighten herself.  And when Jesus saw her,
L    13.12     he called her and said to her, "Woman, you are freed from your infirmity."
L    13.13     And he laid his hands upon her, and immediately she was made straight, and
L    13.14     she praised God.  But the ruler of the synagogue, indignant because Jesus
L    13.14     had healed on the sabbath, said to the people, "There are six days on
L    13.14     which work ought to be done; come on those days and be healed, and not on
L    13.15     the sabbath day."  Then the Lord answered him, "You hypocrites!  Does not
L    13.15     each of you on the sabbath untie his ox or his ass from the manger, and
L    13.16     lead it away to water it?  And ought not this woman, a daughter of Abraham
L    13.16     whom Satan bound for eighteen years, be loosed from this bond on the
L    13.17     sabbath day?"  As he said this, all his adversaries were put to shame; and
L    13.17     all the people rejoiced at all the glorious things that were done by him.
```

62. THE MUSTARD SEED AND THE LEAVEN

Luke 13.18-21

```
L    13.18                       He          said therefore,  "What
M    13.31    Another parable he put before them,  saying,
Mk    4.30    And              he                  said,        "With  what can we


L    13.18    is      the kingdom of God like?  And to what        shall I  compare
M    13.31            "The kingdom of heaven
Mk    4.30    compare the kingdom of God,       or      what parable shall we use for


L    13.19    it?  It is like a grain of mustard seed  which a man took and sowed in
M    13.31         is like a grain of mustard seed  which a man took and sowed in
Mk    4.31    it?  It is like a grain of mustard seed,  which,        when sown   upon


L    13.19    his garden;                                          and
M    13.32    his field; it is the smallest of all    seeds,      but when
Mk    4.32    the ground,   is the smallest of all the seeds on earth; yet when it is


L    13.19         it     grew                                  and became
M    13.32         it has grown     it is      the greatest of     shrubs  and becomes
Mk    4.32    sown it     grows up and becomes the greatest of all shrubs,  and puts


L    13.19              a tree,     and     the birds of the air       made nests
M    13.32              a tree,     so that the birds of the air come and make nests
Mk    4.32    forth large branches, so that the birds of the air       can make nests


L    13.19    in its branches."
M    13.32    in its branches."
Mk    4.32    in its shade."
```

| L | 13.20.21 | And again he said, "To what shall I compare the kingdom of God? It is |
| M | 13.33 | He told them another parable. "The kingdom of heaven is |

| L | 13.21 | like leaven which a woman took and hid in three measures of flour, till |
| M | 13.33 | like leaven which a woman took and hid in three measures of flour, till |

| L | 13.21 | it was all leavened." |
| M | 13.33 | it was all leavened." |

63. THE SAVED ARE FEW

Luke 13.22-30

| L | 13.22 | He went on his way through towns and villages, teaching, and journeying |
| L | 13.22 | toward Jerusalem. |

L	13.23	And some one said to him, "Lord, will those
M	7.14	For the gate is narrow and the way is hard, that leads to life, and those
J	10.0b	he will

L	13.24	who are saved be few?" And he said to them, "Strive to
M	7.14	who find it are few.
J	10.7	So Jesus again said to them, "Truly, truly, I
J	10.9a	be saved,and will go in and out and find pasture. I am the door; if

L	13.24	enter by the narrow door;
M	7.13	"Enter by the narrow gate; for the gate is wide and the way is
J	10.7	say to you, I am the door of the sheep.
J	10.9a	any one enters by me,

| L | 13.24 | for many, I tell you, will seek to enter and will not be able. |
| M | 7.13 | easy, that leads to destruction, and those who enter by it are many. |

| L | 13.25 | When once the householder has risen up |
| M | 25.10 | And while they went to buy, the bridegroom came, and those who were ready |

| L | 13.25 | and shut the door, you will |
| M | 25.11 | went in with him to the marriage feast; and the door was shut. Afterward |

L	13.25	begin to stand outside and to knock at the door, saying, 'Lord,
M	7.21	"Not every one who says to me, 'Lord, Lord,'
M	25.11	the other maidens came also, saying, 'Lord, lord,

L	13.25	open to us.' He will answer you, 'I do not
M	7.21	shall enter the kingdom of heaven, but he who does the will of my Father
M	7.23	And then will I declare to them, 'I never
M	25.12	open to us.' But he replied, 'Truly, I say to you, I do not

L	13.26	know where you come from.' Then you will begin to say, 'We ate and drank
M	7.21	who is in heaven.
M	7.23	knew you; depart from me, you evildoers.'
M	25.12	know you.'

L	13.27	in your presence, and you taught in our streets.'	But	he will
M	7.23		And then	will I
M	25.12		But	he

L	13.27	say,	'I tell	you, I do not	know where you come from;
M	7.23	declare to them,		'I never knew	you;
M	25.12	replied, 'Truly,	I say to you, I do not	know	you.'

L	13.28	depart from me, all you workers of iniquity!'	There you will weep and
M	7.23	depart from me, you evildoers.'	
M	8.12b		there men will weep and
M	13.42b		there men will weep and
M	13.50b		there men will weep and
M	22.13b		there men will weep and
M	24.51b		there men will weep and
M	25.30b		there men will weep and

L	13.28	gnash your teeth,	when you see Abraham and Isaac and Jacob and all
M	8.11b	gnash their teeth."	with Abraham, Isaac, and Jacob
M	13.42b	gnash their teeth.	
M	13.49	gnash their teeth.	So it will be at the close of the age. The angels
M	22.13a	gnash their teeth.'	
M	24.51b	gnash their teeth.	
M	25.30b	gnash their teeth.'	Then the king

L	13.28	the prophets in the kingdom of God	and you
M	8.12a	in the kingdom of heaven,	|while the sons of
M	13.42a		and
M	13.50a	will come out and separate the evil from the righteous,	|and
M	22.13a	said to the attendants, 'Bind him hand and foot,	and
M	24.51a		and will punish
M	25.30a		And

L	13.28	yourselves	thrust out.	
M	8.12a	the kingdom will be thrown		into the outer darkness;
M	13.42a	throw	them	into the furnace of fire;
M	13.50a	throw	them	into the furnace of fire;
M	22.13a	cast	him	into the outer darkness;
M	24.51a	him, and put	him	with the hypocrites;
M	25.30a	cast the worthless servant	into the outer darkness;

L	13.29	And	men will come from east and west, and from north and south,
M	8.11a	I tell you, many will come from east and west

L	13.30	and sit at table in the kingdom of God.	And behold, some	are
M	8.11a	and sit at table		
M	19.30		But many that	are
M	20.16		So	the
Mk	9.35b		"If any one would be	
Mk	10.31		But many that	are

L	13.30	last who will be first, and some are first who will be last."
M	19.30	first will be last, and the last first.
M	20.16	last will be first, and the first last."
Mk	9.35b	first, he must be last of all and servant of all."
Mk	10.31	first will be last, and the last first."

64. LAMENT OVER JERUSALEM

Luke 13.31-35

L	13.31	At that very hour some Pharisees came, and said to him, "Get away from
L	13.32	here, for Herod wants to kill you." And he said to them, "Go and tell
L	13.32	that fox, 'Behold, I cast out demons and perform cures today and tomorrow,
L	13.33	and the third day I finish my course. Nevertheless I must go on my way
L	13.33	today and tomorrow and the day following; for it cannot be that a prophet
L	13.33	should perish away from Jerusalem.'

L	13.34	O Jerusalem, Jerusalem, killing the prophets and stoning those who are
M	23.37	"O Jerusalem, Jerusalem, killing the prophets and stoning those who are

L	13.34	sent to you! How often would I have gathered your children together as
M	23.37	sent to you! How often would I have gathered your children together as

L	13.35	a hen gathers her brood under her wings, and you would not! Behold,
M	23.38	a hen gathers her brood under her wings, and you would not! Behold,

L	13.35	your house is forsaken. And I tell you, you will not see
M	23.39	your house is forsaken and desolate. For I tell you, you will not see

L	13.35	me until you say, 'Blessed is he who comes in the name of the
M	23.39	me again, until you say, 'Blessed is he who comes in the name of the

L	13.35	Lord!'"
M	23.39	Lord.'"

65. A MAN WITH DROPSY

Luke 14.1-6

L	14.1	One sabbath when he went to dine at the house of a
M	12.9	And he went on from there, and entered their synagogue.
Mk	3.1	Again he entered the synagogue,
L	6.6	On another sabbath, when he entered the synagogue

L	14.2	ruler who belonged to the Pharisees, they were watching him. And behold,
M	12.10	And behold,
Mk	3.1	and
L	6.6	and taught,

L	14.3	there was a man before him who had dropsy. And Jesus spoke to the
M	12.10	there was a man with a withered hand. And
Mk	3.2	a man was there who had a withered hand. And
L	6.7	a man was there whose right hand was withered. And the

L	14.3	lawyers and Pharisees, saying, "Is it lawful to heal
M	12.10	they asked him, "Is it lawful to heal
Mk	3.2	they watched him, to see whether he would heal him
L	6.7	scribes and the Pharisees watched him, to see whether he would heal

435

```
L    14.3     on the sabbath,  or not?"
  M  12.10    on the sabbath?"  so that they might        accuse          him.
  Mk 3.2      on the sabbath,   so that they might        accuse          him.
  L  6.8      on the sabbath,   so that they might find an accusation against him.  But


  Mk 3.3                              And he said to the man who had the withered hand,
  L  6.8      he knew their thoughts, and he said to the man who had the withered hand,


L    14.4                                                        But they were
  Mk 3.4b     "Come            here."                            But they were
  L  6.8      "Come and stand here."  And he rose and stood there.


L    14.4     silent.  Then he took him
  M  12.13              Then he
  Mk 3.5      silent.  And he looked around at them with anger, grieved at their
  L  6.10              And he looked around on them all,


  M  12.13                        said to the man, "Stretch out your hand."  And the
  Mk 3.5      hardness of heart, and said to the man, "Stretch out your hand."
  L  6.10                         and said to   him, "Stretch out your hand."  And


L    14.4                       and              healed him, and let him go.
  M  12.13    man stretched it out, and    it  was restored, whole like the other.
  Mk 3.5      He  stretched it out, and his hand was restored.
  L  6.10     he  did so,           and his hand was restored.


L    14.5     And he  said to them, "Which   of you,      having a  son or an ox
  M  12.11        He  said to them, "What man of you, if he has   one sheep     and
  Mk 3.4a     And he  said to them,
  L  6.9      And Jesus said to them,


L    14.5     that has fallen into a well,        will not immediately      pull
  M  12.11    it          falls into a pit on the sabbath, will not lay hold of it and lift


L    14.5     him out
  M  12.12    it   out?  of how much more value is a man than a sheep!  So it is lawful to
  Mk 3.4a                                                      "Is it lawful
  L  6.9                                                 "I ask you, is it lawful


L    14.6              on a   sabbath day?"  And they could not reply to this.
  M  12.12    do good on the sabbath."
  Mk 3.4a              on the sabbath to do good or to do harm, to save life or to kill?"
  L  6.9               on the sabbath to do good or to do harm, to save life or to destroy


  M  12.14         But the Pharisees went out        and            took counsel
  Mk 3.6             The Pharisees went out,     and immediately held counsel with
  L  6.11     it?"  But     they were filled with fury and            discussed     with


  M  12.14              against him, how     to destroy  him.
  Mk 3.6      the Herodians against him, how     to destroy  him.
  L  6.11     one another             what they might do to Jesus.
```

436

Luke 14.7-14

L	14.7	Now he told a parable to those who were invited, when he marked how
L	14.8	they chose the places of honor, saying to them, |"When you are invited
L	14.8	by any one to a marriage feast, do not sit down in a place of honor,
L	14.9	lest a more eminent man than you be invited by him; and he who invited
L	14.9	you both will come and say to you, 'Give place to this man,' and then
L	14.10	you will begin with shame to take the lowest place. But when you are
L	14.10	invited, go and sit in the lowest place, so that when your host comes
T.	14.10	he may say to you, 'Friend, go up higher'; then you will be honored in
L	14.10	the presence of all who sit at table with you.

L	14.11	For every one who exalts himself will be humbled, and he who humbles
M	23.12	whoever exalts himself will be humbled, and whoever humbles
L	18.14b	for every one who exalts himself will be humbled, *but* he who humbles

L	14.11	himself will be exalted."
M	23.12	himself will be exalted.
L	18.14b	himself will be exalted."

L	14.12	He said also to the man who had invited him, "When you give a dinner
L	14.12	or a banquet, do not invite your friends or your brothers or your kins-
L	14.12	men or rich neighbors, lest they also invite you in return, and you be
L	14.13	repaid. But when you give a feast, invite the poor, the maimed, the
L	14.14	lame, the blind, |and you will be blessed, because they cannot repay
L	14.14	you. You will be repaid at the resurrection of the just."

67. THE MARRIAGE FEAST

Luke 14.15-24

L	14.15	When one of those who sat at table with him heard this, he said to him,
L	14.15	"Blessed is he who shall eat bread in the kingdom of God!"

L	14.16	But he said to him,
M	22.1,2	And again Jesus spoke to them in parables, saying, |"The kingdom of

L	14.16	"A man once gave a great banquet, and invited
M	22.2	heaven may be compared to a king who gave a marriage feast for his son,

L	14.17	many; and at the time for the banquet he sent his servant to say to
M	22.3	|and sent his servants to call

L	14.18	those who had been invited, 'Come; for all is now ready.' But they
M	22.3	those who were invited to the marriage feast; but they

L	14.18	all alike began to make excuses. The first said to him, 'I have bought
M	22.4	would not come. Again he sent other servants, saying,

L	14.18	a field, and I must go out and see it; I pray you, have me excused.'
M	22.4	'Tell those who are invited, Behold, I have made ready my dinner, my

```
L    14.19    And another said, 'I have bought five yoke of oxen, and I go to examine
M    22.4     oxen and my fat calves are killed, and everything is ready; come to the


L    14.20    them; I pray you, have me excused.' And another said, 'I have married
M    22.5     marriage feast.' But they made light of it and went off, one to his


L    14.21    a wife, and therefore I cannot come.' So the servant came and
M    22.6     farm, another to his business, |while the rest seized his servants,


L    14.21    reported this to his master.        Then the householder in anger
M    22.7     treated them shamefully, and killed them. The king        was angry,


 M   22.7     and he sent his troops and destroyed those murderers and burned their


L    14.21                         said to his servant,
M    22.8     city. Then he said to his servants, 'The wedding is ready, but those


L    14.21                         'Go out quickly to the streets and lanes of the
M    22.9     invited were not worthy. Go therefore    to the thoroughfares,


L    14.22    city, and bring in the poor and maimed and blind and lame.' And the
M    22.10         and invite to the marriage feast as many as you find.' And those


L    14.22    servant said, 'Sir, what you commanded has been done, and still there
M    22.10    servants


L    14.23    is room.' And the master said to the servant, 'Go   out   to the
M    22.10                                            went out into the


L    14.23    highways and hedges, and compel people to come in,
M    22.10    streets         and gathered all whom they found, both bad and good;


L    14.24    that my house  may be  filled. For I tell you, none of those men
M    22.10    so   the wedding hall was filled with guests.


L    14.24    who were invited shall taste my banquet.'"
```

68. THE COST OF DISCIPLESHIP

Luke 14.25-35

```
L    14.25    Now            great multitudes accompanied him; and  he turned and
M    16.24                                                    Then Jesus
Mk   8.34     And he called to him the multitude  with his disciples,          and
 L   9.23                                                     And  he


L    14.26    said to them,    |"If any one        comes to   me and does not hate
M    10.37                                                    He who loves
M    16.24    told his disciples, "If any man would come  after me,
Mk   8.34     said to them,    "If any man would come  after me,
 L   9.23     said to all,    "If any man would come  after me,
 J   12.25                     He who loves his life loses it, and he who hates
 J   12.26                     If any one      serves     me,
```

438

```
L    14.26    his own father and mother and wife and children and brothers and sisters,
M    10.37              father or mother more than me is not worthy of me; and he who
 J   12.26                                      he must follow me; and where I


L    14.27    yes, and even his own life, he cannot be my disciple.        Whoever does
M    10.38    loves son or daughter more than me is not worthy of me; and he  who does
Mk    8.34                                    let him deny himself  and
 L    9.23                                    let him deny himself  and
 J   12.25                                    let him deny himself  and
 J   12.25                  his      life in this world will keep it for eternal life.
 J   12.26    am, there shall my servant be also;                      if  any one


L    14.27    not bear     his own cross      and come after me, cannot be my disciple.
M    10.38    not take     his     cross      and follow    me  is not worthy of me.
M    16.24         take up his     cross      and follow    me.
Mk    8.34         take up his     cross      and follow    me.
 L    9.23         take up his     cross daily and follow   me.
 J   12.26                                         serves   me, the Father will honor him.


L    14.28    For which of you, desiring to build a tower, does not first sit down and
L    14.29    count the cost, whether he has enough to complete it?  Otherwise, when he
L    14.29    has laid a foundation, and is not able to finish, all who see it begin to
L    14.30    mock him, |saying, 'This man began to build, and was not able to finish.'
L    14.31    Or what king, going to encounter another king in war, will not sit down
L    14.31    first and take counsel whether he is able with ten thousand to meet him
L    14.32    who comes against him with twenty thousand?  And if not, while the other
L    14.33    is yet a great way off, he sends an embassy and asks terms of peace.  So
L    14.33    therefore, whoever of you does not renounce all that he has cannot be my
L    14.33    disciple.


L    14.34                                        "Salt is good;     but if
M     5.13            "You          are         the salt of the earth; but if
Mk    9.49,50   For every one will be salted with fire.  Salt is good;  but if the


L    14.35    salt has lost its taste,    how shall its saltness be restored?  It is
M     5.13    salt has lost its taste,    how shall its saltness be restored?  It is
Mk    9.50    salt has lost its saltness, how will  you season it?              Have


L    14.35        fit neither for the land nor for the dunghill; men throw it away.
M     5.13    no longer good for anything              except to be thrown out and
Mk    9.50    salt in yourselves, and be at peace with one another."


L    14.35                                    He  who has ears to hear, let him hear."
M     5.13    trodden under foot by men.
 M   11.15                                    He  who has ears to hear, let him hear.
 M   13.9                                     He  who has ears,          let him hear."
 M   13.43b                                   He  who has ears,          let him hear.
 Mk   4.9     And he said,                "He  who has ears to hear, let him hear."
 Mk   4.23                                If any man has ears to hear, let him hear."
 Mk   7.16    "If any man has ears to hear, let him hear."
 L    8.8b    As he said this, he called out, "He who has ears to hear, let him hear."
```

439

69. THE LOST SHEEP, THE LOST COIN, AND THE LOST SON

Luke 15.1-32

```
L    15.1     Now
M    9.10     And as       he  sat  at table in the house,                    behold,
Mk   2.15     And as       he  sat  at table in his house,
 L   5.29     And Levi made him a great feast in his house; and there was a large


L    15.1     the          tax collectors and sinners were all drawing near to hear
M    9.10     many         tax collectors and sinners came and sat down          with
Mk   2.16     many         tax collectors and sinners were      sitting          with
 L   5.29     company of tax collectors and others            sitting at table with


L    15.2     him.                                                             And
M    9.11     Jesus and his disciples.                                        And when
Mk   2.16     Jesus and his disciples; for there were many who followed him.  And the
 L   5.30     them.                                                           And
 L   19.7                                                                     And when


L    15.2                  the Pharisees and the    scribes
M    9.11                  the Pharisees            saw this,
Mk   2.16     scribes of the Pharisees, when they saw that he was eating with sinners
 L   5.30                  the Pharisees and their scribes
 L   19.7                  they                     saw it


L    15.2                            murmured,                      saying,         "This
M    9.11          they             said    to   his disciples,    "Why does your
Mk   2.16     and tax collectors, said    to   his disciples,    "Why does
 L   5.30                            murmured against his disciples, saying, "Why do
 L   19.7          they all          murmured,                              "He has gone in


L    15.2     man        receives                              sinners and eats with
M    9.11     teacher    eat           with tax collectors and sinners?"
Mk   2.17     he         eat           with tax collectors and sinners?"
 L   5.30     you        eat and drink with tax collectors and sinners?"
 L   19.7     to be the guest         of a man       who is a sinner."


L    15.2     them."


 M  18.10     "See that you do not despise one of these little ones; for I tell you
 M  18.10     that in heaven their angels always behold the face of my Father who is
 M  18.11     in heaven. For the Son of man came to save the lost.


L    15.3,4   So he told them this parable: "What man of you, having a hundred sheep,
M    18.12    What do you think?        If a man      has    a hundred sheep,


L    15.4     if he has lost one of them,                 does   not leave the ninety-
M    18.12    and              one of them has gone astray, does he not leave the ninety-


L    15.4     nine in the wilderness, and go after      the one which is  lost, until
M    18.12    nine on the mountains   and go in search of the one that went astray?


L    15.5     he finds it? And when he has found it,              he lays it
M    18.13                 And if   he      finds it, truly, I say to you, he
```

L	15.6	on his shoulders, rejoicing. And when he comes home, he calls together
M	18.13	rejoices over it more than over the ninety-nine

L	15.6	his friends and his neighbors, saying to them, 'Rejoice with me, for I

L	15.7	have found my sheep which was lost.' Just so, I tell you, there
M	18.14	that never went astray. So it is not the will

L	15.7	will be more joy in heaven over one sinner who repents than over
M	18.14	of my Father who is in heaven that one of these little ones should

L	15.7	ninety-nine righteous persons who need no repentance.
M	18.14	perish.

L	15.8	"Or what woman, having ten silver coins, if she loses one coin, does
L	15.8	not light a lamp and sweep the house and seek diligently until she finds
L	15.9	it? And when she has found it, she calls together her friends and
L	15.9	neighbors, saying, 'Rejoice with me, for I have found the coin which I had
L	15.10	lost.' Just so, I tell you, there is joy before the angels of God over
L	15.10	one sinner who repents."

L	15.11,12	And he said, "There was a man who had two sons; and the younger of them
L	15.12	said to his father, 'Father, give me the share of property that falls to
L	15.13	me.' And he divided his living between them. |Not many days later, the
L	15.13	younger son gathered all he had and took his journey into a far country,
L	15.14	and there he squandered his property in loose living. And when he had
L	15.14	spent everything, a great famine arose in that country, and he began to
L	15.15	be in want. So he went and joined himself to one of the citizens of that
L	15.16	country, who sent him into his fields to feed swine. And he would gladly
L	15.16	have fed on the pods that the swine ate; and no one gave him anything.
L	15.17	But when he came to himself he said, 'How many of my father's hired ser-
L	15.17	vants have bread enough and to spare, but I perish here with hunger!
L	15.18	I will arise and go to my father, and I will say to him, "Father, I have
L	15.19	sinned against heaven and before you; I am no longer worthy to be called
L	15.20	your son; treat me as one of your hired servants."' And he arose and
L	15.20	came to his father. But while he was yet at a distance, his father saw
L	15.21	him and had compassion, and ran and embraced him and kissed him. And
L	15.21	the son said to him, 'Father, I have sinned against heaven and before you;
L	15.22	I am no longer worthy to be called your son.' But the father said to his
L	15.22	servants, 'Bring quickly the best robe, and put it on him; and put a ring
L	15.23	on his hand, and shoes on his feet; and bring the fatted calf and kill it,
L	15.24	and let us eat and make merry; for this my son was dead, and is alive again;
L	15.24	he was lost, and is found.' And they began to make merry.

L	15.25	"Now his elder son was in the field; and as he came and drew near to the
L	15.26	house, he heard music and dancing. And he called one of the servants and
L	15.27	asked what this meant. And he said to him, 'Your brother has come, and
L	15.27	your father has killed the fatted calf, because he has received him safe
L	15.28	and sound.' |But he was angry and refused to go in. His father came out
L	15.29	and entreated him, |but he answered his father, 'Lo, these many years I
L	15.29	have served you, and I never disobeyed your command; yet you never gave me
L	15.30	a kid, that I might make merry with my friends. But when this son of yours
L	15.30	came, who has devoured your living with harlots, you killed for him the
L	15.31	fatted calf!' And he said to him, 'Son, you are always with me, and all
L	15.32	that is mine is yours. It was fitting to make merry and be glad, for
L	15.32	this your brother was dead, and is alive; he was lost, and is found.'"

L	16.1	He also said to the disciples, "There was a rich man who had a steward,
L	16.2	and charges were brought to him that this man was wasting his goods. And
L	16.2	he called him and said to him, 'What is this that I hear about you? Turn
L	16.2	in the account of your stewardship, for you can no longer be steward.'
L	16.3	And the steward said to himself, 'What shall I do, since my master is
L	16.3	taking the stewardship away from me? I am not strong enough to dig, and
L	16.4	I am ashamed to beg. I have decided what to do, so that people may receive
L	16.5	me into their houses when I am put out of the stewardship.' So, summoning
L	16.5	his master's debtors one by one, he said to the first, 'How much do you owe
L	16.6	my master?' |He said, 'A hundred measures of oil.' And he said to him,
L	16.7	'Take your bill, and sit down quickly and write fifty.' Then he said to
L	16.7	another, 'And how much do you owe?' He said, 'A hundred measures of wheat.'
L	16.8	He said to him, 'Take your bill, and write eighty.' |The master commended
L	16.8	the dishonest steward for his shrewdness; for the sons of this world are
L	16.8	more shrewd in dealing with their own generation than the sons of light.
L	16.9	And I tell you, make friends for yourselves by means of unrighteous mammon,
L	16.9	so that when it fails they may receive you into the eternal habitations.

L	16.10	"He who is faithful in a very little is faithful also in much; and he
L	16.11	who is dishonest in a very little is dishonest also in much. If then
L	16.11	you have not been faithful in the unrighteous mammon, who will entrust to
L	16.12	you the true riches? And if you have not been faithful in that which is
L	16.12	another's, who will give you that which is your own?

L	16.13	No servant can serve two masters; for either he will hate the one and
M	6.24	"No one can serve two masters; for either he will hate the one and

L	16.13	love the other, or he will be devoted to the one and despise the other.
M	6.24	love the other, or he will be devoted to the one and despise the other.

L	16.13	You cannot serve God and mammon."
M	6.24	You cannot serve God and mammon.

L	16.14	The Pharisees, who were lovers of money, heard all this, and they
L	16.15	scoffed at him. But he said to them, "You are those who justify your-
L	16.15	selves before men, but God knows your hearts; for what is exalted among
L	16.15	men is an abomination in the sight of God.

71. THE LAW AND THE PROPHETS

Luke 16.16-18

M	11.11	*Truly, I say to you, among those born of women there has risen no one*
M	11.11	*greater than John the Baptist; yet he who is least in the kingdom of*
M	11.11	*heaven is greater than he.*

L	16.16	"The law and the prophets were until John; since then the
M	11.12	From the days of John the Baptist until now

L	16.16	good news of the kingdom of God is preached, and every one
M	11.12	the kingdom of heaven has suffered violence, and men

```
L   16.16      enters it violently.
M   11.13                    of violence take it by force.  For all the prophets and the law

  M  11.14     prophesied until John; and if you are willing to accept it, he is Elijah
  M  11.15     who is to come.  He who has ears to hear, let him hear.

  M   5.17         "Think not that I have come to abolish the law and the prophets; I have
  M   5.17     come not to abolish them but to fulfil them.

L   16.17      But it is easier        for  heaven and earth to      pass away,
M    5.18      For truly, I say to you, till heaven and earth        pass away, not an
  M 24.34          Truly, I say to you,      this generation  will not pass away
  Mk 13.30         Truly, I say to you,      this generation  will not pass away
  L 21.32          Truly, I say to you,      this generation  will not pass away
  M 24.35                                    Heaven and earth will     pass away,
  Mk 13.31                                   Heaven and earth will     pass away,
  L 21.33                                    Heaven and earth will     pass away,

L   16.17      than  for one dot              of  the law to become void.
M    5.18      iota, not a   dot, will   pass from the law until all                is
  M 24.34                                                till all these things
  Mk 13.30                                            before all these things
  L 21.32                                                till all             has
  M 24.35          but my words will not pass away.
  Mk 13.31         but my words will not pass away.
  L 21.33          but my words will not pass away.

  M   5.19     accomplished.  Whoever then relaxes one of the least of these commandments
  M  24.34     take  place.
  Mk 13.30     take  place.
  L  21.32     taken place.

  M   5.19     and teaches men so, shall be called least in the kingdom of heaven; but
  M   5.19     he who does them and teaches them shall be called great in the kingdom
  M   5.20     of heaven.  For I tell you, unless your righteousness exceeds that of
  M   5.20     the scribes and Pharisees, you will never enter the kingdom of heaven.

  M  19.3      And Pharisees came up to him and             tested him by asking, "Is it
  Mk 10.2      And Pharisees came up          and in order to test  him    asked,  "Is it
  M   5.31                                                  "It was also said,

  M  19.3      lawful          to divorce  one's wife for any cause?"
  Mk 10.3      lawful for a man to divorce his   wife?"  He answered them, "What did
  M   5.31                     'Whoever divorces his   wife,

  M  19.7                          They said to him, "Why then did Moses command
  Mk 10.4      Moses command you?"  They said,              Moses allowed a
  M   5.31                                                         let

  M  19.9      one to give    a certificate of divorce, and to put her away?"  And
  Mk 10.11     man to write   a certificate of divorce, and to put her away."  And
  M   5.32     him   give her a certificate of divorce.'                       But

L   16.18                     "Every one who divorces his wife
M   19.9      I  say  to you:          whoever divorces his wife, except
Mk  10.11     he said to them,         "Whoever divorces his wife
  M   5.32     I  say  to you that every one who divorces his wife, except on the
```

443

```
L    16.18                                    and marries another   commits        adultery,
M    19.9                  for unchastity,    and marries another,  commits        adultery."
Mk   10.11                                    and marries another,  commits        adultery
  M   5.32    ground of unchastity,                                 makes her an   adulteress;


L    16.18                     and he who   marries a woman divorced from her husband
Mk   10.12    against her;     and if she                  divorces      her husband
  M   5.32                     and whoever  marries a divorced woman


L    16.18                                    commits adultery.
Mk   10.12    and marries another, she       commits adultery."
  M   5.32                                    commits adultery.
```

72. THE RICH MAN AND LAZARUS

Luke 16.19-31

```
L    16.19      "There was a rich man, who was clothed in purple and fine linen and who
L    16.20      feasted sumptuously every day.  And at his gate lay a poor man named
L    16.21      Lazarus, full of sores, |who desired to be fed with what fell from the
L    16.22      rich man's table; moreover the dogs came and licked his sores.  The poor
L    16.22      man died and was carried by the angels to Abraham's bosom.  The rich man
L    16.23      also died and was buried; and in Hades, being in torment, he lifted up
L    16.24      his eyes, and saw Abraham far off and Lazarus in his bosom.  And he
L    16.24      called out, 'Father Abraham, have mercy upon me, and send Lazarus to dip
L    16.24      the end of his finger in water and cool my tongue; for I am in anguish in
L    16.25      this flame.'  But Abraham said, 'Son, remember that you in your lifetime
L    16.25      received your good things, and Lazarus in like manner evil things; but
L    16.26      now he is comforted here, and you are in anguish.  And besides all this,
L    16.26      between us and you a great chasm has been fixed, in order that those who
L    16.26      would pass from here to you may not be able, and none may cross from there
L    16.27      to us.'  And he said, 'Then I beg you, father, to send him to my father's
L    16.28      house, |for I have five brothers, so that he may warn them, lest they
L    16.29      also come into this place of torment.'  But Abraham said, 'They have
L    16.30      Moses and the prophets; let them hear them.'  And he said, 'No, father
L    16.30      Abraham; but if some one goes to them from the dead, they will repent.'
L    16.31      He said to him, 'If they do not hear Moses and the prophets, neither
L    16.31      will they be convinced if some one should rise from the dead.'"
```

73. CAUSES OF SIN, FORGIVENESS, AND DUTY

Luke 17.1-10

```
L    17.1      And he said to his disciples, "Temptations to sin          are sure ·
M    18.7      "Woe to the world                for temptations to sin! For it is   necessary


L    17.1      to                    come; but woe to   him by whom      they        come!
M    18.7      that temptations come, but woe to the man by whom the temptation comes!


  M  18.5      "Whoever receives one such child in my name receives me;


L    17.2      It would be better for him if      a        millstone were hung round his
M    18.6b     it would be better for him to have a great  millstone fastened   round his
Mk    9.42b    it would be better for him if      a great  millstone were hung round his
```

444

```
L    17.2    neck and he were cast    into              the sea, than that he should
M    18.6a   neck and    to be   drowned in the depth of the sea.          but whoever
Mk   9.42a   neck and he were thrown  into              the sea.          "Whoever
```

```
L    17.2    cause  one of these little ones                        to sin.
M    18.6a   causes one of these little ones who believe in me to sin,
Mk   9.42a   causes one of these little ones who believe in me to sin,
```

```
M   18.8   And if your hand or your foot causes you to sin, cut it off and throw it
Mk  9.43   And if your hand            causes you to sin, cut it off;
```

```
M   18.8   away; it is better for you to enter life maimed or lame than with two
Mk  9.43        it is better for you to enter life maimed        than with two
```

```
M   18.8   hands or two feet to be thrown into        the eternal      fire.
Mk  9.44   hands           to    go      to hell, to the unquenchable fire, where
```

```
Mk  9.45   their worm does not die, and the fire is not quenched.  And if your foot
Mk  9.45   causes you to sin, cut it off; it is better for you to enter life lame
Mk  9.46   than with two feet to be thrown into hell, where their worm does not die,
```

```
M   18.9                              And if your eye causes you to sin, pluck
Mk  9.47   and the fire is not quenched.  And if your eye causes you to sin, pluck
```

```
M   18.9   it out and throw it away; it is better for you to enter      life
Mk  9.47   it out;                   it is better for you to enter the kingdom of God
```

```
M   18.9   with one eye than with two eyes to be thrown into the hell
Mk  9.48   with one eye than with two eyes to be thrown into      hell, where their
```

```
M   18.9                           of fire.
Mk  9.49   worm does not die, and the fire is not quenched.  For every one will be
```

```
Mk  9.50   salted with fire.  Salt is good; but if the salt has lost its saltness,
Mk  9.50   how will you season it?  Have salt in yourselves, and be at peace with
Mk  9.50   one another."
```

```
L    17.3    Take heed to yourselves; if your brother sins,                  rebuke
M    18.15                       "If your brother sins against you, go and tell
```

```
L    17.3    him,                              and if he repents,
M    18.15   him his fault, between you and him alone.  If he listens to you, you have
```

```
L    17.3    forgive    him;
M    18.16   gained your brother.  But if he does not listen, take one or two others
```

```
M   18.16   along with you, that every word may be confirmed by the evidence of two
M   18.17   or three witnesses.  If he refuses to listen to them, tell it to the
M   18.17   church; and if he refuses to listen even to the church, let him be to
M   18.18   you as a Gentile and a tax collector.  Truly, I say to you, whatever
M   18.18   you bind on earth shall be bound in heaven, and whatever you loose on
M   18.19   earth shall be loosed in heaven.  Again I say to you, if two of you
M   18.19   agree on earth about anything they ask, it will be done for them by my
M   18.20   Father in heaven.  For where two or three are gathered in my name, there
M   18.20   am I in the midst of them."
```

```
L    17.4                                   and if           he
M    18.21   Then Peter came up and said to him, "Lord, how often shall my brother
```

```
L    17.4     sins against you                                    seven times in the day,
M    18.22    sin  against me, and I forgive him?  As many as seven times?"  Jesus


L    17.4                          and turns to you seven times, and says, 'I repent,'
M    18.22    said to him, "I do not say to you seven times, but


L    17.4     you must forgive him."
M    18.22    seventy times seven.


L    17.5              The apostles                        said to the Lord,
M    17.19    Then the disciples came to Jesus privately and said, "Why could we not


L    17.5                                              "Increase our faith!"
M    17.20    cast it out?"  He    said  to them, "Because of your little faith.
     M  21.21                 And Jesus answered them,
     Mk 11.22                 And Jesus answered them,             "Have        faith in God.


L    17.6     And the Lord said,        "If you had  faith as a grain of mustard seed,
M    17.20    For truly, I say to you, if you have faith as a grain of mustard seed,
     M  21.21      "Truly, I say to you, if you have faith and never doubt, you will not
     Mk 11.23      Truly, I say to you, whoever says


L    17.6                                                        you could say
M    17.20                                                       you will  say
     M  21.21   only do what has been done to the fig tree, but even if you       say


L    17.6     to this sycamine tree, 'Be rooted up, and be planted in   the sea,' and
M    17.20    to this mountain,      'Move from here              to       there,' and
     M  21.21   to this mountain,      'Be taken  up  and    cast  into the sea,'
     Mk 11.23   to this mountain,      'Be taken  up  and    cast  into the sea,' and


     Mk 11.23   does not doubt in his heart, but believes that what he says will come to


L    17.6              it would obey you.
M    17.21             it will move; and nothing will be impossible to you."  "But this
     M  21.22          it will be done.                                        And
     Mk 11.24   pass, it will be done for him.                                 Therefore


     M  17.21   kind never     comes  out except by prayer and fasting."
     M  21.22              whatever you ask      in prayer,           you will receive,
     Mk 11.24   I tell you, whatever you ask     in prayer, believe that you have received


     M  21.22       if you have faith."
     Mk 11.24   it, and it  will be yours.


L    17.7         "Will any one of you, who has a servant plowing or keeping sheep, say
L    17.7     to him when he has come in from the field, 'Come at once and sit down at
L    17.8     table'?  Will he not rather say to him, 'Prepare supper for me, and gird
L    17.8     yourself and serve me, till I eat and drink; and afterward you shall eat
L    17.9     and drink'?  Does he thank the servant because he did what was commanded?
L    17.10    So you also, when you have done all that is commanded you, say, 'We are
L    17.10    unworthy servants; we have only done what was our duty.'"
```

Luke 17.11-19

L   17.11   <u>On the way to Jerusalem he was passing along between Samaria and</u>

L   17.12   <u>Galilee.</u> <u>And as he entered   a village,</u>
  M   8.1   <u>When</u> <u>he</u> *came down from the mountain, great crowds followed*
  Mk 1.45b   <u>and</u>   *people came to*
  L   5.12   <u>While</u> <u>he</u> *was in one of the cities,*

L   17.12   <u>he was met by ten lepers, who stood at a distance</u>
  M   8.2   *him;*   *and behold, a* <u>leper</u> *came to him*
  Mk 1.40   *him from every quarter. And*   *a* <u>leper</u> *came to him beseeching him,*
  L   5.12   *there came a man full of* <u>leprosy;</u> *and when he saw Jesus,*

L   17.13 |<u>and lifted up their voices and said,</u>   <u>"Jesus, Master,</u>   <u>have</u>
  M   8.2   <u>and</u> *knelt before him,*   <u>saying,</u>   *"Lord, if you will, you can*
  Mk 1.40   <u>and</u> *kneeling*   <u>said</u> *to him,*   *"If you will, you can*
  L   5.12   *he fell on his face*   <u>and</u> *besought him, "Lord, if you will, you can*

L   17.14   <u>mercy on us."</u>   <u>When he saw</u>
  M   8.2   *make me clean."*
  Mk 1.43   *make me clean." And he sternly charged him, and sent him away at once,*
  L   5.14   *make me clean." And he   charged him*

L   17.14   <u>them he</u>   <u>said to them,</u>   <u>"Go and</u>
  M   8.4   *And Jesus* <u>said to him,</u> *"See that you say nothing to any one; but* <u>go,</u>
  Mk 1.44 |*and*   <u>said to him,</u> *"See that you say nothing to any one; but* <u>go,</u>
  L   5.14   *to tell*   *no one, but* <u>"go and</u>

L   17.14   <u>show yourselves to the priests."</u>
  M   8.4   <u>show yourself</u> <u>to the</u> *priest, and*   *offer*   *the gift*
  Mk 1.44   <u>show yourself</u> <u>to the</u> *priest, and*   *offer*   *for your cleansing*
  L   5.14   <u>show yourself</u> <u>to the priest,</u> *and make an offering for your cleansing,*

  M   8.3   *that Moses commanded, for a proof to the people."*   *And he*
  Mk 1.41   *what Moses commanded, for a proof to the people." Moved with pity, he*
  L   5.13   *as   Moses commanded, for a proof to the people."*   *And he*

  M   8.3   *stretched out his hand and touched him,   saying,   "I will; be*
  Mk 1.41   *stretched out his hand and touched him, and said to him, "I will; be*
  L   5.13   *stretched out his hand, and touched him,   saying,   "I will; be*

L   17.14   <u>And as they went they</u>   <u>were cleansed.</u>
  M   8.3   *clean."* <u>And</u> *immediately his leprosy was* <u>cleansed.</u>
  Mk 1.42   *clean."* <u>And</u> *immediately the leprosy left him, and he was made clean.*
  L   5.13   *clean."* <u>And</u> *immediately the leprosy left him.*

  Mk 1.45   *But he went out and began to talk freely about it, and to spread the*
  L   5.15   *But so much the more the report went abroad concerning him;*

  Mk 1.45   *news, so that Jesus could no longer openly enter a town, but was out in*

  Mk 1.45   *the country; and   people   came   to him from every quarter.*
  L   5.15   *and great multitudes gathered to hear and to be healed of*

  L   5.16   *their infirmities. But he withdrew to the wilderness and prayed.*

```
L   17.15    Then one of them, when he saw that he was healed, turned back, praising
L   17.16    God with a loud voice; and he fell on his face at Jesus' feet, giving
L   17.17    him thanks.  Now he was a Samaritan. |Then said Jesus, "Were not ten
L   17.18    cleansed?  Where are the nine? |Was no one found to return and give
L   17.19    praise to God except this foreigner?"  And he said to him, "Rise and
L   17.19    go your way; your faith has made you well."
```

75. THE KINGDOM OF GOD AND THE SON OF MAN

Luke 17.20-37

```
M   24.19    And alas for those who are with child and for those who give suck in
M   24.20    those days!  Pray that your flight may not be in winter or on a sabbath.
M   24.21    For then there will be great tribulation, such as has not been from the
M   24.22    beginning of the world until now, no, and never will be.  And if those
M   24.22    days had not been shortened, no human being would be saved; but for the
M   24.22    sake of the elect those days will be shortened.
```

```
L   17.20    Being asked by the Pharisees when the kingdom of God was coming, he
L   17.20    answered them, "The kingdom of God is not coming with signs to be
```

```
L   17.21    observed; nor will    they    say,        'Lo,    here it is!'
M   24.23              Then if any one  says to you, 'Lo,    here    is the
Mk  13.21             And then if any one  says to you, 'Look,  here    is the
```

```
L   17.21            or       'There!' for behold, the kingdom of God is in the midst
M   24.24    Christ!' or      'There he is!' do not believe it.  For false Christs
Mk  13.22    Christ!' or 'Look, there he is!' do not believe it.       False Christs
```

```
L   17.22    of you."  And he said to the disciples, "The days are coming when you
M   24.24    and false prophets will arise and show great signs and wonders, so as
Mk  13.22    and false prophets will arise and show       signs and wonders,
```

```
L   17.22    will desire to see one of the days of the Son of man, and you will not
M   24.25    to lead astray, if possible, even the elect.    Lo,      I have told
Mk  13.23    to lead astray, if possible,    the elect.  But take heed; I have told
```

```
L   17.23    see it.                       And    they will say to you, 'Lo, there!'
M   24.26    you             beforehand.  So, if they      say to you, 'Lo, he is in
Mk  13.23    you all things beforehand.
```

```
L   17.23    or 'Lo, here!'   Do not go,
M   24.26    the wilderness,' do not go out; if they say, 'Lo, he is in the inner
```

```
L   17.24            do not follow  them.  For as the lightning flashes
M   24.27    rooms,' do not believe it.     For as the lightning comes from the east
```

```
L   17.24    and lights up the sky from one side to the other, so will
M   24.27    and shines as far as the west,                 so will be the coming
```

```
L   17.25        the Son of man be in his day.  But first he must suffer many things
M   24.27    of the Son of man.
```

| L | 17.25 | and be rejected by this generation. |

M 24.36   *"But of that day and hour no one knows, not even the angels of heaven,*
M 24.36   *nor the Son, but the Father only.*

L 17.26   As it was in the days of Noah, so will it be in the days   of the Son of
M 24.37   As   were   the days of Noah, so will   be   the coming of the Son of

L 17.27   man.   They   ate,   they drank
M 24.38   man.   For as in those days before the flood they were eating and drinking,

L 17.27   they married, they were given   in marriage, until the day when Noah
M 24.38   marrying   and   giving in marriage, until the day when Noah

L 17.27   entered the ark,   and   the flood came and destroyed
M 24.39   entered the ark, |and they did not know until the flood came and swept

L 17.28   them all. Likewise as it was in the days of Lot--they ate, they drank,
M 24.39   them all away,

L 17.29   they bought, they sold, they planted, they built, |but on the day when
L 17.29   Lot went out from Sodom fire and sulphur rained from heaven and destroyed

L 17.30   them all--|so will it be on the day when the Son of man is revealed.
M 24.39   so will   be the coming of   the Son of man.

M 24.15   *"So   when you see   the*
Mk 13.14   *"But when you see   the*
L 21.20   *"But when you see Jerusalem surrounded by armies, then know that its*

M 24.15   *desolating sacrilege spoken of by the prophet Daniel, standing in the*
Mk 13.14   *desolating sacrilege   set up   where*
L 21.20   *desolation has come near.*

M 24.16   *holy place   (let the reader understand), |then let those who are*
Mk 13.14   *it ought not to be (let the reader understand),   then let those who are*
L 21.21   *Then let those who are*

L 17.31   On that day, let him   who is   on the housetop,
M 24.17   *in Judea flee to the mountains;   let him   who is   on the housetop*
Mk 13.15   *in Judea flee to the mountains;   let him   who is   on the housetop*
L 21.21   *in Judea flee to the mountains, and let those who are inside the city*

L 17.31   with his goods in the house, not come down   to take
M 24.17   not go   down   to take
Mk 13.15   not go   down, nor enter his house, to take
L 21.21   *depart, and let not those who are out*

L 17.31   them   away;   and likewise let him who is in the field not turn
M 24.17   what is in his house; and   let him who is in the field not turn
Mk 13.16   anything away;   and   let him who is in the field not turn
L 21.22   *in the country enter it; for these are days of vengeance, to fulfil all*

449

```
L    17.32    back.  Remember Lot's wife.
M    24.18    back to take his mantle.
Mk   13.17    back to take his mantle.
 L   21.23    that is written.


L    17.33         Whoever seeks to gain  his life will lose  it, but whoever loses his
 M   10.39         He who              finds his life will lose  it, and he who  loses his
 M   16.25    For whoever would     save  his life will lose  it, and whoever loses his
 Mk   8.35    For whoever would     save  his life will lose  it; and whoever loses his
 L    9.24    For whoever would     save  his life will lose  it; and whoever loses his
 J   12.25         He who              loves his life      loses it, and he who  hates his


L    17.33    life                         will preserve it.
 M   10.39    life for my sake             will find    it.
 M   16.25    life for my sake             will find    it.
 Mk   8.35    life for my sake and the gospel's will save  it.
 L    9.24    life for my sake,         he will save  it.
 J   12.25    life in this world           will keep    it for eternal life.


L    17.34    I tell you, in that night there will be two              in one bed;  one
M    24.40              Then                        two men will be in the field;  one


L    17.35    will be taken and the other  left.  There will be two women
M    24.41         is taken and    one is left.              Two women will be


L    17.36    grinding together;   one will be taken and the other  left.        Two
M    24.40    grinding at the mill; one      is taken and    one is left.  Then two


L    17.36    men will be in the field; one will be taken and the other  left."
M    24.40    men will be in the field; one      is taken and    one is left.


L    17.37    And they said to him, "Where, Lord?"  He said to them, "Where     the
M    24.28                                                          Wherever the


L    17.37    body is, there the eagles will be gathered together."
M    24.28    body is, there the eagles will be gathered together.
```

76. THE UNJUST JUDGE

Luke 18.1-8

```
L    18.1         And he told them a parable, to the effect that they ought always to
L    18.2     pray and not lose heart.  He said, "In a certain city there was a judge
L    18.3     who neither feared God nor regarded man; and there was a widow in that
L    18.3     city who kept coming to him and saying, 'Vindicate me against my adver-
L    18.4     sary.'  For a while he refused; but afterward he said to himself, 'Though
L    18.5     I neither fear God nor regard man, |yet because this widow bothers me,
L    18.5     I will vindicate her, or she will wear me out by her continual coming.'"
L    18.6,7   And the Lord said, "Hear what the unrighteous judge says.  And will not
L    18.7     God vindicate his elect, who cry to him day and night?  Will he delay
L    18.8     long over them?  I tell you, he will vindicate them speedily.  Never-
L    18.8     theless, when the Son of man comes, will he find faith on earth?"
```

77. THE PHARISEE AND THE TAX COLLECTOR

Luke 18.9-14

L	18.9	He also told this parable to some who trusted in themselves that they
L	18.10	were righteous and despised others: "Two men went up into the temple to
L	18.11	pray, one a Pharisee and the other a tax collector. The Pharisee stood
L	18.11	and prayed thus with himself, 'God, I thank thee that I am not like other
L	18.11	men, extortioners, unjust, adulterers, or even like this tax collector.
L	18.12,13	I fast twice a week, I give tithes of all that I get.' But the tax
L	18.13	collector, standing far off, would not even lift up his eyes to heaven,
L	18.14	but beat his breast, saying, 'God, be merciful to me a sinner!' I tell
L	18.14	you, this man went down to his house justified rather than the other;

L	18.14	for every one who exalts himself will be humbled, but he who humbles
M	23.12	whoever exalts himself will be humbled, and whoever humbles
L	*14.11*	For every one who exalts himself will be humbled, *and* he who humbles

L	18.14	himself will be exalted."
M	23.12	himself will be exalted.
L	*14.11*	himself will be exalted."

78. LET THE CHILDREN COME

Luke 18.15-17

L	18.15	Now they were bringing even infants to him that he might touch
M	19.13	Then children were brought to him that he might lay
Mk	10.13	And they were bringing children to him, that he might touch

L	18.15	them; and when the disciples saw it, they rebuked
M	19.13	his hands on them and pray. The disciples rebuked the
Mk	10.13	them; and the disciples rebuked

L	18.16	them. But Jesus called them to him, saying, "Let
M	19.14	people; but Jesus said, "Let
Mk	10.14	them. But when Jesus saw it he was indignant, and said to them, "Let

L	18.16	the children come to me, and do not hinder them; for to such belongs the
M	19.14	the children come to me, and do not hinder them; for to such belongs the
Mk	10.14	the children come to me, do not hinder them; for to such belongs the

L	18.17	kingdom of God. Truly, I say to you, whoever does not
M	19.14	kingdom of heaven."
Mk	10.15	kingdom of God. Truly, I say to you, whoever does not
M	*18.3*	*and said,* "Truly, I say to you, *unless you turn and*
J	*3.3*	*Jesus answered him,* "Truly, *truly,* I say to you, *unless one is born*
J	*3.5*	*Jesus answered,* "Truly, *truly,* I say to you, *unless one is born*

L	18.17	receive the kingdom of God like a child shall not enter
Mk	10.15	receive the kingdom of God like a child shall not enter
M	*18.3*	*become like children, you will never enter the*
J	*3.3*	*anew, he cannot see the*
J	*3.5*	*of water and the Spirit, he cannot enter the*

L	18.17	<u>it</u>."							
M	19.15		*And he*				*laid*	*his hands on*	
Mk	10.16	it." *And he took them in his arms and blessed them, laying his hands upon*							
M	18.3	*kingdom of heaven.*							
J	3.3	*kingdom of God."*							
J	3.5	*kingdom of God.*							

M	19.15	*them and went away.*
Mk	10.16	*them.*

79. THE PERIL OF RICHES

Luke 18.18-30

L	18.18	<u>And</u>				<u>a ruler</u>		
M	19.16	<u>And</u> behold,				one	came	up
Mk	10.17	<u>And</u> as he was setting out on his journey,		a man	ran	up and knelt
L	10.25	<u>And</u> *behold,*				*a lawyer stood up to put*		

L	18.18			<u>asked him</u>, "<u>Good Teacher, what</u>				<u>shall</u>
M	19.16	to	him,	saying,	"<u>Teacher, what</u> good deed must			
Mk	10.17	before him,	and <u>asked him</u>, "<u>Good Teacher, what</u>			must		
L	10.25	*him to the test, saying,*		"<u>Teacher, what</u>				<u>shall</u>

L	18.19	<u>I do to inherit eternal life</u>?" <u>And Jesus said to him, "Why do you call</u>
M	19.17	<u>I do, to have eternal life</u>?" <u>And he said to him, "Why do you ask</u>
Mk	10.18	<u>I do to inherit eternal life</u>?" <u>And Jesus said to him, "Why do you call</u>
L	10.26	<u>I do to inherit eternal life</u>?" *He* <u>said to him,</u>

L	18.20	<u>me</u>			<u>good? No one</u>		<u>is good but God alone.</u>	|<u>You</u>
M	19.17	<u>me</u> about what is <u>good?</u>		One there is who <u>is good.</u>			If <u>you</u>	
Mk	10.19	<u>me</u>			<u>good? No one</u>		<u>is good but God alone.</u>	|<u>You</u>
L	10.26						*"What is written*	

L	18.20		<u>know the commandments</u>:		
M	19.18	would enter life,	<u>keep the commandments</u>."		He said to him,
Mk	10.19		<u>know the commandments</u>:		
L	10.27		*in the law? How do you read?"*	*And he answered,*	

L	18.20		'Do not commit adultery, Do	not
M	19.18	"Which?" And Jesus said, "You shall <u>not</u> kill,	You shall <u>not</u>	
Mk	10.19		'Do <u>not</u> kill, Do	<u>not</u>
L	10.27	*"You shall love the Lord your God with all*		

L	18.20	<u>kill,</u>	Do <u>not steal</u>,	Do not bear false witness,
M	19.18	commit adultery, You shall <u>not steal</u>, You shall <u>not bear false witness,</u>		
Mk	10.19	commit adultery, Do <u>not steal</u>,	Do not bear false witness,	
L	10.27	*your heart, and with all your soul, and with all your strength, and*		

L	18.20		Honor your father and mother.'"	
M	19.19		|Honor your father and mother, and, You shall love your	
Mk	10.19	Do not defraud, <u>Honor your father and mother</u>.'"		
L	10.27	*with all your mind;*	*and*	*your*

L	18.21		And	he	said,	"All these
M	19.20	neighbor as yourself."	The young man	said to him,		"All these
Mk	10.20		And	he	said to him, "Teacher, all these
L	10.28	*neighbor as yourself."*	And	he	said to him,	*"You have*

452

```
L    18.22    I have observed  from my youth."  And when Jesus heard it,
M    19.21    I have observed; what do I still lack?"  Jesus
Mk   10.21    I have observed  from my youth."  And    Jesus looking upon him loved
 L   10.28    answered right; do this, and you will live."


L    18.22              he said to him, "One thing you still lack.          Sell all
M    19.21                 said to him, "If        you would be perfect,    go,  sell
Mk   10.21    him, and  said to him,              "You       lack one thing; go,  sell


L    18.22    that you have     and distribute to the poor, and you will have treasure
M    19.21    what you possess  and give         to the poor, and you will have treasure
Mk   10.21    what you have,    and give         to the poor, and you will have treasure


L    18.23    in heaven; and come, follow me."  But when         he   heard this
M    19.22    in heaven; and come, follow me."       When the young man heard this
Mk   10.22    in heaven; and come, follow me."  At that saying his countenance fell,


L    18.24       he became    sad,      for he was very  rich.          Jesus
M    19.23       he went away sorrowful; for he had great possessions.  And Jesus
Mk   10.23   and he went away sorrowful; for he had great possessions.  And Jesus


L    18.24    looking at him      said,                              "How
M    19.23                        said to his disciples, "Truly, I say to you, it will
Mk   10.23    looked   around and said to his disciples,             "How


L    18.24       hard it      is for those who have riches   to enter the kingdom of
M    19.23    be hard             for          a rich man to enter the kingdom of
Mk   10.23       hard it will be for those who have riches   to enter the kingdom of


L    18.24    God!
M    19.23    heaven.
Mk   10.24    God!"  |And the disciples were amazed at his words.  But Jesus said to


L    18.25                                                          For it is
M    19.24        Again I tell you,                                   it is
Mk   10.25    them again, "Children, how hard it is to enter the kingdom of God!  It is


L    18.25    easier for a camel to go through the eye of a needle than for a rich man
M    19.24    easier for a camel to go through the eye of a needle than for a rich man
Mk   10.25    easier for a camel to go through the eye of a needle than for a rich man


L    18.26    to enter the kingdom of God."          Those who heard it
M    19.25    to enter the kingdom of God."  When the disciples heard this they were
Mk   10.26    to enter the kingdom of God."  And                     they were


L    18.27                         said,        "Then who can be saved?"  But
M    19.26    greatly     astonished,    saying,   "Who then can be saved?"  But
Mk   10.26    exceedingly astonished, and said to him, "Then who can be saved?"


L    18.27    he                    said,      "What      is impossible
M    19.26    Jesus looked at them and said to them, "With men this is impossible,
Mk   10.27    Jesus looked at them and said,       "With men it   is impossible,
```

L	18.28	with men	is possible with God." And Peter
M	19.27	but with God all things are possible."	Then Peter
Mk	10.28	but not with God; for all things are possible with God."	Peter

L	18.28	said, "Lo, we have left our homes and followed you."
M	19.27	said in reply, "Lo, we have left everything and followed you.
Mk	10.28	began to say to him, "Lo, we have left everything and followed you."

L	18.29	And he said to them, "Truly, I say to you,
M	19.28	What then shall we have?" Jesus said to them, "Truly, I say to you, in
Mk	10.29	Jesus said, "Truly, I say to you,

M	*19.28*	*the new world, when the Son of man shall sit on his glorious throne, you*
M	*19.28*	*who have followed me will also sit on twelve thrones, judging the twelve*

L	18.29	there is no man who has left house or wife or brothers
M	19.29	*tribes of Israel.* And every one who has left houses or brothers
Mk	10.29	there is no one who has left house or brothers
L	*14.26*	*"If any one comes to me and does not hate*

L	18.29	or parents or children, for the
M	19.29	or sisters or father or mother or children or lands, for my
Mk	10.29	or sisters or mother or father or children or lands, for my
L	*14.26*	*his own father and mother and wife and children and brothers and*

L	18.30	sake of the kingdom of God, |who will not receive manifold
M	19.29	name's sake, will receive a hundredfold
Mk	10.30	sake and for the gospel, |who will not receive a hundredfold
L	*14.26*	*sisters, yes, and even his own life, he cannot be my disciple.*

L	18.30	more in this time,
Mk	10.30	now in this time, houses and brothers and sisters and mothers and children

L	18.30	and in the age to come eternal life."
M	19.29	and inherit eternal life.
Mk	10.30	and lands, with persecutions, and in the age to come eternal life.

M	*19.30*	*But many that are first will be last, and the last first.*
Mk	*10.31*	*But many that are first will be last, and the last first."*

80. THIRD PREDICTION OF THE PASSION

Luke 18.31-34

M	*20.17*	*And as Jesus was going up to Jerusalem,*
Mk	*10.32*	*And they were on the road, going up to Jerusalem, and Jesus was*

Mk	*10.32*	*walking ahead of them; and they were amazed, and those who followed were*

L	18.31	And taking the twelve, he
M	20.17	he took the twelve disciples aside, and on the way he
Mk	10.32	*afraid.* And taking the twelve again, he began to

```
L   18.31    said to them,                                    "Behold, we are going
M   20.18    said to them,                                   |"Behold, we are going
Mk  10.33    tell    them what was to happen to him, |saying, "Behold, we are going


L   18.31    up to Jerusalem, and everything that is written of the Son of man by the
M   20.18    up to Jerusalem; and                            the Son of man
Mk  10.33    up to Jerusalem; and                            the Son of man


L   18.31    prophets will be accomplished.
M   20.18            will be delivered to the chief priests and    scribes, and they
Mk  10.33            will be delivered to the chief priests and the scribes, and they


L   18.32                         For he will be delivered    to the Gentiles,
M   20.19    will condemn him to death, |and           deliver him to the Gentiles
Mk  10.33    will condemn him to death,  and           deliver him to the Gentiles;


L   18.33    and        will be mocked and shamefully treated and spit upon; they will
M   20.19           to be mocked                                              and
Mk  10.34    and they will     mock   him,              and spit upon him,    and


L   18.33    scourge him  and kill him,  and on the third day  he will    rise."
M   20.19    scourged     and crucified, and               he will be raised on
Mk  10.34    scourge him, and kill him;  and after  three days he will    rise."


L   18.34    But they understood none of these things; this saying was hid from them,
M   20.19    the third day."


L   18.34    and they did not grasp what was said.
```

81. A BLIND MAN AT JERICHO

Luke 18.35-43

```
L   18.35        As  he    drew near to Jericho,
M   20.29                                    And as they  went out  of    Jericho,
Mk  10.46    And they came       to Jericho; and as he    was leaving    Jericho
 M   9.27                             And as Jesus passed on from there,


L   18.35                                                                      a
M   20.30                        a great crowd followed him.  And behold, two
Mk  10.46    with his disciples and a great multitude,         Bartimaeus, a
 M   9.27                                                                   two


L   18.35    blind man                        was sitting by the roadside begging;
M   20.30    blind men                            sitting by the roadside,
Mk  10.46    blind beggar, the son of Timaeus, was sitting by the roadside.
 M   9.27    blind men                            followed him,


L   18.36    and          hearing a multitude going by, he inquired what this meant.
M   20.30        when they heard
Mk  10.47    And when he    heard
```

L	18.37,38	They told him, "Jesus of Nazareth is passing by." And he				
M	20.30	that Jesus was passing by,				
Mk	10.47	that it was Jesus of Nazareth, he began to				

L   18.37,38   <u>They told him</u>, "Jesus of Nazareth is   passing by."   And he
M   20.30   that   <u>Jesus</u>   was <u>passing by,</u>
Mk   10.47   that it was   Jesus of Nazareth,   he began to

L   18.38   <u>cried</u>,   "Jesus, Son of David, <u>have mercy on me!</u>"
M   20.30   <u>cried</u> out,   "Have mercy on us, Son of
Mk   10.47   cry   out and say, "<u>Jesus, Son of David,</u> <u>have mercy on me!</u>"
   M   9.27   *crying aloud,*   "*Have mercy on us, Son of*

L   18.39   <u>And those who were in front</u> rebuked him, <u>telling him</u> to be
M   20.31   David!" The crowd   <u>rebuked</u> them, <u>telling</u> them to be
Mk   10.48   <u>And</u> many   <u>rebuked him,</u> <u>telling him</u> to be
   M   9.28   *David." When he entered the house,*

L   18.39   silent; <u>but he</u>   cried out all the more, "Son of David, have mercy on
M   20.31   silent; <u>but</u> they <u>cried out</u>   the more, "Lord,   have mercy on
Mk   10.48   silent; <u>but he</u>   cried out all the more, "Son of David, have mercy on
   M   9.28   *the blind men came to him;*

L   18.40   <u>me!</u>"   And Jesus stopped, and   commanded him to be
M   20.32   us, Son of David!" <u>And Jesus stopped</u> <u>and</u>   called   them,
Mk   10.49   me!"   <u>And Jesus stopped</u> <u>and</u> said, "Call   him." And

Mk   10.49   *they called the blind man, saying to him, "Take heart; rise, he is calling*
Mk   10.50   *you." And throwing off his mantle he sprang up and came to Jesus.*

L   18.41   <u>brought to him; and when he came near, he asked</u>   him, |"What do you
M   20.32   saying, "What do you
Mk   10.51   And Jesus said to him, "What do you
   M   9.28   *said to them,* "Do you

L   18.41   <u>want me to do for you?</u>"   He   said,   "Lord,
M   20.33   <u>want me to do for you?</u>"   They <u>said</u> to him,   "Lord,
Mk   10.51   <u>want me to do for you?</u>" And the blind man <u>said</u> to him,   "Master,
   M   9.28   *believe that I am able to do this?" They* <u>*said*</u> *to him, "Yes, Lord."*

L   18.42   <u>let me receive my sight.</u>" And Jesus said to him, "Receive your sight;
M   20.34   <u>let</u> our eyes be opened." And Jesus in pity touched their eyes,
Mk   10.52   <u>let me receive my sight.</u>" And Jesus said to him, "Go your way;
   M   9.29   *Then he*   *touched their eyes, saying*

L   18.43   <u>your faith has made you well.</u>" And immediately he
M   20.34   and immediately they
Mk   10.52   <u>your faith has made you well.</u>" And immediately he
   M   9.30   *"According to* <u>*your faith*</u> *be it done to you." And*   *their eyes*

L   18.43   <u>received his</u>   sight and followed him, glorifying God; and all the people,
M   20.34   <u>received</u> their <u>sight and followed him</u>.
Mk   10.52   <u>received his</u>   sight and followed him on the way.
   M   9.30   *were opened. And Jesus sternly charged them, "See that no one knows it."*

L   18.43   <u>when they saw it, gave praise to God.</u>
   M   9.31   *But they went away and spread his fame through all that district.*

82. ZACCHAEUS

Luke 19.1-10

L	19.1,2	He entered Jericho and was passing through. And there was a man named
L	19.3	Zacchaeus; he was a chief tax collector, and rich. And he sought to see
L	19.3	who Jesus was, but could not, on account of the crowd, because he was
L	19.4	small of stature. So he ran on ahead and climbed up into a sycamore tree
L	19.5	to see him, for he was to pass that way. And when Jesus came to the place,
L	19.5	he looked up and said to him, "Zacchaeus, make haste and come down; for I
L	19.6	must stay at your house today." So he made haste and came down, and
L	19.7	received him joyfully. And when they saw it they all murmured, "He has
L	19.8	gone in to be the guest of a man who is a sinner." And Zacchaeus stood
L	19.8	and said to the Lord, "Behold, Lord, the half of my goods I give to the
L	19.8	poor; and if I have defrauded any one of anything, I restore it fourfold."
L	19.9	And Jesus said to him, "Today salvation has come to this house, since he
L	19.10	also is a son of Abraham. For the Son of man came to seek and to save
L	19.10	the lost."

83. THE POUNDS

Luke 19.11-28

L	19.11	As they heard these things, he proceeded to tell a parable, because
L	19.11	he was near to Jerusalem, and because they supposed that the kingdom of
L	19.11	God was to appear immediately.

L	19.12	He said therefore, "A nobleman went into a far country to receive
M	25.14	"For it will be as when a man going on a journey
Mk	13.34	It is like a man going on a journey, when he leaves

L	19.13	a kingdom and then return. Calling ten of his servants,
M	25.14	called his servants and entrusted
Mk	13.34	home and puts his servants in charge,

L	19.13	he gave them ten pounds,
M	25.15	to them his property; to one he gave five talents, to another two,

L	19.13	and said to them, 'Trade with these till I come.'
M	25.15	to another one, to each according to his ability. Then he went away.
Mk	13.34	each with his work, and commands the doorkeeper to

L	19.14	But his citizens hated him and sent an embassy after him, saying, 'We
M	25.16	He who had received the five talents went at once and traded with them;
Mk	13.34	be on the watch.

L	19.14	do not want this man to reign over us.'
M	25.17	and he made five talents more. So also, he who had the two talents

M	25.18	made two talents more. But he who had received the one talent went and
M	25.18	dug in the ground and hid his master's money.

L	19.15	When he returned, having
M	25.19	Now after a long time the master of those servants came

```
L    19.15    received the kingdom, he commanded these servants, to whom he had given
L    19.15    the money, to be called to him that he might know what they


L    19.16             had gained by trading.     The first
M    25.20    and settled accounts with them.  And he who had received the five talents


L    19.16    came before him,                          saying, 'Lord,
M    25.20    came forward, bringing five talents more, saying, 'Master, you delivered


L    19.17         your pound         has made ten pounds more.'  And he       said
M    25.21    to me five talents; here I have made five talents more.'  His master said


L    19.17    to him, 'Well done, good             servant!  Because you have been
M    25.21    to him, 'Well done, good and faithful servant;       you have been
  L  16.10                                                    "He who  is


L    19.17    faithful in   a very little, you shall have authority over ten cities.'
M    25.21    faithful over a     little, I   will  set you       over much; enter
  L  16.10    faithful in   a very little is faithful also       in  much; and he


L    19.18                                    And the second                came,
M    25.22    into the joy of your master.'  And he also who had the two talents came
  L  16.10    who is dishonest in a very little is dishonest also in much.


L    19.18             saying, 'Lord,                your pound         has
M    25.22    forward, saying, 'Master, you delivered to me two  talents; here I have


L    19.19    made five pounds.'      And he      said to him,
M    25.23    made two   talents more.'  His master said to him, 'Well done, good and


L    19.19                                              'And you
M    25.23    faithful servant; you have been faithful over a little, I will set you


L    19.20    are to be over five cities.'              Then another
M    25.24a            over much; enter into the joy of your master.'  He also who


L    19.20                         came,      saying, 'Lord,    here
M    25.25c    had received the one talent came forward, saying, 'Master, |Here you have


L    19.20          is your pound, which I       kept laid away in a   napkin;
M    25.25b    what is yours.'   |and  I went and hid your talent in the ground.


L    19.21         for I was afraid of you, because you   are a severe man;  you
M    25.25a,24b,d |so  I was afraid,        |I knew you to be a hard  man, |and


L    19.21    take up   what you did not lay down, and reap   what  you did not sow.'
M    25.24c    gathering where you did not winnow;   |reaping where you did not sow,


L    19.22          He     said to him, 'I will condemn you out of your own mouth,
M    25.26a    But his master answered him,
```

458

| L | 19.22 | you wicked   servant! You knew that I was a severe man, |
| M | 25.26a | 'You wicked and slothful servant! You knew that I |

| L | 19.22 | taking up what I did not lay down and reaping what I did not |
| M | 25.26c,b | \|and gather   where I have not winnowed? \|reap   where I have not |

| L | 19.23 | sow? Why then did you   not put   my money into the bank, |
| M | 25.27 | sowed,   \|Then   you ought to have invested my money with the bankers, |

| L | 19.23 | and at my coming I should have collected it   with interest?' |
| M | 25.27 | and at my coming I should have received what was my own with interest. |

| L | 19.24 | And he said to those who stood by, 'Take the pound from him, and give |
| M | 25.28 | So take the talent from him, and give |

| L | 19.25 | it to him who has the ten pounds.' (And they said to him, 'Lord, he has |
| M | 25.28 | it to him who has the ten talents. |

L	19.26	ten pounds!') 'I tell you, that to every one who has will more be given;
M	25.29	For to every one who has will more be given,
M	13.12	For to him who has will more be given,
Mk	4.25	For to him who has will more be given;
L	8.18	Take heed then how you hear; for to him who has will more be given,

L	19.26	but from him who has not, even what he
M	25.29	and he will have abundance; but from him who has not, even what he
M	13.12	and he will have abundance; but from him who has not, even what he
Mk	4.25	and from him who has not, even what he
L	8.18	and from him who has not, even what he thinks

L	19.27	has will be taken away. But as for these enemies of mine, who
M	25.30	has will be taken away. And cast the worthless servant into
M	13.12	has will be taken away.
Mk	4.25	has will be taken away."
L	8.18	that he has will be taken away."

| L | 19.27 | did not want me to reign over them, bring them here and slay them before |
| M | 25.30 | the outer darkness; there men will weep and gnash their teeth.' |

| L | 19.27 | me.'" |

| L | 19.28 | And when he had said this, he went on ahead, going up to Jerusalem. |

84. JESUS APPROACHES JERUSALEM

Luke 19.29-44

L	19.29	When he
M	21.1	And when they
Mk	11.1	And when they
J	12.12	The next day a great crowd who had come to the feast heard that Jesus

459

```
L    19.29   drew near                                to Bethphage and Bethany, at the mount
M    21.1    drew near   to Jerusalem  and came to Bethphage,                   to the Mount
Mk   11.1    drew near   to Jerusalem,            to Bethphage and Bethany, at the Mount
J    12.12   was coming to Jerusalem.


L    19.30   that is called Olivet,        he    sent two of the disciples,    |saying,
M    21.2                 of Olives, then Jesus  sent two           disciples, |saying
Mk   11.2                 of Olives,       he    sent two of his disciples, |and said


L    19.30              "Go into the village opposite,                     where on
M    21.2    to them, "Go into the village opposite you, and immediately
Mk   11.2    to them, "Go into the village opposite you, and immediately as you


L    19.30   entering you will find a  colt tied, on which no one has ever yet sat;
M    21.2             you will find an ass  tied, and a colt with her;
Mk   11.2    enter it you will find a  colt tied, on which no one has ever     sat;


L    19.31   untie it   and bring it   here.  If any one asks            you, 'Why
M    21.3    untie them and bring them to me. If any one says anything to you,
Mk   11.3    untie it   and bring it.         If any one says         to you, 'Why


L    19.31   are you untying it?' you shall say this, 'The Lord has need of it.'"
M    21.3                         you shall say,      'The Lord has need of them,'
Mk   11.3    are you doing this?'         say,        'The Lord has need of it


  M  21.4    and he will send them           immediately."  This took place to fulfil
  Mk 11.3    and    will send it  back here immediately.'"

  M  21.4    what was spoken by the prophet, saying,
  J  12.14b  as it is written,

  M  21.5              "Tell the  daughter of Zion,
  J  12.15             "Fear not, daughter of Zion;

  M  21.5              Behold, your king is coming to you,
  J  12.15             behold, your king is coming,

  M  21.5              humble, and mounted on an ass,
  J  12.15                  sitting on an ass's

  M  21.5              and on a colt, the foal of an ass."
  J  12.15                 colt!"


L    19.32   So   those who were sent went away and found  it   as he      had
M    21.6    The disciples            went       and did        as Jesus had
Mk   11.4    And they                 went away, and found a colt tied at the door out


L    19.33   told      them.                           And as they were untying the
M    21.6    directed them;
Mk   11.5    in the open street; and they untied it.  And


L    19.33   colt, its  owners           said to them, "Why  are you         untying
Mk   11.5          those who stood there said to them, "What are you doing, untying


L    19.34   the colt?"  And they said, "The Lord has need of it."
Mk   11.6    the colt?"  And they told them what Jesus had said; and they let them go.
```

460

```
L   19.35    And they  brought                        it   to Jesus, and throwing their
M   21.7              they  brought the      ass and the colt,            and put       their
Mk  11.7     And they  brought                  the colt to Jesus, and threw        their
J   12.14a   And Jesus found    a young ass


L   19.36    garments on the colt      they set Jesus upon it.  And as he rode along,
M   21.8     garments on         them, and he   sat        thereon.            Most of the
Mk  11.8     garments on         it;   and he   sat        upon it.  And        many
J   12.14a                       and        sat        upon it;


L   19.37    they  spread their garments on the road.  As he was  now drawing near, at
M   21.8     crowd spread their garments on the road,  and others cut          branches
Mk  11.8           spread their garments on the road,  and others spread leafy branches
J   12.13                                               So they    took         branches


L   19.37    the descent of the Mount of Olives,            the whole multitude of the
M   21.9     from the trees and spread them on the road.  And the      crowds that
Mk  11.9     which they had cut from the fields.          And          those who
J   12.13    of  palm trees                               and


L   19.37    disciples began to rejoice and praise God with a loud voice for all the
M   21.9     went before      him and that       followed him shouted,   "Hosanna to
Mk  11.9     went before          and those who followed    cried out, "Hosanna!
J   12.13    went out to meet him,                          crying,    "Hosanna!


L   19.38    mighty works that they had seen, |saying, "Blessed is the King who comes
M   21.9     the Son of David!                          Blessed is      he   who comes
Mk  11.9                                                Blessed is      he   who comes
J   12.13                                                Blessed is      he   who comes


L   19.38    in the name of the Lord!                                    Peace in
M   21.9     in the name of the Lord!
Mk  11.10    in the name of the Lord! Blessed is the kingdom of our father David
J   12.13    in the name of the Lord, even the King of Israel!"


L   19.39    heaven        and glory  in the highest!"  And some of the Pharisees in
M   21.10                   Hosanna in the highest!"  And when he entered Jerusalem,
Mk  11.11    that is coming! Hosanna in the highest!"  And      he entered Jerusalem,
J   12.16                                              His disciples did not under-


L   19.40    the multitude said to him, "Teacher, rebuke your disciples."  He answered,
M   21.11    all the city was stirred, saying, "Who is this?"  And the crowds said,
Mk  11.11    and went into the temple; and when he had looked round at everything,
J   12.16    stand this at first; but when Jesus was glorified, then they remembered


L   19.40    "I tell you, if these were silent, the very stones would cry out."
M   21.11    "This is the prophet Jesus from Nazareth of Galilee."
Mk  11.11    as it was already late, he went out to Bethany with the twelve.
J   12.17    that this had been written of him and had been done to him.  The crowd


J   12.17    that had been with him when he called Lazarus out of the tomb and raised
J   12.18    him from the dead bore witness.  The reason why the crowd went to meet
J   12.19    him was that they heard he had done this sign.  The Pharisees then said
J   12.19    to one another, "You see that you can do nothing; look, the world has
J   12.19    gone after him."
```

461

L	19.41,42	And when he drew near and saw the city he wept over it, |saying,
L	19.42	"Would that even today you knew the things that make for peace! But
L	19.43	now they are hid from your eyes. For the days shall come upon you,
L	19.43	when your enemies will cast up a bank about you and surround you, and
L	19.44	hem you in on every side, |and dash you to the ground, you and your
L	19.44	children within you, and they will not leave one stone upon another in
L	19.44	you; because you did not know the time of your visitation."

85. CLEANSING THE TEMPLE

Luke 19.45-48

J 2.13   *The Passover of the Jews was at hand, and Jesus went up to Jerusalem.*

L	19.45		And he entered the temple
M	21.12		And Jesus entered the temple of God
Mk	11.15	And they came to Jerusalem.	And he entered the temple
J	2.14		In the temple he found those

J 2.14   *who were selling oxen and sheep and pigeons, and the money-changers at*
J 2.15   *their business. And making a whip*

L	19.45	and began to drive out those who sold,
M	21.12	and drove out all who sold and bought in the temple,
Mk	11.15	and began to drive out those who sold and those who bought in the temple,
J	2.15	of cords, he drove them all, with the sheep and oxen, out of the temple;

M	21.12	*and he overturned the tables of the money-changers and the seats of*
Mk	11.15	*and he overturned the tables of the money-changers and the seats of*
J	2.15	*and he poured out the coins of the money-changers*

J 2.16   *and overturned their tables.   And he told*

M	21.12	*those who sold pigeons.*
Mk	11.16	*those who sold pigeons; and he would not allow any one to carry any-*
J	2.16	*those who sold the pigeons,*

L	19.46		saying to them, "It is
M	21.13		He said to them, "It is
Mk	11.17	*thing through the temple.* And he taught, and said to them, "Is it not
J	2.16		"Take these

L	19.46	written, 'My house shall be a house of prayer';
M	21.13	written, 'My house shall be called a house of prayer';
Mk	11.17	written, 'My house shall be called a house of prayer for all the nations'?
J	2.16	things away;

L	19.46	but you have made it a den of robbers."
M	21.13	but you make it a den of robbers."
Mk	11.17	But you have made it a den of robbers."
J	2.16	you shall not make my Father's house a house of trade."

J 2.17   *His disciples remembered that it was written, "Zeal for thy house will*
J 2.18   *consume me." The Jews then said to him, "What sign have you to show us*
J 2.19   *for doing this?" Jesus answered them, "Destroy this temple, and in three*

462

J	2.20	days I will raise it up." The Jews then said, "It has taken forty-six
J	2.21	years to build this temple, and will you raise it up in three days?" But
J	2.22	he spoke of the temple of his body. When therefore he was raised from the
J	2.22	dead, his disciples remembered that he had said this; and they believed
J	2.22	the scripture and the word which Jesus had spoken.

L	19.47	And he was teaching daily in the temple.
M	21.14	And the blind and the lame came to him in the temple, and he healed

L	19.47	The chief priests and the scribes and the principal men
M	21.15	them. But when the chief priests and the scribes saw the wonderful things
Mk	11.18	And the chief priests and the scribes heard it

L	19.48	of the people sought to destroy him; but they did not
M	21.15	that he did, and the children crying out in the temple, "Hosanna to the
Mk	11.18	and sought a way to destroy him; for they feared

L	19.48	find anything they could do, for all the people hung upon
M	21.16	Son of David!" they were indignant; and they said to him, "Do you hear
Mk	11.18	him, because all the multitude was astonished

L	19.48	his words.
M	21.16	what these are saying?" And Jesus said to them, "Yes; have you never
Mk	11.18	at his teaching.

M	21.16	read, 'Out of the mouth of babes and sucklings thou hast brought perfect

M	21.17	praise'?" And leaving them, he went out of the city to Bethany
Mk	11.19	And when evening came they went out of the city.

M	21.17	and lodged there.

86. CONTROVERSIES IN JERUSALEM

Luke 20.1-45

a. The Authority of Jesus

Luke 20.1-8

L	20.1	One day, as he was teaching the people
M	21.23	And when he entered
Mk	11.27	And they came again to Jerusalem. And as he was walking

L	20.1	in the temple and preaching the gospel, the chief priests and the scribes
M	21.23	the temple, the chief priests
Mk	11.27	in the temple, the chief priests and the scribes

L	20.2	with the elders came up | and
M	21.23	and the elders of the people came up to him as he was teaching, and
Mk	11.28	and the elders came to him, | and they

L	20.2	said to him, "Tell us by what authority you do these things, or
M	21.23	said, "By what authority are you doing these things, and
Mk	11.28	said to him, "By what authority are you doing these things, or

463

```
L    20.3    who it is that gave you this authority."          He    answered them,
M    21.24   who          gave you this authority?"       Jesus answered them,
Mk   11.29   who          gave you this authority to do them?" Jesus said  to them,


L    20.3    "I also will ask you a question; now        tell me,
M    21.24   "I also will ask you a question; and if you tell me the answer,    then I
Mk   11.29   "I     will ask you a question;                     answer me, and  I


L    20.4                                                            Was the baptism
M    21.25   also will tell you by what authority I do these things.  The baptism
Mk   11.30        will tell you by what authority I do these things. Was the baptism


L    20.5    of John                  from heaven or from men?"           And they
M    21.25   of John, whence was it? From heaven or from men?"           And they
Mk   11.31   of John                  from heaven or from men? Answer me." And they


L    20.5    discussed it with one another, saying, "If we say, 'From heaven,' he will
M    21.25   argued       with one another,          "If we say, 'From heaven,' he will
Mk   11.31   argued       with one another,          "If we say, 'From heaven,' he will


L    20.6    say,        'Why     did you not believe him?' But if    we say, 'From
M    21.26   say to us, 'Why then did you not believe him?' But if    we say, 'From
Mk   11.32   say,        'Why then did you not believe him?' But shall we say, 'From


L    20.6    men,'               all the people will stone us; for they are convince
M    21.26   men,'   we   are afraid of the multitude;        for all      hold
Mk   11.32   men'?"--they were afraid of the people,          for all      held


L    20.7    that John was a      prophet." So they answered that  they did not know
M    21.27   that John was a      prophet." So they answered Jesus, "We do not know."
Mk   11.33   that John was a real prophet. So they answered Jesus, "We do not know."


L    20.8    whence it was. And Jesus said to them, "Neither will I tell you by what
M    21.27                   And he     said to them, "Neither will I tell you by what
Mk   11.33                   And Jesus said to them, "Neither will I tell you by what


L    20.8    authority I do these things."
M    21.27   authority I do these things.
Mk   11.33   authority I do these things."
```

b. The Wicked Tenants

Luke 20.9-19

```
L    20.9             And he began to tell the people this parable:       "A man
M    21.33            "Hear                        another parable. There was a householder
Mk   12.1             And he began to speak to them    in parables.       "A man


L    20.9         planted a vineyard,
M    21.33   who planted a vineyard, and set a hedge around it, and dug a
Mk   12.1        planted a vineyard, and set a hedge around it, and dug a pit for the
```

```
L    20.9                                           and let it out to tenants, and went
M    21.33    wine press in it, and built a tower, and let it out to tenants, and went
Mk   12.1     wine press,        and built a tower, and let it out to tenants, and went


L    20.10    into another country for a long while.  When the time              came,
M    21.34    into another country.                   When the season of fruit drew
Mk   12.2     into another country.                   When the time              came,


L    20.10          he sent a    servant  to the tenants, that they should give        him
M    21.34    near, he sent his  servants to the tenants,            to get
Mk   12.2           he sent a    servant  to the tenants,            to get from them


L    20.10    some of the fruit of the vineyard;  but the tenants
M    21.35          his fruit;                     and the tenants took his servants and
Mk   12.3     some of the fruit of the vineyard.  And     they    took    him     and


L    20.11    beat him, and sent him away empty-handed.  And   he sent           another
M    21.35    beat one,
Mk   12.4     beat him, and sent him away empty-handed.  Again he sent to them another


L    20.11    servant; him also they beat                    and treated    shamefully,
M    21.35                            killed another,         and stoned another.
Mk   12.4     servant, and       they wounded him in the head, and treated him shamefully.


L    20.12    and sent him away empty-handed.  And   he sent yet a third; this one  they
M    21.36                                     Again he sent   other servants, more than
Mk   12.5                                      And   he sent another, and him        they


L    20.13    wounded and cast out.        Then the owner of that vineyard said, 'What
M    21.36    the first;                   and      they did the same to them.
Mk   12.6     killed; and so with many others, some they beat and some they killed. He


L    20.13    shall I do?  I will send my beloved son;                    it
M    21.37         Afterward he    sent his     son                to them,
Mk   12.6     had still one other,    a beloved son; finally he sent him to them,


L    20.14    may be   they will respect   him.'  But when the  tenants saw    him,
M    21.38    saying, 'They will respect my son.'  But when the  tenants saw the son,
Mk   12.7     saying, 'They will respect my son.'  But        those tenants


L    20.14    they said to themselves,  'This is the heir;       let us kill him, that
M    21.38    they said to themselves,  'This is the heir; come, let us kill him  and
Mk   12.7          said to one another, 'This is the heir; come, let us kill him, and


L    20.15         the inheritance may be ours.'  And they
M    21.39    have his inheritance.'                And they took him
Mk   12.8          the inheritance will be ours.'  And they took him and killed him,


L    20.15        cast him out of the vineyard and killed him.
M    21.40    and cast him out of the vineyard, and killed him.  When therefore the
Mk   12.8     and cast him out of the vineyard.


L    20.15                            What then will the owner of the vineyard do
M    21.40    owner of the vineyard comes, what    will  he                 do
Mk   12.9                             What    will the owner of the vineyard do?
```

L	20.16	to them? He will come and destroy those
M	21.41	to those tenants?" They said to him, "He will put those
Mk	12.9	He will come and destroy the

L	20.16	tenants, and give the vineyard to others." When
M	21.41	wretches to a miserable death, and let out the vineyard to other tenants
Mk	12.9	tenants, and give the vineyard to others.

L	20.17	they heard this, they said, "God forbid!" But he looked at them and
M	21.42	who will give him the fruits in their seasons." Jesus

L	20.17	said, "What then is this that is written:
M	21.42	said to them, "Have you never read in the scriptures:
Mk	12.10	Have you not read this scripture:

L	20.17	'The very stone which the builders rejected
M	21.42	'The very stone which the builders rejected
Mk	12.10	'The very stone which the builders rejected

L	20.17	has become the head of the corner'?
M	21.42	has become the head of the corner;
Mk	12.10	has become the head of the corner;

M	21.42	*this was the Lord's doing,*
Mk	12.11	*this was the Lord's doing,*

M	21.31	*and it is marvelous in our eyes'?*
Mk	12.11	*and it is marvelous in our eyes'?"*

M	21.43	*Therefore I tell you, the kingdom of God will be taken away from you*
M	21.43	*and given to a nation producing the fruits of it."*

L	20.18	Every one who falls on that stone will be broken to pieces; but
M	21.44	"And he *who falls on this stone will be broken to pieces;* but

L	20.18	when it falls on any one it will crush him."
M	21.44	*when it falls on any one,* *it will crush him."*

L	20.19	The scribes and the chief priests tried to lay hands on him at that
M	21.46	But when they tried to arrest him,
Mk	12.12	And they tried to arrest him,

L	20.19	very hour, but they feared the people;
M	21.46	they feared the multitudes, because they held him to be a
Mk	12.12	but feared the multitude,

M	21.45	*prophet. When the chief priests and the Pharisees heard his parables,*

L	20.19	for they perceived that he had told this parable against them.
M	21.45	they perceived that he was speaking about them.
Mk	12.12	for they perceived that he had told the parable against them; so they

Mk	12.12	*left him and went away.*

e. Render to God

Luke 20.20-26

L   20.20   So they watched him, and sent spies, who pretended to be sincere, that
M   22.15   Then   the Pharisees went and took
Mk 12.13   And they   sent to him some of the Pharisees and some of

L   20.20   they might   take hold of what he said, so as to deliver him up to the
M   22.15   counsel   how to entangle him in his talk.
Mk 12.13   the Herodians,to entrap   him in his talk.

L   20.21   authority and jurisdiction of the governor. They
M   22.16   And they sent their disciples to
Mk 12.14   And they came

L   20.21   asked   him, "Teacher, we know that you
M   22.16   him, along with the Herodians, saying,   "Teacher, we know that you
Mk 12.14   and said to him, "Teacher, we know that you

L   20.21   speak   and teach   rightly,   and show   no partiality,
M   22.16   are true, and teach the way of God truthfully, and care for no man; for
Mk 12.14   are true,   and care for no man; for

L   20.21   but truly teach the way of God.
M   22.17   you do not regard the position of men. Tell us, then, what you think.
Mk 12.14   you do not regard the position of men, but truly teach the way of God.

L   20.22   Is it lawful for us to give tribute to Caesar, or not?"
M   22.17   Is it lawful   to pay taxes to Caesar, or not?"
Mk 12.15   Is it lawful   to pay taxes to Caesar, or not? Should we pay them,

L   20.23   But he   perceived their craftiness, and said to them,
M   22.18   But Jesus, aware of their malice,   said,
Mk 12.15   or should we not?" But   knowing their hypocrisy, he said to them,

L   20.24   "Show me a   coin.
M   22.19   "Why put me to the test, you hypocrites? |Show me the money for the tax."
Mk 12.15   "Why put me to the test?   Bring me a   coin, and let me

L   20.24   Whose
M   22.20   And they brought him a coin. |And Jesus said to them, "Whose
Mk 12.16   look at it." |And they brought   one. And he   said to them, "Whose

L   20.24   likeness and inscription has it?" They said,   "Caesar's."
M   22.21   likeness and inscription is this?" |They said,   "Caesar's." Then
Mk 22.16   likeness and inscription is this?" They said to him, "Caesar's."

L   20.25   He   said to them, "Then render   to Caesar the things that are
M   22.21   he   said to them,   "Render therefore to Caesar the things that are
Mk 12.17   Jesus said to them,   "Render   to Caesar the things that are

467

L	20.26	Caesar's, and to God the things that are God's." And they were not
M	22.22	Caesar's, and to God the things that are God's." When they heard it,
Mk	12.17	Caesar's, and to God the things that are God's." And

L	20.26	able in the presence of the people to catch him by what he said; but
M	22.22	they
Mk	12.17	they were

L	20.26	marveling at his answer they were silent.
M	22.22	marveled; and they left him and went away.
Mk	12.17	amazed at him.

d. The God of the Living

Luke 20.27-40

L	20.27	There came to him some Sadducees, those who say that there is no
M	22.23	The same day Sadducees came to him, who say that there is no
Mk	12.18	And Sadducees came to him, who say that there is no

L	20.28	resurrection, |and they asked him a question, saying, "Teacher, Moses
M	22.24	resurrection; and they asked him a question, |saying, "Teacher, Moses
Mk	12.19	resurrection; and they asked him a question, saying, |"Teacher, Moses

L	20.28	wrote for us that if a man's brother dies, having a wife but
M	22.24	said, 'If a man dies, having
Mk	12.19	wrote for us that if a man's brother dies and leaves a wife, but leaves

L	20.28	no children, the man must take the wife and raise up children
M	22.24	no children, his brother must marry the widow, and raise up children
Mk	12.19	no child, the man must take the wife, and raise up children

L	20.29	for his brother. Now there were seven brothers; the first
M	22.25	for his brother.' Now there were seven brothers among us; the first
Mk	12.20	for his brother. There were seven brothers; the first

L	12.29	took a wife, and died without children;
M	22.25	married, and died, and having no children left his wife to
Mk	12.20	took a wife, and when he died left no children;

L	20.30	and the second
M	22.26	his brother. So too the second
Mk	12.21	|and the second took her, and died, leaving no children;

L	20.31	|and the third took her, and likewise all seven left no children and
M	22.26	and third, down to the seventh.
Mk	12.22	and the third likewise; |and the seven left no children.

L	20.32,33	died. Afterward the woman also died. In the resurrection,
M	22.27,28	After them all, the woman died. In the resurrection,
Mk	12.23	Last of all the woman also died. |In the resurrection

L	20.33	therefore, whose wife will the woman be? For the seven
M	22.28	therefore, to which of the seven will she be wife? For they all
Mk	12.23	whose wife will she be? For the seven

L	20.33	had her as wife."
M	22.28	had her."
Mk	12.23	had her as wife."

L	20.34	And Jesus said to them, "The sons of this age marry and are given in
M	22.29	But Jesus answered them, "You are wrong,
Mk	12.24	Jesus said to them, "Is not this why you are wrong,

L	20.35	marriage; but those who are accounted worthy to attain to that age and
M	22.30	because you know neither the scriptures nor the power of God. For
Mk	12.25	that you know neither the scriptures nor the power of God? For

L	20.35	to the resurrection from the dead neither marry nor are given
M	22.30	in the resurrection they neither marry nor are given
Mk	12.25	when they rise from the dead, they neither marry nor are given

L	20.36	in marriage, |for they cannot die any more, because they are equal to
M	22.30	in marriage, but are like
Mk	12.25	in marriage, but are like

L	20.37	angels and are sons of God, being sons of the resurrection. But that
M	22.31	angels in heaven. And as for
Mk	12.26	angels in heaven. And as for

L	20.37	the dead are raised, even Moses
M	22.31	the resurrection of the dead, have you not read
Mk	12.26	the dead being raised, have you not read in the book of Moses,

L	20.37	showed, in the passage about the bush, where he calls the Lord
M	22.32	what was said to you by God, |'I
Mk	12.26	in the passage about the bush, how God said to him, 'I

L	20.38	the God of Abraham and the God of Isaac and the God of Jacob. Now
M	22.32	am the God of Abraham, and the God of Isaac, and the God of Jacob'?
Mk	12.27	am the God of Abraham and the God of Isaac and the God of Jacob'?

L	20.38	he is not God of the dead, but of the living; for all live to him."
M	22.32	He is not God of the dead, but of the living."
Mk	12.27	He is not God of the dead, but of the living; you are quite wrong."

L	20.39	And some of the scribes answered, "Teacher, you have spoken well."
M	22.33	And when the crowd heard it,

L	20.40	For they no longer dared to ask him any question.
M	22.33	they were astonished at his teaching.

e. The Son of David

Luke 20.41-44

L	20.41	But he
M	22.41	Now while the Pharisees were gathered together, Jesus asked them a
Mk	12.35	And as Jesus taught in the
J	7.40	*When they heard these words, some of the people said, "This is really*

L	20.41	said to them, "How can they say that the Christ
M	22.42	question, |saying, "What do you think of the Christ?
Mk	12.35	temple, he said, "How can the scribes say that the Christ
J	7.41	*the prophet."* *Others said, "This is the Christ."*

J	7.41	*But some said, "Is the Christ*
J	7.42	*to come from Galilee? Has not the scripture said that the Christ*

L	20.41	is David's son?
M	22.43	Whose son is he?" They said to him, "The son of David." |He said to
Mk	12.35	is the son of David?
J	7.42	is *descended* from David, *and comes from Bethlehem,*

L	20.42	For David himself
M	22.43	them, "How is it then that David, inspired by the Spirit,
Mk	12.36	David himself, inspired by the Holy Spirit,
J	7.42	*the village* *where* David *was?"*

L	20.42	says in the Book of Psalms,
M	22.43	calls him Lord, saying,
Mk	12.36	declared,

L	20.42	'The Lord said to my Lord,
M	22.44	'The Lord said to my Lord,
Mk	12.36	'The Lord said to my Lord,

L	20.42	Sit at my right hand,
M	22.44	Sit at my right hand,
Mk	12.36	Sit at my right hand,

L	20.43	till I make thy enemies a stool for thy feet.'
M	22.44	till I put thy enemies under thy feet'?
Mk	12.36	till I put thy enemies under thy feet.'

L	20.44	David thus calls him Lord; so how is he his son?"
M	22.45,46	If David thus calls him Lord, how is he his son'? And no one was
Mk	12.37	|David himself calls him Lord; so how is he his son?" And the great

M	22.46	*able to answer him a word, nor from that day did any one dare to ask him*
Mk	12.37	*throng heard him gladly.*

M	22.46	*any more questions.*

Luke 20.45-47

```
L    20.45     And in the hearing of all the people he said                      to
M    23.1      Then                                         said Jesus to the crowds and to
Mk   12.38     And in his teaching                          he said,
 L   11.46     And                                          he said,


L    20.46     his disciples,  |"Beware of the scribes,
M    23.2      his disciples,              |"The scribes and the Pharisees sit on Moses'
Mk   12.38                      "Beware of the scribes,
 L   11.46                      "Woe    to you lawyers also!


 M   23.3      seat; so practice and observe whatever they tell you, but not what they

 M   23.4      do; for they preach, but do not practice. They bind    heavy burdens, hard
 L   11.46                                              for you  load men with burdens  hard

 M   23.4      to bear, and lay them on men's shoulders; but they themselves will not
 L   11.46     to bear,                                  and you yourselves do   not

 M   23.5      move      them    with       their finger. They do all       their deeds
 L   11.46     touch the burdens with one of your fingers.


L    20.46                         who  like to go about                            in
M    23.5      to be seen by men; for they make their phylacteries broad and their fringes
Mk   12.38                         who  like to go about                            in


L    20.46     long robes, and    love salutations in the market places
M    23.7      long,       |and        salutations in the market places, and being called
Mk   12.38     long robes, and to have salutations in the market places
 L   11.43b                and        salutations in the market places.


L    20.46                                  and the best seats in the synagogues
M    23.6b     rabbi by men.               |and the best seats in the synagogues,
Mk   12.39                                 |and the best seats in the synagogues
 L   11.43a    Woe to you Pharisees! for you love   the best seat in the synagogues


L    20.46     and           the places of honor at feasts,
M    23.6a     |and they love the place  of honor at feasts
Mk   12.39     and           the places of honor at feasts,


 M   23.8      But you are not to be called rabbi, for you have one teacher, and you are
 M   23.9      all brethren. And call no man your father on earth, for you have one
 M   23.10     Father, who is in heaven. Neither be called masters, for you have one
 M   23.11     master, the Christ. He who is greatest among you shall be your servant;
 M   23.12     whoever exalts himself will be humbled, and whoever humbles himself will
 M   23.12     be exalted.

 M   23.13        "But woe to you, scribes and Pharisees, hypocrites! because you shut
 M   23.13     the kingdom of heaven against men; for you neither enter yourselves, nor
 M   23.14     allow those who would enter to go in. Woe to you, scribes and Pharisees,


L    20.47                  who devour widows' houses and for a pretense    make
M    23.14     hypocrites! for you devour widows' houses and for a pretense you make
Mk   12.40                  who devour widows' houses and for a pretense    make
```

```
L    20.47    long prayers.        They will receive the greater condemnation."
M    23.14    long prayers; therefore you will receive the greater condemnation.
Mk   12.40    long prayers.        They will receive the greater condemnation."


M    23.15    Woe to you, scribes and Pharisees, hypocrites! for you traverse sea and
M    23.15    land to make a single proselyte, and when he becomes a proselyte, you
M    23.15    make him twice as much a child of hell as yourselves.
```

88. THE WIDOW'S COPPER COINS

Luke 21.1-4

```
L    21.1              He looked up                  and saw     the rich
Mk   12.41    And he sat down opposite the treasury, and watched the multitude


L    21.1     putting their gifts into the treasury;
Mk   12.41    putting        money into the treasury.  Many rich people put in large


L    21.2              and he saw a poor widow        put in two copper coins.
Mk   12.42    sums.  And        a poor widow came, and put in two copper coins, which


L    21.3                                             And he said,
Mk   12.43    make a penny.  And he called his disciples to him, and    said to them,


L    21.3     "Truly I tell   you, this poor widow has put in more than all of them;
Mk   12.43    "Truly, I say to you, this poor widow has put in more than all    those


L    21.4                                        for they all contributed out of
Mk   12.44    who are contributing to the treasury.  For they all contributed out of


L    21.4     their abundance, but she out of her poverty   put in all the living
Mk   12.44    their abundance; but she out of her poverty has put in everything


L    21.4     that she had."
Mk   12.44         she had, her whole living."
```

89. THE END OF THE AGE

Luke 21.5-36

a. The Destruction of the Temple

Luke 21.5-6

```
L    21.5     And as
M    24.1              Jesus left       the temple and was going away, when his
Mk   13.1     And as he     came out of the temple,              one of his


L    21.5     some      spoke
M    24.1     disciples came to point out to him
Mk   13.1     disciples said          to him, "Look, Teacher, what wonderful
```

```
L    21.5                                                   of the temple, how it was adorned
M    24.2                        the            buildings of the temple.
Mk   13.1            stones and what wonderful buildings!"


L    21.6            with noble stones and offerings, he    said,        |"As      for
M    24.2                                 But he    answered them,   "You see all
Mk   13.2                          And Jesus said to him, "Do you see


L    21.6            these things which you see, the days will come when there shall not be
M    24.2            these, do you not?             Truly, I say to you, there will   not be
Mk   13.2            these great buildings?                          There will   not be


L    21.6            left here one stone upon another  that will not be thrown down."
M    24.2            left here one stone upon another, that will not be thrown down."
Mk   13.2            left here one stone upon another, that will not be thrown down."
```

b. Signs of the End

Luke 21.7-36

```
L    21.7            And                                                they
M    24.3                 As he sat on the Mount of Olives,          the disciples
Mk   13.3            And as he sat on the Mount of Olives opposite the temple, Peter and


L    21.7                             asked   him,              "Teacher, when
M    24.3                             came to him privately, saying, "Tell us, when
Mk   13.4            James and John and Andrew asked   him privately,    |"Tell us, when


L    21.7            will this be, and what will be the sign when this        is about to
M    24.3            will this be, and what will be the sign of your coming and of the close
Mk   13.4            will this be, and what will be the sign when these things are all  to


L    21.8                take place?"  And he          said,        "Take heed that you
M    24.4            of the age?"      And Jesus       answered them, "Take heed that no
Mk   13.5            be accomplished?" And Jesus began to say  to them, "Take heed that no


L    21.8            are not led       astray;  for many will come in my name, saying, 'I am
M    24.5            one    leads you astray.   For many will come in my name, saying, 'I am
Mk   13.6            one    leads you astray.       Many will come in my name, saying, 'I am


L    21.9               he!'      and, 'The time is at hand!' Do not go after them. |And
M    24.6            the Christ,' and  they will lead many astray.                  And
Mk   13.7               he!'      and  they will lead many astray.                  And


L    21.9            when you    hear of wars and tumults,        do          not be
M    24.6                you will hear of wars and rumors of wars; see that you are not
Mk   13.7            when you    hear of wars and rumors of wars, do          not be


L    21.9            terrified; for this must first take place, but the end will not be at
M    24.6            alarmed;   for this must       take place, but the end is    not
Mk   13.7            alarmed;       this must       take place, but the end is    not


L    21.9            once."
M    24.6            yet.
Mk   13.7            yet.
```

L   21.10   Then he said to them, "Nation will rise against nation, and kingdom
M   24.7   For nation will rise against nation, and kingdom
Mk 13.8   For nation will rise against nation, and kingdom

L   21.11   against kingdom;   there will be   great earthquakes, and in various
M   24.7   against kingdom, and there will be famines and earthquakes   in various
Mk 13.8   against kingdom;   there will be   earthquakes in various

L   21.11   places   famines and pestilences; and there will be terrors
M   24.8   places: all this is but the beginning of the birth-pangs.
Mk 13.8   places, there will be famines; this is but the beginning of the birth-pangs.

L   21.12   and great signs from heaven. But before all this they will lay their hands
M   24.9   "Then   they will
Mk 13.9   "But take heed to yourselves; for   they will
 M 10.17   Beware of men;   for   they will
 J 16.2   They will

L   21.12   on you and persecute you, delivering you up to the synagogues and prisons,
M   24.9   deliver   you up to   tribulation,
Mk 13.9   deliver   you up to   councils; and you will
 M 10.17   deliver   you up to   councils, and
 J 16.2   put   you out of the synagogues; indeed, the

L   21.12   and you will be brought before kings and
Mk 13.9   be beaten   in   synagogues; and you will   stand   before governors
 Mk 10.17   flog you in their synagogues,
 J 16.2   hour is coming when whoever kills you will think he is offering service

L   21.13   governors for my name's sake. This will be a time for you to bear
Mk 13.9   and kings for my   sake,   to bear
 J 16.2   to God.

L   21.14   testimony. Settle it therefore in your minds, not to meditate beforehand
Mk 13.10   testimony before them. And the gospel must first be preached to all nations

L   21.15   how to answer; for I will give you a mouth and wisdom, which none of your
L   21.16   adversaries will be able to withstand or contradict. You will be
L   21.16   delivered up even by parents and brothers and kinsmen and friends,

 Mk 13.11   And when they bring you to trial and deliver you up, do not be anxious
 Mk 13.11   beforehand what you are to say; but say whatever is given you in that hour,
 Mk 13.12   for it is not you who speak, but the Holy Spirit. And brother will deliver
 Mk 13.12   up brother to death, and the father his child, and children will rise again

L   21.17   and some of you they will put   to death;   you will be hated by all
M   24.9   and   put you to death; and you will be hated by all
Mk 13.13   parents and have them   put   to death; and you will be hated by all
 M 10.22   and you will be hated by all
 J 15.18   "If the world   hates you
 J 15.21   But all this they will do to

L   21.18   for my name's sake. But not a hair of your head will perish.
M   24.10   nations for my name's sake. And then many will fall away, and betray
Mk 13.13   for my name's sake.
 M 10.22   for my name's sake.
 J 15.18   know that it has hated me before it hated you.
 J 15.21   you   on my account, because they do not know him who sent me.

474

M	24.11	*one another, and hate one another. And many false prophets will arise*
M	24.12	*and lead many astray. And because wickedness is multiplied, most men's*
M	24.12	*love will grow cold.*

L	21.19	<u>By</u> <u>your</u> <u>endurance</u> <u>you will</u> <u>gain your lives.</u>
M	24.13,14	But he who endures to the end <u>will</u> be saved. And this gospel of the kingdom
Mk	13.13	But he who endures to the end <u>will</u> be saved.
M	10.22	*But he who endures to the end* <u>will</u> *be saved.*

M	24.14	*will be preached throughout the whole world, as a testimony to all nations;*
M	24.14	*and then the end will come.*
Mk	13.11	*to all nations. And when they bring you to trial and deliver you up, do*

Mk	13.11	*not be anxious before hand what you are to say; but say whatever is given*
Mk	13.12	*you in that hour, for it is not you who speak, but the Holy Spirit. And*
Mk	13.12	*brother will deliver up brother to death, and the father his child, and*
Mk	13.12	*children will rise against parents and have them put to death;*

L	21.20	<u>"But when you see Jerusalem surrounded by armies, then know that its</u>
M	24.15	<u>"So when you see</u> the
Mk	13.14	<u>"But when you see</u> the

L	21.20	<u>desolation has come near.</u>
M	24.15	desolating sacrilege spoken of by the prophet Daniel, standing in the
Mk	13.14	desolating sacrilege set up where

L	21.21	<u>Then let those who are</u>
M	24.16	holy place (let the reader understand), │<u>then let those who are</u>
Mk	13.14	it ought not to be (let the reader understand), <u>then let those who are</u>

L	21.21	<u>in Judea flee to the mountains, and let those who are inside the city</u>
M	24.17	<u>in Judea flee to the mountains;</u> <u>let</u> him <u>who</u> is on the housetop
Mk	13.15	<u>in Judea flee to the mountains;</u> <u>let</u> him <u>who</u> is on the housetop
L	17.31	*On that day,* <u>let</u> *him* <u>who</u> *is on the housetop,*

L	21.21	<u>depart, and let not those who are out</u>
M	24.17	not go down to take
Mk	13.15	not go down, nor enter his house, to take
L	17.31	*with his goods in the house,* *not come down* *to take*

L	21.22	<u>in the country enter it; for these are days of vengeance, to fulfil all</u>
M	24.18	what is in his house; and let him who is in the field not turn
Mk	13.16	anything away; and let him who is in the field not turn
L	17.31	*them away; and likewise let him who is in the field not turn*

L	21.23	<u>that is written.</u> <u>Alas for those who are with child and for</u>
M	24.19	back to take his mantle. And <u>alas for those who are with child and for</u>
Mk	13.17	back to take his mantle. And <u>alas for those who are with child and for</u>
L	17.31	*back.*

L	21.23	<u>those who give suck in those days!</u>
M	24.20	<u>those who give suck in those days!</u> Pray that your flight may not be
Mk	13.18	<u>those who give suck in those days!</u> Pray that it may not happen

L	21.23	<u>For</u> <u>great</u>
M	24.21	in winter or on a sabbath. <u>For</u> then there will be <u>great</u>
Mk	13.19	in winter. <u>For</u> in those days there will be such

```
L    21.24    distress shall be upon the earth and wrath upon this people; they will
M    24.21    tribulation, such as has not been from the beginning of the world
Mk   13.19    tribulation     as has not been from the beginning of the creation


L    21.24    fall by the edge of the sword, and be led captive among all nations;
M    24.22                    until now, no, and never will be.  And if those days
Mk   13.20    which God created until now,     and never will be.  And if the    Lord


L    21.24    and Jerusalem will be trodden down by the Gentiles, until the times
M    24.22    had not been shortened,          no human being would be saved; but for
Mk   13.20    had not     shortened the days, no human being would be saved; but for


L    21.24    of the Gentiles are fulfilled.
M    24.22    the sake of the elect   those days will be shortened.
Mk   13.20    the sake of the elect, whom he chose,  he shortened the days.


M   24.23     *Then if any one says to you, 'Lo,    here is the Christ!' or*
Mk  13.21     *And then if any one says to you, 'Look, here is the Christ!' or 'Look,*

M   24.24     *'There he is!' do not believe it.  For false Christs and false prophets*
Mk  13.22     *there he is!' do not believe it.      False Christs and false prophets*

M   24.24     *will arise and show great signs and wonders, so as to lead astray, if*
Mk  13.22     *will arise and show     signs and wonders,     to lead astray, if*

M   24.25     *possible, even the elect.     Lo,      I have told you*
Mk  13.23     *possible,     the elect.  But take heed; I have told you all things*

M   24.26     *beforehand.  So, if they say to you, 'Lo, he is in the wilderness,' do*
Mk  13.12     *beforehand.*

M   24.26     *not go out; if they say, 'Lo, he is in the inner rooms,' do not believe*
M   24.27     *it.  For as the lightning comes from the east and shines as far as the*
M   24.28     *west, so will be the coming of the Son of man.  Wherever the body is,*
M   24.28     *there the eagles will be gathered together.*


L    21.25    "And                                    there will be signs in sun
M    24.29    "Immediately        after the  tribulation of those days the sun will
Mk   13.24    "But in those days, after that tribulation,      the sun will


L    21.25                    and    moon                    and    stars, and
M    24.29    be darkened, and the moon will not give its light, and the stars will
Mk   13.25    be darkened, and the moon will not give its light, |and the stars will


L    21.25    upon the earth distress of nations in perplexity at the roaring of the
M    24.29         fall    from heaven,
Mk   13.25    be falling from heaven,


L    21.26    sea and the waves, |men fainting with fear and with foreboding of what


L    21.26    is coming on the world; for the powers of the heavens will be shaken.
M  . 24.29                         and the powers of the heavens will be shaken; .
Mk   13.25                         and the powers in the heavens will be shaken.


M   24.30     *then will appear the sign of the Son of man in heaven, and then all the*
```

476

```
L    21.27                                              And then they will see the Son of man
M    24.30    tribes of the earth will mourn, and           they will see the Son of man
Mk   13.26                                              And then they will see the Son of man


L    21.28    coming in a    cloud                with        power and great glory.  Now
M    24.31    coming on the clouds of heaven with        power and great glory;  and
Mk   13.27    coming in      clouds               with great power and          glory.  And


L    21.28    when these things begin to take place, look up and raise your heads,
M    24.31            he will send out his angels with a loud trumpet call, and they will
Mk   13.27    then he will send out the angels,                               and


L    21.28    because your redemption is drawing near."
M    24.31    gather his elect from the four winds, from one end
Mk   13.27    gather his elect from the four winds, from the ends of the earth to the


  M  24.31           of heaven to the other.
  Mk 13.27    ends of heaven.


L    21.29    And he told them a parable: "Look at the fig tree, and all the trees;
M    24.32                                 "From     the fig tree  learn its lesson:
Mk   13.28                                 "From     the fig tree  learn its lesson!


L    21.30    as soon as     they              come out    in  leaf,   you see
M    24.32    as soon as its branch becomes tender and puts forth its leaves, you
Mk   13.28    as soon as its branch becomes tender and puts forth its leaves, you


L    21.31    for yourselves and know that the summer is already near.  So also, when
M    24.33                       know that     summer is          near.  So also, when
Mk   13.29                       know that     summer is          near.  So also, when


L    21.31    you see     these things taking place, you know that the kingdom of God
M    24.33    you see all these things,                 you know that             he
Mk   13.29    you see     these things taking place, you know that                he


L    21.32    is near.                      Truly, I say to you, this generation will
M    24.34    is near, at the very gates.   Truly, I say to you, this generation will
Mk   13.30    is near, at the very gates.   Truly, I say to you, this generation will


L    21.33    not pass away till   all            has taken place.  Heaven and earth will
M    24.35    not pass away till   all these things take  place.  Heaven and earth will
Mk   13.31    not pass away before all these things take  place.  Heaven and earth will
  M   5.18                         For truly, I say to you, till heaven and earth
  L  16.17                         But it is easier for heaven and earth to


L    21.33    pass away, but my words              will not pass away.
M    24.35    pass away, but my words              will not pass away.
Mk   13.31    pass away, but my words              will not pass away.
  M   5.18    pass away, not an iota, not a   dot, will      pass from the law until all
  L  16.17    pass away, than for        one dot             of   the law to become


  M   5.18    is accomplished.
  L  16.17    void.
```

477

```
M   24.36      "But of that day and      hour no one knows, not even the angels of
Mk  13.32      "But of that day or that hour no one knows, not even the angels in

M   24.37      heaven, nor the Son, but      the Father only.  As were the days of Noah,
Mk  13.32      heaven, nor the Son, but only the Father.

M   24.38      so will be the coming of the Son of man.  For as in those days before the
M   24.38      flood they were eating and drinking, marrying and giving in marriage, until
M   24.39      the day when Noah entered the ark, |and they did not know until the flood
M   24.39      came and swept them all away, so will be the coming of the Son of man.
M   24.40,41   Then two men will be in the field; one is taken and one is left.  Two
M   24.41      women will be grinding at the mill; one is taken and one is left.
```

```
L   21.34      "But take heed to yourselves lest your hearts be weighed down with
L   21.34      dissipation and drunkenness and cares of this life, and that day come
L   21.35      upon you suddenly like a snare; for it will come upon all who dwell
L   21.35      upon the face of the whole earth.
```

```
L   21.36              But watch at all times, praying that you may have strength to escape
M   24.42              Watch therefore, for you do not know on    what day your Lord
Mk  13.33      Take heed, watch;          for you do not know    when    the   time
Mk  13.35              Watch therefore--for you do not know       when    the   master
 M  25.13              Watch therefore, for you      know neither the  day nor the
```

```
L   21.36      all these things that will take place, and to stand before the Son of man."
M   24.42                      is   coming.
Mk  13.34                      will come.  It is like a man going on a journey, when he
Mk  13.35      of the house will come, in the evening, or at midnight, or at cockcrow,
 M  25.13      hour.
```

```
M   24.43      But know this, that if the householder had known in what part of the night
M   24.43      the thief was coming, he would have watched and would not have let his
M   24.44      house be broken into.  Therefore you also must be ready; for the Son
M   24.44      of man is coming at an hour you do not expect.

Mk  13.34      leaves home and puts his servants in charge, each with his work, and
Mk  13.34      commands the doorkeeper to be on the watch.

Mk  13.36,37   or in the morning--|lest he come suddenly and find you asleep.  And what
Mk  13.37      I say to you I say to all: Watch."
```

90. DAILY TEACHING IN THE TEMPLE

Luke 21.37-38

```
L   21.37      And every day he was teaching in the temple, but at night      he
M   21.17      And leaving them,                                              he
Mk  11.19      And                                         when evening came they
```

```
L   21.37      went out                           and lodged on the mount called Olivet.
M   21.17      went out of the city to Bethany and lodged there.
Mk  11.19      went out of the city.
```

```
L   21.38      And early in the morning all the people came to him in the temple to
L   21.38      hear him.
```

91. THE PLOT TO KILL JESUS

Luke 22.1-6

L	22.1	Now the feast of Unleavened
M	26.1	When Jesus had finished all these sayings, he said to his disciples,
Mk	14.1	It was now

L	22.1	Bread drew near, which is called the Passover.
M	26.2	"You know that after two days the Passover is coming, and the
Mk	14.1	two days before the Passover and the feast of

M	26.2	*Son of man will be delivered up to be crucified."*
Mk	14.1	*Unleavened Bread.*

J	11.45	*Many of the Jews therefore, who had come with Mary and had seen what*
J	11.46	*he did, believed in him; but some of them went to the Pharisees and*
J	11.46	*told them what Jesus had done.*

L	22.2	And the chief priests and the scribes
M	26.3	Then the chief priests and the elders of the people gathered in the
Mk	14.1	And the chief priests and the scribes
J	11.47	So the chief priests and the Pharisees gathered the

M	26.3	*palace of the high priest,*
J	11.47	*council, and said, "What are we to do? For this man performs many signs.*

J	11.48	*If we let him go on thus, every one will believe in him, and the Romans*
J	11.48	*will come and destroy both our holy place and our nation."*

M	26.3	*who was called Caiaphas,*
J	11.49	*But one of them, Caiaphas, who was high priest that year, said to them,*

J	11.50	*"You know nothing at all; you do not understand that it is expedient*
J	11.50	*for you that one man should die for the people, and that the whole nation*
J	11.51	*should not perish." He did not say this of his own accord, but being*
J	11.51	*high priest that year he prophesied that Jesus should die for the nation,*
J	11.52	*|and not for the nation only, but to gather into one the children of God*
J	11.53	*who are scattered abroad. So from that day on*

L	22.2	were seeking how to
M	26.4	|and took counsel together in order to arrest Jesus by stealth and
Mk	14.1	were seeking how to arrest him by stealth, and
J	11.53	they took counsel how to

L	22.2	put him to death; for they feared
M	26.5	kill him. But they said, "Not during the feast, lest there be a tumult
Mk	14.2	kill him; for they said, "Not during the feast, lest there be a tumult
J	11.53	put him to death.

L	22.2	the people.
M	26.5	among the people."
Mk	14.2	of the people."

L	22.3	Then Satan entered into
M	26.14	Then one of the twelve, who was called
Mk	14.10	Then
J	6.70	*Jesus answered them, "Did I not choose you, the twelve, and one of you*
J	13.2	*And during supper, when the devil had already put it into the heart*
J	13.27	*Then after the morsel, Satan entered into*

479

L	22.3				Judas		called Iscariot, who was of the

```
L    22.3                                    Judas            called Iscariot, who was of the
M    26.14                                   Judas                    Iscariot,
Mk   14.10                                   Judas                    Iscariot, who was
 J    6.71    is a devil?"  He spoke of  Judas the son of Simon  Iscariot, for he,
 J   13.2                         of  Judas            Iscariot, Simon's son,
 J   13.27                              him.  Jesus said to him, "What you are going to


L    22.4     number of the twelve; he went away and conferred with the chief priests
M    26.14                           went                    to    the chief priests
Mk   14.10    one   of the twelve,  .  went                    to    the chief priests
 J    6.71    one   of the twelve,
 J   13.27    do, do quickly."


L    22.5     and officers                       how he might betray  him to them.    And
M    26.15    |and said, "What will you give me if I          deliver  him to you?"    And
Mk   14.11                                       in order to   betray  him to them.    And


L    22.5                           they were glad, and engaged  to give him
M    26.15                          they                  paid            him thirty pieces
Mk   14.11    when they heard it  they were glad, and promised to give him


L    22.6       money.  So he agreed, and                    sought an opportunity
M    26.16    of silver.                 And from that moment he sought an opportunity
Mk   14.11      money.                   And                  he sought an opportunity
 J    6.71                                                       was


L    22.6     to betray him to them in the absence of the multitude.
M    26.16    to betray him.
Mk   14.11    to betray him.
 J    6.71    to betray him.
 J   13.2     to betray him,
```

92. THE PASSOVER MEAL

Luke 22.7-23

```
L    22.7     Then came the        day of Unleavened Bread, on    which            the
M    26.17    Now    on the first day of Unleavened Bread
Mk   14.12    And    on the first day of Unleavened Bread, when they sacrificed the


L    22.8     passover lamb had to be sacrificed.  So Jesus sent Peter and John, saying,
Mk   14.12    passover lamb,


L    22.8     "Go and prepare the passover for us, that we may eat it."


L    22.9          They                 said to him, "Where will you have us
M    26.17    the disciples came to Jesus, saying,     "Where will you have us
Mk   14.12    his disciples         said to him, "Where will you have us go and


L    22.10    prepare                   it?"         He
M    26.18    prepare for you to eat the passover?"      He
Mk   14.13    prepare for you to eat the passover?"  And he sent two of his disciples,


L    22.10         said to them, "Behold, when you have entered the city,     a
M    26.18         said,                       "Go into the city  to  a certain
Mk   14.13    and said to them,                     "Go into the city, and a
```

```
L   22.10   man carrying a jar of water will meet you; follow him into the house which
M   26.18   one,
Mk  14.14   man carrying a jar of water will meet you; follow him, |and wherever


L   22.11   he enters, |and tell   the householder, 'The Teacher says to you, Where
M   26.18              and say to       him,       'The Teacher says,        My time
Mk  14.14   he enters,      say to the householder, 'The Teacher says,       Where


L   22.11   is the guest room, where I am to eat  the passover                    with my
M   26.18   is at hand;              I will  keep the passover at your house with my
Mk  14.14   is my  guest room, where I am to eat  the passover                    with my


L   22.12   disciples?'  And he will show you a large upper room furnished;
M   26.18   disciples.'"
Mk  14.15   disciples?'  And he will show you a large upper room furnished;


L   22.13   there make ready."    And      they              went,
M   26.19                         And the disciples
Mk  14.16   there prepare for us." And the disciples set out and went to the city,


L   22.13   and found it as he    had told    them; and they prepared the passover.
M   26.19      did      as Jesus had directed them, and they prepared the passover.
Mk  14.16   and found it as he    had told    them; and they prepared the passover.


L   22.14   And when the hour came, he sat at table, and the        apostles with
M   26.20       When it was evening, he sat at table  with the twelve disciples;
Mk  14.17   And when it was evening  he came          with the twelve.


L   22.15   him.  And he said to them, "I have earnestly desired to eat this passover
L   22.16   with you before I suffer; for I tell you I shall not eat it until it is


L   22.17   fulfilled in the kingdom of God."  And he took      a  cup, and when
M   26.27                                      And he took      a  cup, and when
Mk  14.23                                      And he took      a  cup, and when
1 C 11.25                                      In the same way also the cup, after


L   22.17   he had given thanks he           said,      "Take this, and divide
M   26.27   he had given thanks he gave it to them, saying,      "Drink of it,
Mk  14.23   he had given thanks he gave it to them, and they all drank of it.
1 C 11.25   supper,                                  saying,


L   22.17   it among yourselves;
M   26.28     all of you;   for this   is my blood of the       covenant, which is
Mk  14.24   And he said to them, "This is my blood of the       covenant, which is
1 C 11.25             "This cup is              the new covenant in my blood.


L   22.18                                         for I tell   you that from
M   26.29   poured out for many for the forgiveness of sins.  I tell  you
Mk  14.25   poured out for many.                 Truly, I say to you,
1 C 11.25   Do this, as often as you drink it, in remembrance of me."


L   22.18   now on I shall not drink      of the  fruit of the vine until
M   26.29             I shall not drink again of this fruit of the vine until that day
Mk  14.25             I shall not drink again of the  fruit of the vine until that day
```

```
L    22.18                                          the         kingdom of God comes."
M    26.29   when I drink it new with you in my Father's kingdom."
Mk   14.25   when I drink it new              in the         kingdom of God."


L    22.19   And
M    26.26   Now as they were eating,
Mk   14.22   And as they were eating,
1 C  11.23   For I received from the Lord what I also delivered to you, that the Lord


L    22.19   he                                    took bread,  and when he had
M    26.26   Jesus                                 took bread,  and
Mk   14.22   he                                    took bread,  and
1 C  11.24   Jesus on the night when he was betrayed took bread, |and when he had
  J  6.48,49                              I am the bread of life.  Your fathers

  J  6.49    ate the manna in the wilderness, and they
  J  6.50    died.                            This is the bread which comes down from
  J  6.50    heaven, that a man may eat of it and not die.
  J  6.51                    I am the living bread which came down from
  J  6.51    heaven;            if any one eats of this bread, he will live for ever;
  J  6.51                             and the bread which I shall give for


L    22.19   given thanks  he broke it  and gave it to      them,      saying,
M    26.26   blessed,   and broke it, and gave it to the disciples and said, "Take,
Mk   14.22   blessed,   and broke it, and gave it to      them,    and said, "Take;
1 C  11.24   given thanks, he broke it,                           and said,


L    22.19               "This is my body which is given for you.  Do this in
M    26.26   eat;         this is my body."
Mk   14.22                this is my body."
1 C  11.24               "This is my body which is      for you.  Do this in
  J  6.52    the life of the world is my flesh."  The Jews then disputed among them-


  J  6.53    selves, saying, "How can this man give us his flesh to eat?"  So Jesus
  J  6.53    said to them, "Truly, truly, I say to you, unless you eat the flesh of
  J  6.53    the Son of man


L    22.20   remembrance of me."  And likewise      the cup  after supper,
M    26.27                        And he took       a  cup,  and when he had given
Mk   14.23                        And he took       a  cup,  and when he had given
1 C  11.25   remembrance of me."  In the same way also the cup,  after supper,


L    22.20                               saying,
M    26.27   thanks he gave it to them, saying,     "Drink of it, all of you;
Mk   14.23   thanks he gave it to them, and they all drank of it.
1 C  11.25                               saying,
  J  6.53                            and drink his blood, you have no


  J  6.54    life in you; he who eats my flesh and drinks my blood has eternal life,
  J  6.55    and I will raise him up at the last day.  For my flesh is food indeed,
  J  6.56    and my blood is drink indeed.  He who eats my flesh and drinks my blood
  J  6.57    abides in me, and I in him.  As the living Father sent me, and I live
  J  6.58    because of the Father, so he who eats me will live because of me.  This
  J  6.58    is the bread which came down from heaven, not such as the fathers ate
  J  6.59    and died; he who eats this bread will live for ever."  This he said in
  J  6.59    the synagogue, as he taught at Capernaum.
```

```
L    22.20                              "This cup  which is poured out for you
M    26.28a,c                 for this            | which is poured out for many for the
Mk   14.24a,c  And he said to them, "This         | which is poured out for many.
1 C  11.25                              "This cup
```

```
L    22.20                        is                 the new covenant in my blood.
M    26.28b   forgiveness of sins. | is my blood of the        covenant,
Mk   14.24b                        | is my blood of the        covenant,
1 C  11.25                         is                 the new covenant in my blood.  Do
```

1 C 11.26   this, as often as you drink it, in remembrance of me." For as often as
1 C 11.26   you eat this bread and drink the cup, you proclaim the Lord's death until
1 C 11.27   he comes. Whoever, therefore, eats the bread or drinks the cup of the
1 C 11.27   Lord in an unworthy manner will be guilty of profaning the body and blood
1 C 11.28   of the Lord. Let a man examine himself, and so eat of the bread and
1 C 11.29   drink of the cup. For any one who eats and drinks without discerning the
1 C 11.30   body eats and drinks judgment upon himself. That is why many of you are
1 C 11.31   weak and ill, and some have died. But if we judged ourselves truly, we
1 C 11.32   should not be judged. But when we are judged by the Lord, we are chas-
1 C 11.32   tened so that we may not be condemned along with the world.

```
L    22.21   But
M    26.21   and as they were            eating, he                        said,
Mk   14.18   And as they were at table eating, Jesus                        said,
J    13.21   When Jesus had thus spoken,        he was troubled in spirit, and testified,
```

```
L    22.21   behold     the hand of  him   who      betrays me        is
M    26.21   "Truly,    I say to you, one of you will betray me."
Mk   14.18   "Truly,    I say to you, one of you will betray me, one who is eating
J    13.21   "Truly, truly, I say to you, one of you will betray me."
```

```
L    22.22   with me on the table.  For the Son of man goes as it has been determined
M    26.24                          The Son of man goes as it is written of him,
Mk   14.21   with me."              For the Son of man goes as it is written of him,
```

```
L    22.22   but woe to that man by whom    he         is betrayed!"
M    26.24   but woe to that man by whom the Son of man is betrayed!  It would have
Mk   14.21   but woe to that man by whom the Son of man is betrayed!  It would have
```

M 26.25   been better for that man if he had not been born." Judas, who betrayed
Mk 14.31   been better for that man if he had not been born."
J 13.30   So, after receiving the morsel, he immediately went

M 26.25   him, said, "Is it I, Master?" He said to him, "You have said so."
J 13.30   out; and it was night.

```
L    22.23   And they began to question                         one
M    26.22   And they           were very sorrowful, and began to say to him one after
Mk   14.19         They began to be        sorrowful, and       to say to him one after
J    13.22   The disciples looked at one another, uncertain of whom he spoke.
```

J 13.23   One of his disciples, whom Jesus loved, was lying close to the breast
J 13.24   of Jesus; so Simon Peter beckoned to him and said, "Tell us who it is
J 13.25   of whom he speaks." So lying thus, close to the breast of Jesus,

483

L	22.23	another, <u>which of them it was that would do this.</u>
M	26.23	another, "Is it I, Lord?" He answered,
Mk	14.20	another, "Is it I?" He said to them, "It is one of the
J	13.26	he said to him, "Lord, who is it?" Jesus answered, "It is

M	26.23	*"He who has dipped his hand in the dish with me, will*
Mk	14.20	*twelve, one who is dipping bread into the dish with me.*
J	13.26	*he to whom I shall give this morsel when I have dipped it." So*

M	26.23	*betray me.*
J	13.26	*when he had dipped the morsel, he gave it to Judas, the son of Simon*

J	13.27	*Iscariot. Then after the morsel, Satan entered into him. Jesus said to*
J	13.28	*him, "What you are going to do, do quickly." Now no one at the table*
J	13.29	*knew why he said this to him. Some thought that, because Judas had the*
J	13.29	*money box, Jesus was telling him, "Buy what we need for the feast"; or,*
J	13.29	*that he should give something to the poor.*

93. A DISPUTE ABOUT GREATNESS

Luke 11.24-30

L	22.24	<u>A dispute also arose among them, which of them was to be regarded as</u>
M	20.20	*Then the mother of the sons of Zebedee came up to him, with*
Mk	10.35	*And James and John, the sons of Zebedee, came forward to him, and*

L	22.24	<u>the greatest.</u>
M	20.20	*her sons, and kneeling before him she*
Mk	10.35	*said to him, "Teacher we want you to do for us whatever we*

M	20.21	*asked him for something. And he said to her, "What do you want?"*
Mk	10.36	*ask of you." And he said to them, "What do you want me to*

M	20.21	*She said to him, "Command that these two sons of*
Mk	10.37	*do for you?" And they said to him, "Grant us*

M	20.21	*mine may sit, one at your right hand and one at your left, in your*
Mk	10.37	*to sit, one at your right hand and one at your left, in your*

M	20.22	*kingdom." But Jesus answered, "You do not know what you are asking.*
Mk	10.38	*glory." But Jesus said to them, "You do not know what you are asking.*

M	20.22	*Are you able to drink the cup that I am to drink?"*
Mk	10.38	*Are you able to drink the cup that I drink, or to be baptized with*

M	20.22	*They said to him, "We are*
Mk	10.39	*the baptism with which I am baptized?" And they said to him, "We are*

M	20.23	*able." He said to them, "You will drink*
Mk	10.40	*able." And Jesus said to them, "The cup that I drink you will drink;*

M	20.23	*my cup, but*
Mk	10.40	*and with the baptism with which I am baptized, you will be baptized; but*

M	20.23	*to sit at my right hand and at my left is not mine to grant, but it is*
Mk	10.40	*to sit at my right hand or at my left is not mine to grant, but it is*

M	20.24	*for those for whom it has been prepared by my Father." And when the*
Mk	10.41	*for those for whom it has been prepared." And when the*

M	20.24	*ten heard it, they were indignant at the two brothers.*
Mk	10.41	*ten heard it, they began to be indignant at James and John.*

```
L   22.25   And he                          said to them,
M   20.25   But Jesus called them to him and said,              "You know that
Mk  10.42   And Jesus called them to him and said to them, "You know that those who


L   22.25            "The kings  of the Gentiles exercise lordship over them; and
M   20.25             the rulers of the Gentiles          lord it  over them, and
Mk  10.42   are supposed to rule over the Gentiles        lord it  over them, and


L   22.25                those in     authority over them are called benefactors.
M   20.25   their great men exercise authority over them.
Mk  10.42   their great men exercise authority over them.


L   22.26   But          not   so with  you; rather          let the greatest
M   20.26       It shall not be so among you; but whoever would be       great
Mk  10.43   But it shall not be so among you; but whoever would be       great
  M  23.11                                    He  who       is      greatest
  J  13.16       Truly, truly, I say to you,  a servant     is not  greater


L   22.26   among you become as the youngest, and the leader as one who serves.
M   20.26   among you                                    must be your servant,
Mk  10.43   among you                                    must be your servant,
  M  23.11   among you                                   shall be your servant;
  J  13.16   than his master; nor is he who is sent greater than he who sent him.


  M  20.27  |and whoever would be first among you must be your slave;
  Mk 10.44  |and whoever would be first among you must be     slave of all.


L   22.27   For which is the greater, one who sits at table, or one who serves?  Is
M   20.28   even as the Son of man      came not to be served   but to serve,  and
Mk  10.45   For    the Son of man also came not to be served   but to serve,  and
  J  13.15   For       I          have given you an example, that you also


L   22.27   it not the one who sits at table? But I am among you as one who serves.
M   20.28   to give his life as a ransom for many."
Mk  10.45   to give his life as a ransom for many."
  J  13.15   should do as I have done to you.


L   22.28                    "You are those who have continued with me in my trials;
  M  19.28      Jesus said to them, "Truly, I say to you, in the new world, when the
  Mk 10.29      Jesus said,        "Truly, I say to you,
  L  18.29   And he      said to them, "Truly, I say to you,


L   22.29,30 and I assign to you, as my Father assigned to me, a kingdom, |that you may
  M  19.28   Son of man shall sit on his glorious throne, you who have followed me


L   22.30   eat and drink at my table in my kingdom, and  sit on        thrones
  M  19.28                                       will also sit on twelve thrones,


L   22.30   judging the twelve tribes of Israel.
  M  19.29   judging the twelve tribes of Israel. And every one who has left houses
  Mk 10.29                             there is no   one who has left house
  L  18.29                             there is no   man who has left house
  L  14.26                             "If any   one comes to me  and
```

485

```
M  19.29          or brothers or sisters or father or  mother         or  children
Mk 10.29          or brothers or sisters or mother or  father         or  children
L  18.29    or wife or brothers         or parents                    or children,
L  14.26      does not hate        his own    father and mother and wife and chidren

M  19.29    or  lands, for my name's sake,                                     will
Mk 10.30    or  lands, for my       sake  and for the gospel    |who will not
L  18.30           for the      sake  of    the kingdom of God, |who will not
L  14.26    and brothers and sisters, yes, and even his own life, he cannot be my

M  19.29    receive a hundredfold,
Mk 10.30    receive a hundredfold now in this time, houses and brothers and sisters
L  18.30    receive   manifold more   in this time,
L  14.26    disciple.

M  19.29                                                        and inherit
Mk 10.30    and mothers and children and lands, with persecutions, and in the age to
L  18.30                                                        and in the age to

M  19.30        eternal life.  But many that are first will be last, and the last
Mk 10.31    come eternal life.  But many that are first will be last, and the last
L  18.30    come eternal life."

M  19.30    first.
Mk 10.31    first."
```

94. PETER'S DENIAL FORETOLD

Luke 22.31-34

```
M  26.30    And when they had sung a hymn, they went out to the Mount of Olives.
Mk 14.26    And when they had sung a hymn, they went out to the Mount of Olives.


L  22.31                          "Simon, Simon, behold, Satan demanded to have you,
M  26.31    Then Jesus said to them, "You will all fall away because of me this night;
Mk 14.27    And  Jesus said to them, "You will all fall away;


L  22.32    that he might sift you like wheat,    |but I have prayed for you that your
M  26.31    for it is written, 'I will strike the shepherd, and the sheep of the flock
Mk 14.27    for it is written, 'I will strike the shepherd, and the sheep


L  22.32    faith may not fail;  and when you have turned again, strengthen your
M  26.32    will be scattered.'  But after I am raised up, I will go before you to
Mk 14.28    will be scattered.'  But after I am raised up, I will go before you to


L  22.33    brethren."  And he    said    to him, "Lord,
M  26.33    Galilee."       Peter declared to him,      "Though they all fall away
Mk 14.29    Galilee."       Peter said    to him, "Even though they all fall away,
 J 13.37              Peter said     to him, "Lord, why cannot I follow you now?


L  22.34                 I am ready to go with you to prison and to death."  He
M  26.34    because of you, I will never fall away."                        Jesus
Mk 14.30                 I will not."                              And Jesus
J  13.38                 I will lay down my life for you."                  Jesus


L  22.34    said,                                              "I tell    you,
M  26.34    said to him,                               "Truly,  I say to you,
Mk 14.30    said to him,                               "Truly,  I say to you,
J  13.38    answered, "Will you lay down your life for me? Truly, truly, I say to you,
```

```
L   22.34   Peter,                     the cock will not crow  this day,  until you three
M   26.34   this very night, before  the cock            crows,             you will
Mk  14.30   this very night, before  the cock            crows twice,       you will
J   13.38                             the cock will not crow,          till you have
```

```
L   22.34   times deny that you know me."
M   26.35        deny          me three times."    Peter said to him, "Even if
Mk  14.31        deny          me three times."  But he    said vehemently,  "If
J   13.38        denied        me three times.
```

```
M  26.35   I must die with you, I will not deny you."  And so     said all the
Mk 14.31   I must die with you, I will not deny you."  And they all said     the
```

```
M  26.35   disciples.
Mk 14.31   same.
```

95. THE TWO SWORDS

Luke 22.35-38

```
L   22.35   And he said to them, "When I sent you out with no purse or bag or san-
L   22.36   dals, did you lack anything?"  They said, "Nothing."  |He said to them,
L   22.36   "But now, let him who has a purse take it, and likewise a bag.  And let
L   22.37   him who has no sword sell his mantle and buy one.  For I tell you that
L   22.37   this scripture must be fulfilled in me, 'And he was reckoned with trans-
L   22.38   gressors'; for what is written about me has its fulfilment."  And they
L   22.38   said, "Look, Lord, here are two swords."  And he said to them, "It is
L   22.38   enough."
```

96. THE MOUNT OF OLIVES

Luke 22.39-46

```
L   22.39   And      he   came out,              and  went, as was his custom,
M   26.30   And when they  had sung a hymn,      they went out
Mk  14.26   And when they  had sung a hymn,      they went out
J   18.1         When Jesus had spoken these words, he   went forth with his
```

```
L   22.39             to    the Mount of Olives;
M   26.30             to    the Mount of Olives.
Mk  14.26             to    the Mount of Olives.
J   18.1    disciples across the Kidron valley, where there was a garden, which he
```

```
L   22.40   and the disciples followed him.  And when he    came        to the
M   26.36                                    Then Jesus went with them  to a
Mk  14.32                                    And     they went         to a
J   18.1    and his disciples entered.
```

```
L   22.40   place
M   26.36   place           called Gethsemane, and he said to his disciples, "Sit
Mk  14.32   place which was called Gethsemane; and he said to his disciples, "Sit
```

```
M  26.37   here, while I go yonder and pray."  And    taking with him Peter and the
Mk 14.33   here, while I          pray."  And he took   with him Peter and
```

```
M  26.37   two sons of Zebedee, he began to be          sorrowful  and troubled.
Mk 14.33   James and John,     and began to be greatly distressed and troubled.
```

```
M   26.38    Then he said to them, "My soul is very sorrowful, even to death; remain
Mk  14.34    And  he said to them, "My soul is very sorrowful, even to death; remain
J   12.27                    "Now is my soul         troubled.


L   22.40                                          he said to them,
M   26.40b   here, and watch with me."  |and he said to Peter, "So,
Mk  14.37b   here, and watch."          |and he said to Peter, "Simon, are you asleep?


L   22.40                                             "Pray that you may not
M   26.41    could you not watch with me one hour?  Watch and pray that you may not
Mk  14.38    Could you not watch         one hour? |Watch and pray that you may not


L   22.40    enter into temptation."
M   26.41    enter into temptation; the spirit indeed is willing, but the flesh is weak."
Mk  14.38    enter into temptation; the spirit indeed is willing, but the flesh is weak."


L   22.41    And he withdrew from them about a stone's throw, and knelt down
M   26.39    And    going              a little farther  he fell on his face
Mk  14.35    And    going              a little farther, he fell on the ground


L   22.41    and prayed,
M   26.39    and prayed,
Mk  14.36    and prayed that, if it were possible, the hour might pass from him.  And
J   12.27                              "Now is my soul troubled.  And what shall


L   22.42            |"Father, if  thou  art willing,      remove this cup
M   26.39        "My  Father, if  it    be possible,      let  this cup
Mk  14.36    he said, "Abba, Father, all things are possible to thee; remove this cup
J    6.38                                                            For I
J   12.27    I  say?        'Father, save me from this hour'?


L   22.42        from me; nevertheless  not      my     will, but              thine,
M   26.39    pass from me; nevertheless, not as   I      will, but as           thou
Mk  14.36         from me; yet          not what I      will, but what          thou
J    6.38    have come down from heaven, not to do my own will, but the will of him
J   12.27                               No, for this purpose I have come to this hour.


L   22.43    be done." And there appeared to him an angel from heaven, strengthening
M   26.39      wilt."
Mk  14.36      wilt."
J    6.38    who sent me;


L   22.44    him. And being in an agony      he          prayed    more
M   26.42         Again, for the second time, he went away and prayed, "My Father,
Mk  14.39         And again                   he went away and prayed,  saying


L   22.44    earnestly; and his sweat became like great drops of blood falling down upon
M   26.42    if this cannot pass unless I drink it, thy will be done."
Mk  14.39    the same words.


L   22.45    the ground. And when he rose from prayer, he came to the disciples and
M   26.40a            And                          he came to the disciples and
Mk  14.37a            And                          he came                   and


L   22.45    found them sleeping for sorrow,
M   26.40a   found them sleeping;
Mk  14.37a   found them sleeping,
```

488

```
M   26.43    And again he came and found them sleeping, for their eyes were
Mk  14.40    And again he came and found them sleeping, for their eyes were very

M   26.44    heavy.  So, leaving them again, he went away and prayed for the third
Mk  14.40    heavy;  and they did not know what to answer him.
```

```
                                                                    and he said
L   22.46    time, saying the same words.  Then he came to the disciples and    said
M   26.45
Mk  14.41                                   And  he came the third time,  and    said
```

```
L   22.46    to them, "Why do you      sleep?  Rise and pray that you may not
M   26.45    to them, "Are   you still sleeping and taking your rest?  Behold,
Mk  14.41    to them, "Are   you still sleeping and taking your rest?  It is enough;
```

```
L   22.46    enter into temptation."
M   26.45    the hour is at hand, and the Son of man is betrayed into the hands of
Mk  14.41    the hour has   come;     the Son of man is betrayed into the hands of
```

```
M   26.46    sinners.  Rise, let us be going; see, my betrayer is at hand."
Mk  14.42    sinners.  Rise, let us be going; see, my betrayer is at hand."
J   14.31b            Rise, let us    go hence.
```

97. JESUS ARRESTED

Luke 22.47-53

```
J   18.2     Now Judas, who betrayed him, also knew the place; for Jesus often met
J   18.2     there with his disciples.
```

```
L   22.47                        While he was still speaking, there came a crowd, and
M   26.47                        While he was still speaking,
Mk  14.43    And immediately, while he was still speaking,
J   18.3                         So
```

```
L   22.47    the man called Judas,                      one of the twelve, was
M   26.47                    Judas              came, one of the twelve, and
Mk  14.43                    Judas              came, one of the twelve, and
J   18.3                     Judas, procuring a band of soldiers and some officers from
```

```
L   22.47    leading them.
M   26.47                           with him a great crowd with swords
Mk  14.43                           with him a       crowd with swords
J   18.3     the chief priests and the Pharisees, went there with lanterns and torches
```

```
M   26.47    and clubs, from the chief priests                and the elders of the
Mk  14.43    and clubs, from the chief priests and the scribes and the elders.
J   18.4     and weapons.  Then Jesus, knowing all that was to befall him, came forward
```

```
M   26.48    people.  Now the betrayer had given them a sign, saying, "The one I shall
Mk  14.44            Now the betrayer had given them a sign, saying, "The one I shall
J   18.5     and said to them, "Whom do you seek?"  They answered him, "Jesus of
```

```
M   26.49    kiss is the man; seize him."                          And
Mk  14.45    kiss is the man; seize him and lead him away under guard."  And when
J   18.5     Nazareth."  Jesus said to them, "I am he."
```

```
L    22.47   He drew near         to Jesus                                                        to
M    26.49   he came         up to Jesus at once  and said, "Hail, Master!"  And he
Mk   14.45   he came, he went up to him   at once, and said,        "Master!"  And he
J    18.5    Judas, who betrayed him, was standing with them.


L    22.48   kiss  him; but Jesus said to him, "Judas, would you betray the Son
M    26.50   kissed him.    │Jesus said to him,  "Friend, why are you here?"  Then
Mk   14.46   kissed him.                                                      And
J    18.6           When he    said to them, "I am he," they drew back and fell


L    22.49   of man with a kiss?"  And when those who were about him saw what would
M    26.50   they came up and laid hands on Jesus and seized him.
Mk   14.46   they          laid hands on him   and seized him.
J    18.6    to the ground.


L    22.49   follow, they said, "Lord, shall we strike with the sword?"


L    22.50   And          one of them
M    26.51   And behold, one of those who were with Jesus stretched out his hand and
Mk   14.47   But          one of those who stood by
J    18.10   Then         Simon Peter,                        having a sword,


L    22.50                  struck the              slave of the high priest
M    26.51   drew his sword, and struck the         slave of the high priest,
Mk   14.47   drew his sword, and struck the         slave of the high priest
J    18.10   drew      it    and struck the high priest's slave


L    22.51   and cut off his right ear.                     But  Jesus said,
M    26.52   and cut off his      ear.                      Then Jesus said
Mk   14.47   and cut off his      ear.   The slave's name was Malchus.  Jesus said
J    18.11   and cut off his right ear.


L    22.51            "No more of this!"  And he touched his ear and healed him.
M    26.52   to him,  "Put your sword back into its place;  for all who take the
J    18.11   to Peter, "Put your sword     into its sheath; shall I not drink the


M   26.53   sword will perish by the sword.  Do you think that I cannot appeal to
J   18.11   cup which the Father has given me?"

M   26.53   my Father, and he will at once send me more than twelve legions of angels?
M   26.54   But how then should the scriptures be fulfilled, that it must be so?"


L    22.52   Then         Jesus said to the chief priests and officers of the temple
M    26.55   At that hour Jesus said to the crowds,
Mk   14.48   And          Jesus said to    them,
J    18.7    Again        he    asked      them,


L    22.52   and elders, who had come out against him, "Have you come out as against
M    26.55                                             "Have you come out as against
Mk   14.48                                             "Have you come out as against
J    18.7                                              "Whom do you seek?"  And they


L    22.53   a robber, with swords and clubs?  When I was with you day after day
M    26.55   a robber, with swords and clubs to capture me?      Day after day I
Mk   14.49   a robber, with swords and clubs to capture me?      Day after day I
J    18.8    said, "Jesus of Nazareth."  Jesus answered, "I told you that I am he;
```

490

```
L    22.53                   in the temple,              you did not lay hands on me.
M    26.55    sat            in the temple teaching, and you did not seize      me.
Mk   14.49    was with you in the temple teaching, and you did not seize      me.
J    18.8     so, if you seek me, let these men go."
```

```
L    22.53    But       this is your hour, and the power of darkness."
M    26.56    But all this has taken  place, that the scriptures of the prophets might
Mk   14.49    But                                    let the scriptures
J    18.9              This was to fulfil        the word which he had spoken, "Of
```

```
M   26.56    be fulfilled." Then all the disciples forsook him and fled.
Mk  14.50    be fulfilled." And           they all  forsook him, and fled.
J   18.9              those whom thou gavest me I lost not one."
```

98. BEFORE THE HIGH PRIEST AND PETER'S DENIAL

Luke 22.54-71

```
L    22.54    Then    they
M    26.57    Then    those who had
Mk   14.53    And     they
J    18.12    So the band of soldiers and their captain and the officers of the Jews
```

```
L    22.54    seized him    and               led him away, bringing him
M    26.57    seized Jesus                    led him
Mk   14.53                                    led Jesus
J    18.13    seized Jesus and bound him.  First they led him to Annas; for he was the
J    18.24                                            Annas then sent him
```

```
L    22.54              into            the high priest's house.
M    26.57              to Caiaphas     the high priest, where   the scribes
Mk   14.53              to              the high priest; and all the chief priests
J    18.14    father-in-law of Caiaphas, who was high priest that year.  It was Caiaphas
J    18.24    bound          to Caiaphas    the high priest.
```

```
J   18.14    who had given counsel to the Jews that it was expedient that one man
J   18.14    should die for the people.
```

```
L    22.54                                              Peter       followed
M    26.58    and the elders                 had gathered.  But Peter     followed
Mk   14.54    and the elders and the scribes were assembled.  And Peter had followed
J    18.15                                         Simon Peter       followed
```

```
L    22.55         at a distance;                    and when they had kindled
M    26.58    him at a distance,
Mk   14.54    him at a distance,
J    18.15    Jesus, and so did another disciple.  As this disciple was known to the
```

```
L    22.55    a fire in the middle of  the courtyard               and sat down
M    26.58              as far as   the courtyard of the high priest, and going
Mk   14.54              right into  the courtyard of the high priest;
J    18.15    high priest, he entered the court     of the high priest along with
```

```
L    22.55    together,    Peter  sat     among   them.
M    26.58    inside       he     sat     with the guards to see the end.
Mk   14.54             and  he was sitting with the guards, and warming himself at the
J    18.16    Jesus, |while Peter  stood outside at the door.  So the other disciple,
```

491

Mk 14.54   *fire.*

J 18.16   *who was known to the high priest, went out and spoke to the maid who kept*
J 18.16   *the door, and brought Peter in.*

L 22.56   Then   a   maid,
M 26.69   Now   Peter was sitting outside in the courtyard. And   a   maid
Mk 14.66   And as Peter was   below   in the courtyard, one of the maids of
J 18.17   The maid who

L 22.56   seeing him as he sat in the light and gazing at
M 26.69   came up   to him,
Mk 14.67   the high priest came; and seeing Peter warming himself,   she looked at
J 18.17   kept the door

L 22.56   him,   said,   "This man also was with him."
M 26.69   and said,   "You also were with Jesus the Galilean."
Mk 14.67   him, and said,   "You also were with   the Nazarene, Jesus
J 18.17   said to Peter, "Are not you also one of this man's disciples?"

L 22.57   But he denied it,   saying, "Woman, I do not   know
M 26.70   But he denied it before them all, saying,   "I do not   know
Mk 14.68   But he denied it,   saying,   "I   neither know nor
J 18.17   He   said,   "I am not."

J 18.18   *Now the servants and officers had made a charcoal fire, because it was*
J 18.18   *cold, and they were standing and warming themselves; Peter also was with*
J 18.18   *them, standing and warming himself.*

L 22.58   him."   And a little later
M 26.71   what you mean."   And when he went out to the porch,   another
Mk 14.69   understand what you mean." And   he went out into the gateway. |And the
J 18.25   Now Simon Peter was standing and warming himself

L 22.58   some one else saw him and   said,
M 26.71   maid   saw him, and she   said to the bystanders, "This
Mk 14.69   maid   saw him, and began again to say to the bystanders, "This
J 18.25   They   said to him,   "Are not

L 22.58   "You also are   one of them."   But   Peter said,
M 26.72   man   was with Jesus of Nazareth." And again he   denied it with an
Mk 14.70   man   is   one of them."   But again he   denied it.
J 18.25   you also   one of his disciples?"   He   denied it and

L 22.59   "Man, I am not."   And after an interval of about an hour still
M 26.73   oath, "I do not know the man." After a little while   the
Mk 14.70   And after a little while   again the
J 18.26   said, "I am not." One of the servants of the high priest, a kinsman of

L 22.59   another insisted,   saying,   "Certainly this man
M 26.73   bystanders came up and   said to Peter, "Certainly   you
Mk 14.70   bystanders   said to Peter, "Certainly   you
J 18.26   the man whose ear Peter had cut off, asked, "Did I not see you

492

```
L   22.60   also was            with him;  for he   is   a Galilean."   But  Peter
M   26.74        are also one of  them,  for  your accent betrays you."  Then he began
Mk  14.71        are          one of  them;  for  you  are  a Galilean."   But  he began
J   18.27   in the garden      with him?"                                        Peter


L   22.60                                      said, "Man, I do not know what
M   26.74   to invoke a curse on himself and to swear,     "I do not know the  man."
Mk  14.71   to invoke a curse on himself and to swear,     "I do not know this man of
J   18.27   again                                  denied it;


L   22.60      you are saying."  And immediately, while he was still speaking, the
M   26.74                        And immediately                               the
Mk  14.72   whom you      speak."  And immediately                             the
J   18.27                        and at once                                   the


L   22.61   cock crowed.  |And the Lord turned and looked at Peter.  And Peter remembered
M   26.75   cock crowed.                                            And Peter remembered
Mk  14.72   cock crowed  a second time.                             And Peter remembered
J   18.27   cock crowed.


L   22.61   the word   of the Lord, how he   had said to him, "Before the cock crows
M   26.75   the saying of    Jesus,                          "Before the cock crows,
Mk  14.72                           how Jesus had said to him, "Before the cock crows


L   22.62   today, you will deny me three times."  And he went  out  and wept bitterly.
M   26.75        you will deny me three times."  And he went  out  and wept bitterly.
Mk  14.72   twice, you will deny me three times."  And he broke down and wept.


L   22.63   Now the men who were holding Jesus mocked him                    and
M   26.67   Then     they          spat in his face,                        and
Mk  14.65   And      some began to spit on      him, and to cover his face, and to
J   18.22   When he had said this, one of the officers standing by


L   22.64   beat   him; they also blindfolded him and asked      him, "Prophesy!
M   26.68   struck him; and some slapped him,          |saying,      "Prophesy to
Mk  14.65   strike him,                         saying to him, "Prophesy!"
J   18.22   struck Jesus with his hand,          saying,       "Is that how


L   22.65                   Who is it that struck you?"  And they spoke many other
M   26.68   us, you Christ! Who is it that struck you?"
Mk  14.65   And the guards received him with blows.
J   18.23   you answer the high priest?"  Jesus answered him, "If I have spoken


L   22.65   words against him, reviling him.
J   18.23   wrongly, bear witness to the wrong; but if I have spoken rightly, why


J   18.23   do you strike me?"


L   22.66   When             day    came,    the assembly    of   the
M   27.1    When             morning came, all the chief priests and  the
Mk  15.1    And as soon as it was morning          the chief priests, with the


L   22.66   elders of the people gathered together, both chief priests and scribes;
M   27.1    elders of the people
Mk  15.1    elders                                                    and scribes,
```

493

L	22.66	<u>and they led him away to their council,</u>
M	27.1	took counsel against Jesus to
Mk	15.1	and the whole <u>council</u> held a consultation; and they bound

M	27.1	*put him to death;*
Mk	15.1	*Jesus and led him away and delivered him to Pilate.*

M	26.59	*Now the chief priests and the whole council sought false testimony against*
Mk	14.55	*Now the chief priests and the whole council sought testimony against*
J	18.19	*The high priest then questioned Jesus about his disciples and his teach*

M	26.60	*Jesus that they might put him to death, |but they found none, though many*
Mk	14.56	*Jesus to put him to death; but they found none. For many*
J	18.20	*ing. Jesus answered him, "I have spoken openly to the world; I have always*

M	26.60	*false witnesses came forward. At last two*
Mk	14.57	*bore false witness against him, and their witness did not agree. And some*
J	18.20	*taught in synagogues and in the temple, where all Jews come together; I*

M	26.61	*came forward |and said, "This*
Mk	14.58	*stood up and bore false witness against him, saying, |"We heard*
J	18.21	*have said nothing secretly. Why do you ask me? Ask those who have heard*

M	26.61	*fellow said, 'I am able to destroy the temple of God,*
Mk	24.58	*him say, 'I will destroy this temple that is made with hands,*
J	18.21	*me, what I said to them; they know what I said."*

M	26.61	*and to build it in three days.'"*
Mk	14.58	*and in three days I will build another, not made with hands.'"*

M	26.62	*And the high priest stood up*
Mk	14.59,60	*Yet not even so did their testimony agree. And the high priest stood up*

M	26.62	*and said, "Have you no answer to make? What is it*
Mk	14.60	*in the midst, and asked Jesus, "Have you no answer to make? What is it*

M	26.63	*that these men testify against you?" But Jesus was silent.*
Mk	14.61	*that these men testify against you?" But he was silent and made no*

L	22.66	and they said,
M	26.63	And the high priest said to him, "I adjure you by the living
Mk	14.61	*answer.* Again the high priest asked him,

L	22.67	|"If you are the Christ, tell us." But he
M	26.64	God, tell us if you are the Christ, the Son of God." Jesus
Mk	14.62	"Are you the Christ, the Son of the Blessed?" And Jesus

L	22.68	said to them, "If I tell you, you will not believe; and if I ask you, you
M	26.64	said to him, "You have said so.
Mk	14.62	said, "I am;

L	22.69	will not answer. But from now on the Son of man
M	26.64	But I tell you, hereafter you will see the Son of man
Mk	14.62	and you will see the Son of man

L	22.69	shall be seated at the right hand of the power of God."
M	26.64	seated at the right hand of Power, and coming on the clouds
Mk	14.62	seated at the right hand of Power, and coming with the clouds

L	22.70	And they all said,
M	26.63b	of heaven." And the high priest said to him, "I adjure you by the
Mk	14.61b	of heaven." Again the high priest asked him,

494

```
L   22.70                        "Are you              the Son of      God, then?"
M   26.63      living God, tell us if you are the Christ, the Son of      God."
Mk  14.61                        "Are you the Christ, the Son of  the Blessed?"


L   22.71      And he    said to them, "You        say that I am."  And           they
M   26.64a,65      Jesus said to him, "You have said so."        Then the high priest
Mk  14.62a,63 And Jesus said,        "I am;                   And   the high priest


L   22.71                        said,                       "What      further
M   26.65      tore his robes,    and said,  "He has uttered blasphemy.  Why do we still
Mk  14.63      tore his garments, and said,                          "Why do we still


L   22.71          testimony do we need? We  have      heard it ourselves from his own
M   26.66      need witnesses?        You  have  now heard his blasphemy. |What is
Mk  14.64      need witnesses?        |You  have       heard his blasphemy.  What is


L   22.71      lips."
M   26.66      your judgment?"     They      answered, "He     deserves death."
Mk  14.64      your decision?"  And they all condemned  him as deserving death.
```

99. TRIAL BEFORE PILATE

Luke 23.1-5

```
L   23.1      Then the whole company of them arose, and brought him
M   27.2      and           they bound him        and led    him   away and delivered
Mk  15.1b     and           they bound Jesus      and led    him   away and delivered
J   18.28     Then          they                     led    Jesus from the house of


L   23.1             before Pilate.
M   27.2      him     to    Pilate the governor.
Mk  15.1      him     to    Pilate.
J   18.28     Caiaphas to the praetorium.  It was early.  They themselves did not enter


J   18.28     the praetorium, so that they might not be defiled, but might eat the pass-
J   18.28     over.


L   23.2      And          they began    to                accuse  him, saying,
M   27.12     But when     he    was                     accused by the chief
Mk  15.3      And the chief priests                      accused him of many
J   18.29     So            Pilate went out to them and said, "What accusation do you


J   18.30     bring against this man?"  They answered him,


L   23.2      "We found this man perverting our nation, and forbidding us to give tribute
M   27.12     priests and elders, he made no answer.
Mk  15.3      things.
J   18.30     "If        this man were not an evildoer, we would not have handed him over."


J   18.31     Pilate said to them, "Take him yourselves and judge him by your own law."
J   18.31     The Jews said to him, "It is not lawful for us to put any man to death."
J   18.32     This was to fulfil the word which Jesus had spoken to show by what death
J   18.32     he was to die.
```

```
L    23.3     to Caesar, and saying that he himself is Christ a king."  And       Pilate
M    27.11                    Now Jesus stood before the governor;   and the governor
Mk   15.2                                                             And       Pilate
J    18.33    Pilate entered the praetorium again and called Jesus,   and


L    23.3     asked    him, "Are you the King of the Jews?"  And he   answered him, "You
M    27.11    asked    him, "Are you the King of the Jews?"  Jesus said to him, "You
Mk   15.2     asked    him, "Are you the King of the Jews?"  And he   answered him, "You
J    18.34    said to  him, "Are you the King of the Jews?"  Jesus answered, "Do   you


L    23.3     have said so."
M    27.11    have said so."
Mk   15.2     have said so."
J    18.34    say  this of your own accord, or did others say it to you about me?"


 J   18.35    Pilate answered, "Am I a Jew? Your own nation and the chief priests have
 J   18.36    handed you over to me; what have you done?" Jesus answered, "My kingship
 J   18.36    is not of this world; if my kingship were of this world, my servants would
 J   18.36    fight, that I might not be handed over to the Jews; but my kingship is
 J   18.37    not from the world." Pilate said to him, "So you are a king?" Jesus
 J   18.37    answered, "You say that I am a king. For this I was born, and for this
 J   18.37    I have come into the world, to bear witness to the truth. Every one who
 J   18.38    is of the truth hears my voice." Pilate said to him, "What is truth?"


L    23.4     And    Pilate       said                 to the chief priests and the
M    27.13    Then   Pilate       said                 to him, "Do    you not
Mk   15.4     And    Pilate again asked                       him, "Have you no answer
J    18.38    After  he     had said this, he went out to the Jews again, and told


L    23.5     multitudes, "I find no crime in this man."  But they were urgent,
M    27.14              hear how many things  they testify against you?"  But he
Mk   15.5     to make? See how many charges they bring   against you."  But Jesus
J    18.38    them,        "I find no crime in     him."


L    23.5     saying, "He stirs up the people, teaching throughout all Judea, from
M    27.14    gave him no          answer, not even to a single charge; so that the
Mk   15.5     made    no further answer,                                 so that


L    23.5     Galilee even to this place."
M    27.14    governor wondered greatly.
Mk   15.5     Pilate   wondered.
```

100. JESUS BEFORE HEROD

Luke 23.6-12

```
L    23.6,7   When Pilate heard this, he asked whether the man was a Galilean.  And
L    23.7     when he learned that he belonged to Herod's jurisdiction, he sent him
L    23.8     over to Herod, who was himself in Jerusalem at that time.  When Herod
L    23.8     saw Jesus, he was very glad, for he had long desired to see him, because
L    23.8     he had heard about him, and he was hoping to see some sign done by him.


L    23.9     So   he           questioned him  at some length;
M    27.13    Then Pilate       said    to him, "Do   you not                       hear how
Mk   15.4     And  Pilate again asked           him, "Have you no answer to make? See how
J    19.8,9   When Pilate heard these words, he was the more afraid; he entered the
```

496

L	23.9		but he	made
M	27.14	many things they testify against you?"	But he	gave
Mk	15.5	many charges they bring against you."	But Jesus	made
J	19.9	praetorium again and said to Jesus, "Where are you from?"	But Jesus	gave

L	23.9	no answer.
M	27.14	him no answer, not even to a single charge; so that the governor
Mk	15.5	no further answer, so that Pilate
J	19.9	no answer.

L	23.10	The chief priests and the scribes stood by, vehemently
M	27.12	wondered greatly. But when he was
Mk	15.3	wondered. And the chief priests

L	23.11	accusing him.	And Herod with
M	27.27	accused by the chief priests and elders, he made no answer.	Then,
Mk	15.16	accused him of many things.	And

L	23.11	his soldiers treated him with contempt and mocked him;	
M	27.27	the soldiers of the governor took Jesus into	the
Mk	15.16	the soldiers led him away inside the palace (that is, the

M	27.27	*praetorium, and they gathered the whole battalion before him.*
Mk	15.16	*praetorium); and they called together the whole battalion.*

L	23.11	then,	arraying him in	gorgeous apparel,
M	27.28	And they stripped him and put		a scarlet robe upon him,
Mk	15.17a	And they	clothed him in	a purple cloak,
J	19.2b	and	arrayed him in	a purple robe;

L	23.12	he sent him back to Pilate. And Herod and Pilate became friends with
L	23.12	each other that very day, for before this they had been at enmity with
L	23.12	each other.

101. CONDEMNED BY PILATE

Luke 23.13-25

L	23.13	Pilate then called together the chief priests and the rulers and the
L	23.14	people, ⌐and said to them, "You brought me this man as one who was
L	23.14	perverting the people; and after examining him before you, behold, I did
L	23.15	not find this man guilty of any of your charges against him; neither did
L	23.15	Herod, for he sent him back to us. Behold, nothing deserving death has
L	23.15	been done by him;

J	19.10	*Pilate therefore said to him, "You will not speak to me? Do you not*
J	19.11	*know that I have power to release you, and power to crucify you?" Jesus*
J	19.11	*answered him, "You would have no power over me unless it had been given*
J	19.11	*you from above; therefore he who delivered me to you has the greater*
J	19.11	*sin."*

L	23.16	I will therefore chastise him and release him."
J	19.12	Upon this Pilate sought to release him, but the Jews cried out,

J	19.12	*"If you release this man, you are not Caesar's*
J	19.12	*friend; every one who makes himself a king sets himself against Caesar."*

497

```
J  19.13    When Pilate heard these words, he brought Jesus out and sat down on the
J  19.13    judgment seat at a place called The Pavement, and in Hebrew, Gabbatha.
J  19.14    Now it was the day of Preparation of the Passover; it was about the sixth
J  19.14    hour. He said to the Jews, "Behold your King!"


L  23.17    Now                          he        was obliged                    to release
M  27.15    Now at the feast the governor was accustomed                          to release for
Mk 15.6     Now at the feast           he        used                            to release for
J  18.39    But                        you       have a custom that I should release


L  23.17                        one man              to   them at the festival.
M  27.17    the crowd any one prisoner          whom they wanted.  So when they had gathered,
Mk 15.8           them     one prisoner for whom they asked.  And the crowd came up and
J  18.39                   one man               for  you  at the Passover;


  M  27.17                                                                        Pilate
  Mk 15.9    began to ask Pilate to do as he was wont to do for them.  And he


  M  27.17    said  to them, "Whom do  you want me to release for you, Barabbas or
  Mk 15.9    answered them,      "Do  you want me to release for you
  J  18.39                        will you have me     release for you


  M  25.18    Jesus who is called Christ?"  For he knew      that it was out of envy
  Mk 15.10    the King of the Jews?"  For he perceived that it was out of envy
  J  18.39    the King of the Jews?"


  M  27.19    that            they      had delivered him up.  Besides, while he was
  Mk 15.10    that the chief priests had delivered him up.


  M  27.19    sitting on the judgment seat, his wife sent word to him, "Have nothing
  M  27.19    to do with that righteous man, for I have suffered much over him today


L  23.18                        But             they all               cried out together,
M  27.20    'in a dream."  Now  the chief priests and the elders persuaded  the
Mk 15.11                        But  the chief priests               stirred up the
J  19.6a                        When the chief priests and the officers saw him,


L  23.18    "Away with this man, and release to  us   Barabbas"--
M  27.20    people        to         ask    for     Barabbas and destroy Jesus.
Mk 15.11    crowd         to have him release for them Barabbas instead.


L  23.19        a man who had been thrown into prison  for an insurrection started
M  27.16    And they had then       a notorious prisoner,
Mk 15.7     And among the rebels         in   prison, who had committed murder
J  18.40b   Now    Barabbas


L  23.20    in the city, and for murder.                          Pilate
M  27.21                                called Barabbas.  The governor again
Mk 15.7     in the insurrection, there was a man called Barabbas.
J  18.40b                   was a robber.


L  23.20    addressed them once more,              desiring to release Jesus;
M  27.21    said  to them, "Which of the two do you want me  to release for you?"  And


  M  27.22    they said,                             "Barabbas."    Pilate       said
  Mk 15.12                                                        And Pilate again said
  J  18.40a    They cried out again, "Not this man, but Barabbas!"
```

```
M  27.22    to them, "Then what shall I do with Jesus  who  is  called   Christ?"
Mk 15.12    to them, "Then what shall I do with the man whom you call the King of the


L  23.21                but they     shouted out,        "Crucify,     crucify him!"
M  27.22                They all said, "Let him be   crucified."
Mk 15.13    Jews?"  And they     cried    out again,, "Crucify him."
J  19.6b                they     cried    out,        "Crucify him, crucify him!"


L  23.22    A third time he     said to them, "Why, what evil has he done?
M  27.22    And         he     said,        "Why, what evil has he done?
Mk 15.14    And         Pilate said to them, "Why, what evil has he done?"
J  19.6b                Pilate said to them, "Take him yourselves and crucify him,


L  23.22        I have found in him no crime deserving death; I will therefore chastise
J  19.7     for I      find      no crime in him."  The Jews answered him, "We have


L  23.23    him and release him."  But they were urgent, demanding with loud cries
M  27.23                      But they shouted all the more,
Mk 15.14                      But they shouted all the more,
J  19.7     a law, and by that law he ought to die, because he has made himself the
J  19.15              They cried out,           "Away with him,


L  23.23    that he should be crucified.  And their voices prevailed.
M  27.23    "Let him       be crucified."
Mk 15.14                   "Crucify him."
J  19.7     Son of God."
J  19.15    away with him,     crucify him!'  Pilate said to them, "Shall I crucify


J  19.15    your King?"  The chief priests answered, "We have no king but Caesar."


L  23.24    So      Pilate gave sentence that their demand should be granted.
M  27.24    So when Pilate saw that he was gaining nothing, but rather that a riot
Mk 15.15    So      Pilate, wishing to satisfy the crowd,


M  27.24    was beginning, he took water and washed his hands before the crowd,
M  27.25    saying, "I am innocent of this man's blood; see to it yourselves."  And
M  27.25    all the people answered, "His blood be on us and on our children!"


L  23.25        He released      the man who had been thrown into prison for insur-
M  27.26    Then he released for them Barabbas,
Mk 15.15             released for them Barabbas;
J  19.1     Then Pilate


L  23.25    rection and murder, whom they asked for; but Jesus  he delivered up
M  27.26                       and having scourged Jesus,     delivered him
Mk 15.15                       and having scourged Jesus, he delivered him
J  19.1                took Jesus and     scourged him.
J  19.16                                      Then he handed    him


L  23.25            to their   will.
M  27.26            to be crucified.
Mk 15.15            to be crucified.
J  19.16    over to them to be crucified.
```

102. CRUCIFIXION AND DEATH

Luke 23.26-49

L	23.26	And as they led him away, they seized one
M	27.32	As they went out, they came upon a man
Mk	15.21	And they compelled a passer-by,
J	19.17	So they took Jesus, and he went out,

L	23.26	Simon of Cyrene, who was coming in from the country, and laid
M	27.32	of Cyrene, Simon by name; this man they compelled
Mk	15.21	Simon of Cyrene, who was coming in from the country, the father of

L	23.27	on him the cross, to carry it behind Jesus. And there
M	27.32	to carry his cross.
Mk	15.21	Alexander and Rufus, to carry his cross.
J	19.17	bearing his own cross,

L	23.27	followed him a great multitude of the people, and of women who bewailed
L	23.28	and lamented him. But Jesus turning to them said, "Daughters of
L	23.28	Jerusalem, do not weep for me, but weep for yourselves and for your
L	23.29	children. For behold, the days are coming when they will say, 'Blessed
L	23.29	are the barren, and the wombs that never bore, and the breasts that
L	23.30	never gave suck!' Then they will begin to say to the mountains, 'Fall
L	23.31	on us'; and to the hills, 'Cover us.' For if they do this when the wood
L	23.31	is green, what will happen when it is dry?"

L	23.32	Two others also, who were criminals, were led away to be put to death

L	23.33	with him. And when they came to the place which is called
M	27.33	And when they came to a place called Golgotha
Mk	15.22	And they brought him to the place called Golgotha
J	19.17	to the place called

L	23.33	The Skull,
M	27.34	(which means the place of a skull), |they offered him wine to drink,
Mk	15.23	(which means the place of a skull). And they offered him wine
J	19.17	the place of a skull, which is called in Hebrew Golgotha.

M	27.34	*mingled with gall; but when he tasted it, he would not drink it.*
Mk	15.23	*mingled with myrrh; but he did not take it.*

L	23.33	there they crucified him, and the
M	27.35a,38	And when they had crucified him, |Then two
Mk	15.24a,27	And they crucified him, |And with him they crucified two
J	19.18	There they crucified him, and with him two

L	23.33	criminals, one on the right and one on the left.
M	27.38	robbers were crucified with him, one on the right and one on the left.
Mk	15.27	robbers, one on his right and one on his left.
J	19.18	others, one on either side, and Jesus between

L	23.34	And Jesus said, "Father, forgive them; for they know not what they do."
J	19.23	them. When the soldiers had crucified Jesus

500

```
L    23.34    And they cast lots to divide  his garments.
M    27.35b          they             divided his garments
Mk   15.24b    and                     divided his garments
J    19.23b          they             took    his garments and made four parts, one for


  J  19.23    each soldier; also his tunic.  But the tunic was without seam, woven from
  J  19.24    top to bottom; so they said to one another, "Let us not

  M  27.35    among them by casting lots;
  Mk 15.24    among them,   casting lots for them, to decide what each should take.
  J  19.24    tear it,  but cast   lots for it   to see   whose it  shall  be."

  J  19.24    This was to fulfil the scripture, "They parted my garments among them,
  J  19.24    and for my clothing they cast lots."

  M  27.36    then they sat down and kept watch over him there.
  Mk 15.25    And it was the third hour, when they crucified him.
  J  19.25a   So  the soldiers did this.


L    23.35    And the   people stood by, watching;
M    27.39,40 And those who    passed by derided him, wagging their heads |and saying,
Mk   15.29    And those who    passed by derided him, wagging their heads, and saying,


  M  27.40       "You who would destroy the temple and build it in three days,  save
  Mk 15.30    "Aha! You who would destroy the temple and build it in three days, |save


L    23.35                                                                      but
M    27.41    yourself! If you are the Son of God, come down from the cross." So also
Mk   15.31    yourself,                    and come down from the cross!"  So also


L    23.35    the rulers                              scoffed at him,
M    27.41    the chief priests, with the scribes and elders, mocked     him,
Mk   15.31    the chief priests                          mocked     him to one


L    23.35                             saying, "He saved others; let him      save
M    27.42                             saying, |"He saved others;   he cannot save
Mk   15.31    another with the scribes, saying, "He saved others;   he cannot save


L    23.35    himself, if he is the Christ of God, his Chosen One!"
M    27.42    himself.  He is            the King of Israel; let him come down now
Mk   15.32a   himself.  Let   the Christ, the King of Israel,      come down now


  M  27.43    from the cross, and we will      believe in him.  He trusts in God; let
  Mk 15.32a   from the cross, that we may see and believe."

  M  27.43    God deliver him now, if he desires him; for he said, 'I am the Son of God.'"


L    23.36                                     The soldiers also mocked him,
M    27.48                         And one of them at once    ran and
Mk   15.36                         And one                    ran and,
J    19.29    A bowl full of vinegar stood there; so       they


L    23.36    coming up     and offering  him    vinegar,
M    27.48    took      a sponge, filled it with  vinegar, and put it on a reed,  and
Mk   15.36    filling a sponge  full   of   vinegar,      put it on a reed   and
J    19.29    put      a sponge  full   of the vinegar           on   hyssop and
```

```
L   23.37                                    |and              saying, "If you are the King of
M   27.49    gave it to him to drink. But the others said,    "Wait, let us see whether
Mk  15.36    gave it to him to drink,                          saying, "Wait, let us see whether
J   19.30a   held it to his mouth.    When Jesus had received the vinegar, he said,


L   23.38    the Jews,         save yourself!"  There was also an inscription
M   27.37    Elijah will come to save him."     And over his head they put
Mk  15.26    Elijah will come to take him down." And            the inscription of
J   19.19               Pilate also wrote a title  and                    put
J   19.30a   "It is finished";


L   23.38            over    him,          "This is              the King
M   27.37    the charge against him, which read, "This is Jesus   the King
Mk  15.26    the charge against him      read,                   "The King
J   19.19        it on the cross;   it    read        "Jesus of Nazareth, the King


L   23.38    of the Jews."
M   27.37    of the Jews."
Mk  15.26    of the Jews."
J   19.20    of the Jews."  Many of the Jews read this title, for the place where Jesus
```

```
J  19.20    was crucified was near the city; and it was written in Hebrew, in Latin,
J  19.21    and in Greek.  The chief priests of the Jews then said to Pilate, "Do not
J  19.21    write, 'The King of the Jews,' but, 'This man said, I am the King of the
J  19.22    Jews.'"  Pilate answered, "What I have written I have written."
```

```
L   23.39    One of the criminals who were hanged             railed at him,
M   27.44    And    the robbers    who were crucified with him also reviled   him in
Mk  15.32b              Those     who were crucified with him also reviled   him.


L   23.40    saying, "Are you not the Christ? Save yourself and us!"  But the other
M   27.44    the same way.


L   23.40    rebuked him, saying, "Do you not fear God, since you are under the same
L   23.41    sentence of condemnation?  And we indeed justly; for we are receiving the
L   23.42    due reward of our deeds; but this man has done nothing wrong."  And he
L   23.43    said, "Jesus, remember me when you come into your kingdom."  And he said
L   23.43    to him, "Truly, I say to you, today you will be with me in Paradise."


L   23.44    It was now about the sixth hour,      and there was darkness over
M   27.45         Now from  the sixth hour          there was darkness over all
Mk  15.33         And when  the sixth hour had come, there was darkness over


L   23.45    the whole land until the ninth hour, |while the sun's light failed;
M   27.46    the         land until the ninth hour.  And about the ninth hour Jesus
Mk  15.34    the whole land until the ninth hour.  And at     the ninth hour Jesus
J   19.28                                          After this                Jesus,
```

```
M  27.46    cried with a loud voice, "Eli, Eli, lama sabachthani?" that is,
Mk 15.34    cried with a loud voice, "Eloi, Eloi, lama sabachthani?" which means,
J  19.28    knowing that all was now finished, said (to fulfil the scripture),

M  27.47    "My God, my God, why hast thou forsaken me?"  And some of the bystanders
Mk 15.35    "My God, my God, why hast thou forsaken me?"  And some of the bystanders
J  19.28    "I thirst."

M  27.47    hearing it said, "This    man is calling Elijah."
Mk 15.35    hearing it said, "Behold, he is calling Elijah."
```

L	23.45	<u>and</u> <u>the curtain of the temple was torn in two.</u>
M	27.51	<u>And</u> behold, <u>the curtain of the temple was torn in two</u>, from top to bottom;
Mk	15.38	<u>And</u> <u>the curtain of the temple was torn in two</u>, from top to bottom.

M 27.52 and the earth shook, and the rocks were split; |the tombs also were
M 27.52 opened, and many bodies of the saints who had fallen asleep were raised,
M 27.53 |and coming out of the tombs after his resurrection·they went into the
M 27.53 holy city and appeared to many.

L	23.46	<u>Then Jesus</u>, <u>crying</u> <u>with a loud voice</u>, <u>said</u>, "Father, <u>into thy hands</u>
M	27.50	<u>And</u> <u>Jesus</u> cried again <u>with a loud voice</u>
Mk	15.37	<u>And</u> <u>Jesus</u> uttered <u>a loud</u> cry,
J	19.30b	and he bowed his head

L	23.46	I commit my spirit!" <u>And</u> having said this he <u>breathed</u> <u>his last.</u>
M	27.50	<u>and</u> yielded up <u>his</u> spirit.
Mk	15.37	<u>and</u> <u>breathed</u> <u>his last.</u>
J	19.30b	<u>and</u> gave up <u>his</u> spirit.

L	23.47	<u>Now when the centurion</u>
M	27.54	<u>When the centurion</u> and those who were with him, keeping watch over
Mk	15.39	And <u>when the centurion</u>, who stood facing him,

L	23.47	<u>saw</u> <u>what had taken place</u>, he <u>praised God</u>,
M	27.54	Jesus, <u>saw</u> the earthquake and <u>what</u> took <u>place</u>, they were filled
Mk	15.39	<u>saw</u> that he thus breathed his last,

L	23.48	<u>and said</u>, "Certainly this man was innocent!" <u>And all the</u>
M	27.54	with awe, <u>and said</u>, "Truly <u>this</u> was the Son of God!"
Mk	15.39	he <u>said</u>, "Truly <u>this man was</u> the Son of God!"

L	23.48	<u>multitudes who assembled to see the sight, when they saw what had taken</u>
L	23.48	<u>place, returned home beating their breasts.</u>

L	23.49	<u>And all his aquaintances and the women</u>
M	27.55	There were also many <u>women</u> there, looking on from afar,
Mk	15.40a	There were also <u>women</u> looking on from afar,
J	19.25b	But standing by the cross of Jesus were his mother, and his mother's

L	23.49	<u>who had followed him</u> <u>from Galilee</u> <u>stood at a distance and saw these</u>
M	27.55	<u>who had followed</u> Jesus <u>from Galilee,</u> ministering to
Mk	15.41	|<u>who,</u> when he was in <u>Galilee,</u> followed him, and ministered to
J	19.25b	sister, Mary the wife of Clopas,

L	23.49	<u>things.</u>
M	27.56	*him; among whom were Mary Magdalene, and Mary the mother of James*
Mk	15.40b	*among whom were Mary Magdalene, and Mary the mother of James the*
Mk	15.41	*him; and also many other women who came up with him to Jerusalem.*
J	19.26	*and* *Mary Magdalene. When Jesus saw his mother, and*

M 27.56 and Joseph, and the mother of the sons of Zebedee.
Mk 15.40b younger and of Joses, and Salome,
J 19.26 the disciple whom he loved standing near, he said to his mother, "Woman,

J 19.27 behold, your son!" Then he said to the disciple, "Behold, your mother!"
J 19.27 And from that hour the disciple took her to his own home.

```
L    23.50              Now
M    27.57              When it was evening,
Mk   15.42      And when          evening had come, since it was the day of Preparation,


L    23.50                        there was  a     man named Joseph from the Jewish
M    27.57                        there came a rich man              from
Mk   15.43      that is, the day before the sabbath,      |Joseph of
J    19.38                        After this             Joseph of


L    23.50      town of Arimathea.  He was a           member of the council, a good and
M    27.57                Arimathea,  named Joseph,
Mk   15.43                Arimathea,         a respected member of the council,
J    19.38                Arimathea,


L    23.51      righteous man, |who had not consented to their purpose and deed, and


L    23.52      he      was         looking for the kingdom of God.        This man went
M    27.58      who also was a disciple of Jesus.                     He   went
Mk   15.43      who was also himself looking for the kingdom of God, took courage and went
J    19.38      who      was a disciple of Jesus, but secretly, for fear of the Jews, asked


L    23.52      to Pilate  and asked for                 the body of Jesus.
M    27.58      to Pilate  and asked for                 the body of Jesus.  Then
Mk   15.44      to Pilate, and asked for                 the body of Jesus.  And
J    19.38        Pilate            that he might take away the body of Jesus,   and


M  27.58      Pilate
Mk 15.44      Pilate wondered if he were already dead; and summoning the centurion, he
J  19.38      Pilate


Mk 15.45      asked him whether he was already dead.  And when he learned from the
Mk 15.45      centurion that he was dead, he


L    23.53                                            Then he
M    27.59      ordered     it to be given to him.     And  Joseph
Mk   15.46      granted the body          to Joseph.  And  he bought a linen shroud,
J    19.38      gave                     him leave.  So   he came and took away his


J  19.39      body.  Nicodemus also, who had at first come to him by night, came
J  19.39      bringing a mixture of myrrh and aloes, about a hundred pounds' weight.


L    23.53            took      it down      and wrapped it  in a      linen shroud,
M    27.59            took   the body,       and wrapped it  in a clean linen shroud,
Mk   15.46      and  taking   him down,          wrapped him in the    linen shroud,
J    19.40      They took   the body of Jesus, and bound   it  in      linen cloths


J  19.41      with the spices, as is the burial custom of the Jews.  Now in the place
J  19.41      where he was crucified there was a garden,


L    23.53      and laid him in  a   rock-hewn tomb, where no one had ever yet been laid.
M    27.60      |and laid it  in  his own new  tomb, which he had      hewn in    the
Mk   15.46      and laid him in  a            tomb which     had been hewn out of the
J    19.41      and in the garden a    new    tomb where no one had ever     been laid.
```

504

```
M   27.60   rock; and he rolled a great stone to        the door of the tomb, and departed.
Mk  15.46   rock; and he rolled a        stone against the door of the tomb.
```

```
L    23.54                                      It was   the        day of Preparation,
M    27.62                   Next day, that is, after the           day of Preparation,
Mk   15.42   And when evening had come, since it was the           day of Preparation,
J    19.42                              So because of the Jewish day of Preparation,
```

```
L    23.54                        and the sabbath was beginning.
M    27.62   the chief priests    and the Pharisees gathered before Pilate
Mk   15.42   that is, the day before the sabbath,
J    19.42   as the tomb was close at hand, they laid Jesus there.
```

```
L    23.55   The women who had come with him from Galilee followed, and saw the tomb,
M    27.61   Mary Magdalene and the other Mary were there,
Mk   15.47   Mary Magdalene and           Mary the mother of Joses      saw
```

```
L    23.56   and how his body was laid; then                         they returned,
M    27.61   sitting opposite the sepulchre.
Mk   15.47   where          he     was laid.
Mk   16.1                             And when the sabbath was past, Mary Magdalene,
J    19.39                                               Nicodemus, also,
```

```
L    23.56                                       and prepared         spices
Mk   16.1    and Mary the mother of James, and Salome,    bought      spices,
J    19.39   who had at first come to him by night, came bringing a mixture of myrrh
```

```
L    23.56                        and ointments.
Mk   16.1    so that they might go and anoint him.
J    19.39                         and aloes, about a hundred pounds' weight.
```

```
L    23.56   On the sabbath they rested according to the commandment.
```

104. THE EMPTY TOMB

Luke 24.1-12

```
L    24.1    But                                 on the first day of the week, at
M    28.1    Now after the sabbath, toward the dawn  of the first day of the week,
Mk   16.1    And when   the sabbath was past,
Mk   16.2                             And very early on the first day of the week
J    20.1    Now                                  on the first day of the week
```

```
L    24.1    early dawn, they                         went to     the tomb,
M    28.1              Mary Magdalene and the other Mary went to see the sepulchre.
Mk   16.1    Mary Magdalene, and              Mary the mother of James, and
Mk   16.2    they                                     went to    the tomb
J    20.1    Mary Magdalene                           came to    the tomb early,
```

```
L    24.1           taking the spices  which  they had prepared.
Mk   16.1    Salome, bought    spices, so that they might go and anoint him.
Mk   16.2    when the sun had risen.
J    20.1    while it was still dark,
```

505

Mk 16.3		*And they were saying to one another, "Who will roll away the stone for*
Mk 16.3		*us from the door of the tomb?"*

L	24.2	And _____ they found __ the stone _____ rolled away from
M	28.2a,c	And behold, there was a great earthquake; |and came and rolled back the
Mk	16.4	And looking up, they saw that the stone _____ was rolled back--it
J	20.1	and _____ saw that the stone ____ had been taken __ away from

L	24.3,4	the tomb, |but when they went in they did not find the body. While
M	28.2c	stone, and sat upon it.
Mk	16.5	was very large. And _____ entering __ the tomb,
J	20.11	the tomb. But Mary stood weeping outside the tomb, and as she wept she

L	24.4	they were perplexed about this, _____ behold, two ____ men
M	28.2b	_____ for an _____ angel of the Lord
Mk	16.5	they _____ saw __ a young man
J	20.12	stooped to look into the tomb; and she saw ____ two _____ angels in white,

L	24.5	stood by them
M	28.3	descended from heaven |His appearance was like lightning, and his raiment
Mk	16.5	sitting _____ on the right side, __ dressed
J	20.12	sitting where the body of Jesus had lain, one at the head and one at the

L	24.5	in dazzling apparel; __ and as they were frightened and bowed their faces
M	28.4	_____ white as snow. __ And for _____ fear of him the guards trembled
Mk	16.5	in a white __ robe; __ and _____ they were amazed.
J	20.12	feet.

L	24.5	to the ground, _____ the men __ said to _____ them
M	28.5	and became like dead men. But the angel said to the women, "Do not be
Mk	16.6a	_____ And __ he __ said to _____ them, __ "Do not be
J	20.13	_____ They __ said to _____ her, __ "Woman, why

M	28.5	*afraid;*
Mk	16.6a	*amazed;*
J	20.13	*are you weeping?" She said to them, "Because they have taken away my*

J	20.14	*Lord, and I do not know where they have laid him." Saying this, she*
J	20.14	*turned round and saw Jesus standing, but she did not know that it was*
J	20.15	*Jesus. Jesus said to her, "Woman, why are you*

L	24.5	"Why __ do you seek the living among the dead?
M	28.5	for I know that _____ you seek Jesus _____ who was crucified.
Mk	16.6a	_____ you seek Jesus of Nazareth, who was crucified.
J	20.15	weeping? __ Whom do you seek?" __ Supposing him to be the gardener, she

J	20.15	*said to him, "Sir, if you have carried him away, tell me where you have*
J	20.16	*laid him, and I will take him away." Jesus said to her, "Mary." She*
J	20.16	*turned and said to him in Hebrew, "Rabboni!" (which means Teacher).*

L	24.6	Remember how he __ told __ you, _____ while
M	28.7	Then go quickly and tell his disciples _____ that he has risen from
Mk	16.7	But go, _____ tell his disciples and Peter that

L	24.7	_____ he was still _____ in Galilee, |that the Son of
M	28.7	the dead, and behold, he is going before you to Galilee; __ there you will
Mk	16.7	_____ he is going before you to Galilee; __ there you will

```
L   24.7     man must be delivered into the hands of sinful men, and be crucified,
M   28.5b    see him. Lo, I have told you."                        who was crucified.
Mk  16.6b    see him, as he    told you."                          who was crucified.


L   24.7              and on the third day rise."
M   28.6     He is not here; for he has risen, as he said. Come, see the place where
Mk  16.6b                     He has risen, he is not here;    see the place where


L   24.8,9            And they remembered his words, |and returning
M   28.8     he    lay.      So  they                 departed quickly
Mk  16.8     they laid him.  And they                 went out and fled
J   20.18             Mary Magdalene                  went


L   24.9     from the tomb
M   28.8     from the tomb  with fear    and great joy,                    and
Mk  16.8     from the tomb; for  trembling and astonishment had come upon them; and
J   20.18                                                                  and


L   24.9     they  told all this to the eleven   and to all the rest.
M   28.9     ran to tell              his disciples.  And behold, Jesus met them and
Mk  16.8     they  said nothing to     any one, for they were afraid.
J   20.18          said          to the disciples, "I have seen the Lord";    and


M   28.9     said, "Hail!"  And they came up and took hold of his feet and worshiped
J   20.17                     Jesus said to her, "Do not hold      me, for I have not
J   20.18    she told them that

M   28.10    him.  Then Jesus said              to them, "Do not be afraid; go and
J   20.17    yet ascended to the Father; but go to my brethren and say to them, I am
J   20.18              he had said these things to her.

M   28.10    tell my  brethren to go to Galilee, and there they will see me."
J   20.17    ascending to my Father and your Father, to my God and your God."


L   24.10    Now it                    was                                   Mary
M   28.1     Now after the sabbath, toward the dawn of the first day of the week, Mary
Mk  16.1     And when   the sabbath was past,                                 Mary
J   20.1     Now                            on the first day of the week    Mary


L   24.10    Magdalene and Joanna and          Mary the mother of James  and the other
M   28.1     Magdalene            and the other Mary
Mk  16.1     Magdalene,           and          Mary the mother of James, and Salome,
J   20.1     Magdalene


L   24.11    women with them who told this to the apostles; but these words seemed to
M   28.1                                         went to see the sepulchre.
Mk  16.1     bought spices, so that they might go and anoint him.
J   20.1                                    came to    the tomb early, while it was


L   24.11    them an idle tale, and they did not believe them.
J   20.2     still dark, and saw that the stone had been taken away from the tomb.  So


J   20.2     she ran, and went to Simon Peter and the other disciple, the one whom
J   20.2     Jesus loved, and said to them, "They have taken the Lord out of the tomb,
J   20.2     and we do not know where they have laid him."
```

L	24.12	*But*	*Peter*	*rose*			*and*	
J	20.3		Peter	then came out with the other disciple,	and	they went
J	20.6	Then Simon	Peter	came, following	him,	and	went

L	24.12			*ran*	
J	20.4	toward the tomb. They both ran, but the other disciple outran Peter and

L	24.12	*to the tomb;*	*stooping and looking in,*	*he saw the linen*
J	20.5	reached the tomb first; and stooping to look in,	he saw the linen
J	20.6	into the tomb;	he saw the linen

L	24.12	*cloths by themselves;*
J	20.5	cloths lying there, but he did not go in.
J	20.7	cloths lying, |and the napkin, which had been on his head, not lying with

J	20.8	*the linen cloths but rolled up in a place by itself. Then the other*
J	20.8	*disciple, who reached the tomb first, also went in, and he saw and be-*
J	20.9	*lieved; for as yet they did not know the scripture, that he must rise*
J	20.9	*from the dead.*

L	24.12	*and*	*he*	*went*	*home wondering at what had happened.*
J	20.10	Then the disciples went back to their homes.

105. TWO TRAVELERS TO EMMAUS

Luke 24.13-35

L	24.13	That very day	two of them	were
Mk	16.12	After this he appeared in another form to two of them, as they were

L	24.13	going to a village named Emmaus, about seven miles from Jerusalem,
Mk	16.12	walking into the country.

L	24.14	|and talking with each other about all these things that had happened.
L	24.15	While they were talking and discussing together, Jesus himself drew near
L	24.16,17	and went with them. But their eyes were kept from recognizing him. And
L	24.17	he said to them, "What is this conversation which you are holding with
L	24.18	each other as you walk?" And they stood still, looking sad. |Then one of
L	24.18	them, named Cleopas, answered him, "Are you the only visitor to Jerusalem
L	24.19	who does not know the things that have happened there in these days?" And
L	24.19	he said to them, "What things?" And they said to him, "Concerning Jesus
L	24.19	of Nazareth, who was a prophet mighty in deed and word before God and all
L	24.20	the people, |and how our chief priests and rulers delivered him up to be
L	24.21	condemned to death, and crucified him. But we had hoped that he was the
L	24.21	one to redeem Israel. Yes, and besides all this, it is now the third day
L	24.22	since this happened. |Moreover, some women of our company amazed us. They
L	24.23	were at the tomb early in the morning |and did not find his body; and they
L	24.23	came back saying that they had even seen a vision of angels, who said that
L	24.24	he was alive. Some of those who were with us went to the tomb,

L	24.24	and found it just as the women had said; but him they did not see."
Mk	16.14	Afterward he appeared to the eleven themselves as they sat at table;

L	24.25	And he said to them, "O foolish men,	and slow	of heart
Mk	16.14	and he upbraided them for their unbelief and hardness of heart, because

```
L    24.26                        to believe  all that the prophets have spoken!  Was it not
Mk   16.14     they had not believed those who saw him after he had risen.


L    24.26     necessary that the Christ should suffer these things and enter into his
L    24.27     glory?"  And beginning with Moses and all the prophets, he interpreted
L    24.27     to them in all the scriptures the things concerning himself.


L    24.28        So they drew near to the village to which they were going.  He appeared
L    24.29     to be going further, │but they constrained him, saying, "Stay with us,
L    24.29     for it is toward evening and the day is now far spent."  So he went in to


L    24.30     stay with them.  When he was at table with them, he took the bread and
J    21.13                         Jesus came           and    took the bread


L    24.31     blessed, and broke it, and gave it to them.  And their eyes were opened
J    21.13                            and gave it to them,  and so with the fish.


L    24.32     and they recognized him; and he vanished out of their sight.  They said
L    24.32     to each other, "Did not our hearts burn within us while he talked to us
L    24.32     on the road, while he opened to us the scriptures?"


L    24.33     And they rose that same hour and returned to Jerusalem; and they found
Mk   16.13     And they                      went back


L    24.34     the eleven gathered together and those who were with them, │who said,
L    24.34     "The Lord has risen indeed, and has appeared to Simon!"


L    24.35     Then they told what had happened on the road, and how he was known to
Mk   16.13     and         told the rest, but they did not believe them.


L    24.35     them in the breaking of the bread.
```

106. APPEARANCES IN JERUSALEM AND ASCENSION

Luke 24.36-53

```
L    24.36     As they were saying this,
Mk   16.14     Afterward
J    20.19     On the evening of that day, the first day of the week,
J    20.26     Eight days later, his disciples were again in the house, and Thomas
J    21.4      Just as day was breaking,


  J  20.19                     the doors being shut where the disciples were, for fear
  J  20.26     was with them. The doors were  shut,


L    24.37                     Jesus himself  stood     among           them.  But
Mk   16.14                     he                       appeared to the eleven themselves as
J    20.19     of the Jews, Jesus came and stood     among           them
J    20.26                 but Jesus came and stood     among           them,
J    21.4                       Jesus         stood     on       the beach;  yet the
```

```
L    24.37      they      were startled and frightened, and supposed that they saw a
Mk   16.14      they sat at table;
J    21.4       disciples did not know that it was Jesus.


L    24.38      spirit.  And  he said   to them,   "Why are you troubled, and why do
Mk   16.14               and  he upbraided them      for their unbelief      and
J    20.19               and     said   to them,   "Peace be with you."
J    20.26               and     said,             "Peace be with you."
J    20.27               Then he said   to Thomas, "Put your finger here,


   J  20.24      Now Thomas, one of the twelve, called the Twin, was not with them when
   J  20.25      Jesus came.  So the other disciples told him, "We have seen the Lord."


L    24.39      questionings rise in your hearts?   See        my  hands  and my  feet,
Mk   16.14      hardness      of        heart, because they had not believed those who
J    20.20      When he had said    this,        he showed them his hands  and his side.
J    20.25      But he      said to them, "Unless I  see     in his hands the print of
J    20.27                                    and see        my  hands; and put out


L    24.39      that it is I myself; handle me, and see; for a spirit has not flesh and
Mk   16.14      saw him after he had risen.
J    20.21      Then the disciples were glad when they saw the Lord. |Jesus said to them
J    20.25      the nails, and place my finger in the mark of the nails, and place my
J    20.27      your hand,                                           and place


   J  20.21      again, "Peace be with you.  As the Father has sent me, even so I send you."
   J  20.22      And when he had said this, he breathed on them, and said to them, "Receive
   J  20.23      the Holy Spirit."  If you forgive the sins of any, they are forgiven; if
   J  20.23      you retain the sins of any, they are retained."


L    24.40      bones as you see that I have."  And when he had said this, he showed them
J    20.25      hand in his side, I will not    believe."
J    20.28      it  in my  side;    do not be faithless, but believing."  Thomas answered


   J  20.29      him, "My Lord and my God!"  Jesus said to him, "Have you believed because
   J  20.29      you have seen me?  Blessed are those who have not seen and yet believe."


L    24.41      his hands and his feet.   And while they still disbelieved for joy, and


L    24.41      wondered, he    said to them,         "Have you anything here to eat?"
J    21.5                  Jesus said to them, "Children, have you any           fish?"


L    24.42,43   They gave him a piece of broiled fish, |and he           took     it
J    21.5       They answered him, "No."
J    21.13                                            Jesus came and took the bread


L    24.43      and ate before them.
J    21.13      and gave it to them, and so with the fish.


L    24.44      Then he said to them, "These are my words which I spoke to you, while
L    24.44      I was still with you, that everything written about me in the law of
L    24.45      Moses and the prophets and the psalms must be fulfilled."  Then he
L    24.46      opened their minds to understand the scriptures, |and said to them,
```

```
L      24.46      "Thus it is written, that the Christ should suffer and on the third day


L      24.47      rise from the dead, |and that repentance and forgiveness of sins should
Mk     16.15                          And he said to them, "Go into all the world and


L      24.47      be preached in his name to    all   nations, beginning from Jerusalem.
Mk     16.16         preach   the gospel  to the whole creation.  He who believes and is
```

Mk 16.16   *baptized will be saved; but he who does not believe will be condemned.*
Mk 16.17   *And these signs will accompany those who believe: in my name they will*
Mk 16.18   *cast out demons; they will speak in new tongues; |they will pick up*
Mk 16.18   *serpents, and if they drink any deadly thing, it will not hurt them;*
Mk 16.18   *they will lay their hands on the sick, and they will recover."*

```
L    24.48,49    You are witnesses of these things.  And behold, I send the promise of
L    24.49       my Father upon you; but stay in the city, until you are clothed with
L    24.49       power from on high."


L    24.50            Then      he led them out as far as Bethany, and lifting up his
Mk   16.19        So then the Lord Jesus, after he had spoken to them,


L    24.51       hands he blessed them.  While he blessed them, he parted from them, and


L    24.52       was carried up into heaven.  And they returned to Jerusalem with great
Mk   16.19       was taken   up into heaven, and sat down at the right hand of God.


L    24.53       joy, |and were continually in the temple blessing God.
Mk   16.20       And they went forth and preached everywhere, while the Lord worked with
```

Mk 16.20   *them and confirmed the message by the signs that attended it. Amen.*

PART IV

THE GOSPEL ACCORDING TO JOHN

26. Seventh Discourse: The Hour Has Come

27. The Foot Washing

28. The Betrayal by Judas

29. Peter's Denial Foretold

30. Last Discourse: Promise of the
                             Counselor

31. Last Discourse: The True Vine

32. Last Discourse: Hatred of the World

33. Last Discourse: I Go to the Father

34. The Prayer of Jesus

35. Jesus Arrested

36. Before the High Priest and Peter's
                             Denial

37. Trial before Pilate

38. Crucifixion and Death

39. The Burial

40. The Empty Tomb

41. The Appearance to Mary

42. Appearances to the Disciples and
                             Thomas

43. The Appearance by the Sea of Tiberias

44. The Charge to Simon Peter

	Page	Parallel Sections in		
		Matthew	Mark	Luke
2.20-50	561			
3.1-20	565			
3.21-35	567			
3.36-38	568	66	62	94
4.1-31	569			
5.1-17	571			
5.18-16.4a	572			
16.4b-33	573			
17.1-26	574			
18.1-11	576	68	64	97
18.12-27	578	69,70	65,66	98
18.28-19.16	581	73	67	99,101
19.17-37	586	74	68	102
19.38-42	589	75	69	103
20.1-10	591	77	70	104
20.11-18	592			
20.19-31	593			106
21.1-14	595			17
21.15-25	597			

16

1. THE PROLOGUE

John 1.1-18

J	1.1	In the beginning was the Word, and the Word was with God, and the Word
J	1.2,3	was God. He was in the beginning with God; all things were made through
J	1.4	him, and without him was not anything made that was made. In him was
J	1.5	life, and the life was the light of men. The light shines in the darkness,
J	1.5	and the darkness has not overcome it.

J	1.6,7	There was a man sent from God, whose name was John. He came for testimony,
M	3.1	In those days came John the Baptist, preaching
Mk	1.4	John the baptizer appeared
L	3.2b	the word of God came to John the son of Zechariah

J	1.8	to bear witness to the light, that all might believe through him. He was
M	3.1	in the wilderness of Judea,
Mk	1.4	in the wilderness,
L	3.3	in the wilderness; and he went into all the region about the Jordan,

J	1.8	not the light, but came to bear witness to the light.
M	3.2	"Repent, for the kingdom of heaven is at hand."
Mk	1.4	preaching a baptism of repentance for the forgiveness of sins.
L	3.3	preaching a baptism of repentance for the forgiveness of sins.

J	1.9	The true light that enlightens every man was coming into the world.
J	1.10	He was in the world, and the world was made through him, yet the world
J	1.11	knew him not. He came to his own home, and his own people received him
J	1.12	not. But to all who received him, who believed in his name, he gave power
J	1.13	to become children of God; who were born, not of blood nor of the will of
J	1.13	the flesh nor of the will of man, but of God.

J	1.14	And the Word became flesh and dwelt among us, full of grace
L	9.32	Now Peter and those who were with him were heavy with sleep, and when

J	1.14	and truth; we have beheld his glory, glory as of the only Son from the
L	9.32	they wakened they saw his glory and the two men who stood with him.

J	1.15	Father. (John bore witness to him, and cried, "This was he of whom I
M	3.11a	"I baptize you with water for repentance,
Mk	1.7	And he preached, saying, "After me
L	3.16a	John answered them all, "I baptize you with water;

J	1.15	said, 'He who comes after me ranks before me, for he was before me.'")
M	3.11a	but he who is coming after me is mightier than I, whose
Mk	1.7	comes he who is mightier than I, the thong of whose
L	3.16a	but he who is mightier than I is coming, the thong of whose

J	1.16,17	And from his fulness have we all received, grace upon grace. For the
M	3.11a	sandals I am not worthy to carry;
Mk	1.7	sandals I am not worthy to stoop down and untie.
L	3.16a	sandals I am not worthy to untie;

J	1.17	law was given through Moses; grace and truth came through Jesus Christ.
J	1.18	No one has ever seen God; the only Son, who is in the bosom of the Father,
J	1.18	he has made him known.

2. JOHN THE BAPTIST: FIRST WITNESS

John 1.19-34

```
J    1.19    And this is the testimony        of John, when the Jews sent priests
M    3.1     In those days            came    John the Baptist, preaching in
Mk   1.4                                       John the baptizer appeared   in
L    3.2b             the word of God came to  John the son of Zechariah    in


J    1.20    and Levites from Jerusalem to ask him, "Who are you?"  He confessed, he
M    3.2     the wilderness                                 of       Judea,
Mk   1.4     the wilderness,
L    3.3     the wilderness; and he went into all the region about the Jordan,


J    1.21    did not deny, but confessed, "I am not the Christ."  And they asked him,
M    3.2                 "Repent,    for the kingdom of heaven is at hand."
Mk   1.4     preaching a baptism of repentance for the forgiveness of sins.
L    3.3     preaching a baptism of repentance for the forgiveness of sins.


J    1.21    "What then? Are you Elijah?"  He said, "I am not."  "Are you the prophet?"
J    1.22    And he answered, "No."  |They said to him then, "Who are you? Let us
J    1.22    have an answer for those who sent us.  What do you say about yourself?"


J    1.23    He said, "I am the voice of one crying in the wilderness, 'Make straight
M    3.3b           "The voice of one crying in the wilderness:  Prepare
Mk   1.3            the voice of one crying in the wilderness:  Prepare
L    3.4b           "The voice of one crying in the wilderness:  Prepare


J    1.23    the way of the Lord,'                              as
M    3.3a    the way of the Lord, make his paths straight."   For this is he who was
Mk   1.2a    the way of the Lord, make his paths straight--"  as  it  is
L    3.4a    the way of the Lord, make his paths straight.    As  it  is


J    1.23                                      the prophet Isaiah        said."
M    3.3a    spoken  of                    by  the prophet Isaiah when he said,
Mk   1.2a    written                       in  Isaiah the prophet,
L    3.4a    written in the book of the words of Isaiah the prophet,


J    1.24    Now they had been sent from the Pharisees.
M    3.5     Then      went out to him Jerusalem and all          Judea  and all
Mk   1.5     And there went out to him           all the country of Judea, and all


J    1.25         They asked him, "Then why are  you baptizing, if you are neither
M    3.6     the region about the Jordan, |and they were baptized by him in the river
Mk   1.5     the people of     Jerusalem;  and they were baptized by him in the river


J    1.26    the Christ, nor Elijah, nor the prophet?"  John answered them,      "I
M    3.11    Jordan, confessing their sins.                                     "I
Mk   1.7a,8a Jordan, confessing their sins.        And he   preached, saying,  |"I
L    3.16                                           John answered them all, "I


J    1.26         baptize      with water; but among you stands one whom you do not know
M    3.11         baptize  you with water for repentance,
Mk   1.7b    have baptize  you with water;                         "After me
L    3.16         baptize  you with water;
```

J	1.27	|even he who comes after me, the thong of whose
M	3.11	but he who is coming after me is mightier than I, whose
Mk	1.7b	comes he who is mightier than I, the thong of whose
L	3.16	but he who is mightier than I is coming, the thong of whose

J	1.27	sandal I am not worthy to untie."
M	3.11	sandals I am not worthy to carry; he will baptize
Mk	1.8b	sandals I am not worthy to stoop down and untie. |but he will baptize
L	3.16	sandals I am not worthy to untie; he will baptize

M	*3.11*	*you with the Holy Spirit and with fire.*
Mk	*1.8b*	*you with the Holy Spirit."*
L	*3.16*	*you with the Holy Spirit and with fire.*

J	1.28	This took place in Bethany beyond the Jordan, where John was baptizing.

J	1.29	The next day he saw Jesus coming toward him, and said, "Behold, the
J	1.30	Lamb of God, who takes away the sin of the world! This is he of whom

J	1.30	I said, 'After me comes a man who ranks before me,
M	3.11b	but he who is coming after me is mightier than I,
Mk	1.7b	"After me comes he who is mightier than I,
L	3.16b	but he who is mightier than I is coming,

J	1.31	for he was before me.' I myself did not know him; but for this I came
J	1.32	baptizing with water, that he might be revealed to Israel." And John

J	1.32	bore witness, "I saw the Spirit descend
M	3.16b	and he now the Spirit of God descending
Mk	1.10b	and the Spirit descending upon him
L	3.22a	and the Holy Spirit descended upon him in bodily

J	1.33	as a dove from heaven, and it remained on him. I myself did not
M	3.16b	like a dove, and alighting on him;
Mk	1.10b	like a dove;
L	3.22a	form, as a dove,

J	1.33	know him; but he who sent me to baptize with water said to me,
M	3.11a	"I baptize you with water for repentance,
Mk	1.8	I have baptized you with water;
L	3.16b	"I baptize you with water;

J	1.33	'He on whom you see the Spirit descend
M	3.16b	and he saw the Spirit of God descending
Mk	1.10b	and the Spirit descending upon him
L	3.22a	and the Holy Spirit descended upon him in bodily

J	1.33	and remain, this is he who baptizes with the Holy
M	3.11c	he will baptize you with the Holy
M	3.16b	like a dove, and alighting on him;
Mk	1.8	but he will baptize you with the Holy
Mk	1.10b	like a dove;
L	3.16c	he will baptize you with the Holy
L	3.22a	form, as a dove,

519

```
J    1.34    Spirit.'  And I have seen and have borne witness that this is the Son of
M    3.11c   Spirit and with fire.
Mk   1.8     Spirit."
L    3.16c   Spirit and with fire.


J    1.34    God."
```

3. THE FIRST DISCIPLES

John 1.35-51

```
J    1.35,36  The next day again John was standing with two of his disciples; and he
J    1.37     looked at Jesus as he walked, and said, "Behold, the Lamb of God!"  The
J    1.38     two disciples heard him say this, and they followed Jesus.  Jesus turned,
J    1.38     and saw them following, and said to them, "What do you seek?"  And they
J    1.39     said to him, "Rabbi" (which means Teacher), "where are you staying?"  He
J    1.39     said to them, "Come and see."  They came and saw where he was staying; and
J    1.40     they stayed with him that day, for it was about the tenth hour.  One of
J    1.40     the two who heard John speak, and followed him,


J    1.40     was Andrew, Simon Peter's brother.
M    4.18c    and Andrew      his      brother,          casting a net into the sea;
Mk   1.16c    and Andrew      the      brother of Simon casting a net in   the sea;
 M  10.2b     and Andrew      his      brother;
 Mk  3.18a        Andrew,
 L   6.14b    and Andrew      his      brother,


J    1.41                             He first found his brother  Simon, and said
M    4.18b    for they were fishermen. he        saw   two brothers,  Simon
Mk   1.16b    for they were fishermen. he        saw                  Simon
 M  10.2a     The       names of the twelve apostles are these: first, Simon,
 Mk  3.16a                                                             Simon
 L   6.13b,14a |whom he named                    apostles;            |Simon,


J    1.42    to him, "We have found the Messiah" (which means Christ).  He brought him
J    1.42    to Jesus.  Jesus looked at him, and said, "So you are Simon the son of


J    1.42    John?  You shall be called Cephas" (which means Peter).
M    4.18b            who      is called                  Peter
 M  10.2a             who      is called                  Peter,
 Mk  3.16a            whom he  surnamed                   Peter;
 L   6.14a            whom he    named                    Peter,


J    1.43    The next day                              Jesus decided to go
M    4.12    Now when he heard that John had been arrested, he        withdrew
Mk   1.14a   Now after          John     was arrested, Jesus          came
L    4.14a   And                                       Jesus          returned


J    1.43                              to Galilee.  And
M    4.12                             into Galilee;
Mk   1.14a                           into Galilee,
Mk   3.18b                                          and
L    4.14a   in the power of the Spirit into Galilee,
L    6.14d                                          and
 M   9.9                                     As      Jesus passed on from
 Mk  2.14a                                   And as  he    passed on,
 L   5.27b                                   After this he went out,
```

```
J     1.43              he found                          Philip
M    10.3a                                                Philip
Mk    3.18b                                               Philip,
L     6.14d                                               Philip,
  M   9.9     there, he saw a man          called Matthew                      sitting at
  Mk  2.14a          he saw                        Levi the son of Alphaeus sitting at
  L   5.27b   and           saw a tax collector, named Levi,                   sitting at


J     1.44                          and      said to him,    "Follow me."   Now Philip was from
M     4.19                          And he   said to them,   "Follow me,    and I will make you
Mk    1.17                          And Jesus said to them,  "Follow me     and I will make you
L     5.10b                         And Jesus said to Simon, "Do not be afraid; henceforth you
  M   9.9     the tax office; and he   said to him,    "Follow me."   And he
  Mk  2.14    the tax office, and he   said to him,    "Follow me."   And he
  L   5.28    the tax office; and he   said to him,    "Follow me."   And he left every-


J     1.45   Bethsaida, the city of Andrew and Peter.  Philip found Nathanael, and said
M     4.19             fishers of men."
Mk    1.17   become   fishers of men."
L     5.10b  will be catching   men."
  M   9.9              rose and followed him.
  Mk  2.14             rose and followed him.
  L   5.28    thing, and rose and followed him.


J     1.45   to him, "We have found him of whom Moses in the law and also the prophets
J     1.46   wrote, Jesus of Nazareth, the son of Joseph." Nathanael said to him, "Can
J     1.46   anything good come out of Nazareth?" Philip said to him, "Come and see."
J     1.47   Jesus saw Nathanael coming to him, and said of him, "Behold, an Israelite
J     1.48   indeed, in whom is no guile!" Nathanael said to him, "How do you know me?"
J     1.48   Jesus answered him, "Before Philip called you, when you were under the fig
J     1.48   tree, I saw you."


J     1.49   Nathanael   answered him,         "Rabbi,
M    16.16   Simon Peter replied,
Mk    8.29b          Peter answered him,
L     9.20b  And   Peter answered,
  J   6.68   Simon Peter answered him,         "Lord, to whom shall we go?  You have the
  J  11.27   She          said to him, "Yes, Lord; I believe


  J   6.69   words of eternal life; and we have believed, and have come to know,


J     1.49          you are           the Son of          God!  You are the King of
M    16.16          "You are the Christ, the Son of the living God."
Mk    8.29b         "You are the Christ."
L     9.20b              "The Christ       of       God."
  J   6.69   that you are the Holy One       of       God."
  J  11.27   that you are the Christ, the Son of       God, he who is coming into


J     1.50   Israel!" Jesus answered him, "Because I said to you, I saw you under
  J  11.27   the world."


J     1.50   the fig tree, do you believe? You shall see greater things than these."
J     1.51   And he said to him, "Truly, truly, I say to you, you will see heaven


J     1.51   opened, and      the angels of God ascending and descending upon the Son
  M   4.11b          and behold, angels         came and ministered to him.
  Mk  1.13b          and       the angels            ministered to him.


J     1.51   of man."
```

4. FIRST SIGN: WEDDING AT CANA

John 2.1-12

J	2.1	On the third day there was a marriage at Cana in Galilee, and the mother
J	2.2	of Jesus was there; Jesus also was invited to the marriage, with his dis-
J	2.3	ciples. When the wine gave out, the mother of Jesus said to him, "They

J	2.4	have no wine." And Jesus said to her, "O woman, what have you
Mk	1.24	and he cried out, "What have you
L	4.33b,34	and he cried out with a loud voice, |"Ah! What have you

J	2.5	to do with me? My hour has not yet come." His mother said to the
Mk	1.24	to do with us, Jesus of Nazareth? Have you come to destroy us? I know who
L	4.34	to do with us, Jesus of Nazareth? Have you come to destroy us? I know who

J	2.6	servants, "Do whatever he tells you." Now six stone jars were standing
Mk	1.24	you are, the Holy One of God."
L	4.34	you are, the Holy One of God."

J	2.6	there, for the Jewish rites of purification, each holding twenty or thirty
J	2.7	gallons. |Jesus said to them, "Fill the jars with water." And they filled
J	2.8	them up to the brim. He said to them, "Now draw some out, and take it to
J	2.9	the steward of the feast." So they took it. |When the steward of the
J	2.9	feast tasted the water now become wine, and did not know where it came from
J	2.9	(though the servants who had drawn the water knew), the steward of the
J	2.10	feast called the bridegroom |and said to him, "Every man serves the good
J	2.10	wine first; and when men have drunk freely, then the poor wine; but you
J	2.11	have kept the good wine until now." This, the first of his signs, Jesus
J	2.11	did at Cana in Galilee, and manifested his glory; and his disciples be-
J	2.11	lieved in him.

J	2.12	After this he went down to Capernaum, with his mother
M	4.13	and leaving Nazareth he went and dwelt in Capernaum by the sea, in
Mk	1.21	And they went into Capernaum;
L	4.31	And he went down to Capernaum, a city of

J	2.12	and his brothers and his disciples; and there they stayed for a few days.
M	4.13	the territory of Zebulun and Naphtali,
Mk	1.21	and immediately on the sabbath he entered the synagogue
L	4.31	Galilee. And he was teaching them on the sabbath;

Mk	*1.21*	*and taught.*

5. CLEANSING THE TEMPLE

John 2.13-25

J	2.13	The Passover of the Jews was at hand, and Jesus went up to Jerusalem.
Mk	11.15	And they came to Jerusalem.

J	2.14	In the temple he found those who were selling oxen and sheep
M	21.12	And Jesus entered the temple of God
Mk	11.15	And he entered the temple
L	19.45	And he entered the temple

| J | 2.15 | and pigeons, and the money-changers at their business.   And making a whip |

J	2.15	of cords, he drove them all, with the sheep and oxen, out of the temple;
M	21.12	and drove out all who sold and bought in the temple,
Mk	11.15	and began to drive out those who sold and those who bought in the temple,
L	19.45	and began to drive out those who sold,

J	2.15	and he poured out the coins of the money-changers
M	21.12	and he overturned the tables of the money-changers and the seats of
Mk	11.15	and he overturned the tables of the money-changers and the seats of

| J | 2.16 | and   overturned their tables.   And   he told |

J	2.16	those who sold the pigeons,
M	21.12	those who sold pigeons.
Mk	11.16	those who sold pigeons; and he would not allow any one to carry any-

J	2.16	"Take these
M	21.13	He said to them, "It is
Mk	11.17	thing through the temple. And he taught, and said to them, "Is it not
L	19.46	saying to them, "It is

J	2.16	things away;
M	21.13	written, 'My house shall be called a house of prayer';
Mk	11.17	written, 'My house shall be called a house of prayer for all the nations'?
L	19.46	written, 'My house shall be a house of prayer';

J	2.16	you shall not make my Father's house a house of trade."
M	21.13	but you make it a den of robbers."
Mk	11.17	But you have made it a den of robbers."
L	19.46	but you have made it a den of robbers."

| J | 2.17 | His disciples remembered that it was written, "Zeal for thy house will |

J	2.18	consume me." The Jews then
M	21.15	But when the chief priests and the scribes saw the wonderful things
Mk	11.18	And the chief priests and the scribes heard it
L	19.47b	The chief priests and the scribes and the principal men of
M	12.38	Then some of the scribes and Pharisees
M	16.1	And the Pharisees and Sadducees came, and to
Mk	8.11	The Pharisees came and began to
L	11.16	while others, to

J	2.18	said to him, "What
M	21.15	that he did, and the children crying out in the temple, "Hosanna to the
Mk	11.18	and sought a way
L	19.47b	the people sought
M	12.38	said to him, "Teacher, we wish to see a
M	16.1	test him they asked him to show them a
Mk	8.11	argue with him, seeking from him a
L	11.16	test him, sought from him a

523

```
J     2.19     sign have you to show us for doing this?"  Jesus answered them,
M     21.16a   Son of David!"  they were indignant;   and they  said  to him, "Do
M     12.38    sign from you."
M     16.1     sign from heaven.
Mk    8.11     sign from heaven, to test him.
L     11.16    sign from heaven.
M     26.61b                                   "This     fellow said, 'I am able
Mk    14.58                                    "We heard him   say,  'I    will

J     2.19     "Destroy this temple,                          and              in three
M     21.16a   you hear what these are saying?"
Mk    11.18    to destroy him; for they feared him,                         because
L     19.48    to destroy him; but they did not find anything they could do, for
M     26.61b   to destroy the  temple of God,          and to build it in three
Mk    14.58      destroy this temple that is made with hands, and         in three
M     12.40                                    For as Jonah was    three

J     2.20     days I will raise it up."  The Jews then said, "It has taken forty-six
Mk    11.18    all the multitude was astonished at his teaching.
L     19.48    all the people       hung upon     his words.
M     26.61b   days.'"
Mk    14.58    days I will build another, not made with hands.'"
M     12.40    days and three nights in the belly of the whale, so will the Son of man

J     2.20     years to build this temple, and will you raise it up in three days?"
M     12.40    be three days and three nights in the heart of the earth.

J     2.21,22  But he spoke of the temple of his body.  When therefore he was raised
J     2.22     from the dead, his disciples remembered that he had said this; and they
J     2.22     believed the scripture and the word which Jesus had spoken.

J     2.23        Now when he was in Jerusalem at the Passover feast, many believed in
J     2.23     his name when they saw the signs which he did;

J     2.24,25  but           Jesus  did not trust himself to them, |because he knew
M     9.4      But           Jesus,                                 knowing
Mk    2.8      And immediately Jesus,                               perceiving
L     5.22     When          Jesus                                  perceived

J     2.25                                    all men and needed no one to bear witness of
M     9.4                     their     thoughts,              said,
Mk    2.8      in his spirit that they thus questioned within themselves, said  to them,
L     5.22                     their     questionings,            he answered them,

J     2.25     man; for he himself knew what was in man.
M     9.4      "Why do you think evil   in your hearts?
Mk    2.8      "Why do you question thus in your hearts?
L     5.22     "Why do you question     in your hearts?
```

6. FIRST DISCOURSE: NICODEMUS

John 3.1-21

```
J     3.1      Now there was a man      of the   Pharisees, named Nicodemus, a
M     22.16    And they   sent             their disciples to him, along  with the
Mk    12.13    And they   sent to him some of the   Pharisees       and some of the
```

524

```
J    3.2      ruler of the Jews.                    This man  came to Jesus by night
M    22.16    Herodians,
Mk   12.14a   Herodians, to entrap him in his talk.  And  they came
L    20.21                                                  They


J    3.2      and said to him, "Rabbi,  we know that you are a teacher come from God;
M    22.16         saying,        "Teacher, we know that you are          true,
Mk   12.14a   and said to him, "Teacher, we know that you are            true,
L    20.21         asked    him, "Teacher, we know that you speak and teach rightly,


J    3.2      for no one can do these signs that you do, unless God is with him."
M    22.16    and teach the way of God truthfully, and care for no man; for you do
Mk   12.14a   and care for no man; for you do not regard the position of men, but
L    20.21    and show    no partiality,                                      but


J    3.3      Jesus answered him, "Truly, truly, I say to you, unless one is born anew,
M    18.3     |and    said,        "Truly,    I say to you, unless you turn and
Mk   10.15                          Truly,    I say to you, whoever does not receive
L    18.17                          Truly,    I say to you, whoever does not receive
M    22.16    not regard the position of men.
Mk   12.14a   truly teach the way of God.
L    20.21    truly teach the way of God.


J    3.3                                      he    cannot   see   the kingdom
M    18.3     become            like children, you will never enter the kingdom
Mk   10.15    the kingdom of God like a child       shall not enter   it."
L    18.17    the kingdom of God like a child       shall not enter   it."


J    3.4      of God." Nicodemus said to him, "How can a man be born when he is old?
M    18.3     of heaven.


J    3.4      Can he enter a second time into his mother's womb and be born?"


J    3.5      Jesus answered, "Truly, truly, I say to you, unless one is born of water
M    18.3     |and    said,        "Truly,    I say to you, unless you    turn and
Mk   10.15                          Truly,    I say to you, whoever does not receive
L    18.17                          Truly,    I say to you, whoever does not receive


J    3.5      and the Spirit,                 he    cannot   enter the kingdom
M    18.3     become            like children, you will never enter the kingdom
Mk   10.15    the kingdom of God like a child       shall not enter   it."
L    18.17    the kingdom of God like a child       shall not enter   it."


J    3.6      of God." That which is born of the flesh is flesh, and that which is
M    18.3     of heaven.


J    3.7      born of the Spirit is spirit. Do not marvel that I said to you, 'You
J    3.8      must be born anew.' The wind blows where it wills, and you hear the
J    3.8      sound of it, but you do not know whence it comes or whither it goes; so
J    3.9      it is with every one who is born of the Spirit." Nicodemus said to him,
J    3.10     "How can this be?" Jesus answered him, "Are you a teacher of Israel,
J    3.11     and yet you do not understand this? Truly, truly, I say to you, we
J    3.11     speak of what we know, and bear witness to what we have seen; but you
J    3.12     do not receive our testimony. If I have told you earthly things and
J    3.12     you do not believe, how can you believe if I tell you heavenly things?
J    3.13     No one has ascended into heaven but he who descended from heaven, the
```

525

J	3.14	Son of man. And as Moses lifted up the serpent in the wilderness, so
J	3.15	must the Son of man be lifted up, |that whoever believes in him may
J	3.15	have eternal life."

J	3.16	For God so loved the world that he gave his only Son, that whoever
J	3.16	believes in him should not perish but have eternal life.

J	3.17	For God sent the Son into the world, not to condemn the world,
M	9.13b	For I came not to call the righteous,
Mk	2.17b	I came not to call the righteous,
L	5.32	I have not come to call the righteous,

J	3.18	but that the world might be saved through him. He who believes in him
M	9.13b	but sinners."
Mk	2.17b	but sinners."
Mk	16.16	He who believes and is
L	5.32	but sinners to repentance."

J	3.18	is not condemned; he who does not believe is condemned
Mk	16.16	baptized will be saved; but he who does not believe will be condemned.

J	3.18	already, because he has not believed in the name of the only Son of God.
J	3.19	And this is the judgment, that the light has come into the world, and
J	3.19	men loved darkness rather than light, because their deeds were evil.
J	3.20	For every one who does evil hates the light, and does not come to the
J	3.21	light, lest his deeds should be exposed. But he who does what is true
J	3.21	comes to the light, that it may be clearly seen that his deeds have
J	3.21	been wrought in God.

7. JOHN THE BAPTIST: SECOND WITNESS

John 3.22-36

J	3.22	After this Jesus and his disciples went into the land of Judea; there he
J	3.23	remained with them and baptized. John also was baptizing at Aenon near
J	3.23	Salim, because there was much water there; and people came and were bap-
J	3.24	tized. For John had not yet been put in prison.

J	3.25	Now a discussion arose between John's disciples and a Jew over purifying.
J	3.26	And they came to John, and said to him, "Rabbi, he who was with you beyond
J	3.26	the Jordan, to whom you bore witness, here he is, baptizing, and all are
J	3.27	going to him." John answered,

J	3.28	"No one can receive anything except what is given him from heaven. You
L	3.15	As the people were in expectation, and all men questioned in their hearts

J	3.28	yourselves bear me witness, that I said, I am not the Christ, but I have
L	3.15	concerning John, whether perhaps he were the Christ,
M	9.15a	And Jesus said to them,
Mk	2.19	And Jesus said to them,
L	5.34	And Jesus said to them,

J	3.29	been sent before him. He who has the bride is the bridegroom; the
M	9.15a	"Can the wedding guests mourn as long as the bridegroom is with
Mk	2.19	"Can the wedding guests fast while the bridegroom is with
L	5.34	"Can you make wedding guests fast while the bridegroom is with

```
J    3.29     friend                          of the bridegroom, who stands and hears him,
M    9.15a    them?
Mk   2.19     them? As long as they have the bridegroom with them, they cannot fast.
L    5.34     them?


J    3.29     rejoices greatly at the bridegroom's voice; therefore this joy of mine
J    3.30     is now full.  He must increase, but I must decrease."


J    3.31        He who comes from above is above all; he who is of the earth belongs
J    3.31     to the earth, and of the earth he speaks; he who comes from heaven is
J    3.32     above all.  He bears witness to what he has seen and heard, yet no one
J    3.33     receives his testimony;  he who receives his testimony sets his seal to
J    3.34     this, that God is true.  For he whom God has sent utters the words of
J    3.34     God, for it is not by measure that he gives the Spirit;


J    3.35         the Father loves the Son,   and has given   all things into his
M    11.26,27a |yea, Father, for such was thy gracious will.  All things have been
L    10.21b,22a |yea, Father, for such was thy gracious will.  All things have been


J    3.36     hand.  He who believes in the Son has eternal life; he who does not
M    11.27a   delivered to me by my Father;
L    10.22a   delivered to me by my Father;


J    3.36     obey the Son shall not see life, but the wrath of God rests upon him.
```

8. SECOND DISCOURSE: WOMAN OF SAMARIA

John 4.1-42

```
J    4.1         Now when the Lord knew that the Pharisees had heard that Jesus was
J    4.2      making and baptizing more disciples than John |(although Jesus himself


J    4.3      did not baptize, but only his disciples),      |he      left Judea and
M    4.12     Now when he heard that John had been arrested, he      withdrew
Mk   1.14     Now after           John     was  arrested, Jesus came
L    4.14a    And                                         Jesus returned in the


J    4.4,5    departed again          to Galilee.  He had to pass through Samaria.  So
M    4.12                       into Galilee;
Mk   1.14                       into Galilee,  preaching the gospel of God,
L    4.14a    power of the Spirit into Galilee,


J    4.5      he came to a city of Samaria, called Sychar, near the field that Jacob
J    4.6      gave to his son Joseph.  Jacob's well was there, and so Jesus, wearied
J    4.6      as he was with his journey, sat down beside the well.  It was about
J    4.6      the sixth hour.


J    4.7         There came a woman of Samaria to draw water.  Jesus said to her,
J    4.8      "Give me a drink."  For his disciples had gone away into the city to
J    4.9      buy food.  The Samaritan woman said to him, "How is it that you, a Jew,
J    4.9      ask a drink of me, a woman of Samaria?"  For Jews have no dealings with
J    4.10     Samaritans.  Jesus answered her, "If you knew the gift of God, and who
J    4.10     it is that is saying to you, 'Give me a drink,' you would have asked
J    4.11     him, and he would have given you living water."  The woman said to him,
J    4.11     "Sir, you have nothing to draw with, and the well is deep; where do
```

J	4.12	you get that living water? Are you greater than our father Jacob, who
J	4.12	gave us the well, and drank from it himself, and his sons, and his
J	4.13	cattle?" Jesus said to her, "Every one who drinks of this water will
J	4.14	thirst again, |but whoever drinks of the water that I shall give him will
J	4.14	never thirst; the water that I shall give him will become in him a spring
J	4.15	of water welling up to eternal life." The woman said to him, "Sir, give
J	4.15	me this water, that I may not thirst, nor come here to draw."

J	4.16,17	Jesus said to her, "Go, call your husband, and come here." The woman
J	4.17	answered him, "I have no husband." Jesus said to her, "You are right in
J	4.18	saying, 'I have no husband'; for you have had five husbands, and he whom
J	4.19	you now have is not your husband; this you said truly." The woman said
J	4.20	to him, "Sir, I perceive that you are a prophet. Our fathers worshiped
J	4.20	on this mountain; and you say that in Jerusalem is the place where men
J	4.21	ought to worship." Jesus said to her, "Woman, believe me, the hour is
J	4.21	coming when neither on this mountain nor in Jerusalem will you worship
J	4.22	the Father. You worship what you do not know; we worship what we know,
J	4.23	for salvation is from the Jews. But the hour is coming, and now is, when
J	4.23	the true worshipers will worship the Father in spirit and truth, for such
J	4.24	the Father seeks to worship him. God is spirit, and those who worship
J	4.25	him must worship in spirit and truth." The woman said to him, "I know
J	4.25	that Messiah is coming (he who is called Christ); when he comes, he will
J	4.26	show us all things." Jesus said to her, "I who speak to you am he."

J	4.27	Just then his disciples came. They marveled that he was talking with
J	4.27	a woman, but none said, "What do you wish?" or, "Why are you talking with
J	4.28	her?" So the woman left her water jar, and went away into the city, and
J	4.29	said to the people, |"Come, see a man who told me all that I ever did.
J	4.30	Can this be the Christ?" |They went out of the city and were coming to
J	4.30	him.

J	4.31,32	Meanwhile the disciples besought him, saying, "Rabbi, eat." But he said
J	4.33	to them, "I have food to eat of which you do not know." So the disciples
J	4.34	said to one another, "Has any one brought him food?" Jesus said to them,
J	4.34	"My food is to do the will of him who sent me, and to accomplish his work.

J	4.35	<u>Do you not say</u>, '<u>There are yet four months</u>, <u>then comes the harvest</u>'?
M	9.37	Then he said to his disciples, "<u>The harvest</u> is
L	10.2	And he said to them, "<u>The harvest</u> is

J	4.35	<u>I tell you</u>, <u>lift up your eyes</u>, <u>and see</u>
M	9.38	plentiful, but the laborers are few; |pray therefore the Lord of the
L	10.2	plentiful, but the laborers are few; pray therefore the Lord of the

J	4.36	<u>how the fields</u> <u>are already white for harvest</u>. <u>He who reaps receives</u>
M	9.38	harvest to send out laborers into his <u>harvest</u>."
L	10.2	harvest to sent out laborers into his <u>harvest</u>.

J	4.36	wages, and gathers fruit for eternal life, so that sower and reaper may
J	4.37	rejoice together. For here the saying holds true, 'One sows and another
J	4.38	reaps.' I sent you to reap that for which you did not labor; others
J	4.38	have labored, and you have entered into their labor."

J	4.39	Many Samaritans from that city believed in him because of the woman's
J	4.40	testimony, "He told me all that I ever did." So when the Samaritans
J	4.40	came to him, they asked him to stay with them; and he stayed there two
J	4.41,42	days. And many more believed because of his word. They said to the
J	4.42	woman, "It is no longer because of your words that we believe, for we
J	4.42	have heard for ourselves, and we know that this is indeed the Savior of
J	4.42	the world."

9. SECOND SIGN: THE OFFICIAL'S SON

John 4.43-54

```
J    4.43    After the two days                                    he     departed
M    4.12    Now when he heard that John had been arrested, he     withdrew
Mk   1.14    Now after           John     was   arrested, Jesus came
L    4.14a   And                                          Jesus returned in the


J    4.43                              to Galilee.
M    4.12                              into Galilee;
Mk   1.14                              into Galilee, preaching the gospel of God,
L    4.14a   power of the Spirit into Galilee,


J    4.44    For Jesus himself testified that       a prophet has no
M    13.57b  But Jesus          said to them,      "A prophet is not without
Mk   6.4     And Jesus          said to them,      "A prophet is not without
L    4.24    And he             said, "Truly, I say to you, no prophet is


J    4.45    honor         in his own country.  So when he came to Galilee, the
M    13.57b  honor  except in his own country                      and in his
Mk   6.4     honor, except in his own country, and among his own kin, and in his
L    4.24    acceptable    in his own country.


J    4.45    Galileans welcomed him, having seen all that he had done in Jerusalem
M    13.57b  own house."
Mk   6.4     own house."


J    4.45    at the feast, for they too had gone to the feast.


J    4.46    So                                                            he
M    8.5     As                                                            he
Mk   2.1     And when                                                      he
L    7.1     After he had ended all his sayings in the hearing of the people he


J    4.46    came again to Cana in Galilee, where he had made the water wine.  And at
M    8.5     entered
Mk   2.1     returned                                                            to
L    7.1     entered


J    4.46    Capernaum there was an official
M    8.5     Capernaum,          a centurion came forward to him, beseeching him
Mk   2.1     Capernaum after some days, it was reported that he was at home.
L    7.2     Capernaum.      Now a centurion had


J    4.46                    whose son              was ill.
M    8.6     |and saying, "Lord, my servant         is lying paralyzed
L    7.2                    a slave who was dear to him, who was sick and at the


J    4.47                    When he heard that Jesus had come from Judea to Galilee,
M    8.6     at home, in terrible distress."
L    7.3     point of death.  When he heard of   Jesus,


J    4.47    he went                     and begged him to come down and heal his
L    7.3     he sent to him elders of the Jews, asking him to xome     and heal his
```

529

J	4.47	son, <u>for he was at the point of death</u>.
L	7.4	slave. And when they came to Jesus, they besought him earnestly, saying,

L 7.5 *"He is worthy to have you do this for him,* |*for he loves our nation, and*
L 7.5 *he built us our synagogue."*

J	4.48	<u>Jesus therefore said to</u> <u>him</u>, "Unless you see signs and wonders you
M	8.7	And he said to him, "I will come and heal him."
L	7.6	And <u>Jesus</u> went with them. When he was not far from the house,

J	4.49	will not believe." <u>The official</u> <u>said</u> <u>to him</u>, "Sir,
M	8.8	But the centurion answered <u>him</u>, "Lord,
L	7.6	the centurion sent friends to him, saying <u>to him</u>, "Lord,

M 8.8   *I am not worthy to have you come under my roof;*
L 7.6 *do not trouble yourself, for I am not worthy to have you come under my roof;*

M 8.8   *but only say the word,*
L 7.7 |*therefore I did not presume to come to you.* But   *say the word,*

J	4.50	<u>come down before my child</u> <u>dies</u>." <u>Jesus</u>
M	8.13	and <u>my</u> servant will be healed. And to the centurion <u>Jesus</u>
L	7.10	and let <u>my</u> servant be healed. And when those who had been

J	4.50	said to him, "<u>Go</u>; your son will live." <u>The man believed the word that</u>
M	8.13	said, "<u>Go</u>; be it done for you as you have <u>believed</u>." And the servant
L	7.10	sent returned to the house, they found the slave

M 8.13 *was healed at that very moment.*
L 7.10   *well.*

J	4.50	<u>Jesus spoke to him and went his way</u>.
M	8.9	For I am a man under authority, with soldiers under me; and I say to
L	7.8	For I am a man set under authority, with soldiers under me: and I say to

J	4.51	<u>As he was going down</u>, <u>his servants met him and told him that his son was</u>
M	8.9	one, 'Go,' and he goes, and to another, 'Come,' and he comes, and to
L	7.8	one, 'Go,' and he goes; and to another, 'Come,' and he comes; and to

J	4.52	<u>living</u>. <u>So he asked them the hour when he began to mend</u>, <u>and they said</u>
M	8.10	my slave, 'Do this,' and he does it." When Jesus heard him, he marveled,
L	7.9	my slave, 'Do this,' and he does it." When Jesus heard this he marveled

J	4.53	to him, "<u>Yesterday at the seventh hour the fever left him</u>." <u>The father</u>
M	8.10	and said to those who followed him, "Truly,
L	7.9	at him, and turned and said to the multitude that followed him,

J	4.53	<u>knew that was the hour when Jesus had said to him</u>, "<u>Your son will live</u>";
M	8.11	I say to you, not even in Israel have I found such faith. I tell you,
L	7.9	"I tell you, not even in Israel have I found such faith."

J	4.54	<u>and he himself believed</u>, <u>and all his household</u>. <u>This was now the second</u>
M	8.11	many will come from east and west and sit at table with Abraham, Isaac,

| J | 4.54 | sign that Jesus did when he had come from Judea to Galilee. |
| M | 8.12 | and Jacob in the kingdom of heaven, \|while the sons of the kingdom will |

| M | 8.12 | *be thrown into the outer darkness; there men will weep and gnash their* |
| M | 8.12 | *teeth."* |

10. THIRD SIGN: THE MAN AT THE POOL BETHZATHA

John 5.1-18

J	5.1	After this there was a feast of the Jews, and
M	9.1	And getting into a boat
Mk	2.1	And when
L	5.17	On one of those days, as he was teaching, there were Pharisees and

L	5.17	*teachers of the law sitting by, who had come from every village of Galilee*
L	5.17	*and Judea and from Jerusalem; and the power of the Lord was with him to*
L	5.17	*heal.*

J	5.2	Jesus went up to Jerusalem. Now there is in Jerusalem
M	9.1	he crossed over and came to his own city.
Mk	2.1	he returned to Capernaum after some days, it was

| J | 5.2 | by the Sheep Gate a pool, in Hebrew called Bethzatha, which has five |
| Mk | 2.2 | reported that he was at home. And many were gathered together, so that |

| J | 5.2 | porticoes. |
| Mk | 2.2 | there was no longer room for them, not even about the door; and he was |

J	5.3	In these lay a multitude of invalids,
M	9.2	And behold, they brought to him a
Mk	2.3	preaching the word to them. And they came, bringing to him a
L	5.18	And behold, men were bringing on a bed a

J	5.4	blind, lame, paralyzed *waiting for the moving of the water; for an angel*
M	9.2	paralytic, lying on his bed;
Mk	2.3	paralytic carried by four men.
L	5.18	man who was paralyzed, and they sought to bring him in and lay him before

J	5.4	*of the Lord went down at certain seasons into the pool, and troubled the*
J	5.4	*water: whoever stepped in first after the troubling of the water was*
J	5.4	*healed of whatever disease he had.*

J	5.5	One man was there, who had been ill for thirty-eight years.
Mk	2.4	And when they could not get near him because of the crowd, they
L	5.19	Jesus; but finding no way to bring him in, because of the crowd, they

| Mk | 2.4 | *removed   the roof above him; and when they had made an opening, they* |
| L | 5.19 | *went up on the roof   and* |

| Mk | 2.4 | *let   down   the pallet on which the paralytic lay.* |
| L | 5.19 | *let him down with his bed through the tiles into the midst before Jesus.* |

531

J	5.6	When Jesus **saw** him and knew that he had been lying there a long time,
M	9.2	and when Jesus **saw** their faith
Mk	2.5	And when Jesus **saw** their faith,
L	5.20	And when he **saw** their faith

J	5.6	he said to him, "Do you want to be healed?"
M	9.2	he said to the paralytic, "Take heart, my son; your sins are forgiven."
Mk	2.5	he said to the paralytic, "My son, your sins are forgiven."
L	5.20	he said, "Man, your sins are forgiven

J	5.7	The sick man answered him, "Sir, I have no man to put me into the
M	9.3	And behold, some of the scribes
Mk	2.6	Now some of the scribes were sitting there,
L	5.21	you." And the scribes and the Pharisees began to

J	5.7	pool when the water is troubled, and while I am going another steps down
M	9.3	said to themselves, "This man is
Mk	2.7	questioning in their hearts, |"Why does this man speak thus? It is
L	5.21	question, saying, "Who is this that speaks

J	5.7	before me."
M	9.4	blaspheming." *But*
Mk	2.8	blasphemy! Who can forgive sins but God alone?" *And immediately*
L	5.22	blasphemies? Who can forgive sins but God only?" *When*

M	9.4	*Jesus, knowing their thoughts,*
Mk	2.8	*Jesus, perceiving in his spirit that they thus questioned within themselves,*
L	5.22	*Jesus perceived their questionings, he*

M	9.5	*said, "Why do you think evil in your hearts? For which is*
Mk	2.9	*said to them, "Why do you question thus in your hearts? Which is*
L	5.23	*answered them, "Why do you question in your hearts? Which is*

M	9.5	*easier, to say, 'Your sins are forgiven,' or to say,*
Mk	2.9	*easier, to say to the paralytic, 'Your sins are forgiven,' or to say,*
L	5.23	*easier, to say, 'Your sins are forgiven you,' or to say,*

M	9.6	*'Rise and walk'? But that you may know that the Son*
Mk	2.10	*'Rise, take up your pallet and walk'? But that you may know that the Son*
L	5.24	*'Rise and walk'? But that you may know that the Son*

J	5.8	Jesus said to
M	9.6	*of man has authority on earth to forgive sins"*--he then said to the
Mk	2.10	*of man has authority on earth to forgive sins"*--he said to the
L	5.24	*of man has authority on earth to forgive sins"*--he said to the man

J	5.8	him, "Rise, take up your pallet, and walk."
M	9.6	paralytic-- "Rise, take up your bed and go
Mk	2.11	paralytic--|"I say to you, rise, take up your pallet and go
L	5.24	who was paralyzed-- "I say to you, rise, take up your bed and go

J	5.9	And at once the man was healed, and he took up his
M	9.7	home." And he rose
Mk	2.12	home." And he rose, and immediately took up the
L	5.25	home." And immediately he rose before them, and took up that

532

J	5.9	<u>pallet</u>	<u>and</u> walked.
M	9.8		<u>and</u> went home. *When the crowds saw it,*
Mk	2.12	<u>pallet</u>	<u>and</u> went out before them all; *so that*
L	5.26		on which he lay, <u>and</u> went home, glorifying God. *And*

M	9.8	*they were*	*afraid,*	*and they glorified God,*
Mk	2.12	*they were all amazed*		*and glorified God,*
L	5.26		*amazement seized them all, and they glorified God and were*	

M	9.8	*who had given such authority to men.*
Mk	2.12	*saying, "We never saw anything like this!"*
L	5.26	*filled with awe, saying, "We have seen strange things today."*

J	5.9,10	Now that day was the sabbath. So the Jews said to the man who was cured,
J	5.11	"It is the sabbath, it is not lawful for you to carry your pallet." But
J	5.11	he answered them, "The man who healed me said to me, 'Take up your pallet,
J	5.12	and walk.'" They asked him, "Who is the man who said to you, 'Take up
J	5.13	your pallet, and walk'?" Now the man who had been healed did not know
J	5.13	who it was, for Jesus had withdrawn, as there was a crowd in the place.
J	5.14	Afterward, Jesus found him in the temple, and said to him, "See, you are
J	5.15	well! Sin no more, that nothing worse befall you." The man went away
J	5.16	and told the Jews that it was Jesus who had healed him. And this was why
J	5.17	the Jews persecuted Jesus, because he did this on the sabbath. But Jesus
J	5.18	answered them, "My Father is working still, and I am working." This was
J	5.18	why the Jews sought all the more to kill him, because he not only broke
J	5.18	the sabbath but also called God his own Father, making himself equal to
J	5.18	God.

11. THIRD DISCOURSE: THE SON AND THE FATHER

John 5.19-47

J	5.19	Jesus said to them, "Truly, truly, I say to you, the Son can do nothing
J	5.19	of his own accord, but only what he sees the Father doing; for whatever he
J	5.20	does, that the Son does likewise. For the Father loves the Son, and shows
J	5.20	him all that he himself is doing; and greater works than these will he
J	5.21	show him, that you may marvel. For as the Father raises the dead and
J	5.22	gives them life, so also the Son gives life to whom he will. The Father
J	5.23	judges no one, but has given all judgment to the Son, |that all may honor
J	5.23	the Son, even as they honor the Father. He who does not honor the Son
J	5.24	does not honor the Father who sent him. Truly, truly, I say to you, he
J	5.24	who hears my word and believes him who sent me, has eternal life; he does
J	5.24	not come into judgment, but has passed from death to life.

J	5.25	"Truly, truly, I say to you, the hour is coming, and now is, when the
J	5.25	dead will hear the voice of the Son of God, and those who hear will live.
J	5.26	For as the Father has life in himself, so he has granted the Son also to
J	5.27	have life in himself, |and has given him authority to execute judgment,
J	5.28	because he is the Son of man. Do not marvel at this; for the hour is
J	5.28	coming when all who are in the tombs will hear his voice

J	5.29	|<u>and</u> <u>come forth,</u> <u>those who have done good,</u> <u>to the resurrection</u>
M	25.46	<u>And</u> they will go away into eternal

J	5.29	<u>of life,</u> <u>and those who have done evil,</u> <u>to the resurrection of judgment.</u>
M	25.46	punishment, but the righteous into eternal life."

```
J   5.30    "I can do nothing on my own authority; as I hear, I judge; and my judg-
J   5.30    ment is just, because I seek not my own will but the will of him who sent
J   5.31,32 me.  If I bear witness to myself, my testimony is not true; there is an-
J   5.32    other who bears witness to me, and I know that the testimony which he
J   5.33    bears to me is true.  You sent to John, and he has borne witness to the
J   5.34    truth.  Not that the testimony which I receive is from man; but I say
J   5.35    this that you may be saved.  He was a burning and shining lamp, and you
J   5.36    were willing to rejoice for a while in his light.  But the testimony
J   5.36    which I have is greater than that of John; for the works which the Father
J   5.36    has granted me to accomplish, these very works which I am doing, bear me
J   5.37    witness that the Father has sent me.  And the Father who sent me has
J   5.37    himself borne witness to me.  His voice you have never heard, his form
J   5.38    you have never seen; and you do not have his word abiding in you, for you
J   5.39    do not believe him whom he has sent.  You search the scriptures, because
J   5.39    you think that in them you have eternal life; and it is they that bear
J   5.40,41  witness to me; yet you refuse to come to me that you may have life.  I
J   5.41    do not receive glory from men.
```

```
J   5.42,43 But I know that you have not the love of God within you.  I have come
L   11.42b  and neglect      justice and the love of God; these you ought to have
```

```
J   5.43    in my Father's name, and you do not receive me; if another comes in his
L   11.42b  done, without neglecting the others.
```

```
J   5.44    own name, him you will receive.  How can you believe, who receive glory
J   5.44    from one another and do not seek the glory that comes from the only God?
J   5.45    Do not think that I shall accuse you to the Father; it is Moses who ac-
J   5.46    cuses you, on whom you set your hope.  If you believed Moses, you would
J   5.47    believe me, for he wrote of me.  But if you do not believe his writings,
J   5.47    how will you believe my words?"
```

12. FOURTH SIGN: THE FIVE THOUSAND FED

John 6.1-15

```
M   14.13   Now when                              Jesus     heard this,
Mk  6.30              The apostles returned to Jesus, and told him all that
L   9.10    On their return the apostles                    told him      what
```

```
Mk  6.31    they had done and taught.  And he said to them, "Come away by yourselves
L   9.10    they had done.
```

```
Mk  6.31    to a lonely place, and rest a while."  For many were coming and going,
Mk  6.31    and they had no leisure even to eat.
```

```
J   6.1     After this Jesus        went                          to the other
M   14.13             he           withdrew from there in a  boat to a   lonely
Mk  6.32    And       they         went     away      in the boat to a   lonely
L   9.10    And       he took them and withdrew apart             to a   city
```

```
J   6.2     side of the Sea of Galilee, which is the Sea of Tiberias.  And
M   14.13   place       apart.                                        But
Mk  6.33    place by themselves.                                      Now
L   9.10    called Bethsaida.
Mk  8.1                                                      In those days,
```

```
J     6.2                    a        multitude                                    followed
M    14.13    when        the      crowds  heard    it,                    they  followed
Mk    6.33                          many saw them going, and knew them, and  they  ran there
L     9.11    When        the      crowds  learned it,                     they  followed
  Mk   8.1    when again a great  crowd    had                                   gathered,


J     6.2     him,
M    14.14    him on foot from      the towns.                                   As he
Mk    6.34       on foot from all the towns, and got there ahead of them.  As he
L     9.11    him;
  M    9.36                                                                      When
  M   15.32                                                  Then Jesus called his
  Mk   8.1    and they had nothing to eat,                       he    called his


  M   14.14   went ashore he saw a great throng; and he had  compassion on        them,
  Mk   6.34   went ashore he saw a great throng, and he had  compassion on        them,
  L    9.11                             and he      welcomed                       them
  M    9.36             he saw the    crowds,      he had  compassion for        them,
  M   15.32   disciples to him    and said,       "I have compassion on the crowd,
  Mk   8.2    disciples to him,    and said to them, |"I have compassion on the crowd,


J     6.2     because they saw the signs which he did on those who were diseased.
M    14.14                                        and healed their sick.
Mk    6.34    because they were                   like sheep without a shepherd;
L     9.11    and spoke to them of the kingdom of God, and cured  those who had need
  M    9.36   because they were harassed and helpless, like sheep without a shepherd.
  M   15.32   because they have been with me now three days, and have nothing to eat;
  Mk   8.2    because they have been with me now three days, and have nothing to eat;


J     6.3     Jesus went up on the mountain, and there sat down with his disciples.
J     6.4     Now the Passover, the feast of the Jews, was at hand.


J     6.5                                    Lifting up his eyes, then, and seeing
M    14.15                                       When it was          evening,
Mk    6.35    and he began to teach them many things.  And when it grew        late,
L     9.12a   of healing.                      Now the day began to wear away;


J     6.5     that a  multitude was coming to him, Jesus said to Philip,
M    14.15          the disciples    came    to him  and   said      "This   is
Mk    6.35          his disciples    came    to him  and   said,     "This   is
L     9.12c   and the twelve        came            and   said to him, |for we are


  M   14.15           a lonely place, and the day  is now over; send the crowds away
  Mk   6.36           a lonely place, and the hour is now late; send    them   away,
  L    9.12b   here in a lonely place."                   |"Send the crowd  away,
  M   15.32                    and    I am unwilling to   send    them   away
  Mk   8.3                     and if I                   send    them   away


  M   14.15   to go into the                 villages
  Mk   6.36   to go into the country and villages          round about
  L    9.12b  to go into the              villages and country round about, to lodge
  M   15.32   hungry,        lest they      faint on the way."
  Mk   8.3    hungry to their homes, they will faint on the way; and some of them have


J     6.5                                            "How   are we  to  buy
M    14.15                                                       and  buy
Mk    6.36                                                       and  buy
L     9.12b                                                      and get
  M   15.33              And the disciples said  to him, "Where are we  to  get
  Mk   8.4    come a long way."  And his disciples answered him, "How  can one feed
```

535

```
J     6.6                        bread, so that these people may eat?"  This he     said
M     14.16                      food for themselves."              Jesus said,
Mk    6.37                       themselves something to eat."  But he      answered
L     9.13a                      provisions;                    But he     said to
  M   15.33                      bread enough in the desert    to feed so great a crowd?"
  Mk  8.4          these men with bread here  in the desert?"


J     6.7         to test him, for he himself knew what he would do.        Philip
M     14.16       "They need not go away; you give them something to eat."
Mk    6.37         them,            "You give them something to eat."  And they
L     9.13a        them,            "You give them something to eat."


J     6.7         answered him,                      "Two hundred denarii would not
Mk    6.37        said to him, "Shall we      go and buy two hundred denarii
L     9.13c                     |unless we are to go and buy


J     6.7         buy enough   bread for each    of them to get a little."
Mk    6.38            worth of bread, and give it to them to eat?"     And he    said to
L     9.13c                    food for all these people."
  M   15.34                                                    And Jesus said to
  Mk  8.5                                                      And he     asked


  Mk  6.38        them, "How many loaves have you? Go and see." And when they had found
  M   15.34       them, "How many loaves have you?"
  Mk  8.5         them, "How many loaves have you?"


J     6.8                     One of his disciples, Andrew, Simon Peter's brother, said to him,
M     14.17                   They                                              said to him,
Mk    6.38        out, they                                                     said,
L     9.13b                   They                                              said,
  M   15.34                   They                                              said,
  Mk  8.5                     They                                              said,


J     6.9         |"There is a lad here who has five barley loaves    and        two
M     14.17       "We     have only        five       loaves here and       two
Mk    6.38                                 "Five,                and        two
L     9.13b       "We     have no more than five       loaves    and        two
  M   15.34                                 "Seven,              and    a few
  Mk  8.7a                                  "Seven."           And they had a few


J     6.10        fish;  but what are they among so many?"        Jesus said,
M     14.18,19a   fish."  And he said, "Bring them here to me."  Then he   ordered
Mk    6.39        fish."                                         Then he   commanded
L     9.14b       fish---                                        |And he   said to his
  M   15.35  small fish."                                        And       commanding
  Mk  8.6    small fish;                                         And he    commanded


J     6.10             "Make the people    sit down."     Now there was much
M     14.19a               the crowds   to sit down           on the
Mk    6.39                 them all to sit down by companies upon the green
L     9.14b       disciples, "Make   them       sit down in companies, about fifty
  M   15.35                 the crowd  to sit down          on the
  Mk  8.6                   the crowd  to sit down          on the


J     6.10        grass in the place; so the men              sat down,
M     14.19a      grass;
Mk    6.40        grass.              So   they               sat down in
L     9.15        each."              And  they did so, and made them all sit down.
  M   15.35       ground,
  Mk  8.6         ground;
```

536

```
J    6.10                                                              in number
M    14.21                              And those who ate                were
Mk   6.44    groups, by hundreds and by fifties.  And those who ate the loaves were
L    9.14a                              For there                        were
  M  15.38                                  Those who ate                were
  Mk 8.9                                And there                        were


J    6.11    about five thousand.                          Jesus then    took   the
M    14.19b  about five thousand men, besides women and children. |and  taking the
Mk   6.41           five thousand men.                            And    taking the
L    9.16    about five thousand men.                             And    taking the
  M  15.36          four thousand men, besides women and children. |he took   the
  Mk 8.6b    about four thousand people.                          |and he took   the


J    6.11          loaves,                                    and when he had
M    14.19b  five loaves and the two fish he looked up to heaven, and
Mk   6.41    five loaves and the two fish he looked up to heaven, and
L    9.16    five loaves and the two fish he looked up to heaven, and
  M  15.36   seven loaves and the      fish,                  and         having
  Mk 8.6     seven loaves,                                    and         having


J    6.11    given thanks,  he                            distributed them to
M    14.19b        blessed, and broke and gave the loaves                to the
Mk   6.41          blessed, and broke          the loaves, and gave      them to the
L    9.16          blessed  and broke          them,       and gave      them to the
  M  15.36   given thanks  he broke            them        and gave      them to the
  Mk 8.6     given thanks  he broke            them        and gave      them to his


J    6.11                                      those who  were seated; so also
M    14.19b  disciples, and the disciples gave them to     the crowds.
Mk   6.41    disciples              to set          before the people; and he divided
L    9.16    disciples              to set          before the crowd.
  M  15.36   disciples, and the disciples gave them to     the crowds.
  Mk 8.6     disciples              to set          before the people; and they set


J    6.11                                        the        fish, as much as they
Mk   6.41                                        the two    fish among them all.
  Mk 8.7   them before the crowd.  And they had a few small fish; and having blessed


J    6.12    wanted.                                                    And when
M    14.20                                                              And
Mk   6.42                                                               And
L    9.17                                                               And
  M  15.37                                                              And
  Mk 8.8    them, he commanded that these also should be set before them.  And


J    6.12    they had eaten their      till, he told his disciples, "Gather up the frag-
M    14.20   they all ate    and were satisfied.
Mk   6.42    they all ate    and were satisfied.
L    9.17         all ate    and were satisfied.
  M  15.37   they all ate    and were satisfied;
  Mk 8.8     they     ate,   and were satisfied;


J    6.13    ments left over, that nothing may be lost."  So  they gathered them up and
M    14.20                                                And they took         up
Mk   6.43                                                And they took         up
L    9.17                                                And they took         up what
  M  15.37                                                and they took        up
  Mk 8.8                                                  and they took        up the
```

```
J    6.13     filled                    twelve baskets       with      fragments from the five
M    14.20                              twelve baskets  full of the broken pieces
Mk   6.43                               twelve baskets  full of      broken pieces and of
L    9.17              was left over,   twelve baskets       of       broken pieces.
 M  15.37                               seven  baskets  full of the broken pieces
 Mk  8.8      broken pieces left over,  seven  baskets  full.


J    6.14     barley loaves, left by those who had eaten.   When the people saw the sign
M    14.20                    left over.
Mk   6.43     the fish.
 M  15.37                    left over.


J    6.14     which he had done, they said, "This is indeed the prophet who is to come
 M  15.39     And     sending   away the crowds,       he got into the boat
 Mk  8.10     And he sent  them away; and immediately he got into the boat with his


J    6.14     into the world!"
 M  15.39                     and went to the region   of Magadan.
 Mk  8.10     disciples, and went to the district of Dalmanutha.


J    6.15        Perceiving then that they were about to come and take him by force to
M    14.23a                                               And after he had dismissed
Mk   6.46                                                 And after he had taken
L    6.12a                                               In these days


J    6.15     make him king,   Jesus withdrew again to the mountain by himself.
M    14.23a        the crowds, he     went up      on the mountain by himself to pray.
Mk   6.46     leave of  them,  he     went up      on the mountain            to pray.
L    6.12a                     he     went out     to the mountain            to pray;
```

13. FIFTH SIGN: WALKING ON THE WATER

John 6.16-21

```
 M  14.23     And after he had dismissed  the crowds, he went up on the mountain by
 Mk  6.46     And after he had taken leave of them,   he went up on the mountain


J    6.16                    When evening came,
M    14.23    himself to pray.   When evening came,
Mk   6.47         to pray.   And when evening came,  the boat was out on the sea,


J    6.16                                                  his disciples
M    14.22        he was there alone,          Then       he made the disciples
Mk   6.45     and he was       alone on the land.   Immediately he made his disciples


J    6.17     went down to the sea, |got into a    boat, and started      across the
M    14.22                           get into the  boat  and go before him to the other
Mk   6.45                            get into the  boat  and go before him to the other


J    6.17     sea    to Capernaum.
M    14.25    side,            while he dismissed the crowds. And in     the fourth
Mk   6.48b    side, to Bethsaida, while he dismissed the crowd.  And about the fourth


J    6.17     It was now   dark, and Jesus had not yet come to them.
M    14.25    watch of the night   he               came to them, walking on the sea.
Mk   6.48b    watch of the night   he               came to them, walking on the sea.
```

J	6.18,19	The sea rose because a strong wind was blowing. When they had	
M	14.24	beaten by the waves; for the wind was against them.	
Mk	6.48a	painfully, for the wind was against them.	

J   6.19   rowed about three or four miles, they   saw Jesus walking on the sea
M 14.26   But when the disciples saw him   walking on the sea,
Mk 6.49 |but when   they   saw him   walking on the sea

J   6.19   and drawing near to the boat.   They   were
M 14.26   they   were
Mk 6.50   they thought it was a ghost, and cried out; for they all saw him, and were

J   6.20   frightened, |but
M 14.27   terrified, saying, "It is a ghost!" And they cried out for fear. But
Mk 6.50   terrified.   But

J   6.20   he said to them,   "It is I; do   not be
M 14.27   immediately he spoke to them,   saying, "Take heart, it is I; have no
Mk 6.50   immediately he spoke to them and said,   "Take heart, it is I; have no

J   6.21   afraid." Then they were glad to take him into the boat,   and
M 14.32   fear." And when they   got   into the boat,
Mk 6.51   fear." And   he   got   into the boat with them and

J   6.21   immediately the boat was at the land to which they were going.
M 14.33   the wind ceased. And those in the boat worshiped him, saying,
Mk 6.52   the wind ceased. And they were utterly astounded, |for they

M 14.33   *"Truly you are the Son of God."*
Mk 6.52   *did not understand about the loaves, but their hearts were hardened.*

14. FOURTH DISCOURSE: THE BREAD OF LIFE

John 6.22-59

J   6.22   On the next day the people who remained on the other side of the sea
J   6.22   saw that there had been only one boat there, and that Jesus had not
J   6.22   entered the boat with his disciples, but that his disciples had gone away
J   6.23   alone. However, boats from Tiberias came near the place where they ate
J   6.23   the bread after the Lord had given thanks.

J   6.24   So when   the people saw that Jesus was not there, nor his disciples,
Mk 1.36,37   And Simon and those who were with him pursued him, |and
L   4.42b   And   the people

J   6.24   they themselves got into the boats and went to Capernaum, seeking
Mk 1.37   they found him and said to him,   "Every one is searching for
L   4.42b   sought

J   6.24   Jesus.
Mk 1.37   you."
L   4.42b   him and came to him, and would have kept him from leaving them;

J	6.25	When they found him on the other side of the sea, they said to him,
J	6.26	"Rabbi, when did you come here?" Jesus answered them, "Truly, truly, I
J	6.26	say to you, you seek me, not because you saw signs, but because you ate
J	6.27	your fill of the loaves. Do not labor for the food which perishes, but
J	6.27	for the food which endures to eternal life, which the Son of man will
J	6.28	give to you; for on him has God the Father set his seal." Then they said
J	6.29	to him, "What must we do, to be doing the works of God?" Jesus answered
J	6.29	them, "This is the work of God, that you believe in him whom he has sent."

J	6.30	So they
M	12.38	Then some of the scribes and Pharisees
Mk	8.11	The Pharisees came and
M	16.1	And the Pharisees and Sadducees came, and
L	11.16	while others,

J	6.30	said to him, "Then what
M	12.38	said to him, "Teacher, we wish to
Mk	8.11	began to argue with him, seeking from him
M	16.1	to test him they asked him to
L	11.16	to test him, sought from him

J	6.30	sign do you do, that we may see, and believe you? What work
M	12.38	see a sign from you."
Mk	8.11	a sign from heaven, to test him.
M	16.1	show them a sign from heaven.
L	11.16	a sign from heaven.

J	6.31	do you perform? Our fathers ate the manna in the wilderness; as it is
J	6.32	written, 'He gave them bread from heaven to eat.'" Jesus then said to them,
J	6.32	"Truly, truly, I say to you, it was not Moses who gave you the bread from
J	6.33	heaven; my Father gives you the true bread from heaven. For the bread of
J	6.33	God is that which comes down from heaven, and gives life to the world."
J	6.34	They said to him, "Lord, give us this bread always."

J	6.35	Jesus said to them, "I am the bread of life; he who comes to me shall
J	6.36	not hunger, and he who believes in me shall never thirst. But I said to
J	6.37	you that you have seen me and yet do not believe. All that the Father
J	6.37	gives me will come to me; and him who comes to me I will not cast out.

J	6.38	For I have come
M	26.39b	"My Father, if it be possible, let this cup pass from
Mk	14.36b	"Abba, Father, all things are possible to thee; remove this cup from
L	22.42	"Father, if thou art willing, remove this cup from

J	6.38	down from heaven, not to do my own will, but the will of him who sent
M	26.39b	me; nevertheless, not as I will, but as thou wilt."
Mk	14.36b	me; yet not what I will, but what thou wilt."
L	22.42	me; nevertheless not my will, but thine, be done."

J	6.39	me; and this is the will of him who sent me, that I should lose nothing
J	6.40	of all that he has given me, but raise it up at the last day. For this
J	6.40	is the will of my Father, that every one who sees the Son and believes
J	6.40	in him should have eternal life; and I will raise him up at the last day."

J	6.41	The Jews then murmured at him, because he said, "I am the bread which

J	6.42	came down from heaven." They said, "Is not this Jesus, the son of Joseph,
M	13.55	Is not this the carpenter's son?
Mk	6.3a	Is not this the carpenter,
L	4.22b	and they said, "Is not this Joseph's son?"

540

```
J    6.42   whose father and mother we know?  How does he now say, 'I have come down
M    13.55          Is not his mother called Mary?  And are not his brothers    James
Mk   6.3a                    the son of Mary    and                 brother of James


J    6.43   from heaven'?"  Jesus answered them, "Do not murmur among yourselves.
M    13.56  and Joseph and Simon and Judas?  And are not all his sisters      with us?
Mk   6.3a   and Joses  and Judas and Simon,  and are not    his sisters here with us?"


J    6.44   No one can come to me unless the Father who sent me draws him; and I will
M    13.56  Where then did this man get all this?"


J    6.45   raise him up at the last day.  It is written in the prophets, 'And they
J    6.45   shall all be taught by God.'  Every one who has heard and learned from
J    6.46   the Father comes to me.  Not that any one has seen the Father except him
J    6.47   who is from God; he has seen the Father.  Truly, truly, I say to you, he


J    6.47   who believes has eternal life.
M    26.26  Now as they were eating,
Mk   14.22  And as they were eating,
L    22.19  And
1 C  11.23  For I received from the Lord what I also delivered to you, that the


J    6.48                                      I am the bread of life.
M    26.26  Jesus                                took bread,  and
Mk   14.22  he                                   took bread,  and
L    22.19  he                                   took bread,  and when he
1 C  11.24  Lord Jesus on the night when he was betrayed took bread, |and when he


J    6.49   Your fathers ate the manna in the wilderness, and they died.
J    6.50                              This is the bread which comes
J    6.51   down from heaven, that a man may eat of it and not die.  I am the
J    6.51   living bread which came down from heaven; if any one eats of this


J    6.51   bread, he will live for ever; and the bread which I shall give for the
M    26.26      blessed,      and broke it, and gave it to the disciples and said,
Mk   14.22      blessed,      and broke it, and gave it to    them,    and said,
L    22.19  had given thanks he broke it  and gave it to    them,    saying,
1 C  11.24  had given thanks, he broke it,                          and said,


J    6.52   life of the world is my flesh."  The Jews then disputed among themselves,
M    26.26  "Take, eat;  this is my body."
Mk   14.22  "Take;      this is my body."
L    22.19          "This is my body which is given for you.  Do this in
1 C  11.24          "This is my body which is      for you.  Do this in


J    6.53   saying, "How can this man give us his flesh to eat?"  So Jesus said to
J    6.53   them, "Truly, truly, I say to you, unless you eat the flesh of the Son


J    6.53   of man
M    26.27              And he took      a  cup, and when he had given
Mk   14.23              And he took      a  cup, and when he had given
L    22.17              And he took      a  cup, and when he had given
L    22.20a  remembrance of me."  And likewise    the cup  after supper,
1 C  11.25   remembrance of me."  In the same way also the cup, after supper,
```

```
J    6.53                                                and drink his blood, you have no
M   26.27    thanks he gave it to them, saying,     "Drink of it, all of you;
Mk  14.24    thanks he gave it to them, and they all drank of it.  And he said to
L   22.17    thanks he                   said,       "Take this, and divide it among
L   22.20a                               saying,
1 C 11.25                                saying,
```

```
J    6.54    life in you; he who eats my flesh and drinks my blood has eternal life,
J    6.55    and I will raise him up at the last day.  For my flesh is food indeed,
J    6.56    and my blood is drink indeed.  He who eats my flesh and drinks my blood
J    6.57    abides in me, and I in him.  As the living Father sent me, and I live
J    6.58    because of the Father, so he who eats me will live because of me.  This
J    6.58    is the bread which came down from heaven, not such as the fathers ate
J    6.59    and died; he who eats this bread will live for ever."  This he said in
J    6.59    the synagogue, as he taught at Capernaum.
```

```
 M 26.28    for     this     is my blood of the     covenant,          which
Mk 14.24    them, "This     is my blood of the     covenant,          which
 L 22.17    yourselves;
 L 22.20c,b         "This cup |is        the new covenant in my blood.  |which
1 C 11.25           "This cup is         the new covenant in my blood.  Do this,
```

```
 M 26.28    is poured out for many for the forgiveness of sins.
Mk 14.24    is poured out for many.
 L 22.15    is poured out for you  |And he said to them, "I have earnestly desired
1 C 11.25    as often as you drink it, in remembrance of me."
```

```
 L 22.16    to eat this passover with you before I suffer; for I tell you I shall
 L 22.16    not eat it until it is fulfilled in the kingdom of God."
```

```
 M 26.29          I tell  you            I shall not drink again of this
Mk 14.25    Truly, I say to you,          I shall not drink again of the
 L 22.18    for   I tell  you that from now on I shall not drink    of the
1 C 11.26    For as often as you eat this bread and drink the cup, you proclaim
```

```
 M 26.29    fruit of the vine until that day when I drink it new with you in my
Mk 14.25    fruit of the vine until that day when I drink it new         in the
 L 22.18    fruit of the vine until                                      the
1 C 11.27    the Lord's death until he comes.  Whoever, therefore, eats the bread
```

```
 M 26.29    Father's kingdom."
Mk 14.25            kingdom of God."
 L 22.18            kingdom of God comes."
1 C 11.27    or drinks the cup of the Lord in an unworthy manner will be guilty of
```

```
1 C 11.28    profaning the body and blood of the Lord.  Let a man examine himself,
1 C 11.29    and so eat of the bread and drink of the cup.  For any one who eats
1 C 11.29    and drinks without discerning the body eats and drinks judgment upon
1 C 11.30    himself.  That is why many of you are weak and ill, and some have died.
1 C 11.31,32 But if we judged ourselves truly, we should not be judged.  But when
1 C 11.32    we are judged by the Lord, we are chastened so that we may not be con-
1 C 11.32    demned along with the world.
```

15. REJECTION AND PETER'S CONFESSION

John 6.60-71

```
J    6.60    Many of his disciples, when they heard it, said, "This is a hard saying;
J    6.61    who can listen to it?"  But Jesus, knowing in himself that his disciples
J    6.62    murmured at it, said to them, "Do you take offense at this?  Then what if
J    6.63    you were to see the Son of man ascending where he was before?  It is the
```

542

```
J    6.63    spirit that gives life, the flesh is of no avail; the words that I have
J    6.64    spoken to you are spirit and life.  But there are some of you that do
J    6.64    not believe."  For Jesus knew from the first who those were that did not
J    6.65    believe, and who it was that would betray him.  And he said, "This is why
J    6.65    I told you that no one can come to me unless it is granted him by the
J    6.65    Father."


J    6.66    After this many of his disciples drew back and no longer went about
M   16.13    Now when           Jesus came                    into the district
Mk   8.27    And                Jesus went on with his disciples, to the villages
L    9.18    Now it happened that as he was praying alone the disciples were


J    6.67    with him.                             Jesus said to the twelve,      "Do
M   16.13    of Caesarea Philippi,          he asked    his disciples, "Who do
Mk   8.27    of Caesarea Philippi; and on the way he asked    his disciples, "Who do
L    9.18    with him;          and          he asked       them,      "Who do


J    6.67    you also wish to go away?"
M   16.14        men    say that the Son of man is?"  And they said, "Some say John
Mk   8.28        men    say that      I      am?"  And they told him,      "John
L    9.19    the people say that      I      am?"  And they answered,      "John


M   16.14    the Baptist,     others say  Elijah, and others Jeremiah or one of the
Mk   8.28    the Baptist; and others say, Elijah; and others          one of the
L    9.19    the Baptist; but others say, Elijah; and others,     that one of the

M   16.15    prophets."          He said to them, "But who do you say that
Mk   8.29    prophets."     And he asked  them, "But who do you say that
L    9.20    old prophets has risen."  And he said to them, "But who do you say that


J    6.68           .   Simon Peter answered him,        "Lord, to whom shall we go?  You
M   16.16    I am?"  Simon Peter replied,
Mk   8.29    I am?"       Peter answered him,
L    9.20    I am?"  And  Peter answered,
J    1.49            Nathanael  answered him,        "Rabbi,
J   11.27            She        said  to him, "Yes, Lord; I believe


J    6.69    have the words of eternal life; and we have believed, and have come to


J    6.69    know, that you are the Holy One       of        God."
M   16.16        "You are the Christ, the Son of the living God."
Mk   8.29        "You are the Christ."
L    9.20        "The Christ       of        God."
J    1.49        you are        the Son of        God! You are the
J   11.27    that you are the Christ, the Son of        God, he who is


J    6.70    Jesus answered them, "Did I not choose you, the twelve, and one of you
M   26.14    Then                        one of the twelve, who was called
Mk  14.10    Then
L   22.3     Then              Satan entered        into
J    1.49    King of Israel!"
J   11.27    coming into the world."


J    6.71    is a devil?"  He spoke of Judas the son of Simon Iscariot, for he,
M   26.14              Judas              Iscariot,
Mk  14.10              Judas              Iscariot, who was
L   22.3               Judas       called Iscariot, who was of the
```

543

```
J    6.71    one     of the twelve,
M    26.14                            went                     to    the chief priests
Mk   14.10   one     of the twelve,   went                     to    the chief priests
L    22.4    number  of the twelve; he went away and conferred with the chief priests
```

M 26.15 |and said, "What will you give me if I   deliver him to you?"   And
Mk 14.11   in order to betray him to them.   And
L 22.5   and officers   how he might betray him to them.   And

M 26.15   they   paid   him thirty pieces
Mk 14.11   when they heard it they were glad, and promised to give him
L 22.5   they were glad, and engaged to give him

```
                                                        was
J    6.71                                              
M    26.16   of silver.        And from that moment he sought an opportunity
Mk   14.11      money.         And                  he sought an opportunity
L    22.6       money.  So he agreed, and             sought an opportunity
```

```
J    6.71    to betray him.
M    26.16   to betray him.
Mk   14.11   to betray him.
L    22.6    to betray him to them in the absence of the multitude.
```

16. THE FEAST OF THE TABERNACLES AT JERUSALEM

John 7.1-13

```
J    7.1     After this Jesus went                              about in Galilee;      he
Mk   9.30                  They   went on from there and passed through Galilee.   And he
```

```
J    7.2     would not go about in Judea, because the Jews sought to kill him.  Now
Mk   9.31a   would not have any one know it; for he was teaching his disciples,
```

```
J    7.3     the Jews' feast of Tabernacles was at hand.  So his brothers said to him,
J    7.3     "Leave here and go to Judea, that your disciples may see the works you
J    7.4     are doing.  For no man works in secret if he seeks to be known openly.
J    7.5     If you do these things, show yourself to the world."  For even his brothers
J    7.6     did not believe in him.  Jesus said to them, "My time has not yet come,
J    7.7     but your time is always here.  The world cannot hate you, but it hates
J    7.8     me because I testify of it that its works are evil.  Go to the feast
J    7.8     yourselves; I am not going up this feast, for my time has not yet fully
J    7.9     come."  So saying, he remained in Galilee.
```

```
J    7.10    But after his brothers had gone up to the feast, then he also went up,
J    7.11    not publicly but in private.  The Jews were looking for him at the feast,
J    7.12    and saying, "Where is he?"  And there was much muttering about him among
J    7.12    the people.  While some said, "He is a good man," others said, "No, he
J    7.13    is leading the people astray."  Yet for fear of the Jews no one spoke
J    7.13    openly of him.
```

17. CONTROVERSIES WITH THE JEWS

John 7.14-52

```
J    7.14    About the middle of the feast Jesus went up into the temple and taught.
```

```
J    7.15        The   Jews                        marveled at it, saying, "How is it
M    13.54b   so that they                were astonished, and said,  "Where did
Mk   6.2b     and      many who heard   him were astonished,     saying, "Where did
L    4.22     And      all spoke well of him, and wondered at the gracious words which


J    7.16     that this man has learning, when he has never studied?"  So Jesus
M    13.54b         this man get    this              wisdom          and these
Mk   6.2b           this man get all this? What is the wisdom given to him? What
L    4.22     proceeded out of his mouth; and they said, "Is not this Joseph's son?"


J    7.17     answered them, "My teaching is not mine, but his who sent me; if any man's
M    13.54b   mighty works?
Mk   6.2b     mighty works are wrought by his hands!


J    7.17     will is to do his will, he shall know whether the teaching is from God
J    7.18     or whether I am speaking on my own authority.  He who speaks on his own
J    7.18     authority seeks his own glory; but he who seeks the glory of him who sent
J    7.19     him is true, and in him there is no falsehood.  Did not Moses give you
J    7.19     the law? Yet none of you keeps the law.  Why do you seek to kill me?"


J    7.20                  The people                        answered, "You have
M    9.34     But          the Pharisees                        said,    "He  casts
M    12.24    But when the Pharisees heard it             they said,    "It  is
Mk   3.22     And          the scribes who came down from Jerusalem said, "He  is
L    11.15    But          some of them                         said,    "He  casts


J    7.20                                      a demon! Who is seeking to
M    9.34     out demons                   by the prince of demons."
M    12.24    only        by Beelzebul,      the prince of demons, that this man casts
Mk   3.22     possessed by Beelzebul, and by the prince of demons          he  casts
L    11.15    out demons by Beelzebul,        the prince of demons";


J    7.21     kill you?" Jesus answered them, "I did one deed, and you all marvel at it.
M    12.24    out      demons."
Mk   3.22     out the demons."


J    7.22     Moses gave you circumcision (not that it is from Moses, but from the
J    7.23     fathers), and you circumcise a man upon the sabbath.  If on the sabbath
J    7.23     a man receives circumcision, so that the law of Moses may not be broken,
J    7.23     are you angry with me because on the sabbath I made a man's whole body
J    7.24     well? Do not judge by appearances, but judge with right judgment."


J    7.25        Some of the people of Jerusalem therefore said, "Is not this the man
J    7.26     whom they seek to kill? And here he is, speaking openly, and they say
J    7.26     nothing to him! Can it be that the authorities really know that this is
J    7.27     the Christ? Yet we know where this man comes from; and when the Christ
J    7.28     appears, no one will know where he comes from."  So Jesus proclaimed, as
J    7.28     he taught in the temple, "You know me, and you know where I come from?
J    7.28     But I have not come of my own accord; he who sent me is true, and him
J    7.29     you do not know.  I know him, for I come from him, and he sent me."
J    7.30     So they sought to arrest him; but no one laid hands on him, because his


J    7.31     hour had not yet come. Yet many of the people    believed in him;
M    9.33b                             and        the crowds   marveled,
M    12.23                             And all   the people were amazed,


J    7.31     they said,   "When the Christ appears, will he do more signs than this
M    9.33b              saying, "Never was anything like this seen in Israel."
M    12.23    and  said,    "Can this be the Son of David?"
```

545

J 7.31   man has done?"

J 7.32   The Pharisees heard the crowd thus muttering about him, and the chief
J 7.33   priests and Pharisees sent officers to arrest him. Jesus then said, "I
J 7.34   shall be with you a little longer, and then I go to him who sent me; you
J 7.35   will seek me and you will not find me; where I am you cannot come." The
J 7.35   Jews said to one another, "Where does this man intend to go that we shall
J 7.35   not find him? Does he intend to go to the Dispersion among the Greeks and
J 7.36   teach the Greeks? What does he mean by saying, 'You will seek me and you
J 7.36   will not find me,' and, 'Where I am you cannot come'?"

J 7.37   On the last day of the feast, the great day, Jesus stood up and pro-
J 7.38   claimed, "If any one thirst, let him come to me and drink. He who be-
J 7.38   lieves in me, as the scripture has said, 'Out of his heart shall flow
J 7.39   rivers of living water.'" Now this he said about the Spirit, which those
J 7.39   who believed in him were to receive; for as yet the Spirit had not been
J 7.39   given, because Jesus was not yet glorified.

J   7.40   When they heard these words, some of the people said, "This is really
M   22.41   Now while the Pharisees were gathered together, Jesus asked them a
Mk 12.35   And as   Jesus taught in the
L   20.41   But   he

J   7.41   the prophet."   Others said, "This is the Christ."
M   2.4   and assembling all the chief priests and scribes of the people, he
M   22.42   question, |saying,   "What do   you   think   of the Christ?
Mk 12.35   temple, he said,   "How can the scribes say   that   the Christ
L   20.41   said to them, "How can   they   say   that   the Christ

J   7.42   But some said,   "Is the Christ to come from Galilee? |Has
M   2.4   inquired of them where the Christ was to be born.
M   22.42   Whose son is   he?"

J   7.42   not the scripture said that the Christ is descended from David, and comes
M   2.5   They   told   him,
L   2.11   for to you is born this day
M   22.42   They   said to him,   "The son   of   David."
Mk 12.35   is the son   of   David?
L   20.41   is   David's   son?

J   7.43   from Bethlehem, the village where David was?" So there was a division
M   2.5   "In   Bethlehem of Judea; for so it is written by the prophet:
L   2.11   in   the city of   David a Savior, who is Christ the Lord.

J   7.44   among the people over him. Some of them wanted to arrest him, but no one
J   7.44   laid hands on him.

J   7.45   The officers then went back to the chief priests and Pharisees, who said

J   7.46   to them, "Why did you not bring him?" The officers answered, "No man
M   7.28   And when Jesus finished these sayings, the crowds
Mk 1.22   And   they
L   4.32   and   they

J   7.47   ever spoke like' this man!" The Pharisees answered them, "Are you led
M   7.29   were astonished at his teaching, |for he taught them as one who had
Mk 1.22   were astonished at his teaching, for he taught them as one who had
L   4.32   were astonished at his teaching, for his word   was with

J	7.48	astray, you also? Have any of the authorities or the Pharisees believed
M	7.29	authority, and not as their scribes.
Mk	1.22	authority, and not as the scribes.
L	4.32	authority.

J	7.49,50	in him? But this crowd, who do not know the law, are accursed." Nicodemus,
J	7.51	who had gone to him before, and who was one of them, said to them, |"Does
J	7.51	our law judge a man without first giving him a hearing and learning what
J	7.52	he does?" They replied, "Are you from Galilee too? Search and you will
J	7.52	see that no prophet is to rise from Galilee."

18. THE WOMAN TAKEN IN ADULTERY

John 7.53-8.11

J	7.53	They went each to his own house,

J	8.1	but Jesus went
M	21.17	And leaving them, he went
Mk	11.19	And when evening came they went
L	21.37	And every day he was teaching in the temple, but at night he went

J	8.1	to the Mount of Olives.
M	21.17	out of the city to Bethany and lodged there.
Mk	11.19	out of the city.
L	21.38	out and lodged on the mount called Olivet. And

J	8.2	Early in the morning he came again to the temple; all the people came to
L	21.38	early in the morning all the people came to

J	8.3	him, and he sat down and taught them. The scribes and the Pharisees
L	21.38	him in the temple to hear him.

J	8.3	brought a woman who had been caught in adultery, and placing her in the
J	8.4	midst |they said to him, "Teacher, this woman has been caught in the act
J	8.5	of adultery. |Now in the law Moses commanded us to stone such. What do
J	8.6	you say about her?" This they said to test him, that they might have
J	8.6	some charge to bring against him. Jesus bent down and wrote with his
J	8.7	finger on the ground. And as they continued to ask him, he stood up and
J	8.7	said to them, "Let him who is without sin among you be the first to
J	8.8	throw a stone at her." And once more he bent down and wrote with his
J	8.9	finger on the ground. But when they heard it, they went away, one by
J	8.9	one, beginning with the eldest, and Jesus was left alone with the woman
J	8.10	standing before him. Jesus looked up and said to her, "Woman, where
J	8.11	are they? Has no one condemned you?" |She said, "No one, Lord." And
J	8.11	Jesus said, "Neither do I condemn you; go, and do not sin again."

19. FIFTH DISCOURSE: WHO JESUS IS

John 8.12-59

J	8.12	Again Jesus spoke to them, saying, "I am the light of the world;
M	5.14	"You are the light of the world.

J	8.12	he who follows me will not walk in darkness, but will have the light of
M	5.14	A city set on a hill cannot be hid.

J	8.13	life." The Pharisees then said to him, "You are bearing witness to
J	8.14	yourself; your testimony is not true." Jesus answered, "Even if I do
J	8.14	bear witness to myself, my testimony is true, for I know whence I have
J	8.14	come and whither I am going, but you do not know whence I come or whither
J	8.15,16	I am going. You judge according to the flesh, I judge no one. Yet even
J	8.16	if I do judge, my judgment is true, for it is not I alone that judge, but

J	8.17	I and he who sent me. In your law it is written that
M	18.16	But if he does not listen, take one or two others along with you, that

J	8.17	the testimony of two men is true;
M	18.16	every word may be confirmed by the evidence of two or three witnesses.

J	8.18	I bear witness to myself, and the Father who sent me bears witness to
J	8.19	me." ⎪They said to him therefore, "Where is your Father?" Jesus answered,
J	8.19	"You know neither me nor my Father; if you knew me, you would know my
J	8.20	Father also." These words he spoke in the treasury, as he taught in the
J	8.20	temple; but no one arrested him, because his hour had not come.

J	8.21	Again he said to them, "I go away, and you will seek me and die in your
J	8.22	sin; where I am going, you cannot come." Then said the Jews, "Will he
J	8.23	kill himself, since he says, 'Where I am going, you cannot come'?" He
J	8.23	said to them, "You are from below, I am from above; you are of this world,
J	8.24	I am not of this world. I told you that you would die in your sins, for
J	8.25	you will die in your sins unless you believe that I am he." They said to
J	8.25	him, "Who are you?" Jesus said to them, "Even what I have told you from
J	8.26	the beginning. I have much to say about you and much to judge; but he who
J	8.26	sent me is true, and I declare to the world what I have heard from him."
J	8.27,28	They did not understand that he spoke to them of the Father. So Jesus said,
J	8.28	"When you have lifted up the Son of man, then you will know that I am he,
J	8.28	and that I do nothing on my own authority but speak thus as the Father
J	8.29	taught me. And he who sent me is with me; he has not left me alone, for
J	8.30	I always do what is pleasing to him." As he spoke thus, many believed
J	8.30	in him.
J	8.31	Jesus then said to the Jews who had believed in him, "If you continue
J	8.32	in my word, you are truly my disciples, ⎪and you will know the truth,

J	8.33	and the truth will make you free." They answered
M	3.8,9	Bear fruit that befits repentance, ⎪and do not presume to say to
L	3.8	Bear fruits that befit repentance, and do not begin to say to

J	8.33	him, "We are descendants of Abraham, and have never been in
M	3.9	yourselves, 'We have Abraham as our father'; for I tell
L	3.8	yourselves, 'We have Abraham as our father'; for I tell

J	8.33	bondage to any one. How is it that you say, 'You will be made free'?"
M	3.9	you, God is able from these stones to raise up children to Abraham.
L	3.8	you, God is able from these stones to raise up children to Abraham.

J	8.34	Jesus answered them, "Truly, truly, I say to you, every one who commits
J	8.35	sin is a slave to sin. The slave does not continue in the house for ever;
J	8.36	the son continues for ever. So if the Son makes you free, you will be
J	8.37	free indeed. I know that you are descendants of Abraham; yet you seek to
J	8.38	kill me, because my word finds no place in you. I speak of what I have
J	8.38	seen with my Father, and you do what you have heard from your father."

J	8.39	They answered him, "Abraham is our
M	3.9	and do not presume to say to yourselves, 'We have Abraham as our
L	3.8b	and do not begin to say to yourselves, 'We have Abraham as our

J	8.39	father."	Jesus said to them, "If you were
M	3.9	father'; for I tell you, God is able from these stones to raise up
L	3.8b	father'; for I tell you, God is able from these stones to raise up

J	8.40	Abraham's children, you would do what Abraham did, |but now you seek to
M	3.9	children to Abraham.
L	3.8b	children to Abraham.

J	8.40	kill me, a man who has told you the truth which I heard from God; this
J	8.41	is not what Abraham did. |You do what your father did." They said to
J	8.41	him, "We were not born of fornication; we have one Father, even God."
J	8.42	Jesus said to them, "If God were your Father, you would love me, for I
J	8.42	proceeded and came forth from God; I came not of my own accord, but he
J	8.43	sent me. Why do you not understand what I say? It is because you can-
J	8.44	not bear to hear my word. You are of your father the devil, and your
J	8.44	will is to do your father's desires. He was a murderer from the begin-
J	8.44	ning, and has nothing to do with the truth, because there is no truth
J	8.44	in him. When he lies, he speaks according to his own nature, for he is
J	8.45	a liar and the father of lies. But, because I tell the truth, you do
J	8.46	not believe me. |Which of you convicts me of sin? If I tell the truth,
J	8.47	why do you not believe me? He who is of God hears the words of God;
J	8.47	the reason why you do not hear them is that you are not of God."

J	8.48		The Jews	answered him,	"Are we
M	9.34	But	the Pharisees	said,	"He
M	12.24	But when	the Pharisees heard it	they said,	"It
Mk	3.22	And	the scribes who came down from Jerusalem said,		"He
L	11.15	But	some of them	said,	"He

J	8.49	not right in saying that you are a Samaritan and have a demon?"		Jesus
M	9.34	casts out demons	by the prince of demons."
M	12.24	is only	by Beelzebul,	the prince of demons,	that
Mk	3.22	is possessed	by Beelzebul,	and by the prince of demons
L	11.15	casts out demons by Beelzebul,	the prince of demons";

J	8.49	answered, "I have not a	demon; but I honor my Father, and you dishonor
M	12.24	this man casts out	demons."
Mk	3.22	he casts out	the demons."

J	8.50	me. Yet I do not seek my own glory; there is One who seeks it and he

J	8.51	will be the judge.	Truly, truly,	I say to you,	if any one
M	16.28		Truly,	I say to you,	there are some
Mk	9.1	And he said to them, "Truly,		I say to you,	there are some
L	9.27		But	I tell you truly, there are some

J	8.52	keeps my word, he will never see	death." The Jews said to him, "Now
M	16.28	standing here who will not	taste death before they see	the Son of
Mk	9.1	standing here who will not	taste death before they see that the
L	9.27	standing here who will not	taste death before they see	the

J	8.52	we know that you have a demon.	Abraham died, as did the prophets; and
M	16.28	man coming in his kingdom."
Mk	9.1	kingdom of God has come with power."
L	9.27	kingdom of God."

549

```
J    8.52     you say, 'If    any one keeps my word, he will never taste death.'
M    16.28b            there are some standing here who will not   taste death before
Mk   9.1b              there are some standing here who will not   taste death before
L    9.27b             there are some standing here who will not   taste death before


J    8.53     Are you greater than our father Abraham, who died?  And the prophets
M    16.28b   they see the Son of man coming in his kingdom."
Mk   9.1b     they see that                   the kingdom of God come with power."
L    9.27b    they see                        the kingdom of God."


J    8.54     died! Who do you claim to be?" Jesus answered, "If I glorify myself, my
J    8.54     glory is nothing; it is my Father who glorifies me, of whom you say that
J    8.55     he is your God.  But you have not known him; I know him.  If I said, I
J    8.55     do not know him, I should be a liar like you; but I do know him and I


J    8.56     keep his word.        Your father Abraham rejoiced that he was to see
M    13.17     Truly, I say to you,    many prophets and righteous men longed  to see
L    10.24     For    I tell    you that many prophets and kings       desired to see


J    8.57     my day;        he         saw it  and was glad."  The Jews then said to
M    13.17     what you see, and did not see it, and to hear what you hear, and did not
L    10.24     what you see, and did not see it, and to hear what you hear, and did not


J    8.58     him, "You are not yet fifty years old, and have you seen Abraham?"  Jesus
M    13.17     hear it.
L    10.24     hear it."


J    8.58     said to them, "Truly, truly, I say to you, before Abraham was, I am."
J    8.59     So they took up stones to throw at him; but Jesus hid himself, and went
J    8.59     out of the temple.
```

20. SIXTH SIGN: THE MAN BORN BLIND

John 9.1-34

```
J    9.1     As   he    passed by,                              he saw a man blind
Mk   8.22    And they came to Bethsaida.  And some people brought to him a blind man,


J    9.2     from his birth.  And his disciples asked him, "Rabbi, who sinned, this
Mk   8.23    and begged him to touch him.  And he took the blind man by the hand,


J    9.3     man or his parents, that he was born blind?"  Jesus answered, "It was not
J    9.3     that this man sinned, or his parents, but that the works of God might be
J    9.4     made manifest in him.  We must work the works of him who sent me, while
J    9.5     it is day; night comes, when no one can work.  As long as I am in the


J    9.6     world, I   am  the light of the world."  As he said this, he      spat on
Mk   8.23    and led him out of the village;              and when he had spit


J    9.6     the ground and made clay of the spittle and anointed the man's eyes with
Mk   8.23                                                  on his   eyes and


J    9.6     the clay,
Mk   8.24    laid his hands upon him, he asked him, "Do you see anything?"  And he
```


Mk 8.25   *looked up and said, "I see men; but they look like trees, walking." Then*
Mk 8.25   *again he laid his hands upon his eyes; and he looked intently*

J 9.7 |saying to him, "Go, <u>wash in the pool of Siloam</u>" (which means Sent).
Mk 8.26   and was restored, and saw everything clearly.   And he <u>sent</u> him

J 9.8   <u>So he went and washed and came back seeing.</u>   <u>The neighbors and those who</u>
M 8.26   away to his home, saying, "Do not even enter the village."

J 9.8   had seen him before as a beggar, said, "Is not this the man who used to
J 9.9   sit and beg?" Some said, "It is he"; others said, "No, but he is like him."
J 9.10   He said, "I am the man." |They said to him, "Then how were your eyes
J 9.11   opened?" He answered, "The man called Jesus made clay and anointed my
J 9.11   eyes and said to me, 'Go to Siloam and wash'; so I went and washed and
J 9.12   received my sight." |They said to him, "Where is he?" He said, "I do
J 9.12   not know."

J 9.13   They brought to the Pharisees the man who had formerly been blind.
J 9.14   Now it was a sabbath day when Jesus made the clay and opened his eyes.
J 9.15   The Pharisees again asked him how he had received his sight. And he
J 9.16   said to them, "He put clay on my eyes, and I washed, and I see." Some
J 9.16   of the Pharisees said, "This man is not from God, for he does not keep
J 9.16   the sabbath." But others said, "How can a man who is a sinner do such
J 9.17   signs?" There was a division among them. |So they again said to the
J 9.17   blind man, "What do you say about him, since he has opened your eyes?"
J 9.17   He said, "He is a prophet."

J 9.18   The Jews did not believe that he had been blind and had received his
J 9.18   sight, until they called the parents of the man who had received his
J 9.19   sight, |and asked them, "Is this your son, who you say was born blind?
J 9.20   How then does he now see?" His parents answered, "We know that this is
J 9.21   our son, and that he was born blind; but how he now sees we do not know,
J 9.21   nor do we know who opened his eyes. Ask him; he is of age, he will
J 9.22   speak for himself." His parents said this because they feared the Jews,
J 9.22   for the Jews had already agreed that if any one should confess him to
J 9.23   be Christ, he was to be put out of the synagogue. Therefore his parents
J 9.23   said, "He is of age, ask him."

J 9.24   So for the second time they called the man who had been blind, and said
J 9.25   to him, "Give God the praise; we know that this man is a sinner." He
J 9.25   answered, "Whether he is a sinner, I do not know; one thing I know, that
J 9.26   though I was blind, now I see." They said to him, "What did he do to
J 9.27   you? How did he open your eyes?" He answered them, "I have told you
J 9.27   already, and you would not listen. Why do you want to hear it again?
J 9.28   Do you too want to become his disciples?" And they reviled him, saying,
J 9.29   "You are his disciple, but we are disciples of Moses. We know that God
J 9.29   has spoken to Moses, but as for this man, we do not know where he comes
J 9.30   from." The man answered, "Why, this is a marvel! You do not know where
J 9.31   he comes from, and yet he opened my eyes. We know that God does not
J 9.31   listen to sinners, but if any one is a worshiper of God and does his
J 9.32   will, God listens to him. Never since the world began has it been heard
J 9.33   that any one opened the eyes of a man born blind. If this man were not
J 9.34   from God, he could do nothing." They answered him, "You were born in
J 9.34   utter sin, and would you teach us?" And they cast him out.

21. SIXTH DISCOURSE: THE GOOD SHEPHERD

John 9.35-10.42

J 9.35   Jesus heard that they had cast him out, and having found him he said,
J 9.36   "Do you believe in the Son of man?" He answered, "And who is he, sir,

```
J    9.37      that I may believe in him?"  Jesus said to him, "You have seen him, and
J    9.38      it is he who speaks to you."  He said, "Lord, I believe"; and he


J    9.39      worshiped him.      Jesus said, "For judgment I came into this world,
M    13.13                     This is why I speak to them  in parables, because
Mk   4.11b,12  but for those outside everything is  in parables; so that they may indeed
L    8.10b     but for others      they      are in parables, so that
  Mk  8.18                                                                    Having


J    9.39      that those who do  not      see may see,  and that those who see may become
M    13.13     seeing     they do  not      see,        and            hearing they do not
Mk   4.12      see        but      not      perceive,    and may indeed hear      but not
L    8.10b     seeing     they may not      see,         and            hearing
  Mk  8.17b               Do   you not yet perceive      or
  Mk  8.18     eyes       do   you not      see,         and  having ears   do  you not


J    9.40      blind."  Some of the Pharisees near him heard this, and they said to him,
M    13.13     hear, nor do they              understand.
Mk   4.12                                     understand; lest they should turn again, and be
L    8.10b              they may not understand.
M    15.14                     Let them alone;
  Mk  8.17b                         understand?  Are your hearts hardened?
  Mk  8.18     hear? And do you        not remember?


J    9.41      "Are   we also blind?"  Jesus said to them, "If you were blind, you would
Mk   4.12      forgiven."
M    15.14     they are      blind guides.        And if a      blind man leads
L    6.39      He also told them a parable:         "Can a      blind man lead


J    9.41      have no guilt; but now that you say, 'We see,' your guilt remains.
M    15.14     a blind man, both           will fall into a pit."
L    6.39      a blind man? Will they not both fall into a pit?


J    10.1      "Truly, truly, I say to you, he who does not enter the sheepfold by the
J    10.2      door but climbs in by another way, that man is a thief and a robber; but
J    10.3      he who enters by the door is the shepherd of the sheep.  To him the gate-
J    10.3      keeper opens; the sheep hear his voice, and he calls his own sheep by name
J    10.4      and leads them out.  When he has brought out all his own, he goes before
J    10.5      them, and the sheep follow him, for they know his voice.  A stranger they
J    10.5      will not follow, but they will flee from him, for they do not know the
J    10.6      voice of strangers."  This figure Jesus used with them, but they did not
J    10.6      understand what he was saying to them.


J    10.7      So Jesus again said to them, "Truly, truly, I say to you, I am the
M    7.13                                              "Enter  by the narrow
L    13.23b,24  And he           said to them,     |"Strive to enter  by the narrow


J    10.8      door of the sheep.  All who came before me are thieves and robbers; but
M    7.13      gate; for the gate is wide and the way is easy, that leads to destruction,
L    13.24     door;                                       for many, I tell you,


J    10.9      the sheep did not heed them.  I am the door; if any one enters by me, he
M    7.13                                    and those who enter  by it are
L    13.24                                    will seek  to enter  and will


  M   7.14     many. For the gate is narrow and the way is hard,     that leads to
  L   13.23a   not be able.  And some one said to him,
```

J	10.9	<u>will</u> <u>be</u> <u>saved, and will go in and out and find pasture.</u>
M	7.14	life, and those who <u>find</u> it are few.
L	13.23a	"Lord, <u>will</u> those who are <u>saved</u> be few?"

J	10.10	The thief comes only to steal and kill and destroy; I came that they may
J	10.11	have life, and have it abundantly. |I am the good shepherd. The good
J	10.12	shepherd lays down his life for the sheep. He who is a hireling and not
J	10.12	a shepherd, whose own the sheep are not, sees the wolf coming and leaves
J	10.13	the sheep and flees; and the wolf snatches them and scatters them. He
J	10.14	flees because he is a hireling and cares nothing for the sheep. I am the

J	10.15	<u>good shepherd; I know my own and my own know me,</u> |<u>as the Father</u>
M	11.27	All things have been delivered to <u>me</u> by my <u>Father</u>; and no one
L	10.22	All things have been delivered to <u>me</u> by my <u>Father</u>; and no one

J	10.15	<u>knows</u> <u>me</u> <u>and</u> <u>I</u> know <u>the Father;</u>
M	11.27	<u>knows</u> the Son except the Father, <u>and</u> no one knows <u>the Father</u>
L	10.22	<u>knows</u> who the Son is except the Father, or who <u>the Father</u> is

J	10.16	<u>and I lay down my life for the sheep. And I have other sheep, that are</u>
M	11.27	except the Son and any one to whom the Son chooses to reveal him.
L	10.22	except the Son and any one to whom the Son chooses to reveal him."

J	10.16	not of this fold; I must bring them also, and they will heed my voice.
J	10.17	So there shall be one flock, one shepherd. |For this reason the Father
J	10.18	loves me, because I lay down my life, that I may take it again. No one
J	10.18	takes it from me, but I lay it down of my own accord. I have power to
J	10.18	lay it down, and I have power to take it again; this charge I have re-
J	10.18	ceived from my Father."

J	10.19	<u>There was again a division among the Jews because of these words.</u>

J	10.20	Many of them said, "He
M	9.34	But the Pharisees said, "He casts out
M	12.24	But when the Pharisees heard it they said, "It is only
Mk	3.22	And the scribes who came down from Jerusalem said, "He is possessed
L	11.15	But some of them said, "He casts out

J	10.20	has a demon, <u>and he is mad; why listen</u>
M	9.34	demons by the prince of demons."
M	12.24	by Beelzebul, the prince of demons, that this man casts out
Mk	3.22	by Beelzebul, and by the prince of demons he casts out
L	11.15	demons by Beelzebul, the prince of demons";

J	10.21	<u>to him?" Others said, "These are not the sayings of one who has a demon.</u>
M	12.24	demons."
Mk	3.22	the demons."

J	10.21	<u>Can a demon open the eyes of the blind?"</u>

J	10.22,23	It was the feast of the Dedication at Jerusalem; it was winter, and
J	10.24	Jesus was walking in the temple, in the portico of Solomon. So the Jews
J	10.24	gathered round him and said to him, "How long will you keep us in sus-
J	10.25	pense? If you are the Christ, tell us plainly." |Jesus answered them,
J	10.25	"I told you, and you do not believe. The works that I do in my Father's

J	10.26	name, they bear witness to me; but you do not believe, because you do
J	10.27	not belong to my sheep. My sheep hear my voice, and I know them, and
J	10.28	they follow me; and I give them eternal life, and they shall never
J	10.29	perish, and no one shall snatch them out of my hand. My Father, who
J	10.29	has given them to me, is greater than all, and no one is able to snatch
J	10.30	them out of the Father's hand. I and the Father are one."

J	10.31,32	The Jews took up stones again to stone him. Jesus answered them, "I
J	10.32	have shown you many good works from the Father; for which of these do

J	10.33	you stone me?"	The Jews	answered
M	9.3	And behold, some of the scribes		said
Mk	2.6	Now some of the scribes were sitting there,		questioning
L	5.21	And the scribes and the Pharisees began to question,		

J	10.33	him,	"It is not for a good work that we stone you but for
M	9.3	to themselves,	"This man is
Mk	2.7	in their hearts,	"Why does this man speak thus? It is
L	5.21	saying,	"Who is this that speaks

J	10.34	blasphemy; because you, being a man, make yourself God." Jesus answered
M	9.3	blaspheming."
Mk	2.7	blasphemy! Who can forgive sins but God alone?"
L	5.21	blasphemies? Who can forgive sins but God only?"

J	10.35	them, "Is it not written in your law, 'I said, you are gods'? If he
J	10.35	called them gods to whom the word of God came (and scripture cannot be
J	10.36	broken), |do you say of him whom the Father consecrated and sent into
J	10.36	the world, 'You are blaspheming,' because I said, 'I am the Son of God'?
J	10.37,38	If I am not doing the works of my Father, then do not believe me; but
J	10.38	if I do them, even though you do not believe me, believe the works, that
J	10.38	you may know and understand that the Father is in me and I am in the
J	10.39	Father." Again they tried to arrest him, but he escaped from their hands.

J	10.40	He went away again across the Jordan to the place where John at first
J	10.41	baptized, and there he remained. And many came to him; and they said,
J	10.41	"John did no sign, but everything that John said about this man was
J	10.42	true." And many believed in him there.

22. THE SEVENTH SIGN: LAZARUS

John 11.1-44

J	11.1	Now a certain man was ill, Lazarus of Bethany, the village of Mary and
J	11.2	her sister Martha. It was Mary who anointed the Lord with ointment and
J	11.3	wiped his feet with her hair, whose brother Lazarus was ill. So the
J	11.4	sisters sent to him, saying, "Lord, he whom you love is ill." But when
J	11.4	Jesus heard it he said, "This illness is not unto death; it is for the
J	11.4	glory of God, so that the Son of God may be glorified by means of it."

J	11.5,6	Now Jesus loved Martha and her sister and Lazarus. So when he heard
J	11.6	that he was ill, he stayed two days longer in the place where he was.
J	11.7	Then after this he said to the disciples, "Let us go into Judea again."
J	11.8	The disciples said to him, "Rabbi, the Jews were but now seeking to stone
J	11.9	you, and are you going there again?" Jesus answered, "Are there not
J	11.9	twelve hours in the day? If any one walks in the day, he does not stumble,
J	11.10	because he sees the light of this world. But if any one walks in the
J	11.11	night, he stumbles, because the light is not in him." Thus he spoke, and
J	11.11	then he said to them, "Our friend Lazarus has fallen asleep, but I go to
J	11.12	awake him out of sleep." The disciples said to him, "Lord, if he has

```
J   11.13    fallen asleep, he will recover."  Now Jesus had spoken of his death, but
J   11.14    they thought that he meant taking rest in sleep.  Then Jesus told them
J   11.15    plainly, "Lazarus is dead; and for your sake I am glad that I was not
J   11.16    there, so that you may believe.  But let us go to him."  Thomas, called
J   11.16    the Twin, said to his fellow disciples, "Let us also go, that we may die
J   11.16    with him."

J   11.17       Now when Jesus came, he found that Lazarus had already been in the tomb
J   11.18,19  four days.  Bethany was near Jerusalem, about two miles off, |and many of
J   11.19    the Jews had come to Martha and Mary to console them concerning their
J   11.20    brother.  When Martha heard that Jesus was coming, she went and met him,
J   11.21    while Mary sat in the house.  Martha said to Jesus, "Lord, if you had been
J   11.22    here, my brother would not have died.  And even now I know that whatever
J   11.23    you ask from God, God will give you."  Jesus said to her, "Your brother
J   11.24    will rise again."  Martha said to him, "I know that he will rise again in
J   11.25    the resurrection at the last day."  Jesus said to her, "I am the resur-
J   11.25    rection and the life; he who believes in me, though he die, yet shall he
J   11.26    live, |and whoever lives and believes in me shall never die.  Do you
```

```
J   11.27    believe this?"  She          said to him, "Yes, Lord; I believe
M   16.16                   Simon Peter replied,
Mk  8.29b                         Peter answered him,
L   9.20b                   And   Peter answered,
  J  1.49              Nathanael  answered him,      "Rabbi,
  J  6.68              Simon Peter answered him,     "Lord, to whom shall we go?
```

```
  J  6.69    You have the words of eternal life; and we have believed, and have come to
```

```
J   11.27         that you are the Christ, the Son of        God, he who is coming
M   16.16         "You are the Christ, the Son of the living God."
Mk  8.29b         "You are the Christ."
L   9.20b            "The Christ          of           God."
  J  1.49          you are          the Son of     God! You are the King
  J  6.69    know, that you are the Holy One    of      God."
```

```
J   11.27    into the world."
  J  1.49    of Israel!"
```

```
J   11.28       When she had said this, she went and called her sister Mary, saying
J   11.29    quietly, "The Teacher is here and is calling for you."  And when she heard
J   11.30    it, she rose quickly and went to him.  Now Jesus had not yet come to the
J   11.31    village, but was still in the place where Martha had met him.  When the
J   11.31    Jews who were with her in the house, consoling her, saw Mary rise quickly
J   11.31    and go out, they followed her, supposing that she was going to the tomb
J   11.32    to weep there.  Then Mary, when she came where Jesus was and saw him, fell
J   11.32    at his feet, saying to him, "Lord, if you had been here, my brother would
J   11.33    not have died."  When Jesus saw her weeping, and the Jews who came with
J   11.34    her also weeping, he was deeply moved in spirit and troubled; and he said,
J   11.35    "Where have you laid him?"  They said to him, "Lord, come and see."  |Jesus
J   11.36,37 wept.  So the Jews said, "See how he loved him!"  But some of them said,
J   11.37    "Could not he who opened the eyes of the blind man have kept this man from
J   11.37    dying?"
```

```
J   11.38       Then Jesus, deeply moved again, came to the tomb; it was a cave, and a
J   11.39    stone lay upon it.  |Jesus said, "Take away the stone."  Martha, the sis-
J   11.39    ter of the dead man, said to him, "Lord, by this time there will be an odor,
J   11.40    for he has been dead four days."  Jesus said to her, "Did I not tell you
J   11.41    that if you would believe you would see the glory of God?"  So they took
J   11.41    away the stone.  And Jesus lifted up his eyes and said, "Father, I thank
J   11.42    thee that thou hast heard me.  I knew that thou hearest me always, but I
J   11.42    have said this on account of the people standing by, that they may
```

J 11.43 believe that thou didst send me." When he had said this, he cried with
J 11.44 a loud voice, "Lazarus, come out." The dead man came out, his hands and
J 11.44 feet bound with bandages, and his face wrapped with a cloth. Jesus said
J 11.44 to them, "Unbind him, and let him go."

23. THE PLOT TO KILL JESUS

John 11.45-55

J 11.45 Many of the Jews therefore, who had come with Mary and had seen what he
J 11.46 did, believed in him; but some of them went to the Pharisees and told them

J 11.47 what Jesus had done. So   the chief priests and the Pharisees
M 26.3   Then the chief priests and the elders of the people
Mk 14.1b   And the chief priests and the scribes
L 22.2   And the chief priests and the scribes

J 11.47 gathered   the council, and said, "What are we to do? For this man
M 26.3 gathered in the palace of the high priest,

J 11.48 performs many signs. If we let him go on thus, every one will believe
J 11.48 in him, and the Romans will come and destroy both our holy place and our

J 11.49 nation." But one of them, Caiaphas, who was high priest that year, said
M 26.3   who was called   Caiaphas,

J 11.50 to them, "You know nothing at all; you do not understand that it is ex-
J 11.50 pedient for you that one man should die for the people, and that the whole
J 11.51 nation should not perish." He did not say this of his own accord, but
J 11.51 being high priest that year he prophesied that Jesus should die for the
J 11.52 nation, ⎰and not for the nation only, but to gather into one the children
J 11.53 of God who are scattered abroad. So from that day on

J 11.53 they took counsel   how   to
M 26.4 ⎰and took counsel together in order to arrest Jesus by stealth and
Mk 14.1b   were seeking   how   to arrest him   by stealth, and
L 22.2   were seeking   how   to

J 11.53 put him to death.
M 26.5 kill him. But they said, "Not during the feast, lest there be a tumult
Mk 14.2 kill him; for they said, "Not during the feast, lest there be a tumult
L 22.2 put him to death;   for they feared

M 26.5 *among the people."*
Mk 14.2 *of   the people."*
L 22.2 *the people.*

J 11.54   Jesus therefore no longer went about openly among the Jews, but went
J 11.54 from there to the country near the wilderness, to a town called Ephraim;
J 11.54 and there he stayed with the disciples.

24. JESUS ANOINTED FOR BURIAL

John 11.55-12.11

J	11.55	<u>Now</u>
M	26.2	"You know that after two days
Mk	14.1a	It was <u>now</u> two days before
L	22.1	<u>Now</u> the feast of Unleavened Bread drew near, which is called

J	11.55	<u>the Passover of the Jews was at hand</u>, and <u>many went up from the country</u>
M	26.2	<u>the Passover</u> is coming, and the Son of man will be delivered up to be
Mk	14.1	<u>the Passover</u> and the feast of Unleavened Bread.
L	22.1	<u>the Passover</u>.

J	11.56	<u>to Jerusalem before the Passover</u>, <u>to purify themselves</u>. <u>They were looking</u>
M	26.2	crucified."

J	11.56	<u>for Jesus and saying to one another as they stood in the temple</u>, "What do
J	11.56	<u>you think? That he will not come to the feast?</u>"

J	11.57	Now <u>the chief priests and the Pharisees</u> had given orders that if any one
M	26.3	Then <u>the chief priests and the</u> elders of the people gathered in the palace
Mk	14.1	And <u>the chief priests and the</u> scribes
L	22.2	And <u>the chief priests and the</u> scribes

J	11.57	<u>knew where he was, he should let them know</u>, so
M	26.4	of the high priest, who was called Caiaphas, |and took counsel together in
Mk	14.1	were seeking
L	22.2	were seeking

J	11.57	<u>that they might arrest him</u>.
M	26.4	order to <u>arrest</u> Jesus by stealth and kill him.
Mk	14.1	how to <u>arrest</u> him by stealth, and kill him;
L	22.2	how to put <u>him</u> to death; for they feared the people.

J	12.1	<u>Six days before the Passover</u>, Jesus came to
M	26.6	Now when Jesus was at
Mk	14.3	And while he was at
L	7.36	One of the Pharisees asked him to eat with him, and he went

J	12.2	<u>Bethany, where Lazarus was</u>, <u>whom Jesus had raised from the dead</u>. There
M	26.6	<u>Bethany</u> in the house of Simon the leper,
Mk	14.3	<u>Bethany</u> in the house of Simon the leper,
L	7.36	into the Pharisee's house,

J	12.2	<u>they made him a supper</u>; <u>Martha served</u>, <u>and Lazarus was one of those at</u>
Mk	14.3	as he sat <u>at</u>
L	7.36	<u>and</u> took his place <u>at</u>

J	12.3	<u>table with him</u>. Mary
M	26.7	|a woman
Mk	14.3	<u>table</u>, a woman
L	7.37	<u>table</u>. And behold, a woman of the city, who was a sinner, when she learned

J	12.3	took a
M	26.7	came up to him with an
Mk	14.3	came with an
L	7.37	that he was at table in the Pharisee's house, brought an

557

```
J    12.3     pound          of      costly    ointment of pure nard
M    26.7     alabaster flask of  very expensive ointment,
Mk   14.3     alabaster flask of             ointment of pure nard, very costly,
L     7.38    alabaster flask of             ointment,  | and standing behind him at


  L   7.38    his feet, weeping, she began to wet his feet with her tears, and wiped
  L   7.38    them with the hair of her head,


J    12.3                              and      anointed    the feet of Jesus and wiped
M    26.7                              and  she poured it on  his head, as he sat at table.
Mk   14.3     and she broke the flask and      poured it over his head.
L     7.38    and     kissed his feet, and      anointed        them


J    12.3     his feet with her hair; and the house was filled with the fragrance of
L     7.38                                                             with


J    12.4     the ointment.  But Judas Iscariot, one of his disciples (he who was to
M    26.8                    But when                    the disciples
Mk   14.4                    But there were            some     who
L     7.39    the ointment.  Now when                  the Pharisee who had invited


J    12.5     betray him),                      said,              | "Why was
M    26.8            saw it, they were indignant, saying,           "Why
Mk   14.4                                        said to themselves indignantly, "Why was
L     7.39    him saw it, he                     said to himself,   "If this


J    12.5                           this ointment not            sold for
M    26.9             this waste?  For this ointment might have been sold for
Mk   14.5     the ointment thus wasted? For this ointment might have been sold for more
L     7.39    man were a prophet, he would have known who and what sort of woman this is


  L   7.40    who is touching him, for she is a sinner." And Jesus answering said to
  L   7.41    him, "Simon, I have something to say to you." And he answered, "What is
  L   7.41    it, Teacher?" "A certain creditor had two debtors; one


J    12.6     three hundred denarii  and given to the poor?" This he said, not
M    26.9     a    large sum,        and given to the poor."
Mk   14.5     than three hundred denarii, and given to the poor." And they reproached
L     7.42    owed five  hundred denarii, and the other fifty. When they could not pay,


J    12.6     that he cared for the poor but because he was a thief, and as he had the
J    12.6     money box he used to take what was put into it.


J    12.7            Jesus          said,          "Let her alone,
M    26.10      But Jesus, aware of this, said to them,
Mk   14.6     her. But Jesus          said,         "Let her alone;
L     7.43    he forgave them both.  Now which of them will love him more?"  Simon


  L   7.43    answered, "The one, I suppose, to whom he forgave more." And he said to
  L   7.44    him, "You have judged rightly." Then turning toward the woman he said


  M   26.10           "Why do you trouble the woman? For she has done a beautiful thing to me.
  Mk  14.6            why do you trouble    her?      She has done a beautiful thing to me.
  L   7.44    to Simon, "Do you see  this woman? I entered your house, you gave me


  L   7.44    no water for my feet, but she has wet my feet with her tears and wiped them
  L   7.45    with her hair. You gave me no kiss, but from the time I came in she has
```

```
J     12.7                                                    let her      keep it
M     26.12                    In pouring this ointment on my body she has done it
Mk    14.8      She has done what she could; she has anointed     my body
L      7.46     not ceased to kiss my feet.  You did not anoint my head with oil, but she


J     12.8      for the day of my      burial.      The poor you always have with you,
M     26.11     to prepare      me for burial.   For you always have the poor with you,
Mk    14.7      beforehand          for burying.  For you always have the poor with you,
L      7.47     has anointed my feet with ointment.  Therefore I tell you, her sins,


J     12.8                                                  but you do    not always
M     26.11                                                but you will   not always
Mk    14.7      and whenever you will, you can do good to them; but you will  not always
L      7.47     which are many, are forgiven, for she loved much; but he who is forgiven


J     12.8      have me."
M     26.13     have me.       Truly, I say to you, wherever this gospel is preached in
Mk    14.9      have me.  And truly, I say to you, wherever the  gospel is preached in
L      7.48     little, loves little."  And he said to her, "Your sins are forgiven."


  M  26.13      the whole world, what she has done will be told in memory of her."
  Mk 14.9       the whole world, what she has done will be told in memory of her."
  L   7.49      Then those who were at table with him began to say among themselves,


  L   7.50      "Who is this, who even forgives sins?"  And he said to the woman,
  L   7.50      "Your faith has saved you; go in peace."


J     12.9          When the great crowd of the Jews learned that he was there, they came,
J     12.9      not only on account of Jesus but also to see Lazarus, whom he had raised
J     12.10     from the dead.  So the chief priests planned to put Lazarus also to death,
J     12.11     |because on account of him many of the Jews were going away and believing
J     12.11     in Jesus.


                        25.  JESUS ENTERS JERUSALEM

                            John 12.12-19

  L  19.28      And when he had said this, he went on ahead, going up to Jerusalem.


J     12.12     The next day a great crowd who had come to the feast heard that Jesus
M     21.1      And when                                                         they
Mk    11.1      And when                                                         they
L     19.29         When                                                         he


J     12.12     was coming to Jerusalem.
M     21.1      drew near  to Jerusalem and came to Bethphage,            to the Mount
Mk    11.1      drew near  to Jerusalem,           to Bethphage and Bethany, at the Mount
L     19.29     drew near                          to Bethphage and Bethany, at the mount


  M  21.2                      of Olives, then Jesus sent two        disciples,    |saying
  Mk 11.2                      of Olives,      he   sent two of his disciples,  |and said
  L  19.30      that is called Olivet,         he   sent two of the disciples,    |saying,

  M  21.2       to them, "Go into the village opposite you, and immediately
  Mk 11.2       to them, "Go into the village opposite you, and immediately as you
  L  19.30                "Go into the village opposite,               where on


                                    559
```

M   21.2   *you will find an ass   tied, and a colt with her;*
Mk 11.2   *enter it you will find a   colt tied, on which no one has ever   sat;*
L   19.30   *entering you will find a   colt tied, on which no one has ever yet sat;*

M   21.3   *untie them and bring them to me. If any one says anything to you,*
Mk 11.3   *untie it   and bring it.   If any one says   to you, 'Why*
L   19.31   *untie it   and bring it here. If any one asks   you, 'Why*

M   21.3   *you shall say,   'The Lord has need of them,'*
Mk 11.3   *are you doing this?'   say,   'The Lord has need of it*
L   19.31   *are you untying it?' you shall say this, 'The Lord has need of it.'"*

M   21.6   *and he will send them   immediately." The disciples   went*
Mk 11.4   *and   will send it back here immediately.'" And they   went*
L   19.32   So those who were sent went*

M   21.6   *and did   as Jesus had   directed them;*
Mk 11.4   *away, and found a colt tied at the door out in the open street; and they*
L   19.32   *away and found   it   as he   had   told   them.*

Mk 11.5   *untied it. And   those who stood there said*
L   19.33   *And as they were untying the colt, its   owners   said*

Mk 11.6   *to them, "What are you doing, untying the colt?" And they told them what*
L   19.34   *to them, "Why   are you   untying the colt?" And they said,   "The*

M   21.8   *Most of the crowd spread*
Mk 11.8   *Jesus had said; and they let them go. And   many   spread*
L   19.36   *Lord has need of it."   And as he rode along, they spread*

J   12.13   So they took   branches of palm
M   21.8   their garments on the road, and others cut   branches from the
Mk 11.8   their garments on the road, and others spread leafy branches which they
L   19.37   their garments on the road. As he was now drawing near, at the descent

J   12.13   trees   and   went
M   21.9   trees and spread them on the road. And the   crowds that   went
Mk 11.9   had cut from the fields.   And   those who   went
L   19.37   of the Mount of Olives,   the whole multitude of the dis-

J   12.13   out to meet him,   crying,   "Hosanna!
M   21.9   before   him and that   followed him shouted, "Hosanna to the Son
Mk 11.9   before   and those who followed   cried out, "Hosanna!
L   19.37   ciples began to rejoice and praise God with a loud voice for all the

J   12.13   Blessed is   he   who comes
M   21.9   of David!   Blessed is   he   who comes
Mk 11.9   Blessed is   he   who comes
L   19.38   mighty works that they had seen, |saying, "Blessed is the King who comes

J   12.13   in the name of the Lord, even the King of Israel!"
M   21.9   in the name of the Lord!
Mk 11.10   in the name of the Lord! Blessed is the kingdom of our father David
L   19.38   in the name of the Lord!   Peace in

J   12.14   And Jesus found   a young ass
M   21.7   Hosanna in the highest!" |they brought the   ass
Mk 11.7   that is coming! Hosanna in the highest!" And they brought
L   19.35   heaven   and glory in the highest!" And they brought

560

J	12.14		**and**
M	21.7	and the colt, and put their garments on them,	and he
Mk	11.7	the colt to Jesus, and threw their garments on it;	and he
L	19.35	it to Jesus, and throwing their garments on the colt	they

J	12.14	<u>sat</u>	<u>upon it</u>;	<u>as it is written,</u>
M	21.4	<u>sat</u>	thereon. This took place to fulfil <u>what was spoken by the</u>
Mk	11.7	<u>sat</u>	<u>upon it</u>.
L	19.35	set Jesus <u>upon it</u>.

M 21.4   *prophet, saying,*

J	12.15	"<u>Fear not, daughter of Zion</u>;
M	21.5	"Tell the <u>daughter of Zion</u>,

J	12.15	<u>behold, your king is coming</u>,
M	21.5	<u>Behold, your king is coming</u> to you,

J	12.15	<u>sitting</u> on an ass's
M	21.5	humble, and mounted <u>on an</u> ass,

J	12.15	<u>colt</u>!"
M	21.5	and on a <u>colt</u>, the foal of an ass."

J	12.16	<u>His disciples did not understand this at first</u>; but when Jesus was
M	21.10	And when he entered Jerusalem, all the city was stirred, saying, "Who
Mk	11.11	And he entered Jerusalem, and went into the temple; and when he had
L	19.39	And some of the Pharisees in the multitude said to him, "Teacher, rebuke

J	12.16	<u>glorified</u>, <u>then they remembered that this had been written of him</u> and
M	21.11	is this?" And the crowds said, "This is the prophet Jesus from Nazareth
Mk	11.11	looked round at everything, as it was already late, he went out to Bethany
L	19.40	your disciples." He answered, "I tell you, if these were silent, the very

J	12.17	<u>had been done to him</u>. <u>The crowd that had been with him when he called</u>
M	21.11	of Galilee."
Mk	11.11	with the twelve.
L	19.40	stones would cry out."

J	12.18	<u>Lazarus out of the tomb and raised him from the dead bore witness</u>. <u>The</u>
J	12.18	<u>reason why the crowd went to meet him was that they heard he had done</u>
J	12.19	<u>this sign</u>. <u>The Pharisees then said to one another, "You see that you</u>
J	12.19	<u>can do nothing; look, the world has gone after him</u>."

26. SEVENTH DISCOURSE: THE HOUR HAS COME

John 12.20-50

J	12.20	Now among those who went up to worship at the feast were some Greeks.
J	12.21	So these came to Philip, who was from Bethsaida in Galilee, and said to
J	12.22	him, "Sir, we wish to see Jesus." Philip went and told Andrew; Andrew
J	12.23	went with Philip and they told Jesus. And Jesus answered them, "The
J	12.24	hour has come for the Son of man to be glorified. Truly, truly, I say
J	12.24	to you, unless a grain of wheat falls into the earth and dies, it

561

```
J   12.24          remains alone; but if it dies, it bears much fruit.


J   12.25          He who           loves his life        loses it, and he who  hates his
M   10.39          He who           finds his life will lose it, and he who  loses his
M   16.25          For whoever would    save  his life will lose it, and whoever loses his
Mk   8.35          For whoever would    save  his life will lose it; and whoever loses his
L    9.24          For whoever would    save  his life will lose it; and whoever loses his
L   17.33          Whoever seeks to gain his life will lose it, but whoever loses his


J   12.25          life in this world              will keep      it for eternal life.
M   10.39          life for my sake                will find  it.
M   16.25          life for my sake                will find  it.
Mk   8.35          life for my sake and the gospel's will save  it.
L    9.24          life for my sake,               he will save  it.
L   17.33          life                            will preserve it.


M  16.24                                                        Then Jesus
Mk  8.34      And he called to him the multitude  with his disciples,            and
L   9.23                                                               And  he
L  14.25      Now                 great multitudes accompanied him; and  he turned and


J   12.26                   If any one      serves    me,
M   10.37                                                       He who loves
M   16.24          told his disciples, "If any man would come  after me,
Mk   8.34          said to them,       "If any man would come  after me,
L    9.23          said to all,        "If any man would come  after me,
L   14.26          said to them,      |"If any one      comes to    me and does not hate


J   12.26                                         he must follow me; and where I
M   10.37                 father or  mother more than me is not worthy of me; and he who
L   14.26          his own father and mother and wife and children and brothers and sisters,


J   12.26          am, there shall my servant be also; if any one serves me, the Father
M   10.38          loves son or daughter more than me  is not worthy of me; and he who  does
M   16.24                                              let him deny himself and
Mk   8.34                                              let him deny himself and
L    9.23                                              let him deny himself and
L   14.27          yes, and even his own life, he cannot be my disciple.        Whoever does


J   12.26          will honor him.
M   10.38          not take     his     cross      and follow   me  is not worthy of me.
M   16.24              take up his     cross      and follow   me.
Mk   8.34             take up his     cross      and follow   me.
L    9.23             take up his     cross daily and follow   me.
L   14.27          not bear     his own cross      and come after me, cannot be my disciple.


J   12.27                   "Now is my soul       troubled.
M   26.38          Then he said to them, "My soul is very sorrowful, even to death; remain here,
Mk  14.34          And  he said to them, "My soul is very sorrowful, even to death; remain here,


J   12.27          And what shall I say?
M   26.39          and watch with me." And going a little farther he fell on his face and praye
Mk  14.36          and watch."         And                    he                        said,


J   12.27             'Father, save me from this hour'?
M   26.39          "My  Father, if  it    be possible,        let   this cup pass from
Mk  14.36          "Abba, Father, all things are possible to thee; remove this cup     from
L   22.42              "Father, if thou  art willing,         remove this cup     from
```

```
J    12.28                                No, for this purpose I have come to this hour. |Father,
M    26.39     me; nevertheless, not as      I  will, but as    thou    wilt."
Mk   14.37     me; yet          not what I  will, but what thou    wilt."
L    22.42     me; nevertheless not         my will, but      thine be done."


J    12.28     glorify thy name." Then    a voice came from          heaven,
M    3.17                         and lo, a voice       from          heaven, saying,
Mk   1.11                         and     a voice came from          heaven,
L    3.22b                        and     a voice came from          heaven,
M    17.5b                        and     a voice       from  the cloud    said,
Mk   9.7b                         and     a voice came out of the cloud,
L    9.35                         And     a voice came out of the cloud, saying,


J    12.28     "I have glorified it, and I will glorify it again."
M    3.17      "This is  my beloved Son, with whom I am well pleased."
Mk   1.11      "Thou art my beloved Son; with thee I am well pleased."
L    3.22b     "Thou art my beloved Son; with thee I am well pleased."
M    17.5b     "This is  my beloved Son, with whom I am well pleased; listen to him."
Mk   9.7b      "This is  my beloved Son;                        listen to him."
L    9.35      "This is  my      Son, my Chosen;                listen to him!"


J    12.29              The crowd standing by heard it and said that it had thundered.
M    17.6      When the disciples          heard this, they fell on their faces, and


J    12.30     Others said, "An angel has spoken to him." |Jesus
M    17.7      were filled with awe.          But Jesus came and touched them,


J    12.31     answered, "This voice has come for your sake, not for mine.  Now is the
M    17.7      saying,   "Rise, and have no fear."


J    12.31     judgment of this world, now shall the ruler of this world be cast out;
L    10.18              And he said to them, "I saw Satan fall like lightning from


J    12.32     and I, when I am lifted up from the earth, will draw all men to myself."
L    10.18     heaven.


J    12.33,34  He said this to show by what death he was to die.  The crowd answered him,
J    12.34     "We have heard from the law that the Christ remains for ever.  How can you
J    12.35     say that the Son of man must be lifted up? Who is the Son of man?" Jesus
J    12.35     said to them, "The light is with you for a little longer. Walk while you
J    12.35     have the light, lest the darkness overtake you; he who walks in the dark-
J    12.36     ness does  not know where he goes.  While you have the light, believe in
J    12.36     the light, that you may become sons of light."


J    12.36     When Jesus had said this, he departed and hid himself from them.


J    12.37     Though he had done                  so many             signs
M    11.20     Then he began to upbraid the cities where most of his mighty works had


J    12.38     before them, yet   they did not believe in him; it was that the word
M    11.20     been done, because they did not repent.
M    13.14                                           With them indeed  is


J    12.38     spoken by the prophet    Isaiah might be fulfilled:
M    13.14     fulfilled the prophecy of Isaiah which says:
```

563

```
J   12.38              "Lord, who has believed our report,
J   12.38               and to whom has the arm of the Lord been revealed?"
J   12.38      Therefore they could not believe.  For Isaiah again said,


  M  13.14                  'You shall indeed hear but never understand,


J   12.40              "He has blinded their eyes
M   13.14               and you shall indeed see but never perceive.


J   12.40              and hardened their heart,
M   13.15              For this people's  heart  has grown dull,


  M  13.15                  and their ears are heavy of hearing,
  M  13.15                  and their eyes they have closed,


J   12.40              lest they should see       with their eyes
M   13.15              lest they should perceive with their eyes,
Mk   4.12b             lest they should


  M  13.15                  and hear with their ears,


J   12.40              and perceive   with their heart,
M   13.15              and understand with their heart,


J   12.40              and turn for me      to heal them."
M   13.15              and turn for me      to heal them.'
Mk   4.12b                 turn again, and be forgiven."


J   12.41                                        Isaiah said this
M   13.16                                        But blessed are your eyes,
L   10.23      Then turning to the disciples he said privately, "Blessed are the  eyes


J   12.41      because he   saw his glory and spoke of him.
M   13.17      for     they see, and your ears, for they hear.  Truly, I say to you,
L   10.24      which       see  what you see!        For   I tell   you that


  M  13.17      many prophets and righteous men longed  to see what you see, and did not
  L  10.24      many prophets and kings         desired to see what you see, and did not


  M  13.17      see it, and to hear what you hear, and did not hear it.
  L  10.24      see it, and to hear what you hear, and did not hear it."


J   12.42      Nevertheless many even of the authorities believed in him, but for fear
J   12.42      of the Pharisees they did not confess it, lest they should be put out of
J   12.43      the synagogue: for they loved the praise of men more than the praise of
J   12.43      God.


J   12.44      And         Jesus cried out and said,        "He who  believes
M   10.40                                                   "He who  receives
M   18.5                                                    "Whoever receives one such
Mk   9.37                                                   "Whoever receives one such
L    9.48a     and                            said to them, "Whoever receives     this
L   10.16                                                    "He who  hears
  J  13.20     Truly, truly, I                say  to you,   he who  receives any one
```

564

```
J    12.44                                    in me,
M    10.40       you              receives  me,                                        and he
M    18.5        child in my name receives  me;
Mk   9.37        child in my name receives  me;                                         and
L    9.48a       child in my name receives  me,                                         and
L    10.16       you              hears     me, and he who rejects you rejects me, and he
  J  13.20       whom I send      receives  me;                                         and he


J    12.44                                   believes not in me but in him who sent me.
M    10.40       who       receives me      receives                 him who sent me.
Mk   9.37        whoever receives me, receives not        me but     him who sent me."
L    9.48a       whoever receives me        receives                 him who sent me;
L    10.16       who     rejects   me       rejects                  him who sent me."
  J  13.20       who     receives me        receives                 him who sent me."


J    12.45,46   And he who sees me sees him who sent me.  I have come as light into the
J    12.47      world, that whoever believes in me may not remain in darkness.  If any
J    12.47      one hears my sayings and does not keep them, I do not judge him; for I
J    12.48      did not come to judge the world but to save the world.  He who rejects
J    12.48      me and does not receive my sayings has a judge; the word that I have
J    12.49      spoken will be his judge on the last day.  For I have not spoken on my
J    12.49      own authority; the Father who sent me has himself given me commandment
J    12.50      what to say and what to speak.  And I know that his commandment is eter-
J    12.50      nal life.  What I say, therefore, I say as the Father has bidden me."
```

27. THE FOOT WASHING

John 13.1-20

```
J    13.1        Now before the feast of the Passover, when Jesus knew that his hour
J    13.1        had come to depart out of this world to the Father, having loved his
J    13.1        own who were in the world, he loved them to the end.


J    13.2        And during supper, when the devil had already put it into the heart of
M    26.14       Then                                     one of the twelve, who was called
Mk   14.10       Then
L    22.3        Then                   Satan entered          into


J    13.2        Judas       Iscariot, Simon's son,
M    26.14       Judas       Iscariot,                                        went
Mk   14.10       Judas       Iscariot, who was      one   of the twelve,      went
L    22.4        Judas called Iscariot, who was of the number of the twelve; he went away


  M  26.15                        to   the chief priests |and said, "What will you give me
  Mk 14.10                        to   the chief priests
  L  22.4        and conferred with the chief priests and officers

  M  26.15       if I         deliver him to you?"  And                they
  Mk 14.11       in order to  betray  him to them.  And when they heard it they were glad,
  L  22.5        how he might betray  him to them.  And                they were glad,

  M  26.16           paid        him thirty pieces of silver.            And from
  Mk 14.11       and promised to give him          money.                And
  L  22.6        and engaged  to give him          money.  So he agreed, and


J    13.2                                      to betray him,
M    26.16       that moment he ·sought an opportunity to betray him.
Mk   14.11                 he sought an opportunity to betray him.
L    22.6                    sought an opportunity to betray him to them in the absence
```

J	13.3	|Jesus, <u>knowing that the Father</u> <u>had given</u> <u>all</u>
M	11.26,27	yea, <u>Father</u>, for such was thy gracious will. <u>All</u>
L	10.21b,22	yea, <u>Father</u>, for such was thy gracious will. <u>All</u>
L	22.6	of the multitude.

J	13.3	<u>things into his hands, and that he had come from God and was going to God,</u>
M	11.27	<u>things</u> have been delivered to me by my Father; and no one knows the
L	10.22	<u>things</u> have been delivered to me by my Father; and no one knows who the

M	*11.27*	*Son except the Father, and no one knows the Father except the Son*
L	*10.22*	*Son is except the Father, or who the Father is except the Son*

M	*11.27*	*and any one to whom the Son chooses to reveal him.*
L	*10.22*	*and any one to whom the Son chooses to reveal him."*

J	13.4	|rose from supper, laid aside his garments, and girded himself with a
J	13.5	towel. Then he poured water into a basin, and began to wash the dis-
J	13.5	ciples' feet, and to wipe them with the towel with which he was girded.
J	13.6	He came to Simon Peter; and Peter said to him, "Lord, do you wash my
J	13.7	feet?" Jesus answered him, "What I am doing you do not know now, but
J	13.8	afterward you will understand." Peter said to him, "You shall never
J	13.8	wash my feet." Jesus answered him, "If I do not wash you, you have no
J	13.9	part in me." Simon Peter said to him, "Lord, not my feet only but also
J	13.10	my hands and my head!" Jesus said to him, "He who has bathed does not
J	13.10	need to wash, except for his feet, but he is clean all over; and you
J	13.11	are clean, but not every one of you." For he knew who was to betray
J	13.11	him; that was why he said, "You are not all clean."

J	13.12	<u>When he had washed their feet, and taken his garments, and resumed his</u>

J	13.13	<u>place, he said to them, "Do you know what I have done to you? You call</u>
M	23.8	But you are not to be called rabbi, for <u>you</u> have

J	13.14	<u>me Teacher and Lord; and you are right</u>, for so I am. <u>If I then, your</u>
M	23.8	one <u>teacher, and</u> you are all brethren.

J	13.14	<u>Lord and Teacher, have washed your feet, you also ought to wash one</u>

J	13.15	<u>another's feet.</u> <u>For I have given you an example,</u>
M	20.28	even as the Son of man came not to be served but
Mk	10.45	For the Son of man also came not to be served but
L	22.27	For which is the greater, one who sits at table, or

J	13.15	<u>that you also should do as I have done to you.</u>
M	20.28	to serve, and to give his life as a ransom for many."
Mk	10.45	to serve, and to give his life as a ransom for many."
L	22.27	one who serves? Is it not the one who sits at table? But I am among you

J	13.16	<u>Truly, truly, I say to you, a servant</u>
L	22.26	as one who serves.
M	10.24	"A disciple
L	6.40a	A disciple
M	20.26	It shall not be so among you; but whoever would
Mk	10.43	But it shall not be so among you; but whoever would
L	22.26	But not so with you; rather

```
J   13.16    is  not greater  than his master;  nor is he who is sent greater than
M   10.24    is  not above        his teacher,  nor  a   servant      above
L   6.40a    is  not above        his teacher,
M   20.26    be      great   among you                                    must
Mk  10.43    be      great   among you                                    must
L   22.26    let the greatest among you become as the youngest, and the leader as
```

```
J   13.17    he who sent him.  If you know these things, blessed are you if you do them.
M   10.24    his master;
M   20.26    be your servant,
Mk  10.43    be your servant,
L   22.26    one who serves.
```

```
J   13.18    I am not speaking of you all; I know whom I have chosen; it is that the
J   13.18    scripture may be fulfilled, 'He who ate my bread has lifted his heel
J   13.19    against me.'  I tell you this now, before it takes place, that when it
J   13.20    does take place you may believe that I am he.  Truly,
```

```
J   13.20    truly, I say to you,  he who  receives any one whom I send      receives
M   10.40                        "He who  receives          you             receives
M   18.5                         "Whoever receives one such child in my name receives
Mk  9.37                         "Whoever receives one such child in my name receives
L   9.48a    and      said to them, "Whoever receives      this child in my name receives
L   10.16                          "He who  hears            you               hears
```

```
J   13.20    me;                           and he who  receives me   receives
M   10.40    me,                           and he who  receives me   receives
M   18.5     me;
Mk  9.37     me;                           and whoever receives me,  receives
L   9.48a    me,                           and whoever receives me   receives
L   10.16    me, and he who rejects you rejects me, and he who  rejects  me   rejects
```

```
J   13.20            him who sent me."
M   10.40            him who sent me.
Mk  9.37  not me but him who sent me."
L   9.48a            him who sent me;
L   10.16            him who sent me."
```

28. THE BETRAYAL BY JUDAS

John 13.21-35

```
J   13.21         When Jesus had thus spoken,  he was troubled in spirit,
M   26.20         When it was evening,          he sat at table  with the twelve
Mk  14.17    And  when it was evening           he came          with the twelve.
L   22.14    And  when the hour came,           he sat at table, and  the apostles
```

```
J   13.21              and                               testified, "Truly, truly,
M   26.21    disciples; and as they were          eating, he   said, "Truly,
Mk  14.18             And as they were at table eating, Jesus said, "Truly,
L   22.21    with him.  But                                        behold
```

```
J   13.21    I say to you, one of you will betray  me."
M   26.21    I say to you, one of you will betray  me."
Mk  14.18    I say to you, one of you will betray  me, one who is eating with me."
L   22.21    the hand of   him   who       betrays me        is        with me on
```

567

J	13.22	The disciples looked at	one another, uncertain of whom he
M	26.22	And they	were very sorrowful, and began to say to
Mk	14.19	They began to be	sorrowful, and	to say to
L	22.23	the table. And they began to question

J	13.23	spoke. One of his disciples, whom Jesus loved, was lying close to the
J	13.24	breast of Jesus; so Simon Peter beckoned to him and said, "Tell us who
J	13.25	it is of whom he speaks." So lying thus, close to the breast of Jesus,

J	13.26	he said to him,	"Lord, who is it?" Jesus answered,	"It is
M	26.23	him one after another, "Is it I,	Lord?" He	answered,
Mk	14.20	him one after another, "Is it I?"	He	said to them, "It is
L	22.23	one	another, which of them it was that would do this.

J	13.26	he to whom I shall give this morsel when I have dipped
M	26.23	"He who has dipped his hand in the dish with
Mk	14.20	one of the twelve, one who is dipping bread into the dish with

J	13.26	it." So when he had dipped the morsel, he gave it to Judas, the son of
J	13.27	Simon Iscariot. Then after the morsel, Satan entered into him. Jesus
J	13.28	said to him, "What you are going to do, do quickly." Now no one at the
J	13.29	table knew why he said this to him. Some thought that, because Judas
J	13.29	had the money box, Jesus was telling him, "Buy what we need for the
J	13.29	feast"; or, that he should give something to the poor.

M	26.24	me, will betray me. The Son of man goes as it is written of him, but
Mk	14.21	me. For the Son of man goes as it is written of him, but
L	22.22	For the Son of man goes as it has been determined; but

M	26.24	woe to that man by whom the Son of man is betrayed! It would have been
Mk	14.21	woe to that man by whom the Son of man is betrayed! It would have been
L	22.22	woe to that man by whom he is betrayed!"

J	13.30	So, after receiving the morsel, he immediately went out;
M	26.25	better for that man if he had not been born." Judas, who betrayed him,
Mk	14.21	better for that man if he had not been born."

J	13.30	and it was night.
M	26.25	said, "Is it I, Master?" He said to him, "You have said so."

J	13.31	When he had gone out, Jesus said, "Now is the Son of man glorified, and
J	13.32	in him God is glorified; if God is glorified in him, God will also glorify
J	13.33	him in himself, and glorify him at once. Little children, yet a little
J	13.33	while I am with you. You will seek me; and as I said to the Jews so now
J	13.34	I say to you, 'Where I am going you cannot come.' A new commandment I
J	13.34	give to you, that you love one another; even as I have loved you, that
J	13.35	you also love one another. By this all men will know that you are my
J	13.35	disciples, if you have love for one another.

29. PETER'S DENIAL FORETOLD

John 13.36-38

J	13.36	Simon Peter said to him, "Lord, where are you going?" Jesus answered,
J	13.36	"Where I am going you cannot follow me now; but you shall follow after-

```
J   13.37   ward."  Peter said    to him, "Lord, why cannot I follow you now?
M   26.33           Peter declared to him,        "Though they all fall away because of
Mk  14.29           Peter said    to him, "Even though they all fall away,
L   22.33   And he        said    to him, "Lord,
```

```
J   13.38        I will lay down my life for you."                      Jesus answered,
M   26.34   you, I will never fall away."                               Jesus said  to
Mk  14.30        I will not."                               And Jesus said  to
L   22.34   I am   ready to go with you to prison and to death."  He      said,
```

```
J   13.38   "Will you lay down your life for me?  Truly, truly, I say to you,
M   26.34   him,                                   "Truly,      I say to you, this
Mk  14.30   him,                                   "Truly,      I say to you, this
L   22.34                                           "I tell   you, Peter,
```

```
J   13.38                      the cock will not crow,          till  you have
M   26.34   very night, before the cock              crows,           you will
Mk  14.30   very night, before the cock              crows twice,     you will
L   22.34                      the cock will not crow this day, until you three times
```

```
J   13.38   denied          me three times.
M   26.35   deny            me three times."     Peter said to him, "Even if I must
Mk  14.31   deny            me three times."  But he      said vehemently, "If I must
L   22.34   deny that you know me."
```

```
 M 26.25   die with you, I will not deny you."  And so        said all the disciples.
Mk 14.3    die with you, I will not deny you."  And they all said      the same.
```

30. LAST DISCOURSE: PROMISE OF THE COUNSELOR

John 14.1-31

```
J   14.1      "Let not your hearts be troubled; believe in God, believe also in me.
J   14.2      In my Father's house are many rooms; if it were not so, would I have told
J   14.3      you that I go to prepare a place for you?  And when I go and prepare a
J   14.3      place for you, I will come again and will take you to myself, that where
J   14.4,5    I am you may be also.  And you know the way where I am going."  Thomas
J   14.5      said to him, "Lord, we do not know where you are going; how can we know
J   14.6      the way?"  Jesus said to him, "I am the way, and the truth, and the life;
J   14.7      no one comes to the Father, but by me.  If you had known me, you would
J   14.7      have known my Father also; henceforth you know him and have seen him."

J   14.8      Philip said to him, "Lord, show us the Father, and we shall be satisfied."
```

```
J   14.9    Jesus said  to him,  "Have I been with you              so  long,
M   17.17   And Jesus  answered,      "O faithless and perverse generation, how long
Mk   9.19   And he     answered them, "O faithless            generation, how long
L    9.41   Jesus  answered,      "O faithless and perverse generation, how long
```

```
J   14.9    and yet you do not know me, Philip?  He who has seen me has seen the Father;
M   17.17   am I to be with you?  How long am I to bear with you?  Bring       him here
Mk   9.19   am I to be with you?  How long am I to bear with you?  Bring       him
L    9.41   am I to be with you              and bear with you?  Bring your son here."
```

```
J   14.10   how can you say, 'Show us the Father'?  Do you not believe that I am in
M   17.17   to me."
Mk   9.20   to me."
```

```
J    14.10     the Father and the Father in me?  The words that I say to you I do not
J    14.10     speak on my own authority; but the Father who dwells in me does his works.
J    14.11     Believe me that I am in the Father and the Father in me; or else believe
J    14.11     me for the sake of the works themselves.


J    14.12     "Truly, truly, I say to you, he who believes in me            will
Mk   16.16                              He who believes and is baptized will be


J    14.12                                                      also do the works
Mk   16.17     saved; but he who does not believe will be condemned.  And these signs


J    14.12     that I do; and greater works than these will he do, because I go to the
Mk   16.17     will accompany those who believe: in my name they will cast out demons;


J    14.13     Father.                        Whatever you
Mk   16.17     they will speak in new tongues;
M    18.19     Again     I say to you, if two of  you agree on earth about anything they
M    21.22     And                            whatever you
Mk   11.24     Therefore I tell  you,    whatever you
L    11.9      And       I tell  you,


J    14.13     ask  in my name,              I  will   do     it, that the Father may
M    7.7       "Ask, and                     it will be given  you; seek, and you will
M    18.19     ask,                          it will be done for them   by my Father in
M    21.22     ask  in prayer,              you will   receive,   if you have faith."
Mk   11.24     ask  in prayer, believe that you have     received it, and it will be yours.
L    11.9      Ask, and                      it will be given  you; seek, and you will


J    14.14     be glorified in the Son;                   if you            ask
M    7.8       find; knock, and it will be opened to you.  For every one who asks
M    18.19     heaven.
L    11.10     find; knock, and it will be opened to you.  For every one who asks


J    14.14     anything in my name, I will do it.
M    7.8       receives, and he who seeks finds, and to him who knocks it will be opened.
L    11.9      receives, and he who seeks finds, and to him who knocks it will be opened.


J    14.15,16   "If you love me, you will keep my commandments.  And I will pray the
J    14.16      Father, and he will give you another Counselor, to be with you for ever,
J    14.17      |even the Spirit of truth, whom the world cannot receive, because it
J    14.17      neither sees him nor knows him; you know him, for he dwells with you,
J    14.17      and will be in you.

J    14.18,19   "I will not leave you desolate; I will come to you.  Yet a little while,
J    14.19      and the world will see me no more, but you will see me; because I live,
J    14.20      you will live also.  In that day you will know that I am in my Father,
J    14.21      and you in me, and I in you.  He who has my commandments and keeps them,
J    14.21      he it is who loves me; and he who loves me will be loved by my Father,
J    14.22      and I will love him and manifest myself to him."  Judas (not Iscariot)
J    14.22      said to him, "Lord, how is it that you will manifest yourself to us, and
J    14.23      not to the world?"  Jesus answered him, "If a man loves me, he will keep
J    14.23      my word, and my Father will love him, and we will come to him and make
J    14.24      our home with him.  He who does not love me does not keep my words; and
J    14.24      the word which you hear is not mine but the Father's who sent me.


J    14.25,26   "These things I have spoken to you, while I am still with you.  But
M    10.20                               for it is not you who speak, but
Mk   13.11b                              for it is not you who speak, but
L    12.12                               for
```

J	14.26	the Counselor, the Holy Spirit, whom the Father will send in my name, he
M	10.20	the Spirit of your Father speaking through you.
Mk	13.11b	the Holy Spirit.
L	12.12	the Holy Spirit

J	14.26	will teach you all things, and bring to your remembrance all that I have
L	12.12	will teach you in that very hour what you ought to say."

J	14.27	said to you. Peace I
M	8.26b	Then he rose and rebuked the winds and the sea;
Mk	4.39	And he awoke and rebuked the wind, and said to the sea, "Peace! Be
L	8.24b	And he awoke and rebuked the wind and the raging waves;

J	14.27	leave with you; my peace I give to you; not as the world gives do I give
M	8.26a	and there was a great calm. And he said to
Mk	4.40	still!" And the wind ceased, and there was a great calm. He said to
L	8.25a	and they ceased, and there was a calm. He said to

J	14.27	to you. Let not your hearts be troubled, neither let them be afraid.
M	8.26a	them, "Why are you afraid,
Mk	4.40	them, "Why are you afraid?
L	8.25a	them, "Where is your

J	14.28	You heard me say to you, 'I go away, and I will come to you.' If you
M	8.26a	O men of little faith?"
Mk	4.40	Have you no faith?"
L	8.25a	faith?"

J	14.28	loved me, you would have rejoiced, because I go to the Father; for the
J	14.29	Father is greater than I. And now I have told you before it takes place,
J	14.30	so that when it does take place, you may believe. I will no longer talk
J	14.30	much with you, for the ruler of this world is coming. He has no power
J	14.31	over me; but I do as the Father has commanded me, so that the world may
J	14.31	know that I love the Father.

J	14.31	Rise, let us go hence.
M	26.46	Rise, let us be going; see, my betrayer is at hand."
Mk	14.42	Rise, let us be going; see, my betrayer is at hand."

31. LAST DISCOURSE: THE TRUE VINE

John 15.1-17

J	15.1,2	"I am the true vine, and my Father is the vinedresser. Every branch
M	15.13	He answered, "Every plant

J	15.2	of mine that bears no fruit, he takes away, and every
M	15.13	which my heavenly Father has not planted will be rooted up.

J	15.3	branch that does bear fruit he prunes, that it may bear more fruit. You
J	15.4	are already made clean by the word which I have spoken to you. Abide in
J	15.4	me, and I in you. As the branch cannot bear fruit by itself, unless it
J	15.5	abides in the vine, neither can you, unless you abide in me. I am the
J	15.5	vine, you are the branches. He who abides in me, and I in him, he it is
J	15.6	that bears much fruit, for apart from me you can do nothing. If a man
J	15.6	does not abide in me, he is cast forth as a branch and withers; and the

```
J    15.7     branches are gathered, thrown into the fire and burned.  If you abide in
J    15.7     me, and my words abide in you, ask whatever you will, and it shall be done
J    15.8     for you.  By this my Father is glorified, that you bear much fruit, and so
J    15.9     prove to be my disciples.  As the Father has loved me, so have I loved
J    15.10    you; abide in my love.  If you keep my commandments, you will abide in my
J    15.10    love, just as I have kept my Father's commandments and abide in his love.
J    15.11    These things I have spoken to you, that my joy may be in you, and that
J    15.11    your joy may be full.
```

```
J    15.12                        "This is my commandment, that you      love one  another
M    22.39    And a    second is like it,                    You shall love your neighbor
Mk   12.31a         The second is this,                      'You shall love your neighbor
L    10.27b   and                                                       your neighbor
```

```
J    15.13    as I have loved you.  Greater love has no man than this, that a man lay
M    22.39    as yourself.
Mk   12.31a   as yourself.'
L    10.27    as yourself."
```

```
J    15.14    down his life for his friends.  You are my friends if you do what I com-
J    15.15    mand you.  No longer do I call you servants, for the servant does not know
J    15.15    what his master is doing; but I have called you friends, for all that I
J    15.16    have heard from my Father I have made known to you.  You did not choose
J    15.16    me, but I chose you and appointed you that you should go and bear fruit
J    15.16    and that your fruit should abide; so that whatever you ask the Father in
J    15.17    my name, he may give it to you.  This I command you, to love one another.
```

32. LAST DISCOURSE: HATRED OF THE WORLD

John 15.18-16.4a

```
J    15.18    "If      the world        hates you, know that it has hated me before
M    10.22a                     and you will be  hated by all
M    24.9b                      and you will be  hated by all
Mk   13.13a                     and you will be  hated by all
L    6.22      "Blessed are you when men hate  you, and when they exclude you and
```

```
J    15.19    it hated you.  If you were of the world, the world would love its own;
M    10.22a                                           for            my name's sake.
M    24.9b                               nations for            my name's sake.
Mk   13.13a                                         for            my name's sake.
L    6.22      revile you, and cast out your name as evil, on account of the Son of man!
```

```
J    15.19    but because you are not of the world, but I chose you out of the world,
J    15.20    therefore the world hates you.  Remember the word that I said to you,
```

```
J    15.20    'A servant  is not greater than his master.'  If they persecuted me,
M    10.24    "A disciple is not above      his teacher,  nor a servant above his
L    6.40      A disciple is not above      his teacher, but every one when he is
```

```
J    15.20    they will persecute you; if they kept my word, they will keep yours also.
M    10.24    master;
L    6.40      fully taught will be like his teacher.
```

```
J    15.21    But all this they will do to you on my account, because they do not know
J    15.22    him who sent me.  If I had not come and spoken to them, they would not
J    15.23    have sin; but now they have no excuse for their sin.  He who hates me
```

```
J   15.24   hates my Father also.  If I had not done among them the works which no
J   15.24   one else did, they would not have sin; but now they have seen and hated
J   15.25   both me and my Father.  It is to fulfil the word that is written in their
J   15.26   law, 'They hated me without a cause.'  But when the Counselor comes, whom
J   15.26   I shall send to you from the Father, even the Spirit of truth, who proceeds
J   15.27   from the Father, he will bear witness to me; and you also are witnesses,
J   15.27   because you have been with me from the beginning.


J    16.1,2   "I have said all this to you to keep you from falling away.  They will
M    10.22b   But he who endures to the end will be       saved.
M    24.13    But he who endures to the end will be       saved.
Mk   13.13b   But he who endures to the end will be       saved.
L    21.19    By   your   endurance      you will gain your lives.


J   16.2    put you out of the synagogues; indeed, the hour is coming when whoever
J   16.3    kills you will think he is offering service to God.  And they will do
J   16.4a   this because they have not known the Father, nor me.  But I have said
J   16.4a   these things to you, that when their hour comes you may remember that
J   16.4a   I told you of them.
```

33. LAST DISCOURSE: I GO TO THE FATHER

John 16.4b-33

```
J   16.4b   "I did not say these things to you from the beginning, because I was
J   16.5    with you.  But now I am going to him who sent me; yet none of you asks
J   16.6    me, 'Where are you going?'  But because I have said


J    16.7     these things to you,  sorrow has filled your hearts.  Nevertheless I
M    17.23b   And they were greatly distressed.
Mk   9.32a    But they did not    understand the  saying,
L    9.45a    But they did not    understand this saying,


J   16.7    tell you the truth: it is to your advantage that I go away, for if I do
J   16.7    not go away, the Counselor will not come to you; but if I go, I will send
J   16.8    him to you.  And when he comes, he will convince the world concerning sin
J   16.9    and righteousness and judgment: concerning sin, because they do not be-
J   16.10   lieve in me; concerning righteousness, because I go to the Father, and
J   16.11   you will see me no more; concerning judgment, because the ruler of this
J   16.11   world is judged.

J   16.12   "I have yet many things to say to you, but you cannot bear them now.
J   16.13   When the Spirit of truth comes, he will guide you into all the truth;
J   16.13   for he will not speak on his own authority, but whatever he hears he will
J   16.14   speak, and he will declare to you the things that are to come.  He will
J   16.15   glorify me, for he will take what is mine and declare it to you.  All
J   16.15   that the Father has is mine; therefore I said that he will take what is
J   16.15   mine and declare it to you.

J   16.16   "A little while, and you will see me no more; again a little while, and
J   16.17   you will see me."  Some of his disciples said to one another, "What is
J   16.17   this that he says to us, 'A little while, and you will not see me, and
J   16.17   again a little while, and you will see me'; and, 'because I go to the
J   16.18   Father'?"  They said, "What does he mean by 'a little while'?  We do not
J   16.19   know what he means."  Jesus knew that they wanted to ask him; so he said
J   16.19   to them, "Is this what you are asking yourselves, what I meant by saying,
J   16.19   'A little while, and you will not see me, and again a little while, and
J   16.20   you will see me'?  Truly, truly, I say to you, you will weep and lament,
J   16.20   but the world will rejoice; you will be sorrowful, but your sorrow will
J   16.21   turn into joy.  When a woman is in travail she has sorrow, because her
```

J   16.21   hour has come; but when she is delivered of the child, she no longer
J   16.22   remembers the anguish, for joy that a child is born into the world. So
J   16.22   you have sorrow now, but I will see you again and your hearts will re-
J   16.23   joice, and no one will take your joy from you. In that day you will ask

J   16.23   nothing of me. Truly, truly, I say to you, if   you
M   18.19   Again   I say to you, if two of you agree on earth
M   21.22   And   whatever you
Mk   11.24   Therefore   I tell   you,   whatever you
L   11.9   And   I tell   you,

J   16.23   ask anything of the Father, he will   give   it
M   7.7   "Ask, and   it will be given
M   18.19   about anything they ask,   it will be done
M   21.22   ask in prayer,   you will   receive,
Mk   11.24   ask in prayer, believe that you have   received it,
L   11.9   Ask, and   it will be given

J   16.24   to you in my name. Hitherto you have asked nothing in my name; ask, and
M   7.7   you; seek, and you will find; knock, and it will be opened to you.
M   18.19   for them by my Father in heaven.
M   21.22   if you have faith."
Mk   11.24   and it   will be yours.
L   11.9   you; seek, and you will find; knock, and it will be opened to you.

J   16.24   you will receive, that your joy may be full.

J   16.25   "I have said this to you in figures; the hour is coming when I shall no
J   16.26   longer speak to you in figures but tell you plainly of the Father. In
J   16.26   that day you will ask in my name; and I do not say to you that I shall
J   16.27   pray the Father for you; for the Father himself loves you, because you
J   16.28   have loved me and have believed that I came from the Father. I came
J   16.28   from the Father and have come into the world; again, I am leaving the
J   16.28   world and going to the Father."

J   16.29   His disciples said, "Ah, now you are speaking plainly, not in any
J   16.30   figure! Now we know that you know all things, and need none to question
J   16.31   you; by this we believe that you came from God." Jesus answered them,
J   16.31   "Do you now believe?

J   16.32   The hour is coming, indeed it has come,   when   you
M   26.31b   for it is written, 'I will strike the shepherd, and the sheep of the flock
Mk   14.27b   for it is written, 'I will strike the shepherd, and the sheep

J   16.32   will be scattered, every man to his home, and will leave me alone; yet
M   26.31b   will be scattered.'
Mk   14.27b   will be scattered.'

J   16.33   I am not alone, for the Father is with me. I have said this to you, that
J   16.33   in me you may have peace. In the world you have tribulation; but be of
J   16.33   good cheer, I have overcome the world."

34. THE PRAYER OF JESUS

John 17.1-26

J   17.1   When Jesus had spoken these words, he lifted up his eyes to heaven and
J   17.1   said, "Father, the hour has come; glorify thy Son that the Son may glorify
J   17.2   thee, |since thou hast given him power over all flesh, to give eternal

J 17.3   life to all whom thou hast given him. And this is eternal life, that they
J 17.4   know thee the only true God, and Jesus Christ whom thou hast sent. I
J 17.4   glorified thee on earth, having accomplished the work which thou gavest
J 17.5   me to do; and now, Father, glorify thou me in thy own presence with the
J 17.5   glory which I had with thee before the world was made.

J 17.6   "I have manifested thy name to the men whom thou gavest me out of the
J 17.6   world; thine they were, and thou gavest them to me, and they have kept
J 17.7   thy word. Now they know that everything that thou hast given me is from
J 17.8   thee; for I have given them the words which thou gavest me, and they have
J 17.8   received them and know in truth that I came from thee; and they have be-
J 17.9   lieved that thou didst send me. I am praying for them; I am not praying
J 17.9   for the world but for those whom thou hast given me, for they are thine;
J 17.10,11 all mine are thine, and thine are mine, and I am glorified in them. And
J 17.11   now I am no more in the world, but they are in the world, and I am coming
J 17.11   to thee. Holy Father, keep them in thy name, which thou hast given me,
J 17.12   that they may be one, even as we are one. While I was with them, I kept
J 17.12   them in thy name, which thou hast given me; I have guarded them, and none
J 17.12   of them is lost but the son of perdition, that the scripture might be
J 17.13   fulfilled. But now I am coming to thee; and these things I speak in the
J 17.14   world, that they may have my joy fulfilled in themselves. I have given
J 17.14   them thy word; and the world has hated them because they are not of the
J 17.15   world, even as I am not of the world. I do not pray that thou shouldst
J 17.15   take them out of the world, but that thou shouldst keep them from the
J 17.16   evil one. They are not of the world, even as I am not of the world.
J 17.17,18 Sanctify them in the truth; thy word is truth. As thou didst send me
J 17.19   into the world, so I have sent them into the world. And for their
J 17.19   sake I consecrate myself, that they also may be consecrated in truth.

J 17.20   "I do not pray for these only, but also for those who believe in me
J 17.21   through their word, |that they may all be one; even as thou, Father, art
J 17.21   in me, and I in thee, that they also may be in us, so that the world may
J 17.22   believe that thou hast sent me. The glory which thou hast given me I
J 17.23   have given to them, that they may be one even as we are one, |I in them
J 17.23   and thou in me, that they may become perfectly one, so that the world
J 17.23   may know that thou hast sent me and hast loved them even as thou hast
J 17.24   loved me. Father, I desire that they also, whom thou hast given me,
J 17.24   may be with me where I am, to behold my glory which thou hast given me
J 17.24   in thy love for me before the foundation of the world.

J 17.25   O righteous   Father, the world has not
M 11.27   All things have been delivered to me by my Father; and   no one
L 10.22   All things have been delivered to me by my Father; and   no one

J 17.25   known thee, but I have known   thee;   and these know
M 11.27   knows   the Son   except the Father, and no one knows the Father
L 10.22   knows who the Son is except the Father, or   who   the Father is

J 17.26   that thou hast sent me. I made known to them thy name,
M 11.27   except the Son and any one to whom the Son chooses to reveal him.
L 10.22   except the Son and any one to whom the Son chooses to reveal him."

J 17.26   and I will make it known, that the love with which thou hast loved me
J 17.26   may be in them, and I in them."

J	18.1	When Jesus had spoken these words, he went forth with his disciples
M	26.30	And when they had sung a hymn, they went out
Mk	14.26	And when they had sung a hymn, they went out
L	22.39	And he came out, and went, as was his custom,
M	26.36a	Then Jesus went with them
Mk	14.32a	And they went
L	22.40a	And when he came

J	18.1	across the Kidron valley, where there was a garden, which he and his dis-
M	26.30	to the Mount of Olives.
Mk	14.26	to the Mount of Olives.
L	22.39	to the Mount of Olives; and the disciples followed him.
M	26.36a	to a place called Gethsemane,
Mk	14.32a	to a place which was called Gethsemane;
L	22.40a	to the place

J	18.2	ciples entered. Now Judas, who betrayed him, also knew the place; for
J	18.2	Jesus often met there with his disciples.

J	18.3	So
M	26.47	While he was still speaking,
Mk	14.43	And immediately, while he was still speaking,
L	22.47	While he was still speaking, there came a crowd, and the

J	18.3	Judas, procuring a band of soldiers and some officers from the
M	26.47	Judas came, one of the twelve, and
Mk	14.43	Judas came, one of the twelve, and
L	22.47	man called Judas, one of the twelve, was leading

J	18.3	chief priests and the Pharisees, went there with lanterns and torches and
M	26.47	with him a great crowd with swords and
Mk	14.43	with him a crowd with swords and
L	22.47	them.

J	18.4	weapons. Then Jesus, knowing all that was to befall him, came forward and
M	26.47	clubs, from the chief priests and the elders of the people.
Mk	14.43	clubs, from the chief priests and the scribes and the elders.

J	18.5	said to them, "Whom do you seek?" They answered him, "Jesus of Nazareth."
M	26.48	Now the betrayer had given them a sign, saying, "The one I shall kiss is
Mk	14.44	Now the betrayer had given them a sign, saying, "The one I shall kiss is

J	18.5	Jesus said to them, "I am he." Judas, who
M	26.49	the man; seize him." And he came
Mk	14.45	the man; seize him and lead him away under guard." And when he came, he
L	22.47	He drew near

J	18.5	betrayed him, was standing with them.
M	26.49	up to Jesus at once and said, "Hail, Master!" And he kissed him.
Mk	14.45	went up to him at once, and said, "Master!" And he kissed him.
L	22.47	to Jesus to kiss him;

J	18.6	When he said to them, "I am he," they drew back and fell to the ground.
M	26.50	⎸Jesus said to him, "Friend, why are you here?" Then they came up and
Mk	14.46	And they
L	22.48	but Jesus said to him, "Judas, would you betray the Son of man with a

M	26.50	*laid hands on Jesus and seized him.*
Mk	14.46	*laid hands on him and seized him.*
L	22.49	*kiss?" And when those who were about him saw what would follow, they said,*

| L | 22.49 | *"Lord, shall we strike with the sword?"* |

J	18.7	Again he asked them,
M	26.55	At that hour Jesus said to the crowds,
Mk	14.48	And Jesus said to them,
L	22.52	Then Jesus said to the chief priests and officers of the temple

J	18.7	"Whom do you seek?" And they
M	26.55	"Have you come out as against
Mk	14.48	"Have you come out as against
L	22.52	and elders, who had come out against him, "Have you come out as against

J	18.8	said, "Jesus of Nazareth." Jesus answered, "I told you that I am he;
M	26.55	a robber, with swords and clubs to capture me? Day after day I
Mk	14.49	a robber, with swords and clubs to capture me? Day after day I
L	22.53	a robber, with swords and clubs? When I was with you day after day

J	18.8	so, if you seek me, let these men go."
M	26.55	sat in the temple teaching, and you did not seize me.
Mk	14.49	was with you in the temple teaching, and you did not seize me.
L	22.53	in the temple, you did not lay hands on me.

J	18.9	This was to fulfil the word which he had spoken, "Of
M	26.56	But all this has taken place, that the scriptures of the prophets might
Mk	14.49	But let the scriptures
L	22.53	But this is your hour, and the power of darkness."

J	18.9	those whom thou gavest me I lost not one."
M	26.56	be fulfilled." Then all the disciples forsook him and fled.
Mk	14.50	be fulfilled." And they all forsook him, and fled.

J	18.10	Then Simon Peter, having a sword,
M	26.51	And behold, one of those who were with Jesus stretched out his hand and
Mk	14.47	But one of those who stood by
L	22.50	And one of them

J	18.10	drew it and struck the high priest's slave
M	26.51	drew his sword, and struck the slave of the high priest,
Mk	14.47	drew his sword, and struck the slave of the high priest
L	22.50	struck the slave of the high priest

J	18.11	and cut off his right ear. The slave's name was Malchus. ⎸Jesus said
M	26.52	and cut off his ear. Then Jesus said
Mk	14.47	and cut off his ear.
L	22.51	and cut off his right ear. But Jesus said,

J	18.11	to Peter, "Put your sword into its sheath; shall I not drink the
M	26.52	to him, "Put your sword back into its place; for all who take the
L	22.51	"No more of this!" And he touched his ear and healed him.

J	18.11	<u>cup which the Father has given me?</u>"
M	26.53	sword will perish by the sword. *Do you think that I cannot appeal to*

M	26.53	*my Father, and he will at once send me more than twelve legions of angels?*
M	26.54	*But how then should the scriptures be fulfilled, that it must be so?*"

36. BEFORE THE HIGH PRIEST AND PETER'S DENIAL

John 18.12-27

J	18.12	<u>So the band of soldiers and their captain and the officers of the Jews</u>
M	26.57	Then those who had
Mk	14.53	And they
L	22.54	Then they

J	18.13	<u>seized Jesus and bound him. First they led him to Annas; for he was the</u>
M	26.57	<u>seized Jesus</u> <u>led him</u>
Mk	14.53	<u>led Jesus</u>
L	22.54	<u>seized</u> him and <u>led him</u> away, bringing him

J	18.14	<u>father-in-law of Caiaphas, who was high priest that year. It was Caiaphas</u>
M	26.57	to <u>Caiaphas</u> the <u>high priest</u>, where the scribes
Mk	14.53	to the <u>high priest</u>; and all the chief priests
L	22.54	into the <u>high</u> priest's house.

J	18.14	<u>who had given counsel to the Jews that it was expedient that one man</u>
M	26.57	and the elders had gathered.
Mk	14.53	and the elders and the scribes were assembled.

J	18.14	<u>should die for the people.</u>

J	18.15	Simon Peter <u>followed Jesus, and so did another disciple. As this</u>
M	26.58	But Peter <u>followed</u> him at a distance,
Mk	14.54	And Peter had <u>followed</u> him at a distance,
L	22.54	Peter <u>followed</u> at a distance;

J	18.15	<u>disciple was known to the high priest, he entered</u> <u>the court</u> <u>of the</u>
M	26.58	as far as <u>the courtyard of the</u>
Mk	14.54	right into <u>the courtyard of the</u>
L	22.55	and when they had kindled a fire in the middle of <u>the</u> courtyard

J	18.16	<u>high priest</u> <u>along with Jesus,</u> |<u>while Peter</u> <u>stood outside at the door.</u>
M	26.58	<u>high priest</u>, and going inside he sat with the guards to
Mk	14.54	<u>high priest</u>; and he was sitting with the guards, and
L	22.66a	and sat down together, <u>Peter</u> sat among them. When

J	18.16	<u>So the other disciple, who was known to the high priest, went out and spoke</u>
M	26.58	see the end.
Mk	14.54	warming himself at the fire.
L	22.66a	day came, the assembly of the elders of the people gathered together,

J	18.17	<u>to the maid who kept the door, and brought Peter in. The maid who kept</u>
J	18.17	<u>the door said to Peter, "Are not you also one of this man's disciples?"</u>
J	18.18	<u>He said, "I am not." Now the servants and officers had made a charcoal</u>
J	18.18	<u>fire, because it was cold, and they were standing and warming themselves;</u>
J	18.18	<u>Peter also was with them,</u> <u>standing and warming himself.</u>

```
J    18.19              The high  priest then questioned Jesus about his disciples and his
M    26.59      Now the chief priests                 and                  the whole council
Mk   14.55      Now the chief priests                 and                  the whole council
L    22.66a          both chief priests and scribes; and they led him away to their council,


J    18.20      teaching.  Jesus answered him, "I have spoken openly to the world; I have
M    26.59      sought false testimony against Jesus that they might put him to death,
Mk   14.55      sought       testimony against Jesus                    to put him to death;


J    18.20      always taught in synagogues and in the temple, where all Jews come together;
M    26.60      |but they found none,   though many        false witnesses came forward.
Mk   14.56       but they found none.  For    many bore false witness against him, and


J    18.21      I have said nothing secretly.  Why do you ask me? Ask those who have heard
M    26.61                         At last two   came forward |and
Mk   14.57      their witness did not agree.  And some stood up     and bore false witness


J    18.21      me, what I said to them; they know what I said."
M    26.61                  said,         "This      fellow said, 'I am able to destroy the
Mk   14.58      against him, saying,     |"We heard him   say, 'I    will    destroy this


   M  26.61     temple of God,                 and to build it in three days.'"
   Mk 14.58     temple that is made with hands, and          in three days I will build

   Mk 14.59     another, not made with hands.'" Yet not even so did their testimony agree.


J    18.22      When he had said this,    one of the officers standing by
M    26.67      Then                      they      spat in his face,
Mk   14.65      And                  some began to spit on    him, and to cover his
L    22.63      Now              the men who were holding Jesus mocked him


J    18.22                  struck Jesus with his hand,          saying,
M    26.68          and     struck him; and some slapped him,   |saying,
Mk   14.65      face, and to strike him,                         saying to him,
L    22.64          and     beat  him; they also blindfolded him and asked    him,


J    18.23      "Is that how you answer the high priest?"  Jesus answered him, "If I have
M    26.68      "Prophesy to us, you Christ! Who is it that struck you?"
Mk   14.65      "Prophesy!"  And the guards received him with blows.
L    22.65      "Prophesy!             Who is it that struck you?"  And they spoke


J    18.23      spoken wrongly, bear witness to the wrong; but if I have spoken rightly,
L    22.65      many other words against him, reviling him.


J    18.23      why do you strike me?"


J    18.24      Annas then                    sent him    to Caiaphas      the high
M    26.57      Then those who had seized Jesus led  him   to Caiaphas      the high
Mk   14.53      And  they                     led  Jesus  to               the high
L    22.54a      Then they          seized him and led  him away, bringing him into the high


J    18.24      priest.
M    26.57      priest, where   the scribes    and the elders              had
Mk   14.53      priest; and all the chief priests and the elders and the scribes were
L    22.54a      priest's house.
```

```
M   26.57        gathered.
Mk  14.53        assembled.


J   18.25        Now Simon Peter was standing and warming himself.
M   26.71        And when he went out  to the porch,    another maid       saw him, and
Mk  14.68b,69    And       he went out into the gateway. And the maid       saw him, and
L   22.58        And a little later                       some one else saw him  and


J   18.25        They          said to him,        "Are not you also         one   of
M   26.71        she           said to the bystanders, "This man    was with Jesus of
Mk  14.69        began again to say  to the bystanders, "This man     is       one   of
L   22.58                      said,                  "You also  are        one   of


J   18.26        his disciples?"       He    denied it and said,     "I am not."  |One of
M   26.72        Nazareth."  And again he    denied it with an oath, "I do not know the
Mk  14.70        them."      But again he    denied it.
L   22.58        them."      But       Peter said,            "Man,  I am not."


J   18.26        the servants of the high priest, a kinsman of the man whose ear Peter
M   26.73        man."  After a little while             the bystanders came up and
Mk  14.70             And after a little while        again the bystanders
L   22.59             And after an interval of about an hour still another insisted,


J   18.26        had cut off, asked,        "Did I not see you in the garden      with
M   26.73                     said to Peter, "Certainly     you       are also one of
Mk  14.70                     said to Peter, "Certainly     you       are        one of
L   22.59                     saying,       "Certainly this man also was          with


J   18.27        him?"                               Peter again
M   26.74        them, for your accent betrays you."  Then he began to invoke a curse on
Mk  14.71        them; for you  are a Galilean."  But  he began to invoke a curse on
L   22.60        him;  for he   is a Galilean."  But Peter


J   18.27                     denied it;
M   26.74        himself and to swear,    "I do not know the   man."
Mk  14.71        himself and to swear,    "I do not know this man of whom you     speak."
L   22.60                     said, "Man, I do not know what           you are saying."


J   18.27        and at once                        the cock crowed.
M   26.74        And immediately                    the cock crowed.
Mk  14.72        And immediately                    the cock crowed a second
L   22.61        And immediately, while he was still speaking, the cock crowed. |And the
```

```
M   26.75                             And Peter remembered the saying of
Mk  14.72        time.                And Peter remembered
L   22.61        Lord turned and looked at Peter.  And Peter remembered the word   of the

M   26.75                Jesus,            "Before the cock crows,       you will
Mk  14.72        how Jesus had said to him, "Before the cock crows twice, you will
L   22.61        Lord, how he   had said to him, "Before the cock crows today, you will

M   26.75        deny me three times."  And he went  out  and wept bitterly.
Mk  14.72        deny me three times."  And he broke down and wept.
L   22.62        deny me three times."  And he went  out  and wept bitterly.
```

John 18.28-19.16

M	27.1	When morning came, all the chief priests and the elders
Mk	15.1	And as soon as it was morning the chief priests, with the elders
L	22.66a	When day came, the assembly of the elders

M	27.1	of the people
Mk	15.1	and scribes, and
L	22.66a	of the people gathered together, both chief priests and scribes; and they

M	27.1	took counsel against Jesus to put him to
Mk	15.1	the whole council held a consultation;
L	22.66a	led him away to their council,

J	18.28	Then they led Jesus from the
M	27.2	death; and they bound him and led him away and
Mk	15.1	and they bound Jesus and led him away and
L	23.1	Then the whole company of them arose, and brought him

J	18.28	house of Caiaphas to the praetorium. It was early. They themselves did
M	27.2	delivered him to Pilate the governor.
Mk	15.1	delivered him to Pilate.
L	23.1	before Pilate.

J	18.28	not enter the praetorium, so that they might not be defiled, but might eat
J	18.29	the passover. So Pilate went out to them and said, "What accusation do
J	18.30	you bring against this man?" They answered him, "If this man were not an
J	18.31	evildoer, we would not have handed him over." Pilate said to them, "Take
J	18.31	him yourselves and judge him by your own law." The Jews said to him, "It
J	18.32	is not lawful for us to put any man to death." This was to fulfil the
J	18.32	word which Jesus had spoken to show by what death he was to die.

J	18.33	Pilate entered the praetorium again and called
M	27.11	Now Jesus stood before the governor;

J	18.33	Jesus, and said to him, "Are you the King of the Jews?"
M	27.11	and the governor asked him, "Are you the King of the Jews?"
Mk	15.2	And Pilate asked him, "Are you the King of the Jews?" And
L	23.3	And Pilate asked him, "Are you the King of the Jews?" And

J	18.34	Jesus answered, "Do you say this of your own accord, or did others
M	27.11	Jesus said, "You have said so."
Mk	15.2	he answered him, "You have said so."
L	23.4	he answered him, "You have said so." And Pilate said to the chief

L	23.4	priests and the multitudes, "I find no crime in this man."

J	18.35	say it to you about me?" Pilate answered, "Am I a Jew? Your own nation
M	27.12	But when he was accused by the chief priests and elders, he made no answer.
Mk	15.3	And the chief priests accused him of many things.
L	23.5	But they were urgent, saying, "He stirs up the people, teaching

L	23.5	throughout all Judea, from Galilee even to this place."
L	23.6,7	When Pilate heard this, he asked whether the man was a Galilean. And
L	23.7	when he learned that he belonged to Herod's jurisdiction, he sent him over
L	23.8	to Herod, who was himself in Jerusalem at that time. When Herod saw Jesus,

```
L   23.8    he was very glad, for he had long desired to see him, because he had
L   23.8    heard about him, and he was hoping to see some sign done by him.


J   18.35   and the chief priests have handed you over to me; what have you done?"
J   18.36   Jesus answered, "My kingship is not of this world; if my kingship were of
J   18.36   this world, my servants would fight, that I might not be handed over to the
J   18.37   Jews; but my kingship is not from the world." Pilate said to him, "So you
J   18.37   are a king?" Jesus answered, "You say that I am a king. For this I was
J   18.37   born, and for this I have come into the world, to bear witness to the truth.
J   18.38   Every one who is of the truth hears my voice." Pilate said to him, "What
J   18.38   is truth?"


J   18.38   After  he had         said this, he went out to the Jews again, and told
M   27.13   Then   Pilate         said                   to him, "Do   you not
Mk  15.4    And    Pilate again  asked                      him, "Have you no answer
L   23.4    And    Pilate        said                   to the chief priests and the


J   18.39   them,      "I find no crime in      him."            But
M   27.15          hear how many things  they testify against you?" Now at the feast
Mk  15.6    to make? See how many charges they bring  against you." Now at the feast
L   23.17   multitudes, "I find no crime in this man."            Now


J   18.39   you      have a custom that I should release               one
M   27.15   the governor was accustomed     to release for the crowd any one
Mk  15.6    he              used            to release for      them     one
L   23.17   he          was obliged         to release                   one


J   18.39   man           for  you  at the Passover;
M   27.17   prisoner      whom they wanted. So when they had gathered, Pilate said   to
Mk  15.9    prisoner for whom they asked.                    And he       answered
L   23.17   man           to   them at the festival.


J   18.39              will you have me   release for you               the
M   27.17   them, "Whom do  you want me to release for you, Barabbas or Jesus who
Mk  15.9    them,       "Do you want me to release for you               the


J   18.39   King of the Jews?"
M   27.18   is called Christ?" For he knew     that it was out of envy that
Mk  15.10   King of the Jews?" For he perceived that it was out of envy that the chief


M   27.19   they      had delivered him up. Besides, while  he was sitting on the judg-
Mk  15.10   priests had delivered him up.

M   27.19   ment seat, his wife sent word to him, "Have nothing to do with that
M   27.19   righteous man, for I have suffered much over him today in a dream."

M   27.20   Now the chief priests and the elders persuaded  the people            to
Mk  15.11   But the chief priests                 stirred up the crowd            to
L   23.18   But          they all                 cried out together, "Away with this

M   27.21           ask      for      Barabbas and destroy Jesus.  The governor again
Mk  15.11   have him releasé for them Barabbas instead.
L   23.20   man, and release to  us  Barabbas"--                   Pilate

M   27.21   said  to them, "Which of the two do you want me to release for you?"
L   23.20   addressed them once more,          desiring to release Jesus;


J   18.40   They cried out again, "Not this man, but Barabbas!" Now
M   27.16   And they said,                       "Barabbas." |And they had then
Mk  15.7                                                     And among the
L   23.19                                                    |a man who had
```

582

M	27.16	*a notorious prisoner,*
Mk	15.7	*rebels in prison, who had committed murder in the insurrection,*
L	23.19	*been thrown into prison for an insurrection started in the city,*

J	18.40	Barabbas was a robber.
M	27.16	called Barabbas.
Mk	15.8	there was a man called Barabbas. And the crowd came up and began to ask
L	23.19	and for murder.

Mk	15.8	*Pilate to do as he was wont to do for them.*

M	27.24	*So when Pilate saw that he was gaining nothing, but rather that a riot*
M	27.24	*was beginning, he took water and washed his hands before the crowd,*
M	27.25	*saying, "I am innocent of this man's blood; see to it yourselves." And*
M	27.25	*all the people answered, "His blood be on us and on our children!"*

J	19.1	Then Pilate
M	27.26	Then he
Mk	15.15	So Pilate, wishing to satisfy the crowd,
L	23.24,25	So Pilate gave sentence that their demand should be granted. He

M	27.26	*released for them Barabbas,*
Mk	15.15	*released for them Barabbas;*
L	23.25	*released the man who had been thrown into prison for insurrection and*

J	19.1	took Jesus and scourged him.
M	27.26	and having scourged Jesus, delivered him to be crucified.
Mk	15.15	and having scourged Jesus, he delivered him to be crucified.
L	23.25	murder, whom they asked for; but Jesus he delivered up to their will.

J	19.2	And the soldiers
M	27.27	Then the soldiers of the governor took Jesus into
Mk	15.16	And the soldiers led him away inside the palace (that

M	27.27	*the praetorium, and they gathered the whole battalion before*
Mk	15.16	*is, the praetorium); and they called together the whole battalion.*

J	19.2	plaited a crown of thorns, and put it on his head,
M	27.29a	him. |and plaiting a crown of thorns they put it on his head, and put a
Mk	15.17b	|and plaiting a crown of thorns they put it on him.

J	19.2	and arrayed him in a
M	27.28	reed in his right hand. And they stripped him and put a
Mk	15.17a	And they clothed him in a
L	23.11b	then, arraying him in

J	19.2	purple robe;
M	27.29b	scarlet robe upon him, |And kneeling before him
Mk	15.17a	purple cloak,
L	23.11a	gorgeous apparel, |And Herod with his soldiers treated him with con-

J	19.3	they came up to him, saying, "Hail, King of the Jews!"
M	27.29	they mocked him, saying, "Hail, King of the Jews!"
Mk	15.18	And they began to salute him, "Hail, King of the Jews!"
L	23.11a	tempt and mocked him;

583

```
J    19.3                                                      and        struck him
M    27.30    And they spat upon him, and took the reed  and        struck him  on the head.
Mk   15.19                                                     And they struck       his head


J    19.4    with their hands. Pilate went out again, and said to them, "See, I am
Mk   15.19   with a      reed, and spat upon him, and they knelt down in homage to him.
L    23.4                    And Pilate                        said to the chief priests


J    19.4    bringing him out to you, that you may know that I find no crime in      him."
L    23.4    and the multitudes,                         "I find no crime in this man."


J    19.5    So Jesus came out, wearing the crown of thorns and the purple robe.  Pilate
J    19.5    said to them, "Behold the man!"


J    19.6    When the chief priests and the officers saw him,
M    27.20   Now  the chief priests and the elders persuaded  the people to
Mk   15.11   But  the chief priests                stirred up the crowd  to have him
L    23.18   But             they all                cried out together, "Away with this


M    27.21              ask      for      Barabbas and destroy Jesus.  The governor again
Mk   15.11              release for them Barabbas instead.
L    23.20   man, and release to us   Barabbas"--                      Pilate


M    27.21   said    to them, "Which of the two do you want me to release for you?"  And
L    23.20   addressed them once more,         desiring to release Jesus;


M    27.22   they said, "Barabbas."  Pilate         said to them, "Then what shall I do
Mk   15.12                     And Pilate again said to them, "Then what shall I do


J    19.6                                                      they        cried    out,
M    27.22   with Jesus   who  is  called    Christ?"          They all said, "Let
Mk   15.13   with the man whom you call the King of the Jews?"  And they    cried   out
L    23.21                                                      but they    shouted out,


J    19.6         "Crucify him, crucify him!"           Pilate said to them, "Take
M    27.23   him be  crucified."              And      he     said,
Mk   15.14   again, "Crucify him."            And      Pilate said to them,
L    23.22       "Crucify,    crucify him!"  A third time he   said to them,


J    19.7    him yourselves and crucify him, for I find no crime in him."  The Jews
M    27.23                      "Why,    what evil has he done?"
Mk   15.14                      "Why,    what evil has he done?"
L    23.22                      "Why,    what evil has he done?"  I have


J    19.7    answered him, "We have a law, and by that law he ought to die, because he
L    23.22   found in him no crime deserving death; I will therefore chastise him and


J    19.7    has made himself the Son of God."
M    27.23                  But they shouted all the more,              "Let him
Mk   15.14                  But they shouted all the more,
L    23.23   release him." But they were urgent, demanding with loud cries that he


M    27.23             be crucified."
Mk   15.14              "Crucify him."
L    23.23   should be crucified.  And their voices prevailed.
```

```
J    19.8,9    When Pilate heard these words, he was the more afraid; he entered the
M    27.13     Then Pilate
Mk   15.4      And  Pilate again
L    23.9      So   he
```

```
J    19.9      praetorium again and said    to Jesus, "Where are you from?"
M    27.13                    said    to him,   "Do      you not
Mk   15.4                     asked   him,     "Have     you no answer to make?
L    23.9                     questioned him     at some length;
```

```
J    19.9                                             But Jesus gave      no
M    27.14     hear how many things  they testify against you?" But he    gave him no
Mk   15.5      See  how many charges they bring  against you."  But Jesus made     no
L    23.9                                               but he      made     no
```

```
J    19.9               answer.
M    27.14              answer, not even to a single charge; so that the governor wondered
Mk   15.5      further  answer,                        so that    Pilate    wondered.
L    19.10              answer.  The chief priests and the scribes stood by, vehemently
```

M 27.14   greatly.
L 23.11   accusing him. And Herod with his soldiers treated him with contempt and

L 23.11   mocked him; then, arraying him in a gorgeous apparel, he sent him back to
L 23.12   Pilate. And Herod and Pilate became friends with each other that very day,
L 23.12   for before this they had been at enmity with each other.
L 23.13   Pilate then called together the chief priests and the rulers and the
L 23.14   people, |and said to them, "You brought me this man as one who was per-
L 23.14   verting the people; and after examining him before you, behold, I did
L 23.15   not find this man guilty of any of your charges against him; neither did
L 23.15   Herod, for he sent him back to us. Behold, nothing deserving death has
L 23.15   been done by him;

```
J    19.10     Pilate therefore said to him, "You will not speak to me?  Do you not know
J    19.11     that I have power to release you, and power to crucify you?"  Jesus an-
J    19.11     swered him, "You would have no power over me unless it had been given you
J    19.11     from above; therefore he who delivered me to you has the greater sin."
```

```
J    19.12     Upon this Pilate            sought       to release him, but the Jews
L    23.16             I will therefore chastise him and release him."
```

```
J    19.12     cried out, "If you release this man, you are not Caesar's friend; every
J    19.13     one who makes himself a king sets himself against Caesar."  When Pilate
J    19.13     heard these words, he brought Jesus out and sat down on the judgment seat
J    19.14     at a place called The Pavement, and in Hebrew, Gabbatha.  Now it was the
J    19.14     day of Preparation of the Passover; it was about the sixth hour.  He said
J    19.14     to the Jews, "Behold your King!"
```

```
J    19.15           They cried out,            "Away with him, away with him,
M    27.23b     But they shouted all the more,          "Let him       be
Mk   15.14b     But they shouted all the more,
L    23.23      But they were urgent, demanding with loud cries that he should be
```

```
J    19.15     crucify him!"  Pilate said to them, "Shall I crucify your King?"  The
M    27.23b     crucified."
Mk   15.14b     "Crucify him."
L    23.23      crucified.  And their voices prevailed.
```

585

```
J    19.15      chief priests answered, "We have no king but Caesar."


M    27.24      So when Pilate saw that he was gaining nothing, but rather that a riot was
Mk   15.15      So        Pilate, wishing to satisfy the crowd,
L    23.24      So        Pilate gave sentence that their demand should be granted.


M    27.24      beginning, he took water and washed his hands before the crowd, saying,
M    27.25      "I am innocent of this man's blood; see to it yourselves."  And all the
M    27.25      people answered, "His blood be on us and on our children!"


M    27.26      Then he released for them Barabbas,
Mk   15.15            released for them Barabbas;
L    23.25      He released       the man who had been thrown into prison for insurrec-


J    19.16                                      Then he handed    him over to
M    27.26              and having scourged Jesus,    delivered him
Mk   15.15              and having scourged Jesus, he delivered him
L    23.25      tion and murder, whom they asked for; but Jesus  he delivered up


J    19.16      them to be crucified.
M    27.26           to be crucified.
Mk   15.15           to be crucified.
L    23.25           to their   will.
```

38. CRUCIFIXION AND DEATH

John 19.17-37

```
J    19.17           So they took Jesus, and he went out,
M    27.32              As they              went out,  they came upon a man
Mk   15.21      And       they                          compelled a passer-by,
L    23.26      And as they led  him       away,  they seized      one


M    27.32           of Cyrene, Simon by name;         this man they compelled
Mk   15.21      Simon of Cyrene, who was coming in from the country, the father of
L    23.26      Simon of Cyrene, who was coming in from the country, and laid


J    19.17                   bearing his own cross,
M    27.32              to carry   his     cross.
Mk   15.21      Alexander and Rufus, to carry   his     cross.
L    23.26                 on him the cross, to carry it behind Jesus.


L    23.27      And there followed him a great multitude of the people, and of women who
L    23.28      bewailed and lamented him.  But Jesus turning to them said, "Daughters of
L    23.28      Jerusalem, do not weep for me, but weep for yourselves and for your
L    23.29      children.  For behold, the days are coming when they will say, 'Blessed
L    23.29      are the barren, and the wombs that never bore, and the breasts that
L    23.30      never gave suck!'  Then they will begin to say to the mountains, 'Fall
L    23.31      on us'; and to the hills, 'Cover us.'  For if they do this when the wood
L    23.31      is green, what will happen when it is dry?"


J    19.17                        to the place       called
M    27.33      And when they came    to a  place       called Golgotha (which
Mk   15.22      And       they brought him to the place       called Golgotha (which
L    23.33      And when they came    to the place which is called


J    19.17           the place of a  skull, which is called in Hebrew Golgotha.
M    27.34      means the place of a  skull),  | they offered him wine to drink, mingled
Mk   15.23      means the place of a  skull).  And they offered him wine       mingled
L    23.33                  The Skull,
```

586

```
 M  27.35a    with gall;  but when he tasted it, he would not drink it.  And
 Mk 15.24a    with myrrh; but                    he did   not take  it.  And


 J  19.18     There they          crucified him,  and with him two others,
 M  27.38     when  they had crucified him,      |Then      two
 Mk 15.27          they      crucified him,      |And with him they
 L  23.32                                         Two others also, who were
 L  23.33     there they          crucified him,  and                     the


 J  19.18                                                    one on either side,
 M  27.38     robbers    were                  crucified  with him, one on the right
 Mk 15.27                                       crucified two robbers, one on his right
 L  23.32     criminals, were led away to be put to death with him.
 L  23.33     criminals,                                   one on the right


 J  19.19     and Jesus between them.   Pilate also wrote a title and
 M  27.37     and one on the left.                        And over his head
 Mk 15.26     and one on his left.                        And            the
 L  23.38     and one on the left.                        There was also an


 J  19.19         put          it on the cross;  it   read,       "Jesus of
 M  27.37     they put      the charge against him, which read, "This is Jesus
 Mk 15.26     inscription of the charge against him          read,
 L  23.38     inscription              over   him,          "This is


 J  19.20     Nazareth, the King of the Jews."  Many of the Jews read this title, for
 M  27.37               the King of the Jews."
 Mk 15.26               "The King of the Jews."
 L  23.38               the King of the Jews."


 J  19.20     the place where Jesus was crucified was near the city; and it was written
 J  19.21     in Hebrew, in Latin, and in Greek.  The chief priests of the Jews then
 J  19.21     said to Pilate, "Do not write, 'The King of the Jews,' but, 'This man
 J  19.22     said, I am King of the Jews.'"  Pilate answered, "What I have written I
 J  19.22     have written."


 J  19.23             When the soldiers had crucified Jesus
 M  27.35     And when       they     had crucified him,
 Mk 15.24     And            they         crucified him,
 L  23.33b,34        there    they         crucified him, |And Jesus said, "Father, forgive


 J  19.23                                            they          took
 M  27.35                                            they          divided
 Mk 15.24                                       and                divided
 L  23.34     them; for they know not what they do."  And they cast lots to divide


 J  19.23     his garments and made four parts, one for each soldier; also his tunic.
 M  27.35     his garments
 Mk 15.24     his garments
 L  23.34     his garments.


 J  19.24     But the tunic was without seam, woven from top to bottom; |so they said


 J  19.24     to one another, "Let us not tear it, but cast    lots for it    to see
 M  27.35                              among them by casting lots;
 Mk 15.24                              among them,   casting lots for them, to decide
```

587

```
J    19.24      whose it shall be." This was to fulfil the scripture
Mk   15.24      what each should take.


J    19.24                "They parted my garments among them,
J    19.24                 and for my clothing they cast lots."


J    19.25      So the soldiers did this.                        But standing by
M    27.36,55   then they sat down and kept watch over him there.  There were also
Mk   15.25,40a  And it was the third hour, when they crucified him.  There were also
L    23.49                                                        And all his


J    19.25      the cross of Jesus were his mother, and his mother's sister, Mary the wife
M    27.55                                          many women there, looking on from
Mk   15.40a                                              women        looking on from
L    23.49      acquaintances                          and the women


J    19.25      of Clopas,
M    27.55      afar,  who had followed Jesus from Galilee,                  ministering
Mk   15.41      afar, |who,      when he was in Galilee, followed him, and ministered
L    23.49            who had followed him   from Galilee  stood at a distance and saw


J    19.26              and           Mary Magdalene.  When Jesus saw his mother, and
M    27.56      to him; among whom were Mary Magdalene, and Mary the mother of James
Mk   15.40b             among whom were Mary Magdalene, and Mary the mother of James the
Mk   15.41      to him; and also many other women who came up with him to Jerusalem.
L    23.48      these things.  And all the multitudes who assembled to see the sight, when


J    19.26      the disciple whom he loved standing near, he said to his mother, "Woman,
M    27.56              and     Joseph, and the mother of the sons of Zebedee.
Mk   15.40b     younger and of Joses,   and Salome,
L    23.48      they saw what had taken place, returned home beating their breasts.


J    19.27      behold, your son!"  Then he said to the disciple, "Behold, your mother!"
J    19.27      And from that hour the disciple took her to his own home.


  M  27.45              Now from  the sixth hour         there was darkness over all
 Mk  15.33             And when  the sixth hour had come, there was darkness over
  L  23.44      It was now about the sixth hour,     and there was darkness over


J    19.28                                           After this          Jesus,
M    27.46      the       land until the ninth hour.  And about the ninth hour Jesus
Mk   15.34      the whole land until the ninth hour.  And at    the ninth hour Jesus
L    23.45a     the whole land until the ninth hour, |while the sun's light failed;


J    19.28      knowing that all was now finished, said (to fulfil the scripture),
M    27.46      cried with a loud voice, "Eli, Eli, lama sabachthani?" that is,
Mk   15.34      cried with a loud voice, "Eloi, Eloi, lama sabachthani?" which means,


J    19.28      "I thirst."
M    27.47      "My God, my God, why hast thou forsaken me?"  And some of the bystanders
Mk   15.35      "My God, my God, why hast thou forsaken me?"  And some of the bystanders


J    19.29              A bowl full of vinegar stood there; so        they
M    27.48      hearing it said, "This  man is calling Elijah."  And one of them at
Mk   15.36      hearing it said, "Behold, he is calling Elijah."  And one
L    23.36                                                       The soldiers also
```

```
J    19.29                        put      a sponge  full       of the vinegar              on
M    27.48   once ran and  took   a sponge, filled it with   vinegar, and put it on
Mk   15.36          ran and, filling a sponge  full     of     vinegar,      put it on
L    23.36   mocked him, coming up        and offering him     vinegar,


J    19.30     hyssop and held it to his mouth.     When Jesus had received the
M    27.49   a reed,  and gave it to him to drink.  But the others said,  "Wait,
Mk   15.36   a reed   and gave it to him to drink,                    saying, "Wait,
L    23.37                               |and              saying, "If you


J    19.30   vinegar, he said, "It is finished";              and  he
M    27.50   let us see whether Elijah will come to save him."      And  Jesus
Mk   15.37   let us see whether Elijah will come to take him down." And  Jesus
L    23.46   are the King of the Jews,        save yourself!"  Then Jesus,


J    19.30   bowed           his head
M    27.50   cried again with a loud voice
Mk   15.37   uttered         a loud cry,
L    23.46   crying      with a loud voice, said, "Father, into thy hands I commit


J    19.30               and               gave  up his spirit.
M    27.50               and               yielded up his spirit.
Mk   15.37               and               breathed  his last.
L    23.46   my spirit!"  And having said this he breathed  his last.


J    19.31                     Since it was the day of Preparation, in
Mk   15.42   And when evening had come, since it was the day of Preparation, that
L    23.54                     It was the day of Preparation,


J  * 19.31   order to prevent the bodies from remaining on the cross on the sabbath
Mk   15.42   is,                              the day before the sabbath,
L    23.54                                        and the sabbath


J    19.31   (for that sabbath was a high day), the Jews asked Pilate that their legs
L    23.54   was beginning.


J    19.32   might be broken, and that they might be taken away.  So the soldiers came
J    19.32   and broke the legs of the first, and of the other who had been crucified
J    19.33   with him; but when they came to Jesus and saw that he was already dead,
J    19.34   they did not break his legs.  But one of the soldiers pierced his side
J    19.35   with a spear, and at once there came out blood and water.  He who saw it
J    19.35   has borne witness--his testimony is true, and he knows that he tells the
J    19.36   truth--that you also may believe.  For these things took place that the
J    19.37   scripture might be fulfilled, "Not a bone of him shall be broken."  And
J    19.37   again another scripture says, "They shall look on him whom they have
J    19.37   pierced."
```

39. THE BURIAL

John 19.38-42

```
J    19.38   After this                           Joseph of
M    27.57   When it   was evening, there came a rich man      from
Mk   15.43                                        Joseph of
L    23.50   Now there was            a    man named Joseph from the Jewish


J    19.38         Arimathea,
M    27.57         Arimathea,    named Joseph,
Mk   15.43         Arimathea,         a respected member of the council,
L    23.50   town of Arimathea.  He was a        member of the council, a good and
```

righteous man, |who had not consented to their purpose and deed, and

J	19.38	who was a disciple of Jesus, but secretly, for fear of the Jews, asked
M	27.58	who also was a disciple of Jesus. He went
Mk	15.43	who was also himself looking for the kingdom of God, took courage and went
L	23.52	he was looking for the kingdom of God. This man went

J	19.38	Pilate that he might take away the body of Jesus, and Pilate
M	27.58	to Pilate and asked for the body of Jesus. Then Pilate
Mk	15.44	to Pilate, and asked for the body of Jesus. And Pilate wondered
L	23.52	to Pilate and asked for the body of Jesus.

Mk 15.44 *if he were already dead; and summoning the centurion, he asked him whether*
Mk 15.45 *he was already dead. And when he learned from the centurion that he was*

J	19.38	gave him leave. So he came and took
M	27.59	ordered it to be given to him. And Joseph
Mk	15.46	dead, he granted the body to Joseph. And he bought a linen
L	23.53	Then he

J	19.39	away his body. Nicodemus also, who had at first come to him by night,
J	19.39	came bringing a mixture of myrrh and aloes, about a hundred pounds'

J	19.40	weight. They took the body of Jesus, and bound it in linen
M	27.59	took the body, and wrapped it in a clean linen
Mk	15.46	shroud, and taking 'him down, wrapped him in the linen
L	23.53	took it down and wrapped it in a linen

J	19.41	cloths with the spices, as is the burial custom of the Jews. Now in the
M	27.59	shroud,
Mk	15.46	shroud,
L	23.53	shroud,

J	19.41	place where he was crucified there was a garden, and in the garden a
M	27.60	|and laid it in his
Mk	15.46	and laid him in a
L	23.53	and laid him in a

J	19.42	new tomb where no one had ever been laid. So because of the
M	27.60	own new tomb, which he had hewn in the rock; and he rolled a
Mk	15.46	tomb which had been hewn out of the rock; and he rolled a
L	23.54	rock-hewn tomb, where no one had ever yet been laid. It was the

J	19.42	Jewish day of Preparation, as the tomb was close at hand, they laid
M	27.61	great stone to the door of the tomb, and departed. Mary Magdalene
Mk	15.47	stone against the door of the tomb. Mary Magdalene
L	23.55	day of Preparation, and the sabbath was beginning. The women who

J	19.42	Jesus there.
M	27.61	and the other Mary were there, sitting opposite
Mk	15.47	and Mary the mother of Joses saw where he
L	23.55	had come with him from Galilee followed, and saw the tomb, and how his body

M 27.61 *the sepulchre.*
Mk 15.47 *was laid.*
L 23.56 *was laid; then they returned, and prepared spices and ointments.*

L 23.56 *On the sabbath they rested according to the commandment.*

40. THE EMPTY TOMB

John 20.1-10

```
J    20.1    Now                                  on the first day of the week
M    28.1    Now after the sabbath, toward the dawn of the first day of the week,
Mk   16.1    And when  the sabbath  was past,
Mk   16.2    And very early                       on the first day of the week
L    24.1    But                                  on the first day of the week,
L    24.10   Now it was
```

```
J    20.1                        Mary Magdalene
M    28.1                        Mary Magdalene      and the other Mary
Mk   16.1                        Mary Magdalene,     and            Mary the mother of
Mk   16.2                        they
L    24.1     at early dawn, they
L    24.10                       Mary Magdalene and Joanna and      Mary the mother of
```

```
Mk  16.1    James, and Salome, bought spices, so that they might go and anoint him.
 L  24.10   James  and the other women with them who told this to the apostles;
```

```
J    20.1    came to      the tomb early, while it was still dark,
M    28.1    went to see the sepulchre.
Mk   16.2,3  went to      the tomb      when the sun had risen.  And they were saying
L    24.1    went to      the tomb, taking the spices which they had prepared.
```

```
Mk  16.3    to one another, "Who will roll away the stone for us from the door of the
Mk  16.3    tomb?"
```

```
J    20.1    and                      saw that the stone
M    28.2    And behold, there was a great earthquake; for an angel of the Lord descended
Mk   16.4    And looking up, they saw that the stone
L    24.2    And           they found     the stone
```

```
J    20.2                   had been taken  away from the tomb.  So she ran, and went
M    28.3    from heaven and came and rolled back the stone, and sat upon it.  His
Mk   16.4                        was  rolled back--it was very large.
L    24.3                        rolled away  from the tomb, |but when they went in
```

```
J    20.2    to Simon Peter and the other disciple, the one whom Jesus loved, and said
M    28.4    appearance was like lightning, and his raiment white as snow.  And for fear
L    24.3    they did not find the body.
```

```
J    20.2    to them, "They have taken the Lord out of the tomb, and we do not know where
M    28.4    of him the guards trembled and became like dead men.
```

```
J    20.3    they have laid him."  Peter then came out with the other disciple, and they
L    24.12              But Peter     rose                                          and
```

```
J    20.4    went toward the tomb.  They both ran, but the other disciple outran Peter
L    24.12                                ran
```

```
J    20.5    and reached the tomb first; and stooping to  look   in, he saw the linen
L    24.12            to the tomb;          stooping and looking in,
```

```
J    20.6    cloths lying there, but he did not go in.  Then Simon Peter came, following
```

591

J	20.7	<u>him</u>, <u>and went into the tomb;</u> <u>he saw the linen cloths lying,</u> |<u>and the napkin,</u>
L	24.12	*he saw the linen cloths by themselves;*

J	20.7	<u>which had been on his head, not lying with the linen cloths but rolled up</u>
J	20.8	<u>in a place by itself.</u> <u>Then the other disciple, who reached the tomb first,</u>
J	20.9	<u>also went in, and he saw and believed;</u> <u>for as yet they did not know the</u>
J	20.9	<u>scripture,</u> <u>that he must rise from the dead.</u>

J	20.10	<u>Then the disciples went back to their homes.</u>
L	24.12	*and he went home wondering at what had happened.*

41. THE APPEARANCE TO MARY

John 20.11-18

J	20.11	<u>But Mary stood weeping outside the tomb,</u> <u>and as she wept she stooped to</u>
Mk	16.5	And entering the tomb,
L	24.4	While they were

J	20.12	<u>look into the tomb; and she</u> saw two angels in white, <u>sitting where the</u>
M	28.2b	for an angel of the Lord descended from
Mk	16.5	they <u>saw</u> a young man <u>sitting</u>
L	24.4	perplexed about this, behold, <u>two</u> men stood by them

J	20.12	<u>body of Jesus had lain,</u> <u>one at the head and one at the feet.</u>
M	28.3	heaven |His appearance was like lightning, and his raiment white as
Mk	16.5	on the right side, dressed in a white robe;
L	24.4	in dazzling

M	28.3	*snow.*
Mk	16.5	*and they were amazed.*
L	24.5	*apparel; and as they were frightened and bowed their faces to the ground,*

J	20.13	They <u>said to</u> her, "Woman, <u>why are you weeping?</u> She said to them,
M	28.5	But the angel <u>said to</u> the women, "Do not be afraid;
Mk	16.6	And he <u>said to</u> them, "Do not be amazed;
L	24.5	the men <u>said to</u> them, "Why

J	20.13	<u>"Because they have taken away my Lord,</u> <u>and I do not know where they have</u>
J	20.14	<u>laid him."</u> <u>Saying this, she turned round and saw Jesus standing,</u> <u>but she</u>
J	20.15	<u>did not know that it was Jesus.</u> <u>Jesus said to her, "Woman, why are you</u>

J	20.15	<u>weeping? Whom do you seek?"</u> <u>Supposing him to be the gardener,</u> <u>she said to</u>
M	28.6	for I know that <u>you seek</u> Jesus who was crucified. He is
Mk	16.6	<u>you seek</u> Jesus of Nazareth, who was crucified. He has
L	24.6	<u>do you seek</u> the living among the dead? Remember how he told

J	20.15	<u>him,</u> "Sir, if you have carried him away, <u>tell me where you have laid him,</u>
M	28.6	not here; for he has risen, as he said. Come, see the place where he
Mk	16.6	risen, he is not here; see the place where they
L	24.7	you, while he was still in Galilee, |that the Son of man must be delivered

J	20.16	<u>and I will take him away."</u> <u>Jesus said to her, "Mary."</u> <u>She turned and said</u>
M	28.7	lay. Then go quickly and tell his disciples that he has risen
Mk	16.7	laid him. But go, tell his disciples and Peter that
L	24.7	into the hands of sinful men, and be crucified, and on the third day rise."

J	20.17	to him in Hebrew, "Rabboni!" (which means Teacher). Jesus said to her,
M	28.7	from the dead, and behold, he is going before you to Galilee; there you
Mk	16.7	he is going before you to Galilee; there you
L	24.8	And they remembered his words,

J	20.17	"Do not hold me, for I have not yet ascended to the Father; but go to my
M	28.7	will see him. Lo, I have told you."
Mk	16.7	will see him, as he told you."

J	20.17	brethren and say to them, I am ascending to my Father and your Father, to
Mk	16.9	Now when he rose early on the first day of the week,
L	24.10	Now it was

J	20.18	my God and your God." Mary Magdalene
M	28.8	So they
Mk	16.8	And they
Mk	16.9	he appeared first to Mary Magdalene, from whom he had cast out seven
L	24.10	Mary Magdalene and Joanna and Mary the mother of

J	20.18	went
M	28.8	departed quickly from the tomb with fear and great joy,
Mk	16.8	went out and fled from the tomb; for trembling and astonishment
Mk	16.10	demons. She went
L	24.9	and returning from the tomb
L	24.10	James and the other women with them

J	20.18	and said to the disciples,
M	28.9	and ran to tell his disciples. And behold,
Mk	16.8	had come upon them; and they said nothing to any one, for they were
Mk	16.10	and told those who had been with him, as they
L	24.9	they told all this to the eleven and to all the
L	24.10	who told this to the apostles;

J	20.18	"I have seen
M	28.9	Jesus met them and said, "Hail!" And they came up and took hold of his feet
Mk	16.8	afraid.
Mk	16.11	mourned and wept. But when they heard that he was alive and had been seen
L	24.9	rest.
L	24.11	but these words seemed to them an idle tale,

J	20.18	the Lord"; and she told them that he had said these things to her.
M	28.10	and worshiped him. Then Jesus said to them, "Do not be afraid; go and
Mk	16.11	by her, they would not believe it.
L	24.11	and they did not believe them.

M	28.10	*tell my brethren to go to Galilee, and there they will see me."*

42. APPEARANCES TO THE DISCIPLES AND THOMAS

John 20.19-31

J	20.19	On the evening of that day, the first day of the week, the doors being
Mk	16.14	Afterward
L	24.36	As they were saying this,

J	20.19	shut where the disciples were, for fear of the Jews, Jesus came and stood
Mk	16.14	he appeared to
L	24.36	Jesus himself stood

```
J    20.19   among them
Mk   16.14   the eleven themselves as they sat at table;
L    24.37   among them.  But they were startled and frightened, and supposed that they


J    20.19                    and   said   to them, "Peace be with you."
Mk   16.14                    and he upbraided them for their unbelief and hardness of
L    24.38   saw a spirit.  And he said   to them, "Why are you troubled, and why do


J    20.20            When he had said this, he showed them his hands and his side.
Mk   16.14   heart, because they had not believed those who saw him after he had risen.
L    24.39   questionings rise in your hearts?  See       my   hands and  my   feet,


J    20.21   Then the disciples were glad when they saw the Lord. |Jesus said to them
L    24.39   that it is I myself; handle me, and see; for a spirit has not flesh and


J    20.21   again, "Peace be with you.  As the Father has sent me, even so I send you."
L    24.39   bones as you see that I have."


J    20.22   And when he had said this, he breathed on them, and said to them, "Receive
M    16.19                            I will give you the keys of the kingdom of
M    18.18                                                      Truly, I say


J    20.23   the Holy Spirit.  If you forgive the sins of any, they are forgiven;
M    16.19   heaven, and whatever you bind on earth        shall be bound in
M    18.18   to you,     whatever you bind on earth         shall be bound in


J    20.23                 if you retain the sins of any, they are retained."
M    16.19   heaven, and whatever you loose on earth        shall be loosed in heaven."
M    18.18   heaven, and whatever you loose on earth        shall be loosed in heaven.


J    20.24      Now Thomas, one of the twelve, called the Twin, was not with them when
J    20.25   Jesus came.  So the other disciples told him, "We have seen the Lord."


J    20.25   But he said to them, "Unless I see in his hands the print of the nails,
L    24.39                              See    my   hands and my feet, that it


J    20.25   and place my finger in the mark of the nails, and place my hand in his
L    24.39   is I myself; handle me, and see; for a spirit has not flesh and bones


J    20.25   side, I will not believe."
L    24.39   as you see that I have."


J    20.26   Eight days later, his disciples were again in the house, and Thomas was
Mk   16.14   Afterward
L    24.36   As they were saying this,


J    20.26   with them.  The doors were shut, but Jesus came and stood among them,
Mk   16.14                              he      appeared    to the eleven
L    24.36                              Jesus himself   stood among them.


J    20.26                            and    said,         "Peace be with
Mk   16.14   themselves as they sat at table; and he upbraided them for their unbelief
L    24.38                            And he said   to them, "Why    are
```

594

```
J    20.27      you."  Then he said to Thomas, "Put your finger here,   and see my hands;
Mk   16.14      and hardness of heart, because they had not believed those who saw him
L    24.39      you troubled, and why do questionings rise in your hearts?  See my hands


J    20.27      and put out your hand, and place it in my side; do not be faithless, but
Mk   16.14      after he had risen.
L    24.39      and my feet, that it is I myself; handle me, and see; for a spirit has


J    20.28,29   believing."  Thomas answered him, "My Lord and my God!"  Jesus said to him,
L    24.39      not flesh and bones as you see that I have."


J    20.29      "Have you believed because you have seen me? Blessed are those who have
J    20.29      not seen and yet believe."

J    20.30      Now Jesus did many other signs in the presence of the disciples, which


J    20.31      are not written in this book; but these are written that you may believe
M    1.1                            The   book        of the genealogy
Mk   1.1                            The   beginning   of the gospel


J    20.31      that Jesus  is the Christ,
M    1.1           of Jesus       Christ,
Mk   1.1           of Jesus       Christ,
L    3.23             Jesus, when he began his ministry, was about thirty years of age, being


J    20.31      the Son                    of God, and that believing you may have life
M    1.1        the Son                    of David,  the son of Abraham.
Mk   1.1        the Son                    of God.
L    3.23       the son (as was supposed) of Joseph, the son of Heli,


J    20.31      in his name.
```

43. THE APPEARANCE BY THE SEA OF TIBERIAS

John 21.1-14

```
J    21.1        After this Jesus revealed himself again to the disciples
M    4.18        As                                                       he
Mk   1.16        And
L    5.1         While the people pressed upon him to hear the word of God, he was


J    21.1                    by the Sea  of Tiberias; and he revealed himself in this way.
M    4.18        walked      by the Sea  of Galilee,            he saw two brothers,
Mk   1.16        passing along by the Sea of Galilee,           he saw
L    5.2         standing    by the lake of Gennesaret.     And he saw two boats by the


J    21.2        Simon              Peter, Thomas called the Twin, Nathanael of Cana in
M    4.18        Simon who is called Peter and Andrew his brother,       casting a net
Mk   1.16        Simon              and Andrew the brother of Simon casting a net
L    5.2         lake;


J    21.2        Galilee, the sons of Zebedee, and two others of his disciples were together.
M    4.18        into the sea; for they were fishermen.
Mk   1.16        in  the sea; for they were fishermen.
L    5.2                     but the       fishermen had gone out of them and were washing
```

595

J	21.3	Simon Peter said to them, "I am going fishing." They said to him, "We
L	5.2	their nets.

J	21.3	will go with you." They went out and got into the boat; but
L	5.3	Getting into one of the boats, which

L 5.3   was Simon's, he asked him to put out a little from the land. And he sat down
L 5.5   and taught the people from the boat. And Simon answered, "Master, we toiled

J	21.3	that night they caught nothing.
L	5.5	all night and took nothing! But at your word I will let down the nets."

J	21.4	Just as day was breaking, Jesus stood on the beach; yet the
L	24.36	As they were saying this, Jesus himself stood among them.

J	21.5	disciples did not know that it was Jesus. Jesus said to them,
L	24.41	And while they still disbelieved for joy, and wondered, he said to them,

J	21.6	"Children, have you any fish?" They answered him, "No." |He said to them,
L	5.4	And when he had ceased speaking, he said to Simon,
L	24.41	"Have you anything here to eat?"

J	21.6	"Cast the net on the right side of the boat,
L	5.4	"Put out into the deep and let down your nets for a catch."

J	21.6	and you will find some." So they cast it, and now they were not
L	5.6	And when they had done this, they

J	21.6	able to haul it in, for the quantity of fish.
L	5.6	enclosed a great shoal of fish; and as their nets were breaking,

J	21.7	That disciple whom Jesus loved said to Peter, "It is the Lord!"
L	5.7a	|they beckoned to their partners in the other boat to come and help them.

J	21.7	When Simon Peter heard that it was the Lord, he put on his clothes, for
L	5.8	But when Simon Peter saw it, he fell down at Jesus'

J	21.8	he was stripped for work, and sprang into the sea. But the
L	5.7b	knees, saying, "Depart from me, for I am a sinful man, O Lord." And

J	21.8	other disciples came in the boat, dragging the net full of
L	5.7b	they came and filled both the boats, so that they began to sink.

J	21.8	fish, for they were not far from the land, but about a hundred yards off.
L	5.9	For he was astonished, and all that were with him, at the catch

L 5.10   of fish which they had taken; and so also were James and John, sons of
L 5.10   Zebedee, who were partners with Simon. And Jesus said to Simon, "Do not
L 5.10   be afraid; henceforth you will be catching men."

J	21.9	When they got out on land, they saw a charcoal fire
L	5.11	And when they had brought their boats to land, they left everything and

596

J	21.10	there, with fish lying on it, and bread. Jesus said to them, "Bring some
L	5.11	followed him.

J	21.11	of the fish that you have just caught." So Simon Peter went aboard and
J	21.11	hauled the net ashore, full of large fish, a hundred and fifty-three of
J	21.12	them; and although there were so many, the net was not torn. Jesus said
J	21.12	to them, "Come and have breakfast." Now none of the disciples dared ask
J	21.12	him, "Who are you?"

J	21.13	They knew it was the Lord. Jesus came and took
L	24.42,43	They gave him a piece of broiled fish, |and he took

J	21.14	the bread and gave it to them, and so with the fish. This was now the
L	24.43	it and ate before them.

J	21.14	third time that Jesus was revealed to the disciples after he was raised
J	21.14	from the dead.

44. THE CHARGE TO SIMON PETER

John 21.15-25

J	21.15	When they had finished breakfast, Jesus said to Simon Peter, "Simon, son
J	21.15	of John, do you love me more than these?" He said to him, "Yes, Lord; you
J	21.16	know that I love you." He said to him, "Feed my lambs." |A second time
J	21.16	he said to him, "Simon, son of John, do you love me?" He said to him, "Yes,
J	21.17	Lord; you know that I love you." He said to him, "Tend my sheep." |He
J	21.17	said to him the third time, "Simon, son of John, do you love me?" Peter
J	21.17	was grieved because he said to him the third time, "Do you love me?" And
J	21.17	he said to him, "Lord, you know everything; you know that I love you."
J	21.18	Jesus said to him, "Feed my sheep. |Truly, truly, I say to you, when you
J	21.18	were young, you girded yourself and walked where you would; but when you
J	21.18	are old, you will stretch out your hands, and another will gird you and
J	21.19	carry you where you do not wish to go." (This he said to show by what
J	21.19	death he was to glorify God.) And after this he said to him, "Follow me."

J	21.20	Peter turned and saw following them the disciple whom Jesus loved, who
J	21.20	had lain close to his breast at the supper and had said, "Lord, who is it
J	21.21	that is going to betray you?" When Peter saw him, he said to Jesus, "Lord,
J	21.22	what about this man?" Jesus said to him, "If it is my will that he remain
J	21.23	until I come, what is that to you? Follow me!" The saying spread abroad
J	21.23	among the brethren that this disciple was not to die; yet Jesus did not
J	21.23	say to him that he was not to die, but, "If it is my will that he remain
J	21.23	until I come, what is that to you?"

J	21.24	This is the disciple who is bearing witness to these things, and who has
J	21.24	written these things; and we know that his testimony is true.

J	21.25	But there are also many other things which Jesus did; were every one of
J	21.25	them to be written, I suppose that the world itself could not contain the
J	21.25	books that would be written.